MARKETING RESEARCH

METHODS AND CANADIAN PRACTICE

MARKETING RESEARCH

METHODS AND CANADIAN PRACTICE

CHUCK CHAKRAPANI
STANDARD RESEARCH SYSTEMS INC.

KENNETH R. DEAL
McMASTER UNIVERSITY

PRENTICE-HALL CANADA INC. SCARBOROUGH, ONTARIO

Canadian Cataloguing in Publication Data

Chakrapani, Chuck
  Marketing research: methods and Canadian practice

Includes index
ISBN 0-13-553298-1

1. Marketing research.   2. Marketing research – Canada
I. Deal, Ken, 1944–   .   II. Title.

HF5415.2.C53 1992   658.8′3   C91-094640-X

Prentice Hall, Inc., Englewood Cliffs, New Jersey
Prentice-Hall International, Inc., London
Prentice-Hall of Australia, Pty., Ltd., Sydney
Prentice-Hall of India Pvt., Ltd., New Delhi
Prentice-Hall of Japan, Inc., Tokyo
Prentice-Hall of Southeast Asia (Pte.) Ltd., Singapore
Editora Prentice-Hall do Brasil Ltda., Rio de Janeiro
Prentice-Hall Hispanoamericana, S.A., Mexico

ISBN 0-13-553298-1

Acquisitions Editor: Jacqueline Wood
Developmental Editor: Linda Gorman
Copy Editor: Mary de Souza
Production Editor: Kelly Dickson
Production Coordinator: Florence Rousseau
Interior Design: Olena Serbyn
Page Layout: Joseph Chin
Cover Design: Derek Chung Tiam Fook
Illustrations: Loates Electronic Design and Illustration

  2 3 4 5 RRD 96

Printed and bound in the U.S. by R.R. Donnelley & Sons

Every reasonable effort has been made to find copyright holders.
The publisher would be pleased to have any errors or omissions
brought to its attention.

Photo Credits: Part 1: Ministry of Industry and Tourism; Part 2: John McNeill;
Part 3: Parmic Task Force, Ottawa/W. McElligott; Part 4: MediaCom;
Part 5: Dick Hemingway.

For
Andrew Ehrenberg

and for
My Mother, Pushpa

–Chuck Chakrapani

For
Barbara, Kent, Jake, Molly, John and Barbie

and for
My Mother, Mary

–Ken Deal

Contents

Preface

The Rationale for this Book

This book grew out of our desire to bridge the growing gap between the theory and the practice of marketing research. One of the authors is a full-time practitioner who teaches extensively; the other is a full-time academic who consults extensively. Our background and experience led us to believe that it is important for the academically trained researcher to understand how research is actually carried out in practice and it is equally important for the practitioner to understand the theoretical basis of techniques and procedures used in marketing research. Most books we have come across tend to fall into one of the two categories: "how-to" books that ignore the theoretical aspects of research and methodological books that walk the reader through an idealized version of research, only a part of which is practiced in real life.

Combining Theory and Practice

Many theoretically sound books in this area tend to ignore how marketing research is actually conducted in practice. For example, an informal review of the 10 most widely used introductory books shows that most of them fail to mention (for example):

- that *sample sizes are seldom decided on the basis of theoretical formulas*. Rather, they are decided on the basis of available resources and the way the information is expected to be used;
- that *many market research studies do not use probability samples;*
- that *qualitative research is a widely used form of research* (many textbooks devote no more than a few pages to discuss qualitative research);
- that *techniques like Baysian Statistics is almost never used in real life market research.*

We believe such differences between theory and practice arise mainly due to practical considerations such as cost and resources available to do a research project. Consequently we believe that anyone learning aspects of marketing research should be aware of how a project is actually done in practice. It is this orientation that led us to eliminate topics like "Baysian Analysis" which we have never seen used in the marketing research context.

EMPHASIS ON NUMERACY

Even a cursory glance at most marketing research books would indicate that data analysis is equated with statistics. We feel data analysis has more to do with numeracy and communication of findings than with statistics. Numeracy is taken for granted because data analysts do it intuitively and are probably not aware of the process by which they extract meaning from data. We believe (like Hans Zeisel and Andrew Ehrenberg before us) that numeracy is a teachable and learnable skill. A special feature of this book is its attempt to teach numeracy to market researchers.

THE STRUCTURE OF THE BOOK

To make the book appealing to readers with varied backgrounds, the book is conceptually divided into three parts: Chapters 1-15 (Parts I & II), Chapters 16-20 (Part III) and Chapters 21-25 (Part IV).

PARTS I AND II

Chapters 1 through 15 form the core of the book. They are written in a straightforward fashion and provide a practical introduction to marketing research. They should be read in sequence.

PART III

Chapters 16 through 20 discuss specialized research areas and may be read partially or fully and in any order.

PART IV

Chapters 21 through 23 deal with some technical aspects of marketing research. Some of the topics are covered in a basic fashion earlier in the book. These chapters are intended for those who require in-depth technical information. Chapters 24 and 25 are intended for every practitioner of marketing research in Canada. Chapters in this part can be read partially or fully and in any sequence.

We suggest that Chapters 1-15 and 24 be included in any basic marketing research course. Any of the remaining chapters may be included or excluded from the syllabus depending on the level of sophistication expected of the student.

CANADIAN CONTENT

The marketing research principles explained in this book are applicable anywhere. However, this is a distinctly Canadian book. A large amount of information contained in this book—such as sources of secondary information, a list of marketing research companies, a list of qualitative research facilities and examples we have used—are Canadian. While this book should be useful to market researchers everywhere, Canadian researchers should find it even more useful.

HOW THE BOOK WAS WRITTEN

We have tried to cover topics that are not normally covered in introductory books and we have tried to cover certain topics in a different way. As the title page indicates this book is a collaborative effort. However, Ken Deal assumed primary responsibility for chapters 3, 4, 7-9, 16, 17, 21-23 while Chuck Chakrapani assumed primary responsibility for chapters 2, 5-6, 10-14, 18-20, 24 and 25.

We would welcome any suggestions for improvement. Please write to us directly or through our publisher, Prentice-Hall Canada.

Chuck Chakrapani, Ph.D.

Kenneth R. Deal, Ph.D.

ACKNOWLEDGMENTS

The delightful Nestlings (the "research birds") cartoons were created by Warren Clements of *The Globe and Mail*. We are grateful for his permission to use them in our book.

The initial draft of this book was based on lecture notes prepared by some of our colleagues in the industry. Many of our friends and colleagues in the marketing research industry were kind enough to go through the final version and offer their helpful comments. In particular, we would like to acknowledge the assistance provided by Peter Atkinson (questionnaire design) of ABM, Don McGrath of Canada Market Research and David Kwechansky of Perception Research Inc. (qualitative research), Don McGrath, and Don Ambrose of Consumer Contact (fieldwork) and Anne Termaten of Thompson Lightstone (fieldwork, coding and tabulation). Professor Andrew Ehrenberg of the London Business School reviewed all numeracy chapters (Part IV) of the book. Their suggestions helped to improve the book immensely. However, since we did not incorporate all their suggestions, we assume the final responsibility for the book. Chris Commins of Commins, Wingrove, and Ruth Jaglowitz of Seneca College provided encouragement during the early stages of this project. We would also like to thank the reviewers: Professor Karen A. Blotnicky of Mount Saint Vincent University, Professor Jack Dart of the University of Saskatchewan, Professor Henry Klaise of Durham College, Dr. John P. Liefeld of the University of Guelph, Dr. Chike Okechuku of the University of Windsor, Professor Tony Schellinck of Dalhousie University, Mr. Dave Tinker of Sheridan College, and Professor Ronald E. Turner of Queen's University.

We are grateful to Mr John Finneran of Newspaper Marketing Bureau, John Chaplin of PMB Print Measurement Bureau, Mr Owen Charlebois of BBM Bureau of Broadcast Measurement, the Field Management Group of the PMRS and A.C. Nielsen for permission to reproduce and paraphrase from their documents. Our thanks also to Statistics Canada and *The Financial Post* for permission to reproduce from their publications.

We have been encouraged and helped by Barbara Deal, Elena Dunn, Rosemary Cliffe and Christine Mole in various ways while the book was in preparation. And we appreciate the patience and dedication shown by Yolanda de Rooy, Jackie Wood, Linda Gorman, Kelly Dickson and others in charge of the production of this book at Prentice-Hall Canada.

CC

KD

ABOUT THE AUTHORS

CHUCK CHAKRAPANI   M.A., M.Sc., Ph.D., F.S.S.

Dr. Chuck Chakrapani is President of Standard Research Systems Inc. and Editor-in-Chief of the *Canadian Journal of Marketing Research*. He has held academic appointments at the London Business School in England and at the University of Liverpool.

He has written over 100 articles and papers which have appeared in journals and magazines throughout the world. In addition, he has written several books including *A History of Marketing Research in Canada* and *Research Techniques For Marketing Decisions* and has edited monographs such as *Market Segmentation* and *Evaluating Advertising Through the Eighties.*

Dr. Chakrapani was president (1985-86) and executive director (1986-91) of the Professional Marketing Research Society. He is currently Fellow of the Professional Marketing Research Society and Fellow of the Royal Statistical Society.

KENNETH R. DEAL   M.B.A., Ph.D.

Dr. Ken Deal is Associate Professor of Marketing and Management Science at McMaster University and is Director of Marketing Decision Research Inc.

His articles, which have appeared in academic and practitioner journals, have focused on marketing research methodology and marketing modelling. He regularly presents executive seminars in marketing research and strategic marketing, especially for the public sector.

Dr. Deal was Chairman of Marketing at McMaster from 1981 to 1985 and was director of education for the Professional Marketing Research Society from 1983 to 1986.

PART 1

What is Marketing Research?

1 / Definition and Scope of Marketing Research

- To appreciate the variety of marketing contributions made by marketing research
- What activities are performed during a marketing research project
- The definition of marketing research
- Who uses marketing research
- Who conducts marketing research
- How marketing research fits into the flow of marketing decision-making
- The difference between primary and secondary research

WHAT IS MARKETING RESEARCH?

Marketing is the set of activities involved in the exchange of goods and services between producers and consumers. To be effective, marketing needs information about consumers. Marketing research provides that information.

Producers of goods and services need information about the market. For example, the manufacturer of a breakfast cereal may want to know about the potential buyers, their ability to pay a given price, their breakfast habits, their likes and dislikes; the manufacturer of computer software may want to know the requirements of a given type of business so that efficient computer programs can be written and marketed.

Marketing research deals with the collection, processing and analysis of information with regard to people's attitudes, feelings, intentions and behaviour towards products and services. One commonly accepted definition of marketing research is that

> Marketing research is the function which links the consumer, customer, and public to the marketer through information—information used to identify and define marketing opportunities and problems; generate, refine, and evaluate marketing actions; monitor marketing performance; and improve understanding of marketing as a process (American Marketing Association, 1987).

In more specific terms, marketing research:

- specifies the information required to address the marketing issues
- designs the method for collecting information
- manages and implements the data collection process
- analyzes the results
- communicates the findings and their implications

This and other similar definitions try to characterize marketing research from an academic perspective. However, marketing research is not a discipline that fits into neatly defined boundaries. Nor is its scope clearly defined. The subject matter can and usually does include diverse areas such as social research, psychological research, advertising research, political polling, and analysis of historical data records. Students of marketing research can get a better idea of what marketing research is by understanding what market researchers do. The purpose of this book is to explore what market researchers do and the tools and techniques they use.

The Daily Interest Savings Account idea came out of a sophisticated marketing research study undertaken by the Bank of Montreal. The study not only identified the need for this product but accurately predicted market share gains that the Bank of Montreal would achieve and the impact on market shares when the Royal Bank launched a similar service. The launch of the daily interest savings account service resulted in massive revenue gains for the Bank of Montreal (Brian Cockle, personal communication).

The bulk of marketing research is carried out with a view to marketing goods and services. To assess the scope of marketing research, consider the problems that are routinely handled by market researchers, as listed in Exhibit 1.1. Marketing research can contribute important information to all the situations described in Exhibit 1.1. In addition, there are hundreds of other situations in which marketing research can be used. Additional examples of marketing research projects are used throughout the book.

Exhibit 1.1   Some Typical Marketing Research Problems

You are a manufacturer and would like to introduce a new kind of perfume:
- You want to find out if consumers would find the perfume desirable.
- You would like to know that the market is large enough for a new brand.
- You want to estimate the price that the consumer would be willing to pay.
- You want to make sure that your advertisement is not offensive to the consumer.
- You would like to know if the market is growing or declining.
- You would like to understand what image your corporation has among the public.
- You want to know what people like about your corporation.
- You would like to explore what they dislike about your corporation.
- You want to explore the reasons for their likes and dislikes.
- You want to find out how your corporation compares with other similar corporations.

You are associated with a political party and would like to predict the election results:
- You want to know which party is viewed more favourably.
- You want to know whether any party is gaining or losing popularity.
- You want to know the factors that are likely to influence the voters.
- You want to know who the undecided voters are and why they are undecided.

You are a publisher of a magazine and would like to know more about your readership:
- You would like to know the demographics of your readers.
- You would like to know their likes and dislikes.
- You would like to know what motivates a person to subscribe to your magazine.
- You would like to know their lifestyles.

You are with the federal government and would like to know about the current trends in public thinking:
- You would like to know what the voters think about capital punishment.
- You would like to know whether Canadians would support a free trade deal with the United States.

Who Uses Marketing Research?

Marketing research is used by marketing managers, product managers, media planners, advertising executives, educational institutions, governments, political parties, non-profit organizations and, in fact, by any organization which needs information from the public.

The bulk of commercial marketing research is conducted for firms that market products to the public through retail operations. However, during recent years an increasing amount of research has been done for pharmaceutical firms, financial institutions, and firms that provide other services.

60% of all Canadian adults have a VCR in the household

28% of all Canadian adults aged 18-24, own a compact disc player

15% of Canadians make three or more transactions per week using their automatic bank teller cards

29% of high-end sports car owners in Canada own or lease a cellular telephone

80% of all Canadian government bond owners read a Saturday and/or Sunday edition of a daily newspaper

5% of Canadians took an overnight business trip to an American city last year (*Playback Strategy*, 1990).

The various levels of government are responsible for a very large amount of marketing research. Statistics Canada alone accounts for a tremendous volume of marketing research studies. Provincial governments typically conduct research to understand the tourism market better. Metropolitan governments conduct marketing research to assess the social and economic impact of large public development projects; while private land developers conduct marketing research in order to show municipal planning committees that the public is not opposed to the type of development that they propose.

"A *Good Statistics Guide* would never make the best-seller lists. More's the pity. Official statistics steal headlines, wipe billions off shares and defeat governments, yet all too often the numbers are ropey. Britain's national accounts, for example, are so riddled with holes and revisions that the true state of its economy is anybody's guess . . .

"How might Britain's record be improved? Look at the world's best official statisticians: Canada, followed closely by Australia, Sweden and Holland. These countries' systems are centralised with most numbers collected by a single body whose independence is guaranteed by law." (©1990 The Economist Newspaper Ltd. Used with permission).

Industry associations such as the Canadian Institute for Steel Construction, the Canadian Manufacturers' Association, the Society for Management Accountants and others conduct marketing research studies from time to time to make a base level of market information available to all of their members. Some of the member organizations might then decide to conduct their own studies to gain information that might provide them with a competitive advantage.

Sales representatives for newspapers and other media use readership and listening studies to show prospective advertisers the profiles of those who read the newspaper or listen to the radio station, so that the advertiser can decide if the target market can be reached by the publication (see, for example, the advertisement for *The Toronto Sun* in Exhibit 1.2). Media planners in agencies must determine how to spend their clients' advertising budgets for maximum impact. To do this they use marketing research from the Bureau of Broadcast Measurement to identify the time slots, programs, and stations that will achieve the best coverage of the targeted markets.

Apart from these obvious uses, marketing research is also used to prove and disprove points of views for legal or competitive purposes. For example, a manufacturer may commission a research project with a view to isolating certain facts that can be used in an advertising campaign: "Two out of three consumers preferred drink A over B." Here the direct purpose of the research project is not so much to collect information for decision-making as to provide input to advertising claims so that they can pass the scrutiny of government regulatory agencies.

Marketing research is sometimes used to support the arguments in legal cases. There is a case on record in which Revenue Canada carried out a study to find out the meaning of *dentifrice*, because a particular company claimed that its toothpaste was a health product and deserved a tax break. Marketing research was also used in the "Ontario Champagne Case" in the Supreme Court of Ontario by the Champagne producers of France. They wished to establish that when people in Ontario heard the word *champagne*, they thought of the sparkling wine called "Champagne," produced in the Champagne region of France. In fact, the marketing research was unable to prove this and France lost the case.

WHO CARRIES OUT MARKETING RESEARCH?

Marketing research is usually carried out by companies that specialize exclusively in marketing research. Some marketing research houses, such as Canadian Facts, ISL and Market Facts of Canada, are so large that they undertake to execute almost any type of marketing research project. At the other

Exhibit 1.2   The Colour of Our Collars is Changing

THE COLOUR OF OUR COLLARS IS CHANGING

They're less blue than they've ever been. Decidedly more white. And that's not just a tough little paper talking. It is the fact according to NADBANK: 53% of Sun readers are now white collar workers. As well, 53% are over 35 and, you guessed it, 53% generate household incomes of over $50,000 annually. All this with a 13% increase in readership in 18 plus.* It's enough to make a broadsheet green with envy.
*Based on 1990 NADBANK figures.

SOURCE: NADbank 90, *Playback Strategy*, October 22, 1990. Reproduced by permission of **The** Newspaper Marketing Bureau and *The Toronto Sun*.

end of the spectrum are companies that concentrate on very specific areas of research, such as political polling or policy research, panel research or new product research. Other companies specialize in some functional aspect of research, such as group discussions, computer tabulation of the data, special statistical analysis of the data, or fieldwork interviewing. Exhibit 1.3 gives examples of various types of research houses. Even research firms that specialize in one area will often carry out research in almost any other area if they have the resources and expertise to do so, or if they can hire the expert consultants needed. For instance, prominent political polling companies, such as Goldfarb Consultants and Decima Research, claim to derive only about 10 to 20 per cent of their revenue from political polling.

Exhibit 1.3 Examples of Research Houses

Type	Some Examples[1]
Full Service	Canadian Facts, Market Facts, Thompson Lightstone
Political Polling	Goldfarb Consultants, Decima Research, Angus Reid
Panel Data	A.C. Nielsen, ISL, Karom
New Products	Product Initiatives, Camelford Graham
Fieldwork	Consumer Contact, RIS Christie, Research House
Special Analysis	Applied Marketing Statistics, Standard Research Systems
Qualitative	Kwechansky Marketing Research, Catherine Fournier Inc.

[1] The firms listed here are just examples. They are not chosen on any criterion except that they are representative of their category. Some firms listed under specialities also conduct general studies and other special studies.

While a marketing research firm might have an excellent capability to execute general level marketing research projects, it might lack the expertise to conduct very specialized studies. For example, a research firm that is good at interviewing consumers may lack the skill or the personnel to interview opinion leaders on the impact of free trade.

Specialists in specific areas of research such as political pollsters, social researchers and policy researchers may not consider themselves market researchers. Such specialists may even take exception to market researchers including their areas of expertise under the term *marketing research*. However, the techniques used in different areas of specialization have a common logic, structure and procedures. Firms that specialize in marketing research have the infrastructure and, in most cases, the expertise to tackle

problems in related fields. In cases where the research firm has the capability to complete the physical aspects of the project but not enough technical expertise to design or analyze the study, it may employ consultants for guidance.

Currently, there are more than a dozen major full-service marketing research organizations in Canada. In addition, there are quite a large number of small (often one-person) research consultants and qualitative research specialists.

There are also many marketing, management, economic, and engineering consulting firms which advertise that they do marketing research. Some do, but most would subcontract the marketing research to a marketing research specialist if such a job were obtained.

Advertising agencies also say that they do marketing research. Mostly, the marketing research personnel in advertising agencies act in the same manner as marketing research managers in manufacturing firms: they determine what research their advertising clients want, help with the initial design of the project, subcontract the execution of most of the actual marketing research, and then assist the client to understand and interpret the findings.

Very few marketing firms in Canada carry out marketing research using only, or even primarily, their own internal resources. When credibility is a problem, firms are well advised to utilize outside suppliers instead of their in-house facilities. In some cases, it is hard to measure your own company's performance objectively. Outside sources may also be used when in-house facilities lack the capacity to conduct the research, when special competencies are required, or when they may be cheaper. For example, it may be cheaper to use a market research firm based in the actual market to conduct a telephone survey, instead of trying to do it from an in-house, centralized marketing research department located in the head office of the manufacturing firm.

MARKETING RESEARCH AND MANAGEMENT DECISION-MAKING

Marketing research information is used by management as an aid to making decisions; for example:

- Should a company introduce a new product?
- Will a given advertisement antagonize the consumer?
- What media are most suited for a given message?
- What appeals would be most effective to change the corporate image?

Of course, marketing research information is only one component in the marketing decision-making process. For example, even if research indicates that there is a market for a new product, the development, marketing and management of that product are very challenging tasks that go far beyond the bounds of marketing research. The product, if launched, may not succeed; or, it might achieve a greater market position than initially projected. These actual results do not come about because of or in spite of the marketing research. The marketing management would receive the laurels or the blame for the product's success or failure.

The key factor influencing the brand's position could be any of the following marketing activities: pricing, product formulation, product distribution, the competence of the sales force, the effectiveness of the advertising campaign, the activities of competitors and other such factors. So, it is important to remember that marketing research must not dictate management decisions. It can only guide the decision-maker by providing valuable information and insight upon which to make decisions.

It is often stated that the value of marketing research lies in its contribution to reducing the risks of making bad marketing decisions. There are considerable risks involved in making decisions without the information that can be provided by marketing research. Many studies have found that the main reason for new product failure is the lack of adequate marketing research (Cooper, 1987).

Ideally, research inputs should assist firms at all levels in the marketing planning process, from goal-setting, planning and implementation, through to evaluation of the efforts. Such a process ensures that firms have the information to get the expertise to accurately determine the success of their marketing plans. It is the responsibility of the researcher to make sure that research information is valid, reliable, and suitable for its intended use.

Once again, the main value of marketing research is to provide information on which better marketing decisions can be based. The marketing decisions, in turn, are components of the comprehensive strategy for the organization. Many firms and public organizations have strategic planning processes that require marketing decisions to be made at appropriate points and to be based on expert judgment and sound information.

One of the best ways of appreciating the breadth of information that marketing research can provide to an organization is to follow the strategic planning process through its many phases. By asking "How do you know that?" and "What information do you need in order to make that decision?", many marketing research tasks can be identified that would enhance the strategic plan.

Strategic planning is a process designed to result in the best allocation of resources within the organization to achieve its objectives. Strategic planning is a continuing process of assessing the organization's resources, determining the current state of the organization's affairs, diagnosing its current situation, forecasting its position in the future, developing a set of alternative strategic directions, choosing a strategy, implementing that strategy and providing for the strategic and tactical control of that plan.

As an example of the variety of marketing research projects which could be used to provide input to an organization's strategic plan the *strategic planning path* shown in Exhibit 1.4 was proposed for the Hamilton Central Public Library. This was part of a study to assess the needs of those living within the Regional Municipality of Hamilton-Wentworth for library resources and services. The strategic planning process is a flow that cycles through the assessment, strategy development, implementation and control phases. Marketing research can play as valuable a role in measuring the needs and desires of the public for library resources and services as it can in private business in assessing the needs of new features for home carpet cleaning, or for microwavable frozen entrees.

The "current planning gap" identifies the distance between where the organization thought it would be at a point in time and where that organization actually is at that time in terms of several key indicators. This might be stated in terms of the difference between the number of requests for books and the number borrowed, or in terms of sales or market share for a private company. Marketing research and research of the organization's operations should provide substantial input to this gap analysis. The organization's "mission" would have specified what the organization ideally intends to achieve. The "objectives" are more practical manifestations of what the organization strongly desires to achieve at particular points of time. The "strategic market audit" is an investigation of the capabilities and resources of the organization to plan strategically and to execute those plans.

Once the current gap is identified, the reasons for the gap's existence ("diagnosis") and the prediction of the gap's implications for the organization ("prognosis") are studied. The "future planning gap" can then be estimated. This specifies that if the organization continues with its present strategy for

Exhibit 1.4   Proposed Strategic Planning Process Hamilton Central Public Library

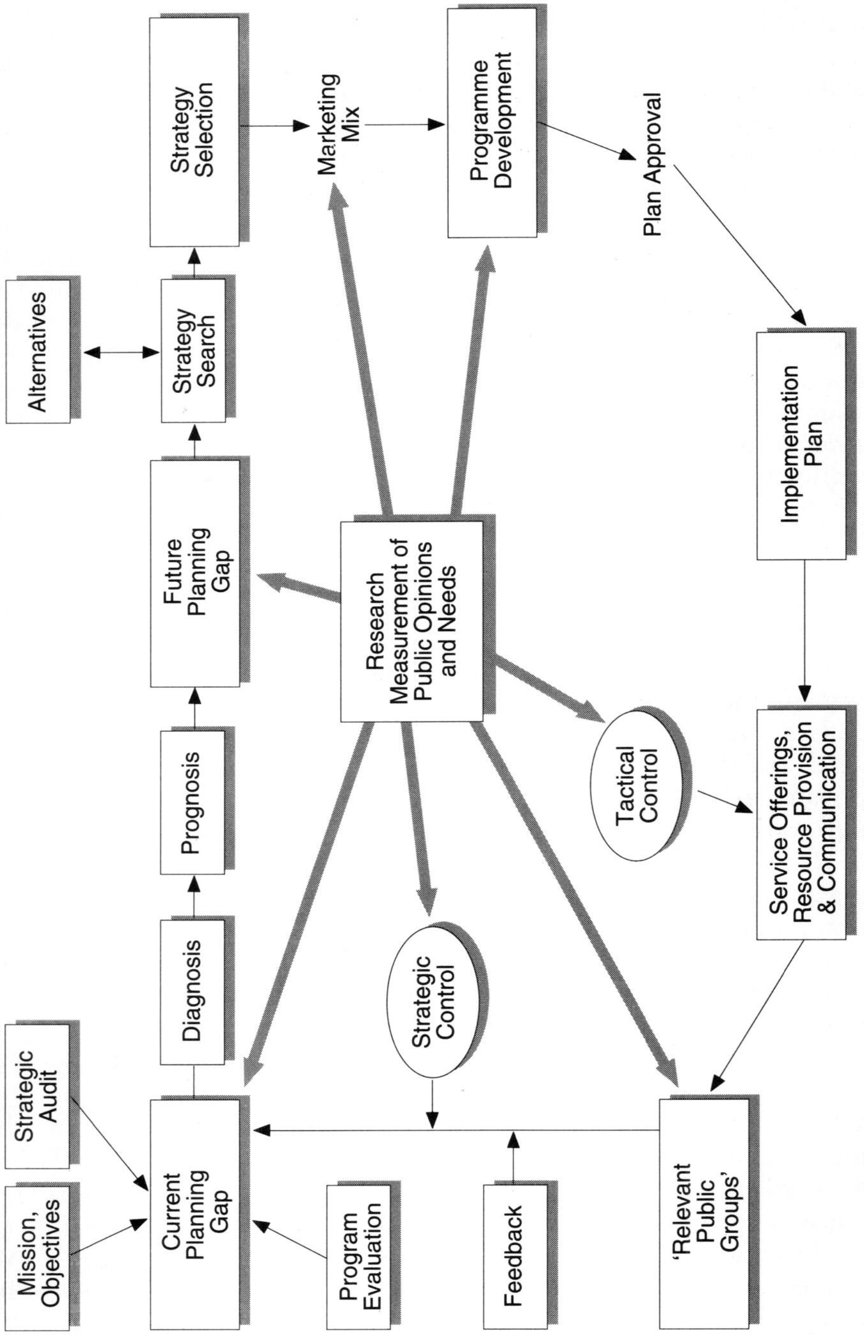

the next year, for example, then the gap between objectives and achievement will be of a certain size. Rather than changing strategy based on the current planning gap, the organization needs to project the effects of its strategy for a long enough period of time to see whether the strategy is perhaps correct but the timing was a bit too ambitious. Maybe the organization just has to wait another year and everything will be fine. Or, of course, the reverse might be true. Marketing research can be helpful at this state to estimate the likely response of the public to current marketing strategies during the next year or so.

If it is determined that a change of strategy is needed, then "alternatives" must be identified and assessed. The organizational and marketing strategies will foster a reformulation of the marketing actions of the firm through the development of a new or modified "marketing mix." To determine new service and product directions, changes to existing services and products, revised pricing, more effective advertising and distribution that better meets the needs of the organization's public, the needs and wants of that public must be measured through marketing research. Similarly, the development of "programs" to inform and motivate the public to make better and more effective use of the organization's services and resources should be the subject of marketing research.

After the strategic plan is "approved," the plan for the "implementation" of the strategy is developed. Then the services and resources that the marketing research identified as needed and desired are "offered" to the public through communication and distribution. It is important at this stage that "tactical control" mechanisms are established to measure the effectiveness of the organization's day-to-day mechanisms in providing the resources and services. In parallel, the "public's opinions and behaviour" must be sensitively measured to identify their reactions to those resources and services, and the manner in which they are provided by the new strategies.

It is nearly impossible to get any strategy working exactly right without "monitoring" the market and organizational activities, adjusting those activities, and, perhaps, "refining" the strategies in a sensitive manner as quickly as possible.

At the end of the planning cycle is the detailed "evaluation"of the strategic plan in terms of objective measures on internal and external performance criteria. Naturally, marketing research is again needed to identify the reactions of the several segments of the public to the many facets of the strategic plan and its implementation.

It is fairly easy to see that there are many opportunities for marketing research to contribute to the more effective provision of library resources and services as proposed in Exhibit 1.4. The strategic planning path for a private manufacturing company would be very similar to that diagrammed in Exhibit 1.4, and the opportunities for improving marketing decisions through good marketing research are at least as diverse.

PRIMARY AND SECONDARY RESEARCH

There are several ways of characterizing marketing research. One of those ways pertains to the intention and source of the research. For the sake of convenience in this section, we will classify research projects as being of two types: primary and secondary.

Primary research refers to those projects that are executed to obtain information to meet the specific objectives of a current marketing problem. This type of research always generates new data and information. Whether the research is a survey or a focus group, it produces primary data. Two weeks after the primary research project is finished, someone else might retrieve and use that data for a slightly different purpose and they are then called secondary data.

Secondary research refers to the search, retrieval, use and analysis of information not collected specifically for the purpose at hand. In other words, secondary research works with old or second-hand data that were part of a project executed at some time in the past for some reason other than the one that is motivating the current research. Secondary research is also called "desk research" because the researcher can very often call for the data and perform the analysis without getting up from the desk.

HOW TO USE SECONDARY RESEARCH

Most secondary data come from three basic sources:

- Company records of sales, advertising expenditures, special promotions, etc.
- Syndicated surveys like A.C. Nielsen, Predicasts and Frost & Sullivan in which information on products and brands in general is collected and distributed free or for a fee
- Information that is collected by large organizations such as Statistics Canada, *The Financial Post* or *The Globe and Mail* (InfoGlobe) and distributed free or for a fee

Such information can be extremely valuable. Many marketing problems can be answered very effectively through the analysis of secondary data. For example, suppose the sales of your brand have been going down, then:

- Company records might indicate that your distribution has become weak over the past several years; or
- A syndicated study like A.C. Nielsen might indicate that cheaper products are gaining ground at the expense of your brand; or
- Your brand may have a greater appeal to younger people. Statistics Canada figures might indicate that the current population trend is such that there are fewer younger people today than there were 10 years ago.

Analysis of secondary data may sometimes provide a complete solution to a marketing problem. Basic feasibility studies sometimes use only secondary data. For instance, suppose you are in the retail business selling expensive imported perfumes and would like to open a store in a given town. Demographic analysis of published data (e.g., Statistics Canada figures) may alert you to the fact that the income level of the people in that town is too low to support such a store.

Unfortunately, the utilization of secondary data is not as extensive as it should be. One of the main reasons for this, apart from simple oversight, could be that many people are unaware of the existence, sources, and value of such information. Besides, such information does not usually solve the marketing research problem directly and sometimes it is not in a readily usable format. It requires experience to identify and organize such data. Sometimes one may have to "stretch" the secondary data, since some questions that need answering for the current project might not coincide with the format in the secondary database.

Therefore, in practice, secondary data are relegated to a supporting role. There are few attempts to solve a marketing problem with the aid of secondary data. Nevertheless, it should be emphasized that in certain sectors of business, such as store location research, the initial stages of a feasibility study, expansion of distribution of an industrial product to foreign markets, secondary research is used very extensively. Chapter 24 provides a detailed account of information available in Canada. Exhibit 1.5 shows some common secondary sources of information that may prove useful from time to time.

Exhibit 1.5 Commonly Used Sources of Secondary Information

Statistics Canada

The Conference Board of Canada

Economic development departments of regional and municipal governments

Marketing research firms specializing in syndicated industry studies

Various trade associations, e.g., Canadian Institute for Steel Construction

Professional organizations, e.g., The Society of Management Accountants

Information disseminated by lobby groups (sometimes biased)

Commercial directories, e.g., Scott's Directory, Taylor's Directory

The U.S. Bureau of the Census

U.S. Department of Agriculture

SUMMARY

1. Marketing research is the systematic gathering, recording and analyzing of data about problems relating to marketing of goods and services. In practice, market researchers are called upon to solve problems that pertain to other areas such as political polling, social trends, policy research, etc.

2. Marketing research is also used to create and support advertising claims and advocacy advertising.

3. The bulk of marketing research is carried out by marketing research firms, independent research consultants and large organizations which have their own research facilities.

4. Marketing research is a component of the management information system. Because research can be a vital component of the management information system, the researcher should make sure that the research data are valid, reliable, and error-free.

NOW THINK ABOUT THIS

1. Which area of business are you most interested in? Imagine that you have a position as the first marketing research manager in a company operating in that area of business. The company has never done any marketing research before and really doesn't know what it is. Take the definition used in this chapter and adopt the definition for use within your company to inform others of the nature of marketing research and its benefits.

2. Statistics Canada is mentioned in the chapter. Go to your library and ask the librarian in the government documents section to show you where the Statistics Canada publications are kept. Find the occupational and ethnic profiles of the town in which you live.

3. Go to the Yellow Pages for your town (or the closest large town) and look for the ads under marketing research. What did you find?

4. Look in today's issue of a newspaper and find an ad which refers to marketing research findings. Why are these pertinent? If you can't find any, see if the results of any political polls are reported in the newspaper. Why are these uses of marketing research important?

5. Refer to Exhibit 1.4. List five questions which would be pertinent to the *Tactical Control* part of that diagram.

6. While in your library investigating question 2, ask the librarian if there are any syndicated marketing reports. Look through one. Find the library's copy of Scott's Directory and copy the information for two prominent manufacturers in your community.

REFERENCES

American Marketing Association
1987 "New Marketing Research Definition Approved." *Marketing News,* American Marketing Association, January 2, 1987.

Cooper, Robert G.
1987 *Winning at New Products.* Toronto: Gage Publishing Co.

The Economist
1990 "Numbers not worth crunching." *The Economist,* July 28, 1990, p. 15.

Playback Strategy
1990 "NADbank numbers." NADbank 90, *Playback Strategy,* October 22, 1990, p. 14.

PART 2

How to Design a Marketing Research Project

2 / Defining the Problem

- Why marketing research problems may not be defined properly
- How to define the marketing problems and the marketing research problems
- How to distinguish betwen manifest and latent variables
- The differences between the scope and the objectives of the study
- The steps in defining the marketing research problem

RESEARCH AND PROBLEM SOLVING

Marketing research provides information that should help marketers to better solve marketing problems. Therefore, it is important to define the marketing problem precisely so that the information obtained from the marketing research relates specifically to the initial problem. This seems obvious. Yet, in practice, it is not unusual to find research studies in which the definitions are not clear. When this happens, the information collected tends to be unreliable or irrelevant for decision-making purposes. Inadequate problem definition also results in the collection of information that is extraneous to marketing decision-making. Unproductive research is typically due to the problem's not being defined properly, the sample's not being chosen properly, the questionnaire's not being interpreted precisely, and conclusions not being made relevant to the problem at hand.

WHY PROBLEMS ARE NOT DEFINED PROPERLY

Most difficulties with regard to problem definition arise mainly from three basic factors:

- the failure to distinguish between the marketing objectives and the marketing research objectives
- trying to identify latent behaviour patterns by direct questioning
- confusing the objectives with the scope of the study

FAILURE TO DISTINGUISH MARKETING AND MARKETING RESEARCH OBJECTIVES

The marketing decision-maker thinks in terms of marketing objectives and problems and may phrase them as follows:

- How can I outsmart the competition?
- Why is the market share of my product going down?
- What can I do to increase the sales of my product?

After listening to such marketing objectives, a researcher may be tempted to define the marketing research objectives in similar terms:

- To assess the factors contributing to competitive edge
- To find out why the market share of Product X is going down
- To find out how the sales of Product X may be increased

The main problem with such objectives is not that they are wrong, but that they cannot necessarily be solved by marketing research. Specific problems for a research project should be defined in such a way that they can be directly answered to a substantial degree by the study. For instance, in the example above, the research may or may not be able to find out how the sales of Product X may be increased. The marketing research might identify that Product X's advertising is less likable than Product Y's commercials. If so, the total advertising process would involve formulating the advertising strategy and tactics to improve Product X's advertising, and then executing and placing that advertising. This goes well beyond marketing research. The objective defined is too broad to be a research problem. If the researcher were to analyze the problem more closely, research objectives could be derived from marketing objectives. For example:

Marketing problem: Why is our market share going down?

Factual information and analysis:

1. Consumers buy less of the brand than they did before.
2. This could be the result of fewer consumers buying the brand or the same consumers buying in smaller quantity or both.
3. A research project may be designed to find out information on aspects such as:
   a. whether consumers increasingly feel that the brand is inferior;
   b. the rate at which consumers buy the product;
   c. the rate at which consumers buy the brand;
   d. whether consumer brand perceptions have changed;
   e. whether consumers tend to use another product as a substitute;
   f. what proportion of buyers exist in different demographic groups; or
   g. whether there is any change in claimed usage.

   The aspects listed in 3 above can be answered directly by research. These, in effect, become the marketing research objectives. Achieving these research objectives may or may not fully solve the main marketing problem. The important point is that the research objectives must pertain to the consumer, the subject of the research. While there may be other relevant variables, the research will provide information to the decision-maker as to the probable causes of his or her marketing problem, if the project is designed properly (see Chapter 3).

   Let us analyze another marketing problem to see how it can be translated into manageable research objectives.

Marketing problem: We would like to increase the price of our brand of soap, but we want to make sure that this will result in increased profitability.

Factual information and analysis:

1. An increase in the unit price would increase the unit profit. This is purely a maneuver to increase the profit margin and has nothing to do with the

cost of production.

2. However, if people buy less or switch to other brands then our total profitability will decrease rather than increase. Therefore, we need to know how the consumers—in particular the current users of our brand—would react to a price increase.

3. A research project can be designed to determine the following objectives:

   a. whether consumers in this category are price conscious;
   b. whether consumers in this category are price sensitive;
   c. whether users of our brand are price sensitive;
   d. whether users of our brand are brand loyal;
   e. to what extent our brand users will remain loyal (continue to buy our brand) when the price is increased;
   f. whether the current users will switch to a competitive brand or simply consume less if they find the price increase unacceptable.

These initial research objectives may be sharpened, extended, and modified depending on how much information is already available from other sources. Another major consideration is the availability of sufficient resources to accomplish all the research objectives. When resources are limited, some research objectives (judged to be less important) may be sacrificed.

CONFUSING LATENT VARIABLES WITH MANIFEST VARIABLES

At a more subtle level, unreliable results are obtained when the researcher tries to measure something directly that cannot be so measured. Let us consider the case in which the researcher is trying to determine the rate at which consumers buy the product. It seems to be a fairly straightforward objective that can be achieved by direct questioning such as, "How many units of Product X do you buy every month?" Unfortunately, it is difficult to obtain an accurate measure of a consumer's *rate of purchase* by asking a direct question. Rate of purchase is not a directly observable behaviour. It is inferred from the actual purchases reported by the consumer over a period of time (e.g., "How many units of Product X did you buy last week?"), which is a directly observable behaviour. When we let consumers infer answers to questions, we not only make the answers less accurate, but we also run into the risk of uneven interpretation of questions. In the example above, some consumers may exclude purchases carried out during the Christmas season because it is an unusual time and does not reflect their true rate of purchase; others may include it because it is a part of their rate of purchase.

An even more complicated situation would be one in which subtle motivational factors play a dominant role. If we are designing a research project to understand why people buy a highly expensive perfume or an over-priced car, direct questioning of the consumers would hardly provide us with any major insights. It is highly unlikely that users of these products who are motivated by status through the use of prestige brands will admit to such motivation. An even more serious threat to validity is that they may not even be aware of the real reasons for their purchase behaviour.

Two basic types of variables are inherent in most marketing research projects, *manifest variables* and *latent variables*. The values of manifest variables are obtained by directly observing the behaviour of consumers or by direct, structured, and undisguised questions. Manifest variables are associated with behaviour which is directly observable and about which respondents can be expected to provide direct, truthful, and accurate answers. Examples of manifest variables include the sex of a person, the model of car owned by a person, etc.

Some consumer characteristics cannot be directly observed. In other instances, consumers cannot or will not answer questions about the characteristics referred to as *latent variables*. As indicated earlier, inferred and calculated variables, like rate of purchase and motivational factors, fall into the category of latent variables. Potentially serious problems can arise if the researcher tries to identify latent variables by direct questioning.

Some examples of latent variables:

- Reasons for consuming alcohol:
    Respondent: "To relax with friends"
    Latent behaviour: Alcohol dependency
    Solution: Use an indirect research method, e.g., projective techniques
        (see Chapter 5)
- Reading frequency:
    Respondent: "I read one book a month."
    Latent behaviour: Difficult to ascertain
    Solution: Ask, "How many books did you read last month?"

CONFUSING THE OBJECTIVES WITH THE SCOPE OF THE STUDY

The third problem is that of confusing the objectives with the scope of the study. The *objectives* are the problems for which solutions are sought, while the *scope* is the context and the extent of the information required for that purpose. For example, if your objective is to identify the target market for a new brand of detergent, the scope of the project may include identifying the target market in terms of its demographic, socio-economic, behavioural, and media usage characteristics. However, if the objectives have not been defined clearly, then we cannot define the scope of the project very clearly either, since the scope of the study follows from the objectives. This usually results in a confused study in which many aspects that appear irrelevant are included, while some other aspects that are relevant are excluded.

A PRACTICAL GUIDE TO DEFINING MARKETING RESEARCH PROBLEMS

Most marketing research objectives can be defined by using the four-step procedure given below:

Step 1: State the marketing problem:
The sales are not going up.

Step 2: Explicitly state the factual information implied in the marketing problem:
Consumers are buying the same quantity as they did the year before.

Step 3: State the possible causes that might have led to this problem:
- *Market has expanded, but not to our benefit.*
- *Market has shrunk but not to our detriment.*
- *Market has shrunk to our detriment.*
- *Market is static, so are our sales.*

Step 4: List what you would like to know about the market:
You may want to test one of the four causes listed above or you may already know which one of the four is the problem. Depending on the state of your knowledge, you may list the type of information that can be obtained through marketing research.
These will be the research objectives.

STEPS IN DEFINING THE PROBLEM

The essence of defining the objectives for a marketing research study is identifying the components of a marketing problem that can be answered by a research study. The scope of the study is defined by the objectives and modified by the resources available to carry out the study.

Answering the following questions will help clarify the objective and scope of the project:

1. What is the marketing problem for which a solution is sought? (What marketing decision will be based directly on the information to be collected?)
2. What information is required to solve the problem?
3. What are the different sources that can provide the required information?
4. Can any part of this information be obtained from consumers directly?
5. What resources are available for this purpose?
6. What specific information should it be? (This would include decisions on latent variables. For instance, if the required information cannot be obtained directly from consumers (latent behaviour), what information, if collected, would provide a reasonable approximation?)
7. Once this information becomes available how can it be used to solve the initial problem on hand?
8. What additional information should be collected? (The reason for collecting additional information can be twofold: to augment the primary information to be collected as outlined in step 6 above; and to maximize the benefit to be derived from the project—the marginal cost of asking a few additional questions is likely to be small compared to the total cost of the project.)

The scope of the study includes all the information to be collected (i.e., both steps 6 and 8 above), whether or not such information is absolutely required to fulfill the objectives satisfactorily. The objectives of the study are less negotiable than its scope. A competent researcher would give first priority to accomplishing the objectives of the study rather than to covering its scope, if there were a conflict between the two due to cost, timing, or other factors.

The formalizing of information needs, as detailed above, clarifies the problem, sets realistic goals for research, and defines the scope of research very clearly by weeding out information that is not relevant to decision-making.

SUMMARY

1. Marketing research is a problem-solving process. The marketer has a problem and the marketing researcher attempts to solve it through marketing research methods. In doing so, the researcher should bear the following in

mind:

- Distinguish marketing problems from marketing research problems. Marketing research problems are those aspects of a marketing problem that can be solved directly by research.
- Distinguish between manifest and latent variables. Certain aspects of consumer behaviour cannot be measured directly. Defining research problems in terms of data to be collected may alert us to critical latent variables that should be taken into account at the design stage.
- Distinguish between the objectives and the scope of the study. The scope of the study is defined by the objectives. The scope of a well-designed study includes everything that is needed to adequately cover the objectives, no more, no less.

2. There are four basic steps in defining research objectives:
   1. State the marketing problem.
   2. Explicitly state the factual information implied in the marketing problem.
   3. State the possible causes that might have led to this problem.
   4. List what you would like to know about the market. These will be the research objectives.

3. Many variables that we want to measure cannot be measured directly. Variables that can be measured directly (for example, the number of movies seen by a consumer last week) are called *manifest variables*, while variables that cannot be measured directly (such as the consumer's reason for going to the movie *Blue Velvet*) are called *latent variables*.

   Any variable for which direct questioning is unlikely to provide a reasonably correct answer is a latent variable. For instance, any self-incriminating question, such as asking a person whether he is normally rude to others, is unlikely to provide a reasonable measure of such a behaviour. Special techniques may be necessary when latent behaviour is being studied.

   We should first identify the latent variables to understand their inferred status and psychological position within the consumer frame of reference. Only then will we be in a position to construct manifest variables that can be used as proxy measures of corresponding latent variables.

4. Research *objectives* are those aspects of the problem that can be effectively answered by a research study. The *scope* of the project is defined by the objectives and modified by the resources available. The scope is the context, the environment, the breadth, and depth of the project.

5. All research data needed as a result of asking the following questions are

related to the objectives of the project:

- What is my marketing or advertising objective? (What marketing decision needs the research information?)
- What information do I need to achieve this objective?
- How much of this information can be provided by marketing research?
- In what form do I need the information?
- Once I get this information, exactly how am I going to use it to make decisions?
- Alternatively, if I do not have this information, to what extent will it affect my decision?

All other information to be collected—either to understand the market better or for cost efficiency reasons—should be considered as falling within the scope of the study.

NOW THINK ABOUT THIS

Think about any article that you have bought in a grocery store during the past month. List five questions that the manufacturer of that product might ask grocery shoppers about the article to provide marketing information.

1.1 Define the marketing problem which those questions address.

1.2 State the marketing research problem which those questions could be part of.

1.3 For each question, identify the manifest variable(s) and/or the latent variable(s).

1.4 Justify your reasons for classifying those variables as manifest or latent.

1.5 Be a bit expansive and state the objectives and the scope for the study.

3 Designing the Research Project

- About the different types of marketing research problems
- How to identify exploratory, descriptive and causal information requirements
- The difference between qualitative and quantitative research
- The pros and cons of different field methodology
- How to question a survey research study

MARKETING RESEARCH PROBLEMS

The research design specifies the path and the methodology for solving the marketing research problem. It can be as simple as a plan for a basic descriptive study involving seven-minute telephone interviews among the general population, or as complex as an elaborate experimental design for testing a marketing theory. Naturally, for any given problem, some designs are more appropriate than others. When deciding on the design of marketing research projects, the following three components of the design task must be fully specified:

1. the type of marketing research problem
2. the information requirements
3. the field methodology

Marketing problems are often characterized as particular types of marketing research projects. For example, if sales are down, we do a *usage and attitude study*. If we need to evaluate various new product ideas, we do a *concept test*, and when the best of those ideas has been identified, we test for some suitable brand names. If the type of identification is done correctly, then the critical second step of the marketing research project has been successfully completed. From Chapter 2, step one was correct definition of the problem and step two was identifying the information needed to solve the problem. Some common types of marketing research projects are presented in Exhibit 3.1.

Exhibit 3.1   Common Types of Marketing Research Projects

- Usage and Attitude Studies
- Concept Tests
- Tracking Studies
- Segmentation Studies
- Product Testing
- New Product Testing
- Test Marketing
- Advertising Research
- Name Testing
- Package Research

Many problems can be translated quickly and with accuracy into one of the standard research designs outlined in Exhibit 3.1. However, there are cases where premature labelling of a marketing problem as a specific type of marketing research project results in the wrong type of information being collected and the original need for information not being properly addressed.

Each of the research studies detailed in Exhibit 3.1 can progress through the three information phases of exploratory, descriptive and causal research. Although most studies tend to be defined as descriptive research, many would benefit from more careful consideration of the exploratory stage and extension to the causal research phase. In practice, the distinction between exploratory, descriptive and causal research is not always made.

Some of the above studies are typically conducted using a specific type of fieldwork; for example, concept tests are usually conducted in face-to-face interviews. However, most of the research types are flexible enough to accommodate the fieldwork procedure that is most appropriate given the specific domain of the study at hand. Accurate research design is essential for the proper execution of the marketing research project and for supplying the right information for the marketing problem. There are three essential components to the marketing research design task. Exhibit 3.2 presents the different combinations of problem type, information requirements and field methodology which might be employed in any one project.

Exhibit 3.2 Designing the Marketing Research Project		
Type of Marketing Research Problem	*Information Requirements*	*Field Methodology*
Usage and Attitude Studies	Exploratory Information	Depth Interviews
Concept Tests	Descriptive Information	Focus Groups
Tracking Studies	Causal Information	Personal Interviews
Segmentation Studies		Telephone Interviews
Product Testing		Mall Intercepts
New Product Research		Self-Administered Questionnaires
Test Marketing		
Advertising Research		
Name Testing		
Package Research		

Exhibit 3.3 shows another way of deciding on the possible design considerations for methods used to collect information. Given a problem, the researcher will want to decide on the best possible approach to answer the following questions:

- Is the problem better solved by quantitative rather than qualitative methods?
- Do I have to design a special study to solve the problem or can I make use of an omnibus study or an ongoing panel?
- Does the study call for personal interviews or can I use alternative, less expensive methods like telephone or mail surveys?
- Can the interviews be carried out in a shopping mall?

By answering questions like these, the researcher can arrive at one or more research designs appropriate to the problem. An experienced researcher often arrives at suitable research designs by mentally eliminating the inappropriate ones and evaluating the pertinent designs according to a set of constant criteria. The final design chosen would depend on several factors, such as:

- the suitability of the design for the given problem
- cost considerations
- the level of accuracy desired
- timing constraints
- other variable project-specific aspects

Although the designs are shown as alternatives in Exhibit 3.3, they are not mutually exclusive. Few problems require unique research designs. Thus, for example, a research study may include a qualitative phase using focus groups, followed by an ad hoc quantitative stage using both telephone interviews and face-to-face, mall-intercept interviews.

Exhibit 3.3   Classification of Research Methods

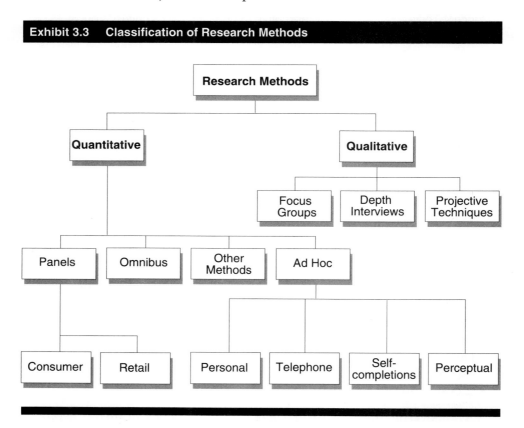

STANDARD RESEARCH DESIGNS

One of the most critical things to understand in marketing research is that the primary aim of a research design is to answer the research questions, and subsequently the marketing questions, in an effective way while keeping the costs at a reasonable level. In practice, the marketing scope, the marketing research objectives, and the costs of the study determine the research design. Listed in Exhibit 3.4 are the most commonly encountered marketing research project designs and some of the marketing problems that each is intended to address.

Exhibit 3.4 Marketing Problems and Research Techniques

Marketing Problem/Issue	Research Technique
Who and how many use the product category/brands?	**Usage and attitude Studies**

Marketing Problem/Issue — *Research Technique*

Who and how many use the product category/brands?

What are the differences between heavy and light users?

What are the main features of their behaviour and habits—frequency of purchase, brand loyalty, what do they mix it with?

What are their attitudes, beliefs, values to existing brands?

What are their product requirements?

What are the brand's strengths and weaknesses?

Tell me everything I ever wanted to know about ...!

Usage and attitude Studies

Which of a number of alternative new product ideas has the most appeal?

Is the idea easy to understand?

What expectations and associations does it generate?

Do you perceive distinct benefits for this product over those products currently on the market?

Are the claims about this product believable?

Would you buy this product?

Would you replace your current brand with this new brand?

Would this product meet a real need?

What improvements can you suggest in various attributes of the concept?

How frequently would you use the brand?

Who would use the brand?

What share potential does it have?

If I reposition my brand this way, will it work?

Concept Tests

Which is the preferred prototype?

How much is the "improved" formulation liked?

Will consumers buy a "cost-reduced product"?

Is our product acceptable to consumers?

Product Testing

continued

Is our product marginally or much
better or worse than the competition?

Can we get away with substituting carob
for chocolate?

Does the product we've developed deliver its promise?

Which brand is better - ours or P&G's?

How does the market segment (demographics, psychographics, behaviour, attitudes, lifestyles)?	**Segmentation Studies**

How large are the segments?

What's the potential of the segments?

How can each segment be reached with ads?

Can I improve my brand's current positioning?

Are there any gaps in the market that can be
exploited?

What are the levels of brand and advertising awareness over time?	**Tracking Studies**

What are the progressing levels of trial
and purchase?

Is there any conversion to occasional and
regular usage?

Is the advertising communicating, compared to
last quarter, last year, etc.?

How have attitudes towards the brand changed?

How has our brand's image changed relative to
that of competitive brands?

How believable is our advertising?	**Advertising Research**

How relevant is our advertising to the
target consumers?

How much do the target consumers
like our advertising?

How much power does our advertising
have over the receivers?

To what does our advertising appeal?

Does our advertising provide the information
that the consumers want?

Has our advertising shifted consumer attitudes?

How will our new brand fare in an actual market situation?	**Test Marketing**

How well does the new brand gain retailer
interest?

continued

How does the new brand do against real competition?

Is the marketing plan strong enough to gain initial trial?

Does repeat purchase build as expected after initial trial?

Which is the best name out of the alternatives?

Which name connotes the benefits that consumers want most?

Is the name easily pronounced?

Does the name have any secondary meanings?

Is the name remembered?

Do the target consumers like the name?

Name Testing

Which package communicates best on the shelf?

Which package is most visually appealing?

Which package is most useful to consumers?

Which package produces the best imagery of the brand to consumers?

Package Research

How effective is our advertising in building awareness of the new brand?

Which brands will our new brand compete against?

How effective is our marketing plan in encouraging initial trial?t

Will the brand characteristics entice consumers to repeat purchase?

How strong is the likability of the brand?

How can we answer all of the above as inexpensively as possible?

New Product Research

LEVEL OF INFORMATION REQUIREMENTS

Although practical marketing research projects don't often characterize studies according to their information requirements, it's often very helpful to view projects from this perspective. A common way of referring to the information requirements of marketing research projects is as follows:

- exploratory studies
- descriptive studies
- causal studies

EXPLORATORY STUDIES

Suppose that a company has identified a marketing problem significant enough that the marketing research staff has been called to a meeting to discuss the options. It's important that someone at that first meeting recognize that the marketing issue and the marketing research problem are not understood well enough to enter immediately into a full survey project. At the beginning of a new research project, a company needs to explore the basic nature of the marketing issue that's facing it in order to plan an effective fact-gathering mission (a survey). Since exploratory studies are conducted at the very beginning of a project, there's little more to rely upon than the experience of the marketing managers, the firm's marketing research manager, and the consulting marketing research project director.

There is always a great temptation to charge the marketing and research staff with the task of defining the project completely and of getting on with the descriptive or causal study. When this acceleration of the project occurs, the information gathered by that study might not coincide with the real need to solve the marketing problem. The research team might be so frantic to get something done, that it loses its focus on the problem. A project that is improperly designed at the early stages cannot be saved through later manipulations. The design must be done sensitively right from the beginning.

The main output from an exploratory study is a solid understanding of the nature of the marketing problem and a set of hypotheses which can be tested through survey research.

DESCRIPTIVE RESEARCH

Descriptive research constitutes the bulk of marketing research activities. A descriptive study begins with a good understanding of the marketing problem and of the marketing research problem. This understanding is based on experience, knowledge of how the study will be executed, and on a set of hypotheses that describe the relationships between the variables in the study. The difference between exploratory and descriptive research is that descriptive studies have well defined hypotheses of relationships between variables, while exploratory studies contain basic intuitive hypotheses, at best.

In large firms, there's typically no lack of experience on the topic being researched since the current project is sometimes a re-creation of some past study on the same topic. At the very least, the marketing manager or, especially, the marketing research consultants have executed similar studies on other brands many times in the past. For example, concept tests are executed several times each year at most of the large packaged goods companies around Toronto. Consequently, somebody in the marketing research depart-ment or among the marketing management staff has had experience of that type of study. However, a particular firm might never actually have executed a simulated-test-market study (STM) for a new product, even though several people in the firm might have substantial understanding of the nature and value of STMs. The expertise necessary to conduct an STM, for example, is available from consultants at firms such as The Creative Research Group, Burke International Research, Thompson-Lightstone & Company, and Canadian Facts.

The end report of a descriptive study provides a portrait of the type of people who are heavy users of a product, for example. These descriptions would be fairly complete and the relationships between some of the variables would be tested through standard statistical hypothesis testing procedures.

In practice, the exploratory, descriptive, and causal stages are not singled-out for specific identification during a project. In fact, most projects would be called descriptive. If asked, many researchers would say that "standard" marketing research projects (i.e., descriptive studies) contain information that leads to conclusions regarding cause-effect relationships. To some extent, they'd be right. However, the term *causal study* is reserved for more formal studies specifically designed to test causal hypotheses.

CAUSAL RESEARCH

Naturally, causal research is directed at investigating and establishing the cause of some phenomenon. The behavioural effects of consumers' attitudes and states as represented by several marketing variables are the concentra-tion of many causal studies. For example, a soap manufacturer might be interested in whether the advertising or the pricing for brands of soap is more instrumental in causing shifts in the demand for the brands within the cate-gory. Or a dog food manufacturer might need to determine whether media advertising or acceptability to the pet is more effective in causing shifts among category brands.

While causal research is potentially the most beneficial type of research, it's also the most difficult to gain approval for and to execute. Causal research is usually the most expensive type to carry out because of

- the great care needed in designing the project;
- the requirement for very highly qualified project directors, analysts and interpreters of the findings; and
- higher field costs resulting from the more intricate designs.

Causal hypotheses are directed at proposing and testing relationships between more variables than are descriptive hypotheses. The intention with causal hypotheses is to be able to conclude specific cause-effect relationships that can be used to direct the highest-level marketing decisions. The ideal would be to provide the advertising manager, for example, with information that would allow for the achievement of specific sales figures based on the total advertising budget and the placement and timing of that budget.

Unfortunately, causal research has not been spectacularly impressive in its contribution to marketing practice. However, academic researchers have been paying increasing attention to this area during the past 10 years.

DATA COLLECTION METHODOLOGY

Regardless of the type of marketing problem, the methods used for obtaining information may be quite diverse. Although marketing research is often equated with a survey, this is not always the case. Sometimes qualitative information is best suited to the needs of a marketing problem, while in other cases a large cross-Canada survey is absolutely necessary. It's often difficult to indicate where one project begins and another ends. And since projects can have all three information components, exploratory, descriptive and causal, the breadth of data collection can be extensive.

QUALITATIVE RESEARCH

Qualitative research is the term used to refer to studies that obtain information in the form of verbatim comments resulting from unstructured conversations with a relatively small number of respondents. The best known types of qualitative research are focus groups and in-depth personal interviews. While focus groups are normally conducted with eight to twelve people, in-depth personal interviews are face-to-face conversations between the researcher and one respondent. The findings from focus groups and in-depth personal interviews are typically summaries of the comments of the respondents, punctuated with their verbatim quotes.

Qualitative research is used most often to obtain information for exploratory studies. However, occasionally qualitative research is used to obtain clarifications of the findings of descriptive and causal research. From time to time, quantitative findings can't be effectively assessed by the researchers. A focus group presented with those same research results might illuminate the findings and give them substantial usefulness. Qualitative research is explored in considerable detail in Chapter 5.

Exhibit 3.5 When Qualitative Research is Useful

A qualitative research design is chosen when our main interest is in:

- obtaining background information
- understanding consumer language and vocabulary
- tracing salient behaviour patterns, attitudes and motivations
- exploring alternative concepts
- investigating suspected problem areas
- screening contenders for large-scale studies
- piloting or amplifying quantitative studies
- generating hypotheses for further testing

For some of the situations described in Exhibit 3.5, it is also possible to use quantitative research. Therefore, these guidelines cannot be used as criteria for determining whether one should do a qualitative study. However, as one gains experience in research, it becomes an easier task to determine the appropriateness of qualitative research for a given problem.

QUANTITATIVE RESEARCH

The bulk of marketing research uses quantitative techniques. The term *quantitative research* is used to describe virtually any research project in which the interpretation depends on the numbers and percentages obtained from the investigation. Qualitative and quantitative research complement and strengthen each other when used to solve well defined research problems.

Quantitative research, when used in a formal sense, refers to studies that yield results with known accuracy. For example, if the results indicate that 20% of the consumers use brand X, the analyst will be able to state the margin of error on this percentage along with the likelihood of error because these are aspects that can be mathematically calculated. (This topic will be covered in Chapters 14 and 21.)

Compared to qualitative studies, quantitative studies use larger numbers of respondents and generally ask questions to which the respondent can give a one- or two-word answer rather than one or several sentences. Representative samples (especially in large-scale studies), structured interviews, and formal questionnaires generally characterize quantitative studies. The interpretation of the results is based more on the numbers obtained rather than on the intuition of the researcher.

Exhibit 3.6 Characteristics of Quantitative Studies

- Studies where the findings are presented in numerical fashion, e.g., in tables, graphs or equations
- Numerical data are based on large numbers of data points
- May be based on secondary sources of data or on surveys conducted with structured questionnaires
- Formal findings from quantitative surveys can be stated with known accuracy
- Quantitative studies are used more for measuring and evaluating rather than for investigating and exploring
- Most quantitative surveys use telephone or personal interviews or rely on mailed questionnaires

Qualitative study interviewers (or moderators) often have substantial experience in quantitative marketing research as well. Thus, qualitative moderators are often capable of interpreting the findings from a qualitative study and drawing relevant implications for related quantitative projects. However, the typical interviewer in a quantitative study specializes in survey interviewing and is not usually trained or experienced in other aspects of research. Consequently, he or she might not appreciate the full importance of qualitative research to the understanding of the marketing problem and the success of the project.

Quantitative studies are used more for measuring and evaluating rather than for investigating and exploring. Most research studies are assumed to belong to this category, even when they do not fulfill the stringent criteria to deserve the title. Most of this book, therefore, is devoted to understanding the mechanics of doing what is loosely described as quantitative research.

Quantitative studies collect information through interviews with samples of people from the target audience or through investigating existing data obtained from various sources. However, the method of collecting information may differ from study to study. Most quantitative surveys use either telephone or personal interviews. Some studies (e.g., mail surveys) use self-completion techniques by asking the respondents to fill-in their answers to questions on printed questionnaires. Others use observational techniques where, for example, the behaviour of shoppers when selecting popping corn at supermarkets would be watched by hidden researchers. Once they have made their selections, the subjects may then be interviewed.

PERSONAL INTERVIEWS

Personal interviews can take place in the home, on the street, in shopping malls, in pre-arranged locations (e.g., a large meeting room where respondents can participate in a taste test) or in places people congregate with a specific purpose (e.g., a polling station or football game).

IN-HOME PERSONAL INTERVIEWS   The method in which the interviewer personally visits the homes of the respondents for the purpose of collecting information is called the in-home interview technique. In-home interviews allow for accurate selection of respondents since the interviewer can ask to speak to a specific person. For this reason, they are particularly well suited for large-scale quantitative studies. The main advantages of in-home interviews are listed in Exhibit 3.7.

Exhibit 3.7 Main Advantages of In-Home Interviews

- Compared to other forms of interviews, the respondents are, in general, more cooperative
- Interviewers can establish a higher degree of rapport with the respondents
- A relatively more complex and lengthy questionnaire can be administered with greater ease
- Prompting and probing can be done more effectively
- Personal interviews allow for the presentation of visual aids and stimuli during the course of the interview

On the negative side, in-home interviews can be relatively more expensive, especially when carried out in non-urban areas. In some cases, due to restrictions on transportation, availability of interviewers, and the availability of respondents at any given time, personal interviews may be difficult to execute. Another problem associated with in-home interviewing is that only a minimal degree of control can be exercised over interviewers in remote locations. If an interviewer does not understand the proper questioning process, this might not be caught until several of the completed questionnaires are edited. Even then, subtle problems might never be identified. Also, when the subject matter includes personally sensitive and potentially embarrassing topics, personal interviews might result in more distorted responses since there is no direct observation of an interviewer's diplomacy with regard to delicate matters and, therefore, no opportunity of correcting any interviewing faults.

MALL OR CENTRAL LOCATION PERSONAL INTERVIEWS   In mall or central location personal interviewing, the respondents are invited to a central location, such as a shopping mall, theatre, auditorium or meeting room, where an interview can be held. Typically, respondents for these studies are recruited using shopping mall intercept procedures and, to a lesser extent, through telephone screening interviews. In the mall-intercept technique, potential respondents are intercepted in shopping malls by interviewers for preliminary information gathering. If the respondents qualify, they are invited into an auditorium, an interview room, a van or a screened-off area to participate in further tests. The advantages are listed in Exhibit 3.8.

Exhibit 3.8   Mall Intercepts or Central Location Personal Interviewing

Central location interviewing is particularly useful when:
- The tests require bulky or elaborate material or use gadgets
- Commercials are to be judged by respondents
- Taste tests need to be conducted
- The tests involve different sensory modalities
- Statistical accuracy is not important
- The study involves simulated shopping behaviour

Many research houses have permanent interviewing facilities in shopping malls. Although phrases such as "ABC Research bought Brightside Mall" are fairly commonly used by marketing research practitioners, this really means that ABC leased space in the mall and has exclusive rights to conduct survey research in Brightside during the term of their lease. Sometimes a research house will rent out its time in the mall when it has no study being fielded. Also, some fieldwork firms generously allow student groups to use their mall rights for short course projects.

The main advantages of central location interviews are that they offer all the advantages of personal interviews discussed earlier, are cheaper than in-home interviews, can handle unwieldy stimulus materials and equipment and can be relatively fast. Mall intercepts provide the flexibility of combining interviewer-administered questions and self-completion questions within a cohesive framework and relatively short time period. The main disadvantages of this method are that the respondents are seldom representative in a statistical sense, that the response rate can be low and that respondents may not want to participate in a lengthy test when they are in the middle of their shopping.

Current and Future Challenges for Mall Interviewing

"Mall intercepts have replaced much door-to-door interviewing, once a standard technique. Money is the reason. While other techniques can yield more representative and projectable samples, door-to-door interviewers are expensive to hire, and telephone interviewing precludes face-to-face interaction that is required in some product and advertising testing.

"Ninety-five percent of all American households shop at malls at least once a year; two thirds go once every two weeks. Compared to total population proportions, however, mall customers tend to be more affluent, and on weekdays more seniors and teens are present.

"Increasingly, critics maintain that mall shoppers are not representative of the larger population, making survey results unprojectable. The sample might not be representative of the people who shop in the mall, depending on selection criteria. Even within a mall, more low-income respondents are found near entrances close to bus stops than near entrances close to parking lots.

"In textbooks, mall-shopper samples are considered non-probability samples with 'no theoretical basis for estimating population characteristics', so public opinion surveys are seldom done in malls. Academic researchers have studied the biases and suggest weighting frequent mall shoppers so they are not overrepresented and randomly placing interviewers proportionate to pedestrian taffic.

"Practitioners seem to have fewer qualms than academics. Market Facts of Chicago found in October 1988 that 89 percent of the 140 largest USA product and service companies used mall intercepts and that 58 percent of these spent more on this technique than on any other. Mall intercepts are said to be quick, easy and inexpensive. Florence Skelly says that enough data exist on specific malls' shoppers across the USA to create slightly biased random population samples.

"Perhaps it is mall owners who will end mall interviewing. Managers are growing skittish about allowing interviewers on their premises, apparently from a civil rights point of view: if they allow non-lessee researchers onto their premises, are they bound to accept religious groups?"

SOURCE: Gray Hammond, "International Intelligence", *PMRS Imprints* (Toronto: Professional Marketing Research Society), November 1989, p.26.

TELEPHONE INTERVIEWS

In recent years, telephone ownership has become sufficiently high in some parts of the world to make the telephone an adequate medium for collecting representative opinion on many subjects. Therefore, a large proportion of marketing research depends on telephone interviews as a method of data collection. In addition to being an alternative method of data collection, telephone interviews have some special advantages, which are presented in Exhibit 3.9

Exhibit 3.9   How Telephone Interviews Are Useful

- For contact screening for main studies
- For measuring the immediate recall of commercials and advertisements
- For assessing the immediate impact of a newly announced government policy
- For continuous political polling

Telephone surveys in larger cities are conducted from central locations. This allows for the interviews to be monitored by field supervisors. In addition, Central Location Telephone interviewing (CLT) can be computer assisted as will be described in Chapter 8 (Computer Assisted Telephone Interviewing or CATI). In several small centres, however, telephone interviews are carried out by interviewers from their own homes, with virtually no supervision. Substantial inconsistencies among the work of the interviewers may develop and never be identified except by a particularly sensitive field supervisor.

One of the main differences between marketing research in Canada and in the United States pertains to telephone interviewing locations. In the U.S., telephone interviewing is more often conducted from central facilities than it is in Canada. The reason for this contrast lies primarily in the differences in telephone charges. In the U.S., the WATS (Wide Area Telecommunications Service) line charges are less costly than they are in Canada and research budgets can more easily cover the costs of central location interviewing, with all of its advantages of control and speed. Consequently, in the U.S. the extreme of CLT is quite common, i.e., where all of the telephone interviewing for a cross-U.S. study would be conducted from one central facility in, say, Chicago. Some cross-Canada studies are conducted from one central location, e.g., Toronto. However, the incidence of these studies is less than in the U.S.

Exhibit 3.10 Advantages and Disadvantages of Telephone Interviews

Telephone interviews offer several advantages over other forms of interviews, in particular, personal interviews:

- Telephone interviews are less expensive
- They are faster
- They are better controlled (in central locations)
- They have (in practice) fewer restrictive sample frames
- When they are computer assisted, complex questionnaires can be administered with relative ease

Disadvantages associated with telephone interviews include:

- Problems of screening
- Easy refusals
- Limited rapport between interviewer and respondent
- Inability to do physical checks or present visual stimuli
- Restrictions on open-ended questions due to constraints on the time available for recording answers.

MAIL SURVEYS

The mail survey is a classic example of the self-completion technique. In mail surveys, questionnaires are mailed to selected respondents (or to the members of a panel) who are asked to complete and return them within a specified time. Such surveys are particularly useful where a list of the names and addresses of the target respondent audience is available.

Exhibit 3.11 Common Uses of Mail Surveys

- Surveys of the membership of an organization
- Surveys of subscribers to magazines
- Study of customers of a small retail outlet or a financial institution
- Buyers of a given product or service

Mail surveys can be low cost and they seem deceptively simple to execute. Consequently, many inexperienced people tend to write self-completion questionnaires without realizing their true complexities and that there are major differences between mail surveys and interviewer-administered surveys.

A great deal of care must be taken with the development of a self-completion questionnaire. Remember, this is the only type of questionnaire that is actually seen by the respondents. Consequently, not only must the questions and answers be perfect, but the physical placement of the questions on the page and the overall visual appearance of the questionnaire must motivate the respondent to begin, continue, complete and return the questionnaire. (The procedures for developing and executing successful mail surveys will be presented in a subsequent chapter.) For example, the following question could cause considerable confusion and non-valid responses.

Q.17   Could you tell me the number of rolls of toilet tissue which you've bought during the past year?

0–10 _____   10–20 _____   20–30 _____   30–40 _____
50–60 _____   60–100 _____   100–150 _____   150–200 _____

However, the question could be reconstructed and rephrased in the following way:

Q.17   How many rolls of toilet tissue, in total, were bought for use in your household during the past month?

[   ] 0–2
[   ] 3–4
[   ] 5–7
[   ] 8–10
[   ] 11–15
[   ] 16–20
[   ] 21 or more

One advantage of mail surveys is that the questionnaires are all printed in the same format. Each respondent receives a questionnaire that is exactly the same as that received by every other respondent. And since no interviewers are involved, there's no concern about interviewing inconsistencies and other fieldwork difficulties that might somewhat alter what one respondent hears compared to what another might hear. The fact that no interviewers or field supervisors are needed to carry out the study ensures the respondent's anonymity (just omit the name and address questions). In addition, respondents can give considered responses at their own pace.

However, the lack of an interviewer is a major drawback, as well as a major benefit, of mail surveys. One of the main difficulties is that there is no interviewer present to clarify, probe, ensure that skip patterns (e.g., instructions for skipping from question 4 to question 8 if the answer to question 4 is "yes", but continuing to question 5 if the answer to question 4 is "no") are followed correctly and that the information provided is internally consistent. One of the jobs of the field supervisor is to ensure that interviewers are consistent in the way in which they read the questions, record answers, probe, present visual and audio stimuli, and so on.

Most mail surveys (especially the ad hoc variety) suffer from several shortcomings. Complex skip-patterns cannot usually be accommodated and the researcher cannot withhold anything from the respondents to be revealed at a specific stage of the questioning. Brand awareness questions are most effectively used where an unaided awareness question (e.g., "Please tell me the names of all the brands of chocolate candy bars that you're aware of") is followed by an aided awareness question (e.g., "Have you ever heard of Skor chocolate bar, or not?"). Unfortunately, this sequence can't be used in self-completion questionnaires because respondents will usually look ahead and find the brand names to fill in the unaided question. Further problems arise when the respondent consults with his or her family and friends before responding to a question.

The speed of completion of mail surveys is almost totally in the hands of the respondents. Consequently, the total time span of the fieldwork can be quite long. However, in most surveys cut-off dates are used to limit the response period. Also, the response rate in a mail survey (unless it is a panel) can be very poor. It can be as low as 20% or 30% or as high as 60% to 70%. Low interest surveys can have response rates lower than 10%.

Field Procedures to Increase Response Rates in Mail Studies

The following procedures can coax the response rates above 50% and can accelerate the response time:

- The survey is of special interest to the respondents (most marketing research does not fall under this category)
- There is negative reinforcement for not responding (e.g., "Your name will not be included in the membership directory unless you return the questionnaire before October 1")
- There is a high-interest, positive reinforcement for responding (e.g., "All those who respond before October 1 will be eligible for a draw for a two-week vacation in Acapulco")
- Financial incentives, usually a dollar, are enclosed with the questionnaires
- The respondents are followed up through reminders (this is particularly effective if done by telephone)

PERCEPTUAL METHODS

Perceptual methods include the use of eye-movement cameras, tachisto-scopes, psychogalvanometers, and related technological equipment. They appear quantitative in their orientation as a result of all the gadgetry and readings involved in their implementation. Yet, there is no clear-cut scientific proof, apart from their apparent face validity, that they are effective.

OMNIBUS STUDIES

An omnibus study is a marketing research survey where questions are asked on topics pertinent to several clients. Each client has his or her own information needs; thus, most omnibus projects are studies in which the costs of sampling, the fixed costs of the survey, and collection of the demographic information are shared by all participating clients. Each omnibus sponsor pays costs that are proportional to his or her information requirements. Since the costs of sampling and collecting demographic information can be substantial, shared-cost studies tend to be much less expensive than specially designed custom studies.

Omnibus studies are offered by several large research houses on a regular basis. Participants are usually charged on the basis of the number and the nature of questions they want included. In some cases there may also be a flat fee. Omnibus studies usually provide data tables with minimal or no interpretation. Further analysis and interpretation, if required, are done for an additional fee.

Omnibus studies can be highly specialized. There are omnibus studies that specialize in groups such as teenagers, children, motorists, mothers of babies and infants, etc. Because special groups are expensive to isolate for a sample, shared-cost omnibus studies are particularly valuable when information is needed from these groups.

Omnibus studies can and do achieve considerable cost savings over studies conducted for just one company at a time. The studies are planned well in advance and therefore the total elapsed time to complete the study is relatively short. Because the sample is usually large and well designed, the results tend to be reliable. Another attractive feature of omnibus studies is that they enable the users to track market trends over time.

There are, however, some disadvantages attached to omnibus studies. Most will allow only a limited number of questions per client. Sometimes 10 or 15 questions are more than enough to complete a study, while in other cases this small number would be completely inadequate. Since costs are shared, each sponsor must work within constraints that don't exist in custom-designed, single sponsor studies. The negative aspects of omnibus surveys include:

- less flexibility in questionnaire layout and design
- more restrictions on the visual material that can be shown to respondents
- more rigidity in the precise timing of the study
- the nature of reporting is predetermined

CONSUMER PANELS

Consumer panels are composed of groups of respondents from whom information is collected on a regular basis for use by one specific company. These respondents are recruited and the sample is maintained to represent the population that is of interest for the particular study. The main objective of a panel is to track consumer behaviour over time on a continuous basis.

Consumer panels can be conducted either through *home audits* or *diaries*. In home audits, the interviewer visits the participant on a regular (e.g., weekly) basis and checks the stocks of relevant products, identifies old products from new, checks discarded packs and wrappers, and obtains information on new purchases (e.g., outlet type, price, etc.). In the diary method, panel members record the details of all purchases of relevant products in a pre-printed diary. The diary is returned periodically (e.g., weekly) by mail to the auditing company.

The comments made earlier about mail surveys by and large do not apply to mail panels. In mail panels, respondents are recruited to represent the target audience, usually the general population. Often, substantial efforts are made to maintain the panel members' interest by sending regular incentives, newsletters, conducting contests and sending birthday cards. Because of initial agreement to cooperate (and partly because their panel membership is reinforced), the response rate in mail panels can be very high.

Members of the mail panel can be used for continuous research as well as for one-time studies. Thus, mail panels have all the advantages of custom mail studies while sharing few of the shortcomings associated with one-shot, ad hoc mail surveys.

Problems associated with panels revolve around the sample design and selection, the need for reserve respondents to replace drop-outs, panel profile maintenance, questionnaire restrictions, family influences, etc. The panel may also be conditioned over a period of time to respond to questions in a specific way. Exhibit 3.12 lists some of the typical marketing research questions that can be answered through mail panels.

Exhibit 3.12 Types of Questions Answered by Consumer Panels

- How many people are buying my product?
- Who are these people?
- How much do they buy and in what pack sizes?
- Is this proportion increasing or decreasing?
- Who are our competitors?
- What is the state of their business?
- Who are we gaining business from?
- Who are we losing business to?
- What is the extent of brand loyalty in the market?
- What is the frequency of purchase?
- What is the response to promotions?
- How does performance vary by area and outlet type?

RETAIL AUDIT PANELS

Retail audits provide a continuous measure of the effect on consumer purchases, retailer stocks and distribution of short- and long-term sales and marketing activities. This is done through auditing retail outlets for stocks, purchases, and sales. The rationale for retail audits is that company sales records and wholesale figures are somewhat out of step with actual consumer purchases.

Most audit data are derived from large, national samples, operated on a syndicated basis (e.g., A.C. Nielsen). Test audits may be syndicated or exclusive. Large, national audits use stratified samples such that all types of retail outlets are adequately represented. They usually represent distinct product groups like confectionery or tobacco. Retail audits are based on panels of stores that are audited on a regular basis. Current sales are obtained by using the formula: *Sales = Previous Stocks + Deliveries – Current Stocks*. These data are accumulated and projected to the population within each stratum.

The major problem associated with retail panels is obtaining the cooperation of selected, representative stores, especially retail chains, and other large organizations where such additional record-keeping would be an onerous task. Also, the cost of some syndicated studies is quite high.

Exhibit 3.13 shows the principal data obtained through panels and their uses. Retail audits provide valuable information to the marketer. Their limitations usually arise from a lack of cooperation from some outlets, the sample's becoming out-of-date over time, introduction of new non-conventional outlets, and other such factors. The data are also subject to auditing errors.

Exhibit 3.13 Retail Audit Panels

Principal Data

- Consumer purchases—in total and by brand—volume/shares
- Retailer purchases—in total and by brand—volume/shares
- Retailer stocks—in total and by brand—volume/shares
- Distribution—% handling/% in stock/% out-of-stock
- Average purchases and average stocks per outlet
- Stock cover—number of day's supply
- Displays and facings
- Average prices

Uses

- Tracking your own competitive sales performance
- Monitoring stock levels
- Checking distribution and out-of-stocks
- Analyses by region and by outlet type
- Evaluating test market

Data Collection Methodology

The procedures for obtaining information from respondents are very diverse in marketing research. Choosing the most appropriate method depends on the type of marketing research problem, the information requirements, the accuracy desired, the project budget, the geographical area, the culture of the respondents and many other things. The data collection methodologies used most often include the following:

Qualitative Research

- In-depth personal interviews
- Focus group interviews

Quantitative Research

- In-home personal interviews
- Mall intercept and central location personal interviews
- Telephone interviews
- Self-administered surveys, including mail surveys
- Perceptual methods
- Omnibus studies
- Consumer panels
- Retail audit panels

SUMMARY

The ability to design a marketing research study to achieve the project objectives is an essential ability of any professional marketing researcher. This chapter introduced the design of marketing research from the perspective of the type of marketing research problem, the information requirements and the field methodology useful for collecting that information.

1. The types of marketing research problems were described as usage and attitude studies, concept tests, product testing, segmentation research, tracking research, advertising research, test marketing, name testing, package research and new product research. Although many other types exist, these 10 span a range of problems that capture the scope of marketing research.

2. The information requirements of a marketing research project might be exploratory, descriptive or causal. Exploratory research is conducted when little is known objectively about a marketing problem area or about a group of people. Talking in depth to customers and patrons might unearth much more valuable information than that obtained from conducting a survey based on questions that are not well formulated because of the researchers' lack of understanding of how customers approach the purchase or usage situation.

   Descriptive research includes most marketing research projects. The research is conducted on problems that are fairly well understood, among customers who can be identified clearly and recruited fairly easily, to provide marketing information for decisions that are well defined except for some lack of market information.

   Causal studies aim to establish the reasons why people do things within the social or market segment important to the marketers. These projects are typically the most sophisticated and challenging in marketing research. They often involve recruiting experimental and control samples and comparing the difference in attitudes and behaviour between the two when the experimental group is exposed to the marketer's message or product.

3. The sources of marketing research information and variety of ways of collecting that information are quite extensive. There is the basic difference between qualitative and quantitative studies, but also there are the specific needs and benefits of each of the many ways of conducting the data collection task. These include personal interviews in people's homes or work or in a central location such as a shopping mall. Telephone interviews are used extensively in marketing research because of their speed, versatility and cost. Mail surveys also have their place in collecting information

from large numbers of people when long questionnaires must be used. Procedures such as perceptual methods, omnibus studies, consumer panels and retail audit panels play important roles in collecting data for many specialized information needs of marketing.

Proper research design must be a natural part of every marketing researcher's working life. However, it's also an area that requires continuing education and refinement of the researcher's knowledge as well as skills based on experience.

NOW THINK ABOUT THIS

1. You're the manager of marketing research for a large beverage manufacturer (alcoholic or non-alcoholic), adapt the usage and attitude questions from Exhibit 3.4 to that context.
2. Take one of the questions which you wrote for question 1 and write it for an exploratory study and also for a causal study.
3. Suppose that you're the director of a project pertaining to canned soup. In-home personal interviews will be conducted to collect the data. List three questions that could be asked using personal interviews but could not be asked in a mail questionnaire.
4. List three benefits of using mall-intercept interviews over telephone interviews.
5. What are two key benefits of a panel?
6. Why does additional care have to be taken when conducting public sector marketing research?

APPENDIX 3A

The preceding discussion of research design in this chapter is pertinent to almost any application area of marketing research. However, every business or social area that uses marketing research has its own particular perspective of what marketing research design should be.

THE PUBLIC USE OF MARKET AND OPINION RESEARCH

Because of the sometimes very prominent use of marketing research in public issues, there is substantial pressure from outside the industry for very high quality work. The following excerpt from the Advertising Research Foundation (1987) confirms the need for attention to proper design and execution of research studies.

Research is being used increasingly for public purposes:
- as evidence in legal cases;
- as evidence in testimony in government and other public hearings;
- in support of advertising or publicity claims for product, candidates or causes;
- as support for news stories and features which appear in the press and other media.

These public purposes can and do impact broadly on our lives and our institutions. They are creating a new role for research and a need for new ways to assess its soundness and value.

Research used for public purposes is different from internal or private research in its implications and in its quality requirements. *Research used internally* by companies, individuals or governments only has to meet the requirements of its sponsor, and while it is often done to exacting specifications, it may also be done to standards that are less demanding than those required for public research. It may be useful to its sponsors even though it is selective in its orientation, or based on very limited cases, tests or opinions.

However, *when research is put to public purpose* the situation is different. This research can affect the interests of people and organizations who have neither solicited it nor supported it. Once it is published or reported it may come to be put to purposes for which it was not intended, and the public use may impute authority to the research not anticipated by those who designed and conducted it. It may lend an importance that the research itself does not warrant.

Given the potential fallout from research that is put to public use, it is essential that such research be conducted carefully and judged critically.

This is not to say that the standards for such research should be dogmatic or unrealistic. Few absolute standards of quality ever apply to market and opinion research. Decisions about what to do and how many cases to study, and what words to use to communicate what meaning are often pragmatic and, on occasion, somewhat arbitrary.

The realities of the field make compromise inevitable and perfection impossible. Nonetheless, when research is put to public use, it is essential that it be fairly and competently conducted and that it be honestly reported.

Listed below are a number of factors which affect the quality of research. All of them must be considered when the research is judged:

a. Origin—What is behind the research—intent and background.

b. Design—The concept and the plan—the universe, method and measures used.

c. Execution—Collecting and handling the information—competence and conscientiousness.

d. Stability—Sample size and reliability—overall accuracy.

e. Applicability—Generalizing the findings—providing the context.

f. Meaning—Interpretations and conclusions—rigorous objectivity and sound judgment.

g. Candor—Open reporting and disclosure—direct, simple and free of distortions.

A good deal of information is needed to assess how research results may legitimately be used. Those who do the research should provide whatever is needed to judge it. If needed information is not supplied, and the users of the research cannot secure it on their own inquiry and initiative, an assumption that the information would reflect negatively on the study is probably justified.

SOURCE: *Guidelines for the Public Use of Market and Opinion Research*, Public Affairs Council of the Advertising Research Foundation, as reprinted in PMRS (British Columbia Chapter) Newsletter, February 1987.

POLL REPORTING IN NEWSPAPERS

Newspapers have become increasingly important in the dissemination of marketing research findings. In order to help reporters to ask the questions important to the accurate reporting of survey research findings, the American Newspaper Publishers Association (1980) published the following guide.

Newsroom Guide To Polls & Surveys
Specific Questions to Ask About Polls or Surveys

The Guide attempts to help journalists ask critical questions about polls and to understand and evaluate them. These critical questions include the standards for disclosure of the American Association of Public Opinion Research (AAPOR) and the National Council on Public Polls (NCPP).

Journalists should ask these questions about polls and surveys, and the answers to many of them should appear in news stories (or sidebars) about polls:

a. Who sponsored (paid for) the poll and who conducted it?

b. What were the actual questions asked, including the response choices offered the persons answering? (We strongly urge that the actual wording of the key questions be printed along with the news story.)

c. What was the population (or universe) which was sampled?

d. Was a probability (random) sample used? (If not, don't generalize to a larger group of people.)

e. What was the size of the total sample? Of subsamples or specific groups (such as registered voters) analyzed in the poll results?

f. (If a probability sample was drawn) What is the estimated sampling error for the total sample? For any subsamples or specific groups?

g. What was the completion rate (response rate)? How many persons were interviewed from the total sample?

h. What results (if any) are based on only part of the total sample?

i. Was any weighting technique used to make the sample more representative of the population? (Note: This is a fairly common practice among survey researchers and does not imply anything "wrong" with the data.)

j. Are there any data available on population characteristics to compare with sample characteristics (such as percentages of blacks, males, females, registered Democrats, etc.)? Was such a comparison done?

k. How were the interviews done? (Face-to-face in the respondent's home, by telephone from a central location, by mail, etc.)

l. When were the interviews done? What was happening at the time of the interviewing which might have influenced people's answers?

m. Could you as a journalist answer the questions in the survey? Were the questions clear and unambiguous?

n. What do other polls on the same subject say?

o. What is the purpose of the survey or poll? Who is going to use the results for what purpose?

p. What else was found? Is the poll sponsor releasing data selectively, avoiding disclosure of less flattering results from other questions?

SOURCE: *Newsroom Guide to Polls and Surveys*, Bloomington: Indiana University Press, 1990.

4 The Marketing Research Proposal

WHAT YOU WILL LEARN IN THIS CHAPTER

- How a formal proposal, proposal to formalize, and a letter proposal differ
- Which projects to bid on and which to pass
- How to write a formal marketing research proposal
- The importance of a proposal
- How a proposal can be used as a working project plan

THE COMMUNICATION FUNCTION OF THE MARKETING RESEARCH PROPOSAL

The most critical function in any area of consulting is clear and effective communication. The attractive message gets attention, the clear message gets read, the message containing the right promise gets acted upon, and the author of the message that gives true and good advice gets asked back to do another project.

When a client has been served successfully several times by a consultant, then the communication process between the two parties becomes more natural and easier. This is because of the client's familiarity with the role of marketing research and with the consultant's work in particular. However, when a client is considering his or her first marketing research project, the consultant has a responsibility to inform the client about the general practice of marketing research as well as about the specific task to be performed. Documents should always be written in a style that clearly informs the research buyer of the exact nature of what's being proposed and about the consultant's qualifications.

The term *research proposal* is often used as if its nature is fully known. However, there are actually three types of research proposals:

1. the formal proposal;
2. the proposal to formalize; and
3. the outline or letter proposal.

The primary intention of the formal marketing research proposal is to convince a prospective client that the consultant is the most capable to conduct the marketing research project described in the terms of reference. The consultant's competence is usually established by presenting a plan for executing the project that abides by the terms of reference, and shows solid knowledge of the relevant literature and practice. The purpose of this chapter is to help improve the writing of proposals.

The intention of the proposal to formalize is more modest than that of the formal proposal. The proposal to formalize is written after the consultant has been selected and the basic parameters of the project have been informally agreed upon by the consultant and the client. The proposal puts down on paper the points already agreed upon and states the specifics of the project, such as the sample size, the sampling procedure, the field methodology, any special analysis procedures, the completion date, any intermediate reporting dates, and the budget.

The letter proposal states in a less formal fashion the nature of the project that will be undertaken by the consultant. For example, the letter might state that a concept test will be conducted in three specified shopping malls, among a specified number of people, and will begin on such a date with the top-line report to be available within one week of the conclusion of the fieldwork and the final report to be presented within two weeks.

From time to time, you'll be in the advantageous position of submitting a *quote* (i.e., the price for conducting the study) rather than the full proposal described here. At the quote stage, your attention is focused on providing one number—the one that denotes value to your prospective client. Although a brief description of your plan might be necessaary, it will be much shorter than the one presented here.

The principal concentration of this chapter will be on the formal proposal because it encompasses the other two forms. However, while the formal proposal is the typical proposal type used in public sector projects, the proposal to formalize and the letter proposal are the dominant forms used in private company marketing research.

"The problem with most salespeople is that they don't understand their job. They try to take the horse to water and make him drink. Their job is to make the horse thirsty."

Anonymous

Developing a winning research proposal isn't a hard task. In most marketing research projects, if you are asked to submit a proposal, then you are considered to be a qualified and responsible supplier. Don't reduce your chances of success by providing a proposal that is not sound and that doesn't sell your services effectively.

To the new marketing researcher, the placement of this chapter on proposal writing so early in the text might seem somewhat confusing, but we hope it will also be helpful. Some frustration might occur because some of the terms used in referring to parts of marketing research projects may not yet be fully understood. But, if you're a student in a course that has a full field project as its principal focus, you will be required to write a proposal at this stage so that:

1. your professor can approve your project;
2. your prospective client organization can approve your project, understand what you want to study and confirm your project budget; and
3. you can develop a plan of action that you and your project colleagues understand and can follow from now until project completion.

SELECTING PROJECTS TO BID ON

You will not bid or submit a proposal in response to every request for proposals (RFP) that you read. Many marketing research firms consider themselves to be all-purpose and will tend to bid on a wide variety of projects. However, other marketing research consultants have a targeted approach to business development. After having identified the niche that they intend to occupy, they avoid the temptation of proposing to execute projects that might lead them outside their niche strategy. As in any line of endeavour, some projects are just not worth bidding for on financial grounds. Administrators who have never put together an RFP before often fill the terms of reference so full of research wishes that the objectives can't be met by any research firm that has to pay a reasonable per diem fee to its consultants.

Experienced marketing research consultants are usually very capable of costing the project. However, some projects are so large and complex that a formalized scheduling approach can be helpful in developing the timing of project tasks as well as in the costing of the project. This is particularly true for less experienced researchers. Small projects and routine projects don't need a formalized scheduling procedure. However, large projects can be planned most effectively by scheduling the study using the critical path method (CPM), the project evaluation and review technique (PERT), or a Gantt chart. While these techniques are not often used for private-sector research projects, proposals for government contracts must frequently contain a formal project schedule chart. By the use of these methods, personnel fees and project costs can be easily integrated into the schedule to arrive at a total budget. Computer programs, such as MacProject and Micro Planner Plus for the Apple Macintosh computer, provide convenient and attractive ways of planning marketing research projects.

Other problems beyond the financial dimension can make proposal writing nothing more than something you "chalk up to experience." Sometimes, a prospective client is not firmly committed to conducting the project. If this is the case, that client should be honest enough to inform the prospective consultants that the project might never see the light of day. A direct approach to the potential project will be met by professional consultants with honesty in return.

Some consultants will genuinely be too busy to sit down with prospective clients and discuss projects that might never be put to tender. However, many consultants will see this as an opportunity to develop goodwill that might pay off in substantial dividends down the road. Of course, this is just an application of one of the basic principles of human psychology as expressed by Robert Conklin (1979), "To the degree you give others what they want, they will give you what you want! That is the key to persuading, leading, motivating, selling, supervising, influencing, guiding others—getting people to do things for you... For instance, you must *first* give others what they want. Then they give you the things you want. Most people have that twisted around."

Reprinted from *How to Get People to do Things* by Robert Conklin. Copyright ©1979 by Robert J. Conklin. Used with permission by Contemporary Books, Inc.

Clients often return to the same consultant time and time again. This relationship might seem like preferential treatment to the consultant who is trying to win a project from the company. However, it's simply the result of loyalty based on a feeling of comfort and safety which the consultant exudes because of competence, timely reporting and good service over several projects.

THE PROPOSAL OUTLINE

A standard research proposal contains a number of elements, as listed in Exhibit 4.1.

Exhibit 4.1 The Proposal Outline

Cover Letter—(not really part of the proposal, but the proposal submission would seem incomplete without it.)

Title Page

1. **Background Information**

   About the client, the industry and the problem area.

2. **The Marketing Problem/Opportunity**

   This is a clear and comprehensive statement of the marketing problem, opportunity or issue, and the marketing research problem. It is the binding direction of the project.

3. **The Marketing Research Objectives** of the project and the working hypotheses

   This should list the objectives and hypotheses for discussion and consensus. The findings will be expected to address these.

4. **The Proposed Field Methodology**

   This should be explained as fully as possible. However, change might be necessary as the project moves further along.

5. **The Proposed Analysis Procedures**

   In basic projects these are very simple. However, if special techniques are needed, they should be explained.

6. **The Project Schedule**

   Include at least the starting and completion dates, probably milestone dates and maybe a CPM, PERT or Gantt chart.

7. **The Project Budget**

   This is the total fee quote for private projects, more detail for public projects.

8. **The Terms of Agreement and Agreement Form**

   This includes the project conditions for both parties.

9. **Biographical Profiles of Principal Members of the Study Team**

   Clients want to know who's working on the project.

THE BACKGROUND

Since the title page and the cover letter are straightforward, the first stage to be explained is the background. This section should include a brief description of the environment of the problem that precipitated the proposal. The placing of the problem within its business context is often critical to understanding the importance of the problem and the value of the proposed research. In straightforward projects, the background necessary for understanding the formal proposal should not take more than one page. However, in a formal proposal on a large and complex project, the background section might take several pages. In proposals to formalize, the background section will probably be one short paragraph; while one or two sentences are all that's necessary to explain the background in a proposal letter.

The best source of background information is the client. Asking a lot of questions is the way to discover a great deal about the prospective client's business, the competition and the industry. Find out if there are other research reports on the same and related topics that you can read. Try to get permission to study sections of the firm's strategic marketing plan that are relevant to the project. Determine if there's an industry or trade association in the prospect's industry and if the firm is a member. If the answer to those two questions is yes, then get association documents, industry data and research reports.

Trade journals can be a tremendous help in understanding the industry and gaining intelligence about the competition. Is there an industry conference being planned for the near future? If there is and if the project is of a large enough size, then attend that conference and do some firsthand fact (and rumour) gathering among the participants.

Government sources, trade commissions, boards of trade and other business associations can be helpful in completing your initial profile of the firm and its industry. Also, if the firm is of a medium or small size, pay particular attention to the information available from economic development departments in the firm's geographic areas.

THE MARKETING PROBLEM/OPPORTUNITY

The marketing problem section of the proposal is the key justification for the research project. Remember that the purpose of marketing research is to provide information for making better marketing decisions. Consequently, the marketing decision must be important enough to justify the research expenditure. Although some textbooks propose a study to determine the expected value of sample information to be generated by the study and a comparison of that value to the proposed budget prior to approving the proposal, in practice this analysis is very rarely done.

Examples of the marketing problems that can motivate a marketing research proposal were presented in Chapters 1 and 3. Basically, anything that can be considered to be part of marketing (i.e., the four P's of promotion, product, price and place) can legitimately generate a marketing research project that can lead to more effective marketing decisions and increased profit for the firm. A statement of the marketing research problem should be included along with the depiction of the marketing problem.

THE MARKETING RESEARCH OBJECTIVES

The marketing research objectives must be stated succinctly and clearly. These are the key points on which the researcher will be evaluated. As in any task, you will need to achieve the project objectives in order to be judged as having met your responsibility to your client. Usually five or fewer objectives are all that one marketing research project can accomplish.

Exhibit 4.2 Examples of Marketing Research Objectives

- Estimate market share of a new product
- Determine the sensitivity of the brand demand to price changes
- Segment the market based on category usage
- Identify which of three advertising copy proposals generates the greatest interest
- Determine which of two product formulations is most preferred by category users based on actual usage in the home

---

THE PROPOSED FIELD METHODOLOGY

The proposed field methodology describes the sampling and data collection plans. Exhibit 4.3 lists the typical components of the field methodology section of the proposal. The nature of the detailed information typically contained in this section of the proposal will be described in later chapters. An overview of the ways of describing the field function of marketing research was presented in Chapter 3. An in-depth explanation of data collection methodology is presented in Chapter 8.

Exhibit 4.3 Typical Topics Explained Under Proposed Field Methodology

- The size of the total sample and of sub-samples
- How the sample will be selected
- Whether the questionnaire will be self-administered or interviewer-administered
- How the interviewing will be done, or how the mailing will be conducted
- Requirements imposed on the collection of data.

THE PROPOSED ANALYSIS PROCEDURES

The proposed analysis procedures' section is used when special analysis techniques are needed to extract information of importance from the data. Techniques such as factor analysis, discriminant analysis, correspondence analysis, conjoint analysis, price sensitivity meter, multidimensional scaling, simulated test marketing and others should be briefly described in this section in terms of the reasons for using the techniques and the benefits to be derived from each. (These are discussed in Chapters 22 and 23.)

Clients pay to get information and to solve problems; they rarely pay just so that a particular high-tech analysis procedure can be used to analyze their data. Consequently, concentrate the justification of the statistical analysis on problem solution rather than complication for the sake of complication.

THE PROJECT SCHEDULE

Naturally, the project schedule indicates the expected length of the project together with the milestones that are important to the client. For example, the dates for finalization of the questionnaire, beginning the fieldwork, completing the fieldwork, availability of top-line findings and report submission are all strong candidates for inclusion.

Although the project schedule can be submitted simply as a listing of dates, some proposals may include a critical path method, project evaluation and review technique, or a Gantt chart, or another diagram that can be much more informative than an enumeration of dates.

THE PROJECT BUDGET

Naturally, the budget is extremely important—especially in cases where there are competitive bids. In those situations, it is helpful to know that the project is being tendered by more than one firm. The Code of Ethics and Good Practice of the Professional Marketing Research Society requires that firms submitting proposals be advised by the prospective client that competing bids are being considered for the project.

The costing of projects can either be very quick or quite a lengthy procedure. The effort needed depends on the size of the project, the requirements of the prospective client and the researcher's experience with similar projects. On relatively routine descriptive projects, such as usage and attitude studies, concept tests, and certain types of advertising testing, both the consultant and the client usually have a fairly good idea of the cost after a very short discussion. Sometimes an oral quote is given and later firmed up after some detailed calculations on a few of the cost components.

The costing of large projects depends on many details and can differ substantially among the many types of marketing research projects. Because of this diversity, and since costing is often not done by the beginning researcher, this topic will not be explained in detail here. Exhibit 4.4 lists the most important factors that influence the cost of projects.

Exhibit 4.4 Project Costing—Major Influencing Items

- Type of project
- Sample size
- Field methodology (method of data collection)
- Incidence rate of qualified respondents in population
- Location of the research and the number of locations
- Type of respondent (average person versus executive in company)
- Detail of analysis required
- Sophistication of analysis desired
- Type of final report required
- Whether formal presentation of findings desired
- Speed of execution
- Special services

THE TERMS OF AGREEMENT

The terms of agreement and the agreement form are not always used; however, these pages can be critical to continuing good relations between the research parties. The terms of agreement help to eliminate the problems of misinterpretation of the research contract, and they enhance the joint understanding of the responsibilities of the research consultant and the client. If the terms of agreement exist, the deliverables of the project are often specified in that section (for example, whether reporting must be done at several stages of the project, whether a top-line report is needed and when, the type of final report, or whether a formal oral presentation of the findings is needed).

BIOGRAPHICAL PROFILES

Every client wants to know who is actually going to be supervising the project and conducting the research. The complaint is sometimes heard that juniors are assigned to the project after it is "sold-in" by the experienced researcher who is assumed by the client to be the future project director but who sometimes is rarely seen again.

Provide one- or two-paragraph profiles of the experience and educational backgrounds of the principal consultants. Include the type of product and service experience of the researchers and any specialties that they have developed and that might be beneficial to the project. Also, list the research firm's major projects and clients and, if possible, describe some projects similar to that being bid on to highlight the earned expertise of the firm.

THE IMPORTANCE OF THE PROPOSAL

It's easy to underestimate the value of the research proposal. However, serious professional consultants and research buyers understand the critical position that the proposal occupies in the life of a project. Robert Joselyn (1977) clearly spells out that importance in the following list of functions of a research proposal in Exhibit 4.5

Exhibit 4.5 Implications of a proposal

1. *The research proposal is a formal plan of action.* As with any formal plan, the proposal forces the research team to consider all vital elements of the project as well as to make a number of methodology decisions. In other words, a formal proposal encourages disciplined planning.

2. *The research proposal is a "communication checkpoint" between the research team and the client.* One component of the written proposal is a description of the problem and a specified scope of the proposed project. The researcher may find his view of the problem, or objectives of the project, differing from those held by the client (again assuming they are not one and the same). It is hoped that such a discrepancy will be encountered earlier, but if not, the written proposal provides one last formal check. Obviously, it is much better to discover such points of conflict at this point rather than when a final report is submitted.

3. *The research proposal is a sales device for the research team.* Although often overlooked, the proposal is very much like a brochure used to sell any service. It is unique because it is really custom-designed for selling the proposed marketing research to the client contact and to other influential client representatives.

   A word of caution is necessary. Selling a proposed marketing research project should not imply any lack of professional objectivity on the part of the researcher. Only if he is totally convinced that the research effort will be worth the investment should the researcher try to sell it to the client. Selling a useless research project would be as professionally improper as trying to sell a product which would not meet the client's needs.

4. *The research proposal should be viewed as a binding contract between the research team and the client.* To be complete, a marketing research proposal should specify the obligations of both the research team and the client. Obligations of the research team include what is to be done, how it will be done, and the time and cost requirements for completion. Obligations of the client include specification of costs to be incurred, the payment schedule, and any help that must be given to the research team.

   It is recommended that every proposal be concluded with a page signed by both the research director and the client representative, thereby making the proposal a legal contract and emphasizing the preparation and presentation of a marketing research proposal as serious business.

SOURCE: Robert W. Joselyn, *Designing the Marketing Research Project*. New York: Petrocelli/Charter, 1977, pp. 136-7.

THE PROPOSAL AS A WORKING PROJECT PLAN

The formal proposal can be used as the master plan for the project if no major alterations are made after the original proposal is written. The details of the field methodology, sampling, and analysis might be excluded from the proposal to avoid bulk and overly lengthy explanation. This is particularly true of proposals to formalize and proposal letters. However, the details not included in the proposal are planned and costed during the proposal preparation state. Go back to those details and flesh out the proposal to the point where the project tasks can be described and transmitted to field staff, the data entry staff, the analysts, the subcontractors and the other research staff involved.

An indirect benefit of a well written and annotated formal proposal will be realized at the report writing phase of the project. Most of the front end of the proposal can be used again in the initial sections of the project report. Don't ever underestimate the time needed to write the final report—or its importance. One quarter to one third of the total project time is usually spent writing the final report (Kelley, 1981: 153). You'll appreciate being able to abbreviate the report writing task by including some of the well prepared formal proposal.

SUMMARY

The marketing research proposal can take four basic forms:

1. The Formal Proposal
2. The Proposal to Formalize
3. The Letter Proposal
4. The Quote

For most projects conducted for private companies, the last three forms of the research proposal are adequate. The formal proposal is used most often for large private projects and for public sector projects.

The formal proposal is used to:

• convince the prospective client of the capability of the consultant;
• communicate and formalize the approach to the research; and
• act as a plan of action after approval, and alteration, by the client.

This chapter provided a focus and an outline for developing the proposal, especially the formal proposal. The differences between the types of proposals were explained.

A recurring problem in marketing research firms is whether a bid should be developed for a project. The strategic position of those projects is important to the development and health of the firm and must be justified on objective grounds.

The proposal outline was discussed within the context of the background information, the marketing problem/opportunity, the marketing research objectives, the proposed field methodology, the proposed analysis procedures, the project schedule, the project budget, the terms of agreement and the biographical profiles of study team members.

The importance of the proposal as a working plan for the project as well as a sales document was also discussed.

NOW THINK ABOUT THIS

1. Write down three uses of a marketing research proposal.

2. The program evaluation and review technique is mentioned in this chapter. Find out what that procedure is and draw a short PERT chart for a hypothetical project.

3. Take a well documented project report, read its table of contents and executive summary and then, if possible, match those to the proposal which was developed for the project.

4. Read *The Globe and Mail* or your local newspaper for several days or weeks and identify the announcement of public consulting projects. Call to receive the terms of reference for those projects. Read them and try to develop at least a viable outline for that project.

5. Go to the public documents section of your local library and ask to see the reports for any marketing research or social research consulting projects which have been conducted for your municipality during the past three to five years. Identify whether the proposals for the projects were included in the appendices. If not, ask the municipal department for which the project was conducted for a copy of the proposal.

REFERENCES

Conklin, Robert
1979　*How to Get People To Do Things*. Chicago: Contemporary Books, Inc.

Joselyn, Robert W.
1977 *Designing the Marketing Research Project.* New York: Petrocelli/Charter, pp. 136-7.

Kelley, Robert E.
1981 *Consulting: The Complete Guide to a Profitable Career.* New York: Charles Scribner's Sons, p. 153.

PART 3

How to Implement a Marketing Research Project

5 / Qualitative Research

WHAT YOU WILL LEARN IN THIS CHAPTER

- To identify research problems for which qualitative research is suited
- The general and specific skills needed to be a good moderator
- The various techniques used by the focus group moderator
- How to verify the data collected through focus groups
- To analyze the data and write reports
- Related techniques, such as depth interviews, repertory grids and laddering

INTRODUCTION

Qualitative research techniques are among the most widely used exploratory procedures. The purpose of qualitative research is to explore in depth the full extent of opinions on a given subject, rather than to seek to establish a statistical framework for measuring specific and limited aspects of the full extent, as is done in survey work. To achieve this purpose, a qualitative researcher relies on semi-structured, or even unstructured, probing of the opinions of representatives from a given population, in contrast to the fully structured nature of a survey.

Qualitative research aims to obtain insights into consumer behaviour rather than to draw precise conclusions. The opinions so gathered are typically used to generate hypotheses that may be further tested and confirmed by quantitative research procedures.

The end product of quantitative research is literally public opinion; while in qualitative research the end product is the researcher's reasoned interpretations and presumptions about public opinion.

Qualitative study structures almost always involve the use either of focus groups or of individual depth interviews. Qualitative techniques mostly involve direct and oblique questioning, and projective techniques. In this chapter, some of these procedures will be outlined.

THE FOCUS GROUP

Focus groups are by far the most frequently used form of qualitative research. In a typical focus group, eight to ten people whose opinions are relevant to the subject are assembled in a central location to be interviewed over the course of two hours, or so, by a moderator trained in the special skills required for working with such groups.

No set questionnaire is used to elicit opinions. The moderator works from an outline of the topic areas he or she wants to cover, usually referred to as a discussion guide. While a discussion guide represents an advance best-guess as to how the discussion flow ought to go, it is often the case that once groups are actually underway a better way of exploring the subject emerges. When this happens, ad hoc adaptation is required. Hence, a discussion guide is not hard and fast in the sense that a questionnaire is, but more a jumping off point into possibly uncharted waters.

The rigid structure of a questionnaire defines both the information it will elicit and the information it will leave out. A question not asked is a question not answered. The on-going adaptability of qualitative research is what makes it pliable to exploring all issues, whether anticipated or not.

Focus groups are recorded onto audio tapes for later transcription. In some cases, they are videotaped as well, though this is seldom necessary. The interview room is equipped with a one-way mirror to facilitate client viewing of the interviews. The participants are made aware of both the tapings and the presence of observers behind the one-way mirror, but for evident reasons of bias prevention, the specific identity or connections of the observers are not specified. They are normally only described as people relevant to the topic, and anxious to hear the respondents' comments firsthand.

The ambience of a focus group is informal, since it is essential that the participants be at ease in order to establish rapport. Partly for this reason too, participants in a focus-group discussion are generally compatible with one another in terms of demographics and in sharing a common topic-related interest.

DEPTH INTERVIEWS

Although focus groups are the most widely used form of qualitative research, individual interviews are also a common qualitative method. Individual depth interviews are conceptually similar to focus groups, but the moderator talks to one respondent at a time rather than to a group of people. The interviews tend to be somewhat more structured than is true for groups, with more need for moderator intervention. They last about 20 to 40 minutes, but can last longer when there is enough "meat" in the topic to keep the attention of the respondents.

In some instances it is preferable to have individual interviews instead of focus groups. Such instances would include occasions in which a person's opinion can easily be coloured by others in the group, or when certain opinions are not likely to be expressed in a group because they are too personal, sensitive or embarrassing in nature. In addition, when it is as important to learn what people don't know about a subject as what they do know, the individual interview is the best approach. In a group setting, more knowledgeable respondents quickly teach less knowledgeable ones, making it very difficult or impossible to explore areas of ignorance or misperception. Sometimes, there is no choice but to conduct individual interviews; for example, when interviewing executives from competing firms, who won't open up in front of each other, and may even intentionally make misleading statements.

QUALITATIVE RESEARCH SHOULD BE USED SELECTIVELY

Qualitative research should be used when it is the right approach to the problem at hand. Although relatively inexpensive and quick compared to quantitative methods, it should not be used for time or budgetary reasons when a survey is what is really called for. Some of the specific research applications to which qualitative is well suited include:

- brand or service positioning exploration
- new product or advertising concept screening and refinement
- assessment of brand or corporate imagery, or general competitive environment assessment
- packaging and graphic design development

More generally, qualitative research works when:

1. There is an information vacuum which needs to be filled before the topic can be meaningfully and effectively researched by quantitative methods.

2. There is a need to understand the basis of consumer motivations, priorities, anxieties, hidden agendas, patterns of perceptions, desires and so forth which may not emerge fully when investigated quantitatively.

3. Boiling down of several initial possibilities to the more workable and promising few is required.

4. It is used as input to the creative process.

5. The subject matter is too subtle to create efficient direct questions for use in standard survey research techniques.

THE MECHANICS OF FOCUS GROUPS

RECRUITING THE RESPONDENTS

As for any opinion study method, qualitative respondents are methodically drawn from the target market group. Criteria for respondent selection are normally specified by the client, working in collaboration with the moderator, and then passed on to recruiters who specialize in assembling respondents to take part in qualitative studies. While determined recruiters can usually find respondents who will fulfill almost any set of criteria, complex recruitment criteria should be avoided, if possible, because they prolong the recruitment time, increase the cost, and may result in erroneous respondent selection. It is therefore important to test each criterion and restriction for importance and relevance. The larger the size of the defined universe being recruited from, the more successful the process is likely to be. Recruitment procedures take at least a week (or several weeks if criteria are complex) and this should be taken into account when deciding on recruitment criteria.

CRITERIA FOR SELECTING RESPONDENTS

Qualitative research is not bound by the same rigorous sampling rules that govern major quantitative surveys. It is not expected that respondents will be as strictly random and representative as they should be for a survey. However, this does not imply that one can recruit participants in a haphazard way. It is especially important that recruitment procedures be designed to control the introduction of unintended recruitment-related bias. To ensure this, good recruitment follows a number of guidelines. Some of these guidelines are:

- Respondents in any group should not be known to the moderator, and should be strangers to one another. Friends tend to act as a social unit of their own and this can inhibit the global interaction process. Within reason, persons who know each other may take part in back-to-back groups on the same day, but not in ones on different days, due to the likelihood of the one participating earlier briefing the one to participate later.

- Respondents should not be regular participants in focus group discussions. Respondents who have participated in too many groups, almost always with the collaboration of an unethical recruiter, are called professionals. They become wise to the ways of moderator questioning and cease responding as lay consumers. Some come to see themselves as amateur moderators, and try to help out by asking probing questions. The general rule is that participation is permitted just once a year, or five times in total, and never twice on the same subject. In Toronto, there is a computerized data bank to control this participation rate. Elsewhere, the ethics of recruiters must be relied upon.

- As far as is feasible, respondents should be unaware in advance of the discussion details. A primed respondent is less likely to be a representative one. Screening questionnaires can be designed to incorporate spurious criteria to deliberately keep respondents off guard.

- Respondents should be sufficiently skilled in the language so that they do not misunderstand the moderator and vice versa. Linguistically disadvantaged respondents are usually non-participatory, and can also inhibit the free flow of dialogue.

- Respondents should not be closely connected, either personally or through their families, with advertising, marketing research, or industries related to the topic of discussion. The latter exclusion is both to assure lay rather than informed response, and to guard against revealing confidential information to competitors.

- Respondents should not be recent immigrants to the country (less than five years), or to the city (less than two years). This is because until they get used to their new environment, their point of reference continues to be the place they came from.

These are not rigid rules but guidelines to be used when no specific criteria are set. For example, although respondents who know one another should be avoided, there are occasions in which it may be permissible. In small cities, it is all but inevitable that some respondents will know each other, even if not recruited by friend-to-friend reference.

When there is a potential for one part of the group to restrict the comments of another part, it may be necessary to keep different sub-groups separate. For example, if a teen group were composed of respondents ranging from 13 to 18, the younger ones could easily be intimidated by the older ones, and defer to them. Users and non-users may conflict by one's being deferential to the other, but unpredictably as a result of the force of personalities on each side.

Whenever the budget permits, the study structure should include at least two groups in each project specification category. This is to guard against any one group's being atypical, and leading the researchers astray. This precaution is no different than for any other inherently small-sample research.

Mixing respondents of opposing views (such as in political or social matters) for the purpose of creating a confrontation has evident theoretical appeal, but does not work very well in practice. The presence of strong and unbridgeable disagreement among a group of strangers is likely to induce silence and discomfort for all concerned rather than spirited and constructive debate.

TWO METHODS OF RECRUITING

Respondents for focus groups may be recruited by two methods, by the random method and the referral method. In the *random* method, respondents are chosen using mechanical statistical procedures. In many ways this is an ideal procedure because it eliminates human judgmental errors that may result in bias. In practice, however, this method is seldom used because it requires over-recruitment and it can be frustrating to the recruiters. Both of these drawbacks stem from the inherent skepticism in our culture. Potential respondents tend to doubt the innocence of the invitation to participate, and possibly to be concerned about their own security as well. The refusal rate is very high. Moveover, a disturbing proportion of such random recruits do not show up, or are very much on guard when they do. Above all, it has yet to be demonstrated that the random method is appreciably better than the referral method to warrant the additional time and expense.

Therefore, in practice, the most commonly used method is the *referral* method. It is a snowball or pyramid technique in which respondents are recruited on the basis of being referred by others. Recruiters build up data banks of past participants and of potential references known to past participants. This technique is relatively inexpensive and respondent reliability is usually good. The reason is that skepticism is greatly reduced since a recruiter can say that such and such a person whom they know has participated in a study before has recommended them. The persons contacted can quickly and independently verify that nothing untoward is involved. The referring friend will probably encourage them to take part. Respondents almost always enjoy the experience. They are flattered to know someone values hearing their opinion, learn from the interchange with others, and like the sense of having been admitted to the inner sanctum of the marketing world.

SCHEDULING CONSIDERATIONS

There are no hard and fast rules with regard to the scheduling of group interviews. The following suggestions may, however, be useful:

- Customarily, two groups are conducted per evening, at 6:00 and 8:00. Daytime female groups tend to exclude working women and, for that reason, may be suitable only if non-employed or part-time employed housewives are to be the respondents.
- As many as three group discussions can be carried out in a day. More than three a day is too draining on moderators and observers alike.
- Friday evenings or evenings before a statutory holiday are a poor choice for group discussions. No-show problems are at their worst then. For the same reason, scheduling should take into consideration sports play-off series of special interest in a city to be a research site, major television events, etc.
- Respondents are paid an incentive for participating in the group discussion. (During early 1991, the standard incentives were $30-$35 for most respondents, a little less for teens, and for rare and difficult to motivate respondents, $100 or more was common. Examples of the latter would be doctors, owners of luxury cars, business executives, and so on.)

CRITERIA FOR LOCATIONS

It is almost always desirable for clients to observe the focus group sessions as they happen. In fact, this is one of the main spin-off benefits of qualitative research. The opportunity for marketing people to play "fly on the wall" and learn firsthand what their customers (or those of the competition) are thinking can provide invaluable exposure and insight. This is the reason for having special focus group facilities equipped with one-way mirrors.

Having the client present is also invaluable to the moderator, at least for the first few sessions, in order to ensure that he or she is working to the ends the client desires. Frequently, procedural modifications are made as a result of client observation.

A good focus group location should have neutral and relaxing decor. There should be a host or hostess to control comings and goings, look after hospitality, attend to the recording equipment, and ensure that all respondents are on the attendance list. Sometimes, respondents will try to bring along friends, not knowing this isn't permitted, or knowing but hoping to get them into the group anyway.

The facility may offer an open, living-room-style seating arrangement or a boardroom-style table. The layout is not too important, although some moderators feel more comfortable with one than the other. Boardroom arrangements are by far the more common of the two types.

The number of observers should be kept down, and limited to persons with a direct reason for being present. Experience has shown that the more observers there are, the more they interact among themselves and the less attentive they are to the job of observing. Generally, more than five observers can become problematic.

In Canada, there are observation facilites in Toronto, Halifax, Quebec City, Montreal, Ottawa, London, Winnipeg, Calgary, Edmonton and Vancouver. In towns where there are no observation facilities, a suite in a major, centrally located hotel is used instead. A living room and adjoining bedroom with separate entrances (rather than a meeting room) works best. Clients can listen to the proceedings via audio hookup into the adjoining room. Video hookup can be used as well, though a passive, fixed camera usually adds very little enhancement. The camera can be panned and zoomed by an operator to produce a more interesting video; but, this can be very distracting for the respondents. The camera itself is no longer much of an inhibitor, as the proliferation of camcorders has made video equipment fairly commonplace now.

Depending on the arrangement of the hotel space, one or two observers can sit off to the side in the group room. It is very important that such observers remain quiet and unobtrusive, and do nothing to interfere with the moderator's control of the group. The moderator customarily introduces such observers as research colleagues who alternate the job of moderating and note-taking, and collaborate on the eventual report, even if the "colleague" is the president of the client company.

HOW MANY GROUPS?

An important decision to be made is how many groups (or individual interviews) should be used for a given study. Obviously, the more segmented the market is, the larger the number of groups needed. The best test for determining the number of groups is to identify how many segments are necessary in order to elicit all major motivational perspectives related to the subject. The law of diminishing returns also applies. While increasing the number of groups increases one's chances of finding new material that is relevant to the product category, increasing the number of groups beyond a certain number is counter-productive. Conducting groups beyond that number merely produces more of the same.

What is the magical number of groups beyond which the insight generated by respondents is no longer new? This depends on a number of factors such as:

- Are there major regional variations in attitudes towards the product?
- Do different socio-economic groups buy the product for different reasons?
- Are there distinct age segments in the target group with different needs?
- Is the target market highly heterogeneous?
- Are the motivations of segments incompatible?
- Are heavy users different from light users?
- Should own users and competitive users be dealt with separately?

The way in which these issues must be dealt with will indicate whether a small or large number of groups is needed. For example, if both younger and older male and female response must be elicited, and the marketing environment is known to be different in Vancouver than in Toronto, at least eight groups (four per city) will be needed. If the key target segment is younger, then at least these two segments should be replicated, resulting in six groups per city. The number of groups can really mushroom if users and non-users must be dealt with separately, and if there are several strong regional differences. However, if the target is simply female users and non-users, of a wide age range, four groups in one city should be quite adequate. In this example, twelve groups would be far past the point of diminishing returns, while in the first example, twelve groups would make sense.

In addition to the above, there are other considerations which deal with the smooth functioning of groups. There are:

- *Age Range*: Use separate groups for younger and older people, in order to assure creation of a sense of participating among one's peers. Among teenagers, an age span of two years is advisable; among the under 30's, 5-10 years; among older adults, 20-25 years. Most studies are confined to people under 50 years of age, but this is due to marketing target definition, not to any inherent age-related impediment. When their input is pertinent, groups of the elderly can be just as productive as younger segments.
- *Demographics*: It is best to keep white/blue collar, higher/lower educated, upscale/downscale groups apart. People do not tend to open up in the presence of their social opposites when affluence or sophistication are involved in the subject.
- *Gender*: It is not advisable to mix males and females in the same group, though it can be done if budgetary constraints make it necessary. Mixed groups tend to be less relaxed and less productive. Moreover, gender-related issues will usually not emerge, since both genders will avoid the risk of possibly demeaning or stereotyping the other (though such stereotypes can provide highly valuable insight). The problem can be particularly acute if the respondents are teens—giggling and squirming might well be the only result of such a mixed group.

WHAT THE MODERATOR NEEDS TO KNOW

Since in qualitative research there is no set questionnaire, it is difficult to determine in advance the course that group discussions may actually take. It is therefore imperative that the moderator be thoroughly briefed beforehand. This allows him or her to make ad hoc adaptations intelligently as required, and to sense unexpected but potentially valuable additional avenues to follow. The poorly briefed moderator will be ill-equipped to be adaptive in this way. Naturally, the more familiar the moderator is with the category, the less general briefing he or she will need. Briefing should take into account the following aspects:

- the marketing environment of the product or service being investigated, how the proposed intervention fits within this, and the tactical expectations for it;
- the range of subjects and issues to be investigated;
- the format, kind and degree of finish, etc., of display materials, if such are to be used during the interview. Examples of display material are samples of existing products, prototypes of new ones, advertisements and commercials, concept boards, etc. (The moderator may have some suggestions as to the suitability of these various forms of display material.)

One subject that clients should avoid while briefing the moderator is revealing team biases regarding favoured concepts, political pressures, or desired results. This may put pressure on the moderator's essential role of impartiality. Another temptation to resist is the tendency to include every aspect of the subject, especially aspects that are only marginally relevant but time-consuming to explore; worse are add-on subjects not relevant to the actual topic. The time available is basically limited to two hours by scheduling needs and respondent patience. Marginal topics reduce the amount of time available for discussing important ones.

MODERATING SKILLS

Because of the nature of qualitative research, the skills that are required to be a good moderator involve a high degree of sensitivity to others, lateral thinking, and the ability to be a catalyst rather than an influence. The aim of this chapter is to familiarize you with some of the tools that are available to moderators, without trying to be exhaustive. Almost all the skills described here are also relevant to individual depth interviews. In fact some of the skills (e.g., creating rapport using matching and mirroring) are much more effective in individual depth interviews than in focus groups.

PUTTING RESPONDENTS AT EASE

The first priority of the moderator is to put the participants at ease. This is done by first explaining the purpose of the discussion in an informal and non-technical way, and then by establishing a relaxed and permissive climate conducive to getting the respondents to open up. The moderator talks to the respondents at their own level to aid in establishing rapport, and should be dressed accordingly. Moderating a group of blue collar workers while wearing a business suit may send the signal that the moderator wants the respondents to know he isn't one of them, imperiling the creation of rapport. Jeans can be entirely appropriate business dress for a moderator.

Skilled moderators follow several explicit and implicit rules of conduct, except when they deliberately stray from them to achieve a certain goal. In qualitative research, much more than in quantitative research, it is critical for the moderator to develop rapport quickly and effectively with the respondents. Most good qualitative researchers do this intuitively, even subconsciously. Recent developments in the fields of socio-linguistics, hypnotic patterns, psychology and Neuro-Linguistic Programming (NLP) have identified explicit patterns that can help the researcher establish rapport with respondents.

CONTROLLING GROUP DYNAMICS

Whenever two or more people interact, two conflicting motives propel their interaction, power and solidarity. One wants to be heard (power), but is socialized to make room for other views (solidarity). Different people have different balances of power and solidarity. Most people balance the two well, although it is to be expectd that the balance is imperfect. When a group has one person with an extreme power orientation and seven others with high solidarity orientation, the power-oriented person will tend to dominate the discussion. The main danger in this case is not that person's domination *per se*, but the acquiescence of the remaining participants for reasons of solidarity. In other words, they may simply agree with the dominant person, although they have their own opinions on the subject.

The challenge to moderators is to control the dominant person(s), without appearing to do so, while at the same time enhancing their communication links with the others. In fact, whether power-solidarity conflict is a problem or not, it is important for moderators to keep all their links open throughout, and always to make it clear that conflicting views are not only welcome but also essential to their purpose in learning all facets of the subject.

CREATING RAPPORT

The ability to create a feeling of rapport lies in being able to enter someone else's world and to communicate in such a way as to make the other person feel that he or she is understood, and that his or her views (mainstream or not) are important to the moderator. This leads the other person to trust the moderator, which in turn results in an uninhibited flow of information. When rapport is established, the respondent becomes less self-conscious and guarded, and thus is in a position to more openly provide valuable information.

However, it is important to note that maintaining rapport does not mean surrendering control of the group to the respondents. In fact, if this happens, the moderator will have failed in one of his or her most important tasks.

UNDERSTANDING SURFACE MESSAGES AND METAMESSAGES

When we communicate with another person, two types of messages are sent out, surface message and metamessage. Suppose you say to your assistant, "Have you finished the report?", the surface message is the information that is sought in the literal sense: whether the report is finished or not. The metamessage might be, "I don't think you have," implying incompetence.

Metamessages are conveyed through the intonation, pitch, and facial and bodily expressions that accompany the words. It appears that words account for only 7 per cent of the meaning, while 38 per cent is accounted for by tonality and 55 per cent of the communication is through body posture. Thus the most powerful part of the communication is through metamessages that are picked up and responded to subconsciously by the other person.

Because metamessages are so important in communication, it is quite common to observe that people almost always react to metamessages. For example, if you ask your assistant if he has finished the report he might not say no, instead he might respond, "It's almost finished"; "I would have finished it by now but the computer crashed for a couple of hours this morning." A person who buys a notably non-prestigious brand may offer a defensive explanation of his purchase without even being asked.

Breakdown in communication is often the result of misunderstood metamessages. Consider this conversation between two acquaintances:

John: Let's have lunch sometime.

Joe: How about next Monday?

John: Okay.

Both of them feel trapped into going to a lunch which neither of them may have wanted, as shown in the following interpretation of the implicit messages.

Surface message	Intended Metamessage	Received Metamessage
"Let's have lunch sometime"	Friendliness with no commitment	Let's consolidate our friendship
"How about next Monday?"	Reciprocation of intended friendship even though Joe is not really keen	Being trapped

Both of them wanted to be nice to each other, but neither of them wanted to get any closer. But because metamessages were misunderstood, both of them ended up in a situation that neither of them wanted to be in.

Metamessages are important in all forms of human communication. They become particularly critical in face-to-face situations between strangers, as is mostly the case with focus groups and depth interviews. A straightforward question such as, "What wine do you drink?" can send out any of the following (or other) metamessaages to the respondent:

- I expect any normal person to drink wine.
- The wine you drink will tell me how sophisticated you are.
- You look like a person who would drink wine.
- I'll bet you drink cheap wines.
- You look sophisticated enough to drink wine.

The respondent's answer will vary depending on the metamessage he or she thought was received. The metamessage would depend, among other things, on the tone and context in which the question was asked. The moderator should be aware of the metamessages he or she might be sending by the way a question is asked and the context in which it is asked. Perhaps there is no more important a skill for a moderator to cultivate than how to ask a question without at the same time seeming to have made an unintended statement or to have inadvertently suggested a desired avenue of response.

MAINTAINING RAPPORT

Socio-linguists, psychologists, hypnotists and NLP specialists have identified many ways in which rapport is created between people and have offered a number of guidelines for creating and maintaining it in the shortest possible time.

One major premise in creating rapport is that we are quickly in rapport with people who are similar to us. Similarity can be created through three main methods: 1) physiology; 2) speech patterns; and 3) framing. The techniques described here can be used effectively in focus groups.

PHYSIOLOGY: MATCHING AND MIRRORING   If we observe people in a social setting, we find that close friends tend to mirror each other. If one of them leans forward, the other leans forward as well; if one tilts his head, so does the other. This process can be used deliberately to create rapport. Thus, if you want to create rapport with someone, you can mirror the body posture, breathing pattern, tonality of voice, etc., of the other person. If the person you are talking to is a slow talker, talking to him fast is not conducive to establishing rapport.

Rapport is created to make the respondents feel that the moderator is one of them. In terms of physiology, oneness is created by the moderator's mirroring the physical behaviour of the participants. If the participants relax, a relaxed moderator has a better chance of creating rapport than a tense moderator. If most participants lean forward, a moderator who leans back in his or her chair is not likely to create rapport. Of course, there are situations in which there is no consistent pattern in the group. In such cases, the moderator may not be able to use his or her physiology to create rapport. However, there are other means of creating rapport.

Neuro-linguistic programmers (NLPers) hold that when we speak we use a dominant mode. It may be visual, auditory, kinesthetic, or even olfactory or gustatory. Greater rapport is created when we follow the speaker's modality. Let us review the following conversation:

Participant: I don't see how this new concept fits into the whole picture.

Moderator: Listen to this carefully. What I was saying was ...

Participant: It's still fuzzy to me.

The participant is obviously looking at a mental picture and trying to make sense of that. The moderator, on the other hand, is talking in terms of listening, which at this point is like speaking to the participant in a foreign language. Moreover, in this example there is a concealed metamessage that the respondent is either imperceptive or not very bright. NLPers hold that such mismatch is destructive to maintaining rapport. If the moderator had matched the participant in the following way:

Participant: I don't see how this new concept fits into the whole picture.

Moderator: Let us look at it this way. If you observe...

Then perhaps the participant might have responded:

Participant: Oh, I see what you mean.

The second conversation above in which the moderator matched the participant's dominant modality would have created a powerful rapport between the moderator and the participant.

When the conversation is not one-on-one as described above, the moderator may have to use the dominant modality of the group, while also reiterating his talk in other modalities.

Even when participants do not use modality-specific words (such as *see*, *hear*, *perspective*, etc.), it is possible to know how they are processing information. Our eye movements are correlated with the mode in which we operate. For example, when we try picturing something, our eyes go up, and we feel angry, we look down to the right. By observing the eye movements of the participant, it is possible to know how she or he has processed the information. The pictures in Exhibit 5.1 show some common eye movement patterns associated with information processing.

Exhibit 5.1   Eye Movement Patterns Associated with Information Processing

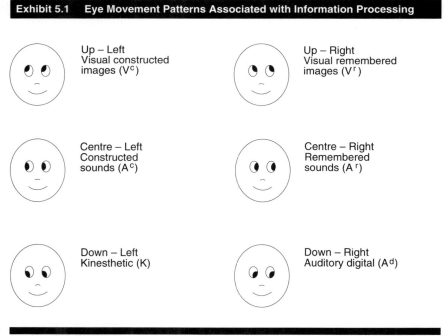

Up – Left
Visual constructed
images (V^c)

Up – Right
Visual remembered
images (V^r)

Centre – Left
Constructed
sounds (A^c)

Centre – Right
Remembered
sounds (A^r)

Down – Left
Kinesthetic (K)

Down – Right
Auditory digital (A^d)

Note: You are looking at another person.

SPEECH PATTERNS   The second method of creating rapport is through following the speech patterns of the participants. Speech patterns vary in different dimensions:

- Speed
- Tempo
- Tonality
- Words

To a slow speaker, a fast speaker may appear rude and self-centred. A fast speaker in turn may perceive a slow speaker as less sharp-witted. Whether a given tone is perceived to be firm and friendly or bossy and offensive would depend on the background of the participants. What is bossy and offensive to people from one part of the country may simply be normal to people from another part of the country. Extensive use of colloquial expressions may be perceived as coarse by members of some socio-economic groups, while absence of colloquial expressions may be perceived as stuffy and pompous by other groups. A good moderator is aware (consciously or subconsciously) of such speech patterns and adjusts his or her speech to suit that of the group.

When the groups are distinct, it is enough to identify the suitable speech patterns. However, a good sensory acuity is needed to assess the physiological and language patterns when the groups are not very distinct. Some rapport almost always develops within the group and with the moderator (assuming that he or she is competent). The real challenge to the moderator is to elevate the level of rapport as much as possible by being very perceptive of the subconscious signals generated by participants through the course of the discussion.

FRAMING AND REFRAMING   Framing is a way of creating a context. This is done to guide the participants to change the topic or to give up their current orientation while maintaining rapport. Sometimes framing can also be used to create rapport. Consider a situation in which the discussion has moved into areas that are outside the scope of the study and the moderator's attempts to steer the conversation have not been very successful. The moderator can completely reframe the mindset of the participants by asking something like: "That is very interesting. Now suppose you are in a store and you have only $5. Which brand of product X, would you buy?" Such a frame is specific and therefore requires the participants to abandon their earlier frame. Yet it is non-offensive in that it does not ask them not to discuss what they were discussing before. However, the indirect result is that the participants have no logical way of returning to their earlier frame.

Reframing can also be used to change someone's orientation while maintaining rapport. Consider a situation in which a participant believes that he has superior knowledge and is bent on exhibiting it by straying into areas that are of no consequence either to the moderator or to the other participants. (This is one of the key reasons for screening our respondents with inside knowledge of the industry under discussion.) The moderator may reframe the participant's orientation with something like, "That is a very sophisticated view. We may even have another group discussion on that subject. Now, if you were to deal with the issue at a more common level what would you say about ...?" Here, by acknowledging the participant as sophisticated, the moderator maintains rapport by in effect patting the respondent on the back, but at the same time making it clear that another frame is required. The respondent cannot ignore the fact that his previous frame of reference and that of the moderator are at odds.

BREAKING RAPPORT

While it is absolutely critical for a moderator to create and maintain rapport, he or she may also want to break the rapport from time to time by not following some of the procedures described above. Here is an example: The group rapport may be so high that they start interacting with each other with exuberance. To regain order, the moderator may temporarily break rapport with the group by (for instance) reframing. One must also remember that the group is being recorded and observed. When the proceedings break down into cross-currents of babble, the tape will become unintelligible and the observers will be lost. This is part of the challenge to the moderator of maintaining rapport with participants without ceding control to the group itself, or becoming personally involved in the discussion.

SPECIFIC MODERATING SKILLS

In the previous section we discussed rapport and how to create and maintain it. In addition to creating and maintaining rapport, the moderator should be:

- capable of maintaining firm but quiet control
- non-critical and non-judgmental of the opinions expressed, and able to keep their own biases out of it entirely
- alert and interested without showing emotion
- even-handed in seeking equal participation
- encouraging of respondents, especially of the reticent who may need special attention and stroking to be forthcoming
- able to keep the topic reasonably on track
- credibly naive, so as to induce discussion of key fundamentals that respondents may otherwise assume are self-evident
- sensitive to undercurrents and disagreements
- flexible, adaptable, and able to improvise
- observant of cues from body language
- able to interact, probe and bring out feelings and emotions

When a moderator asks a question, he or she does not settle for the first answer, but probes over and over again to get at deeper levels of perception. The ability to uncover such material is one of the most important differences between qualitative and quantitative research. The moderator achieves this in several different ways: by encouraging the respondents to expound on their views in greater detail; by feigning non-comprehension; by deliberately playing the devil's advocate; by reframing; by questioning body language; and by questioning without words, with looks, gestures, etc. A good moderator never takes anything for granted. Moderators have to think on their feet. Unlike survey researchers, they do not have the luxury of pre-testing questions to refine their effectiveness. Every moderator miscue or error may potentially affect the respondents, and influence results.

The moderator's toolbox consists of a wide variety of tools which enables them to achieve their objectives. We shall examine some of these tools in the following sections.

INVENTING HYPOTHETICAL SCENARIOS   If the discussion is about alcoholic beverages, the moderator may introduce several scenarios such as dinner at home, dinner in a restaurant, relaxing in the afternoon on a weekend, etc. Such scenarios put the participants in particular situations that can make the discussion more realistic, and shed light on how different products are perceived under different usage circumstances.

REGRESSION   When participants get stuck, removing them from the present and putting them in a different context might aid the discussion to go forward. Such questions as, "What did you think about smoking cigarettes when you were young?" may also be used to gather additional information about participants' attitudes towards a product.

SILENCE   In our culture, whenever people interact, a level of discomfort quickly develops if there is a long pause in conversation, as often happens. The moderator can use this pause to ask another question, but someone in the group is bound to talk eventually, simply to fill the gap. Forcing respondents to fill the vacuum when the group seems to be running out of steam is one way to induce a fresh approach. However, the moderator should be careful not to let the silence go on too long, lest someone say, "I guess we're done, then," when they aren't at all.

NEGATIVE QUESTIONS   Using negative questions is a way of eliciting less apparent distinctions that exist in the particpant's mind. Suppose a participant states that she never goes to supermarkets. The moderator might simply ask "What would happen if you did?" This type of negative questioning is likely to focus the participant's thinking on the specific reasons for a given behaviour.

PROJECTIVE TECHNIQUES   In addition to the techniques described above, a moderator can use projective techniques. Projective techniques are an indirect way of gleaning insights into human behaviour. These techniques are based on the work of psychoanalysts who claim that we attribute our less socially acceptable feelings, emotions and motives to others. For example, we may be too embarrassed to admit (or may not even know at the conscious level) that we are highly concerned about our appearance. Yet, if we are asked to write a story based on a photograph, we may freely project our concerns onto the person in the story and state that he or she seems highly concerned with his or her appearance. Such projective techniques include the following:

PERSONIFICATION   This is a commonly used method. In this technique, respondents are asked to assume that a product is a person; can the respondent describe this person? For example, if a Toyota and a Jaguar are people, what human characteristics would you attribute to them?

Personification is relatively easy to interpret and to understand. Due to its reasonably common reference points, it is widely used. However, it only lends itself to subjects in which it is reasonable to assume that respondents will be able to carry it out because the product has a well-established and distinctive image. Trying to personify such products as two obscure brands of allergy remedy would be asking too much. The test for the appropriateness of any projective technique is for the researchers to ask themselves whether or not they could respond fairly to the question themselves. A question that leaves researchers uncertain how to answer it is bound to leave respondents scratching their heads.

TRANSPOSED VOCABULARY   In this technique, which is similar to personification, respondents are asked to assume that a given product is actually a different product. How would they describe them? For example, what if Ivory Liquid and Palmolive Liquid were not detergents but clothing stores. What would they look like? What lines would they carry? How would they arrange their displays? Who would shop there? How would they advertise? Such transposition is expected to remove the respondents' mental blocks and release them from rational and linear thinking, thereby providing valuable insights to the researcher.

TRANSFERENCE   Similar in psychological roots to projection, this technique is particularly suitable for socially sensitive issues. An example of the use of this technique would be the question, "That is very interesting, but I bet you know people who wouldn't share your viewpoints. What do you know of the way others think about this?" Thus, by removing from the respondent the responsibility for the opinions expressed, the researcher may be able to obtain a less inhibited view of the underlying motives behind the consumer's behaviour. There is a danger here: it may be impossible to know whether the respondent shares the transferred views, or is merely being a good reporter.

SENTENCE COMPLETION   Here the respondent is given an incomplete sentence and is asked to complete it. The theory is that, in so doing, the respondent will reveal his or her biases, preferences and hidden motives. An example of this technique would be, "From what I've seen, people who only fly with Air Canada are ..." (The respondent is expected to complete the sentence.) There are several variations of this technique. Though respondents may be quick to recognize this for the manipulation it in fact is. More sophisticated respondents may refuse to play along by pointedly doing no more than reiterating what they have said before, to dissuade the moderator from trying again. They may also become annoyed. However, these drawbacks can be true of any projective technique.

HALF QUESTIONS   This is a variation of the sentence completion technique—except that here the respondents do not know that they are filling in a sentence or a question. For example, the researcher may state, "If I understand you correctly this commercial is getting at ...", and then seems to draw a blank. As the researcher fumbles for words, the respondent tries to help out with a suitable completion, without realizing that the researcher had no intention of finishing the sentence in the first place. This approach is much less likely to be problematic with sophisticated respondents, who may even think their wisdom has come to the rescue of the moderator.

Here, too, discretion is called for. Doing this more than once or twice in a group can convey the metamessage that the moderator might be daydreaming, or has trouble understanding what is being said, to the detriment of rapport.

OTHER TECHNIQUES   The above are known as projective techniques because the respondent projects his or her own ideas when presented with half-questions, incomplete sentences or personification. There are several other related techniques, although most of them are not used on a regular basis. (Projective techniques as a whole are in fact only used when merited, not as a regular part of group conduct.) Some may be helpful with certain groups of people. For example, techniques based on drawings and cartoons can be helpful when dealing with children. When respondents are locked into some form of linear thinking, thus providing no new insights into the problem, fantasy or hypothetical scenarios may be helpful in reorganizing their perceptions.

It may be productive to try role-playing techniques with teenagers who can be very shy and hard to motivate to get into a subject. Role playing can be helpful with adults as well, especially when dealing with inherently interactive situations. For example, it may be an ideal way to probe customer-salesperson relations.

Free-choice rankings of products can also provide much insight. Here the respondents are presented with an assortment of related products that are to be arranged according to any criterion chosen by a given respondent; subsequent rankings by others are to be based on different criteria. One can even use masking tape to create a product segmentation grid on the discussion table, and allow the group to place actual products on it as a reflection of how they perceive them.

USE PROJECTIVE TECHNIQUES WITH CAUTION   There are several things that one should bear in mind when using projective techniques. First, the interpretation of what the respondent says is not always clear cut. The statements may be open to more than one interpretation, and in such a case, it is almost impossible for the moderator to keep his or her own biases out of it. Second, some respondents may not want to respond to projective technique type questions; they may even be dissuaded from further participation. Third, projective techniques leave room for client observers to each overlay their own biases in the way they interpret the responses, resulting in conflict in later trying to decide what it all meant. Notwithstanding all these limitations, projective techniques can be very effective if used properly.

WRITING EXERCISES   During the course of the discussion a moderator can make use of writing exercises or their substitutes. Writing exercises are used when the moderator would like to know the uninfluenced opinions of each member of the group on a pivotal point. For example, after viewing a commercial, each respondent may be asked to complete a simple questionnaire before the floor is turned over to open discussion once again. There is no intent to tabulate such data. They are collected and scanned by the moderator as an opinion snapshot of the group, providing guidance on where to proceed with questioning.

When less precaution is needed, a close equivalent of a show-of-hands may be used. The round-robin question is a similar technique in which each respondent's bottom-line response is obtained serially, each being for a yes or no, for ratings from 1 to 10, etc. Although serial questioning tends to make the respondents passive, a few round-robins, done quickly, cause no harm and aid the goal of equal participation.

USE OF DISPLAY MATERIALS   Many discussions involve display materials, like package or ad designs, product samples, concept statements, etc. When the goal is to assess the relative impact of these materials, they are presented simultaneously. When relative impact is not important, but maximum depth of response to each piece of design is important, serial presentation is more appropriate. However, in serial presentation, sequence bias may be involved. This should be minimized by careful *a priori* sequencing of the materials and by proper rotation procedures between groups.

BIAS IN QUALITATIVE RESEARCH

Bias in qualitative research is of two types, study-related and moderator-related. The study-related biases arise out of incorrect problem definition, improper recruitment, poor display material, restrictions on proper rotation of display material, an inappropriate research location, excessive subject matter, and unrealistic timing provisions.

The moderator-related biases arise out of factors such as the moderator's inability to remain dispassionate, moderator incompetence and inability to control, insensitivity to cross-currents and subtleties, political pressures that are brought to bear on the moderator, and inadequate briefing. When biases are detected, they can sometimes be adjusted for, provided they are not very serious.

ANALYZING AND REPORTING

CLASSIFICATION AND PATTERN IDENTIFICATION

Focus groups are analyzed using a wide variety of techniques and tactics. The tapes are nearly always listened to by either the moderator or a trained analyst, or a transcript is made. Moderators usually also make analytical use of the notes they took during the group. In addition, their own recall of the dynamics and non-verbal aspects of the groups plays an important part. The two common modes of analysis are classification and pattern identification.

CLASSIFICATION   The moderator examines every quotation and analytical note and classifies them under various categories derived from the study objectives. A study outline may yield ten or more main classifications, each divided into sub-classifications—there may be dozens, depending on how fine the breakdowns are and on the complexity of the subject matter.

PATTERN IDENTIFICATION   In this critical phase, the moderator looks for patterns among groups and tests the data with the following questions:

- Which groups reacted one way, which another? Why?
- Were there correlations by group structure or not? Why?
- On what did the groups agree or disagree? Why?

From this process, which seeks not simply to describe the responses but to explain them, come the hypotheses that qualitative research generates. The experienced moderator does not interpret the results in isolation, but judiciously takes into account past experience in the category as well.

FORMAL ANALYSIS PROCEDURES

We can also use a more elaborate and formal scheme for analyzing qualitative data. Such formal schemes often require that the analyst be aware of the analysis to be performed from the very beginning because some necessitate that the researcher conduct group interviews in a certain way. One such scheme is proposed by David Snell (1987):

1. *Use content analysis for relevant analysis*: This is the basic form analysis in which the moderator goes through his or her notes/tapes to identify responses to relevant questions. We can also create quantitative indices such as likes and dislikes or positive and negative statements.

2. *Identify categories or themes*: In this type of analysis we go a step further and create categories of information by sorting through the focus group transcript. Such categories can be created in three ways:
   - actual comments by the respondents
   - analyst's interpretation of the interview content
   - *a priori* information

Other forms of content analyses include sorting through key themes and identifying contradictions and complexities.

3. *Use relational and causal analysis*: This type of analysis is used to identify the causal links between different responses provided by the respondents. To accomplish this one can use cross-reference matrices (Godet, 1979) which is a way of relating different elements. The analyst first creates a matrix of different elements and uses the data from transcripts to think about the relationships between the two or three items in the cell. If the analyst decides that they are related, he or she then explores the strength of the relationship. The laddering technique described later in this chapter is a more formalized exploration of this technique.

   Some analysts prefer to use holistic judgment (Patton, 1980). They find the formal exploration described in the previous section rather restrictive and may prefer to use their prior knowledge and experience to interpret what a given set of responses means.

4. *Identify symbolic meanings*: Symbolic meaning is created when a consumer interprets a product—what does this product mean to me? The underlying assumption is that the users are saying something about themselves and about the relationship of the product to themselves when they use it and when they talk about it.

Respondents may generate comments that may be designated as binary oppositions (Levy, 1981). Such concepts would include descriptions of a product as masculine or feminine, low status or high status, etc. Respondents may also have product boundaries (Leach, 1976), and define products accordingly. Products have different meanings depending on the boundaries. For instance, drinking alone has a different meaning compared to drinking socially, and the type of clothing you wear might depend on the context. The job of the analyst who is interested in product boundaries is to look for references to such boundaries in respondents' lives, seek the associated meanings and relate the product to these boundaries. Yet another way to analyze the data is to look for signals, signs and symbols (Dugaree, 1986) a product stands for. A product signals something if it is causally related to it (e.g., exercising makes you fit); a product is a sign of all things that are associated with the full context that goes with the object (e.g., driving a BMW as a sign of being a yuppie). Symbols are an attempt to link two unrelated things, such as eating at McDonald's as an American way of life.

5. *Use deformalization procedures*: Deformalization is a strategy of understanding what a word actually means to a respondent. Often people hide meaning under formalization and nominalization. A statement like, "Big business does not care about the environment," is a formalization of specific discontents. For instance, what is the "environment?" Is the respondent referring to overpackaging for some products? Or does it have anything to do with chemical pollution? Similarly, what is "big business?" An exploration (deformalization) may reveal that the respondent is simply dissatisfied with one aspect of the product/service/corporation but has generalized it to a whole category by formalizing and nominalizing it.

In practice, the researcher can use any or all the above methods, in any combination he or she chooses.

VERIFICATION PROCEDURES

The findings arrived at by the analysis of notes and transcripts need to be verified for two reasons. First, it is a means of increasing one's confidence in the validity of the findings. Second, it increases the confidence of the user in the quality of the findings. There are several methods by which the analyst can verify his or her findings. All these methods are themselves tenuous. Some of those suggested are not even feasible in all cases. Nevertheless, verification through some of these and other methods should be preferred to analysis that uses no means of verification.

1. *Frequency of occurrence*: If two concepts are strongly related, they are likely to recur in several contexts during the discussion, possibly from different participants. Tentative relationships are likely to be mentioned in passing.

2. *Rival explanations*: Is there another explanation for the findings than the one arrived at by the analyst? Can the findings be explained by another hypothesis that would contradict the current one? If this is the case, why should this explanation be preferred?

3. *Negative cases*: When patterns and trends are identified, are there participants who contradict the pattern? If so, why? Why should a contradictory pattern be given less weight? Are we emphasizing exceptions? Are we emphasizing current trends rather than emerging ones? What is our bias?

4 *Triangulation*: This is a way of comparing two or more independent sources of information to see if they match. When they do, we can place greater reliance on our findings. For example, does the conventional analysis agree with the projective technique findings? Is it in line with current social trends as measured by other sources? Does it agree with quantitative research findings (if they are available)? Obviously, if other sources of perfect information were available, we would probably not be doing qualitative research. In triangulation, all we are trying to do is to see if the findings are generally in line with those observed elsewhere.

   Triangulation can also be achieved by comparing notes taken by different observers during the focus group session. While some focus group moderators may find this statement heretical (i.e., comparing his or her notes with those of a lay observer), sometimes it may be a good way of confirming one's thoughts or of looking at things from a different perspective. A variation of this theme is to present the findings to respondents for their reactions at a later date. While the moderator aims to go beyond what is explicitly stated by participants, it may be instructive to find out what the participants feel about the analysts' conclusions.

5. *Design checks (Keep methods and data in context):* Qualitative research design is subject to three sources of errors:
   - *Respondent sampling deficiencies.* The majority of the chosen respondents may belong to a group that does not form the target group for the product under consideration. Or they may be professional respondents—those who attend a number of focus groups. Trying to generalize from such groups is fraught with the potential for making misleading interpretations.
   - *Time sampling deficiencies.* For instance, if a focus group on a political subject is held immediately after a political scandal, the results will be influenced to a large extent by that scandal. If our aim is not to assess the immediate effect of the scandal, our findings are likely to be biased since they are unduly influenced by what is likely to be a short-term reaction to a random event.
   - *Situation sampling constraints.* Because of time constraints, focus groups may have to omit discussion of certain areas or perspectives. If the areas actually covered are not broad enough (if salient situations

are inadvertently left out), then the findings will not adequately reflect the true state of affairs.

Exhibit 5.2 shows different types of focus groups and the analytical and verification strategy that can be used with each type.

Exhibit 5.2 Focus Group Design and Analysis Model			
Research Type	**Focus Group Type**	**Analytical Strategy**	**Verification Strategy**
Hypothesis Generation	Exploratory	Content Analysis for Relevant Information; Content Analysis for Key Themes	Frequency and Strength of Occurrence, Design Checks; A Quantitative Study
Questionnaire Pre-Testing	Exploratory	Content Analysis for Relevant Information	Frequency and Strength of Occurrence, Design Checks
Communications Effectiveness Testing	Enumerative	Content Analysis for Relevant Information	Frequency and Strength of Occurrence, Design Checks
New Product Development	Enumerative	Content Analysis for Relevant Information	Frequency and Strength of Occurrence, Design Checks
Consumer Food Problem Detection	Enumerative	Content Analysis for Relevant Information; Content Analysis for Key Themes	Frequency and Strength of Occurrence, Design Checks
Brand Image and Meaning Study	Phenomenological	Content Analysis for Symbolic Meaning; Content Analysis for Key Themes; Deformalization	Triangulation—Multiple Observers and Analysts, Presenting Analysis Results to Respondents, Rival Explanations, Negative Cases
Motivational Analysis	Clinical/ Motivational	Content Analysis for Key Themes; Relational and Causal Analysis	Triangulation—Multiple Observers and Analysts, Presenting Results to Respondents, Rival Explanations, Negative Cases, Design Checks
Social Segment/ Social Trend Analysis	Phenomenological plus Clinical/ Motivational	Content Analysis for Key Issues; Relational and Causal Analysis	Triangulation—with Quantitative Data, Triangulation—Multiple Observers and Analysts, Negative Cases, Design Checks

Source: David A. Snell, "Focus Groups: Theory and Analysis." *Canadian Journal of Marketing Research*, 1987,6.

WRITING THE REPORT

On the basis of the analysis as outlined, the moderator prepares the final report which is a mixture of analytical and descriptive text with illustrative verbatim quotes. It should be logically ordered and clearly expressed just as any research report should be. The report appraises and interprets the findings, relates them to the study objectives, and may also provide recommendations.

INTERPRETING THE RESULTS

The results obtained through qualitative research are descriptive of the group(s) and not projectable to the population in the formal sense that applies to survey data. However, decision-makers can put considerable faith in qualitative research when the following conditions are met:

- The client already has a substantial research background in the subject and familiarity with its workings
- The results seem sensible and reasonable when evaluated against this background, with no inexplicable or untoward surprises
- There was much more consistency than disagreement between groups, relative to their composition
- Recruiting was accurate and appropriate
- The moderator was known to be sufficiently familiar with the subject not to be led astray by spurious responses.

Even under these conditions, the results are still hypotheses, but in all reasonable likelihood, valid ones. Such hypotheses nearly always need to be validated by confirmatory, quantitative studies. Modest variation may be found in the proportion of the universe that holds the various views, but almost never in terms of whether the views are legitimate and meaningful.

OTHER QUALITATIVE TECHNIQUES

Although individual and group depth interviews are by far the most commonly used qualitative techniques, there are other powerful qualitative techniques. We will describe two such techniques, repertory grid analysis and laddering. Both these are based on principles of psychology and are considerably more structured than focus groups.

REPERTORY GRID ANALYSIS

Repertory grids assume that we see our lives and purchasing choices in terms of constructs that are relevant to us. The task of the researcher, then, is to elicit these constructs on which people evaluate a product. This technique is described in Chapter 17, Communication Research.

MISUSE OF QUALITATIVE RESEARCH

By now it should be obvious that qualitative research can be a powerful tool, if used appropriately and carried out by a competent researcher. However, qualitative research is very often misused. Many neophyte research buyers tend to think that qualitative research tells them all they want or need to know. Another tendency is to increase the number of groups unnecessarily and use them as a substitute for quantitative research. Some research buyers have an inadequate understanding of quantitative research because of its technical nature and feel comfortable with qualitative research, even when it is not quite appropriate or adequate. All such misuse eventually diminishes the usefulness of qualitative research by forcing it to do things that it is not designed to do.

SUMMARY

1. **What is qualitative research?** Qualitative research aims to obtain insights into consumer behaviour rather than to draw precise conclusions. The opinions so gathered are typically used to generate hypotheses, which may be further tested and confirmed by quantitative research procedures.

2. **Focus group and depth interviews**. In a typical focus group, eight to ten people whose opinions are relevant to the subject are assembled in a central location, and are interviewed over the course of two hours or so by a moderator trained in the special skills required for working with such groups. Individual depth interviews are conceptually similar to focus groups, but the moderator talks to one respondent at a time rather than to a group of people.

3. **When to use focus groups?** Focus groups may be useful under the following conditions:

    • There is an information vacuum which needs to be filled before the topic can be meaningfully and effectively researched by quantitative methods.

- There is a need to understand the basis of consumer motivations, priorities, anxieties, hidden agendas, patterns of perceptions, desires, and so forth which may not emerge fully when investigated quantitatively
- There is a need to "boil down" several initial alternatives to the more workable and promising few
- We need input to the creative process
- The subject matter is too subtle to create efficient direct questions for use in standard survey research techniques

4. **Criteria for selecting respondents** (general guidelines):

- Respondents should not be known to the moderator, and they should be strangers to one another
- Respondents should not be regular participants in focus group discussions
- As far as is feasible, respondents should be unaware in advance of the discussion details
- Respondents should be sufficiently skilled in the language so that they do not misunderstand the moderator and vice versa
- Respondents should not be closely connected to each other or the research and advertising industry in general

5. **Two methods by which respondents are chosen**: In the *random* method, respondents are chosen using mechanical statistical procedures. In the *referral* method respondents are recruited on the basis of being referred by others.

6. **How many groups to use**? The more segmented the market is, the larger the number of groups needed. The best test for determining the number of groups is to identify how many segments are necessary in order to elicit all major motivational perspectives related to the subject.

   While increasing the number of groups increases one's chance of finding new material that is relevant to the product category, increasing the number of groups beyond a certain number is counter-productive. Conducting groups beyond that number merely produces more of the same.

7. **What the moderator needs to know**:

- The marketing environment
- The range of subjects and issues to be investigated
- The format, kind and degree of finish, etc., of display materials, if such are to be used during the interview.

8. **Moderating skills**: Moderators need two types of skills to be successful: general skills and specific skills.

   General skills: These include the following abilities:

- To put the respondents at ease
- To control the group dynamics

- To create and maintain rapport
- To understand what is communicated
- To understand implied meanings
- To understand and respond to respondents' physiological states and speech patterns
- To use framing and reframing
- To break rapport with respondents when required

Specific skills: Familiarity with standard techniques such as:
- Inventing hypothetical scenarios
- Regression
- Silence
- Negative questions
- Personification
- Transposed vocabulary
- Transference
- Sentence completion
- Half questions
- Writing exercises
- Using display materials

9. **Formal procedures for analyzing group interviews:** The two common modes of analysis are classification and pattern identification. Formal analysis procedures include:
   - Using content analysis for relevant analysis
   - Identifying categories or themes
   - Using relational and causal analysis
   - Identifying symbolic meanings
   - Using deformalization procedures

10. **Verification procedures:** A moderator can use a variety of techniques to verify his or her focus group findings:
    - Frequency of occurrence
    - Rival explanations
    - Negative cases
    - Triangulation
    - Design checks:
      - respondent sampling deficiencies
      - time sampling deficiencies
      - situation sampling constraints.

11. Other qualitative techniques:

- *Repertory Grid Analysis*: Aims to explore the constructs which a consumer used to make distinctions between different products, brands or services.

- *Laddering*: The respondents are repeatedly probed to lead them from surface attitudes to consequences to end values (called ACV model). The moderator probes the respondent until ends values are arrived at.

NOW THINK ABOUT THIS

You are the marketing research manager of a bank. You would like to know what your customers think of the quality of service you offer.

1. What factors would influence your decision on how many focus groups to conduct? On what basis would you decide who the focus group participants should be? Are projective techniques relevant to this problem? If so which ones? Why?

2. Is laddering a suitable technique for this purpose? Discuss the pros and cons of this technique in relation to the above problem.

3. Write a discussion guide for the moderator.

REFERENCES

Dugaree, J.F.
1986   "Richer Qualitative Findings." *Journal of Advertising Research*, 25(6), pp. 29-37.

Godet, M.
1979   *The Criteria in Forecasting and the Emergence of the Forecasting Approach*. New York: Pergamon Press.

Goldman, Alfred E., and Susan S. McDonald
1987   *The Group Depth Interview*. NJ, Englewood Cliffs: Prentice-Hall.

Gutman, Jonathan
1982   "A Means-End Chain Model Based on Consumer Categorization Processes." *Journal of Marketing*, 46, 2, pp. 60-72.

Leach, Edmund R.
1976   *Culture and Communication*. New York: Cambridge University Press.

Levy, J.
1981   "Interpreting Consumer Mythology: A Structural Approach to Consumer Behaviour." *Journal of Marketing*, Summer.

Patton, M.Q.
1980   *Qualitative Evaluation Methods*. CA: Sage Publications.

Reynolds, Thomas, and Jonathan Gutman
1988   "Laddering Theory, Method, Analysis and Interpretation." *Journal of Advertising Research*, 28(1), pp. 11-31.

Snell, David A.
1987   "Focus Groups: Theory and Analysis." *Canadian Journal of Marketing Research*, 6.

APPENDIX 5A

What the Focus Group Observers Should Know

If you are taking part in a focus group study as an observer, there are some aspects of this role that you should sensitize yourself to. The most obvious one is to conduct yourself in a serious and business-like manner, and to influence others to do the same. This is both to enhance your own learning from the process, and to facilitate that of others. Pay attention, take notes, and cultivate the virtue of patience.

People are able to process information much more quickly than they can articulate it. That's why the discussion process may at times seem plodding to you, a passively listening non-participant. Teach yourself to resist the "get-on-with-it syndrome" of wishing the moderator would hurry up. What may seem slow behind the mirror, especially after four hours or more, may seem adequately animated and productive from the moderator's chair.

While some good-natured bantering and light hearted moments are to be expected behind the glass, a party atmosphere is inappropriate. Not only does this subvert the rationale for having observers present, but the muffled sounds of commotion that will come through even the best soundproof mirror will be disruptive to moderator and respondents alike. Moreover, you will be telling the moderator that you aren't interested enough to pay attention.

Bear in mind that the respondents should not know the specific identity of the client. For that reason, be very discreet when asking the hostess for directions to the observation room if you are at an unfamiliar facility. Don't say, "I'm Mary Smith from ABC Corp. and I'm here to watch the focus groups." Respondents may be in the waiting area, overhearing you. Instead, just ask for the moderator by name. The hostess will immediately understand, and anonymity will be preserved. Also, don't take a break from the back room with a colleague and chat about the progress of the groups where early arrivals for the next group may overhear you. If you must make a business-related phone call where respondents may overhear, try to by cryptic.

If you intend to discuss certain last minute issues with the moderator, arrange to meet at the facility an hour ahead. Don't bring substantive new issues to the project at the last moment. This can confuse things more than help them, and if such eleventh hour re-briefing runs on, as it tends to do, the group may start late. A group that is running behind schedule must not only be rushed to end on time if there is another one to follow, but also begins with testy respondents who have been kept waiting, and who may feel more combative than cooperative.

If there are a number of observers, avoid having everyone arrive en masse at the last minute. The sight of a half-dozen people with briefcases marching through their midst (which is often the way it happens) can be disconcerting to the respondents sitting and waiting. If it is impossible for you to arrive a half hour early, then arrive ten minutes late. You will miss little or nothing, and the group will not be disrupted by your arrival. Facilities that keep respondents and observers separate, which is the ideal, remove this constraint.

Quite often an important point occurs to the observers that the moderator seems to have missed, or that was not on the original agenda. If absolutely necessary, you can arrange to have the hostess take in a note, but remember that this is highly disruptive to the flow of the discussion and to the moderator's train of thought. It is better to arrange in advance that the moderator visit the observers' room on a pretext midway during the group to pick up such questions, or to do so ten minutes or so before the end. Don't necessarily assume that the moderator has missed a point, just because he didn't deal with it when you thought he should have done. The moderator may well have picked it up, but be keeping it for later in anticipation of a more propitious moment.

Remember that if you have done your job of briefing the moderator properly, it is then incumbent on you to let him or her do the job properly. Show confidence, and try to resist the urge to closely stage-manage what is done. Your consideration will be repaid by an increased eagerness to work hard for you. If you send the message that you don't trust the moderator to do the job, he or she will hardly be eager to work with you again, and may well decline.

6 / Sampling

WHAT YOU WILL LEARN IN THIS CHAPTER

- To define and understand sample surveys
- The terms population, sampling unit and sample frame
- To distinguish between estimates and parameters
- To distinguish between sampling and non-sampling errors
- The characteristics of the main types of probability samples: single stage, multistage samples, telephone interviews
- To distinguish probability samples from non-probability samples
- To calculate the sample required for a given degree of precision

SAMPLE SURVEYS

A marketing research survey is the collection of information about characteristics of interest from some or all units of a population using well defined concepts, methods and procedures, and further compilation of such information into a useful summary form. If we were to get such information from all the units in our population (whether we're talking about Hamilton or all of Canada), we would be conducting a census survey. However, in most market research studies, we restrict ourselves to a portion of that population and the result is a sample survey. In general, market researchers would prefer to do census surveys, that is, asking everyone what they think about this or that concept or product. However, the restrictions imposed by cost, time and resources, nearly always result in sample surveys—asking only a representative group what they think and then projecting their answers to the rest of the population which was not asked. The selection of a representative group of subjects for a survey is what is known as sampling.

What is a representative group? How large should a sample be? What is the relationship between sample size and accuracy of results? This chapter attempts to answer these questions.

"Data! Data! Data!" he cried impatiently. "I can't make bricks without clay."

Sherlock Holmes

SAMPLE DESIGN

Every sample has certain defined characteristics. The *sample design* is a description of these characteristics. A sample design should specify the following: the population, the frame, the size of the sample and the methods for selecting the sample.

POPULATION (THE UNIVERSE)

In marketing research we are interested in a specific group of people. For example, we may be interested in all beer drinkers in Canada, undergraduates who hold part-time jobs, or people who drive Cadillacs. The group of interest is called the *population* or the *universe*. Definitions of population can encompass any feature of individuals that are under scrutiny. Some typical examples are

- adults 18+
- home owners
- doctors practising in Ontario

However, population definitions can also be very specific such as:

- men who drink at least 20 cans/bottles of beer per week
- home owners who have electric heating
- doctors currently practising psychiatry in Ontario

It is important to note that the target population (for which information is required) and the survey population (from which information is actually obtained) may be quite different, though a researcher's efforts should be concentrated on ensuring that they are identical. For example, you may want to know about the behaviour of adults in Canada. However, you may have neither the time nor the resources to conduct interviews in the Yukon. Therefore, the Yukon will be excluded from your survey population though the results will be projected to the entire population of Canada. Wherever such gaps arise, they should be pointed out to the client.

SAMPLING UNIT

A *sampling unit* is the smallest unit of a sample that will constitute one unit in analysis. If your survey is of Canadian adults, "Canadian adult" is your sampling unit. A sampling unit can be an individual, a household, a corporation.

SAMPLE FRAME

The sample frame is the means by which the population is physically accessed. Many market research studies depend on various types of lists, computer records, telephone directories, tapes and texts for listings of prospective respondents. To be effective, a sample frame should fulfill several conditions.

- **Comprehensiveness:** A good sample frame should include everyone in the population. In practice, this is seldom the case. For example, you may use telephone directories as a frame to reach households in a city. But this frame would exclude households with unlisted numbers and people who had recently moved. The usefulness of any frame depends on the nature and size of the omissions.

- **Precision of definition**: There are associations that represent people in a certain profession but their membership requirements are so broad that anyone who can pay the membership fee can become a member. If you are interested in doing a survey among members of this profession, using this association's membership list as your frame is likely to yield a number respondents who are not really in your target group.

In most cases, it is simply not possible to list our target audience. The most common procedure in such cases is to rely heavily on *area frames*. Area frames are geographical areas such as CMAs (Census Metropolitan Areas). EAs (Enumeration Areas), etc. These areas are defined by Statistics Canada.

Exhibits 6.1 and 6.2 show the Canadian geographic units. An EA, for example, may consist of 200 households within clearly defined boundaries. A researcher may select 100 EAs at first and then select eight households within each EA. While each resident in an EA may not be actually listed in a current listing somewhere, the physical city blocks remain as a solid record of who lives there. Frames can also be combined for further population definition,

Exhibit 6.1   Demographic Divisions

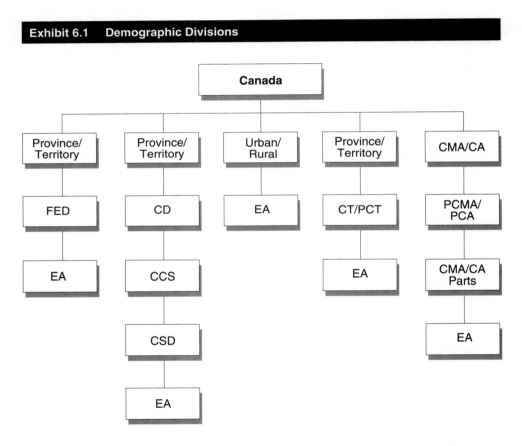

Demographic segmentation should not only take into account the current consumption structure and future growth patterns, but also the geographical variations in those patterns. For instance, when we project population growth over the next 10 years, we need to remember that the growth is not likely to be even across the country. Prosperous regions are likely to attract more people than depressed regions of the country. Demographic information is available at various levels as indicated in this chart.

Exhibit 6.2 Standard Census Geographic Units

Abbre-viations	Standard Census Geographic Units	Capsule Description	Coverage	
			No. of Units in Canada 1986	Size (based on 1981 population counts
CA	Census Agglomerations	Labour market areas with an urbanized core of at least 10 000 population, based on the previous census	114	From 10 000 to over 115 000 persons
CCS	Census Consolidated Subdivisions	Grouping of contiguous subdivisions	2 628	Less than 100 to around 2 000 000 persons
CD	Census Divisions	General term applying to census divisions, counties, regional districts, regional municipalities and five other types of areas made up of census subdivisions	266	5 000 to over 2 000 000 persons
CMA	Census Metropolitan Areas	Main labour market areas of urban areas (urbanized cores) of at least 100 000 population, based on previous census	25	From 100 000 to over 3 000 000 persons
CMA/ CA Parts	Census Metropolitan Area and Census Agglomeration Parts	Three types of areas— urbanized core, urban fringe and rural fringe within CMAs and CAs	359	From around 1 000 to almost 3 000 000
CSD	Census Subdivisions	General term applying to cities, towns, villages, Indian Reserves and settlements and unorganized territories	6 009	Less than 100 to around 1 000 000 persons
CT	Census Tracts	Permanently defined areas within large	3 776	About 4 000 persons

continued

urban communities

Abbre-viations	Standard Census Geographic Units	Capsule Description	Coverage	
			No. of Units in Canada 1986	Size (based on 1981 population counts
EA	Enumeration Areas	The basic area for which data are collected and the building block of all standard census geographic areas	44 080	About 600 persons
FED	Federal Electoral Districts	Areas that return a member to the House of Commons	282	About 85 000 persons
PCA	Primary Census Agglomerations	Labour market sub-region within a larger consolidated census metropolitan area (CMA) or consolidated census agglomeration (CA)	21	From 10 000 to about 115 000
PCMA	Primary Census Metropolitan Areas	Labour market sub-region within a larger consolidated census metropolitan area	12	From 100 000 to almost 3 000 000 persons
PCT	Provincial Census Tracts	Permanently defined areas outside large urban communities	1 837	About 5 000 persons
PR	Province/Territory	The major political division of the country	12	From almost 22 000 to over 9 000 000
UA	Urban Areas	An area with a population of 1 000 or more and a population density of 400 or more per square km	940	From 1 000 to almost 3 000 000

Counts are as of November 14, 1986. PCMAs and PCAs have been introduced for the first time as part of the 1986 Census.

such as EAs that have a higher proportion of high income earners.

Whichever method is used to determine the sample frame, it must be adequate to define the sample. If a list is used, it must be accurate, current and consist of unduplicated units. For example, if we are selecting doctors by their specialty from a list, we need to make sure that each doctor is listed only once. If the same doctor is listed more than once (under different specialties), it would a) give some doctors a greater chance of being included in the sample, and b) result in some doctors appearing twice in the sample.

ESTIMATES AND PARAMETERS

Suppose you are interested in knowing how many Canadian adults use your product. You conduct a study using a sample of 1000 Canadian adults. Your results show that 33 per cent of those surveyed use your product. This result—33 per cent users obtained through a sample survey—is called an *estimate*. What would the result be if you had collected this information by actually asking all Canadian adults rather than a sample of just 1000? Intuitively we feel that the results obtained by asking everyone in the population (called the *parameter*) are likely to be somewhat different from the sample estimate that we obtained. But different by how much? How close are our results to the true values or parameters? We try to estimate parameter values through sample estimates. The basic sampling questions are:

- Do sampling estimates track the parameter values closely?
- If they do, how closely?
- What factors can distort the relationship between sample estimates and parameter values?

At this stage, we would like to provide simple answers to the above questions.

- **Do sampling estimates track the parameter values closely?** Sampling estimates can track the parameter values closely, if two conditions are met: a) the sample is chosen using a set of procedures known as probability sampling, and b) the sample size is large enough.
- **If they do, how closely?** Provided the sample is chosen according to statistical principles, the closeness between the sample estimates and parameter values depends on the sample size.
- **What factors can distort the relationship between sample estimates and parameter values?** Uncontrolled or uncontrollable variables often enter a study and can create biases. The effect of biases (which tend to distort the relationship between parameter values and sample estimates) is often difficult to estimate. Variables such as a respondent's refusal to answer the survey, language problems, misunderstanding of questions posed, etc., are examples of biases that can distort the survey results.

SAMPLING ERRORS

When we use probability sampling procedures, we can assess the parameter values with consistency. However, *sampling errors* will be attached to the estimates we obtained through sampling. Sampling error results from studying only a small portion of the population. It therefore follows that the larger the sample, the smaller the sampling error. Sampling error can also arise when the characteristics studied are too varied (a wide variety of possible responses to the same question) for general conclusions—another function of limited sample size.

Without repeating the study in a census format, sampling error can be mathematically measured, but only if probability sampling methods were utilized in the sampling design.

A survey, for example, may show that 40% of the people favour the Liberal party, but the actual figure (if we measured everyone in the population) could be somewhere between 35% and 45% or 40% $\pm$ 5%. This is called *the confidence interval* (or *margin of error* or *precision of the estimate*) and it can be estimated using statistical formulas. Every confidence interval has a confidence level attached to it. Thus we can make statements such as "results are accurate within $\pm$ 5 percentage points (p.p.) 90% of the time." Our confidence interval or margin of error is $\pm$ 5 p.p. and the confidence level is 90%. In other words, if the study were repeated, the results would be the same within plus or minus 5 p.p. in 90 out of a hundred times. We shall see how this is arrived at in a later chapter.

NON-SAMPLING ERRORS

Non-sampling errors are more common than sampling errors and are inherent in nearly all sample (and census) surveys. This type of error is caused by a wide variety of factors including:

- Unclear questionnaire wording or skip patterns
- Poor interviewing or sampling procedures
- Respondent fatigue
- Language problems
- High level of non-response
- Omission of eligible units from the frame
- Incorrect data collection or data processing techniques

Non-sampling errors are non-statistical in nature and cannot be easily measured. Non-sampling errors can create biases in the study.

PROBABILITY SAMPLING

There are two sampling methods, probability sampling and non-probability sampling. The former, as its name implies, is based on the principle of randomness. *Random* means that each unit in the population has an equal, or at least measurable, chance of being included in the sample. The principle of randomness provides a sound theoretical basis for projecting the results to the general population.

A sample can be *single stage* or *multistage*. In single stage sampling we choose our sample directly from all sampling units in our frame. In multistage sampling, we go through several stages. For example, we may first choose the cities, then specific blocks within the city, and then households within each selected block, etc., before selecting a specific person to be interviewed. This procedure is called multistage sampling because the sample is not chosen directly from all available sampling units, but sampling is carried out at different levels of generalization (hence *multistage*) before the final sample unit is chosen.

SINGLE STAGE SAMPLING

SIMPLE RANDOM SAMPLING   Simple random sampling is a procedure in which every member of the population has an equal chance of being selected and included in the sample. If your objective were to collect information on customer satisfaction among bank customers with more than $3000 in their chequing accounts and you had a complete list of such customers (this would be the population), you could use a simple random sample. Here are two ways you could make the selection:

- Write each name on a separate piece of paper, mix up all the slips of paper, then draw out the number of names you require for your sample. This becomes difficult if you have hundreds of names to mix up. In practice, this procedure would be used only when the population is very small. In marketing research this procedure is rarely used.

- Another method is to use a table of random numbers. First, number each name on your list, then choose any column from the table of random numbers (see table in Exhibit 6.3).

If your population consisted of 20 000 customers and you had to select a sample of 2000 from it, you would select a five digit number from the table (because 20 000 has five digits and will accommodate the outermost limit of your population) and proceed in any direction from that number until 2000 numbers under 20 000 had been chosen. The numbers correspond to customer

Exhibit 6.3 Table of Random Numbers

53 74 23 99 07	61 32 28 69 84	94 62 67 86 24	98 33 41 19 95	47 53 53 38 09
63 38 06 86 54	99 00 65 26 94	02 82 90 23 07	79 62 67 80 60	75 91 12 81 19
35 30 58 21 46	06 72 17 10 94	25 21 31 75 96	49 28 24 00 49	55 65 79 78 07
63 43 36 82 69	65 51 18 37 88	61 38 44 12 45	32 92 85 88 65	54 34 81 85 35
98 25 37 55 26	01 91 82 81 46	74 71 12 94 97	24 02 71 37 07	03 92 18 66 75
02 63 21 17 69	71 50 80 89 56	38 15 70 11 48	43 40 45 86 98	00 83 26 91 03
64 55 22 21 82	48 22 28 06 00	61 54 13 43 91	82 78 12 23 29	06 66 24 12 27
85 07 26 13 89	01 10 07 82 04	59 63 69 36 03	69 11 15 83 80	13 29 54 19 28
58 54 16 24 15	51 54 44 82 00	62 61 65 04 69	38 18 65 18 97	85 72 13 49 21
34 85 27 84 87	61 48 64 56 26	90 18 48 13 26	37 70 15 42 57	65 65 80 39 07
03 92 18 27 46	57 99 16 96 56	30 33 72 85 22	84 64 38 56 98	99 01 30 98 64
62 95 30 27 59	37 75 41 66 48	86 97 80 61 45	41 53 04 01 63	45 76 08 64 27
08 45 93 15 22	60 21 75 46 91	98 77 27 85 42	28 88 61 08 84	69 62 03 42 73
07 08 55 18 40	45 44 75 13 90	24 94 96 61 02	57 55 66 83 15	73 42 37 11 61
01 85 89 95 66	51 10 19 34 88	15 84 97 19 75	12 76 39 43 78	64 63 91 08 25
72 84 71 14 35	19 11 58 49 26	50 11 17 17 76	86 31 57 20 18	95 60 78 46 75
88 78 28 16 84	13 52 53 94 53	75 45 69 30 96	73 89 65 70 31	99 17 43 48 76
45 17 75 65 57	28 40 19 72 12	25 12 74 75 67	60 40 60 81 19	24 62 01 61 16
96 76 28 12 54	22 01 11 94 25	71 96 16 16 88	68 64 36 74 45	19 59 50 88 92
43 31 67 72 30	24 02 94 08 63	38 32 36 66 02	69 36 38 25 39	48 03 45 15 22
50 44 66 44 21	66 06 58 05 62	68 15 54 35 02	42 35 48 96 32	14 52 41 52 48
22 66 22 15 86	26 63 75 41 99	58 42 36 72 24	58 37 52 18 51	03 37 18 39 11
96 24 40 14 51	23 22 30 88 57	95 67 47 29 83	94 69 40 06 07	18 16 36 78 86
31 73 91 61 19	60 20 72 93 48	98 57 07 23 69	65 95 39 69 58	56 80 30 19 44
78 60 73 99 84	43 89 94 36 45	56 69 47 07 41	90 22 91 07 12	78 35 34 08 72
84 37 90 61 56	70 10 23 98 05	85 11 34 76 60	76 48 45 34 60	01 64 18 39 96
36 67 10 08 23	98 93 35 08 86	99 29 76 29 81	33 34 91 58 93	63 14 52 32 52
07 28 59 07 48	89 64 58 89 75	83 85 62 27 89	30 14 78 56 27	86 63 50 80 02
10 15 83 87 60	79 24 31 66 56	21 48 24 06 93	91 98 94 05 49	01 47 59 38 00
55 19 68 97 65	03 73 52 16 56	00 53 55 90 27	33 42 29 38 87	22 13 88 83 34
53 81 29 13 39	35 01 20 71 34	62 33 74 82 14	53 73 19 09 03	56 54 29 56 93
51 86 32 68 92	33 98 74 66 99	40 14 71 94 58	45 94 19 38 81	14 44 99 81 07
35 91 70 29 13	80 03 54 07 27	96 94 78 32 66	50 95 52 74 33	13 80 55 62 54
37 71 67 95 13	20 02 44 95 94	64 85 04 05 72	01 32 90 76 14	53 89 74 60 41
93 66 13 83 27	82 79 64 64 72	28 54 96 53 84	48 14 52 98 94	56 07 93 89 30
02 96 08 45 65	13 05 00 41 84	93 07 54 72 59	21 45 57 09 77	19 48 56 27 44
49 83 43 48 35	82 88 33 69 96	72 36 04 19 76	47 45 15 18 60	82 11 08 95 97
84 60 71 62 46	40 80 81 30 37	34 39 23 05 38	25 15 35 71 30	88 12 57 21 77
18 17 30 88 71	44 91 14 88 47	89 23 30 63 15	56 34 20 47 89	99 82 93 24 98
79 69 10 61 78	71 32 76 95 62	87 00 22 58 40	92 54 01 75 25	43 11 71 99 31
75 93 36 57 83	56 20 14 82 11	74 21 97 90 65	96 42 68 63 86	74 54 13 26 94
38 30 92 29 03	06 28 81 39 38	62 25 06 84 63	61 29 08 93 67	04 32 92 08 00
51 29 50 10 34	31 57 75 95 80	51 97 02 74 77	76 15 48 49 44	18 55 63 77 09
21 31 38 86 24	37 79 81 53 74	73 24 16 10 33	52 83 90 94 96	70 47 14 54 36
29 01 23 87 88	58 02 39 37 67	42 10 14 20 92	16 55 23 42 45	54 76 09 11 06
95 33 95 22 00	18 74 72 00 18	38 79 58 69 32	81 76 80 26 92	82 80 84 25 39
90 84 60 79 80	24 36 59 87 38	82 07 53 89 35	96 35 23 79 18	05 98 90 07 35
46 40 62 98 82	54 97 20 56 95	15 74 80 08 32	16 46 70 50 80	67 72 16 42 79
20 31 89 03 43	38 46 82 68 72	32 14 82 99 70	80 60 47 18 97	63 49 30 21 30
71 59 73 05 50	08 22 23 71 77	91 01 93 20 49	82 96 59 26 91	66 39 67 08 60

numbers on your listing. While selecting these 2000 names, you would auto-matically discard numbers that exceeded 20 000 since your population does not have any customer with a number greater that 20 000.

In market research, commercially produced tables and computer- generat-ed random numbers are used to choose random samples. Computer-generated random numbers are particularly common in telephone surveys *(RRD or Random Digit Dialling)* where random telephone numbers are generated for the telephone exchanges in existence for the population covered by the survey.

SYSTEMATIC SAMPLING   Systematic sampling is similar to simple random sampling, but instead of selecting numbers or units at complete random they are chosen at a given interval. Using the previous example, if we want to select 200 doctors from a list of 4000, we would choose every twentieth doc-tor on the list. Therefore, our *sample interval* would be 20. As long as the list does not have a pattern (e.g., every twentieth customer is a surgeon), system-atic sampling will yield results comparable to random sampling. Usually, systematic samples will have a random start: the first person will be chosen at random and then the sample interval will be added to that number repeat-edly to select the rest of the sample. Thus in our example, if we choose a ran-dom number such as 3, we will select doctor number 3 and then keep adding 20 to this number until we get the required number: 3, 23, 43, 63, 83, 103, 123, and so on.

STRATIFIED SAMPLES   There are times when you want to be sure that your research sample represents several segments or sub-groups in your popula-tion. If you use a random sample, it is possible to miss an entire sub-group. Just as a simple random sample allows everyone an equal chance of being chosen, it also allows an equal chance of being excluded. The following examples describe situations in which a stratified sample might be used.

- **A research survey of staff in a multi-level organization**: You might choose to do group interviews with different levels of staff to assess their perception and needs. It is unlikely that there will be uniformity in the way they perceive things. Therefore, a study that stratifies and then samples each stratified group is likely to yield more useful results.

- **Surveying different ethnic groups**: Whenever a survey relates to a special characteristics of the population—be it ethnicity or income—it is more efficient to stratify the population according to the characteristic of interest first. This would ensure that each group of interest is adequate-ly represented in the final sample.

Now let's work through an example to see how to create a stratified sam-ple. Suppose we want to assess how a bank's customers react to the services provided by the bank. We find from our records that its customers are divided into the following categories:

a.	Customers with a balance of $50 or less	10%
b.	Customers with a balance of $50-$499	70%
c.	Customers with a balance of $500-$999	10%
d.	Customers with a balance of $1000-$1999	5%
e.	Customers with a balance of $2000+	5%

Let us assume that we want each one of these groups represented in the same proportion in our sample. Then we can use the following steps to stratify the sample so that every sub-group will be represented (in this case, in the same proportion as in the population):

1. Divide your population into the sub-groups identified above.

2. Determine the size of the sample needed for the population (this is explained later). Suppose you have decided on a sample size of 500.

3. Stratify your total sample into the same proportions that exist in the population. That is, multiply the number in the sample by the proportion of the population in each strata.

Type		Sample Size
a. 10% x 500	=	50
b. 70% x 500	=	350
c. 10% x 500	=	50
d. 5% x 500	=	25
e. 5% x 500	=	25
Total		500

4. Separate your total population list into separate lists, one for each group (stratum). Or, go through the total population list and indicate the appropriate sub-group beside each name.

5. Draw a random sample from each sub-group. If you've made a separate list for each sub-group, draw the required number of names at random from each list. If you are working from a master list, it is easiest to do one sub-group at a time.

Choose 50 people from group a
Choose 350 people from group b
Choose 50 people from group c
Choose 25 people from group d
Choose 25 people from group e

These 500 names from the five lists will represent the whole population of customers. You will be able to generalize any conclusions you draw back to the population of customers. In other words, stratified sampling uses relevant information about the population to define the sample to increase efficiency.

PPS AND DISPROPORTIONATE SAMPLES   The above procedure in which we selected the sample groups in the same proportions as the population is known as *PPS* or *probability proportional to size* or *proportionate sampling*. PPS procedures are not always efficient because we get a small number of respondents from smaller groups. This might make it very difficult to make generalizations about such groups. In the above example, two groups in our sample had only 25 people each. If we are particularly interested in those groups, the small sample sizes would make it very difficult for us to draw any conclusions regarding these groups. In such cases, an equal number of respondents may be drawn from each stratum so that each stratum is properly represented (*disproportionate sample*). When a disproportionate sample is used, the figures are adjusted to the proper proportion at the tabulation/analysis stage.

The use of the disproportionate sample is very common in marketing research. Suppose we decide to interview 1000 adults across the country. If we use PPS sampling, the sample will be distributed as follows:

	Population %	Sample Size (PPS)
Atlantic	17	170
Quebec	15	150
Ontario	19	190
Prairies	33	330
BC	16	160

In the above example, the four Atlantic provinces collectively get a sample of only 170 respondents. Again, if we want to understand upper income consumers in Quebec, the sample could be reduced to a small number (for example, if the upper income group is 20% of the Quebec population, then, we will have a sample of only 30 respondents in this group in our sample. To avoid this happening, we may assign a sample of 200 per region irrespective of it size. This will enable us to analyze the data in each region more satisfactorily. In the above example, the effect is not very dramatic. Even so, an evenly distributed sample is better suited for sub-group analysis in smaller regions.

It is important to realize that, from a statistical point of view, PPS has no special appeal. Once the sample is less than 10% of the population (which is the case in almost all market research surveys), *it is the actual sample size and not the size of the population that determines the accuracy of the results.*

Another important point to remember is that the results obtained using disproportionate sampling should be *weighted* to bring everything into proportion before combining the groups to arrive at total estimates. (This procedure is described in detail in Chapter 21, Sampling Methods.)

OVERSAMPLING   Oversampling is a special case of proportionate sampling. In this method, initial sampling is done using the PPS method. We then augment the sample by adding more respondents to groups that are small. For example, if you are doing a large scale study on toothpaste usage you may start with a PPS sample. Assume further than you are especially interested in Toothpaste A which has only a 3% market share. Even if your sample is as large as 1000, you may still be left with only 30 users of Toothpaste A and you would like at least 100 users. In such cases, you may decide to increase the number of Toothpaste A users by continuing the survey simply to identify and interview another 70 users. These 70 will not form a part of the main sample of 1000. But whenever users of A are analyzed, the 70 will be combined with the 30 obtained from the main sample. Oversampling procedures are commonly used in marketing research.

MULTISTAGE SAMPLING

How do we select a random sample in marketing research? In general we can use the single stage selection procedures described in the previous section. However, there are several problems such as

- There is no sample frame (list of all Canadians, suitably numbered) from which we can select the sample.
- If there were such a frame, it is quite possible that some respondents might live some 800 km away from any other respondent. It might not be feasible to travel 800 km to interview one single respondent.

To avoid these problems, we use a procedure known as multistage sampling. In a typical survey using random sampling procedures across Canada, the country is first divided into several regions. Each region is then divided into cities of different population sizes. For each region, a few cities representing each size group are drawn at random. Within each of these selected cities, a number of smaller areas called enumeration areas (EAs) are once again drawn at random. Within each EA a certain number of households are chosen and a person is drawn at random from the selected households and interviewed. (Refer to Exhibit 6.1 which shows the geographic areas commonly used in multistage sampling.)

CLUSTER SAMPLING   You can use cluster sampling when:

- your population is spread over a large geographic area

- your research plan calls for face-to-face interviewing or direct observations of people (or their houses, or recreation equipment, etc.).

If you wanted to study a sample of people who are seniors and who live alone, you would realize immediately that seniors are spread out over the entire city. If you drew a random sample (if you could obtain lists of all seniors who live alone), it is likely that the addresses would be so scattered that to reach them all would make travel costs prohibitive.

In cluster sampling, you minimize the number of areas that have to be visited by choosing only some areas for study. The first step in cluster sampling is to select at random a number of different locations in the city or in the province depending on the scope of your research and population. You can do this first step in two ways. The first way is to number every city block, or area of the province, then use a table of random numbers to select specific areas. The second way involves using maps that divide a geographic area with a grid, and then a table of random numbers is used to select specific areas for study.

The last step of cluster sampling is to choose a random sample of names or houses within the selected area. When names and addresses are not available, an interviewer can be instructed to go to every third, fourth (or whatever) house, depending on the sample size needed.

Cluster sampling maintains the principle of random selection of respondents so researchers can generalize results from a sample to the population, but it cuts down the final costs of interviewing. Locations are randomly chosen first, then respondents are randomly chosen in each location. Almost all personal interview studies use cluster sampling. Thus, once an EA or block is chosen as a sampling point, four to eight interviews may be carried out at the same sampling point. This is to avoid the excessive cost associated with carrying out interviews in locations that are spread out.

REPLICATED SAMPLING   In replicated sampling, to do a survey with 1000 respondents, you select your sample as though you are doing two surveys with 500 respondents each. This method is one way of determining the accuracy of your study results, since each replicate can be used to confirm the results obtained with the other replicate. In larger studies several replicates may be used.

TELEPHONE INTERVIEWS

As we discussed earlier, we use clustering procedures in personal interviewing for practical reasons. Telephone interviewing, on the other hand, does not have such restrictions. Calling a number next door is the same as calling a number across the town or across the country. In this sense, telephone samples can be superior to door-to-door samples. However, telephone samples are subject to their own problems:

- **Wastage:** A large number of phone numbers selected may belong to businesses or may be hooked up to fax machines.
- **Non-availability of respondents**: An increasing number of people use answering machines as a call screening device.
- **Refusals**: Many people find it easier to refuse an interview or discontinue the interview when the interviewer is just an anonymous voice at the other end. They find it harder to say no or to discontinue when the interviewer is seen in person.

There are three common ways in which telephone interviews are carried out. These are:

1. using white pages as the sample frame

2. using Random Digit Dialling

3. using seed samples/Plus *n* procedures

USING WHITE PAGES   In this technique, we simply choose the sample from the telephone directory (white pages). For practical purposes, you may decide to sample a few pages from a telephone directory and then randomly choose a number from each selected page. This procedure has several drawbacks. First, people who have unlisted numbers cannot be reached by this method. Second, most telephone directories have a lag ranging from 6 to 18 months. It is estimated that an average North American moves every five years. If we assume an average lag of 12 months between a directory's data collection, about 20% of the population cannot be reached by this method.

RANDOM DIGIT DIALLING   In the random digit dialling (RDD) method, all live exchange numbers (the first three digits of telephone numbers) are input in the computer. The computer randomly selects the last four digits thus providing a completely randomized sample.

While RDD is a very good method from a statistical point of view, it is very wasteful. It does not eliminate business numbers, fax numbers and numbers not in service. There is also the additional problem that it can include unassigned numbers. Suppose 923 is a live exchange currently in operation, but all the numbers starting with 923 may not yet have been assigned. (It could be a new exchange.) Yet the computer has no way of knowing how many numbers are actually assigned. Therefore, RDD will consist of numbers that are not assigned to anyone yet. In fact, a very high proportion of numbers selected by the RDD procedure tend to get wasted. While this does not affect the integrity of the sample, it does add to the cost of the study considerably. Many procedures are available to reduce such wastage, but RDD continues to be the most wasteful (although theoretically the best) method of selecting telephone samples.

SEED SAMPLES/PLUS N METHOD   This is a compromise between the theoretically less defensible white page sampling and the highly wasteful RDD sampling procedures. In seed sampling procedures, we make up a set of telephone numbers that are known to exist (they can come from the white pages). Then instead of using the numbers so chosen, we add a number (say 100) to the chosen number. For example, if our seed number is 555-1483, we add 100 to this number and it becomes 555-1583, and this is the number we dial. This procedure has several advantages:

- Since the new number may be listed or unlisted, we get potential access to unlisted numbers.
- It might be a number that was not in existence when the directory went to press and thus might include people who have recently moved.
- Because we are just adding a number to existing numbers, we are not likely to find too many unassigned numbers. For example, if exchange 555 has assigned only 1000 numbers, adding 100 to the number selected within this range is likely to pick up newly assigned numbers. If only the first 1000 numbers are assigned in this exchange, the Plus n method (unlike the RDD method) will not generate numbers in the 2000 to 9000 series.

While the Plus n method is not as theoretically sound as the RDD method, given the cost-savings and its near equivalence to the theoretical model, Plus n should be seriously considered as an effective alternative to RDD.

NON-PROBABILITY SAMPLING

A large number of marketing research surveys use non-probability sampling procedures. Considerations of cost and timing are the main reasons for the use of non-probability samples. Furthermore, in certain diagnostic areas of research—such as the acceptability of the taste of a proposed product or the offensiveness of a new commercial—it may not be critical to have probability samples. Some non-probability samples are described below.

PURPOSIVE SAMPLE

This is a fairly common way of selecting people to respond to a survey or to be interviewed about issues. In purposive samples, the choice of an individual depends on someone's judgment of who is and who isn't a typical representative of the population. Sometimes, people are selected because of their reputations, or because they are publicly visible, or because they hold some position in an organization.

Purposive samples (e.g., talking to the presidents of organizations, to the executive directors, or chairmen of councils, etc.) are perfectly legitimate ways of collecting information. However, no claims should be made that the views of these people represent the views of the population. The people are chosen because of their role in an organization that might well represent their group to government but in a true (sampling) sense their opinions are not representative of the population they come from.

ACCIDENTAL SAMPLE

This is the weakest type of sample, but it is the easiest to get. "Man-in-the-street" interviews are typical of accidental samples. The researchers simply uses the first five, or ten (or whatever number) people who happen along and are willing to talk. There are enormous chances for bias in accidental sampling. For example, suppose you were doing a survey of community recreational needs and you decided to interview 100 households. If the interviewers went to selected addresses and talked to whoever answered the door, the sample would be accidental. Children, mothers, fathers, babysitters, etc., could have answered the door and been interviewed. It's possible that the majority of respondents would have been children or teenagers—neither of whom represent the whole of the community.

Accidental sampling produces results that can lead to accidents in drawing conclusions and making decisions.

QUOTA SAMPLING

Quota sampling is sometimes used when two conditions are present: 1) you have limited resources; and 2) in spite of your limited resources you want to be certain that your sample mirrors, as closely as possible, the gross features of your population. For example, you may decide that your research budget will allow interviews with a sample of only 60 people. Let's say you are interested in the view of a group of recent immigrants about recreation opportunities in their neighbourhood, and you are also interested in the views of specific sub-groups. Even though you can't afford to do a stratified sample of the size required to make precise generalizations, you can construct a sample of 60 in which you specify how many persons of different characteristics should be included.

Let's say your population of adult newcomers had the following characteristics:

Sex	Males	60%
	Females	40%
Age	21-34	25%
	35-54	45%
	Over 55	30%

If you want your sample of 60 to be as much like the population as possible, then it should be constructed to fit these known percentages. With a total sample size of 60, you will need 36 males (60% of 60) and 24 females (40% of 60). Among the male sub-sample, you will want 9 in the 21-34 age group (25% of 36), 16 in the 35-54 age group (45% of 36) and 11 in the over 55 age group (30% of 36).

This procedure will give you a miniature of the population in a very small sample. In general, this type of sample will give you a quick reading on the population, but there may be a large margin of error because sample members are not selected at random.

When the interviewer goes out, he or she will interview an adult from among the newcomers in the area, note which category that person fits into, then go on to the next address until all of the required numbers of people have been interviewed. That is, until the quota for each sub-group in the sample has been filled.

Many market research studies (taste testing, reactions to some print advertisements, etc.) are often carried out in shopping malls. Since the researcher does not have any control over who happens to enter a shopping mall, he or she tries to control the respondent characteristics, usually though the use of quota sampling procedures.

GENERALIZING FROM A SAMPLE

Suppose we want to find out the percentage of teenagers in Canada who smoke. We can carry out a survey among 1000 teenagers in Canada. But how do we know that our results, based on just these 1000 teenagers, are really representative of all teenagers in Canada? How do we know that the results obtained through a sample will represent the universe (population)? This is the fundamental sampling problem. (The true answer is called the *parameter* and the result obtained by us is called the *estimate*.)

"While the individual man is an insoluble puzzle, in the aggregate he becomes a mathematical certainty. You can, for example, never foretell what any man will be up to, but you can say with precision what the average number will be up to. Individuals vary, but percentages remain constant."
Sherlock Holmes (Sir Arthur Conan Doyle, *The Sign of Four*, 1899).

To make any statement about the population from a sample, we must first make sure that our sample is chosen scientifically. This means that our sample should have been drawn using random sampling procedures: it can be a simple random sample, multistage random sample, or cluster sample using random sampling procedures.

Provided we choose our sample using random procedures, certain generalizations can be made. It can be shown that, if we plot all the means of all possible samples from a population, it will follow a bell-shaped curve called the *normal probability curve*. This result is called the *central limit theorem*. The practical implication of this finding is that it is possible to estimate how close our results are to the true mean. This in turn generates what are known as confidence intervals and margins of error. These aspects are discussed in Chapter 14, Reckoning. Here we will simply provide a formula for determining the sample size without any explanation.

HOW LARGE SHOULD THE SAMPLE BE?

In practice, the sample size for any study depends on a number of factors:

- The importance of the study for management decision-making: A study on which multimillion dollar decisions are to be based warrants a larger sample size than one which is a general fact-finding study.
- The range of sample size generally used for such studies: Many shopping mall studies use a sample size of 100, while a national, full-scale usage and attitude study is likely to use a sample size in the region of 1000-2000 respondents.
- Resources available for the study: Within the acceptable range, the actual sample size to a large extent depends on the resources available for the study.
- How many sub-groups are to be studied and in what detail: If it is important that your conclusions be valid for each sub-group (such as each region of the country) rather than for the population in general (such as Canada as a whole), then you would need a larger sample size.

Statistical criteria for selecting the sample also exist, although they are less routinely used in practice compared to the criteria listed above. The statistical arguments will be developed later (Chapter 21), here we will simply provide a formula for calculating the sample size.

If we choose the sample according to statistical criteria, we need to specify two parameters:

- the margin of error acceptable to us; and
- the degree of certainty required.

For example, we may want a sample large enough to fulfill the following requirements: the results should not have a margin of error greater than plus or minus four percentage points and we want to be certain that this requirement will be met with 95% certainty. This means that if the results of our survey showed that 30% of the respondents use our products, then the range between 26% and 34% (30%+ or −4%) would include the "true mean," or the percentage we would have obtained if we had measured everyone in the population. If we carried out a large number of surveys with the same sample size and made a similar statement with regard to each survey result thus obtained, the margin of error would include the true mean in 95% of the surveys.

To specify the sample size, you need two pieces of information:

- margin of error acceptable to you
- the degree of certainty required

Degree of certainty	Confidence coefficient
99%	2.56
95%	1.96
90%	1.56

Sample size is computed by the formula

$$2500 \div (\text{Margin of error/Confidence coefficient})^2$$

Note:
2500 is derived from the formula P(100-P), where P is the percentage expected from the survey results. For example, if the survey expects to find that the usage of a product is likely to be 30%, then P=30. Since the researcher is seldom interested in a single result, in practice it is assumed P=50, which yields a conservative estimate.

When P=50, P(100-P)= 50 x 50 = 2500. This point is explained in Chapter 22.

Examples:

A. We need our results to be accurate within ± 4% at 95% level of confidence.

1. The margin of error = 4%
2. The confidence coefficient corresponding to 95% level = 2 (actually, 1.96)
3. Substituting this in our formula,

$$\text{Sample Size} = 2500/(4 \div 2)^2 = 2500/4 = 625$$

(Using more precise calculations, we would have obtained a sample size of 601.)

B. We need our results to be accurate within ± 4 percentage points at 90% level of confidence.

1. We want the results to be accurate within ± 4%
2. The confidence coefficient corresponding to 90% level = 1.65
3. Substituting,
    Sample Size = $2500/(2.4)^2 = 434$

DESIGN FACTORS

The formulas given above are based on the assumption that a simple random sample is used (i.e., no clustering). Except in certain forms of telephone interviewing, this never happens. To allow for this, a design factor should be used.

Methods exist for calculating the design factor. However, often judgment has to be used. For example, some researchers assume an arbitrary design factor such as 1.6. If the parameter you are studying is associated with things that you know to be highly correlated within geographical areas, (e.g., income, ethnic origin, voting habits), a higher design factor would be appropriate.

If your sample is one of large clusters and a small number of sampling points, the design factor will be higher. This is discussed in greater detail in Chapter 21.

SUMMARY

1. Every sample has certain defined characteristics. The *sample design* is a description of these characteristics. A sample design should specify the following: the population, the frame, the size of the sample and the methods for selecting the sample.
    - The group that a researcher is interested in (the target group) is called the *population* or the *universe*.
    - A *sampling unit* is the smallest unit of a sample that will constitute one unit in analysis, e.g., a respondent.
    - The *sample frame* is the means by which the population is physically accessed, e.g., a phone directory, a list of doctors, etc. It should be comprehensive and precise.

2. If we measure everyone in the population, our measurements will be called *parameters*. Instead, when we use a sample, our measurements are called *estimates*. In other words, we try to estimate parameter values through sample estimates.

3. The use of *probability sampling procedures* enables us to assess the parameter values with consistency. However, *sampling errors* will be attached to the estimates we obtained through sampling. Sampling error

results from studying only a small portion of the population. Therefore, the larger the sample, the smaller the sampling error.

4. *Non-sampling errors* are non-statistical in nature (e.g., poorly designed questionnaire, biased sample, etc.) and cannot be easily measured. Non-sampling errors can create biases in the study.

5. There are two sampling methods: *probability sampling* and *non-probability sampling*. A sample can be *single stage* or *multistage*. In single stage sampling, we choose our sample directly from all sampling units in our frame. In multistage sampling, we go through several stages.

6. *Simple random sampling* is a procedure in which every member of the population has an equal chance of being selected and included in the sample.

7. *Stratified sampling* is a procedure in which we divide the sample into homogeneous sub-samples and draw separate samples from these sub-groups. For example, we may divide Canada into five regions and select an independent sample from each of these regions.

8. In *multistage sampling*, samples are chosen at different levels. For example, we can choose telephone numbers from the directory; once we reach a given household, then we can choose a member of the household. Thus, in this case, a sample is chosen using the multistage procedure involving two stages. In personal interviewing, we often use cluster samples.

9. In *cluster samples*, we cluster the sampling units for reasons of cost efficiency. For example, once a block is chosen, the interviewer may interview (for instance) four respondents in the same block rather than just one.

10. There are three common ways in which telephone interviews are carried out. These are:
    • using white pages as the sample frame
    • using Random Digit Dialling (RDD)
    • using seed samples/Plus *n* procedures

    Although RDD is theoretically the best method, it is very expensive and wasteful. White pages sampling is the least wasteful of the three methods; but it can have serious limitations. Using seed sampling or the Plus *n* method provides a reasonable compromise.

11. *Non-probability sampling*: A large number of marketing research surveys use non-probability sampling procedures. Considerations of cost and timing are the main reasons for the use of non-probability samples. Some frequently used non-probability sampling procedures are:

- purposive sample
- accidental sample
- quota sample

12. Sample size is computed by the formula:

    2500 ÷ (Margin of error/Confidence coefficient)^2

13. In practice, the sample size of any study depends on a number of factors:
    - The importance of the study for management decision-making
    - The range of sample size generally used for such studies
    - Resources available for the study
    - How many sub-groups are to be studied and in what detail

14. *The design factor* adjusts for the fact that our samples are not truly random.

NOW THINK ABOUT THIS

1. You are designing a large-scale study to understand the drinking habits of Canadians. What is the population and what is the sampling unit? Can you define your sample frame?

2. Distinguish between sampling and non-sampling errors.

3. Outline the characteristics of different sampling procedures.

4. If the acceptable margin of error is 4% and if you are willing to be wrong 5 times out of 100, what is the sample size you need?

7 Designing the Questionnaire

WHAT YOU WILL LEARN IN THIS CHAPTER

- The process of questionnaire design
- How to relate the project objectives to the questionnaire
- How to write the screening questions
- How to use the funnelling approach
- What to do and what not to do in composing a questionnaire
- How to word sensitive questions to get the maximum response rate
- How to format a questionnaire properly on the page (page layout)
- How to develop effective skip patterns
- The difference in layout between self-administered and interviewer-administered questionnaires
- What makes a questionnaire easy or difficult to answer
- How people respond to various types of questions
- How to measure respondents' attitudes

THE QUESTIONNAIRE IS THE BASIC TOOL OF MARKETING RESEARCH

All quantitative marketing research studies use formal questionnaires to collect information. A questionnaire is simply a set of questions arranged in a sequence with the following elements:

- space for recording the answers
- instructions to the interviewer
- space for the coder
- information for the keypuncher

Constructing a questionnaire, however, is not necessarily a simple proposition. When one considers that the questionnaire is the medium through which the researcher hopes to accomplish the objectives of the study, its importance becomes obvious. Furthermore, even a simple questionnaire affects a number of people from the time it is constructed to the time the information is transformed into a report (see Exhibit 7.1). It is therefore essential that a questionnaire be constructed properly and this necessitates a thorough understanding of the issues involved. Each question should have a definite purpose and be directly related to the research objectives and scope. There are some specific rules that govern the construction of a questionnaire. Before discussing these principles, we need to understand the process of constructing a questionnaire.

Exhibit 7.1 People Affected by a Questionnaire

- *It affects the interviewer:* who has to understand the instructions and ask questions.
- *It affects the respondent:* who may find the questionnaire too boring, tedious, personal or ambiguous.
- *It affects the coder:* who may find the questionnaire too confusing.
- *It affects the keypuncher:* who may make keypunch (data entry) errors because of a badly laid out questionnaire.
- *It affects the researcher:* who cannot solve the research problem if the questionnaire does not measure what it purports to measure.
- *It affects the decision-maker:* to whom a poorly designed questionnaire may give misleading information.

BASIC STEPS OF QUESTIONNAIRE DESIGN

Every area of study and practice has a set of principles which help to guide practitioners in their activities. Questionnaire design is no exception. This section is a combination of guidelines, rules and examples directed at helping readers to develop better questionnaires.

IDENTIFY INFORMATION NEEDS

The main purpose of a questionnaire is to provide information relating to the objectives and the scope of the study. The first step in designing a questionnaire, therefore, is to make a list of items to be covered, based on the objectives and the scope. In some studies a formal set of hypotheses is established in advance. These hypotheses provide an effective driving force for designing the questionnaire: the researcher must design the questionnaire to ensure that the data necessary for testing the hypotheses are obtained from the field-work. In those projects where explicit hypotheses are not pre-determined, the researcher should develop the questions based on the objectives of the study and the informal hypotheses that are a natural consequence of any research endeavour.

One benefit of having fully specified hypotheses is that each of the questions can be justified relative to the hypotheses. Also, dummy tabulations can be formatted so that the implications of the data analysis plan can be considered when developing the final questionnaire.

When the questionnaire is thought to be complete, it should be scrutinized to determine whether all the hypotheses can be tested and the objectives met, and whether questions have been included, that don't relate to any of the hypotheses or objectives. If seemingly superfluous questions are encountered, the reason for their inclusion should be ascertained. If they are found to serve no specific purpose, they should be omitted.

SEQUENCE THE QUESTIONS

One of the common errors made by inexperienced researchers is to sequence the questionnaire according to their information needs. This may result in a questionnaire that is disjointed and that appears to the respondents to have an illogical flow. It is important to remember that the sequence of the questions has little to do with their individual importance.

Some people might suggest that questions should be "jumbled up" to reduce bias. When reading a novel would you like to read chapter 8 first, then chapter 4, then chapter 15 and then chapter 1? Of course not. Neither do respondents!

SCREENING   Screening (or filtering) questions that determine whether a consumer is eligible to take part in a survey are always placed first. For example, if only heads of households who are over 18 years of age, who are primarily responsible for their household's grocery shopping, and who use shampoo at least once a week are to be included in the study, then these characteristics will be screened for at the beginning of the interview.

Screening questions are very important. They're needed to ensure that you speak to the right people. But they have to be written very carefully since you shouldn't turn off a respondent right at the beginning.

FUNNELLING   The most common way of sequencing a questionnaire is by funnelling. The funnelling technique starts with generalized questions and proceeds to more and more specific questions. Thus, for example, if you would like to find out the brands of anti-dandruff shampoo used by consumers, the questionnaire is not likely to start with the question "Which brand of anti-dandruff shampoo do you use most often?" It is more likely that there are several questions leading up to the targeted information, as shown in Exhibit 7.2. The main advantages of the funnelling approach are that 1) it gradually orients the respondents to the information needs of the researcher, and 2) it puts consumers' responses into proper perspective. There are, of course, situations in which the use of the funnelling approach is inappropriate.

Exhibit 7.2   An Example of Funnelling

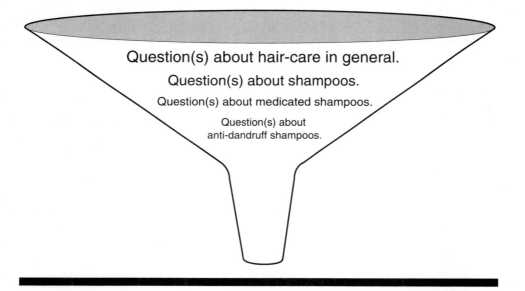

Question(s) about hair-care in general.

Question(s) about shampoos.

Question(s) about medicated shampoos.

Question(s) about
anti-dandruff shampoos.

INVERTED FUNNELLING   There are instances where a general question may distort the response to specific questions and an inverted funnel approach is used. In such instances specific questions are asked before the general question. These situations also arise when the respondent might not have thought enough about the general question in order to provide a considered response. In these cases, the respondent is asked a series of questions about important details of the object or situation before being asked the general question which might pertain to "general liking" or "overall intention to buy." An example of this would be asking a person a series of questions regarding the most recent service obtained at a particular garage, prior to the main question of whether the respondent would return to that garage for service. For example:

What servicing was done when you had your car serviced at Firestone the last time?

When was the work done?

Was that the first time that you had any automotive servicing done at a Firestone store?

What was the approximate cost of that service?

What prompted you to have the most recent service done at Firestone?

A battery of agree-disagree questions:

All services were done correctly. (Agree-disagree)

The mechanic was courteous.

The car did not run well afterwards.

The work was done on time.

The service manager was trustworthy.

The bill was unreasonably high.

The waiting area was comfortable.

. . .

They provided prompt attention.

How likely are you to take your car back in the future to Firestone for servicing or repairs?

[　]1　DEFINITELY WOULD TAKE BACK TO FIRESTONE

[　]2　PROBABLY WOULD TAKE BACK

[　]3　MIGHT OR MIGHT NOT TAKE BACK

[　]4　PROBABLY WOULD NOT TAKE BACK

[　]5　DEFINITELY WOULD NOT TAKE BACK

PRECEDENCE OF EASIER AND MORE INNOCUOUS QUESTIONS   To establish rapport with the respondent, easier questions should precede the difficult ones and innocuous questions should precede the more sensitive ones. At times this principle may override the funnelling approach. The following might be asked of respondents attending the Canadian National Exhibition (CNE) in Toronto, for example:

Have you been here at the CNE earlier this summer?

Did you come last year?

How long have you been on the CNE grounds today?

Did other members of your family come with you today?

Who came?

Which buildings have you been in so far?

And which exhibits did you like best?

The acid test for any questionnaire is whether it reads like a book or like an income tax form. The respondent wants it to read like a good book. Don't provide an income tax form nightmare.

CHECK QUESTIONNAIRE FLOW

This aspect is related to sequencing. After all the necessary questions have been included and the questionnaire has been sequenced, it should be checked for ease of administration, from the viewpoints of both interviewer and respondent. Points to be considered at this stage are

- Is the filtering as easy as possible for the interviewer?
- Can the interviewer move forward with ease through the questionnaire if questions are to be omitted?
- Can the interviewer easily refer back to an answer if the need to ask a particular question is dependent on the response to an earlier question?
- Does everything appear to the respondent to be in logical order?
- At any point, does the respondent have information that you don't want him or her to have?

When conducting personal interviews, be sure that the respondent does not see anything that's written on the questionnaire. This would bias and invalidate the questionnaire.

It is important in many studies to determine if respondents mention the name of the brand being studied without any prompting whatsoever (unaided awareness), and then whether subjects say that they recognize the brand name when it's read to them by the interviewer (aided awareness). For example, suppose that respondents are to be asked to name brands of frozen dinners, and that if they don't mention Swanson Frozen Dinner they will then be asked, "Have you heard of Swanson Frozen Dinner?" In order for this question sequence to work properly, the interviewer must make sure that the respondent does not see any pre-coded list of names that are printed as possible answers to the unaided question; nor, must the respondent see the statement of the aided question.

This care about what respondents see is also pertinent when investigating a product category that is a subset of a larger category. Consider a study that is primarily concerned with beer but that also sets out to investigate the use of beer in the context of the consumption of other alcoholic beverages.

The more general questions regarding alcoholic beverage consumption should be asked before the questions specifically about beer, otherwise the respondents will conclude that the study is about beer and the responses to the more general questions will inevitably have a beer focus.

One final point to be considered when checking the questionnaire flow is will the questionnaire hold the respondent's interest? This is one of the most important points for achieving high response rates. When boredom sets in, the respondent is much more likely to terminate. Also, the likelihood of providing an inaccurate or inappropriate answer is increased. Thirty-one per cent of those surveyed recently by Gallup Canada (1990) said that they had at some time lost interest in an interview and had simply answered mechanically without thinking very much about their answers.

CHECK QUESTIONNAIRE LENGTH

The length of the questionnaire affects the cost of the study and the analysis time. In many cases, the length also affects respondent cooperation. Therefore, it is important to check the questionnaire and if it is excessively lengthy to shorten it to a reasonable length (see below). The response rate to a questionnaire depends greatly on the length of the questionnaire; however, length is not the only factor that determines respondent cooperation. It's often stated that a telephone interview should last for 10 to 15 minutes at the longest; but interviews of 30 to 45 minutes (sometimes even longer) have been conducted with high response rates when the subject matter was of special concern to the respondents and when the questionnaire was well written and interesting.

When excessive length has been identified in a questionnaire, each question should be justified relative to the objectives of the study. If a question does not help to achieve one of the objectives and, consequently, would not be used to test one or more of the hypotheses, then it should be seriously considered for elimination.

EDIT RIGOROUSLY

Even when questions are constructed based on information needs, it is not always possible to sort out productive questions from unproductive ones. The first draft of the questionnaire may, therefore, contain several superfluous questions. The inclusion of such questions not only wastes resources but actually makes the job of the interviewer more difficult — lengthy questionnaires reduce respondent cooperation. In addition, the final report may lack cohesion because the responses to non-relevant questions cannot be related to the objectives of the study. Therefore, superfluous questions should be rigorously edited

out. Be careful of "wouldn't it be nice to know" questions. They often serve no purpose other than unnecessarily lengthening the questionnaire.

The fundamental criterion that determines whether a question should be included is the usefulness of the response to the decision-maker. Can the answer to this question, either by itself or in combination with other information, help the decision-maker to arrive at a better marketing decision? If you cannot think of a reasonable way in which the specific response can be used in decision-making, the question is probably superfluous. When editing out, a good rule to use is to ask the question, "How will I use the data I've collected?" and if you can't visualize the answers in a table or what you're going to do with the information, you should probably not be asking the question (Anne Termatten, personal communication, 1990).

The questionnaire should also be checked for questions that are redundant. On occasion, more than one question might be used to investigate one particular point or objective; however, redundancy will create an unnecessarily long questionnaire that might bore the respondent and/or result in a reduced response rate.

PRE-TEST THE QUESTIONNAIRE

Pre-testing the questionnaire might mean administering it to a small sample of the target respondents or just trying it out on a few colleagues. The more important the study, the more critical the pre-test. Questionnaires for many small, run-of-the-mill studies do not undergo any form of pre-testing. This is somewhat unfortunate because a proper pre-test can identify problem areas fairly quickly and at a low cost. (This important topic is treated in more detail in Chapter 8.)

WHAT TO CONSIDER IN WRITING A QUESTIONNAIRE

When developing questionnaires and field methodology, keep in mind the following truism: Respondents' behaviour is motivated by whether they expect the rewards to outweigh the costs of participating in a survey. One of the most important jobs of the researcher is to eliminate the debilitating costs of boredom, irritation, embarrassment, possible misinterpretation and difficulty of understanding that might be present when respondents read a self-completion questionnaire or when respondents are interviewed.

USE SIMPLE WORDS

The following words of advertising copywriter Arthur Kudner to his teenage son, who was struggling with a high school essay, underline the importance of using simple words:

> Never fear big, long words. Big, long words name little things. All big things have little names. Such as life and death, peace and war, dawn, day, night, hope, love and home. Learn to use little words in a big way. It's hard to do, but they say what you mean. When you don't know what you mean, use big words. They often fool little people.

It should be realized that even simple words can be open to interpretation. For example, the following five-word question composed of single syllable words can be read, heard and interpreted in five different ways, depending on the words accented most strongly and on the intonation of the interviewer (Payne, 1951:204).

WHY do you say that?

Why **DO** you say that?

Why do **YOU** say that?

Why do you **SAY** that?

Why do you say **THAT**?

DON'T BE VAGUE, BE SPECIFIC

Keep a dictionary handy when designing a questionnaire. It's amazing how many meanings one word can have depending on the context and usage, cultural background of the subject and so on.

Stanley Payne (1951:210) provides an excellent example of why the vague phrase "how much" should not be used in questions because it leads to such a variety of responses. For example, while holding up a bottle of orange-drink, the interviewer asked respondents, "How much orange juice do you think it contains?" Some of the answers which that imprecise question elicited are:

One orange and a little water and sugar.

Twenty-five per cent orange and 75 % carbonated water.

Juice of one-half dozen oranges.

Three ounces of orange juice.

Full-strength.

A quarter cup of orange juice.

Not much.

A small amount of orange juice.

A pint.

Had the question been stated as follows, it would have drawn much more precise and comparable answers from the respondents: "This bottle holds sixteen ounces of a drink. How many ounces of that would you say is orange juice?"

Using words that express an idea precisely is of little value, if those words are not the same as the ones used by consumers to express that idea. The main problem here is that, in most cases, comprehension errors cannot be detected. Few consumers will volunteer the information that your questions are less than comprehensible. For example, the following question may not mean very much to someone who is not used to terms like *peripheral devices*: "If you buy a home computer, what peripheral devices would you consider buying at the same time?"

It's important to learn how consumers speak about a topic. For this reason, focus groups are particularly beneficial prior to the questionnaire design.

AVOID FACTUAL QUESTIONS THAT CANNOT BE ANSWERED ADEQUATELY

If interest is centred on factual information (as opposed to impressions), it is better to avoid questions that are not within the respondent's recall capabilities or sphere of knowledge. Questions such as: "How much money was spent on groceries for your household in the last month?" and, "How many movies did you see in the last year?" might cause the respondent to feel as if a completely accurate answer is needed. The respondent might provide an approximate answer, which is what the questionnaire should have sought.

But some respondents will stop answering the questionnaire when they encounter an accuracy question because they feel as if they can't answer the question precisely enough, or will, at best, give an unhelpful "don't know" response. Other respondents will actually try to calculate the amount of money spent on groceries during the past month. Some might never return to the question in a self-administered questionnaire because their attention is diverted elsewhere, or they might become frustrated and give up. The potential for losing a respondent is increased when a question that appears to require accuracy is asked.

AVOID DOUBLE-BARRELLED QUESTIONS

Questions that have two parts with provision for only one answer fall into this category and should be avoided, since there is no way of telling which of the two parts is being answered. For example, in the following question, "Would you agree or disagree that although this brand is expensive, it is good value for the money?", if the respondent says he disagrees, his disagreement may be with the part that says "this brand is expensive," or with the part that says, "it is good value for the money," or with both parts.

AVOID AMBIGUOUS QUESTIONS

Avoid questions that can be open to different interpretations; for example:

"How much money was spent on groceries for your household in the last month?"

- What is meant by "groceries"? Does it include cleaning products, pet foods, and sundries?

"How many movies did you see in the last year?"

- What is meant by "movies"? Does it include theatre, video, T.V.? How do we define a movie on T.V.?
- What do we mean by "see"? Does it mean that the whole movie was watched, at least half, or what proportion?
- Are in-home and out-of-home to be included?

"Do you read the New York Times?" Does that mean:

- Have you ever read the New York Times?
- Do you read the New York Times on a regular basis?
- Do you read it now and then?
- Do you have any objection in principle to reading the New York Times?

Each question must be precise in its meaning to the respondent. Even people who feel competent enough in the English language to write a lengthy report will often find it necessary to consult a dictionary in order to write precise and unambiguous questions.

AVOID LEADING AND LOADED QUESTIONS

Questions worded in such a way as to elicit a particular answer in preference to another should be avoided; for example: "Do you agree with the policy of this government that has been responsible for our huge deficit burden?" Unless the respondent has strong views on politics and economy, the chances of his answering yes to this question are minimal. Also "deficit burden" must be defined for the respondent.

Unscrupulous researchers could get any desired answer by loading the question with bias or leading the respondent.

Another question that is often used to illustrate the ultimate in loaded questions is, "Have you stopped beating your wife yet?" Both possible answers of yes and no are incriminating.

The following excerpt from Haller (1983: 131-2) illustrates the dangers inherent in question phrasing:

> It is common knowledge that a questionnaire must be free of bias and ambiguity that could invalidate the whole study. Most researchers can avoid commonsense blunders, but few ever rise to the plateau where they can guarantee a questionnaire, plus instructions to the interviewers, that are totally unbiased.
>
> *Example:*
>
> The research alumni of a famous midwestern consumer goods company, so the story goes, share a recurring nightmare where their boss calls them on the carpet for sabotaging a test market by forgetting to include the phrase *or not* in a study.
>
> Why would they have these strange dreams, any sensible person would ask; what makes putting *or not* at the end of a question loom so large in their lives? Why do the folks that work for this one company (name on request) feel that survey results can be invalidated by the omission of a phrase many researchers consider an affectation?
>
> In yes-or-no questions more respondents have a strong impulse to give you a *yes* answer. Now, intelligent readers are going to think this a lost of nonsense, so here are a few reasons why this happens:
> • Once they've agreed to be interviewed, respondents are curious about what you're going to ask them. A lot of the initial screening

questions in an interview are dichotomous; too many negative answers could—they think to themselves—terminate the interview before it gets very far. To satisfy their curiosity they have to keep the questions coming by feeding you positive responses.

- For some types of questions many interviewees are simply incapable of giving a negative response unless it is absolutely clear that it will be acceptable. The positive one is generally thought to the *right one.* Both possibilities have to be clearly presented. "Do you ever use the Yellow Pages?" would produce a far greater number of affirmative answers than the proper "Do you ever use the Yellow Pages, or not?"

- Questions that drop the *or-not* produce inaccurate information. It is not unusual in actual experiments to have the *or-not* query produce 20 to 30 points fewer affirmative answers than the same query without the suffix. Comparisons to independent data sources, such as purchase diary panels, characteristically reveal that the *or not* question produces the more reliable information.

- The pull toward the positive response is even more extreme among certain language groups. Hispanics, for example, are notorious yea-sayers. Unfortunately, they will try to tell you that *or not* is also a lot more awkward to say in Spanish ("o no") than it is in English. In fact I don't know of any foreign language where the purists enjoy using the phrase. That's too damn bad, but it is still a vital point and if you want reliable information from foreign consumers you must instruct the field personnel in these basic facts of life. Most foreign tongues, with the exceptions of Greek and Latin and modern German, are too loose to produce the kind of ultraprecision we need in marketing research interviewing without major transfusions of American English syntax. In the less developed countries (LDC's) there will be a big split in the vernacular between those who have virtually no education (the consumers) and those with a college education (the researchers). The latter will insist on phrasing their questions in some classical or literary version of the language more suitable to eighteenth century drawing rooms than to the mud huts their respondents usually live in. Needless to say most denizens of the Third World have only passing familiarity with the polished phrases of the Enlightenment. We can thank our lucky stars, those of us who work in the United States, that we do not have this problem. (This is because the educated in the United States are not all that literate.)

SOURCE: Terry Haller, *Danger: Marketing Researcher at Work.* (Westport, CT: Quorum Books), 1983.

AVOID BLACK-AND-WHITE QUESTIONS WHEN ANSWERS MIGHT BE GREY

Consumers have opinions that are different shades of grey. Yes or no type questions are inappropriate when the answer may lie anywhere in between; for example, "Do you agree with Brian Mulroney's policies?" The respondent may agree with some policies and not with others, or the respondent may agree with Mulroney's policies with some qualifications. This type of question is very frustrating to the respondent who really wants to provide an answer, but can't because of the limited nature of the answers allowed by the questionnaire.

BE CAREFUL WHEN WORDING SENSITIVE AND PERSONAL QUESTIONS

If possible, sensitive and personal questions should be avoided. If it is necessary to ask such questions, a proper foundation should be laid, either through suitable explanations or by other questions, so that they are seen in context.

A few questionnaire design books address the problem of asking very sensitive questions. In some cultures, almost anything can be asked of strangers while in others great care must be taken in order not to scandalize the respondent. Researchers who have a better understanding of human nature are often able to avoid writing questions that are unacceptable to many respondents.

Asking people about their income can often produce embarrassment or hostility in the respondent. Consider a man and his 15-year-old son who have been stopped in a shopping mall. If the interviewer were to ask the man to indicate which category includes his income, he might not want to answer because he doesn't want his son to know his income. This problem can be overcome by using a response card that lists the seven income categories of interest. Each category has a letter next to it, in scrambled order; for example,

Household Income for 1991	
LESS THAN $20 000	P
$20 000 TO $29 999	F
$30 000 TO $39 999	A
$40 000 TO $49 999	Q
$50 000 TO $59 999	W
$60 000 TO $79 000	H
$80 000 OR MORE	S

The interviewer hands the card to the man and asks him to indicate the letter that approximates his total household income. The embarrassment has been greatly reduced and the answer is much more likely to be provided.

Response cards can be used for many sensitive questions. They are also effective when the respondent must answer on a scale with many descriptors and when he or she must consider five or more brands of the product and indicate which three are liked best.

CONSIDER POSSIBLE WAYS IN WHICH A QUESTION MAY BE ANSWERED

Respondents may at times provide answers that are consciously or unconsciously distorted. Such distortions are usually based on one or more of the motivations listed below:

- **Desire to impress or to give an answer that is believed to be socially the "right" answer.** "Did you give any money to the Salvation Army during its Red Kettle campaign during this past Christmas season?" will be answered "yes" by many more people than actually did donate.

- **Desire to please or to be polite.** Brand ratings or higher intention to purchase the brand might be inflated by some respondents to please the interviewer.

- **Desire to tell you what the respondent believes you want to know rather than what you actually want to know.** When asked, "Which brand of coffee did you buy last time?" respondents might tend to provide the name of the brand they buy most often because they think that's what you want.

- **Desire to report major rather than minor events**. The question, "How often did you eat a meal in a restaurant last month?" might be answered with the number 2 even though the respondent ate out 12 times. The 2 given referred to two meals in good restaurants, whereas the other 10 times were at fast-food restaurants.

The researcher should take steps to reduce the potential for distortion in the following ways:

- By changing the sequence of the questions to minimize the impact of a given question
- By changing the wording to make the question neutral and precise
- By eliciting the information through indirect questioning
- By collecting comparative data and such other means

There is a natural tendency for respondents to over-report the incidence of their doing socially more acceptable actions and to under-report their activities in socially unacceptable areas. For example, a much higher percentage of Canadians say that they have voted in a national election than actually ever vote; and a much lower percentage report after an election that they voted for the losing parties. Similarly, very few people will mention that they have cheated on their income taxes and that they drive when intoxicated. These are just manifestations of human behaviour of which the researcher must be aware when developing a questionnaire.

VARIOUS TYPES OF QUESTIONS

A questionnaire may contain several types of questions. A classification of these types is given in Exhibit 7.3.

Exhibit 7.3   Question Types

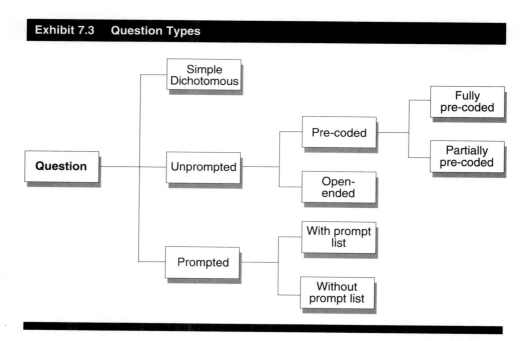

SIMPLE DICHOTOMOUS PRE-CODED QUESTIONS

These questions can be answered with a simple *yes* or *no, have* or *haven't,* etc. They are simple to administer and work well for non-sensitive, factual items.

Examples (self-completion questions):

Do you currently own a motorcycle, or not?

      [ ]1   YES
      [ ]2   NO

Did you buy any meals at a restaurant last week, or not?

      [ ]1   YES
      [ ]2   NO

UNPROMPTED PRE-CODED QUESTIONS

These are unprompted in that the questions themselves do not incorporate the range of possible answers. They are pre-coded in that some (or all) of the potential responses are pre-printed for the interviewer to circle the ones mentioned.

Examples (self-completion questions):

How often do you read a daily newspaper?

      [   ]1   EVERY DAY, OR FIVE DAYS OUT OF FIVE
      [   ]2   FOUR OUT OF FIVE DAYS
      [   ]3   THREE OUT OF FIVE DAYS
      [   ]4   TWO OUT OF FIVE DAYS
      [   ]5   ONE OUT OF FIVE DAYS
      [   ]6   FIVE OUT OF TEN TO ONE OUT OF TEN DAYS
      [   ]7   LESS THAN ONE OUT OF TEN BUT MORE OFTEN
               THAN ONCE A MONTH
      [   ]8   ONCE A MONTH OR LESS OFTEN

Which newspapers do you read at least once a week?

      [ ]1   GLOBE & MAIL
      [ ]2   THE TORONTO STAR
      [ ]3   THE TORONTO SUN
      [ ]4   OTHER _____

Example (interviewer-administered):

What is your favourite leisure time activity?

        INDOOR SPORTS   1
        OUTDOOR SPORTS   2
        NON-SPORTS ACTIVITIES   3   (43)
        NONE IN PARTICULAR   4

The area to the right of the vertical bar in this question is the **coding strip**. If the respondent says "outdoor sports," then the "2" is circled by the interviewer. The "43" in parentheses in the coding strip indicates that the data entry person types the answer 2 into column 43 of the data record for this respondent. For some data entry procedures, the variable name would be put in the coding strip instead of the column number.

Questions like those listed above can produce a number of answers. The questions are **fully pre-coded** in that all possible answers are printed on the questionnaire, as in the first question above. (The numbers to the right of the boxes in the first and second examples and in the coding strip of the third example are the numerical codes which will be entered into the computer for data analysis.) Pre-coding simplifies the work of the interviewer and that of the coder. However, when there are too many potential answers to a question, it may be partially pre-coded. As in the second example above, this is done by pre-coding the answers that are likely to be most frequently given and providing space to write in other answers.

You will have noticed that the examples used to illustrate types of questions don't all have the same formats. The use of various ways of printing the questions on the questionnaire page will be discussed in a following section.

PROMPTED CLOSED-ENDED QUESTIONS

For prompted questions, a range of potential answers is given to the respondent along with the question. The respondent is required to choose one of the answers given. If the prompts are not read to the respondent, then anything that pops into the subject's head will be given as the answer. If this is the case, and the interviewer was expecting one of four listed answers, then the interviewer may harbour a lot of resentment toward the questionnaire designer.

Examples:

> *How likely is it that you will buy a brand new car during the next six months; do you think that you'll definitely buy a new car, probably will, probably will not or definitely will not buy a new car?*

DEFINITELY WILL NOT	1	
PROBABLY WILL NOT	2	
MIGHT OR MIGHT NOT	3	(56)
PROBABLY NOT	4	
DEFINITELY WILL	5	

If the question were asked in open-ended format as:

> Do you think that you'll buy a new car during the next six months?, then the respondent might say "yes" or "probably" or "Yea, I'd really like to buy a new RX-7 and I'll probably be able to if I can just get the promotion that I've been gunning for."

The question above is an example of a scaled attitude question. The scale is comprised of five points with a middle category. More will be mentioned about scaled questions in a following section and in Appendix 7A.

> Which of the following brands do you like the most: Brand X; Brand Y; or Brand Z?

BRAND X	1	
BRAND Y	2	(75)
BRAND Z	2	

When designing prompted questions with a prompt list, the researcher should make sure that all the important answers are on the list. In addition, the list should be rotated (presented in different order to different respondents) to avoid potential bias. It has been shown, for example, that the first mentioned and last mentioned answers are often preferred by respondents. (Scaled responses are not rotated but are sometimes reversed.) It is also important to ensure that the list is not too long: at most, a list can contain 12 to 15 items in a self-administered questionnaire, and 5 to 7 for an interviewer-administered telephone survey. In a face-to-face interview, prompt cards should be used for a list of more than five items.

OPEN-ENDED QUESTIONS

Open-ended questions let the respondent decide the scope of the answer. The answers given by the respondent are recorded verbatim by the interviewer. These answers are grouped into logical categories at the coding stage. Sometimes the interviewers are asked to probe. This is usually done by a simple question, like "what else?" after the respondent gives his or her initial answer to an open-ended question.

> *Example:*
>
> *What do you like about this new brand of toothpaste?*
>
> _____
>
> _____
>
> *(PROBE: What else?)* _____
>
> _____

Open-ended questions are expensive to administer and to code. Interviewers vary in their ability to probe effectively and respondents vary in their ability to verbalize their thoughts without specific guidance. (More information on how to administer open-ended questions is in Chapter 8.) Because of these factors, it is difficult to draw consistent conclusions from open-ended questions. However, it should be remembered that, in many instances, open-ended questions are an effective tool for eliciting answers that are not apparent to the researcher when the questionnaire is designed. For instance, a researcher may concentrate on product attributes and may overlook the possibility that the real problem with the product is, in fact, the inconvenient size of the package. In some studies, open-ended questions will supply the high points and will help to give meaning to the statistical analysis.

Open-ended questions tend to be relatively ineffective in self-completion questionnaires. While interviewers can probe and draw out responses in interviewer-administered questionnaires, the respondent can easily ignore open-ends in the self-completion format.

Care should be taken when applying the guidelines given in this chapter. Not all of the above comments are applicable to all situations. Although the basic principles of questionnaire construction do not change, specific details may vary depending on several factors. For example, it is not practical to provide a prompt list to a respondent in a telephone interview; it is not practical in a mail survey to persuade the respondent not to look through the whole questionnaire before answering.

SCALES

In market research, almost all questionnaires measure some aspect of consumer attitudes. Attitudes include the constructs of consumer awareness, knowledge, liking, preference, conviction, and intentions. Researchers are always trying to discover what consumers are interested in, to what extent, and why. While open-ended questions are useful in obtaining qualitative responses, they are not very useful for comparing different consumers or different groups of consumers. To facilitate comparison among consumers, we need some kind of measurement or scale. Such scales are particularly useful in measuring the strength of attitudes. Scales can be constructed in different ways. Examples are given below, but several other variations are possible.

Examples:

> *How likely is it that you will buy Brand A during the next 7 days? Do you think that you definitely will buy Brand A, probably buy Brand A, probably will not buy, or definitely will not buy Brand A?*

DEFINITELY WILL BUY	5	
PROBABLY WILL BUY	4	
MIGHT OR MIGHT NOT BUY	3	(82)
PROBABLY WILL NOT	2	
DEFINITELY WILL NOT	1	

Or

How likely is that you will buy Brand A during the next 7 days? On a scale of 1 to 10 where 10 means you definitely will buy and 1 means that you definitely will not buy, how likely are you to buy Brand A in the next 7 days?

DEFINITELY WILL NOT BUY 1 2 3 4 5 6 7 8 9 10   DEFINITELY WILL BUY | (44)

(You can also use other numbers like 7 or 5 instead of 10 as the high end point for the scale. These are commonly referred to as ten-point scales, five-point scales and so on.)

Or

Would you say that the Canadian content of CBC television at this time is too much, too little or about right?

TOO MUCH	1	
ABOUT RIGHT	2	(27)
TOO LITTLE	3	

Please note that in the third example, both ends of the scale are undesirable. Hence, it is not unidirectional. You should be careful in interpreting the findings if you assign scale values to a scale like this. Appendix 7A explores attitude scaling in more depth.

Questions frequently pondered by marketing researchers are, how many points should be used on the scale, and should there be an even number of points on the scale or an odd number of points which will accommodate a neutral category? Unfortunately, there are no pat answers to those questions. Researchers often argue these points and don't always reach conclusions which are acceptable to all concerned.

Sometimes the consulting marketing researcher might prefer an agree-disagree scale with an even number of points, while the client might want the scale to have an odd number of points. Probably neither of the two is absolutely correct. Research has shown that when respondents are presented with a neutral category, the incidence of non-committal or neutral answers increases significantly. Some practitioners feel that it is preferable in opinion questions to give the respondents an even number of scale points, thus encouraging the expression of negative or positive attitude.

Although the neutral and don't know categories are not given as options by the interviewer, if the respondent provides either of those answers it is coded. (See Appendix 7A.)

INTERPRETING SCALE VALUES

The researcher should be careful in interpreting scale values. Is a purchase intent score of 7 on a 10-point scale good or bad? Does an average score of 7 mean the same thing in Quebec as it does in Ontario? There are no reliable answers to these questions. What we do know is that these numerical values are relative. Thus, some product categories receive a higher rating than other categories, although the attitudinal intensity for both categories is the same; some groups tend to give higher ratings, although they do not necessarily view the product as any more superior than other groups do. Experienced researchers will often state that females tend to give more positive answers to attitude questions in comparison to males. This tends to be true of French Canadians as well.

LIFESTYLE AND PSYCHOGRAPHICS

Most questionnaires ask for the following types of information:

- **Respondent characteristics** (demographic and socio-economic factors such as age, sex, income, education, mother tongue, etc.)

- **Respondent's relation to the subject under consideration** (there could be questions relating to the respondent's frequency of usage of the brand and other competing brands)

- **Respondent's evaluation of the subject** (respondent's evaluation of brand characteristics)

- **Respondent's attitude to the subject** (rating of the brand, likes and dislikes)

In addition, some questionnaires also collect consumer's *lifestyle* characteristics, *psychographic* profiles and the like. This is done in order to relate respondents' usage and attitudes regarding brands and product categories to how "green," economy-minded, home-oriented, sociable, experimental, liberal, etc. they are. These relationships may help to explain the respondents' purchase behaviour and attitudes. The examples below illustrate the type of questions that may be included:

Examples:

- *Which outdoor sports do you participate in during the winter?*

- *How many times last month did you eat dinner at a restaurant?*

Answers to lifestyle/psychographic questions are usually collected using rating scales and interpreted using complex statistical procedures for grouping respondents. While psychographics is a useful tool for analyzing data, it is also an extremely specialized and relatively new aspect of marketing research. Therefore, it will not be fully explored within the context of this book.

PAGE LAYOUT, QUESTION SEQUENCE AND QUESTION FORMAT

As we explained in the earlier sections of this chapter, the intelligent and sensitive development of pertinent questions is of paramount importance in effective questionnaire design. However, in order to ensure that the well developed questions are communicated properly to respondents and that the answers are stated accurately by the respondents or the interviewers, it is necessary to pay careful attention to the physical appearance of the pages of the questionnaire. The physical appearance can have a substantial effect on response rate, the reduction of boredom and the accompanying bias in self-administered questionnaires. The remainder of this section will present and illustrate several important rules of questionnaire layout. Although the preferred layout will vary among researchers, the following suggestions will provide the basics for proper communication of survey research questions and answers.

The well designed questionnaire has many similarities to the well produced creative commercial. The questionnaire should read almost like a short story. It should be pleasant, informative and interesting. The respondent should notice a basic logical sequence to the series of questions. Confusion on the part of the reader should be reduced as much as possible by not jumping back and forth among several topics during the interview. You would immediately stop reading a novel that began with chapter 5 then chapter 2 followed by chapter 8 and then chapter 1 and so on. Many respondents would do the same thing to a similarly poorly designed questionnaire. Although the respondent should not be able to guess what the next question will be, there should be a natural flow to the interview. It should seem to the respondent and to the interviewer that they are participating in a structured conversation, not in a linguistic tug-of-war.

A natural flow can be maintained by grouping together those questions that pertain to a particular topic. Questions regarding past purchases could be put in a section together; queries about perceptions of competing products should generally be together; the demographic questions are normally grouped in the last section of the questionnaire, and so on. In addition, within each of the sections, the writer should identify those questions that might be objectionable to the respondent and consider placing them last within the section. This is almost always done with the income and age questions in the last section of the questionnaire, but can also produce benefits if treated carefully in the earlier sections. If income, age, and other sensitive questions are asked in a proper and clever manner, very high levels of response will be obtained.

Most introductions to interviewer-administered questionnaires and most cover letters for self-administered, mailed questionnaires mention that the study is important. The respondent is therefore prepared for question pertaining to important issues as the questioning begins. The researcher would also like to begin in this fashion, but often there are other tasks that must be dealt with before the main questionnaire can begin. For example, an overriding consideration at the beginning of the interview is whether the respondent is qualified to be part of the study. Suppose that the project is directed to obtaining information from university-educated women who work full-time in management positions in the Toronto area, who are between the ages of 35 and 55, who have at least two children between the ages of 13 and 19, and a husband who also works full-time, who travels for business purposes, and takes at least one vacation each year with the family. There would, of course, have to be a series of questions at the beginning of the questionnaire that would identify those who fit the description of qualified respondents and screen-out those who don't fit the requirements. These questions will not appear to be important or relevant to the respondent, but just a nuisance.

This extreme example points out the problem which screening questions must address. If you can't get the correct respondent, pass up the interview.

Exhibit 7.4 provides a basis for establishing the order of the questions. However, please realize that the following are guidelines and are not meant to be unbreakable rules. If good sense suggests that a guideline can't be followed in a particular situation, perhaps it's best to follow another path through the questionnaire.

Exhibit 7.4 Questionnaire Design: Points to Watch in Ordering the Questions

1. Start with questions that determine whether the respondent has the qualities or characteristics needed for the study purpose in order to continue with the interview (screener).

2. At least some of those questions which the respondent would see as most socially useful or important should come early.

3. Ensure that earlier questions do not give the respondent information that he/she should not have prior to the asking of later questions, e.g., making it clear too soon that a particular brand is the prime concern of the study.

4. Group questions that are similar in content together and, within content areas, by type of question.

5. Build a sense of flow and continuity by taking advantage of natural relationships and ties that respondents are likely to make among groups of questions.

6. Questions within any topic area that are likely to be difficult or objectionable to respondents should come after rapport has been built up to encourage a thoughtful and frank response.

The physical format of the questionnaire can have a substantial impact on the response rate for self-administered questionnaires and on the accuracy and ease of recording and data entry for interviewer-administered questionnaires.

There are substantial differences between the layout of questionnaires for the two administration types. With self-administered questionnaires, great care must be taken to ensure that any qualified respondent can read, understand, and respond to all the questions. The questionnaire writer must always consider the respondent who has qualified according to the screening questions, but whose vision is somewhat impaired, or who has poor hearing, or a relatively low level of intelligence, or is not fully conversant with the English language. These people should either be screened out at the beginning of the questionnaire or the questionnaire must be developed so that they feel comfortable in reading and answering the questions.

Don't make the respondents figure out how to physically answer the question. Their only job should be to determine their answer mentally and then speak it or write it effortlessly. An example of an extremely poor format for a question is as follows:

1. *How would you rate the general health of Canadians today?*

very good health____ good health ____ fair health ____ poor health ____ very poor health ____

A greatly improved version of this question for a self-administered question-naire is:

1. How would you rate the general health of Canadians today?

    [ ]1   VERY GOOD HEALTH
    [ ]2   GOOD HEALTH
    [ ]3   FAIR HEALTH
    [ ]4   POOR HEALTH
    [ ]5   VERY POOR HEALTH

The second format gives the following advantages:

- Respondents can clearly see where and how to indicate their answers to the questions. In the first version, the respondent might have to study the sequence of answers and spaces carefully before feeling comfortable in answering.
- As the respondent progresses through the questionnaire, it becomes more or less routine that when capital letters are seen, then it's time to check a box to answer a question.

Capital letters usually most clearly differentiate the answers from the questions. However, italics and bold type can be used to accomplish the same purpose.

- The respondent feels a sense of accomplishment in the second format since the vertical column of answers establishes a flow which seems to get one more quickly through the pages and the questionnaire. The questionnaire also looks much less cluttered when the vertical flow is used.
- In some questions, when the respondent gives one of the answers, then directions are given for skipping to a question further down the page, or even several pages further ahead in the questionnaire. When these skip patterns are used, the vertical placement of the answers allows for a much cleaner indication of which question(s) should be skipped to next.

The interviewer-administered version of the question above is presented below:

1. First of all, would you rate the general health of Canadians as very good, good, fair, poor or very poor?

VERY GOOD HEALTH	1	
GOOD HEALTH	2	
FAIR HEALTH	3	(45)
POOR HEALTH	4	
VERY POOR HEALTH	5	

Many of the same benefits listed for the self-administered questionnaire are also relevant for the interviewer-administered format. However, the respondent does not see this version of the question, so a bit more liberty can be taken with the format of the page. Although the questions are kept in lower case, the answers are in upper case and placed in a vertical column, there are still major differences between the two forms. These are motivated by a desire to simplify and improve the interviewing and data-entry processes in the interviewer-administered version.

Notice that the answers in the self-administered questionnaire were left-justified to a position just slightly indented to the right of the question. However, the interviewer-administered questionnaire was written so that the answers are right-justified allowing a margin for data entry purposes. One objective in writing a self-administered questionnaire is to keep the amount of ink on the page to a minimum so that it appears clean and easy to read. The respondent should never see the interviewer-administered question-naire, so information that will make the jobs of interviewing, editing, coding, and data entry easier can be included on the interviewer-administered ques-tionnaire without fear of impeding the respondent's understanding and moti-vation. With the answers right-justified and the inclusion of the coding strip, the tasks of editing, coding and data entry are simplified. The answers that are circled by the interviewer are reviewed by the editor. The data-entry staff can then key-in the data directly from the edited and coded questionnaires. Not only are costs reduced but a potential source of error can be avoided. (See a complete questionnaire in this format in Appendix 7C.)

Another technique for developing good questionnaires is to provide infor-mation and directions on how to skip questions. Arrows and boxes should be used either alone or in conjunction with statements to direct respondents and interviewers clearly to the next question in sequence. The following illustrates this technique:

Who decided where the car should go for this most recent service?
(Please check box.)

[   ] I DID

[   ] 2 ANOTHER HOUSEHOLD MEMBER DID
[   ] 3 A FAMILY MEMBER WHO DOES NOT LIVE IN MY HOME DID
[   ] 4 SOMEONE OUTSIDE OF MY IMMEDIATE HOUSEHOLD AND FAMLY DID

GO TO QUESTION 2

*What prompted you to have this **most recent** service done at Firestone? (Check all boxes that apply.)*

Check all that apply

[ ] BEST VALUE FOR THE MONEY
[ ] PREVIOUS GOOD EXPERIENCE AT FIRESTONE STORES
[ ] DISCOUNT BECAUSE OF AUTO CLUB MEMBERSHIP
[ ] TV ADVERTISING
. . .
[ ] THE FIRESTONE NAME HAS A GOOD REPUTATION

Other suggestions are to keep each question and its corresponding answers on one page. Don't start a question on one page and then continue it onto the next page. This is too difficult for the respondent to read in self-administered questionnaires and it interrupts the conversational style of the interview in interviewer-administered questionnaires.

When passing from one distinct section of questions to another section, it's often helpful to the respondent if there is just a short sentence or two to explain the next set of questions and to act as a smooth transition into a state of mind suitable for answering those questions. (Never apologize before asking the demographic questions. This acts as a red flag to respondents, their guard will be up and their mouths closed.) That transition is often similar to, "Now just a few more questions to help us divide our interviews into groups," or "Now I have to ask just a few more questions for statistical purposes." Other comments could include the following:

Section 5

"It's important to our study to be able to relate what people have experienced, what they believe to be true, and their opinions.

1. Many people have definite opinions about automotive service in general. We'd like to know your opinions . . .

Using the current jargon of computer-based writing, Exhibit 7.5 lists nine basic rules of page layout for questionnaires. These are rules that will definitely improve the quality of a questionnaire and should be adhered to strictly.

Exhibit 7.5 Questionnaire Design: Page Layout, Question Format and Question Sequence

1. Use lower case letters for questions, UPPER CASE (or **bold** or *italics*) for pre-coded answers and interviewer instructions.

2. Identify answer categories on *left* for self-administration, identify answer categories on *right* for interviewer-administration.

3. Establish a *vertical flow*.

4. Provide *directions* for answering or recording the answer.

5. Special procedures for items in a series:
   - ask *one* question at a time
   - use *words* for answer choices on self-administered questionnaires (sometimes not for scaled responses)
   - show the *connection* between items and answers

6. Use *multiple column* technique to conserve space.

7. Show how to *skip* questions.

8. Make questions *fit* each page.

9. Use *transitions* for continuity.

Exhibit 7.5.1 Identify Answer Categories on the Left for Self-administration

1. How would you rate the general health of Canadians today?

[   ] 1   VERY GOOD HEALTH
[   ] 2   GOOD HEALTH
[   ] 3   FAIR HEALTH
[   ] 4   POOR HEALTH
[   ] 5   VERY POOR HEALTH

Exhibit 7.5.2 Identify Answer Categories on the Right for Interviewer-administration

1. First of all, would you rate the general health of Canadians today as very good, good, fair, poor or very poor?

VERY GOOD HEALTH	1	
GOOD HEALTH	2	
FAIR HEALTH	3	(45)
POOR HEALTH	4	
VERY POOR HEALTH	5	

In the above, the interviewer circles the answer, which is later typed into column 45 of the data record.

Exhibit 7.5.3 Formulating the Pages: Establish a Vertical Flow

Don't Ever Do This

1. *How would you rate the general health of Canadians today?*

____ very good health   ____ good health   ____ fair health
____ poor health   ____ very poor health

This format is confusing and leads to unintentional errors in answering since the answers and the lines for ticking are so close together.

Rather, Choose the Following:

1. *How would you rate the general health of Canadians today?*

[   ] 1 VERY GOOD

[   ] 2 GOOD

[   ] 3 FAIR

[   ] 4 POOR

[   ] 5 VERY POOR

Here, the answers are presented in an orderly fashion with answer boxes clearly evident. The capitalization of the answers establishes a perceptual cue that leads the respondent to expect to provide an answer when capital letters are read. Also, the vertical placement on the pages allows the respondent to move down the page more quickly, giving a feeling of achievement.

The different field methodologies (interviewer-administered or self-administered) place special requirements on the questionnaire. For example, since the self-administered questionnaire is handled and read by the respondent, special care must be taken to ensure that its visual appearance is pleasing and effective. Exhibit 7.6 lists several suggestions to improve the impact of self-administered questionnaires.

Exhibit 7.6   General Suggestions for Self-administered Questionnaires

1. It's usually best not to number the questions sequentially from the beginning to the end of the questionnaire. The respondent might balk at the large number of questions even though the time needed for completion might be quite short. This problem can be avoided by numbering questions sequentially within sections.

2. The font (type face) and size must be legible enough for people with less than perfect vision.

3. If the questionnaire is longer than three pages, consider formatting it as a booklet in a size less than the standard 8.5" x 11" sheet of paper. Often, a standard sheet of paper folded in half and turned sideways makes a good size for a booklet. Both sides of the pages would be printed.

4. If possible, put a diagram or a line drawing on the first page to enhance the attractiveness and heighten interest.

5. For mail surveys:

   • follow a three wave technique —

      wave 1. the cover letter, questionnaire, stamped self-addressed envelope and incentive

      wave 2. follow-up post-card one-and-a-half weeks after wave 1 to encourage cooperation

      wave 3. a reminder letter, questionnaire and stamped self-addressed envelope one-and-a-half weeks after wave 2

   • be sure to check the questionnaires carefully as soon as they are returned from the printer

   • a financial incentive, such as a $1 coin or $2 bill, enhances cooperation substantially

6. Don't crowd the questions together. Some open space makes for a more appealing questionnaire — one that will be more inviting to respondents.

7. Reduce the amount of ink on the page as much as possible. Only the questions, the answer categories and instructions to the respondents should be on the page. If any coding information appears on the questionnaire, reduce it to a bare minimum.

8. Keep open-ended questions to a minimum. People are usually reluctant to record lengthy responses.

Exhibit 7.7 Special Considerations for Interviewer-administered Questionnaires

1. Since the interviewer-administered questionnaire is not seen by the respondent, the objective is to make the printed page as helpful to the interviewer, the editor and the data-entry people as possible.

2. Provide coding information on the questionnaire to reduce the difficulty of the coding task and to reduce the errors of data entry. A **coding strip** down the right-hand margin of the page can be very effective. This area will indicate in which columns in the data file the answers should be entered or which variable relates to the answer. Because of the many revisions through which most questionnaires pass, it's often wise to wait until the final draft to insert the column numbers. If variable names are used instead of column numbers, they can be inserted at any stage.

3. Use the column numbers or variable names from the coding strip to prepare dummy tabs to make sure that the division into columns is done properly *before* the questionnaire is printed.

4. For difficult or sensitive questions in face-to-face interviews, hand cards with answer categories to respondents. This allows the respondent to see the several categories on a scaled question or to read off the number of brands from which they must choose the one they like best. Also, sensitive questions, such as income level may achieve a higher response rate if the respondent can answer with a letter indicating income category. (See Appendix 7C.)

Naturally, most questionnaires contain questions on fairly standard topics that are encountered in respondents' everyday lives. Most questionnaires also tend to ask for the same kinds of information. The most common varieties of questions are listed in Exhibit 7.8.

Exhibit 7.8 Types of Primary Data Which Need to be Captured by Questions

1. Attitudes/opinions
2. Awareness/knowledge
3. Motivation
4. Intentions
5. Behaviour
6. Demographic and socio-economic characteristics

Care should be taken with the overall look of the questionnaire. Those that are longer than two or three pages can be set up in a booklet format. Coloured paper can also increase interest.

QUESTIONNAIRE ADMINISTRATION IS ERROR PRONE

The entire operation of administering the questionnaire is highly error prone. Errors can occur at different levels.

THE RESPONDENT

Although it is tempting for the researcher to consider the respondents as not being very thoughtful when answering questions, the fact is that some questionnaires are not very well designed. They fail to take into consideration several obvious things:

- A respondent's mental set is abruptly interrupted by the interviewer.
- What is important to the researcher is often trivial to the respondent.
- The questionnaire is influenced by the researcher's cultural background (although the researcher would like to believe that it is the respondent's cultural background that is the problem).
- The fine distinctions that a researcher makes in wording the questionnaire may have no counterpart in the respondent's repertory of experience. (Can a housewife who is interrupted by an interviewer in a shopping mall really tell the difference between coffee that has body and coffee that has strength? After having distinguished these two attributes, can she really evaluate a brand on each of these attributes on a 7-point scale?)

Very little is being done about these aspects of questionnaire administration since they are seldom brought to the attention of the researcher. This is unfortunate because ignoring these challenges can result in gradually declining response rates. Thus, the first source of questionnaire error can be attributed to the respondent, although the researcher, rather than the respondent, is the cause of the problem in most cases.

THE INTERVIEWER

A special relationship must exist between the respondent, the interviewer and the field supervisor. The supervisor must ensure that the interviewers are properly trained, motivated and disciplined. Even under stringent field control, there is substantial threat of error in administration of the questionnaire.

THE CODER AND THE DATA-ENTRY PERSON

Both the coder and the data-entry person do tedious and repetitive jobs. The nature of their jobs is such that errors cannot be easily avoided and, in some cases, cannot even be detected. Computer Assisted Telephone Interviewing (CATI) and data entry programs are helping to reduce these errors.

Because the entire operation is error prone, the researcher cannot hope to eliminate errors completely. The main objective of the researcher is to provide as little scope as possible for error on the part of anyone involved in the chain of questionnaire administration. This has to be accomplished without compromising, in any major way, the information needs of the study.

WHAT MAKES A QUESTIONNAIRE DIFFICULT TO ANSWER?

William Belson (1981: 24–27), a British researcher, identified some of the factors that make it difficult for a respondent to answer questions posed by the researcher. They are reproduced below and are a good basis for thought about improving questionnaire design.

CATEGORIES OF QUESTION DIFFICULTY

(Category 1 occurs most frequently and category 13 least frequently.)

1. Instances of two questions presented as one (e.g., questions offering two long and rather cumbersome alternatives that could be difficult for a respondent to hold in mind while making a decision between them; questions in which there is overlap between the alternatives offered; questions in which the alternatives, separated by the word "or," do not cover all the possibilities)

Examples:
   (a) Did you, personally, get our letter of invitation to come here tonight or did you come as a guest of someone else who got our letter of invitation?

   (b) Do you think there are enough job opportunities for a person like you in this district or do you think there are better jobs elsewhere?

   (c) Do you usually get it from the shop or do you usually have it delivered?

   (d) Which brand do you use or do you change brands frequently?

2. Questions that contain a lot of meaningful words (possibly quite simple ones) in a short space and in which each contributes an element of meaning necessary to the question

Examples:

(a) Can you estimate the proportion of your sales accounted for by this brand?

(b) How many of each sized packet have you bought?

(c) How many hours do you usually watch TV on a weekday?

(d) Did you buy any . . . in the last 7 days?

3. Questions that conclude with a qualifying clause or phrase

Examples:

(a) Have you bought any chocolates in the last 7 days, not counting today?

(b) Do you ever buy something other than X because X is not available?

(c) Have you ever bought any paint to use for home decorating?

4. Questions that contain multiple ideas or subjects

Examples:

(a) Can you give me some idea of the number, makes and sizes of each that you have sold to date or have in-stock at the moment?

(b) Amongst the different brands of cigarettes that you know well, which ones do you like?

(d) Which of these have you heard of or shopped at?

5. Questions that contain difficult or unfamiliar words

Examples:

Informal/constituency/excluding/merit/to-date/vary/antiseptic/ failure/availability/experimenting/nonfrozen/impartial/periodical/proportion/associate/property/estimate/impressions/appropriate/consider/solvent.

6. Questions that contain one or more instructions to the informant

Examples:

(a) Have you bought any chocolates in the last 7 days? Do not include today's buying in your answer.

(b) Which of these words applies to ...'s toothpaste? Look at the words in the list and choose the ones that apply. It doesn't matter how many you choose.

7. Questions that start with words meant to soften the question's impact or its seeming harshness or directness

Examples:

(a) Would you mind telling me how old you are?

(b) Do you happen to know the names of any brands of X?

(c) Can you give me some idea of when you last bought X?

8. Difficult phrases in questions

Examples:

Is there any advantage in having . . . /brand name associations/ taking everything into consideration/ display material/ would you be inclined to . . . /of these same qualities/which classes of people/what is the appropriate alternative to

9. Questions that contain conditional or hypothetical clauses

Examples:

(a) Supposing I were to take you into a shop and show you a television set and say, "That's what I call a really good-looking TV set"—what would it look like?

(b) If you were buying a refrigerator, what would be the qualities you would most want it to have?

10. Questions that are dependent in character in the sense that they are linked to a master question without which they would not make sense

Examples:

(a) Have you seen any booklets on safety in the home? . . . Which were they? . . . Where did you get them?

(b) Was last week's copy of . . . delivered to your home? Where is it now? . . .

(c) During the last week did you buy any chocolates? How much did you get then? . . . On the last occasion, where did you do your buying?

11. Questions that have a negative element

Examples:

(a) Is there any particular reason why you do not use coal?

(b) Why have you not bought X since then?

12. Sentences that are inverted

Examples:

(a) The ones you bought last time, what were they?

(b) The car you have now, did you buy it new or second hand?

13. Questions that include the term "if any" or "if at all"

Examples:

(a) Which of these, if any, have you ever bought?

(b) How much, if at all, do you think that the brand of your gas matters?

14. Examples of other types of difficulty are the following:

- Questions that are very long
- Questions in which both the present and the past tense are used
- Questions in which both the singular and the plural are used (Belson, p.24–7)

It should be noted that it may not always be possible to avoid questionnaire difficulty. In cases where unavoidable complexity is involved, it is best to use the simplest and most explicit language.

RESPONDENT MISUNDERSTANDING AND MISINTERPRETATION

When a question is difficult to answer (or even when it is not), a respondent may delete, distort or generalize the question. Although there is no definitive answer to help the researcher avoid these problems, it helps to know the nature and causes of respondent misunderstanding. William Belson (1981: 370-387) proposed a set of 15 hypotheses covering the most likely distortions that might occur. These are listed below along with examples and interpretations which are the responsibility of the authors. While going through the hypotheses, try to think of additional examples of questions and possible distortions that might occur when the respondents do not understand the questions.

1. When a respondent finds it difficult to answer a question, he is likely to modify it in such a way as to be able to answer it more easily.

Examples:

- If an executive who travels abroad extensively is asked,

  How often in a week do you read the Star?,

  he may reply "every day", meaning everyday he is in Canada.

• If a shift-worker is asked,

Do you watch the 11 o'clock news every day?,

he may reply in the affirmative, meaning that he watches the 11 o'clock news, provided he is not at work.

The problem in the above examples is that the respondents do not necessarily make their interpretation clear to the interviewer. In both cases, if the researcher is attempting to estimate audience for the medium, he or she will end up with an overestimate.

2. If a broad term or concept is used, there will be a strong tendency for respondents to interpret it less broadly.

Examples:
• How many hours of TV did you watch yesterday?

It might be interpreted by the respondent to include only those programs selected by her.

• Do you ever read *Time* magazine?

The respondent may answer "no", although he had seen it while waiting for his dentist; as far as the researcher is concerned, the respondent has indeed read the magazine.

3. Under certain circumstances a term or concept may be widened.

Examples:
• What do you think of radio commercials?

If the respondent has a lot to say about commercials in general, he or she may widen the scope to include TV commercials, without making this clear to the interviewer.

• What do you think of multinationals operating in Canada?

If the respondent has complaints against other companies that are not multinationals, he or she may offer opinions on all corporations.

4. Part of a question may be overlooked under certain conditions as set out below. The respondent might distort the question or delete phrases when they seem to be superfluous, when words might be misheard and when one long alternative phrase overshadows another.

Examples:
• Do you think that children suffer any ill-effects from watching programs with violence in them, other than ordinary police shows?

Respondents may ignore the qualifying clause and include police shows as well.

- How many times did you drink coffee last week, excluding the after-dinner occasions?

Respondents might well include all instances of coffee drinking.

5a. A respondent may distort a question to fit his own situation, position or experience.

Examples:
- Do you usually watch the TV news?

This may be interpreted by a respondent who keeps irregular hours, as "Do you sometimes . . ."

- Do you make over $50 000 in your job?

This may be interpreted by an electrician to mean, "Did you ever make over $50 000 . . ."

5b. A respondent may distort a question because he wants to create an opportunity to express an opinion, perhaps strongly held.

Examples:
How many people work in your office?

Oh, about half of them, I should say.

5c. A respondent may distort the question so as not to admit anything that puts him in a poor light.

Examples:
- A respondent may underestimate the time he spends watching TV, if he feels that it puts him in an unfavourable light.
- A respondent may exaggerate the number of times he goes to the theatre.

6a. The general context, or setting of a term, in a question may wrongly influence the way that term is interpreted (context being the question and/or the questionnaire within which the term is set).

Examples:
- When a question refers to "political programming," the respondent may interpret news as a political program.

  Do you watch documentaries on TV?

This might be interpreted by the respondents to include docudramas, which look like documentaries.

6b. Specific words or clauses which are meant to define or qualify a wider term, may lead to the misinterpretation of that wider term.

Examples:

• A question pertaining to the effect of TV viewing on moral behaviour may be interpreted by the respondent to include only sexual morality.

How often during the week, on the average, do you go to a bar?

In this example, the respondent may exclude all times he goes to a bar on special occasions, because they are not "average" occasions.

7. A respondent may answer what he regards as the spirit or sense of the question, rather than its actual words, and so perhaps misinterpret the question.

Examples:

• When a respondent is asked whether he changes from channel to channel or just watches one or two programs an evening, the respondent may interpret this as asking whether he is discriminating in what he watches and answer the question accordingly.

• Do you contribute to charities?

This may be interpreted by the respondent as a value-ridden statement. Consequently, he may reply that he does, meaning that he might contribute to charities.

8. A question may be wrongly interpreted if it includes difficult words or words which mean different things to different people.

Examples:

• For some respondents, "weekdays" may include Saturdays.

Is your phone unlisted?

The respondent could interpret it in either of the following two ways and give an answer:

The respondent has a phone number which is deliberately unlisted

The respondent got his number too late to be included in the current directory.

9a. A word or part of a word may not be heard properly and so lead to erroneous interpretation of the question in which it occurs.

9b. A respondent may, because he misses part of a question, reconstruct the question from those parts of it that he has heard.

9c. When a question has in it a lot of information carrying words, it is specially open to misinterpretation.

Example:

In the past week, by that I mean Monday to Friday only, how many issues of *The Star* did you personally happen to read or look into either at home or elsewhere?

Because there are too many information-carrying words, the respondent may distort the question.

10. The word "you" is prone to be interpreted collectively (e.g., as "you and others") where it refers to behaviour in which the respondent is involved with others.

Example:

Did you buy any household detergent last month?

Here the "you" could refer to the respondent in particular or the household in general. Different respondents may interpret the question differently. Often phrases such as "you personally" and "you yourself" are used to get the respondent to realize that the question pertains to himself or herself.

11. A respondent may add to a question in order to be able to enlarge or to qualify his answer.

Examples:

- A question that relates to U.S. government policies may be enlarged by the respondent to include his opinion of President George Bush.
- If a respondent is asked to comment on the Meech Lake Accord, he or she may extend his or her answer to comment on all government policies.

12. Where a question is ambiguous, a respondent may select one of the two possible interpretations, without the interviewer necessarily being aware that this has happened.

Example:

Do you eat in expensive restaurants?

This could mean (1) Do you ever eat in expensive restaurants? or (2) Do you normally eat in expensive restaurants? or (3) Would you eat in expensive restaurants, should the occasion arise?

13. A qualifying clause may interfere with the consolidation of the respondent's grasp of preceding elements of the question (see also hypothesis 9c).

14. When a concept is presented to a respondent that seems odd, he may well normalize it.

Example:

"Cartoon advertisements" may become "cartoons" or "cartoon programs"; "advertising time" may become "the timing of advertisements."

15. When a complex or thought-demanding question is followed by a simple choice of answers (e.g., yes/no), the respondent is likely to give less care to his consideration of the detail of the question and so is less likely to interpret the question as intended.

Example:

Let us assume that the government deficit is so high that the only sensible way out is through taxation. When you take this into account in conjunction with the restrictive monetary policy, are you in favour of increased taxes or not?

[ ]1 YES
[ ]2 NO

Here respondents may ignore the deficit and monetary policy parts of the question because they don't understand those concepts and may simply respond to the question of whether they are in favour of increased taxes.

SUMMARY

This chapter on questionnaire design has presented both the conceptual and practical sides of a marketing research activity that is central to achieving high quality answers to the formalized marketing questions.

The development of questions that capture the essence of the marketing investigation and provide for uninhibited responses by the respondents is an art-form that is developed through experience. The suggestions made in this chapter can be very helpful in accelerating the development of this knowledge and skill.

The questionnaire design activity involves:

• identifying information needs
• composing the questions
• sequencing the flow of the questions
• laying out the pages for maximum comprehension and efficiency

- editing
- pretesting

Questions must be written so that they can be understood precisely by all respondents, even those who might have reading, seeing, hearing and comprehending difficulties. All questions must be edited so that none are biased, have double meanings, are two questions in one, or don't provide for complete and comfortable answering by respondents. Researchers must be quite creative at times to devise questions which reduce the willingness of respondents to complete the questionnaire.

The researcher should be concerned about the content of the individual questions as well as with the physical layout of the pages of the question- naire. Self-administered and interviewer-administered questionnaires have different layouts which facilitate their usage by the respondents and the interviewers, respectively. The logic behind those styles and the mechanism for their construction should be fully understood and implemented in order to increase comprehension, reduce the questionnaire answering time, reduce errors in recording and to ease the editing and data entry processes.

Questions that attempt to measure the attitudes of the sample are typi- cally quite challenging to compose and to test. While researchers must strive for valid and reliable measurements, they must also make the questions comprehensible and easy to answer but not so repetitive that they become boring. Scaled responses are often developed to measure attitudes. Some of the scales are fairly standard. However, researchers often develop scales for new applications when the standard scales are felt to be too limiting.

NOW THINK ABOUT THIS

1. Develop both self-administered and interviewer-administered versions of a questionnaire to determine when the respondent last visited the donut shop that they are sitting in right now; how often they visit that particu- lar store; how often they visit any donut shop; the name and location of their favourite donut shop; their order at the time; the amount of money spent; their liking of the shop; their intention to return; and simple demo- graphics.

2. Use the interviewer format for the questionnaire developed in question 1, interview someone and then revise your questionnaire. Provide both the original and the revised questionnaire. Interview one more person with the revised questionnaire and revise again.

REFERENCES

Belson, William A.
1981 *The Design and Understanding of Survey Questions*. Aldershot, Hants, England: Gower Publishing Co. Ltd., pp. 370-387.

Crask, Melvin R. and Richard J. Fox
1987 "An exploration of the internal properties of three commonly used marketing research scales: a magnitude estimation approach." *Journal of the Marketing Research Society*, Volume 29, No. 3, 317-339.

Gallup Canada, Inc.
1990 *Canadians' Attitudes Toward Survey Research: Where does Our Industry Stand?* Toronto: Gallup Canada, Inc., May 1990.

Haller, Terry
1983 *Danger: Marketing Researcher at Work*. Westport, CT: Quorum Books.

Loken, Barbara, Phyllis Pirre, Karen A. Virnig, Ronald L. Hinkle and Charles T. Salmon
1987 "The use of 0-10 scales in telephone surveys." *Journal of Market Research Society*, Volume 29, No. 3, 353-362.

Mullet, Gary M.
1983 "Itemized Rating Scales: Ordinal or Interval?" *European Research*, April, 1983, 49-52.

Payne, Stanley L.
1951 *The Art of Asking Questions*. Princeton, NJ: Princeton University Press.

APPENDIX 7A

Attitude Measurement

It is difficult to imagine the discipline of marketing research without attitude measurement. Not only is attitude measurement key to the basic business value of marketing research, but it also imparts much of the interest and excitement to the discipline. The challenge of capturing peoples' attitudes by constructing a question which appears simple and straightforward to respondents is not trivial. The question must also appear to be valid to critics and to give the appearance of providing reproducible information from study to study and group to group.

In developing questionnaires, it is helpful to keep in mind the hierarchy of affects which is often used in understanding the purposes of advertising. A somewhat extended hierarchy of effects is shown in Exhibit 7A.1.

The hierarchy of effects model is one of many ways of conceptualizing the relationship among the supposed components of attitudes. The formulation of the hierarchy of effects in Exhibit 7A.1 is somewhat extended but it is presented here to allow the reader to consider a wider set of possible attitude questioning areas. The model assumes that a person must first become aware of a brand before an eventual purchase of that brand can transpire. After becoming aware of the brand, the person acquires some knowledge about the brand, then a level of liking, and so on. The stages of awareness, knowledge, liking, preference, conviction and post-purchase influences are normally considered to be parts of the formation and influence of attitudes. Very often, within one particular questionnaire, attitudinal questions are drawn from each level in this hierarchy, or at least from several of the levels in Exhibit 7A.1.

The hierarchy of effects steps are often grouped under three major components of attitudes:

- Cognitive: includes the person's awareness of an object, the person's knowledge, beliefs and specific levels of information regarding the object
- Affective: emotions or feelings about the object
- Conative: intended action toward the brand

Exhibit 7A.1 Hierarchy of Effects

Unaware

Aware

Knowledge

Liking

Preference

Conviction

Purchase

Post-Purchase

These stages of the hierarchy of effects are often looked upon as the several tasks of advertising.

Awareness

Creating awareness of a brand or service is the most basic objective of marketing communication. Conventional wisdom tells us that unless a person is aware of the brand, that person can't be expected to decide consciously to purchase the brand or not to purchase it. Awareness means that the name of the brand is in the person's memory and that the person is able to state the name of that brand, either without any help (unaided awareness), or with prompting from the interviewer (aided awareness).

The following example illustrates the use of an interviewer-administered, unaided question to help identify whether the respondent is aware of the brand. The unaided question is followed by an aided question.

Please tell me the names of all the brands of dog food that you're aware of.

FIRST MENTION _____

SECOND MENTION _____

THIRD MENTION _____

IF PAL NOT MENTIONED, THEN ASK:

Have you ever heard of Pal dog food?

> YES   1
>
> NO   2

The unaided version of the awareness question is considered by some to be more effective in identifying actual awareness than is the aided question. The reason for this is that a percentage of the respondents will "yea-say" in response to a question regarding whether they were aware of Pal dog food or any other brand of a product. It's human nature to want to appear intelligent and aware of the outside world and its components. Consequently, a higher percentage of the respondents will state awareness of Pal if they are provided with the Pal brand name than will supply the Pal brand when asked to list brands of dog food. On the other hand, the unaided question assumes that the memories of all respondents are equally good in recalling those most familiar brands names. In response to the unaided question above, the respondent might not mention Kibbles 'n Bits dog food. However, when asked the aided question "Have you ever heard of Kibbles 'n Bits?", the respondent might say "Of course, the ad with the little dog jumping over the bulldog", indicating not only awareness but also recall of the contents of the commercial.

KNOWLEDGE

Awareness of a brand technically means that the person knows that the brand exists. However, knowledge in attitude measurement implies that the respondent has some level of understanding of some characteristic(s) of the brand beyond its basic identity. Naturally, the range and depth of knowledge questions are very extensive. The appropriate level of detail of knowledge depends on the project requirements, the survey methodology and the abilities of the respondents to answer various types of questions.

Consider the following questions as asking only for a very basic level of knowledge. (These are intended to illustrate various ways of asking knowledge questions, not as being part of one questionnaire, necessarily.)

Now, please tell me which of those dog foods you just mentioned are canned dog food?

_____

_____

_____

Which are semi-moist dog food?

_____

_____

_____

And which are dry dog food?

_____

_____

_____

IF MORE THAN ONE CANNED DOG FOOD BRAND MENTIONED, ASK:

Of the canned dog food brands which you just mentioned, which one do you think has the highest percent of protein?

_____

What percent protein does that brand have?

_____%

If price were no consideration at all, what percent protein should a canned dog food have to be best for your dog?

_____%

Now, of the three canned dog foods, Alpo, Derby and Pal (ROTATE), which two do you think are the most alike in nutrition?

_____

_____

Which two of Alpo, Derby and Pal do you think are most different in nutrition?

_____

_____

Would you rate the nutritional content of Pal canned dog food as excellent, very good, good, fair, poor, very poor or terrible?

EXCELLENT	7
VERY GOOD	6
GOOD	5
FAIR	4
POOR	3
VERY POOR	2
TERRIBLE	1

Compared to Alpo canned dog food, would you say that the nutrition of Pal canned dog food is much better, a little better, a little worse, much worse or about the same?

MUCH BETTER	5
BETTER	4
ABOUT SAME	3
WORSE	2
MUCH WORSE	1

LIKING

Liking of a brand or an object can be measured in several ways. A useful way of questioning is to ask the respondent to choose the most liked brand out of a group. Then to choose the second most liked, and so on. This is a task in assigning *rank orders* to the brands. There is quite a broad range of procedures for analyzing rank-ordered data, from simply obtaining the overall rank positions from a sample based on the average ranks to using Friedman's Analysis of Variance (see Chapter 21), multidimensional scaling, or other high level techniques.

A.1 Of the three brands of canned dog food, Pal, Alpo and Dr. Ballard, which do you like the best?

_____

A.2 Which of the three do you like second best?

_____

Some researchers attempt to get respondents to indicate their degree of liking for brands of a product by asking them to answer scaling questions such as the following.

B. Would you please tell me how much you like Pal canned dog food by giving me a number between 0 and 10, where 10 means that you like it very much and where 0 means that you dislike it greatly.

$$0 \quad 1 \quad 2 \quad 3 \quad 4 \quad 5 \quad 6 \quad 7 \quad 8 \quad 9 \quad 10$$

C. Overall, would you say that your dog likes Pal dog food very much, likes it somewhat, dislikes it somewhat or dislikes it very much?

LIKES VERY MUCH	4
LIKES SOMEWHAT	3
DISLIKES SOMEWHAT	2
DISLIKES VERY MUCH	1

Notice that the above two ways of asking questions about the respondent's degree of liking for the brand are quite different. Question A asks the respondent simply to name a brand as best liked, second best liked and third best liked. That type of questioning is referred to as comparative because the liking is expressed relative to other brands in the product category. The second type of liking question above, questions B and C, is a non-comparative attitude scaling question. The respondent is asked to assign one number out of eleven numbers or one level of liking to the degree of liking for the brand in isolation from all other brands. Both types of questions are used in marketing research practice. However, the researcher must always determine which type of attitude question is most appropriate to any specific research task; which form of the question is most likely to capture the true level of liking of the brand(s) (*validity*); and which form would be most likely to elicit answers that would be reproducible should the question be asked again under the same conditions (*reliability*). Validity and reliability will be defined and discussed later.

Another point to note is that in question B, two of the eleven points on the scale are described by words or *anchored*. In question C, each point is anchored by the phrase that is read to the respondent.

The comparison approach can be combined with scaling in some types of projects by asking questions such as the following.

Compared to Derby canned dog food, would you say that your dog likes Pal canned dog food much more, somewhat more, somewhat less, or much less?

MUCH MORE	5
SOMEWHAT MORE	4
ABOUT THE SAME	3
SOMEWHAT LESS	2
MUCH LESS	1

PREFERENCE

The measurement of preference can take a wide variety of forms. Preference measurement can use some of the scaling procedures illustrated for liking in the previous section. For example, one might ask the following question which is almost identical to a question above:

Please indicate which of the following brands of ice cream you prefer the most, prefer second most, third most and fourth most by **writing the brand letter in the appropriate preference position to the right.**

A Sealtest Parlor Ice Cream	_____ BRAND MOST PREFERRED
B Beatrice Classic Ice Cream	_____ BRAND 2ND MOST PREFERRED
C Neilson Ice Cream	_____ BRAND 3RD MOST PREFERRED
D President's Choice Ice Cream	_____ BRAND 4TH MOST PREFERRED

Preference information can also be collected by asking *paired comparison* judgments.

Below you'll find several pairs of brands of ice cream. For each pair, put a check mark in the box that indicates which of the two paired brands of ice cream you prefer the most.

[   ] SEALTEST PARLOR ....or..............[   ] BEATRICE CLASSIC

[   ] SEALTEST PARLOR ....or..............[   ] NEILSON

[   ] SEALTEST PARLOR ....or..............[   ] PRESIDENT'S CHOICE

[ ] BEATRICE CLASSIC ....or..............[ ] NEILSON

[ ] BEATRICE CLASSIC ....or..............[ ] PRESIDENT'S CHOICE

[ ] NEILSON ....or..............[ ] PRESIDENT'S CHOICE

In some cases, the procedure of *constant sum* is used, in which a numerical value or points are distributed over two or more brands to indicate the preference among the brands.

Please indicate your preference for the following four brands of ice cream by dividing 100 points among the four brands listed below. Out of the 100 points write in the number which indicates how much you prefer one brand of ice cream among the four listed. Make sure that the points add up to 100.

[   ] SEALTEST PARLOR

[   ] BEATRICE CLASSIC

[   ] NEILSON

[   ] PRESIDENT'S CHOICE

The two procedures above can be combined to provide a very effective way of obtaining respondent preferences for a number of brands on a numerical scale. The following technique is called *constant sum paired comparisons*.

Now, we'd like you to indicate your preference for several brands of ice cream. Imagine that you have 11 poker chips that you can pile in front of two brands of ice cream to indicate your relative preference. If you like one brand much more than you like the other, then you might write 10 in the box to the left of the more preferred brand and 1 in the box to the left of the less preferred brand. If you liked two brands about the same, but one just a little more than the other, then you'd give one brand 6 chips and the other brand 5 chips.

[ ] SEALTEST PARLOR	[ ] BEATRICE CLASSIC
[ ] SEALTEST PARLOR	[ ] NEILSON
[ ] SEALTEST PARLOR	[ ] PRESIDENT'S CHOICE
[ ] BEATRICE CLASSIC	[ ] NEILSON
[ ] BEATRICE CLASSIC	[ ] PRESIDENT'S CHOICE
[ ] NEILSON	[ ] PRESIDENT'S CHOICE

CONVICTION

Conviction measurement produces a type of question that tries to determine which brand the respondent would buy if he or she were in the store at the time of the interview. The marketer must be careful with this type of information since a lot can transpire between the time of the interview and when the respondent is actually in the position of buying the product. The following questions illustrate conviction-type questions.

> If you needed to buy a can of dog food right now, which would you buy, Pal, Dr. Ballard or Alpo?

> _____

> Regarding your purchase of Pal canned dog food, would you say that you definitely would buy Pal, probably would buy Pal, probably would not buy Pal, definitely would not buy Pal, or might or might not buy Pal?

DEFINITELY WOULD	5
PROBABLY WOULD	4
MIGHT OR MIGHT NOT	3
PROBABLY WOULD NOT	2
DEFINITELY WOULD NOT	1

The questions listed above provide examples that are intended to measure various aspects of attitude. When working in the area of attitude measurement, it is important to realize that an attitude can't be seen and empirically tested. It only exists as a hypothetical construct. Because the existence and degree of existence of the attitude can't be confirmed, great responsibility is placed on the researcher to develop a question with a corresponding scale that elicits a verbalization of the attitude from the respondent.

THE BASIC PROBLEM OF ATTITUDE MEASUREMENT

Suppose that it's hypothesized that a person's intention to buy a Macintosh computer is related to the person's conviction that the Mac is easiest to learn. Two constructs have been created:

Construct A—a perception of the ease of learning to use a Macintosh computer

Construct B—an intention to buy a Macintosh

A hypothesis can also be advanced that those people who feel that the Macintosh is easy to learn will have a higher intention to buy a Macintosh computer.

The constructs A and B are represented by circles in Exhibit 7A.2. The true nature of these constructs will never be known. We'll never be able to see either of these attitudes and will never be able to measure them 100 per cent accurately. The best that can be done is to develop questions which we hope measure the constructs' validity and reliably (see the next section for the definitions of validity and reliable). These questions are portrayed as X

Exhibit 7A.2   Grounding Concepts to the Real World with Data

and Y in the diagram. The hypothesis linking the constructs A and B is denoted by the line connecting the circles A and B.

In order to test the hypothesis, the theory must be grounded, i.e., data must be collected from pertinent respondents and the hypothesis must be tested in a statistical sense. The double lines falling from the circles to the ground represent this grounding of the theory in the real world.

Our argument rests on four separate propositions:

- The constructs of perceived ease of learning to use a Macintosh (A) and intention to buy a Macintosh (B) exist and relate to one another.
- The scale X provides a measure of A.
- The scale Y provides a measure of B.
- The measurements from scale X and the measurements from scale Y correlate positively and strongly.

However, the weakness of attitude measurement rests on the fact that only the fourth proposition can be directly examined with empirical data to establish the validity of the hypothesis. If the measurement process is not designed and executed effectively, the measurements resulting from scales X and Y may not provide the desired information about constructs A and B. Researchers must be constantly diligent regarding their capabilities and achievements in measuring the attitudes of the public.

VALIDITY AND RELIABILITY

In presenting the attitude measurement procedures above, the correctness of the measurement and the reproducibility of the score were mentioned. The correctness of an attitude measurement is referred to as *validity* and the reproducibility is referred to as *reliability*.

Essentially, validity means that the question(s) in fact measure what the researchers had intended to measure. Whereas, reliability just means that whatever measurement value was garnered earlier will be obtained again under similar situations with similar or identical respondents.

Validity and reliability mean two different things. However, if a researcher is able to establish that a question is valid, then that question is also reliable. If the question is shown not to be reliable, then it is not valid. But, if the question is shown to be reliable, then it might or might not be valid.

To illustrate a reliable question that might or might not be valid, let's take a real case which happened several years ago at the Canadian National Exhibition. The CNE management commissioned a survey to obtain information from people who were visiting the Ex during the summer of 1982. Management did not want any potentially embarrassing questions asked of the respondents and so excluded all questions to do with age. However, management did want to know the age profile of the interviewed visitors. Consequently, the interviewers were asked to determine visually the age category within which a respondent fell and to indicate that age category on the questionnaire, without mentioning anything about age to the respondent. Seven interviewers were used to conduct approximately 2500 interviews. The frequency distributions for age turned out to be extremely close among the seven interviewers. In fact, the greatest difference in age categories from one interviewer to another was one percentage point. Most of the frequency distributions were identical over most of the categories. It can be concluded that the visual identification of age was reliable in that survey. However, there was no way of identifying whether the actual age categories recorded by the interviewers were correct or valid.

APPENDIX 7B

Questionnaire Layout

An Example of Introductory Dialogue for an Interviewer-administered Questionnaire

My name is _____. I'm working with the CNE this summer to find out people's opinions of the Exhibition and why they came.

Keep the introductory dialogue as short as possible. The sooner you get a respondent to answer a question, the sooner he or she is hooked and won't terminate.

An Example of Using the Multiple Column Technique to Conserve Space in Interviewer-administered Questions

13. What is the <u>one</u> thing that you want to do <u>most</u> at the CNE?

1 GRANDSTAND	12 CENTENNIAL SQUARE
2 AIR SHOW	13 SPORTS CANADA
3 CARLSBERG BUILDING	14 LABATT'S AQUA '82
4 DAILY PARADES (CRUSH)	15 MOLSON LUMBERJACKS
5 CANADA PAVILION	16 ALBERTA EXHIBIT
6 COKE-IS-IT THEATRE	17 HORTICULTURE
7 BETTER LIVING BUILDING	18 AGRICULTURAL EXBTS
8 FOOD BUILDING	19 RIDES
9 INTERNAT'L BUILDING	20 MIDWAY
10 WARRIORS' DAY PARADE	21 ONTARIO PLACE
11 FASHION EXHIBITS	

OTHER: _____ [26 27]

(WRITE IN)

PROBE: Please tell me just one more thing that you're going to do.

An Example of Some Typical Demographic Questions (Interviewer-administered Questionnaire)

The next few questions are just to help us divide our interviews into groups.

14. What was the year of your birth? 19___

15. What was the highest level of formal education you completed?

GRADE 8 OR LESS..........................1
GRADES 9 TO 13 2
COLLEGE......................................3
SOME UNIVERSITY 4
UNIVERSITY GRAD OR MORE 5

16. How many people live in your household?   [   ]

17. Was your household's 1990 total income before taxes

$35 000 or more   or   was it less than $35 000?
          V   V

IF $35 000 OR MORE >> ASK...   IF LESS THAN $35 000 >> ASK

..was it under $45 000........3   ...was it over $20 000.......2
..   or over $45 000 >> ASK   ...   or under $20 000.......1

IF OVER $45 000 >> ASK...
...was it under $55 000....4
..   or over $55 000....5

My supervisor will check back with some of the people in this study for accuracy purposes. So that she can do this, will you please give me your name?

• • • •Thank you for your help• • •   R'S SEX FEMALE...1
                                                           MALE.......2

An Example of Some Typical Demographic Questions (Self-administered Questionnaire)

17. What was the highest level of formal education which you completed?

[ ]1 GRADE 8 OR LESS   [ ]5 SOME UNIVERSITY
[ ]2 SOME HIGH SCHOOL   [ ]6 COMPLETED COLLEGE
[ ]3 COMPLETED HIGH SCHOOL   [ ]7 COMPLETED UNIVERSITY
[ ]4 SOME COLLEGE   [ ]8 GRADUATE STUDIES

18. What is your present occupation?

[ ]1 PROFESSIONAL OR SEMI-PROFESSIONAL
[ ]2 WHITE COLLAR, MANAGERIAL, ADMINISTRATIVE
[ ]3 WHITE COLLAR, CLERICAL, SALES, SERVICE
[ ]4 BLUE COLLAR, SKILLED OR UNSKILLED LABOUR, FACTORY, FARM WORK

[ ]5 STUDENT
[ ]6 HOUSEWIFE - NOT EMPLOYED OUTSIDE HOME
[ ]7 NOT EMPLOYED/RETIRED/DISABLED

19. Is your job full-time or part-time?

[ ]1 FULL-TIME
[ ]2 PART-TIME

20. Please check the range below which includes your age.

[ ]1 17 or younger   [ ]6 35 to 39
[ ]2 18 to 20   [ ]7 40 to 49
[ ]3 21 to 24   [ ]8 50 to 59
[ ]4 25 to 29   [ ]9 60 to 69
[ ]5 30 to 34   [ ]10 70 OR OVER

21. Which of the following categories includes your total household
income for 1990 (before taxes)?

[ ]1 UNDER $10 000   [ ]5 $40 000 TO $49 999
[ ]2 $10 000 TO 19 999   [ ]6 $50 000 TO $59 999
[ ]3 $20 000 TO $29 999   [ ]7 $60 000 TO $69 999
[ ]4 $30 000 TO $39 999   [ ]8 $70 000 OR MORE

APPENDIX 7C

Sample Questionnaire—
Face-to-Face Intercept Interview

The questionnaire appearing on the following pages was developed for the
Ontario Ministry of Tourism and Recreation, Marketing Branch, Tourism
Research Section. It was designed as an exit survey and interviews were con-
ducted with people who had visited and were leaving Old Fort William in
Thunder Bay, Ontario. Information gleaned from the survey was used as
input for an economic impact analysis of the financial effect that Old Fort
William has on the Region of Thunder Bay. The project was conducted by
Econometric Research Ltd. and Marketing Decision Research Inc.

RANDOMLY INTERCEPT PEOPLE 15 YEARS OLD OR OLDER BY SIGHT

Hello, I'm _____ from ERL/MDR, a marketing research firm, and I'm doing a study that will help this tourist site in the future. I need to ask a broad sample of people a few questions about their visit to Old Fort William. I'd be very grateful if you would help me. Your answers will be kept confidential and anonymous.

READ OUT LOWER CASE ONLY -- ** DO NOT READ OUT UPPER CASE **

Are you 15 years of age or older?

YES   NO ————— Thank you very much. But I need to interview people who are at least 15. I hope that you had a good time today. Bye.

1. First, how many people, **including yourself**, are travelling together in your immediate travel party?

GO TO Q.4 ————————————————— ONE 1

_____ MORE THAN ONE 2   [___ ___]

(WRITE IN #)   16   17

2. **In addition to yourself**, how many other members of your household are here today with you?

GO TO Q.4 ————————————— NO OTHERS WITH R... 00..   [___ ___]

————————————— WRITE IN # OF PERSONS   18   19

2.1 Are you one of the heads of your household?

GO TO Q.3 ———————————————————— YES   1

NO   2   [___]

20

2.2 Is either of the heads of your household, whether male or female, here at Old Fort William?

GO TO Q.3 ——————— NO

——————— YES

2.3 I'd like to speak to the heads of your household, are they close by?

GO TO Q.3 ——————— NO

——————— YES

[IDENTIFY THE HEAD OF THE HOUSEHOLD]

IF ONE HEAD PRESENT	IF TWO HEADS PRESENT: ASK HEADS
	To help in selecting someone to interview, whose birthday comes next?

ASK SELECTED HOUSEHOLD HEAD-- START AGAIN AT HELLO:

3. **Including yourself,** how many members of your household travelling on this trip are ...

...15 years of age or older ____ ____   [___ ___]

21   22

How many are 7-14 years of age ____ ____   [___ ___]

23   24

How many are under 7 years old? ____ ____   [___ ___]

25   26

ASK EVERYONE:

4. How many miles (kilometres) did you travel from your home to get here to Old Fort William?

LESS THAN 25 MI (40KM) 1   [___]

25 MI (40KM) OR MORE 2   27

5. What mode of transportation did you use to get here to Old Fort William today?

PERSONAL CAR, VAN, LIGHT TRUCK, MOTORCYCLE 1

RECREATIONAL VEHICLE, CAMPING VEHICLE 2

IF CAR MENTIONED, ASK: "IS THAT A RENTAL CAR"

BICYCLE, WALKING 3

BUS 4   [___]

RENTAL CAR 5   28

OTHER _____ 7   CRUISE SHIP 6

6. Where is your regular place of residence? (NEAREST CITY/TOWN) _____

                     (PROVINCE/STATE) _____

                     (COUNTRY) _____

29	30	31
32	33	34
35	36	37

7. How many nights in total are you going to be away from home on this trip?

NONE-DAY TRIP 00   [___ ___]

#NIGHTS ____ ____   *39 40

** (HAND MAP TO R)

8. This map indicates the boundaries of the Region of Thunder Bay. By the time you return home from this trip, how many nights in total will have been spent in the Thunder Bay Region? ____ ____

[___ ___] 41 42

9. How many nights in total will have been spent in the City of Thunder Bay?

NO NIGHTS   00

\# OF NIGHTS ____ ____

[___ ___] 43 44

** (HAND YELLOW CARD TO R)

10. Now, thinking of the (READ # OF NIGHTS IN Q.9) night(s) you will have spent in the City of Thunder Bay, please look at the card and tell me where you will have stayed overnight and the number of nights you will have spent in each type of accommodation.

with friends or relatives .... # NIGHTS ____ ____	45	46
in a hotel .... # NIGHTS ____ ____	47	48
a motel with a restaurant .... # NIGHTS ____ ____	49	50
a motel without a restaurant .... # NIGHTS ____ ____	51	52
a resort, lodge, or rented cottage .... # NIGHTS ____ ____	53	54
bed and breakfast .... # NIGHTS ____ ____	55	56
camping or trailer .... # NIGHTS ____ ____	57	58
marina or organized anchorage ...... # NIGHTS ____ ____	59	60
other (SPECIFY) .... # NIGHTS ____ ____	61	62

BE SURE TOTAL ALL NIGHTS IN Q.10 ADD TO TOTAL IN Q.9

** (TAKE BACK YELLOW CARD) **

11. What was your main reason for taking this trip?

VISIT OLD FORT WILLIAM 1
VISIT FRIENDS AND RELATIVES 2
JUST FOR A RIDE 3
VISIT SOME OTHER ATTRACTION 4
PART OF TRAVEL (VACATION) PLANS 5
DAY TRIP FROM THE COTTAGE 6
OTHER _____ 7

[___] 63

12. Thinking about your entire trip, what is the main destination of your trip away from home? (EX., TOURIST ATTRACTION, RESORT, CITY, ETC.)

_____ _____ _____
(NEAREST CITY/TOWN/MAIN ATTRACTION) (PROVINCE/STATE) (COUNTRY)

[___ ___ ___] 64 65 66
[___ ___ ___] 67 68 69

13. What other destinations will you have visited during this trip away from home? EX., OTHER ATTRACTIONS, BEACH, RESORT, TOWNS, CITIES, PARKS, ETC.

_____

_____

_____

70	71	72
73	74	
75	76	
77	78	

14. About how long have you been at Old Fort William today?

        # Hours _____ _____   # Min _____ _____

                                                                       79 80 81

15. Please give me your best estimate of all <u>on-site</u> expenditures in Canadian $ which have been made by you and by the other members of your household while travelling on this trip in the Region of Thunder Bay area as shown on the map. Please include all spending <u>at this attraction site only</u> whether paid by cash, travellers cheque or credit card in Canadian dollars.

    How much has been spent for
      food and beverage? $ _____ _____ _____ _____ $ _____ _____ _____ _____
                                                        82 83 84 85
    How much has been spent for
      souvenirs and for retail purchases? $ _____ _____ _____ _____ $ _____ _____ _____ _____
                                                          86 87 88 89
    How much has been spent for
      entrance to the park? $ _____ _____ _____ _____ $ _____ _____ _____ _____
                                                           90 91 92 93

    IF RESPONDENT CANNOT PROVIDE EXPENDITURES IN CANADIAN $,
    INDICATE OTHER CURRENCY USED HERE _____   [_____]
                                                                  94 95

    ** HAND PINK CARD TO R **

16. Please look at the card and give me your best estimate of all off-site expenditures in Canadian $ which will have been made by you and by the other members of your household while travelling on this trip in the Region of Thunder Bay area as shown on the map. Please include all spending in this area whether paid by cash, travellers cheque or credit card.

    How much will have been spent for accommodation? $ _____ _____ _____ _____
      (MOTEL, HOTEL, CAMPSITE, ETC.) $ _____ _____ _____ _____
                                                          96 97 98 99
    How much will have been spent for travelling by
    public transportation? $ _____ _____ _____ _____
      (BUS, TAXI,ETC.) $ _____ _____ _____ _____
                                                     100 101 102 103
    How much will have been spent for travelling in a
    private vehicle? $ _____ _____ _____ _____
      (GASOLINE, PARKING, ETC.) $ _____ _____ _____ _____
                                                     104 105 106 107
    How much will have been spent for food and beverage
    in restaurants? $ _____ _____ _____ _____
      (RESTAURANTS, FAST FOOD, TAKE OUT) $ _____ _____ _____ _____
                                                 108 109 110 111
    How much will have been spent for entertainment,
    attractions and sightseeing? $ _____ _____ _____ _____
      (ALSO RENTALS FOR RECREATION) $ _____ _____ _____ _____
                                                  112 113 114 115
    How much will have been spent for souvenirs, retail
    purchases and shopping?   ┌──────┐ $ _____ _____ _____
                                                  116 117 118 119
      IF RETAIL/SHOPPING MORE THAN $300, ASK:

         16.1 Will you have purchased any individual   NO 1   [_____]
            items which cost more than $300?   YES 2   120

    IF R UNWILLING TO OR CANNOT BREAK DOWN TOTAL
    EXPENDITURES, ASK: Please just give me your best estimate of $ _____ _____ _____ _____
    the total amount you will have spent while visiting this area?
                                                       121 122 123 124
    IF RESPONDENT CANNOT PROVIDE EXPENDITURES IN CANADIAN $,
    INDICATE OTHER CURRENCY USED HERE. _____   [_____]
                                                       125 126

17. Thinking of the 6 months prior to this visit, do you recall seeing or hearing any advertising for Old Fort William?

        Go to Q.19 ──────────────────── NO 1
                ┌──────────────────── YES 2   [_____]
                │   127

  **HAND GREEN CARD TO R **

18. Please look at this card and tell me where that advertising
    was seen or heard? (PROBE: Where else? Anywhere else?)

	YES	NO		
Magazine advertising	1	0	[____]	128
Newspaper advertising	1	0	[____]	129
Booklet/Supplement in Newspaper	1	0	[____]	130
Radio advertising	1	0	[____]	131
Television advertising	1	0	[____]	132
Billboard advertising	1	0	[____]	133
Brochure at an Ontario Visitor Information Centre	1	0	[____]	134
Brochure Someplace Else	1	0	[____]	135
Highway Signs (not Billboards)	1	0	[____]	136
Word-of-mouth (told by someone)	1	0	[____]	137
Other (WRITE IN) _____	1	0	[____]	138
DON'T KNOW	1	0	[____]	139

** TAKE BACK CARD **

19. Have you yourself visited Old Fort William before this trip?

                                                          NO   1   [____]
                                                          YES 2   140

    19.1 In which year was that previous trip? 19 ___ ___   [_____]
                                                               141 142

20. In terms of your satisfaction with today's visit to Old Fort
    William, would you say that you are very satisfied,
    somewhat satisfied, somewhat dissatisfied, or very
    dissatisfied with this attraction?
                                        VERY SATISFIED 4
                                    SOMEWHAT SATISFIED 3
                                 SOMEWHAT DISSATISFIED 2
                                     VERY DISSATISFIED 1   [____]
                                            DON'T KNOW 9   143

21. How likely is it that you will return to visit Old Fort William
    during the next 2 years? Do you think that you definitely
    will return, probably will return, probably will not return or
    definitely will not return?
                                       DEFINITELY WILL 4
                                         PROBABLY WILL 3
                                     PROBABLY WILL NOT 2
                                   DEFINITELY WILL NOT 1   [____]
                                            DON'T KNOW 9   144

22. Did your visit to Old Fort William cause you to extend
    your stay in the area or not?   YES 1
                                                     NO   2   [____]
                                                              145

Now, I need to ask just a few more questions for statistical purposes.

23. What was the highest level of formal education which
    you have completed?   ELEMENTARY OR GRADE SCHOOL 1
                                        SOME HIGH SCHOOL 2
                                   GRADUATED HIGH SCHOOL 3
                         COMMUNITY COLLEGE/TECH SCHOOL 4
                                          SOME UNIVERSITY 5
                                    GRADUATED UNIVERSITY 6
                                   SOME GRADUATE SCHOOL 7   [____]
                                                 REFUSED 9   *147

** HAND TAN CARD TO R **

24. Please look at this tan card and give me the letter that best
    indicates your age group.
                             15 TO 19 YEARS .... G   1
                             20 TO 24 YEARS .... K   2
                             25 TO 34 YEARS .... J   3
                             35 TO 44 YEARS .... B   4
                             45 TO 54 YEARS .... R   5
                             55 TO 64 YEARS .... F   6
                             65 YEARS OR OLDER...... A   7   [____]
                                                  REF 9   148

**TAKE BACK TAN CARD **
**HAND BLUE CARD TO R **

25. Please look at this blue card and tell me the letter that indicates the total income of your household during 1988 before taxes? Just tell me the appropriate letter.

E	LESS THAN $19,999	1
R	$20,000 TO $29,999	2
F	$30,000 TO $39,999	3
I	$40,000 TO $49,999	4
Q	$50,000 TO $59,999	5
W	$60,000 TO $79,999	6
O	$80,000 TO $99,999	7
B	$100,000 OR MORE	8
	DON'T KNOW	9
	REFUSED	0

[___]
149

** TAKE BACK CARD **

26. In total, how many people contributed to that income in 1988?

WRITE IN NUMBER [_____ _____]

[___ ___]
150 151

27. What is the occupation of the highest income earner in your household? (If retired: What was his/her occupation before retirement?)

_____

TYPE OF JOB

[___ ___]
152 153

What is the occupation of the second highest income earner in your household?

_____

TYPE OF JOB

[___ ___]
154 155

*** Thank you for your help ***

SMATH	1
HNME	2
OFW	3

[___]
156

My supervisor may want to call you to verify that I conducted this interview. At what phone number can you usually be reached?

___ ___ ___ - ___ ___ ___ - ___ ___ ___ ___

(AREA CODE)   (-------- PHONE NUMBER --------)

And what's your first name? _____

"I HEREBY CERTIFY THAT THIS INTERVIEW WAS CONDUCTED ACCORDING TO THE QUESTIONNAIRE AND THE INSTRUCTIONS FOR THIS STUDY AND THAT THE ANSWERS RECORDED ARE AS GIVEN TO ME BY THIS RESPONDENT.

ALSO, I REALIZE THAT A PROPORTION OF MY WORK WILL BE CHECKED BACK FOR VERIFICATION."

_____   _____

(INTERVIEWER'S NAME--PRINT)   (INTERVIEWER'S SIGNATURE)

8 / Fieldwork: Asking the Right People the Right Way

INTRODUCTION

Fieldwork is the "opening night" of marketing research. There's a dress rehearsal, the pre-test, and the opening night—the actual beginning of the main interviewing. It's the acid test of whether the work done during the preceding stages was worthwhile or not. And its results will also have an impact on whether the remaining stages produce anything of value to the client.

Although fieldwork is often invisible in the final report, its execution is critical to the value of the research project and it is a fascinating topic to study on its own. As a stand-alone, researchable topic, fieldwork can give insight into the dynamics of large project management; the training, testing and education of large numbers of people; and the psychology of extracting specific information from (sometimes unwilling) respondents.

WHO ARE THE PLAYERS IN MARKETING RESEARCH FIELDWORK?

The principal participant is the respondent. All the policies, procedures and guidelines of fieldwork have evolved from fieldworkers' understanding of the supreme importance of the respondent. In fact, the respondent is often described as being the most important person in the life of the researcher, besides family members and close personal friends. It's considered to be the responsibility of each fieldworker to satisfy the needs of the respondents and to encourage their cooperation.

The importance of the respondent is further advocated by the survey respondent's "Constitutional Rights" developed by George Gallup (1989):

1. The right to know the true purpose of the survey and how the results will be used;

2. The right to be assured that one's responses are important;

3. The right to have one's privacy respected and not violated by tasteless questions or obnoxious interviewing;

4. The right to have an interesting and stimulating experience in an interview;

5. The right to have one's survey responses held in strictest confidence and to have the guarantee of anonymity;

6. The right to be treated in the interview in a thoroughly professional manner; and

7. The right to have one's time respected.

As Exhibit 8.1 shows, each phase of the marketing research process involves an input, an expenditure of effort, a transformed input and a reward for the effort and the transformation. The input to the fieldwork function is the questionnaire and the fieldwork directions. These directions include specification of those characteristics of respondents which qualify them to

Exhibit 8.1   The Transformation of Fieldwork

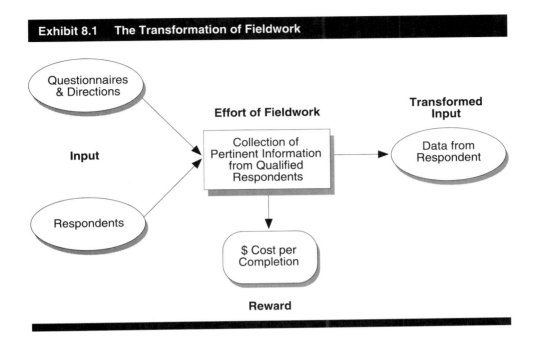

provide answers to the questionnaire, and instructions for executing the survey. The effort of fieldwork is the collection of pertinent information from qualified respondents. The transformed input or output of the fieldwork phase is data from the respondents. This is the meat of marketing research. The function of the field director and staff is to organize and execute this transformation in the most effective and efficient fashion.

The latter phases of fieldwork are devoted to analyzing and reporting the information content of these data. But, without valid and unbiased data there would be nothing to analyze and to report. Well, that's not quite correct: any data can be analyzed and reported; however, if the fieldwork function isn't done properly, the analysis and reporting is meaningless, at best. At worst, it's incorrect and could lead the client to make disastrous decisions.

The reward of the fieldwork function is often quoted in dollars per completion (i.e., completed questionnaire) and is also stated as the total project cost. This cost can vary substantially. For one study recently put to tender, the submitted quotes ranged from $19 000 to $85 000, approximately. Naturally, one reason for this wide range of prices was misinterpretation of the study parameters by the bidders. However, there were also some significant variations in the field costs for similarly specified studies.

HOW IS FIELDWORK ORGANIZED?

The organization of the fieldwork function is typically a very simple, five-level structure, even though hundreds of fieldworkers could be involved (see Exhibit 8.2). Field directors and field supervisors provide the critical management and quality control functions for the actual field execution phase of marketing research.

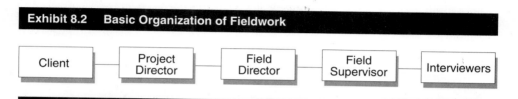

Exhibit 8.2   Basic Organization of Fieldwork

Client — Project Director — Field Director — Field Supervisor — Interviewers

Naturally, all parties to the fieldwork function are extremely important to the success of the project. However, during the preparation and execution phases, the field director is the critical figure. The field director is the essential link between the interviewers and the project. Although project directors and clients only visit field operations very occasionally, their visits are intended as a check to see if the directions were translated to the field properly and that the key aspects of the fieldwork are working correctly.

The Field Management Group of the Professional Marketing Research Society (1986:39) describes the field supervisor as follows: "A good supervisor requires understanding and tact, tenacity and the ability to accept responsibility. The good supervisor also requires initiative, the ability to make certain decisions, and last, but certainly not least, professionalism and good common sense."

Essentially, the field director takes on the duties of the project director during the fieldwork phase. The detailed management of staff is critical to ensure that the interviewers are properly motivated, that they follow proper interviewing practice, that the project directions are translated into effective interviewing activities, and that accurate records are kept.

THE STAGES OF FIELDWORK EXECUTION

The field stage of marketing research involves the following main stages:

1. Receive the questionnaire and field directions
2. Prepare price quotation (if necessary)
3. Prepare interviewer manual
4. Allocate (hire) field staff
5. Brief field staff
6. Receive or prepare list of sample contacts
7. Pre-test questionnaire in face-to-face interviews
8. Provide pre-test information to the project director and assist with revising questionnaire.
9. Prepare for main study
10. Mobilize field study and execute fieldwork
11. Implement quality control
12. Edit incoming questionnaires
13. Code questionnaires
14. Transmit field output to data entry staff
15. Debrief project director on field study

Points 13 through 15 are not part of fieldwork, but are included to give a feeling for the field process and related tasks.

RECEIVE THE QUESTIONNAIRE AND FIELD DIRECTIONS

There is specialization of labour in most marketing research projects. Typically, it is the responsibility of those involved with the earlier stages of the research process to develop the questionnaire to the point where it is a finely tuned survey instrument. Sometimes, the questionnaire that is accepted by the field operation is in need of improvements before good information can be obtained. In those cases the project director should be able and willing to rely on the field staff for suggestions and testing of question forms. The project director should monitor the field operation closely through the field director.

PREPARE PRICE QUOTATION

If the fieldwork is to be performed by a field-house, then a quotation of the fee for the data collection must be developed and presented to the client for approval. However, if the fieldwork is to be performed by a division of the research consulting firm, then the costing must still be worked out but the isolated field costs are typically expressed as a component of the total project cost rather than as a separate quotation. Although in full-service research firms the price quotation is most often prepared by the project director, the assistance of the field director is essential, especially in large and complicated projects.

PREPARE INTERVIEWER MANUAL

A key concern of the project director and the field director is the consistency of operating practices among the field staff. In order to provide a common basis for the fieldwork, a manual must be provided to inform and direct the fieldworkers. The manual provides administrative instructions, sample selection requirements, interviewing instructions and respondent management directions. This manual is often very detailed, even down to suggested answers to commonly asked questions and to indicating how many pencils to take to the interviews. The reason for this is, of course, to provide guidance and thereby ensure consistency.

The detail of interviewer manuals varies among marketing research firms. Some firms believe that the questionnaire should stand by itself, i.e., if a competent interview can't be conducted from the questionnaire, then the questionnaire should be revised rather than instructions added to the manual. For these firms, the manual concentrates more on the selection of sample respondents than on instructions for conducting the interview.

ALLOCATE (HIRE) FIELD STAFF

Although field-houses have some interviewers who work as regular full-time staff, many of the interviewing staff work whenever there's a project but are occasional part-time employees. In many cases, when the firm begins a particularly large job it's necessary either to recall part-time staff or to hire new interviewers. Sometimes during high demand periods, even relatively large marketing research firms may have to subcontract some of their fieldwork to other research firms. Although there's a great deal of competition during the bidding phase, marketing research firms cooperate professionally to get projects completed.

Certain types of jobs require interviewers with different talents. Projects that require the interviewing of executives within large firms must be allocated to highly proficient, senior interviewers. Other projects that specify anyone from the general population as being qualified to respond can utilize interviewers with a less qualified background.

BRIEF THE FIELD STAFF

Remember that each project is unique—even if only in a minor way—so each field venture must be treated as a stand-alone project. This means that each project must be preceded by a briefing to familiarize the supervisors and the interviewers with the special requirements of the study and with the questionnaire. Although some briefings might take less than half an hour, others might consume one half to one full day of preparation, plus practice interviewing. In general, it's highly recommended that in difficult, long and complicated studies the field director brief all interviewers operating outside the head office territory. This helps with consistency and also lends an importance factor to the briefing.

> It is extremely important that all interviewers are working EXACTLY the same way, asking the same questions EXACTLY (verbatim), and that the supervisor is briefing the questionnaire in EXACTLY the same way. (Field Management Group, 1986:8)

The project director, the field director and the field supervisor are responsible for the quality of the field staff. Surely, some incompetent interviewers are to be found working on projects. However, it's the supervisor's job to minimize and strive to eliminate this source of bias in data collection. The supervisor will be briefed by the field director and will subsequently brief the interviewers in the same manner. The questionnaire is read through step by step by the supervisor, with the interviewers practising after the supervisor is finished. If questionnaire problems arise at this stage, they should be reported to the project director immediately.

As mentioned earlier, many research houses feel that the questionnaire is the key to field quality. In cases where time and expertise have been devoted to developing a high quality questionnaire, the field briefing can be very much abbreviated. In fact, some research firms feel so strongly about this that they will hold no briefings for the pre-test. They will use the pre-test and an extensive debriefing to provide an acid test of the questionnaire. The end result should be a questionnaire that stands on its own and needs no briefing *per se*.

RECEIVE OR PREPARE LIST OF SAMPLE CONTACTS

In some cases the list of names to be contacted from the sample frame (see Chapter 6) is provided to the field unit. In other situations, the field personnel are instructed in how to pull the sample and then perform that function themselves. In either case, dial sheets must be prepared for the telephone interviewers to work from (see Exhibit 8.3); area sampling plans must be developed so that house-to-house interviewers are able to conduct their function in a prescribed, orderly and verifiable manner; and sample selection procedures need to be provided to shopping mall interviewers. Mailing lists and labels will be provided for the clerical staff involved in posting self-administered mail questionnaires.

Dial sheets vary only slightly from firm to firm. They serve the dual purpose of providing the interviewers with names and numbers and also constitute a record of contact history for survey administration and field reporting. In addition to the working dial sheet, in many studies a contact sheet should be attached to each questionnaire to indicate the occurrences during the process of trying to get that person to be part of the survey. Other versions of these forms are provided later in this chapter.

PRE-TEST QUESTIONNAIRE IN FACE-TO-FACE INTERVIEWS

WHY IS PRE-TESTING VITAL TO PROJECT SUCCESS? The answer to this question is the same as the answer to: Why do we have to rehearse? In fact, the reasons for pre-testing go beyond the purposes of rehearsing. Pre-testing is a test of the script and of the performers.

Researchers are prone to falling into the trap of knowing the respondent too well. Sometimes the researchers and marketing client get so close to the project that they feel as if they know everything about the topic before the field work is even started. They know the problems, they know the questions to ask, and they might think that they know the answers that the public will give. Why conduct the research at all? In fact, if the research team does not step back from the project and pre-test its work, the project often should not continue. The chance of not catching the mistakes of questionnaire design is just too high.

From a practical position, many questionnaires are so basic that with proper attention from an experienced, capable and sensitive project director and field director, and perhaps someone else in the office, they can often go into the field with no formal pre-testing.

Exhibit 8.3 Example of Dial/Recording Sheet

DIAL/RECORDING SHEET

City _____
Project # _____
Area Code _____
Project Name _____
Sample # _____

Interviewer: _____ **FIRST ATTEMPT** Date _____ Time _____

Interviewer: _____ **SECOND ATTEMPT** Date _____ Time _____

Interviewer: _____ **THIRD ATTEMPT** Date _____ Time _____

#	Telephone Number	Name (Last, First)	I.D. #	N	BZ	R	Ref	Bus	Lang	Disc	Term at	Comp	N	BZ	R	Ref	Bus	Lang	Disc	Term at	Comp	N	BZ	R	Ref	Bus	Lang	Disc	Term at	Comp
				C		N	A						C		N	A							C		N	A					
1																															
2																															
3																															
4																															
5																															
6																															
7																															
8																															
9																															
10																															
11																															
12																															
13																															
14																															
15																															
16																															
17																															
18																															
19																															
20																															
21																															
22																															
23																															
24																															
25																															

Although pre-testing does not have to be expensive nor very time consuming, sometimes the crunch of meagre budgets and demanding time schedules just does not leave time for this important function.

THE DESIGN OF A PROPER PRE-TEST   The pre-test will be your dress rehearsal as writer, director and performer. You want to design the pre-test to get the maximum input from the fieldwork. How should this be done? There's only one way! Face-to-face interviews must be conducted for any project to be fully pre-tested.

Whether the project design calls for telephone interviews, self-administered, mailed questionnaires, panel data or whatever, always test the questionnaire through personal interviews. Only when the respondent is sitting in front of you can you see that smile that means the question is silly; or the frown resulting from not seeing the right answer in the list of alternatives.

Grunts, Giggles and Guffaws. The value of facial expressions, body language, grunts, groans and giggles cannot be overstated. The pre-test procedure produces the maximum amount of humiliation for the researcher at a time when action can be taken to correct a potentially devastating final result. If the errors are caught because of the pre-test, you can still be a hero. If they are not caught, you could suffer the worst of fates—humiliation, embarrassment and non-payment of your invoice. Take time for the pre-test.

QUESTIONNAIRE FORM FOR THE PRE-TEST   The form of the interviewer-administered questionnaire is quite different from the self-administered form. Of course, if your intention is to conduct a face-to-face or telephone interview, the pre-test should be conducted as a face-to-face interview. Once more, the personal interview provides the opportunity to probe based on physical expressions of the respondent as well as oral response. This can help to unearth some question problems which might never be discovered during a telephone interview. After the face-to-face test of the telephone questionnaire, a small *pilot* sample pre-test should be conducted in order to test the refined questionnaire through its natural medium—the phone. The following presents a convincing argument to include the telephone phase as part of the pre-test.

It is absolutely essential that telephone questionnaires be tested over the telephone. Having respondents fill it out themselves or reading it to them in a face-to-face situation, does not provide an adequate pre-test. If fact, it may do more harm than good. The face-to-face situation results in both the interviewer and respondent relying on visual cues; the questionnaire deficiencies may be missed. Asking someone

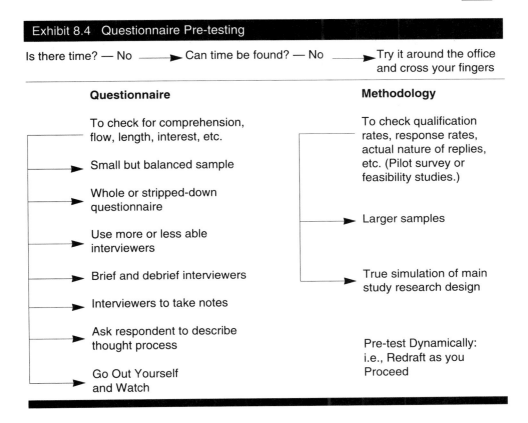

Exhibit 8.4   Questionnaire Pre-testing

Is there time? — No ——▶ Can time be found? — No ——▶ Try it around the office and cross your fingers

Questionnaire

To check for comprehension, flow, length, interest, etc.

Small but balanced sample

Whole or stripped-down questionnaire

Use more or less able interviewers

Brief and debrief interviewers

Interviewers to take notes

Ask respondent to describe thought process

Go Out Yourself and Watch

Methodology

To check qualification rates, response rates, actual nature of replies, etc. (Pilot survey or feasibility studies.)

Larger samples

True simulation of main study research design

Pre-test Dynamically: i.e., Redraft as you Proceed

to self-administer a telephone questionnaire often results in suggestions (e.g., more parsimony and layout changes) that make a questionnaire more, rather than less, difficult to comprehend over the telephone. Testing over the telephone means that such things as normal line noise and the respondent's ability to concentrate while completely dependent on a verbal oral message are components of the test situation, as should be the case (Dillman, Don A., *Mail and Telephone Surveys: The Total Design Method* (New York: John Wiley & Sons, Copyright ©1978), p.229).

If your design calls for a self-administered questionnaire, there are three options that can be used in the pre-test:

1. Conduct the pre-test of the self-administered questionnaire *completely in the face-to-face interview format.* In many cases, the questionnaire will have to be designed in the interviewer-administered form for the pre-test and then re-written in the self-administered form after pre-testing. However, in some cases the self-administered form can be accommodated in the personal interview.

2. *Self-administration with interviewer accompaniment.* Although this is a rather unnatural mode of questionnaire administration, it does provide for the questionnaire to be used in its final self-administered form. Also, the advantage (requirement) of direct visual and oral feedback from the respondent to the interviewer is achieved. In this pre-test format, the respondent self-completes the questionnaire with the interviewer looking on and probing on a question-by-question basis. In this way, immediate responses to questions are received from the respondents. This is sometimes referred to as the *protocol* method (Hunt et al., 1982).

3. *Self-administration with interviewer debriefing.* In this mode, the respondent completes the whole questionnaire without interviewer discussion. After completion, the interviewer reviews the whole questionnaire with the respondent. The interviewer discusses each question with the respondent to identify whether the respondent actually understood the questions, the answers, the flow and so on.

THE IMPLEMENTATION OF A PRE-TEST   The pre-test preparation should be treated as seriously as the beginning of the main fieldwork. In fact, many feel that a bit more time should be taken to prepare the interviewers for the sensitive and important task of testing the questionnaire.

A common temptation at the pre-test stage is to use the best interviewers, since they are more perceptive and sensitive and will pick up more of the errors in the phraseology and execution of the questionnaire. Very highly qualified interviewers may be used to test the questionnaire in a small preliminary pre-test. However, the use of only top-notch, pre-test interviewers will reduce the reliability of the full pre-test as a precursor to the actual fieldwork, unless all of the interviewers in the main study are to be of the same high quality as those used in the pre-test.

Every attempt should be made to ensure that the pre-test is a microcosmic version of the main study. This often means using a variety of interviewers. It might be found that the best interviewers can handle anything thrown at them, but that the less capable interviewers struggle with some of the phraseology of the pre-test version of the questionnaire. Better to find the difficult wording in the pre-test than in the full study. The only possible difference between the pre-test and the main study will be the interview method and the added probing which the interviewers will use during the actual interviews.

THE USE OF PRE-TEST FINDINGS   The beneficial results of the pre-test are seen in an improved questionnaire and field methodology. Sometimes there are relatively few changes in the wording of questions and the sequence of those questions; sometimes there are major alterations. In fact, it does happen that the field methodology changes completely based on information found during the pre-test. There are cases in which it has been specified that studies will be executed through self-administered, mail questionnaires, but as a result of the pre-test they have been changed to interviewer administration by telephone.

Use the pre-test to check the following points:

- **Question wording**: clarity, understandability, bias, errors, double-barrelled, ambiguity, phraseology, length of the questions, as well as length of the words within questions
- **Answer wording:** relevant alternatives, understandable phrasing, non-overlapping categories, proper administration of answers, proper use of closed-end and open-end questions
- **Flow of the questions:** follows logically, does not appear haphazard
- **Skip patterns:** apparent to the respondent and are easy to execute for the interviewer
- **Screening questions:** adequate to eliminate non-qualifying respondents and to include all qualified respondents
- **Format:** conducive to the interviewer's presentation style and is natural and interesting to the respondent
- **Overall length and general feasibility of the questionnaire** (This is another important reason for pre-testing.) Trying the questionnaire out in the office can be very misleading. Professional researchers become used to the ways in which their profession operates. Question types which might give the typical respondent difficulty will be handled easily by the office staff, resulting in no improvement to the questionnaire.
- **Boredom factor**

Of course, the above points (as well as the many others that could be mentioned) are also addressed during the questionnaire development stage by those who are responsible for the questionnaire design. The project director should solicit thoughtful input from office colleagues as well as from the users of the survey findings. It's not possible to overemphasize the importance of thoughtful questionnaire design. Without a well designed questionnaire, the remaining components of the research project are without real value.

> Most people are educated in writing material that will be read by others. In developing an interviewer-administered questionnaire, one must write words that will be spoken to others—normal writing will sound too formal and non-conversational.

Provide Pre-test Information to Project Director and Assist with Revising Questionnaire

A follow-up stage after the pre-test is to provide the project director with the information needed to refine the questionnaire. In most cases, revision of the questionnaire is a quick process of rephrasing a few questions. However, in some cases where questions just did not work, a substantial revision might be necessary, along with another pre-test.

> Some research firms will encourage the client to attend the pre-test debriefing of interviewers so that suggestions for changes are communicated directly by those who had to administer the less-than-perfect questionnaire. This practice can be very helpful to the whole field process.

Prepare for Main Study

In addition to the allocation and briefing of staff, tasks such as securing interview locations, scheduling the project among several other projects which will depend on the same field staff, and planning the future steps of the study are necessary for the success of the project.

Mobilize Field Study and Execute Field Work

The maintenance of a high level of professionalism and quality throughout the execution stage is vital to the success of the project. If the preparation work was done properly, then the mobilization and execution should run smoothly. As the survey is expedited, certain administrative and clerical duties, such as counting contacts, attempts, and completions, assume importance. Other essentials for thorough fieldwork, such as the fulfilment of quotas, require special attention from the supervisor.

Answering Machines Threaten Survey Research

The number of U.S. households with a telephone-answering machine is exploding. This could present a serious obstacle to survey research users in the 1990s.

Consider these data from a recent survey (96 761 respondents) conducted by the mail panel of NFO Research Inc., Toledo, Ohio: 36% of all U.S. households now have phone-answering machines, and more than half of those were acquired during the last two years.

About 17% of those with answering machines use them to screen *all calls* and then selectively return those they wish. This is the electronic barrier that telephone surveys must break through to get representative samples. Twenty-four percent of single males under 25 screen all their calls.

That's the general picture, but it's the segment data that provide the real scare.

For instance, with families (households where members are related by blood or marriage) with a head of household under 30 years old, the penetration rate is 42%. With households of singles or unrelated people living together in the under-35 age group, the penetration rate is 64%.

In short, penetration is extremely high among younger people. The use of answering machines is an integral part of their lifestyles and probably will continue to be through life.

The penetration rate is 73% for young people, urban apartment or condo dwellers, with incomes above $50 000.

Ironically, the survey research industry, which has invested so much in electronic innovations in recent years to automate telephone interviewing—CATI systems and automatic dialing are examples—will find itself increasingly in a situation where its electronic paraphernalia is interacting with a respondent's electronic paraphernalia, and flesh-and-blood consumers become more elusive than ever (Honomichl, 1990:11).

SECURITY AND CONFIDENTIALITY   As mentioned earlier, the respondent has a right to security, confidentiality and anonymity. Also, the client has a similar right.

The client's identity should not be disclosed to anyone, unless prescribed by the client. On some occasions, it might seem to the interviewer that the client's identity is obvious to the respondent. However, this assumption is often incorrect and no information should be provided by the interviewer that is not specifically approved in the questionnaire or in the interviewer manual. Of course, in many cases the field interviewers don't know the client's identity—only the study number will appear on the questionnaire. In this way, there can be no conscious or subconscious biasing by the interviewers. Also when asked by the respondent for the name of the client, the interviewers can honestly say that they don't know. In any case, the interviewer should never confirm a respondent's supposed or voiced suspicion for the following reasons:

- It could be very damaging for a client if a competitor were to become aware of the nature of the study at any time.
- It may introduce bias into a respondent's replies if it is implied that a study is being conducted for a particular company or organization.
- It could be damaging to the marketing research company if the client's identity is known (Field Management Group, 1986:4).

Remember, one can never be sure of the possible connections between the client and the person being interviewed. Questions from persistent respondents should be directed to the supervisor or head office. If the client should happen to visit the interview site unexpectedly, the supervisor should be informed immediately (Field Management Group, 1986:5).

Since large firms often have several studies being fielded at one time, a client in the phone bank could have access to questionnaires of other companies which could be valuable information to competitors.

Equally important is the *respondent's identity*. The people who are interviewed must be made to feel comfortable and free to express their honest opinions without fear that their name, phone number or address will be released. All information given by a respondent is held in confidence between the respondent and the marketing research company. No person outside the survey research firm will see any individual respondent's replies.

On most occasions the client is provided with a report and computer tabulations; the client rarely sees the actual questionnaires. If this does happen, the names, phone numbers and addresses of the respondents must be removed.

An interviewer must never reveal to anyone except the field staff what an individual may have said during the course of an interview. Each interviewer is responsible for the confidentiality of the respondent.

Lastly, *all* materials provided are the property of the marketing research company and are to be returned to its head office on completion of the study. Care must be taken not to leave material —whether complete or not—where any unauthorized person can see it (Field Management Group, 1986:6).

QUALITY CONTROL

The field supervisor provides for the continual monitoring of interviewers and the retraining or firing of inadequate interviewers. This monitoring is achieved at central location telephone facilities through listening to the interviewer's conversations with respondents. When the supervisor identifies an interviewer who has not been fully trained, who is tired, ill-mannered to the respondent, is not following skip patterns properly or having other problems, then the supervisor must remove the interviewer from the phone. The nature of the problem must be determined and the interviewer retrained and remotivated, or dismissed.

CAMRO NEWS

CAMRO Industry Survey 1988

Hot off the press is CAMRO's recently completed annual survey of full service marketing research organizations. The purpose of this survey is to collect key industry financial data on the operations of CAMRO companies.

Of the 27 firms reporting, billings totalled $104.0 million, a gain of 10.9% over the 1987 figure. Quantitative research accounted for 87% of the 1988 billings, with qualitative research making up 12%...virtually no change from the 1987 billing breakdowns.

Revenues from door-to-door surveys are down slightly in 1988, declining from 23% of billings in 1987 to 20% last year. Telephone surveys still dominate, however, as the most popular interviewing method, retaining 46% of total industry billing in 1988, exactly the same as in 1987.

On an industry sector basis, research expenditures were most heavily concentrated in the private sector (73%), with government departments and agencies totalling 10% for government, and 7% for crown corporations. Ad agencies were split out as a separate category and together, they account for 6% of total industry revenue, unchanged from 1987 (Calhoun, 1989:12).

Another part of quality control in fieldwork pertains to the post-interview verification. A requirement of the Canadian Association of Marketing Research Organizations is that at least 10% of every interviewer's work must be verified. This entails the following three steps.

1. During the normal interviewing process, each respondent is asked for his or her name and telephone number so that a contact can be made. The phone number should be requested even if the interview was conducted by telephone, in case the number was dialled incorrectly. Although an inexperienced person might feel that respondents will not provide this information, almost all respondents will give their names and phone numbers.

Exhibit 8.5 shows the verification data that often appear at the end of the questionnaire.

Exhibit 8.5   Request for Name for Verification Follow-Up

My supervisor may want to call you to verify that I conducted this interview. At what phone number can you usually be reached?

_____

And what's your name?   _____

or

My supervisor might have to check over some of my work. So that she can do that would you please give me your name?

_____   _____
FIRST NAME   LAST NAME

And your phone number please?   _____

The interviewer is also required to sign a statement similar to the one shown in Exhibit 8.6.

Exhibit 8.6

"I HEREBY CERTIFY THAT THIS INTERVIEW WAS CONDUCTED ACCORD-ING TO THE QUESTIONNAIRE AND THE INSTRUCTIONS FOR THIS STUDY AND THAT THE ANSWERS RECORDED ARE AS GIVEN TO ME BY THIS RESPONDENT.

"ALSO, I REALIZE THAT A PROPORTION OF MY WORK WILL BE CHECKED BACK FOR VERIFICATION."

_____
INTERVIEWER'S NAME—PRINT

_____
INTERVIEWER'S SIGNATURE

---

2. The respondents selected for verification must be phoned and re-interviewed in total or on a few selected questions.
3. The verified interviews for each interviewer are reconciled with the origi-nal interviews. If problems are identified, the likely causes are recorded and followed-up with the interviewer as soon as possible.

When a telephone interview is monitored by a field supervisor, it is considered to be verified. However many field researchers feel that separate callback verification should be conducted as part of the total verification. These call-backs should be conducted by a separate field group with reporting through channels that cannot be scrutinized by the original interviewers and supervisors.

In addition to the requirement of verification, monitoring can be very helpful in advising the interviewers on their telephone styles, thus improving their performance as well as the quality of the fieldwork.

FIELD-EDIT THE INCOMING QUESTIONNAIRES

As the questionnaires are completed and returned to the base office, they must be scrutinized for adequate completion, consistency and understanding of the questionnaire. The questionnaires must also be examined for legibility of responses to open-ended questions. Only after the questionnaires are edited at the interview site can they be sent to the head office.

CODE QUESTIONNAIRES

(This task and the following are not formally part of the fieldwork but are included here for completeness.)

Coding is the function that translates the answers to the questions into numerical or alpha-numerical codes to be entered into a computer for analysis. In most cases, the coding is found directly on the questionnaires. However, for open-ended questions, the verbatim answers must be scrutinized and codes assigned so that the data tabulation can be conducted. The coding function is changing due to Computer Assisted Telephone Interviewing (CATI) and data entry computer programs. (See Chapter 9 for an explanation of coding and coding sheets.)

TRANSMIT FIELD OUTPUT TO DATA ENTRY STAFF

The actual entry of the survey data into the computer might be done by the field operation. However, it is normally conducted as a separate function. There are firms that specialize in data entry. This transmitting function involves sending the coded questionnaires or the coding sheets to the data entry staff, either internally or externally.

DEBRIEF PROJECT DIRECTOR ON FIELD STUDY

The last function of the field director is to debrief the project director on the field execution. The debriefing will include informing the project director of the response rate, completion rate, quota fulfilment, special problems encountered and other insights that the field director can provide to help interpret the findings and explain the data.

An incidence report is usually filed by the field director shortly after the fieldwork is completed. A typical incidence report is shown in Exhibit 8.7.

Exhibit 8.7 Incidence Report			
Total Contacts	**3955**	**100%**	
Refused	3211	81.2%	
Language Barrier	19	0.5%	
Ineligible—Non-Base Population	**233**	**5.9%**	**100%**
Q.1a Under 18 yrs of age/over 49	44	1.1%	18.9%
Q.1b Not responsible for family grocery shopping	107	2.7%	45.9%
Q.1c Employed/family member in a sensitive occupation	82	2.1%	35.2%
Base Population—Main Grocery Shopper Sample Frame (Eligible)	**492**	**12.4%**	**100.0%**
Concept Acceptors—Target Population	303	7.7%	61.6%
Definitely buy it	66	1.7%	13.4%
Probably buy it	237	6.0%	48.2%
Concept Rejectors	189	4.8%	38.4%
Might/Might not buy it	109	2.8%	22.2%
Probably not buy it	48	1.2%	9.8%
Definitely not buy it	32	0.8%	6.5%

Also important are several ratios which result from the interviewing process and its success or failure.

$$\text{Response Rate} = \frac{\text{Number of Completed Interviews}}{\text{Number of Sample Units Contacted}} = \frac{492}{3955} = 8\%$$

$$\text{Contact Rate} = \frac{\text{Number of Sample Units Contacted}}{\text{Number of Sample Units Identified}}$$

$$\text{Completion Rate } = \frac{\text{Number of Completed Interviews}}{\text{Number of Sample Units Identified}}$$

$$\text{Incidence Rate } = \frac{\text{Number of Sample Units Who Qualify}}{\text{Number of Sample Units Contacted and Cooperative}}$$

Only the response rate can be calculated for the above example since the number of names on the dial sheets was not identified. These rate equations are presented above in their most basic form, they often need to be more detailed (Wiseman and McDonald, 1980:4).

These "production rate" ratios are needed both at the planning stage for costing of the project and at the reporting stage for information and for quality control.

One problem that arises with these ratios is deciding when they can be estimated with some level of accuracy. Of course, after the interviewing they can be calculated from the data. But accurate estimates of the ratios are particularly helpful at the project planning and costing stage. The estimated cost of the study and the corresponding bid price are directly related to the above four ratios, especially the incidence and response ratios. In cases where a similar type of study is not part of a firm's repertoire, then educated guesses of ranges of likely incidence and response might be all that a firm can rely on. Large research firms are able to draw on their extensive experience to help them establish very tight estimates of field costs when the parameters of the study are well formulated.

FIELDWORK TECHNIQUES

FIELD OPERATIONS MUST BE MANAGED CAREFULLY

Fieldwork is the operations stage of marketing research. It is akin to the factory floor in the manufacturing process of a product. The key difference (in most cases) is that the fieldwork for a marketing research project is done only once, whereas the factory keeps producing multiple units of the same product for a long time. The collection of usable data is usually a large one-time project that must be scheduled and executed in much the same way as a large construction project. In fact, the critical path method, the project evaluation and review technique and Gantt charts, procedures for scheduling large projects, are sometimes used when scheduling very large marketing research projects, including the fieldwork. These formal scheduling techniques are used more frequently on government projects which often require very detailed reporting.

While scheduling the work on large field projects is a difficult task, there are many more activities that must be managed effectively. One of the most important of the field director's duties is to ensure that the field operations are executed with consistently high quality across all segments and phases of the project. In other words, respondent interviewing must be done in the same high quality manner in every study city and by every interviewer. That same high quality must also be maintained across the pre-testing, main field, editing and coding phases.

FIELD INTERVIEWING: CONDUCTING A CONTROLLED STRUCTURED CONVERSATION

Although some marketing research is conducted through self-administered mailed questionnaires, most fieldwork is executed through telephone and face-to-face interviews. This function is the "production mode" of marketing research. Although the principal output of marketing research is a report (or at least computer tabulations), the function that produces the raw input is the fieldwork.

One important part of the telephone interviewing function is finding a respondent, i.e., dialling until someone answers and is willing to talk. There are various ways to speed up this task. Once technology goes by the generic name of *predictive dialling.* "A predictive dialler works by assigning a group of telephone numbers to each group of interviewers working on the project. The predictive dialler then dials ahead simultaneously on multiple lines for each project. The dialler is designed to detect whether it has reached a busy signal, telephone company message, ringing phone, or voice. Only when a call is answered is it passed along—instantly—to an available interviewer, thus screening out unproductive diallings ... What makes a predictive dialler 'predictive' is that it statistically predicts how fast it must dial to keep interviewers occupied" (CATI News, 1990:2). Claims are made that "up to one third of the interviewing costs of a telephone study can be saved with predictive dialling" (CATI News, 1990:1). This technique is used very little presently but is being integrated into CATI systems and might find extensive usage in the future.

Source: "More on Predictive Dialing," *CATI News* (Sawtooth Software), Vol. 3, No. 2 (Fall 1990), p.6. "Predictive Dialing," *CATI News* (Sawtooth Software), Vol. 3, No. 1 (Spring 1990), p.8.

It is practically impossible to analyze the interviewing scientifically to determine what characterizes good and bad interviewers. Interviewing is more of an artistic activity, such as acting, than it is mechanical and scientific. It's purely the art of carrying on a *structured conversation* that is recorded after each verbal exchange between the interviewer and the respondent. Most theatrical plays are presented to an audience which sees and hears but usually does not participate. Interviewers speak the script of the questionnaire to the individual audiences who must then respond to complete the play.

Interviewers are the only direct contact between the research team and the target respondents. The are the eyes and the ears of marketing research. It is their job to make the respondents understand what's needed from them, to ask questions of the respondents and to report accurately, without bias or personal opinions, what the respondent answered.

Interviewers need to think on their feet, listen to themselves as well as to respondents, be capable of self-discipline, plus have the ability to adjust to many different types of respondents. Competent interviewers rely on trained, disciplined judgment, based on a thorough understanding of the interviewing function and the project questions at hand. The competent interviewer should be able to answer the following questions for each project:

Do I understand **why** I'm asking this question?

Do I understand the **meaning** of this question, that is, what information I'm seeking to obtain?

Do I understand **why** I am asking the questions in this **order**?

Do I understand **how** all of these **questions fit** together to make a meaningful interview?

Interviewers who understand the questionnaire and the nature of the project can usually provide more effective interviews. Consideration of the interviewers usually provides substantial benefits to the project.

COMMUNICATION GAPS   How does it happen that we have so much trouble getting answers when we supposedly all speak the same language? One of the reasons is quite simple. People hear different things within the context of the same statement or question. The more you observe and listen to people, the more you'll find that:

- Respondents try to please and give the answers they think interviewers want to hear (14% told Gallup Canada that they had done this (Gallup Canada, 1990)).
- People have pride and don't want to give the wrong answer, so often they will pretend they don't understand the question.
- The same word may mean different things to different people.

- Respondents are in different frames of reference from those of the interviewer.
- The respondent wants to get rid of the interviewer and will say almost anything to get off the hook.
- Respondents lose interest in an interview and start to answer mechanically without much thought (31% reported doing this in a recent Gallup Poll (1990)).
- Respondents are sometimes confused by survey questions and guess the answer rather than seeking clarification (16% reported doing this in a Gallup Canada study (1990)).

The above are just a few observations, there are many more. However, to acknowledge them and to anticipate them requires the interviewer to possess several key characteristics essential to receiving and recording information accurately. While several of the essential characteristics that are expected of an interviewer are qualitative and undefinable, the following five tend to be generally accepted:

- Sensitivity to the respondent
- Verbal flexibility (for probing)
- Good rapport, delivery and control
- Verbal accuracy (for recording)
- Recording accuracy

While it is unrealistic to expect all interviewers to have all the characteristics listed above, good interviewers should possess most of them to a substantial degree. During a structured conversation, the interviewer has to both *hear* and *listen* in order to filter and sort responses so that she or he can *retain* and *record* accurately what is essential for accurate data retrieval. The following section discusses these and other important aspects of fieldwork in depth.

FIELD INTERVIEWING TECHNIQUES

Field interviewing is a difficult topic to explain in written form. Almost all interviewers learn how to interview through on-the-job-training under experienced and knowledgeable supervisors. The Field Management Group of the Professional Marketing Research Society has prepared written instructions for interviewing. That material has been rephrased for use in this book and is presented with permission. The perspective of this section is generally that of the field interviewer, the field supervisor and the field director. The project director can design and control studies much better if the tasks of the field director, the field supervisor and the interviewers are well understood and appreciated.

RULES FOR OPEN-ENDED QUESTIONS—PROBING AND CLARIFYING   The purpose of marketing research is to provide information that will aid marketers to make better marketing decisions. The basic source of that information is the answers to questions. The field interviewer has a key role to play in the marketing research process. The interviewer must read the questions clearly and then accurately record the respondent's answers. If the questions are closed-ended or scaled, there's very little, if any, chance for misinterpretation of the answers when the questionnaires are reviewed some time after the interviewing. This is because the respondent is allowed to give only one of five pre-coded responses, for example, or to say that he or she doesn't know the answer or to refuse to answer. In any case, there is a limited set of specific answers and they are almost never subject to misinterpretation.

Open-ended questions present a more substantial challenge for the interviewer and for later analysis. Open-ended questions give the respondent the opportunity to provide a complete and rich answer to the question. This can reveal respondents' thoughts much better than can closed-ended questions. In some interviews, the respondents will go to great lengths to answer the question and then to explain or justify the answers. In other cases, the answers are cryptic and uninformative.

Open-ended answers are recorded on the questionnaire exactly as the respondent phrases them. By their very nature, open-ended questions are answered in the words of the respondents. Sometimes those words are very few and the interviewer's job is to draw a complete answer out of the respondent (probing). In other cases, the respondent might provide many answers but those words might not be specific enough to provide enough background or insight into what the respondent truly thinks about the object (clarification). The interviewer's role does not involve *interpreting* the respondent's answers in order to assist with the making of the marketing decision. That's a task reserved for the project director and the client.

Probing and clarifying techniques are used to obtain responses to open-ended questions in which respondents are asked to give their own opinions about a subject or product from pre-listed choices. When a respondent does not understand just what the researcher needs to know, the answer to the question will often be very general. The respondent will feel that the answer was sufficient and will want to move on to the next question. It's the interviewer's job in these situations to draw a complete and understandable answer from the subject.

By probing and clarifying, the interviewer gives the respondent the opportunity to communicate more fully, thus enlarging on what has been said. Therefore, what was originally a general response becomes a specific and detailed response. *Probing* is basically the technique of asking "what else?" until the interviewer feels that he or she has elicited all the respondent's answers to the question. Probing is conducted by asking the respondent for more answers to a question in addition to those already given. It continues until a respondent indicates there is nothing more to add.

Question	What do you like about this cheese?
1st answer	It is very moist in my mouth.
PROBE	What else do you like about this cheese?
2nd answer	It doesn't cost a lot.
PROBE	What else do you like about this cheese?
3rd answer	The package is easy to open because it has the zip-open strip on the end.
LAST PROBE	What else do you like about it?
4th answer	Nothing else.

Clarification is the technique of asking a respondent to explain in detail an answer previously given. The interviewer wants to know specifically what the respondent meant by an answer. It's necessary to make the respondent's answers more precise in order that they can be used for marketing input.

Question	What do you like about this cheese?
1st answer	It tastes good.
CLARIFICATION	What do you mean "it tastes good"?
2nd answer	I like the taste of this cheese. It's just the way I like it.
CLARIFICATION	What do you mean "it's just the way I like it"?
3rd answer	It has just the right amount of salt in it.

An interview with another respondent might go as follows:

Question	What do you like about this cheese?
1st answer	It's good.
CLARIFICATION	What do you mean "good"?
2nd answer	It tastes good.
CLARIFICATION	It tastes good in what way?
3rd answer	It tastes smooth, not biting, and has a nutty flavour.

From a general answer of "It's good," the interviewer has been able to extract a specific answer of "tastes smooth, not biting" and "has a nutty flavour" by clarification.

HOW TO PROBE AND CLARIFY   The probing technique is usually used after the respondent has given the initial answer to the question. Since the interviewer's job is to obtain all the information possible from the respondent, the interviewer will keep asking probe questions until the respondent cannot think of anything else. Some examples of general probe questions are:

What else?

Please tell me more.

What other reasons?

Any other reason? (This probe should be used only at the very end since it tends to solicit a "no other reasons" response.)

The clarifying technique is used to obtain the details that are missing from all general or vague responses to open-ended questions. Since respondents often do not realize that phrases such as "It is good," "I like it," or "It's a nice idea," can mean different things to different people, the interviewer will need to clarify those responses until the respondent gives specific phrases as answers.

Only neutral unbiased questions should be used when clarifying:

1. Interviewers should never suggest answers to the respondent. A suggested answer will almost always be played back by the subject as his or her own answer.

2. Many respondents wish to be helpful. If the respondent can tell how the interviewer feels about the subject, he or she may formulate an answer intended to please the interviewer. However, it's the respondent's answers that are wanted, not those of the interviewer.

Following are examples of questions useful when clarifying a respondent's vague answers:

What do you mean by that?

Why do you say that?

What are your reasons for saying that?

How do you mean (REPEAT RESPONDENT'S EXACT WORDS)?

In what way would it be (REPEAT RESPONDENT'S EXACT WORDS)?

How do you notice it was (REPEAT RESPONDENT'S EXACT WORDS)?

Please describe what you mean by (REPEAT RESPONDENT'S EXACT WORDS).

Why, what, when, where and *how* should be used in the same manner as they would be by a newspaper reporter trying to get the details of a news story or by a detective trying to pick up clues about a crime.

Following are two examples of how to probe and clarify.

NOTE THAT TWO DIFFERENT TECHNIQUES CAN BE USED:

1. The first way is to clear up incomplete answers before asking probe questions.

Question:	What did you dislike about your new Brand M automobile?
Respondent:	I don't know. It's really terrible. (TOO GENERAL; SHE HASN'T TOLD YOU ANYTHING SPECIFIC.)
CLARIFICATION:	What do you mean by `it's really terrible'?
Respondent:	It sounds like an old tin truck. (BETTER, BUT STILL NOT DETAILED ENOUGH.)
CLARIFICATION:	In what way does it `sound like an old tin truck'?
Respondent:	It rattles a lot and is very noisy.
PROBE:	What else do you dislike about your new Brand M automobile? (ASKING FOR MORE ANSWERS TO THE ORIGINAL QUESTION)
Respondent:	Nothing else. (STOP PROBING, SINCE RESPONDENT HAS STATED ALL OF HER REASONS.)

2. The second way is to ask all probe questions before clarifying incomplete answers.

Question:	What did you dislike about your new Brand M automobile?
Respondent:	I don't know. It's really terrible.
PROBE:	What else do you dislike about your new Brand M automobile?
Respondent:	Nothing else.

CLARIFICATION: What do you mean `it's really terrible'? (GO BACK TO CLARIFY INCOMPLETE ANSWER.)

Respondent: It sounds like an old tin truck.

CLARIFICATION: In what way does it sound like an old tin truck?

Respondent: It rattles a lot and is very noisy.

SUGGESTIONS FOR ASKING OPEN-ENDED QUESTIONS   Since open-ended questions require significantly more care than most closed-ended questions, we will provide several examples of good interviewer practice.

1. Interviewers should read questions from questionnaires word for word as they are written. If the respondent doesn't seem to understand a question, it should be repeated exactly as it was written on the questionnaire. Since the research analyst will combine and treat the data collected in all the interviews statistically, the data must be collected in a uniform manner for all respondents and all people in a sample must be asked the same questions in the same way.

   a) If the respondent (R) does not understand, she should be asked to interpret the question as she thinks it is meant.

   b) If R says "What do they mean by...?, the reply should be "Whatever you think it means." or "Whatever it means to you."

   c) Since exactly the same questions must be asked of each respondent, no changes in the phrasing of the questions should be made by the interviewers. Words should not be changed for any reason, even if it appears that the question could be made clearer.

   • Do not leave out part of a question.

   • Do not change some of the words.

   • Do not add a few words at the end of the question in an effort to be conversational.

   Examples:

   Asking printed questions as worded:

   Where do you get the majority of your news about current events in this country—from the radio, the newspaper, TV or talking to people?

   Response: TV

If the question is not read out as it is printed on the questionnaire, the respondent may provide answers which don't coincide with any of the precoded choices.

Variation 1:	Where do you get the majority of your news about current events in this country? (LEFT OFF CHOICES— RESPONDENT SAYS THE ONE HE THINKS OF FIRST.)
Response:	Time Magazine
Variation 2:	Where do you get the majority of your news—from the radio, the newspaper, TV or talking to people? (LEFT OFF THE TYPE OF NEWS.)
Response:	That depends on if it's local news, national news or just current stuff.
Variation 3:	Where do you get most of your news about current events in this country—from the radio, the newspaper, TV or talking to other people? That is, which one do you rely on the most? (THE LAST QUESTION IS NOT THE QUESTION WE WANT ANSWERED.)
Response:	I think the newspapers are the most accurate.

By changing the wording of a question, the respondent may be answering a different question than all other respondents on the survey. The information given is worthless.

---

2. The voice tonality of the interviewer should be absolutely matter-of-fact, with no indication of feelings about the question by voice or expression. The interviewers are to be *impartial* recorders of opinions.

Example:

Question:	Do you think the United Nations is doing all it can to help keep peace in the world, or not?

Asked in a normal manner, this easily permits a straightforward answer. By changing voice inflection, however, the interviewer can do all kinds of tricks with it. If the word "all" is emphasized, a higher than normal percentage of negative responses might result. If "United Nations" is stressed, it's likely to elicit a higher percentage of positive answers.

When reading a list of answers to the respondent, the interviewer must maintain an even tonality throughout the list. Otherwise, variations in the interviewer's voice might underline the answer that the interviewer wants to elicit from the respondent and bias the response. The interviewer must also read the complete list, even though the respondent indicates an answer part way through the list.

3. Leading questions should not be asked when probing or clarifying— respondents may be led in a direction they would not normally take.

Examples:

a. Wrong	You say you don't like it? What about the taste don't you like? (TASTE NOT PREVIOUSLY MENTIONED.)
b. Right:	You say you don't like it? Why is that?
Question:	How do you think things are going in the world today, specifically our relations with other countries?
Response:	Well, I don't know too much about our relations with foreign countries. (QUESTION HAS NOT BEEN ANSWERED, REQUIRES CLARIFICATION.)
Correct Clarification:	There are no right or wrong answers on things like this, of course. I'd just like to have your opinion. (REPEAT THE QUESTION HERE.)
Response:	Well, it seems as if most other countries look at us as a constant source of financial and military support.
Leading/ Wrong Clarification:	You mean like in our relations with Latveria?

The respondent now considers any answer she might give in terms of the developed relationship with Latveria, a subject she herself has not mentioned at all but was introduced by the interviewer. It will be impossible to find out what the respondent really thought about "our relations with other countries" in general.

Correct Clarification:	Please tell me more about that.

4. An answer should not be suggested to a respondent, even if the interviewer senses what the respondent intends to say.

Examples:

Wrong:	You don't like the taste? Is that because it tastes too strong?
Right:	You don't like the taste? What is there about the taste that you don't like?
Question:	What was the major benefit in purchasing your Brand Y automobile when compared with Brand T?
Respondent:	Really, both cars were comparable in style, comfort, gas mileage and standard factory-installed features.
Suggestive/ Wrong Clarification:	Do you think the price was too high on Brand T?
Correct Clarification:	But what do you feel was the major benefit in purchasing?

5. The interviewer should not put words in the respondent's mouth. If she does not know the answer, that is still an answer. (RECORD AS DON'T KNOW "DK".)

    Examples:

Wrong:	You don't like the taste? Oh, you mean the strong taste?
Right:	You don't like the taste? What is there about the taste that you do not like?
Question:	What do you like least about your new Brand T car?
Respondent:	Well, the apple red isn't exactly the shade of red I was expecting from the colour chart.
Suggestive/ Wrong Clarification:	Oh, I see... You mean the colour was more like tomato soup than like apples?
Correct Clarification:	What was there about the apple red that was different from the colour chart?

6. Some clarifications should never be used. "Could you be more specific?" should never be used because it insults the respondent since he or she thinks the answer is as specific as possible. Also, any probe or clarification containing "could you" or "would you" begs for a yes answer—i.e., the respondent is able to respond, but will he? Maybe not.

7. The interviewer should never insert his or her own ideas or otherwise bias the interview. Care must be taken by the interviewer not to encourage the respondent with reactions to answers such as "that's good" or "that's right."

    Examples:

Wrong:	You don't like that taste? I don't either.
Right:	You don't like that taste ... let me record that.
Question:	And what do you dislike about pay television?
Respondent:	There are never any commercials during the movies so I don't get a chance to raid the refrigerator without missing a part of the plot.
Interviewer (Wrong):	Oh, I know what you mean. I've solved that by turning the television around so I can see it from the kitchen.

8. The questions were developed to be asked in the order presented in the questionnaire. The interviewer should not change the order of asking questions; it may disrupt the respondent's train of thought or bias the answers. The sequence is planned for continuity and promoting a conversational atmosphere. Earlier questions are structured so they will not affect the respondent's answers to later questions.

9. Every question specified in the questionnaire must be asked as indicated. A questionnaire with unanswered questions may be thrown out and not counted. In answering one question, a respondent will sometimes also answer another question appearing later in the interview. However, it is the interviewer's responsibility to make certain that the respondent is fully exposed to each question specified in the questionnaire, even if it seems as though some points are being repeated. If this case arises, the interviewer should try using the following procedure:

a) Write down the initial answer under the question when it occurs.

b) Then ask the partially answered question when it occurs in the questionnaire, but preface it with some remark which will show the respondent that his or her earlier answer wasn't forgotten or rejected. Such a remark might be: "You may have mentioned this before, but let me ask you..." or "We're asking people on this survey about each of these, and I'd like to make sure how you feel about each one separately..." or "Even though you may have already told me..." or "Just to check...".

c) In those few cases where the question has been clearly answered, the interviewer might say, "You've told me something about this, but this next question asks...?" Assuming the respondent has already answered a question is a dangerous practice. Every question must be asked, even when it might seem as if it has been previously answered.

Example:

Question 1a:	Generally speaking, do you think you personally will be earning more money within the next year, or not?
Answer:	I should be making more.
Question 1b:	Why is that?
Answer:	I'm scheduled for a raise in salary on Sept. 1.
Question 2:	Overall, do you expect your total family income to be more next year than it is at present, less or just what? You've already told me you expect a raise...? (EXPECTANT PAUSE)
Answer:	Yes, but my wife will no longer be working, so actually we will be bringing in even less than we are making now.

If the answer to Q.2 had been assumed to be "more" because of the raise, the recorded answer would have been incorrect. All questions must be asked.

A NOTE ON DEMOGRAPHIC/BASIC DATA QUESTIONS   Basic data, demographic or classification questions are all questions dealing with personal characteristics of the respondent, such as age, education, income, etc. These types of questions usually make up the last section of the questionnaire.

Basic data questions are very important because respondents' answers are grouped by demographic characteristics for purposes of analysis. The demographic questions should always be treated as just another part of the interview. Embarrassment or hesitation on the interviewer's part may lead to the respondent's refusal to answer such questions. The respondent should be assured that the demographic questions are being asked in order to group the interviews, or for statistical purposes, or for validation purposes—whatever the questionnaire says.

Obtaining and confirming the respondent's name and telephone number for validation purposes is a requirement of most studies. If necessary, the respondents can be assured that their names will not be put on a mailing list and that no further contact other than validation by a supervisor will be made. It is important that the name, telephone number and address be *printed* clearly so that the correct person is contacted when validating.

MECHANICS OF RECORDING AN INTERVIEW

Legibility is of paramount importance in filling out the questionnaire. The interviewer must always print or write clearly. It's important that the interviewer always takes time at the end of each interview to scan the questionnaire. Anything that may be difficult for someone else to read should be crossed out and rewritten. Legibility is one of the first things which the field supervisor looks for when editing.

Short forms are generally not acceptable on a completed interview. Whenever abbreviations are used during recording, the interviewer must go back and fill them in once the interview is completed. The phrase "same as above" or ditto (") marks, should not be used. Interviewers should use their interviewing skills to obtain the respondent's complete answer to each question. In turn, those complete answers to each question should be on each questionnaire.

The written responses should not be erased. If an error is made or the respondent changes an answer, it should be slashed or crossed out. The interviewer should make a notation in the margin of the questionnaire of what happened to cause the change noted. If the respondent cannot answer a question or is interrupted, it should be noted in the margin at that point.

The interviewer must be careful to record the respondent's full name (including Mr., Mrs., Miss or Ms.) so there can be no mistake in contacting the designated respondent when verifying. For verification purposes, full address information (including postal code, when required,) needs to be obtained. The telephone number should also be confirmed. All classification data must be *printed* clearly.

RECORDING RESPONSES TO CLOSED-ENDED QUESTIONS   A closed-ended question is a question with an answer code (number) to be circled, or a box to be marked as indicated. One of the pre-coded answers must be used. There is no provision for any handwritten answers.

Exhibit 8.8   Recording of Dichotomous Closed-ended Questions (Interviewer Administered)

Example One:	**Correct Recording**	**CODING**
A "Do you own a car?" CIRCLE <u>ONE</u> CODE	YES ....① NO 2	[___] 21
	Incorrect Recording	
B. "Do you own a car?" CIRCLE <u>ONE</u> CODE	⬭YES⬭ ....① NO 2	[___] 21

The instruction calls for one code to be circled, that means that a 1 or 2 will be circled. The word should not be circled and only one code should be circled.

Exhibit 8.9   Recording of Scaled Closed-ended Questions (Interviewer Administered)

Example Two:	**Correct Recording**	**CODING**
A. "Would you rate the cake you just tasted as poor, fair, good or excellent?" "X" ONE BOX	EXCELLENT ...... ☐ - 1 VERY GOOD ..... ☒ - 2 GOOD .... ☐ - 3 FAIR .... ☐ - 4 POOR .... ☐ - 5 REF.................... ☐ - 7 DK .... ☐ - 8 NA .... ☐ - 9	[___] 35
	Incorrect Recording	**CODING**
B. "Would you rate the cake you just tasted as poor, fair, good or excellent?" "X" ONE BOX	EXCELLENT ...... ☐ - 1 VERY GOOD ..... ☒ ② GOOD .... ☐ - 3 FAIR .... ☐ - 4 POOR .... ☐ - 5 REF .... ☐ - 7 DK .... ☐ - 8 NA .... ☐ - 9	[___] 35

The instructions ask that an "X" be put in one box. An "X" should be used and care should be taken so that it is contained in just one box. No codes are to be circled, according to the instructions above.

There are differences of opinion surrounding the inclusion of missing value codes of *refused, don't know* and *not applicable*. Some researchers feel that each pre-coded question should provide for any possible reasonable answer. This means that if a person says "I don't know", then the interviewer should see that answer on the questionnaire. However, other researchers feel that providing a DK answer on the questionnaire encourages the interviewer to accept a *lazy don't know*, without at least trying to elicit an answer. The interviewer should say "I have to mark a *yes* or *no*. Which one would you have me mark?"

RECORDING RESPONSES TO OPEN-ENDED QUESTIONS   The most basic rule of interviewing is that the questions must be read as printed and the interviewer is to record the answers *verbatim*. The interviewer should record exactly what the respondent says, word-for-word.

If the respondent talks too quickly, the interviewer should say, "One moment please, I'm writing this down...", or "The last thing I have recorded is...", or "What did you say after...?". This indicates to the respondent that his or her opinions have been written down verbatim. It also reminds the respondent of what he or she has just said and the respondent will be kept on topic. The respondent usually slows down when this is done.

Another way of slowing the dialogue down is for the interviewer to tell the respondent that every answer is very important and that it's necessary to be sure to get every word down correctly.

In the case where a respondent doesn't seem to understand the question, the interviewer should repeat the question to the respondent, slowly, but should not reword the question or interpret its meaning.

When more than one product is referred to, the interviewer should always indicate which product the respondent is describing so that there can be absolutely no doubt which statement applies to which product.

1. The answers should be recorded in the exact words the respondent uses (first person, verbatim).

    Examples:

a. Wrong:	She say she likes the colour of the car.	
Right:	I like the colour of the car.	
b. Wrong:	He thinks it tastes like chocolate.	
Right:	It tastes like chocolate.	

Open-ended questions are where respondents' comments are recorded *verbatim* with *probing* and *clarifying* as indicated. Indicate every probe with a '(P)'.

Examples:

<u>Correct Recording:</u>

Questions: What did you like about the soup you tried?

The taste (P) Natural tasting (P) Not artificial. You could taste real chicken and vegetables (P). That's all.

<u>Incorrect Recording:</u>

Question: What did you like about the soup you tried?
                    (Field Management Group, 1986).

– taste
– natural
– not artificial

2. The spoken responses should not be summarized or shortened.

    Examples:

    a. Wrong: It would be a good idea.
       Right: Oh, I think it might be a good idea if it is done carefully.

    b. Wrong: It tastes nutty.
       Right: It has a taste kind of like walnuts and almonds.

3. Slang and other expressions which often vividly reveal a respondent's true feelings should be written down with the rest of the answers.

    Example: It was a real macho-looking car, definitely classy.

4. Ditto marks or "same as above" should not be used when recording answers; the answer should be re-recorded if it is the same as one given earlier in the questionnaire.

5. Responses should be recorded during the interview; interviewers should never try to remember what was said and write it later.

6. Answers should be written legibly using a black graphite pencil. A pen should not be used unless specified, such as for recording on validation sheets.

Record Sheets   On each survey, the interviewer must keep a record of all attempted contacts made with every possible respondent. This record must be kept accurately and returned to head office correctly completed.

Accuracy in keeping a record of contact is very important in providing information about the study. For example, this tells us how many people were screened to find the quota of eligible respondents. Typical record or contact sheets are shown in Exhibits 8.10 and 8.11.

Exhibit 8.10   Cover Sheet for Each Contact

ECONOMETRIC RESEARCH LTD./MARKETING DECISION RESEARCH INC.
SALMONID STUDY (THUNDER BAY RESIDENTS) – **MTR – JAN. 1990**

( )   -

R. NAME   R. PHONE #

ADDRESS: CITY:

PROV: POSTAL CODE:

DATE:_____ TIME STARTED:_____TIME ENDED: _____

VERIFIED BY:_____   DATE: _____ CHECKED BY SUPERVISOR:_____

"I hereby certify that this interview was conducted following the questionnaire attached and according to the instructions for this study. I also certify that the answers recorded by me are as given to me by this respondent. I acknowledge that a proportion of my work will be verified by having a supervisor of Econometric Research Ltd./Marketing Decision Research Inc. contact the respondent identified in this questionnaire."

CALLBACK	DATE											
	INTERVIEWER											
No answer/recorder		1	1	1	1	1	1	1	1	1	1	1
Busy		2	2	2	2	2	2	2	2	2	2	2
Qualified Respondent not available		3	3	3	3	3	3	3	3	3	3	3
- Callback arranged for (Date/Time)												

DEAD NUMBER

Not in service/ disconnected	4	4	4	4	4	4	4	4	4	4	4	
No ring	5	5	5	5	5	5	5	5	5	5	5	
Not Residential Listing	6	6	6	6	6	6	6	6	6	6	6	
Incorrect listing	7	7	7	7	7	7	7	7	7	7	7	
(Correct # above)												
No longer in residence	8	8	8	8	8	8	8	8	8	8	8	
Terminated at Q. _____	9	9	9	9	9	9	9	9	9	9	9	
Refused to answer screener	10	10	10	10	10	10	10	10	10	10	10	
Other [SPECIFY]	11	11	11	11	11	11	11	11	11	11	11	
Terminate D	12	12	12	12	12	12	12	12	12	12	12	
Complete	13	13	13	13	13	13	13	13	13	13	13	

Exhibit 8.11 Call Record Sheet

Call Record Sheet

Project #: _____

Interviewer: _____

City: _____

1. No answer/Not in service
   Business Number
2. Busy/No answer
3. Refusal
4. Language Barrier
5. Person answering is not resident of household
6. Respondent not available

7. Discontinued during interview
8. Q.A. -- Fewer than 2 health problems
9. Over quota (SPECIFY IN MARGIN)
10. Completed Interview

Phone Number	Respondent's Full Name (If Completed Interview)	Final Result
		1 2 3 4 5 6 7 8 9 10
		1 2 3 4 5 6 7 8 9 10
		1 2 3 4 5 6 7 8 9 10
		1 2 3 4 5 6 7 8 9 10
		1 2 3 4 5 6 7 8 9 10
		1 2 3 4 5 6 7 8 9 10
		1 2 3 4 5 6 7 8 9 10
		1 2 3 4 5 6 7 8 9 10
		1 2 3 4 5 6 7 8 9 10
		1 2 3 4 5 6 7 8 9 10
		1 2 3 4 5 6 7 8 9 10
		1 2 3 4 5 6 7 8 9 10
		1 2 3 4 5 6 7 8 9 10
		1 2 3 4 5 6 7 8 9 10
		1 2 3 4 5 6 7 8 9 10
		1 2 3 4 5 6 7 8 9 10
		1 2 3 4 5 6 7 8 9 10

> Although clients don't usually scrutinize call record sheets, these documents do constitute part of the study records and an important part of quality control and should be easily available to the client.

HOW TO RECORD ON A RECORD OR CONTACT SHEET

1. The interviewer's name, city, date, study number and time, when applicable, should be recorded.
2. There will be a column for all possible results. A result must be recorded for each attempted contact.
3. For telephone interviews, results must be recorded in different columns for each attempted interview.
4. On door-to-door studies, the address of each house or apartment attempted and the result must be recorded.
5. The result of each attempt is recorded by using the appropriate code for each attempt as required by the individual study.
6. Any call-back information is recorded, e.g., "Respondent will be home at 5 p.m. today, July 11".

SUMMARY

Fieldwork is the heart of marketing research. However, it's not often seen directly by clients and those trying to appreciate marketing research from outside the profession. The need for confidentiality of the respondents and the clients makes this observation difficult if not inadvisable. Also, many onlookers might feel that getting people to answer questions is quite a simple and direct task. This is anything but the case in fieldwork practice.

Fieldwork is a marketing research activity which requires:

- Expertise
- Experience
- Excellent organizational skills
- Attention to detail
- Commitment to quality
- Thorough professionalism

These requirements can be met better if all who are involved in the project understand an support the fieldwork function.

NOW THINK ABOUT THIS

1. Refer back to question 1 in Chapter 7. Now that you've interviewed two people using the questionnaire, have two of your classmates interview you. After each interview, critique their technique and work to improve the quality of the interview using the guidelines provided in this chapter.

2. Write a short questionnaire to determine the opinions of fellow students towards a well-known politician. Make the questions primarily open-ended. Interview five people with no probing or clarification and another five with extended probing and clarification. Now compare the differences in the answers that you obtained. Comment on the likely impact of these two levels of fieldwork on the final report of a study.

REFERENCES

Calhoun, Douglas
1989   "CAMRO News"—Standards." *Imprints: PMRS Newsletter.* Toronto: Professional Marketing Research Society, April 1989, p.10.

Calhoun, Douglas
1989   "CAMRO News." *Imprints: PMRS Newsletter.* Toronto: Professional Marketing Research Society, June, 1989, p.12.

CATI News
1990   "Predictive Dialing." *CATI News* (Sawtooth Software), Vol. 3, No. 1 (Spring 1990), p.8.

CATI News
1990   "More on Predictive Dialing." *CATI News* (Sawtooth Software), Vol. 3, No. 2 (Fall 1990), p.6.

Dillman, Don A.
1978   *Mail and Telephone Surveys: The Total Design Method.* New York: John Wiley & Sons.

Field Management Group
1986   *Supervisor and Interviewer Training Manual.* Toronto: Professional Marketing Research Society.

Gallup Canada, Inc.
1990   "Canadians' Attitudes Towards Survey Research: Where Does Our Industry Stand?" Unpublished report, May 1990.

Gallup, George
1989   "The Constitutional Rights of Survey Respondents." *Imprints: PMRS Newsletter*, November 1989, p.16.

Honomichl, Jack
1990   "Answering Machines Threaten Survey Research." *Marketing News*,
        August 6, 1990, p.11.

Hunt, Shelby D., Richard D. Sparkman, Jr., and James B. Wilcox
1982   "The Pretest in Survey Research: Issues and Preliminary Findings."
        Journal of Marketing Research, 19 May 1982, pp. 269-73.

Tomany, Denis
1989   "CAMRO News." *Imprints: PMRS Newsletter.* Toronto: Professional
        Marketing Research Society, December 1989, p. 11-12.

Wiseman, Frederick, and Philip McDonald
1980   "Movement Begins Toward Much Needed Response Rate Standards."
        Marketing News, 13, January 11, 1980, p.4.

APPENDIX 8A

CAMRO STANDARDS

One of the principal aims of the Canadian Association of Marketing Research Organizations (CAMRO) is to promote high standards of quality and professionalism in the market research industry. A key requirement of membership in CAMRO is the agreement to enforce a code of standards for all research projects conducted by member companies.

The standards to which all CAMRO members adhere cover the following areas:

A. VALIDATION OF INTERVIEWS

1. A minimum of 10% of each interviewer's work must be validated. If on-site supervision is provided (e.g., central location telephone interviewing), a minimum of 10% of all interviews must be directly monitored.
2. In the event of non-validation, all of the interviewer's work must be rejected and/or replaced.
3. The validation procedure and outcome must be described in the report.
4. Evidence of validations must be kept on file for a minimum of six months.

B. THE REPORT

The report must include the following:

1. A full description of the sample, sample design and its execution.
2. A summary of all contacts made in the survey execution.

3. A copy of the questionnaire(s) used.

4. Copies and/or descriptions of any exhibits used during the interview.

The supplier must also be prepared to provide the client with information about:

- When, how, and by whom fieldwork was conducted.
- Who tabulated and/or processed the data.

These validation and report procedures must always be followed by a CAMRO member unless explicitly agreed upon with the client. In the event of such agreement, this must be clearly stated in the report.

C. INTERVIEWER IDENTIFICATION

1. For personal interviewing: all interviewers must carry company I.D. with an expiry date.

2. For all interviewing: the name of the research company must be clearly identified at the start of the interview.

D. AUDIO/VISUAL RECORDING OR OBSERVATION

1. Electronic recording is not permitted without the knowledge of respondents.

2. Where a one-way mirror is present, respondents must be made aware of this and the possibility that there may be viewers.

E. CONFIDENTIALITY

1. The confidentiality of the respondent must be assured.

2. Except in the case of a syndicated study, the client is assured that his project is held in complete confidence by the research agency.

3. Market survey reports are normally for use within the client's own organization. If a wider circulation of the whole, or any part, of the report is required, the market research agency is entitled to be consulted and to approve the exact form of publication. Furthermore, if the client divulges the whole, or any part, of the report without prior authorization, the agency is then entitled to answer all bona fide enquiries about the survey they have conducted.

F. STORAGE OF RESEARCH MATERIALS

The supplier must keep original questionnaires for a period of 12 months and the survey data in the form of cards or tape for 24 months following the end of fieldwork. After these periods, such material may be destroyed unless special arrangements have been made with the client.

To ensure compliance with these standards, CAMRO conducts audits of its member companies (Calhoun, 1989:10).

APPENDIX 8B

Refusal Rates Investigated by CASRO

The Council of American Survey Research Organizations (CASRO) undertook a study called the Your Opinion Counts 1988 Refusal Study for the U.S.A. The study was undertaken to determine the trend and level of refusal rates on "general purpose quantitative consumer research studies". It was conducted through the participation of survey research firms who are members of CASRO. These companies provided information for each cluster/location on all studies they conducted during September 1985 and September 1988.

Prior to discussing the key findings, it is appropriate to explain how the refusal rate was calculated in this CASRO study. Five categories of outcome for each contact were established.

A. INITIAL REFUSAL

Respondent refuses to participate in interview before or during introduction.

B. REFUSED TO CONTINUE

. . . "Break off" . . . respondent refuses to continue with questions after introduction has been read and screening questions have begun.

C. QUALIFIED REFUSED

Respondent has answered all qualifying questions but refuses at any point after that.

D. INELIGIBLE

Inappropriate response to qualifying questions.

E. COMPLETED

Acceptable full interview.

The Refusal Rate is defined as the Total Refused (A + B + C) as a percentage of the Total Asked (A + B + C + D + E). The appropriateness of including ineligible respondents (D) within the total is a contentious issue. The argument for including them is that they were contacted and asked the qualifying questions. They had, therefore, the opportunity to refuse at initial contact. On the other hand, this means that many respondents who may have been asked a few brief screening questions are included with the "Total Asked" category. While the appropriateness of this has been debated within CASRO, the fact remains that this is how the Refusal Rate is calculated and presented in the Your Opinion Counts Refusal Rate Survey for the U.S. The method of calculation is, of course, consistent for the two years for which data are available.

According to the study results, the overall level and nature of refusals did not change in the U.S. between 1985 and 1988. In both years, the Refusal Rate was 38%.

Furthermore, the primary problem continues to be initial refusal. In the 1988 study, approximately 90% of all refusals fell into this category.

Refusal Rate in U.S.	1985	1988
Total Contacts	(1 387 000)	(1 687 000)
Total Refusals	38%	38%
–Initial Refusals	32%	34%
–Refused to Continue	4%	1%
–Qualified Refused	2%	3%

Refusal Rate in U.S. By Interviewing Method in:		
Telephone Interviews	30%	32%
–Listed Numbers	25%	26%
–Random Digit Dialling	38%	40%
Personal Interviews—Mall	56%	54%
Personal Interviews Door-To-Door	29%	36%

The study results suggest that in 1988 the Refusal Rate is similar for telephone interviewing (32%) and door-to-door interviewing (36%), but considerably higher for mall intercept interviewing (54%). Within telephone interviewing it appears that a considerably higher Refusal Rate is encountered when using an RDD sample (40%) than when using a sample of listed numbers (26%).

The report offered a number of suggestions which it urged the research industry to implement, whenever possible, to help reduce refusal rates. These are listed below.

- Exercise courtesy when considering what hours of the day to call into a respondent's home. "Your Opinion Counts" believes a good guideline would be calling during the hours between 9 a.m. and 9 p.m.
- When mall respondents indicate it is not a convenient time, make an appointment to do the interview at a later time.
- Data collectors should routinely administer interviewer training programs. Data collection firms need to ensure their people are effective at their jobs at all times.

- The subject matter should be revealed to the participant if it can be done without biasing the data. The more information a person is provided, the less reason he has to be suspicious.
- Researchers should consider limiting questionnaires to a reasonable length for both phone and personal interviews. We must discipline ourselves in this area and educate our clients as to the importance of this issue relative to refusal rates.
- Strive to make the interviewing process as pleasant and appealing as possible to encourage repeat participation.
- Support the "Your Opinion Counts" Public Education Program by using YOC Consumer Brochure, spreading the message through speaking engagements, college seminars and community activities, and closing every survey with "Your Opinion Counts" (Tomany, 1989: 11-12).

APPENDIX 8C

The Interview Manual

RAPID TRANSIT STUDY
Personal Interview
Interviewer's Manual
September 3, 1981

1. <u>What company are you with?</u>

We are with MDR. MDR is a research firm in Hamilton. We are involved in a wide range of studies and surveys of social importance.

2. <u>Who are you doing the study for?</u>

The study is being conducted for the Rapid Transit Project Office and has the support and encouragement of the Regional Council of Hamilton-Wentworth.

3. <u>How did you get my name?</u>

You live on the route of the proposed alignment and it is important to interview everyone who lives on the route.

4. <u>Why are you doing the study?</u>

It is important to understand how different people feel about the proposed Rapid Transit System.

5. Will I get the results?

The results of our study will be made public when the report is given to Regional Council.

6. Why don't you talk to my husband/wife/son, etc?

In this interview, we would like the opinions of (both) the head(s) of the household. However, we will be pleased to interview just one if it is inconvenient for both to be present.

7. How can I be sure that the information will be confidential?

Everything you tell me is confidential and anonymous. Your name will not appear on the questionnaire. Your answers will be combined with the answers of other people and presented as statistics.

8. How long will the interview take?

The time varies from person to person, but on the average it takes about an hour.

9. How can I be sure the study is legitimate?

You can call the Rapid Transit Project Office at _____ and check with them.

Our office number is _____. You can ask to speak to Mr. _____ or Mr. _____

MATERIALS

Bring the following materials with you to each interview:
a. Interview Manual
b. 1 Questionnaire
c. 1 deck of sorting cards
d. 1 picture
e. 1 I.D. card
f. pencils
g. 1 copy of Flash Cards

THE QUESTIONNAIRE

1. Read all questions exactly as worded.
2. Read out everything in regular type.
3. Be sure to record the I.D. number.
4. Be sure to record time begin and time end.
5. Use neutral probes only, don't bias responses.

RESPONDENT SELECTION: VERIFY ADDRESS BEFORE INTERVIEW

We require a completed interview from every address on the assignment. If the name or phone number on the interviewer assignment is not correct, then a personal visit to the household must be made to set up the appointment. It is the people living at the designated address that must be interviewed even though the name is different or the phone number has changed.

MOST IMPORTANT!

Do not express your own opinions or ideas about the Rapid Transit System. If a respondent asks you a question, your answer is "We have been instructed not to give our own feelings or answers during the interview. Can we wait until the interview is over? We don't want to influence anyone's answers one way or another."

At the end of the interview you can say "I really don't know all of the details of the study—if you would like more information you can call the Rapid Transit Project Office at _____."

It is critical that we accept no substitutes. We must attempt to complete an interview with every person in the sample. This may require 6 call-backs, but we must do this and more if necessary to get the completion!

PRE-INTERVIEW CONTACT

Everyone in the sample has received a letter ahead of time and one-half have received a fact sheet on the Rapid Transit System. See the attached fact sheet and letters as follows:

RT-1 Personal interview with fact sheet—even number I.D.
RT-2 Personal interview—no fact sheet—odd number I.D.

Note:

For personal interviews, if you have not been provided with the phone number to make the appointment, try the telephone directory, then call Directory Assistance if you need to. We have no other way of getting a number for you. You may have to knock on the door to try and arrange the appointment (or collect the interview).

We will accept the interview with the adult head of household at the designated address even if the name is incorrect. It is the persons living at that address we are interested in.

HANDOUT PICTURE

If the respondent says something about a driver or attendant in the picture, you can say that there has been no decision made yet as to whether or not there will be an attendant on the vehicle.

9 / Data Reduction, Processing and Tabulation

WHAT YOU WILL LEARN IN THIS CHAPTER

- Editing, coding and tabulation comprise a substantial and important part of marketing research
- How to edit and code for maximum quality
- About the coding of answers that is necessary prior to data entry
- About data entry programs and computer assisted telephone interviewing (CATI)
- About the importance of quality control in the eliciting and analysis of survey responses
- The meaning of stubs, banners and marginals
- The basics of beginning a tabulation of survey responses

AFTER THE FIELDWORK

One of the most frustrating phases of marketing research is to have several huge stacks of questionnaires piled on one table and a computer on another table. Now you think, if only there were a slot on the computer where I could feed these in. Well, there isn't, and there are only two ways to get the answers into the machine. You could have had the fieldwork done by a firm that uses computer assisted telephone interviewing (CATI). Then the responses would have been entered into the computer as they were spoken. However, if you're staring at all of those questionnaires, now is not the time to think about the things you could have done. Just call in the coding and data entry people and set them to the task. Or send the questionnaires out to a data entry firm.

CATI is a system in which the interviewing process is automated. The questionnaire is read off the computer screen and the answers are typed on the computer keyboard. The questionnaire sequence is controlled automatically through the computer. The typed answers immediately become part of the study data base.

DATA REDUCTION

Several stages of marketing research can remain hidden from and ignored by those who read marketing research textbooks but who don't actually conduct marketing research. However, those phases of the project suddenly leap out of the shadows when you have to get the work done—especially that niggling task of getting the information from the questionnaires into a form which can be analyzed by computer.

These intermediate steps of marketing research are also mainly invisible to most marketing research clients. Clients need to feel comfortable that these operations are properly handled by their suppliers. They should be able to take it for granted that the data reduction and data processing are done correctly.

From the research consultants' side, these steps are really not the things that take up much discussion time with the client. There are more important issues for client meetings. However, the consultant must ensure that the process of data reduction is done properly. This is an important task. Some firms pride themselves on having excellent data reduction (editing and coding) departments that reduce or eliminate any errors that might find their way into the data through sloppy or incomplete operations. (These errors would be categorized as non-sampling errors.) As we'll see later in this chapter, some editing and coding errors can be caught during the tabulation phase. However, many of the editing and coding errors become invisible after the computer data file has been constructed and are never caught.

FIELD EDITING BY THE INTERVIEWERS

Editing involves scrutinizing the questionnaire and, if advisable, making any corrections. Field editing begins as soon as a questionnaire is completed in an interviewer-administered survey and as soon as a self-administered questionnaire is received by one of the survey firm's staff. As noted in Chapter 8, the interviewer should review the questionnaire as soon as the phone is hung up. The editing is continued by the field supervisor and then by the editing staff when the questionnaires are received at the head office.

The purpose of this stage of the editing is for the interviewer to make sure that every piece of information provided by the respondent was written accurately and in the words of the respondent for open-ended questions. The interviewer should also provide clarifying notes for any changes in initial responses which were written down and then changed in any way.

Sometimes, the interviewer completes an interview but then feels uncomfortable with it. In most cases, this discomfort arises because the respondent just didn't seem credible or seemed to be "clued-out." This is usually due to a lack of understanding, lack of intelligence on the part of the respondent, or a language problem. The questionnaire should have been developed so that it could be understood by anyone with a basic level of intelligence, in most studies. This should include the design of screening questions. Lack of understanding shouldn't be a problem during the fieldwork.

In most surveys, there's a potential for language or cultural problems to arise. The field specifications should have directed whether the interviewing was to be conducted in English, French or any other language, and how long the respondent was to have lived in the area. However, there are respondents who at the outset of the interviewing seem to understand the language of the survey, but part-way through a problem of comprehension arises. There will be occasions when the interviewer has a hard time deciding whether to terminate because of language problems or to continue. If in doubt, she'll usually try to complete the interview. Afterwards, she might decide that the questionnaire needs greater scrutiny for usability by the field supervisor or by the editing staff and will note this on the questionnaire and bring it to the attention of the field supervisor. A lack of adequate intelligence on the part of the respondent is a similar problem to that of language comprehension. Sometimes it's obvious, but often the interview is completed and then the supervisor is notified. This a basic level of editing, but still editing.

FIELD EDITING BY THE FIELD SUPERVISOR

The field supervisor plays an important role in editing since he or she is the closest management person to the actual interview. In addition to picking up problems noted by the interviewers as described in the last section, the field supervisor does a quick sight edit of the questionnaires to weed out those that are incomplete; to identify responses that were not adequately entered or annotated by interviewers; to find questions that are causing persistent problems and weren't picked up by the pre-test; and to identify interviewers who are not executing their functions properly.

Naturally, in order to perform the editing function effectively the supervisor must have proper directions. Just as the interviewers are provided with an interview manual, the supervisors and other staff involved in editing are given editing manuals. The more specific the editing manual, the more efficiently the job will be performed. A good set of editing instructions will also speed up the process. The conscientious supervisor will tend to place quite a few phone calls to the head office editing supervisor or field director if he or she is finding problems and needs clarification of what course of action to take.

Manual Editing by the Head Office Staff

The quick and thorough sight editing of the first questionnaires received from the field is critical. The first few hours or days of interviewing are the time to pick up any remaining problems with the questionnaire, with the interviewing, and with the supervision. The editing or coding supervisor or the project director should have a good feeling of whether the first questionnaires are working by scrutinizing them in complete detail. If problems exist with any parts of the field process, the earlier they are detected, the better. The basic problems can then be fixed immediately. However, if a significant problem exists with the questionnaire, the sample or the type of interviewers, then the project must be stopped until the appropriate adjustments are made. This is why the editing of the first few questionnaires is so vital.

Editing the questionnaire can detect quite a few problems. While some of these are obvious, others need specific instructions from the project director to be resolved.

INCOMPLETENESS   Almost any study will have questionnaires that contain a few incomplete answers which end up being classified as *missing values*. Sometimes people refuse to answer a particular question; or they really don't know the answer; or the question was not asked, either by design or by mistake. The occasional blank answer can be accommodated. However, in most cases the interviewer should supply the reason for the missing value. The reason for not answering should then be assigned a code. For example, the code could be 7 for *refused to answer*, 8 for *don't know* or 9 for *not applicable* or *skipped according to directions*.

Most questionnaires have some planned *skip patterns*. For example, if the respondent didn't shop at Sobeys, then don't ask how she like shopping at Sobeys. These gaps in the answers to the questionnaire are not a sign of incompleteness. In fact, the interviewer should note that the skipped questions were *not applicable* to the respondent. They might be denoted by a code 9.

Sometimes skips are made when they shouldn't be. This can be an honest mistake by the interviewer; a lack of understanding by the interviewer; improper questionnaire design; or a deliberate attempt by the interviewer to shorten the interview. If several improper skips appear, these should be traced to the interviewer and the problem rectified either by a reminder, an explanation, further training or dismissal.

In mail surveys, the editing staff can only rely on what's on the printed page of the questionnaire. Some respondents return the questionnaire totally blank, sometimes with the monetary incentive. Others will fill in part of the questionnaire but leave other parts unanswered. Still others will leave a note explaining why they didn't answer. The project director and the coding supervisor should provide specific directions regarding the maximum quantity of blank answers to be allowed and still have the questionnaire included in the total count. This criterion will vary among studies and sometimes the decision on individual questionnaires will be left to the judgment of the supervisor.

There is also the problem of a questionnaire that is too complete. When the interviewer ignores the skip directions and just continues blindly to the next question regardless of the answer given by the respondent, then there's too much data. Sometimes the respondent will correct the interviewer when something seems obviously wrong ("Why are you asking me this? I just told you I never eat those."), but many will simply continue with the interview. The problem here is to figure out which branch of questions the interviewer should have taken and then to eliminate the data arising from the other branch. (Sometimes this is done automatically with the data entry program in the computer. The "Skip & Fill" component of SPSS/PC+ Data Entry II handles these problems nicely.)

INCONSISTENT OR ERRONEOUS ANSWERS   Sometimes respondents get confused during an interview and provide answers that don't make any sense given the flow of answers that preceded the one in question. This can also happen because of interruptions while the respondent is on the phone or while filling in the questionnaire. It's not the function of the editor to read the mind of the absent subject and then provide the supposedly logical answer. However, there are a few rare situations where the logic of the responses leading up to the answer in question is such that only one answer could have been correct. In these cases, the supervisor should decide whether to insert the right answer.

FRIVOLOUS RESPONSES   In self-administered surveys, some respondents don't have anything better to do than to play with a questionnaire and provide crazy answers. Sometimes these creative replies can be caught, but often they are easy to loose in the mass of several hundred or thousand questionnaires being edited by too few people under a lot of pressure. When these questionnaires are identified, they should be scrapped. (This situation happens only rarely in interviewer-administered surveys.)

AMBIGUOUS ANSWERS   Have you ever been tempted to put your check mark between the 3 box and the 4 box on a five-point attitude question? So have many other people, and some of them give in to the temptation. In these cases, what should be done by the editor or coder? A rule has to be established at the beginning of the coding duty; it could be always to mark the lower number, or the higher number, or to give it a blank or missing value code, or to put all of those questionnaire aside and alternate in giving a higher or a lower code to average out the responses.

COMPUTER EDITING

There are computer programs that provide for the partial editing of the questionnaire data both as they are being entered and after entry is complete. However, even though these programs do eliminate some of the tedious inspection of questionnaires, they can't be relied upon to spot all those errors that can be identified by manual coding. SPSS/PC+ Data Entry II is one such program which will help with the editing task. It has two components, "Skip & Fill" and "Clean," that allow the analyst to program various editing tasks. Consider the sequence of three questions shown in Exhibit 9.1. If the subject answers "three stores" to question 10, then the interviewer should skip to question 12 and not ask question 11. So the code for question 11 should be 0.

In SPSS/PC+ Data Entry II Skip & Fill, the logic would be written so that whenever the code 1 was typed for the answer to question 10 (see Exhibit 9.1), the code 0 would automatically be filled in for question 11 and the field would be advanced and be ready to accept the code for the answer to question 12.

Automatic cleaning can be also be accommodated within SPSS/PC+ Data Entry II. For example, in question 10 (Exhibit 9.1) the answer typed into the computer must be either 1 or 2. If the data entry clerk were to type 4 by mistake, the computer would beep and indicate on the screen that an incorrect code had been entered. A permissible code could then be typed and the program would progress to the next answer.

Some firms rely substantially or mainly on computer programs for editing the responses. They feel that the logic checking, filling of missing values for skipped questions and the time saving provide substantial benefits over manual editing.

CODING

Coding is another area that is largely hidden from the view of the client. It is also another area where non-response errors can enter the data if proper quality is not maintained. Basically, coding involves assigning a number to every

Exhibit 9.1   Example of Skip Patterns

10. Did you do all of that last grocery shopping at one store or did you go to more than one store?

GO TO Q.12	TWO OR MORE	1
GO TO Q.11	ONE STORE	2

11. At which store did you do your last main grocery shopping?

FORTINOS	1
SUPERCENTRE	2
A&P	3
MIRACLE MART	4
FOOD CITY	5
IGA	6
MR. GROCER	7
NEW DOMINION	8
OTHER	9
REF/DK/NA	0

GO TO Q.16

12. At which store did you spend the most amount of money on groceries last time?

FORTINOS	1
SUPERCENTRE	2
A&P	3
MIRACLE MART	4
FOOD CITY	5
IGA	6
MR. GROCER	7
NEW DOMINION	8
OTHER	9
REF/DK/NA	0

answer provided by the respondent, assigning that number to a specific column (or variable location) in the data record, and preparing the coded documentation for entry into the computer.

Before the questionnaire information can be entered into the computer, each possible answer to each question must have a numeric code. For example, in question 11, in Exhibit 9.2, only those ten answers pre-coded on the questionnaire from zero through 9 can be entered into the computer.

Exhibit 9.2   Pre-coding of Answers to an Open-ended Question

Q.11 At which store did you do your last main grocery shopping?

FORTINOS	1
SUPERCENTRE	2
A&P	3
MIRACLE MART	4
FOOD CITY	5
IGA	6
MR. GROCER	7
DOMINION	8
OTHER	9

Although there are exceptions to using completely numeric coding, these will not be discussed here.

CODING SELF-ADMINISTERED QUESTIONNAIRES

This used to involve transcribing every answer (or potential answer) from the questionnaire onto sheets of paper containing column numbers. These column numbers were used to indicate the proper positions for the data entry staff to type the coded answers into a computer file. A coding manual or code book was prepared and typed and the coding staff instructed in the proper coding procedure. This task was treacherous because of the high likelihood of transcribing errors, typing errors and, sometimes, the misinterpretation of coded data.

A small excerpt of a coding manual for an interviewer-administered study is presented in Exhibit 9.3. A coding manual for a self-administered questionnaire would look the same. For simple closed-ended questions such as "gender" and "distance travelled," the coding is very direct and one might wonder why a code book is really necessary. In fact, many research firms no longer use a formal code book for pre-coded questions except for special studies. Often an annotated questionnaire works as well as a complete code book and is substantially less expensive to develop and sometimes less cumbersome to use. However, open-ended questions such as that shown for variable ATT1 in Exhibit 9.3 require a coding manual so that errors can be reduced to the minimum.

The coder is often the only person who actually reads the completed self-administered questionnaires. With respect to both self-administered and interviewer-administered questionnaires, failure to assure that the coder is familiar with the background of the product or of the study may accidentally result in misinterpretation and incorrect coding of comments resulting in the true meaning of this information being lost forever (Jan Lockwood, personal communication).

Exhibit 9.3	Coding Manual Economic Impact Study Ste-Marie Among the Hurons/ The Historic Naval and Military Establishments/Old Fort William The Ministry of Tourism and Recreation—The Government of Ontario

Column	Variable	Codes	Instructions
1-4	ID	Sequential ID Numbers 0### = Ste-Marie 1### = The Establishments 2### = Old Fort William	As entered on Q with leading digits indicating sites
5	Blank	Blank	Spacer
6	SEX	1Male 2 Female 9 REF/DK/NA	Respondent's Sex
27	DISTANCE	1 = Less than 25mi (40km) 2 = 25mi (40km) or more 9=REF/DK/NA	Distance travelled from home to tourist site
28	MODE	1 = Personal car, van, light truck, motorcycle 2 = RV, camping vehicle 3 = Bicycle, walking 4 = Bus 5 = Rental Car (V.IMPORT) 6 = Cruise ship 7 = Other (non-specific) 9=REF/DK/NA	Mode of transportation taken to the tourist site on the day of the interview. Be careful to enter rental car if indicated
64-66	ATT1	001 = Thunder Bay 002 = Midland or Ste-Marie 003 = Penetanguishene or Establishments 004 = Muskoka Area 005 = Georgian Bay Area - Manitoulin 006 = Wasaga Beach 007 = Awenda Provincial Park 008 = Provincial Parks in Ontario 009 = Cottage Country - Cottage 010 = Touring-Driving - Travelling 011 = Huronia	The main destination of their trip away from home which includes their present site visit Wide variety of potential responses. Code as closely as possible to the list.

continued

Column	Variable	Codes	Instructions
		012 = Ontario or Southern Ontario	
		013 = Barrie	
		014 = Orillia	
		015 = Niagara	
		016 = Boat Cruise	
		017 = Wye Marsh	
		018 = Algonquin	
		019 = Parry Sound	
		020 = Shrine	
		021 = Toronto	
		022 = Moosinee	
		023 = Kawarthas	
		024 = Victoria Harbour	
		025 = Metro Zoo	

A coding sheet is shown in Exhibit 9.4. The coders take each question-naire and then transcribe each answer for respondent one (ID# 1) in the columns indicated in the coding manual. For Exhibit 9.3, the identification number 0001 would be entered in the first four columns, then a blank in column 5, then a 1 in column 6 if the respondent were male, and so on.

Exhibit 9.4   A Coding Sheet for the Transcription of Answers from Self-Administered Questionnaires

Column numbers

ID#	1	2	3	4	5	6	7	8	9	10	11	12	13	14	15	16	17	18	19	20	21
1																					
2																					
3																					
4																					
5																					
6																					
7																					
8																					
9																					
10																					

In the past, many researchers felt that typing coding column numbers onto self-administered questionnaires might influence the respondent or present an overly complicated visual format. Some researchers continue to feel that the self-completed questionnaire should be as clean as possible and contain only information important for the respondent's understanding of the questions and for registering the answers.

The computer literacy of the general population has increased dramatically with the diffusion of personal computers through our society. (There are even prime-time television commercials that mention the type of CPU chip in the PC.) Because of this increased acceptance of the computer and familiarity with forms which elicit data for computer entry, many researchers feel comfortable in placing the coding column numbers directly on self-administered questionnaires. The use of these column numbers and the ability to have the questionnaire format appear on the computer screen while the interviewer is keying in the data facilitate data entry directly from the self-completed questionnaire. This process avoids the expensive and error-prone intermediate step of transcribing responses onto coding sheets.

CODING INTERVIEWER-ADMINISTERED QUESTIONNAIRES

This is much less complicated than coding self-administered questionnaires, if the proper questionnaire format is used (see Chapter 7). The main coding tasks with interviewer-administered questionnaires are the coding of open-ended questions and editing the questionnaire to ensure that the coding is consistent and does not lead to obviously incorrect sequences of answers. Even though the effort is reduced, a compete coding manual must still be prepared.

CODING OPEN-ENDED QUESTIONS

This must be performed with particular attention to understanding the content of the responses and with accuracy in assigning the correct codes to answers. Many feel that open-ended questions are much more valuable than closed-ended questions because of the opportunity the respondent has for answering in his or her own words, rather than conforming to a pre-designed scale developed by the researcher.

Question: What are the most serious concerns or issues that Canada as a country is facing today?

Answer: I could talk to you for hours on this matter, but right now nothing comes to mind (Lockwood, 1990: 18).

During the coding process, the most frequently appearing answers are assigned code numbers, which are then entered into the computer and tabulated. The more specific and detailed the answer obtained from the respondent, the more chances of having meaningful (codable) answers.

Example:

"It's good" is one general, nonspecific code.

"It's smooth," "It's not biting" and "has a nutty flavour" might be three specific codes among several others, as shown below.

The questionnaire format for the question "What do you like about this cheese?" might be pre-coded and look somewhat like the questionnaire in Exhibit 9.5.

Exhibit 9.5   Example of Coding for Open-ended Question (Partly Pre-coded)

What do you like about this cheese?	CODES	
IT TASTES GOOD	1	
SMOOTH	2	
NUTTY FLAVOUR	3	
NOT BITING	4	
GOOD QUALITY	5	
NO ADDITIVES	6	
ALWAYS FRESH	7	
OTHERS	8	[37]

_____

_____

_____

_____

_____

Note that some researchers would take exception to Exhibit 9.5 because of the partial pre-coding of the open-ended question. These researchers contend that if pre-codes are provided, and if the respondent gives one of the answers, say "It tastes good," then the interviewer will have the tendency to circle the answer code and continue rather than clarifying what the answer means to that respondent.

The pre-coded categories in the questionnaire in Exhibit 9.5 would have been derived based on common sense, on prior surveys or on focus group information. The interviewer must be careful not to force-fit the subject's answer into one of the pre-coded categories for convenience. If the clarification process produces an answer on the list, then the appropriate code should be circled. However, if the respondent's answer is even a little different from those on the list, then the answer should be written verbatim on the lines provided.

The first step in coding open-ended questions is to develop the coding scheme. The researcher can write down a number of responses that the respondent is thought to be most likely to give. Let's say that the researcher comes up with 14 of these most likely responses. The coding supervisor or senior coder will then code 50 to 100 of the questionnaires using these 14 codes and will add to this list as answers are encountered that depart from the first 14 pre-coded answers.

Question: What is there in the description of the product (shampoo) that you find hard to believe?

Answer: It's hard to believe that it brings out the *natural* highlights when most people dye their hair.

Question: How likely are you to buy cereal?

Answer: I'll buy it if you arrange for the girl in the commercial to deliver it. (Lockwood, 1990:16)

It's important to make sure that the questionnaires used for the coding of open-ended questions are representative of the whole sample. If the first hundred are all from Toronto, those answers might be substantially different from answers given by respondents in the Maritimes.

Eventually, a list of answers comprising those initially anticipated plus those actually encountered will be developed. A decision is then made by the coding supervisor (possibly in consultation with the project director) as to how many of the codes represent reasonable and important responses and how many occur so infrequently that they should be relegated to the "other" category. At this point, the coding scheme for the open-ended questions is completed and it becomes part of the code book for the questionnaire. In some cases there can be from 50 to 100 code numbers for one question. The coding for the variable ATT1 in the coding manual presented in Exhibit 9.3 illustrates the translation of the answers to an open-ended question into 25 specific codes, which were then entered into the computer in fields 64, 65 and 66 of each respondent's data record.

The coding process itself slows down considerably for each open-ended question. The coders must first read and interpret the answer, then find the code that best reflects the respondent's intended meaning and finally transcribe this code onto the coding sheet. Naturally, the cost of a project increases with the number and complexity of open-ended questions.

In research firms which use a CATI system or a data entry program, the open-ends would be handled primarily within the computer program. One procedure is to type the verbatim comments directly into the computer, initially without concern for coding. At the end of the day these comments would be printed out and the coding supervisor would then assign codes, which would be entered into the computer file as part of each respondent's record of answers.

PRE-CODE ON THE QUESTIONNAIRE TO REDUCE ERRORS AND TIME

In consumer surveys, most of the questions direct the respondents to provide one answer out of a fixed number of alternatives. In most cases, those alternatives are read off to the subject as part of the question. These are closed-ended questions with pre-coded answers. Usually, the coding of these questions is very easy. In fact, in most cases it's obvious since the number indicating the answer is on the page of the questionnaire in black-and-white.

The pre-coding indicates the code number for each allowable response, as well as the column number for interviewer-administered questionnaires. The questions in Exhibit 9.6 from an interviewer-administered questionnaire illustrate this procedure.

Exhibit 9.6   Pre-coded Questions

4. In evaluating that training session, do you feel that it was excellent, good, fair, poor or very poor?

	CODE	COL#
EXCELLENT	5	
GOOD	4	
FAIR	3	
POOR	2	[10]
VERY POOR	1	

12. About how many people from your organization attended public training sessions during the past twelve months?

WRITE IN # GIVEN >> _ _ _   [_ _ _]
                                    10 11 12

If the pre-coding is not done as illustrated in Exhibit 9.6, then the coding task becomes an even more difficult procedure since each code number and column number must be looked up before the coding is done.

When respondents are asked to provide the names of several brands which they've heard of or use often, then special considerations must be used. There are two ways of providing for the coding of this type of question, the multiple variable format or multipunch format.

MULTIPLE VARIABLE PROCEDURE   This occurs when the answers to one question produce information for two or more variables rather than the customary situation where one question generates data for one variable. This occurs very often when a question asks the respondent to select two or more brands from his or her memory or from a list of brands read out by the interviewer (See Exhibit 9.7).

Exhibit 9.7   Multiple Variables (Responses) for One Question (Column Coding)

Please tell me all the brands of canned soup which you've eaten at home during the past two months? (PROBE) What others? (PROBE) Any others?

CODING

1ST MENTIONED _____   [_]
                                      51

2ND MENTIONED _____   [_]
                                      52

3RD MENTIONED _____   [_] ·
                                      53

Each of the mentioned brands will be coded as a separate variable. In this case there will be three variables, one for the brand mentioned first, one for second mention and one for third.

If the data entry were being done by using a database program, such as dBase or FoxBASE+, or by using special data entry programs, such as SPSS Data Entry II or PC Punch, then the variable names rather than the column numbers would be used. This format is shown in Exhibit 9.8. Also, in the illustration in Exhibit 9.7, at the tabbing stage variable names such as those used in the form shown in Exhibit 9.8 would be assigned to each of the column ranges. For example, the numerical code representing the brand of soup mentioned first would be entered in column 51 and would be labelled BRAND1 (meaning brand mentioned first) in the computer program, the answer in column 52 would be named BRAND2, and so on.

Exhibit 9.8   Multiple Variables (Responses) for One Question (Variable Coding)

Please tell me all the brands of canned soup which you've eaten at home during the past two months? (PROBE) What others? (PROBE) Any others?

CODING

1ST MENTIONED _____   [_____]

BRAND1

2ND MENTIONED _____   [_____]

BRAND2

3RD MENTIONED _____   [_____

BRAND3

If Heinz soup were mentioned first, and if its code were 2, then the number 2 would be written in the box above the variable name of BRAND1.

MULTIPUNCH FORMAT   This is used for the same types of questions as the multiple variable procedure. In fact, the multipunch format can give information on each of several brands mentioned as answers to the question. Multipunch data were popular when survey data were stored on computer punch cards. In an effort to have space (columns) on the cards, the data were compressed to fit into one column.

In the multipunch format, the codes for each of the three mentioned brands of soup are all entered in the same column as three separate numbers (such as column 51 in Exhibit 9.9). Consequently, the ordinal relationships of the first, second and third mentions can no longer be identified after the data entry is completed. Only the fact that three different brands were mentioned can be retrieved during the data analysis.

Not all data entry procedures or programs allow multiple punches in a column. Consequently, it's best to use the multiple column format or to be certain that a multipunch-friendly data entry program is available for the project. Although data entry programs which will handle multipunches are used at most marketing research firms and tab houses, they are often not available at most universities because of their very high cost. Also, not all statistical analysis programs can use multipunch data.

In the near future, coding will become much easier. In fact, much of the normal coding function will disappear when widespread use is made of the electronic questionnaire or Computer Assisted Telephone Interviewing (CATI).

Exhibit 9.9 Multiple Variables (Responses) for One Question (Multipunch Coding)

Please tell me all the brands of canned soup which you've eaten at home during the past two months? (PROBE) What others? (PROBE) Any others?

		CODING
CAMPBELLS	1	[__]
HEINZ	2	51
LIPTON	3	
KNORR	4	
A&P	5	

OTHER _____

OTHER _____

In this CATI procedure, the interviewer reads the question from a computer screen and enters the response on the computer keyboard. After the answer is typed, the computer verifies that the answer (code) is permissible and then automatically enters the code in the correct field of the data record. If the answer is not allowed, then the computer either audibly prompts the interviewer to correct the entry or provides both an audible alarm and screen instructions to re-ask the question and then key-in a correct and permissible answer. When the correction has been made, the next appropriate question appears on the screen and the process continues.

The potential advantages of CATI surpass the benefit of easier reading of the questions from the computer screen and easier handling of skip patterns. The separate data entry stage is eliminated, since the typed-in answers are automatically entered into the study data file. Also, data editing is greatly

---

CATI has several advantages:

1. CATI automatically brings up on the screen the next relevant question for a given respondent. This eliminates the interviewer searching through the questionnaire for the next appropriate question to ask.

2. CATI brings up one question at a time. Thus interviewer does not have to turn pages of the questionnaire and thereby lose time.

3. CATI allows for multiple and instantaneous checks on the study to keep it on track (Chakrapani, 1990).

simplified. Instead of having editors and coders manually perform those tasks, the computer can be programmed to check on all aspects of the data quality. As mentioned earlier, the electronic questionnaire will not allow the entry of numbers that do not fall within pre-specified permissible ranges. If questions are not answered because of proper following of the skip patterns, then designated missing value codes are automatically entered into the appropriate answer fields by the computer. Also, certain logic sequences can be specified. For example, if the respondent says that he is responsible for the main grocery shopping for the household and says that he did the main grocery shopping last Wednesday, then he should not give a *don't know* response when asked the name of the store in which he shopped. The computer can be programmed to pick up this logical sequence error and not allow the *don't know* response.

TRANSFORMATION OF VARIABLES   Sometimes, the questions that appear in the questionnaire are not used in exactly the same format for the data analysis. One situation in which this occurs is when a battery of scaled questions are asked. Each of the questions would be important in its own right and could be analyzed in various ways. However, they might also be combined so as to produce a summed index, which can be used in further analyses.

The questionnaire in Exhibit 9.10 was used in a study for Firestone Canada during 1980. The 13 Likert scaled questions (agree-disagree) were analyzed separately and were also combined in an index of Firestone service competence. (Notice that the third, sixth, and eighth statements are phrased in the negative.) To form the index, the scales for those negatively phrased questions were changed to positive and the answers provided by each individual were added together to provide a total measure of the attitude of the respondent regarding the overall competence of the Firestone store operation.

DATA PROCESSING

Data entry is a very simple task requiring only basic skills. The data entry staff must, of course, know the basics of the computer; however, the required level of knowledge is typically very modest.

There are several formats for data entry software. Some tabulation packages have internal provisions for the entering of data. SPSS Data Entry II for SPSS/PC+ and the Editor within SYSTAT are two programs for personal computers which both simplify data entry and, especially in the case of SPSS Data Entry II, make the cleaning of data much easier. However, many word-processing programs, such as WordPerfect, Word Star and Word, can be used for data entry, as can many spreadsheet and data base management programs.

Exhibit 9.10 Forming An Index from Likert Scaled Questions

2. Remembering back to this most recent service or purchase occasion at a Firestone store, please check the boxes below which indicate the amount that you agree or disagree with each of the following statements.

	Strongly Agree 5	Somewhat Agree 4	Neither Agree Nor Disagree 3	Somewhat Disagree 2	Strongly Disagree 1
All services were done correctly.	❑	☒	❑	❑	❑
The mechanic was courteous.	❑	❑	☒	❑	❑
Car did not run well afterwards.	❑	❑	❑	❑	☒
Work was done on time.	☒	❑	❑	❑	❑
Service manager was trustworthy.	❑	❑	☒	❑	❑
The bill was unreasonably high.	❑	❑	☒	❑	❑
The waiting area was comfortable.	❑	☒	❑	❑	❑
Staff was courteous and helpful.	❑	☒	❑	❑	❑
The location was inconvenient.	❑	❑	☒	❑	❑
The mechanic was competent.	☒	❑	❑	❑	❑
Excellent credit terms.	❑	❑	❑	☒	❑
Convenient business hours.	❑	☒	❑	❑	❑
They provided prompt attention.	☒	❑	❑	❑	❑

For the respondent who checked the boxes in the example above, the total index value is 50. The maximum is 65 and the minimum is 13, if all statements were answered.

In fact, just about any software that can produce a raw data or ASCII file can be used for data entry. If a program is used which produces a raw data file, then one additional step must be completed to set-up a usable data file in the programm that will be used for the data analysis. When the data are entered via SPSS Data Entry II or SYSTAT's Editor, the resulting data file is ready to be analyzed by SPSS/PC+ or by SYSTAT, respectively.

> Data base management programs offer the benefit of being able to establish valid ranges for the entered data. For example, if numbers between 1 and 5 are valid answers, the data base program will signal if an 8 happens to be typed by mistake. The entry clerk will then be able to correct the value prior to the entry of the next value. This checking is also part of data entry programs and CATI.

DATA CLEANING

Although the data entry programs and the data base programs have the benefit of catching data that are outside the permissible range of values, they do not pick up mistakes made in typing values that are incorrect but still permissible. For example, codes one through five might be allowable for a particular answer. If the data entry clerk were to type a seven, then the data entry program would signal that a mistake had been made. However, if the correct answer indicated on the questionnaire were a two and the clerk had entered a five, the error would be accepted. Some programs provide for logical editing or cleaning. For example, if the only logical answer to Q.6 was code 2 when the answer to Q.5 was 1, but *don't knows* were also allowed (coded 8), then a five would be rejected if typed in for Q.6.

However, logical relationships can't be used for all answers in a questionnaire since logical linkages don't exist between all sequences of questions and for all answers to each question. The only way of catching all mistakes in typing within range is through careful attention to the typing task and by verification. Often, ten per cent or more of the cases are retyped from scratch by a different entry clerk. The data in the fields for those retyped records are then compared either visually or automatically by the program. This is one of the important quality control stages of marketing research. Errors which occur during this stage are classed as non-sampling errors—they're in the data but might never be caught after the data file has been passed through the data entry department and sent on for data analysis.

DATA TABULATION

The project leader and the client are always anxious to get a quick first look at the data in a basic analysis format. If this analysis goes to the client, it's called a *top-line report*. The first quick look at the data might simply involve a set of frequencies for the key survey questions. For example, a client might want to know who the winner was in a paired taste test before he wants the complete set of computer tables. This first printout might be somewhat disappointing since there are usually a few data entry errors. After the frequencies are run out, the data errors are cleaned and a new set of frequencies are prepared. This cleaning should involve tracing any wild codes back to the offending questionnaires for verification of the coded answers.

The analysis will progress from this simple beginning to perhaps a simple ending or maybe a very complicated conclusion. The word *tabulation* is a shortened version of the term cross-tabulation, which is the next stage of data analysis after frequency distribution analysis. Tabulation, or tabbing, has become a catch-all word which includes most aspects of basic data analysis.

As with most of the functions in marketing research, tabulation is a task that is sometimes done within the project director's firm and sometimes subcontracted, in this case to a tab-house. Occasionally, the data analysis is performed by analysts within the client's own organization. Regardless of where the tabulation is done, computer software is needed to execute the analysis and to produce presentable tables. There are two types of software capable of performing tabulation. For what is traditionally known as tabulation (cross-tabs and frequency distribution), the special purpose tabulation packages are the best. These include special purpose programs, such as UNCLE or SumQuest, but they sometimes are included in comprehensive packages, such as the STAR system. Although cross-tabs can be done by statistical analysis packages, the output form might not provide the most effective medium for presentation nor for conserving space on paper.

The tabulation analysis can be done on main frame computers, on mini computers and on desktop personal computers. Personal computers can provide adequate service for many marketing research projects. In fact, with the increasing power of personal computers and the availability of tab packages, wider use will be made of micros for almost any size of tabulation task.

Jargon tends to be developed for almost any technical task over a period of time and tabulation is no exception. *Stubs, banners, banner points, breaks* and *marginals* are the five key terms for tabulation. These terms can best be illustrated through an example. Exhibit 9.11 investigates the potential of a relationship between purchase intention and age and between purchase intention and income. Typically, this analysis would be performed with purchase intention as the stub and with age and income as two variables or breaks in the banner, each with several columns or banner points.

The *banner* spans the width of the cross-tab page and can contain several variables. It's often said that the stub is broken down by the banner variables or *breaks*. In Exhibit 9.11, the *stub* is "Purchase Intention" and the banner variables or *breaks* are "Age" and "Income." The table has a total of five *banner points*, three for "Age" and two for "Income." In most commercial tab packages, the table would have also contained the frequencies for each cell in addition to the cell percentages. Some tab packages have a number of options for table formatting and also options for basic statistical analysis.

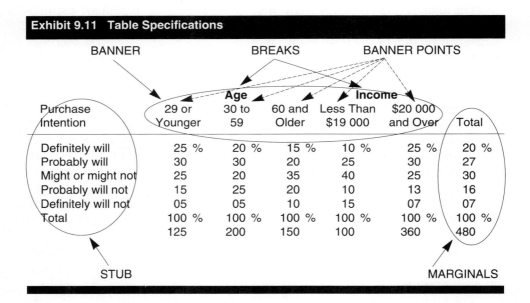

Exhibit 9.11 Table Specifications

Purchase Intention	Age — 29 or Younger	Age — 30 to 59	Age — 60 and Older	Income — Less Than $19 000	Income — $20 000 and Over	Total
Definitely will	25 %	20 %	15 %	10 %	25 %	20 %
Probably will	30	30	20	25	30	27
Might or might not	25	20	35	40	25	30
Probably will not	15	25	20	10	13	16
Definitely will not	05	05	10	15	07	07
Total	100 %	100 %	100 %	100 %	100 %	100 %
	125	200	150	100	360	480

FREQUENCIES

The first step in data analysis is to get a basic feeling for the answers provided by the respondents. Before jumping into cross-tabs or some higher data analysis, frequencies or marginals should be obtained on all of the variables represented in the questionnaire. The frequency distributions will allow the analyst to see the data for the first time in a summary fashion and will provide the ideas that will lead to more sophisticated analysis. In addition, if there are any remaining obvious coding and data entry problems, these will be discovered when the frequencies are reviewed.

Some of the data findings will be so obvious that visual inspection of the data often allows the analyst either to draw an immediate conclusion or, at least, to identify where some analysis problems might lie. When data patterns are not quite so obvious, i.e., when patterns might be interpreted differently by different people, statistical tests can be used.

In many commercial studies, a first run of marginals is not done. The client and the project director will know which cross-tabs they want prepared even before the fieldwork is begun. In fact, this is quite essential to the best questionnaire development. There's no sense in executing the study if the marketing answers can't be provided because the questions which would produce the responses that would be tabbed are not asked in the correct way. Consequently, dummy tabs should always be specified prior to finalization of the questionnaire. The tab-specifications (tab-specs) would then be waiting for the data rather than vice-versa. Because of this sequence, standard banners would be specified and run on all of the other variables as the first computer run and running the marginals might not be necessary. As an example, consider the mail survey in Exhibit 9.12 which was conducted for Firestone Canada Inc. in 1981.

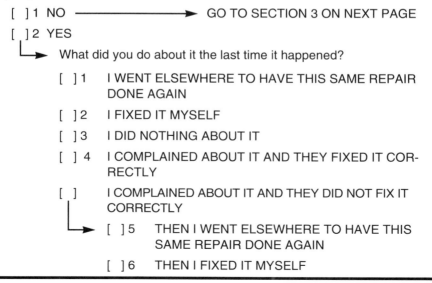

Exhibit 9.12 Actions Caused by Poor Automobile Service

In the past, did <u>you</u> ever experience the situation where your car was serviced incorrectly by <u>any</u> automative service outlet?

[ ] 1 NO —————————————▶ GO TO SECTION 3 ON NEXT PAGE

[ ] 2 YES

   ▶ What did you do about it the last time it happened?

    [ ] 1 I WENT ELSEWHERE TO HAVE THIS SAME REPAIR DONE AGAIN

    [ ] 2 I FIXED IT MYSELF

    [ ] 3 I DID NOTHING ABOUT IT

    [ ] 4 I COMPLAINED ABOUT IT AND THEY FIXED IT CORRECTLY

    [ ]   I COMPLAINED ABOUT IT AND THEY DID NOT FIX IT CORRECTLY

      ▶ [ ] 5 THEN I WENT ELSEWHERE TO HAVE THIS SAME REPAIR DONE AGAIN

        [ ] 6 THEN I FIXED IT MYSELF

Exhibit 9.13

Q.2-6   What did you do about it (poor automotive service) the last time it happened?

Reaction to poor service	Observed From survey	
	Number	*Percent*
Went elsewhere	97	18%
Fixed myself	43	8
Did nothing	16	3
Complained and fixed correctly	279	52
2nd complaint, then went elsewhere	79	15
2nd complaint, then I fixed it myself	22	4
Total	536	100%

A reasonable hypothesis based on the question in Exhibit 9.12 is that the reaction of most people to poor servicing of their cars would be to complain and then the problem should be fixed. It's obvious from the frequency distribution that 52% of the respondents (the mode) reacted in the expected manner and that the hypothesis has been confirmed. The findings are so overwhelming that no statistical analysis is needed in this case. It can also be seen that no *wild codes* (those not allowed by the question coding) can be seen in the distribution. Further, since the numbers of people who "did nothing" or who "complained again and then fixed it themselves" was so small, those groups could not easily be investigated further. Further analysis could be done on the distribution in Exhibit 9.13. For example, the distribution could be tested to see if the frequency of answers forms a uniform distribution, i.e., all of the answers occurred with the same frequency and no pattern exists in the data. (This is done for illustrative purposes in Chapter 21.) However, since the frequency of the modal response is so much greater than the others, visual inspection leaves little room for doubt in this case—except doubt of the value of further statistical analysis regarding the shape of the distribution.

CROSS-TABULATION

Although statistical analysis of the shape of the frequency distribution presented in Exhibit 9.13 is probably not worthwhile, other analysis could be enlightening. For example, the following questions could be asked:

- Do men and women react in the same manner to poor automotive service?
- Do younger people and older people react in the same manner?
- Do younger females react differently than older males to poor automotive service?
- Do higher income and lower income react the same to poor auto service?

There are often scores of questions that could follow from one frequency distribution. A good first step in answering these questions is to present the data in a *cross-tab,* a table that presents both variables in such a way that some obvious conclusions can be drawn. In many cases, additional statistical analysis helps to investigate the extent of the relationships, especially in those cases where there are no obvious conclusions.

Exhibit 9.14

Consumers' Reactions to Poor Automative Service Broken Down by Gender

	Gender		
Reaction to Poor Service	*Male*	*Female*	*Total*
Went elsewhere	17%	21%	18%
Fixed it myself	8	8	8
Did nothing about	3	3	3
Complained and they fixed it	53	49	52
2nd complaint, then went elsewhere	14	16	15
2nd complaint, then I fixed it myself	5	3	4
Total	100.00%	100.00%	100.00%
Base	381	143	524

Inspection of Exhibit 9.14 indicates that each of the reactions was attributed to about the same percentage of males and females. There are some differences, but they don't look too large. To identify whether these small differences are "significantly large" or "non-significantly small," in a statistical sense, a procedure called a chi-square analysis can be performed on the table as a whole or a z-test can be executed on pairs of percentages, e.g., are 53% and 49% significantly different or essentially the same? This procedure will be illustrated in Chapter 22.

Many marketing research projects process the data through the cross-tabulation stage and never get into any higher level statistical analysis. The client might not have a desire for the analysis or the budget might be too small to fund such an undertaking. There is nothing inherently wrong with

stopping at this stage of investigation. Each project has a certain level of sophistication which will be found during its life. More important than level of sophistication in statistics is level of understanding and ability to communicate that knowledge to the clients. These topics will be investigated in the following chapters.

SUMMARY

The stages of translating the information contained on the study questionnaires to a format that can be interpreted by non-technicians is an important, although often invisible, step in the research process. These stages are:

1. The editing and coding of answers to survey questions

2. The inputting of those answers into a computer

3. The production of computer tables

These tasks require tight quality control in order to preserve the integrity of the data that have been obtained from respondents.

Many marketing research firms place substantial emphasis on this function and take great pride in their high quality products. Although the basic concepts of this topic area can be learned fairly easily, to become fully competent in editing, coding, data entry and tabulation requires a substantial amount of experience.

NOW THINK ABOUT THIS

1. Take any questionnaire that you can conveniently put your hands on and develop a set of codes for the questions on the first two pages of the questionnaire. Write these codes down in a code book format. Now write down the cross-tabs which should be run on this data file.

2. Take a sequence of five to ten questions which have at least two skip patterns within the group. Whether or not you've had any experience with CATI or a data entry program, write down a sequence of statements that you could hand to a person who would be charged with the job of entering the answers into a data file. Make sure to indicate the missing value codes, such as *refused, don't know,* and *not applicable.* Also, determine if there is any inherent logic to a sequence of questions that would naturally cause some of the answers to the last question in the sequence to be "invalid" or "highly unlikely to occur" and others to be labelled "most likely to occur." Integrate this logic into your set of instructions. When you finish you'll have a complete set of coding and data entry instructions. Realize that these instructions could be converted fairly easily into a computer program for computerized data entry using a stand-alone data entry program or a CATI data entry program.

REFERENCES

Chakrapani, Chuck
1990   "New Specifications Improved NADbank '90." *Playback Strategy,* October 22, p.7.

Lockwood, Jan
1990   "Coders' Corner." *Imprints.* Toronto: Professional Marketing Research Society, September 1990, p.18.

Lockwood, Jan
1990   "Coders' Corner." *Imprints.* Toronto: Professional Marketing Research Society, October 1990, p.16.

PART 4

How to Analyze the Data and Communicate the Results

10 Looking: The Art of Global Understanding

WHAT YOU WILL LEARN IN THIS CHAPTER

- To visually scan and "chunk" numerical data into meaningful units
- To improve your understanding of data through techniques such as using summary figures, ordering, and reversing rows and columns
- To understand why double spacing distorts visual perception
- To use external data to understand the data better
- To elicit patterns and exceptions in numerical data
- To construct better numerical tables

SCANNING AND ORGANIZING

Once the survey is completed, the researcher is confronted with a set of computer-generated tables, usually several hundred pages long. The researcher's task at this stage is twofold: to understand the data and to communicate the results to others who might be interested.

All data analysis in marketing research can be reduced to finding patterns and exceptions in data. The task of the researcher is to identify these patterns and exceptions, add explanations and communicate them to the decision maker. Computer tables often come in a form that makes understanding difficult. A researcher can do a number of things to facilitate his or her task of understanding the data. A typical market research table is shown in Exhibit 10.1.

Exhibit 10.1 Sales Figures in Four Regions for Eight Quarters

City	Q I	Q II	Q III	Q IV	Q V	Q VI	Q VII	Q VIII
Toronto	97.49	88.51	94.94	91.15	98.98	91.49	97.18	93.12
Vancouver	37.74	34.26	36.75	35.28	37.54	35.64	37.84	36.27
Montreal	91.20	82.80	109.81	85.27	90.72	83.72	89.04	85.24
Ottawa-Hull	25.16	22.84	54.50	23.52	25.03	23.09	24.56	23.51

If you were asked to interpret the table in Exhibit 10.1, what would your conclusions be? How would you begin to analyze the table? Although the table is small with just 32 numbers, it is still daunting. To a casual observer or to a decision maker in a hurry, this table does not communicate anything meaningful. Our objectives here are to:

1. Improve the layout of the table

2. Understand the patterns and exceptions present in the table

3. Communicate the results effectively to others

These objectives can be achieved to a substantial degree by following some simple procedures.

VISUALLY SCAN AND "CHUNK"

Our first objective is to understand the structure of the information presented. When we scan the table, we find sales figures for four Canadian cities for eight quarters (two years). One thing is obvious at this stage: the table lacks both visual and conceptual focus. Visually, headings are not separated from the body of the table. Conceptually, two years' data are presented as a single unit. However, it is easier and more logical to analyze one year of data at a time and then to confirm that finding with the following year's data. To do this, we "chunk" the table by drawing lines in logical places as in Exhibit 10.2

Exhibit 10.2 Scanning and "Chunking" the Table

City	Q I	Q II	Q III	Q IV	Q V	Q VI	Q VII	Q VIII
Toronto	97.49	88.51	94.94	91.15	98.98	91.49	97.18	93.12
Vancouver	37.74	34.26	36.75	35.28	37.54	35.64	37.84	36.27
Montreal	91.20	82.80	109.81	85.27	90.72	83.72	89.04	85.24
Ottawa-Hull	25.16	22.84	54.50	23.52	25.03	23.09	24.56	23.51

Chunking: Chunking divides information into visual and logical units. In the example in Exhibit 10.2, the table is chunked between headings and body, between one year's data and the next. Such division makes tables more readable and understandable.

Remember that most computer tables are produced with no grids or visual aids to facilitate our understanding of the numbers.

ROUND TO TWO EFFECTIVE DIGITS

In the next step, we isolate the basic unit of analysis (one year's data) and then concentrate on the information in that unit. Our first concern is to make comparison within that unit as easy as possible. Patterns in data are easier to find when the numbers are rounded. The rule here is to round all numbers to two effective digits. *Effective digits are those digits that can vary from one number to another.* In our example, both the first digit and the second digit vary from city to city. Therefore, we can eliminate the decimal places.

Exhibit 10.3 Basic Analysis Unit (Rounded 1990 Data)

City	Q I	Q II	Q III	Q IV
Toronto	97	89	95	91
Vancouver	38	34	37	35
Montreal	91	83	110	85
Ottawa-Hull	25	23	55	24

Rounding: By isolating the basic unit of analysis and eliminating extra digits, we simplify our analysis. Such simplification helps us to do mental arithmetic. It is also less intimidating to the analyst and the reader. The general rule is to round to two effective digits.

There is some error associated with rounding numbers to two effective digits. But in most cases, such errors will be in the 1% to 2% range, less than the margin of error (explained later) for most figures in marketing research. Any potential loss in accuracy is more than compensated for by substantial improvement in comprehension. There are two primary reasons for this.

First, it is not easy mentally to manipulate numbers with more than two digits. For instance, it is more difficult to understand the relationship between 14.89 and 31.16 than to understand the relationship between 15 and 31 (about twice as large). Secondly, when we look at numbers such as 13.89 or 28.16, the second part of the number i.e., .89 or .16 is likely to be fresh in our memory; yet the second part is much less important (in most cases irrelevant) to our understanding of the meaning of the table.

> The first few times my controller sent me a report with figures rounded to the nearest $1000, I felt very uneasy. The report seemed lacking and incomplete. Now that I have grown used to the shorter figures, I find I round mentally all figures I look at down to two or three digits (R.A. Golde, "Sharpen Your Number Sense." *Harvard Business Review*, July-August 1966.)

USE SUMMARY FIGURES

The table still lacks focal points. There are 16 numbers in the table, but what are we comparing with what? One of the most common focal points is the average. If we compute the averages for rows and columns, then we can understand the data better. Row averages will tell us whether the sales are stable from quarter to quarter, and column averages will tell us whether sales figures are comparable from city to city.

Exhibit 10.4 Row and Column Averages/1990 Data					
City	Q I	Q II	Q III	Q IV	Average
Toronto	97	89	95	91	93
Vancouver	38	34	37	35	36
Montreal	91	83	110	85	92
Ottawa-Hull	25	23	55	24	32
Average	63	57	74	59	63

Row and Column Averages: Row and column averages provide focal points, benchmarks against which individual figures can be compared. In the table in Exhibit 10.4, it is obvious that sales figures do not vary much from one quarter to another, but vary a great deal from city to city.

PUT APPROXIMATELY CONSTANT FIGURES IN COLUMNS

When we scan Exhibit 10.4, we can see that the numbers in each row are approximately constant. For example, all numbers in row 1—97, 89, 95, 91—are around 93, the row average; in row 2, all numbers—38, 34, 37, 35—are around 36, the row average. This is not true of numbers in columns. For instance, the average of the first column, is 63, but the numbers in the column—97, 38, 91, 25—deviate from the average very widely. When this happens, the data can be presented more effectively by putting approximately constant numbers in columns rather than in rows. Exhibit 10.5 presents the information by interchanging rows and columns.

Exhibit 10.5 Approximately Constant Columns					
1990	**Toronto**	**Vancouver**	**Montreal**	**Ottawa-Hull**	**Average**
Q I	97	38	91	25	**63**
Q II	89	34	83	23	**57**
Q III	95	37	110	55	**74**
Q IV	91	35	85	24	**59**
Average	**93**	**36**	**92**	**32**	63

Constant Columns: It is easier to see patterns and exceptions in data in columns rather than in rows. Approximately constant figures are understood and interpreted better when presented in columns rather than in rows. When we read each column we see that the sales figures do not vary much from one quarter to another, but they do vary from city to city. Exceptional figures (Q III in Montreal and Ottawa-Hull) stand out when constant figures are presented in columns.

It is easier to detect patterns and exceptions in columns than in rows. For example, the third quarter figures in Montreal and Ottawa-Hull stand out very clearly as exceptional figures. There are reasons why this procedure results in better pattern/exception identification. We traditionally write figures one below another whenever we do basic calculations such as addition, subtraction, multiplication, or division and we are trained to read figures vertically. More importantly, when figures are written one below the other, our perception is not interrupted by blank spaces, i.e., our eyes do not have to scan: *97 blank 89 blank 95 blank 91 blank* and so on, they can take in a column as a unit. (This is demonstrated in the following section.)

AVOID DOUBLE SPACING

It is not an uncommon practice for researchers to use double spacing in research reports. This is particularly true of summary reports presented to management. The assumption is that such a layout is attractive and easy on the eye.

Exhibit 10.6 Rows in Double Spacing					
1990	Toronto	Vancouver	Montreal	Ottawa-Hull	Average
Q I	97	38	91	25	63
Q II	89	34	83	23	57
Q III	95	37	110	55	74
Q IV	91	35	85	24	59
Average	93	36	92	32	63

Avoiding Double Spacing: When data are presented in a double spaced format, they lose their impact because eyes are not guided to travel in any one direction. The insertion of spaces between numbers makes it difficult for the reader to see the patterns and exceptions in the data.

Unfortunately, the visual gains made thus far are lost when we use double spacing. The patterns and exceptions are less easy to see when numbers are double spaced. With this layout, each column is not seen as a single unit but as a series of numbers interrupted by blank spaces reading downwards: *97 blank 89 blank 95 blank 91 blank* and so on.

ORDER BY SIZE

Ordering the figures by their average size (in this case by column averages) lends a clearer structure to the data as seen in Exhibit 10.7. Now that we know the averages decrease as we move from left to right, we can see if the same relationship holds for each quarter. Ordering the figures is almost always helpful, but it can be crucial when we compare a large group of numbers, as, for example, the data from as many as 10 provinces.

Exhibit 10.7 Columns Arranged in Order of Average Size				
1990	**Toronto**	**Montreal**	**Vancouver**	**Ottawa-Hull**	**Average**
Q I	97	91	38	25	**63**
Q II	89	83	34	23	**57**
Q III	95	110	37	55	**74**
Q IV	91	85	35	24	**59**
Average	**93**	**92**	**36**	**32**	**63**

Ordering by Average Size: Rearranging columns in order of their average size enables us to see the patterns more clearly. Exceptions also stand out better. There are cases where such ordering may not make sense. However, whenever relevant, both columns and rows should be arranged in order of their average size.

TREAT EXCEPTIONS AS EXCEPTIONS

From our analysis so far we can tentatively infer the following:

1. Sales figures vary from city to city in the following order: Toronto, Montreal, Vancouver and Ottawa-Hull.

2. Sales figures do not generally vary much from one quarter to another.

3. There are two exceptions to the above: in the third quarter of 1990, Montreal and Ottawa-Hull registered sharp increases in sales.

What we do not know at this stage is whether sales go up in Montreal and Ottawa the third quarter of every year or whether some exceptional circumstances caused the increase in 1990. Because our data set is small, exceptional figures can distort the average figures to a substantial degree (e.g., Q III average of 74). To understand the patterns in our data, we tentatively exclude them from our averages and at the same time highlight the exceptions. Exhibit 10.8 shows the adjusted figures. From this exhibit we see that the sales figures for Toronto are 93±4, Montreal 86±5, Vancouver 36±2 and Ottawa 24±1. As noted, there are two exceptions: the sales figures for Montreal and Ottawa in the third quarter.

Exhibit 10.8 Adjusted Regional Averages

1990	Toronto	Montreal	Vancouver	Ottawa-Hull	Average
Q I	97	91	38	25	63
Q II	89	83	34	23	57
Q III	95	110 *	37	55 *	66
Q IV	91	85	35	24	59
Average	93	86	36	24	60

* Excluded from averages

Excluding Exceptional Figures: When a data set is small, using exceptional figures in calculating averages makes them unrepresentative. In preliminary data analysis, eliminating exceptional figures from averages (while highlighting this fact) aids our understanding.

USE PRIOR KNOWLEDGE

Now we have to resolve the issue of the exceptional figures in Montreal and Ottawa. If this is the only set of data we have, we may have to ask for additional information such as what actually happened in Montreal and Ottawa in the third quarter of 1990. Was there a special promotion during this time in those cities? Did the competitor have distribution problems around this time? Fortunately, in our case, we have additional data available to us. We have 1991 data that can be used to corroborate the 1990 results. Exhibit 10.9 sets out the 1991 figures.

Exhibit 10.9 1991 Data

1991	Toronto	Montreal	Vancouver	Ottawa-Hull	Average
Q I	99	91	38	25	63
Q II	91	84	36	23	59
Q III	97	89	38	25	62
Q IV	93	85	36	24	60
Average	95	87	37	24	61

Exhibit 10.9 shows that the 1991 third quarter figures for Montreal and Ottawa are not different from those of the other quarters. Exhibit 10.10 compares the two years.

Exhibit 10.10 1990 and 1991 Averages Compared

	Toronto	Montreal	Vancouver	Ottawa-Hull	Average
1987	93	86 *	36	24 *	**60**
1988	95	87	37	24	**61**
Average	**94**	**87**	**37**	**24**	**61**

* Excluding Q III

Using Prior Knowledge: Our conclusions can be supported and extended by the use of prior knowledge. In this case, the 1991 data confirmed that the Q III figures for Montreal and Vancouver in 1990 were probably exceptional.

The comparability of the two years' data (when we eliminate the two exceptional figures) would lead us to believe that, in all probability, the 1990 third quarter figures for Montreal and Ottawa are exceptional and not recurring.

USE EXTERNAL INFORMATION, WHERE AVAILABLE

So far it appears that there are no seasonal variations in sales, but sales vary from city to city. Can we go further and explain why sales vary from city to city? One possible explanation is the population size of the cities: Toronto is slightly larger than Montreal, nearly three times as large as Vancouver and about four times as large as Ottawa. That could account for the differential sales volume in these cities. When we divide the sales figures by the population figure, we obtain the per capita consumption as shown in Exhibit 10.11.

This leads to a very simple conclusion: the per capita consumption is 30. Neither cities nor seasons have any significant influence on consumption. Thus, after starting with a table of numbers that are difficult to understand, we have arrived at a model that is simple and memorable. That is not to say that every table will lead us to such simple solutions. The important point to remember is that most data contain patterns and exceptions; the procedures described in this chapter will help you identify these patterns clearly and communicate them effectively.

Exhibit 10.11 The Regional Averages and Population (in millions)					
	Toronto	Montreal	Vancouver	Ottawa-Hull	Average
Ave. Quarter	94	87	37	24	**61**
Population	3.1	2.9	1.2	0.8	**2.0**
Per Capita	**30**	**30**	**30**	**30**	**30**

Using External Information: External information can often clarify the reasons for the observed patterns and exceptions in data. A data analyst should be willing to look into relevant external information while interpreting research data.

Although all the procedures discussed in this chapter are deceptively simple, they can have considerable impact on our understanding and communication. To illustrate, let us go back to our original table.

Exhibit 10.12 Exhibit 1 Revisited								
City	Q I	Q II	Q III	Q IV	Q V	Q VI	Q VII	Q VIII
Toronto	97.49	88.51	94.94	91.15	98.98	91.49	97.18	93.12
Vancouver	37.74	34.26	36.75	35.28	37.54	35.64	37.84	36.27
Montreal	91.20	82.80	109.81	85.27	90.72	83.72	89.04	85.24
Ottawa-Hull	25.16	22.84	54.50	23.52	25.03	23.09	24.56	23.51

Criterion of a Good Table: In a good table, the readers should be able to observe easily the patterns uncovered by the analyst. The patterns in this table are difficult to observe, even if you explain them to someone. Tables like these fail the test for good tables.

We have analyzed the table at great length. Perhaps we can see all the patterns now because we know what they are. But could we have identified all these patterns when the table was presented to us in the original form? For instance, could we have seen that quarterly figures within each city do not vary very much? Or that there are only two exceptional figures in the table? More importantly, could we communicate our understanding to others? Probably not.

Not all the principles discussed can be applied to all tables. But applying as many of these principles as possible to numerical tables is likely to increase our comprehension and our ability to communicate the results.

SUMMARY

1. The research analyst is expected to understand and communicate numerical data. He or she does this by identifying the patterns and exceptions that are present in numerical tables. A table can be better understood if one follows a few rules.

   - Visually scan and "chunk" data
   - Round figures to two effective digits
   - Use summary figures
   - Put approximately constant figures in columns
   - Avoid double spacing
   - Order by size
   - Treat exceptional figures as such
   - Use prior knowledge
   - Use external information, where relevant

2. **Criterion of a good table:** In a good table, the readers should be able to observe easily the patterns uncovered by the analyst. The patterns in many tables are difficult to observe, even if the analyst explains what they are. When this happens, the tables have failed the test for good tables.

NOW THINK ABOUT THIS

1. Go to a marketing research report that you or someone else has written recently, to the statistics textbook that you used previously, or to some other book or report and pick out a table. Criticize that table in the context of scanning and chunking, rounding, organizing rows and columns, proper spacing, and comparison to similar information. If the table does not weather the criticism, re-write it using the principles explained in this chapter.

2. Obtain a copy of *Business Week*. Suggest how the "Figures of the Week" section could be improved using the principles discussed in this chapter.

REFERENCES

Chakrapani, Chuck
1976   "Numerical Information Processing." Paper presented at the Poster Session, British Psychological Society Annual Conference.

Chakrapani, Chuck
1982   "Data Analysis and Statistics." Paper presented at Statistics Canada/PMRS joint conference.

Chakrapani, Chuck
1985   "Numeracy." In N. Kotz and N.L. Johnson (eds.) *Encyclopedia of Statistical Sciences.* New York: John Wiley.

Ehrenberg, A.S.C.
1975   *Data Reduction.* New York: John Wiley.

Ehrenberg, A.S.C.
1982   *A Primer in Data Reduction.* New York: John Wiley.

Zeisel, Hans
1985   *Say It With Figures.* 6th ed. New York: Harper & Row.

11 Comparing: The Art of Using Comparison Indices

WHAT YOU WILL LEARN IN THIS CHAPTER

- To identify the difference between percentages and percentage points
- To apply percentages, percentage points and special ratios in the right contexts
- To understand how ceiling effect works and when and how to use it
- To dramatize numbers, when appropriate

USING COMPARISON INDICES

Once we have scanned and organized our data, the next step is to construct indices for comparing numbers within the table. Percentage figures are widely used as comparison indices in marketing research as well as in other contexts. Their widespread use attests to their usefulness. Yet they are not always used or interpreted correctly. Let us start with the common market research table in Exhibit 11.1.

You will note that Exhibit 11.1 gives both the actual numbers and the percentages. Percentages facilitate the perception of certain relationships in data. There are, however, several nuances to the use of percentages, some of which are explored in this chapter.

Exhibit 11.1 Overall Liking of Bobbins Ice Cream		Men	Women	Total
Like Bobbins	N	127	324	451
	%	49	44	45
Don't like	N	133	416	549
	%	51	56	55
Sample base	N	260	740	1000
	%	100	100	100

In most marketing research tables, percentages accompany actual numbers. Percentages facilitate comparisons by providing an index.

PERCENTAGES FACILITATE SUB-GROUP COMPARISONS

In Exhibit 11.1, 324 women out of a total of 740 women and 127 out of 260 men interviewed preferred Bobbins ice cream. The question whether women like Bobbins more than men cannot be directly answered if we simply look at the raw numbers. Whenever we compare two or more sub-groups, we need an index that would make such comparisons easy and meaningful. The most obvious and widely used index of comparison is the percentage. Because percentages are used so widely as an index of comparison, statements such as, "twice as many men as women like the product," can be made on the basis of percentages and are easy for readers to understand.

WAYS OF COMPARING

Two or more numbers can be compared in any number of ways. The most commonly used indices of comparison include:

- percentages
- percentage points
- special ratios

These are discussed in greater detail in the following sections. Much of the discussion in this chapter is inspired by two brilliant books: Hans Zeisel's *Say it with Figures*, which has been in print for over 40 years, and Andrew Ehrenberg's *Data Reduction* which was published in 1975.

PERCENTAGES AND PERCENTAGE POINTS

If Bobbins was used by 5% of families last year and by 10% of families this year, we can say that the usage has gone up by 5 percentage points. Or we can say that the usage has gone up by 100% (i.e., if 5 = 100%, then 10 = 200% and the increase is 200-100 = 100%).

DECIDING BETWEEN PERCENTAGES AND PERCENTAGE POINTS

How do we decide whether to use percentages or percentage points? Consider the figures in Exhibit 11.2.

Exhibit 11.2 Market Share of Bobbins and Dagenhas		
	1986	*1987*
	%	%
Use Bobbins Ice Cream	5	10
Use Dagenhas Ice Cream	20	30

Which brand is growing faster? If you use percentage points, Dagenhas is growing faster than Bobbins. If you use percentages, Bobbins is growing faster.

Given the above figures, you may state:

- Bobbins's usage has increased by 5 percentage points while the usage of Dagenhas has increased by 10 percentage points. Dagenhas's usage is growing faster.

or

- Bobbins's usage has gone up by 100% in one year while Dagenhas's usage has gone up by only 50% during the same period. Bobbins is growing at a faster rate than Dagenhas.

These two statements apparently contradict each other. Which brand shows the stronger growth? Unless the researcher is trying to twist the interpretation, this question can be answered only by setting up a meaningful criterion for the word "faster." For instance, it is easier for a product to double its market share if it has a small share to begin with. It is unrealistic for a product with a market share of 40% to double its share in the normal course of events.

Therefore, whether one should use percentages or percentage points would depend on the context and the meaningfulness of the two approaches within that context. There are no set rules, but the following guidelines may be useful.

USE PERCENTAGE POINTS UNDER COMPARABLE CONDITIONS

Whenever there are stable conditions in the market, whenever the increase and decrease indicate a trend rather than an immediate change, percentage points are meaningful. Consider the market share of a product over five years as shown in Exhibit 11.3.

Exhibit 11.3 Market Share of Nelson	
1983:	33.8%
1984:	32.4%
1985:	33.7%
1986:	34.1%
1987:	33.9%

In Exhibit 11.3 we are interested in our share of the market rather than the actual sales volume. For instance, our actual sales may go up even when our market share stays steady, if the total market is in a growth mode.

It may not be particularly meaningful to say that the market share declined 4% between 1983 and 1984 [(32.4 - 33.8) ÷ 33.8] or that it increased 4% between 1984 and 1985 [33.7 - 32.4) ÷ 32.4]. A more meaningful inference would be that the market share has been fairly stable over the 5 year period observed: 33±1 percentage points. Exhibit 11.4 shows the stable nature of Nelson's market share between 1983 and 1987.

Whenever conditions are volatile (and the underlying per cent is small), relatively small differences in figures can result in large changes in percentages without altering the market conditions in any meaningful way. Percentage points may be more meaningful in these situations. Compare the interest rates of two banks: Robem Commercial Bank gives 10% and Blynde Business Bank gives 11%. It is less confusing to state that Blynde Business Bank's interest rate is 1 percentage point higher than Robem's, than to state that Blynde Business Bank's interest rate is 10% higher [(1 ÷ 10) x 100]. However from the bank's point of view, it may be more meaningful to state that it paid out 10% more in interest than did its competitor. It should be borne in mind that the *context* is important in deciding whether to use percentages or percentage points.

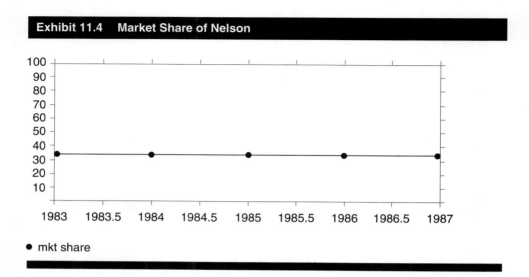

Exhibit 11.4   Market Share of Nelson

• mkt share

USE PERCENTAGES FOR CAUSAL CONNECTIONS

Percentages are meaningful when causal connections are implied. For instance, if sales went up from $3 million to $3.3 million as a result of a 5% increase in the advertising expenditure, it may be meaningful to state that a 5% increase in advertising expenditure resulted in a 10% increase in sales.

USE PERCENTAGES FOR SMALL PROPORTIONS

When the proportions are small but the underlying numbers large, percentage figures may hide the impact of small percentage changes. An example is given in Exhibit 11.5

Exhibit 11.5 Insurance Claims

| | Insurance companies | |
| | Janus | Gemini |
	%	%
Non-claimants	98.4	98.9

The percentage of non-claimants appears to be more or less the same for both companies. But what is of relevance is the percentage of claimants, which is 1.6% for Janus (100 - 98.4 = 1.6) and 1.1% for Gemini (100 - 98.9 = 1.1). When we analyze the claimant figures the chances are that Gemini is far more profitable than Janus, because Janus pays out 45% more [{(1.6 - 1.1) ÷ 1.1} x 100] in claims. Assuming that the size of the average claim is about the same for both companies, the actual percentages rather than percentage points provide more meaningful comparisons.

CAUSE AND EFFECT RELATIONSHIPS

In marketing research tables, we often use percentage figures to facilitate comparisons. In a typical marketing research table, how should we use percentages? Should we use percentages in columns or in rows, or both? There are four basic options that are available in many computer packages such as SPSS. These options are given in Exhibit 11.6.

Exhibit 11.6

In a survey, 1500 consumers were asked how many dollars per month they spent in restaurants.

Actual Numbers

$ spent/month in restaurants	Income			
	Under $20 000	$20-50 000	$50-75 000	$75 000+
Under $200	590	280	120	10
Over $200	80	140	180	100

A. Option 1: Row percentages

$ spent/month in restaurants	Income				Total
	Under $20 000	$20-50 000	$50-75 000	$75 000+	
Under $200 (%)	59	28	12	1	100% (1000)
Over $200	16	28	36	20	100% (500)

continued

B. Option 2: Column percentages

$ spent/month in restaurants	Income			
	Under $20 000 %	$20-50 000 %	$50-75 000 %	$75 000+ %
Under $200	88	67	40	9
Over $200	12	33	60	91
Total	100%	100%	100%	100%
Sample base	670	420	300	110

C. Option 3: Two-way percentages

$ spent/month in restaurants	Income				Total
	Under $20 000	$20-50 000	$50-75 000	$75 000+	
Under $200	590	280	120	10	
Row %	59	28	12	1	100% (1000)
Column%	88	67	40	9	
Over $200	80	140	180	100	
Row %	16	28	36	20	100% (500)
Column %	12	33	60	91	
Total	100%	100%	100%	100%	
Sample base	670	420	300	110	

D. Option 4: Total percentages

$ spent/month in restaurants	Income			
	Under $20 000 %	$20-50 000 %	$50-75 000 %	$75 000+ %
Under $200	39	18	8	1
Over $200	5	9	12	7
		Sample base (1500)		

Although four options are provided in Exhibit 11.6, not all of them are appropriate for presentation purposes. First let us eliminate the less effective options — Option 3 and 4. Option 3 presents both row and column percentages in the same table. In its present form, it helps neither the analyst nor the reader. The analyst is confronted with too many numbers and the reader is not guided to look at them in any particular way. Even if the analyst had no problem coping with this type of table, it should not be presented in this form to the reader. Option 4 presents percentage figures for the total sample ignoring the basic structure of the table. The basic structure of the table includes both rows and columns and they may have different patterns. Consequently, neither the analyst nor the reader is helped by total percentages.

That leaves us with two choices: either present the percentages in rows or in columns. How do we decide between the two? To answer this question, let us go back to the structure of a table. The general rule is that *percentages should be presented in the direction of the causal factor*. In most cross-tabulations, we look at two variables at a time. In Exhibit 11.6, for instance, we are looking at the relationship between the amount spent on restaurants and the income level of a consumer. In *very broad terms*, we can consider income as the potential cause of expenditure in restaurants, but not the other way round, i.e., the income level of a consumer is not *caused* by the amount he or she spent in a restaurant. The percentages should therefore be within each income group (the causal variable), rather than within each expenditure group (the effect variable). The column percentages are more appropriate here. They show the relationship between a person's income and his or her expenditure in restaurants. This relationship cannot be understood from a table that has only row percentages.

(A note on cause and effect: Please note that the terms *cause* and *effect* are used loosely here. Higher income is not really the cause and spending more money in restaurants is not really the effect. Not all people who earn large incomes spend more on restaurant meals; conversely, some consumers whose incomes are low spend a large amount in restaurants. It is more likely that "higher income probably enables a consumer to spend more on restaurant meals." We cannot make a similar statement if the variables are reversed. A statement such as "higher expenditure in restaurants probably *causes* higher income" or "higher expenditure in restaurants probably *enables* a consumer to earn a higher income" are wrong. Therefore we designate higher income as the "cause" and higher expenditure as the "effect.")

Going back to Exhibit 11.6, is the table that presents row percentages of any use at all? The answer to this depends on the objective of the analysis. Consider the situation in which our main aim is *not to identify the relationship* between income and restaurant expenditure but to *understand the structure* of the market. Row percentages may become meaningful enabling us to make statements like, "56% of all people who spend over $200 per month in restaurants earn at least $75 000 per year."

Whether the percentages should run row-wise or column-wise therefore depends on what we are trying to communicate. However, it is important to remember the general principle that *unless there is a specific reason for doing otherwise, percentages should be calculated in the direction of the causal factor.*

Some researchers believe that causality is hard to establish and the analyst should concentrate on the way the data vary and trends co-vary. For an elegant exposition of this point of view see Ehrenberg (1975).

WHEN TO USE SPECIAL RATIOS

WHEN SMALL PROPORTIONS ARE INVOLVED

Consider your chance of winning LotoLoto lottery. Let us assume that it is 0.0001% (or one in one million). Now let us consider another lottery, TripleLoto, in which your chance of winning is 0.00009%. How do you compare the two numbers? The leading zeros and the number at the end make it very difficult to assess the relative magnitude of these numbers. In such situations percentages are not an effective tool. The above information can be better summarized as shown in Exhibit 11.7.

Exhibit 11.7 Chances of Winning a Lottery

Lottery	# of chances in 10 million
LotoLoto	10
TripleLoto	9

Whenever the calculated proportion is very small (as in winning the lottery), special ratios should be preferred to percentages or percentage points. Using large numbers such as 100 000 or millions rather than one hundred as the basis for calculation is quite common wherever small proportions (e.g., murder rate, number of millionaires, etc.) are concerned.

WHEN COVERAGE IS IMPLIED

Sometimes our interest is in knowing how well we compare with others in terms of coverage. For instance, we may want to know:

- How our distribution network compares with that of our competitors

- How many doctors there are in Canada compared to other countries
- The ratio of men and women in different countries

In all these cases, percentage figures are less illuminating. To say that 0.0001% of the Canadian population are doctors, or that 51.3% of the population in Vancouver are women hardly makes the numbers come alive or makes them understandable. In these cases, we can use special ratios (Exhibit 11.8).

Exhibit 11.8 Examples of Special Ratios

Example 1

Average number of residents served by a store

In Winnipeg	11 000
In Montreal	10 000

Example 2

Number of patients per doctor

In Canada	120
In the U.S.	150

Using such ratios make the numbers more understandable. The following relationships are obvious:

- *Example 1:* Winnipeg stores serve more people (per capita) than Montreal stores.
- *Example 2:* An average doctor in the U.S. has 25% more patients than an average doctor in Canada.

Whenever large numbers are involved (as in examples 1 and 2 in Exhibit 11.8), it is preferable to round them off. Exhibit 11.9 reports the actual averages.

Exhibit 11.9 Unrounded Numbers

Example 1 (not rounded)

Average number of residents served by a store

In Winnipeg	11 073
In Montreal	9 986

When numbers are not rounded, it is difficult to see the relationships. It is not immediately obvious from Exhibit 11.9 that Winnipeg stores serve about 10% more people compared to stores in Montreal.

THE CEILING EFFECT

COMPLEX RELATIONSHIPS

Let us consider the following paradigm. You are a philanthropist and have $1 000 000 to give away to a charity, but you do not want to give it all at once. Whenever the charity is in need, you decide to give it 50% of what you have. Thus, when the charity requests your help for the first time, you give away $500 000 and are left with $500 000. When it approaches you the next time, you once again give 50% of what you have and are left with $250 000. When the charity approaches you the third time, it gets $125 000, or half of what you have at that time, and so on. In the above paradigm, we see that although the charity receives 50% of what you have everytime it approaches you, the amount the charity receives diminishes. What is left over is related to what has already been utilized. This paradigm can be called the ceiling effect paradigm.

Let us see how the concept of the ceiling effect can be used in marketing research. Three advertisements appeared in two consecutive issues of the same magazine. A readership study was carried out for each issue. The readership figures (in percentages) are given in Exhibit 11.10.

Exhibit 11.10 Comparing the Readership

| Advertisement for | % Seen the advertisements in | |
	Issue 1	Issue 2
Bobbins	40	58
Dagenhas	30	51
Nelson	20	44

Exhibit 11.10 shows that the readership has increased in each case when the advertisement was repeated for the second time. Exhibit 11.11 shows the increase both in terms of percentages and percentage points.

However, the increase in readership for the second exposure does not appear to be consistent in terms of absolute percentages or in terms of percentage points. It would appear that the increase in readership when the advertisement was released for the second time depends on the advertisement. Here is the problem: is there a consistent relationship between readership and the number of issues in which the advertisement was placed?

Exhibit 11.11 Hidden Relationships

| | % Seen the ad in | | Increase in | |
Advertisement	Issue 1 (A)	Issue 2 (B)	%*	Percentage points **
Bobbins	40	58	45	18
Dagenhas	30	51	70	21
Nelson	20	44	120	24

* Issue 2 readership increase expressed as a percentage change from Issue 1 readership. [(B-A)÷A] x 100

** The difference in percentage points in readership between Issues 1 and 2. [B-A].

If you recall the example of giving your money to the charity, you will remember that whenever some money was given out, you had less money to give the next time. Let us apply this analogy to the problem on hand. The Bobbins advertisement was read by 40% of the people when it was released for the first time. This means 60% had not read the ad the first time. When it was released for the second time, the percentage of people who read it increased by 18 percentage points. In other words, we reached 30% (18÷60) of those who had not seen it in the first issue.

Similarly, the Dagenhas advertisement was read in the first issue by 30% of the people. This means 70% had not read the ad in that issue. When the advertisement was released for the second time, the percentage of people who read it increased by 21 percentage points. Again, we reached 30% (21÷70) of those who would not have seen it in the first issue. The Nelson advertisement also reveals a parallel relationship. These are summarized in Exhibit 11.12.

Exhibit 11.12	The Ceiling Effect Model			
Advertisement	(A) Seen	(B) Not Seen (100-A)	(C) 30% of 'Not-Seen' (B x 0.30)	(D) Seen in Issue 2 (A+C)
Bobbins	40%	60%	18%	58%
Dagenhas	30%	70%	21%	51%
Nelson	20%	80%	24%	44%

It appears that there is a consistent relationship between the readership of the advertisement when we compare the first and second exposure to an advertisement. About 30% of the non-readers of the advertisement would read the ad when it appears for the second time.

The ceiling effect is based on the principle that the higher the starting percentage, the less room there is for improvement. Therefore, percentages are calculated on the basis of potential for improvement rather than on current figures.

DRAMATIZING THE NUMBERS

Sometimes the figures can be made more interesting by putting them in a much broader context. The technique that is commonly used for this purpose takes something that appears insignificant (such as one cola per year or one cigarette a day) and turns it into something that is mind boggling (such as 1.2 billion bottles of cola or $92 million in revenue). Examples of such statements are:

- If every person in China were to consume just one cola per year, the total sales would be 1 200 000 000 bottles annually.

- "If [the health lobby] caused every smoker to smoke one less cigarette a day, our company would stand to lose $92 million in sales annually" (William Hobbs, Chairman, RJR Reynolds in Kidron and Segal, 1987).

Dramatization of numbers is pertinent for communication of numbers within the firm and to the outside world through the press. Judiciously used, it clearly points out what is at stake. The dramatization technique works well in oral presentations and in instances where implications of certain events are not obvious because of the cumulative nature of the effect.

SUMMARY

To compare two or more numbers, it is advantageous to use percentage figures or ratios.

1. **Percentage points:** These are generally used when comparing relatively stable or trending figures over a period of time. For example, if your market share was 10% last year and 12% this year, your percentage point increase in market share is 2%, i.e., 12-10 = 2%.

2. **Percentages:** These use a given figure as the standard (i.e., as 100%) and measure increases and decreases from the standard. Percentages are useful when the incidence is small and minor changes may have substantial impact on the corporation or the market. Percentages are also meaningful when causal connections are implied. For example, if your market share was 10% last year and 12% this year, your percentage increase in market share is 20%, i.e., 2÷10 = 20%. In this example, last year's sales of 10% is used as the standard and the increase of 2% is expressed as a percentage of 10%.

3. **Percentage of the potential:** Sometimes the correct percentage to be computed is based on the potential figures rather than on the current figures. This strategy can be used whenever ceiling effect is in evidence.

4. **Small proportions:** When the incidence of a given characteristic is too small in a population, we usually express the incidence per 100 000 or 1 000 000 population rather than as a percentage (e.g., murder rate per 100 000 population). Sometimes we can also express the relationship as "units per one" (e.g., in Montreal, one doctor serves about 250 patients).

5. **Dramatizing the numbers:** This technique takes something that appears insignificant and turns it into something that is mind boggling (e.g., if every person in China were to consume just one cola per year, the total sales would be 1.2 billion bottles annually). The dramatization technique works well in oral presentations and in instances where implications of certain events are not obvious because of the cumulative nature of the effect.

NOW THINK ABOUT THIS

1. Go to your university or metropolitan library and obtain a report that has been written on some project area. Find two cases where percentages have been used in tables and two cases where percentage points have been used. Write a short criticism on why the percentages and percentage points were or were not used properly.

2. Consider the ceiling effect described in this chapter. Draw a graph that illustrates the ceiling effect portrayed in Exhibits 11.10 and 11.12. Find or make up at least one other example of the ceiling effect in business.

REFERENCES

Ehrenberg, A.S.C.
1975   *Data Reduction.* New York: John Wiley.

Kidron, M., and Segal, R.
1987   *The Book of Business Money and Power.* London: Pan Books Limited.

Zeisel, Hans
1985   *Say it with Figures.* 6th ed. New York: Harper & Row.

12 / Telescoping: The Art of Sub-group Analysis

WHAT YOU WILL LEARN IN THIS CHAPTER

- To ask the right questions about the data
- How to start with a global understanding of the data
- To carry out sub-group analysis systematically
- To uncover hidden relationships in data
- How sub-group analysis can contradict initial findings

TWO ASPECTS OF DATA ANALYSIS

The researcher receives the results of market research in the form of cross-tabulations (commonly called cross-tabs). Cross-tabs are simply the results of the study tabulated systematically by different sub-groups of the sample. Thus, for example, each question in a survey may be tabulated by age, sex, income group and so on. A typical set of cross-tabs consists of all questions tabulated by all relevant demographic groups. At this stage you, as a researcher, have two functions. One, you should be able to understand the implications of any such table; two, you should be able to answer the question: when you put it all together, what does it mean?

TEASING THE MEANING OUT OF DATA

ASKING QUESTIONS ABOUT THE DATA

Under normal circumstances, your client would expect you to answer a few questions through your analysis. Such questions are generally related to the objectives of the study. But usually there are no guidelines as to what interpretation a report should contain. Hence, it is the analysis, interpretation and presentation that distinguish a good researcher from a mediocre one. A mediocre researcher simply tries to answer the questions posed by the client, sometimes without even understanding the implications of the numbers. A good researcher constantly carries out an internal dialogue with himself or herself trying to understand the meaning and implications of the data that are being interpreted.

You should try to ask more questions of yourself and provide more interpretation than has been strictly requested by the client. To the extent that data analysis is an art, it cannot be fully taught. However, in the example provided below, some questions that may be asked by a good analyst are given in boxes. You may want to add your own questions at various stages or substitute other questions.

BEGINNING WITH THE TOTAL COLUMN

Data analysis starts with broad conclusions based on the total sample. These conclusions are revised and expanded as the analysis is extended to subgroups of the population. The starting point of any data analysis in marketing research is a set of straightforward tables or cross-tabs. As mentioned earlier, in standard cross-tabs, answers to each question are tabulated by different groups of people. As an example, let us analyze the table below. We begin with the "total" column in Exhibit 12.1.

Exhibit 12.1 The Total Column	
Prefer	*Total %*
Brand A	50
Brand B	50
Sample base	*1000*

When you start analyzing data, you should first understand the global patterns. The total column is a good place to begin.

You can use the information in Exhibit 12.1 to describe the market at the time of the interview and to predict the future, i.e., if nothing drastic happens, you would expect to find the same patterns of preference for a while to come.

Looking at the total column in Exhibit 12.1, your first tentative conclusion is that both brands are equally preferred. Yet, this information is only the beginning of data analysis. To really understand the data you need to go much further with cross-tabs and often beyond, to other analysis.

At this stage, you may want to think about issues such as:

Are the two brands really equally popular? Are their market shares comparable? Are people who prefer Brand A very different from those who prefer Brand B, or are they similar?

EXTENDING THE ANALYSIS TO SUB-GROUPS

The next step is to see whether this pattern holds for different sub-groups in the population. For example, do consumers belonging to different gender groups, age groups, and income groups prefer Brand A equally? If so, do they prefer it to the same extent as the total population? Look at the tabulation by sex presented in Exhibit 12.2.

Exhibit 12.2 Extending the Analysis

Prefer	Total %	Men %	Women %
Brand A	50	60	40
Brand B	50	40	60
Sample base (N)	1000(100%)	500(100%)	500(100%)

The second step in data analysis is to extend the initial findings to sub-groups. Initial findings may or may not hold for sub-groups.

Now we begin to modify our tentative conclusion. There are measurable preferences between products, but they differ depending on the sex of the consumer. Men prefer Brand A much more than do women; women prefer Brand B far more than do men.

At this stage, you may want to think about issues such as:

Is this the traditional pattern of preference? Why does Brand A appeal more to men than to women? Is it because your brand has some special features that appeal more to women? Is it because of your advertising campaign? Something else?

It appears from Exhibit 12.3 that as a person's income increases, his or her preference for Brand A also increases. How about different income groups?

Exhibit 12.3 Introducing an Alternative Variable

Prefer	Total	Personal Income		
		<$20 000	$20-50 000	$50 000+
	%	%	%	%
Brand A	50	45	52	56
Brand B	50	55	48	44
Sample base: 1000(100%)		*400(100%)*	*400(100%)*	*200(100%)*

Additional variables are introduced into the analysis in a systematic way.

At this stage, you may want to think about issues such as:

What is it about Brand A that appeals to higher income groups? Is Brand A expensive? Is it available only in exclusive outlets? Does it have anything to do with the marketing or advertising strategy adopted by Brand A?

Following the above example, you may continue to analyze the data with other breakdowns.

MISLEADING ALTERNATIVE BREAKDOWN ANALYSIS

The analysis of data by a series of alternative breakdowns such as sex, income group, etc., forms the basis of cross-tabulation analysis. Yet using alternative breakdowns exclusively can lead to an incomplete and, at times, even misleading interpretation.

Let us look at the example above. We concluded that Brand A is preferred by men. We also concluded that there is a relationship between a person's income and brand preference. Are these preferences unrelated to each other? Is it possible that the preference is related to sex but *not* to income?

ADDITIONAL FACTORS CAN ALTER OUR INTERPRETATION

Consider the following table which breaks down the income groups by the sex of the respondents (Exhibit 12.4). Now a different picture is beginning to emerge. Although looking at the income groups we concluded that higher income groups prefer Brand A, breakdown of income groups by sex suggests that the preference is constant across different income groups.

Exhibit 12.4 Combining Explanatory Variables

Men

Prefer	Total %	<$20 000 %	$20-50 000 %	$50 000+ %
Brand A	60	60	60	60
Brand B	40	40	40	40
Base	500	100	240	160

Women

Prefer	Total %	<$20 000 %	$20-50 000 %	$50 000+ %
Brand A	40	40	40	40
Brand B	60	60	60	60
Base	500	300	160	40

To understand the interrelationships, we need to consider more than one variable at a time. In the above example, sex and income are considered together.

The apparent increase in preference for Brand A in higher income groups that we saw earlier is the result of a higher proportion of men (who prefer Brand A) in these groups. It is likely that this factor, rather than the *income level* of the respondents, determines the preference. Because, in our example, there are proportionately more women in the lower income groups, it initially appeared that income is directly related to preference.

Introducing an additional variable can thus alter our conclusions: sometimes we may find a hidden relationship, sometimes we may find that an apparent relationship disappears, and at other times we may find that the strength of a relationship has changed.

Whenever you see the apparent influence of several variables, you may want to think about issues such as:

Are the influencing variables really independent? Is it likely that the relationship in some cases is just incidental? Which variable is really related to the variable under consideration?

THE ROLE OF EXPERIENCE

How will an analyst know which variable to use for further breakdown? It is neither possible nor desirable to try various combinations. It is not possible because the number of combinations of variables will be too many; it is not desirable because the analysis will become time consuming, mechanical and, in all probability, confusing.

In practice, breakdowns of the data by different variables are obtained based on past experience or the researcher's hypotheses as to the nature of the underlying relationship. Although there is no real substitute for experience, a beginning data analyst should constantly be asking himself or herself whether there is yet another way of looking at the data.

THE ART OF DISTRUSTING THE OBVIOUS

APPEARANCE AND REALITY

Suppose a survey of motorists reveals two facts:

- 70% of all accidents are caused by 5% of drivers
- Over 85% of all accidents happen within 8 kilometres of the driver's residence or place of work.

On the basis of these two findings, a researcher can recommend the following courses of action:

- A small group of drivers (5%) are responsible for most of the accidents (70%). If we can identify these drivers and make it difficult for them to renew their licences, we will be in a position to decrease the number of accidents.
- Since most of the accidents happen within 8 kilometres of a driver's residence or place of work, it is even more important to use seat belts for shorter trips than for longer trips.

Such conclusions appear logical, but they can be wrong.

Vanishing Relationships

Whenever our analysis shows strong relationships, it is important to consider other variables that might have generated such relationships.

In the first example, although there is a relationship between some drivers and accidents, it may have nothing to do with those drivers being careless or incompetent. It is even possible that they are safer drivers than those who were not involved in any accident. Let us consider the possibility that accidents are related to the number of kilometres driven—you are more likely to be involved in an accident if you drive 80 000 km a year rather than 8000 km during the same period. Since only a small proportion of drivers are likely to drive a large number of kilometres, it follows that a small proportion of drivers would be involved in a large number of accidents. If, on the average, a person is likely to be involved in an accident for every 32 000 km driven, a driver who drives 32 000 km a year is likely to be involved in an accident every year, while a person who drives only 3200 km may not get involved in an accident for 10 years. The real relationship may be between the number of road kilometres and accidents rather than between certain individuals and accidents.

In the second example, short trips are considered particularly accident prone because 85% of all accidents happen on short trips. But this statistic may reflect that most trips *are* short. Fewer accidents happen on long trips simply because most of us take fewer long trips.

Emerging Relationships

There are instances where preliminary results show no relationship between two variables. Yet when we identify a third variable that is confounding the relationship, a new picture emerges. Suppose a study reveals that households that consume large quantities of junk food are about as healthy as households that consumer small quantities of junk food.

Exhibit 12.5 Junk Food Consumption and Health

Household consumption of junk food*	Average health score**
20 or more	77
10-19	78
9 or less	79

* Score on "Junk food consumption index"
** Higher scores mean more healthy

It would appear from Exhibit 12.5 that people who eat junk food are about as healthy as those who don't. A closer look at our problem shows that junk food consumption and health score should be studied at the individual level and not the aggregate household level. It is the individuals—not the households—that consume junk food. Therefore we need to relate the health scores to individual consumption of junk foods, rather than to household consumption. It we adjust the household "junk food consumption index" by the number of members in that household, we get the individual per capita consumption of junk food. Retabulation of results shows the patterns in Exhibit 12.6.

Exhibit 12.6 Using the Appropriate Units

Junk food per person*	Health score
20 or more	65
10 - 19	74
9 or less	86

* Score on "Junk food consumption index"
When we use inappropriate units for comparison, we are likely to get misleading results.

How did this reversal happen? Let us start with the hypothesis that people who live alone are likely to consume more junk food than those who live in larger households. However, larger households are likely to consume more junk food simply because they have more household members. Higher consumption of junk food in single-person households is thus counterbalanced by the greater number of consumers in larger households. When we take into account the household size, the effect of the *confounding factor* (the effect of the number of persons in a household) is eliminated and the true relationship emerges.

LATENT EFFECTS OF CONFOUNDING VARIABLES

In all of the above examples, the introduction of an additional factor changed the nature of the initial relationships observed. When this happens, the additional factor (commonly called the confounding variable) is said to have had a *latent effect* on the true relationship. Because their effect is latent, confounding factors are not always easy to identify. Also, if data have not been collected on the latent effect variables, then their effect cannot be measured. Constant questioning of apparent relationships and prior experience contribute to the identification of confounding variables' effects.

CAUSAL IMPLICATIONS

Let us consider the following two propositions:

1. Those who own cottages tend to buy more insect repellents.
   The reason: Cottages are located in areas that attract insects.

2. Widowed people tend to have greater health problems.
   The reason: Widowed people are, on the average, older. Older people tend to have more health problems.

In both instances, the introduction of an additional variable provides an additional explanation of the relationships found initially. Yet in the first example the relationship is real while in the second example the relationship is spurious. Let us explore this further.

In example 1, the relationship can be expressed as follows:

Going to the cottage ——> Facing insects ——> Buying repellents

In example 2, the nature of the relationship is different:

Growing older ——> Higher probability of being a widowed person

Growing older ——> Higher probability of having health problems

In other words, while facing insects is the cause of greater use of insert repellents, being a widowed person is not the cause of increased health problems. Becoming a widowed person and having health problems are both caused by old age. To understand the difference between the two examples consider this: The person who faces insects when he goes to his cottage will be rid of the problem if he stops going to the cottage, but a widowed person having health problems will not be rid of them if he or she remarries (except perhaps for the psychological effect that marriage has on one's physical condition). Hence the relationship between a person's marital status and health is called *spurious*.

It is possible to make profitable marketing decisions based on spurious relationships. However, doing so is risky for the following reasons:

1. Since the spurious relationship is only a proxy to the real relationship, marketing efforts–even when profitable–will be less focused.

2. When marketing conditions change, lack of understanding of the real relationships among marketing variables can lead to serious errors in judgment.

SUMMARY

1. In data analysis, our first priority is to understand the data from a global perspective. The analyst uses his or her global findings as working hypotheses for further analysis.

2. Using sub-group analysis can substantially alter our initial conclusions:
   • In some cases, the observed relationships can disappear
   • In other cases, new relationships can emerge.

   Such hidden relationships are call *latent relationships.*

3. If the relationship between two variables disappears when we take into account a third variable, the initial relationship is called *spurious*. To make proper marketing decisions, it is important to understand whether the obtained relationships are real or spurious.

NOW THINK ABOUT THIS

1. Produce a cross-tabulation table from a data set available to you, or select a table from a report or book. For the tables, hypothesize the hidden relationships that might lurk behind the variables presented in the table. These hidden relationships are sometimes referred to as concomitant variation. In the table you produced from the data file, perform other cross-tabs to tease out the meaning of the data.

2. Go to a library and select an annual report for an organization. As discussed in the section on distrusting the obvious, write a list of questions which you would like answered relative to one or two tables that appear in the report.

13 Anchoring: The Art of Using Simple Paradigms

WHAT YOU WILL LEARN IN THIS CHAPTER

- How the anchoring process works
- To use a variety of anchoring procedures such as
  - objectives anchoring
  - accountability anchoring
  - polarity anchoring
  - triangulation anchoring

LOOKING FOR RELEVANCE: THE UNTAUGHT ART

Experienced data analysts know what to look for in raw data. However, they may not be able to describe the process by which they are able to find patterns and exceptions in data. A beginning data analyst is at a distinct disadvantage since experienced data analysts do not–often cannot–describe the process by which they arrive at conclusions based on a set of data. Books on data analysis appear to concentrate on the statistical treatment of the data rather than on the organizing and understanding of the data that should precede statistical tests.

Inexperienced data analysts tend to resort to one of two ways of coping with such a situation. They simply follow the sequence in which the questions are asked in the questionnaire and interpret consumer responses to each question; or they interpret each computer table in the order in which it is generated. Both these methods are either sterile or meaningless or both. When analysts follow the questionnaire sequence, they ignore the fact that the questionnaire sequence is related more to the ease with which a set of questions can be answered than to how the data should be analyzed or presented. When analysts follow the sequence presented in computer tables, the overall meaning of the survey is usually lost. It is difficult to make sense of reports that, page after page, summarize the computer tables in words.

What is an inexperienced data analyst to do? While there can be no substitute for experience, a beginning data analyst can benefit from using simple paradigms and models of reality. While models do not necessarily add anything to our understanding of the data, they are very good heuristic devices for new data analysts (and at times are useful even for the experienced). They help the analyst to focus on the central themes of the research project. These models anchor analysts to basic analytic structures and enable them to look for relevance.

OBJECTIVES ANCHORING

The most logical way to start the analysis is by relating it to the study objectives. Once this is done, the analysis is expanded around that central theme with supporting evidence, related facts and limiting circumstances. This is known as objectives anchoring. As was seen earlier, the study objectives were critical to the initiation of the project. The objectives were also vital to the design of the questionnaire. Because of this flow, it makes perfect sense that the data analysis process be focused on the objectives and hypotheses stated at the beginning of the project design process.

Let us consider a project for which one of the objectives is to estimate the market share of Nelson. The analyst may want to proceed as follows (questions that the analyst would or should naturally ask are given in italics):

What is the estimated market share of Nelson?
The market share of Nelson is 14%.

Who are the closest competitors?
Dagenhas with 12% market share and Bobbins with 10% market share compete most closely with Nelson. The rest of the market is fragmented with less than a 3% share each.

Are all brands strong in all regions of the country?
Dagenhas has a strong presence in Quebec with a 25% market share, while Bobbins dominates the Western market with a 23% share. Nelson's market share is more or less the same across the country.

Are there demographic differences in usage?

Bobbins is very popular with younger people. No distinct demographic patterns are evident for the other brands.

Is usage related to the price of the product?

Bobbins is the most expensive product in the market followed by Nelson and Dagenhas. The prices of other brands also vary widely. When we compare the prices and market shares of different brands, no relationship is evident between the price of a product and its market share. Either this product category is not price sensitive or the range of prices is not significant for the consumer. (Alternative explanations are possible. As the analyst gains experience, he or she is likely to come up with a greater number of alternative explanations and choose the most plausible one.)

Who is gaining, who is losing?

Dagenhas's market share appears to have declined to 12% from 15% two years ago, while Bobbins seems to be steady at 10% for the past two years. Nelson has gained 2 percentage points—from 12 to 14%—over two years. (Please note that it may be necessary to use information collected outside the present study—such as market shares two years ago—to interpret numbers obtained in a given study meaningfully.)

As the above example shows, for every objective there are several implicit questions that need answering. The implicit questions are the hooks that are anchored to the main theme, which in this case is one of the objectives of the study.

This type of analysis can be continued until the relevant questions are exhausted for the first objective. Then another objective of the study can be chosen and the process repeated. Once all the appropriate information is thus consolidated, the report can be organized around the objectives of the study and presented with supporting tables.

THE ART OF ASKING QUESTIONS

The beginning data analyst may wonder how to think up a series of questions that are relevant to the study objectives. Again, there are several heuristics devices that can be used to arrive at relevant questions:

1. Ask what, who, why, where, when and how of the central themes.

What: *What are the market shares of Nelson and its competitors?*

Who: *Who are the users (heavy, medium and light)? Is the market segmented?*

Why: *Why are the market shares the way they are?*

Where: *Where are they strong? Where are they weak?*

When: *When did they achieve their share? Are they growing or declining?*

How: *How do we account for these shares? What are the relevant factors?*   *(Price, quality, etc.)*

2. Assume the role of the decision-maker and think of the questions you may want answered by the researcher. Think of being at the presentation meeting. What questions will your client's boss want answered first?

3. When analyzing an objective, go through the questionnaire and list all the questions that have a bearing on the objective. Then formulate marketing questions based on the available information.

ACCOUNTABILITY ANCHORING

In most surveys, we collect information on consumers at various levels: demographics, product attribute judgments, likes and dislikes, etc. In addition, we have information on seasonality, availability and other extraneous factors. We can use accounting anchors to understand the data. Consider the purchase of expensive cars. Suppose our survey shows the data in Exhibit 13.1.

Exhibit 13.1 Distribution of Ownership of Expensive Cars	
Age group	*%*
18-24	15
25-49	40
50 +	45
Total	100%

Ownership of expensive cars is about three times higher in the older age group than in the younger age group. But why? How do we account for our results? One of the most obvious explanations is that there are more people in the older age group than in the younger age group. Exhibit 13.2 presents the population distribution to account for the differential ownership of cars.

There appears to be some relationship between the number of people in a group and the ownership of expensive cars. This becomes evident when we combine the two tables in Exhibit 13.3.

Exhibit 13.2 Population Distribution

Age group	%
18-24	28
25-49	34
50 +	38
Total	100%

Exhibit 13.3 Population Distribution and Ownership of Expensive Cars

Age group	Ownership %	Population %
18-24	15	28
25-49	40	34
50 +	45	38
Total	100%	100%

Population counts account for some of the discrepancies in ownership; the 18-24 age group has fewer people and fewer owners of expensive cars. But the accounting is by no means complete. It is obvious that the ownership is proportionately greater among the higher age group than in the younger age group. In any case, if the ownership is directly related to population size then there is nothing more of interest to the marketer.

To eliminate the effect of the size of the above groups, we can recompute the percentages *within* each group to show the incidence of expensive car ownership within each group (see Exhibit 13.4).

Exhibit 13.4 Ownership Within Age Groups

Age Group	Owners	Non-owners	Total
18-24	5%	95%	100%
25-49	12%	88%	100%
50 +	12%	88%	100%

From Exhibit 13.4 it is obvious that the differences in ownership between the age groups 25-49 and 50+ have disappeared once the size of the group has been taken into account. In other words, we have accounted for part of the difference initially found in the data, but we still have to account for the fact that ownership of expensive cars is indeed low among the younger age group.

If we continue with our accounting anchors, we may hypothesize several reasons for the cause of this discrepancy:

- Young people are turning away from ostentation these days; they do not buy expensive cars.
- Expensive cars are considered old-fashioned and are therefore not popular among young people.
- Young people cannot afford expensive cars.

Looking at the results once again, no real trend in the data appears: people in the 25-49 age group have the same level of ownership as the 50+ age group. It is likely that people under 25 may not have adequate income to buy and support an expensive car. We now try to account for the differential results by income. We retabulate the results to find out if income is indeed a factor (see Exhibit 13.5).

Exhibit 13.5   Ownership of Expensive Cars Per 10 000 Adults

	Income	
	$40 000 or Less	*Over $40 000*
Per 10 000 consumers	9	50

The results indicate that ownership is indeed a function of income. Ownership of expensive cars is five times higher among those who earn over $40 000 than among those who earn under $40000. It also appears reasonable to hypothesize that people in the 18-24 age group are low income earners. We can retabulate the income category by age groups (see Exhibit 13.6).

Exhibit 13.6   Car Ownership, Age and Income

Age Group	*Income*		*Total*
	$40 000 or less	*Over $40 000*	
18-24	95%	5%	100%
25+	70%	30%	100%

Two groups (25-49 and 50+) are combined since the results showed that there is no evidence of differential ownership in these two groups.

In Exhibit 13.5 we saw that for every 9 expensive cars owned by the lower income group, the higher income group owned 50 such cars. Let us apply this relationship to each sub-group (Exhibit 13.7)

Exhibit 13.7 Expensive Car Ownership Per 1000 Adults			
Age	Income		Total
Group	$40 000 or less	Over $40 000	ownership
18-24	0.95 x 9 +	0.05 x 50 =	11.05
25+	0.70 x 9 +	0.30 x 50 =	21.30

The analysis in Exhibit 13.7 shows that the ratio of ownership between the two groups is approximately 11 to 21. This compares well with the earlier relationship we found between the two groups which was 10 to 24 (or 5 to 12 as noted in Exhibit 13.4). You might want to note that even when we take income into account, ownership is still relatively high in the higher age group.

At this stage the analyst can accept income as the explanatory variable since it explains most of the variations among the sub-groups or he may look for more variables to explain remaining variations.

SELECTING VARIABLES FOR ACCOUNTING ANCHORS

Once we identify the relevant variables for accountability analysis, it is a fairly simple task to incorporate them into the analysis. But how do we know which variables are relevant? For example, we could have started our analysis in the previous example with the sex of consumers rather than with the age of consumers. In fact, in a typical marketing research project, data are collected on a number of variables and if one's hypotheses prove to be false, one could spend a considerable amount of time analyzing data. Most data analysts select the appropriate variables based on experience. The beginning data analyst can use the following criteria in selecting suitable variables for analysis:

1. What factors are most likely to influence the variable under consideration? (List all the variables that are considered relevant. Are they within the scope of the study?)
2. Among these, which ones are the most important? (Order them by their importance—use study objectives as the guide.)
3. Which ones are concrete? (If two or more variables are about equally important, choose the variable that is concrete or directly measurable.)

The third criterion is an important one. It states that our explanations should be parsimonious and should not hypothesize complex concepts when simple ones will do. For example, if the income level of a consumer can explain his or her buying behaviour we should not use a complex explanation such as the psychological make-up of the consumer. (This principle has its origins in *Occam's razor*, formulated by William of Occam, a Franciscan scholastic philosopher of the 14th century, who suggested that entities of thought ought not be multiplied except through necessity.)

POLARITY ANCHORING

Most marketing research is aimed at providing input for marketing. Marketing, in turn, is aimed at manipulating marketing variables to achieve a given objective. For example, marketing research can provide reasons that explain why the market share of a given brand is going down. Marketing can use this information to halt the slide and perhaps increase the market share. To make the research results more meaningful to the marketer, the researcher may want to use the polarity anchoring model.

The polarity anchoring model suggests that there are factors that attract (positive) and there are those that repel (negative). The resultant effect determines consumer behaviour. Let us consider the problem confronted by the marketing manager of Nelson ice cream (see Exhibit 13.8).

Exhibit 13.8 Polarity Anchoring: An Example	
Problem	Nelson ice cream is losing its share to Dagenhas
Negative factors	• Nelson is too sweet • Nelson is not widely available
Positive factors	• Dagenhas is expensive • Dagenhas's advertising is not very persuasive

Exhibit 13.8 can be further expanded to include positive factors for Nelson and negative factors for Dagenhas. (Please note that what is negative for Dagenhas is positive for Nelson and vice versa.) The marketer has greater control over the negative factors than over the positive factors. It is easier to make Nelson less sweet than to make Dagenhas less expensive.

The negative factors of competitors can also be the positive factor for your brand, but this is not automatic. The negative factors of competitors can be used to your advantage only if a marketing strategy is developed to take advantage of those factors. Conversely, the positive factors of your competitors cannot be negated simply by emulating them. As mentioned before, specific strategies are required to lure customers away from the competition.

The polarity anchoring model focuses the researcher's thinking and provides actionable input for the marketer.

TRIANGULATION ANCHORING

Many marketing research studies are based on small samples, high non-response rates, imprecise questionnaires and other imperfections. They are carried out once, with one sample and in one place. It is neither feasible nor cost-effective to carry out perfect studies to understand the underlying marketing factors. To add greater weight to our conclusions we may use a procedure known as *triangulation*.

Triangulation refers to the confluence of evidence from two or more independent sources. Each of these sources in itself may not be strong enough to support the conclusion drawn, but together they add support to the finding.

Consider the research finding that people claim to drink more light beer these days compared to two years ago. If the finding has come from a research study that surveyed a small number of people, it is subject to a large margin of error and we will want to look for evidence from other sources.

- **From industry statistics**: Is more light beer brewed now than it was two years ago?

- **From health surveys**: Are people more careful about their weight now than they were two years ago?

- **From published surveys**: Is there any other published study that would confirm the finding?

If all the evidence points in the expected direction, we can have greater faith in our results. One advantage of triangulation is that each study in itself need not be perfect. It is only necessary that each go in the same direction.

Two cautionary notes about using the triangulation technique:

1. Resist the temptation to ignore contrary evidence.

2. The *evidence should be independent*. If a conclusion drawn on the basis of a survey is supported in three other places in the same survey, it will not be independent and cannot be used as the basis for triangulation. The study can be faulty and the same fault might have given rise to similar faculty conclusions in three different places.

WHEN TO USE DIFFERENT ANCHORING TECHNIQUES

The data analyst should always start with the objectives anchoring model, using the study objectives as central themes. This will guarantee that the analysis will fulfill the minimum requirement of any study: accomplish the primary study objectives. During the course of such analyses, the analyst may want to use the accountability anchoring model to make sure that the obtained results can be adequately explained.

Whenever there is evidence of competing factors—such as likes and dislikes for a given brand—the polarity anchoring model is appropriate. The polarity anchoring model is particularly useful when we analyze the competitive marketing environment.

The triangulation anchoring model is useful when we are not sure of our results because of sampling and non-sampling errors (to be discussed later) or the results appear to contradict our expectations. It is also useful when major marketing decisions have to be based on the research results.

SUMMARY

1. Anchoring is a heuristic device that enables the data analyst to view the data in a clearly focused way. Anchoring can be done in several different ways, the most common of which are given below.

2. **Objectives Anchoring:**
   - Choose a few important central themes for your analysis. (Study objectives are a good place to start.)
   - Ask a series of questions (hooks) that will explain and expand the chosen themes.

3. **Accountability Anchoring:**
   - When you analyze the data, you may want to account for the results by finding the variables that explain the results.
   - The variables for this purpose are chosen on the basis of experience, logic and simplicity.

4. **Polarity Anchoring:**
   - In understanding research results, the analyst should attempt to understand both negative and positive factors. Such factors should be understood in terms of the product under consideration and its competitors.

5. **Triangulation Anchoring:**
    - Triangulation is the process of gathering evidence from two or more different sources to confirm the research results obtained independently.

NOW THINK ABOUT THIS

Select an important table from an analysis which you have recently conducted. What accountability anchors did you use or could you have used? How would you resolve contentious issues arising out of accounting for variation if you didn't have these anchors?

   a. Identify triangulation anchors that could be used. How would you use them?
   b. Identify polarity anchors that can be used.

14 Reckoning: The Art of Data Reduction

WHAT YOU WILL LEARN IN THIS CHAPTER

- How to calculate the averages, mean, median and mode
- How to calculate the variability measures, range, mean absolute deviation, variance, and standard deviation
- The meaning of standard error and how to determine the margin of error
- To determine whether two groups are different from a statistical point of view

NUMERACY AND STATISTICS

As a market researcher, you are expected to interpret information contained in numbers. If 20% of the people use your product, what does it mean? Is an overall average of 5.6 good or bad? If a competitive brand scores an overall average rating of 5.9 should you be worried? In order to interpret these numbers, market researchers make use of several tools of their trade. These tools include prior knowledge, background information, and statistics.

Many people seem to think that one should be mathematical to understand and communicate the implications of data. This is not true. Mathematics or statistics play only a minor role in numeracy. Statistics is only one of the several tools available to the researcher. Blind application of statistics to data analysis will do more harm than good. A sound knowledge of basic statistical principles is a prerequisite for any marketing researcher. But it should be understood that it is no substitute for numeracy. A researcher should develop statistical skills in addition to—and not as a substitute for—numeracy.

DEVELOPING FOCAL POINTS

Market research data are most commonly presented in tables produced by computer-based data analysis programs. Quite often these tables are overwhelming. Because of this, there is a tendency among researchers to go through the tables one by one, commenting on interesting or significant differences. This approach usually results in poor reports. When we look at each table individually, we tend to miss the significant patterns that may be present in the data. The use of statistics in such cases will often only help to obscure any possible underlying patterns. Market research tables also tend to be voluminous. As a result, it may not be possible to summarize all data onto one single page in order to understand the patterns. The first step in data analysis is to develop focal points.

As an example, let us assume that one of the objectives of your study is to understand the attribute ratings of your brand compared to other brands. This can be your first focal point—understanding the ratings globally. On a single page, write the average ratings of different attributes for different brands. Do not worry about sub-group differences. Look at these ratings to see if anything stands out. If something looks exceptional, can you explain it? Is it logical? Is it consistent with earlier studies? The next step is to understand the consistency of results. Does the same pattern hold for men and women? English- and French-speaking consumers? older and younger consumers? and so on.

DEPENDENT AND INDEPENDENT VARIABLES

Any numerical information pertaining to an individual can be defined as a variable. Thus, a person's age, the overall rating of a product, the number of magazines read in the previous week, are all examples of variables. An attribute is also a variable, but the word is often used to describe a special type of variable for which the data are expressed in terms of the presence of a certain characteristics, e.g., young, old, male, female, etc. Thus *female* is an attribute of a consumer, while the amount spent by her on clothes is a variable. In marketing research, we are primarily interested in the relationship among attributes and variables:

- Is purchase intention related to sex (male/female)?
- Is age related to smoking?
- Is readership related to socio-economic characteristics?

Suppose we try to examine the relationship between purchase intention and product ratings. In this case our hypothesis states that purchase intent *depends* on how a consumer rates a product. Purchase intent is therefore the *dependent variable* and the product attributes are the *independent variables*. Other examples are:

- Expenditure *depends* on income: Expenditure is dependent and income is independent.
- Smoking *causes* lung cancer: Lung cancer is dependent and smoking is independent.
- Higher education *leads* to better jobs: Better jobs is dependent and higher education is independent.

According to the context, the same variable may be a dependent or an independent variable. For example, a person who has got a better job may enroll himself or herself in an evening course to obtain an MBA. In this case, the better job is the independent variable and higher education is the dependent variable.

When we plot the relationship onto a graph, the independent variable is on the horizontal axis and the dependent variable on the vertical axis. Thus, in order to demonstrate the pattern that expenditure is related or dependent on income, the graph is plotted as shown in Exhibit 14.1.

Exhibit 14.1 Dependent and Independent Variables: An Example

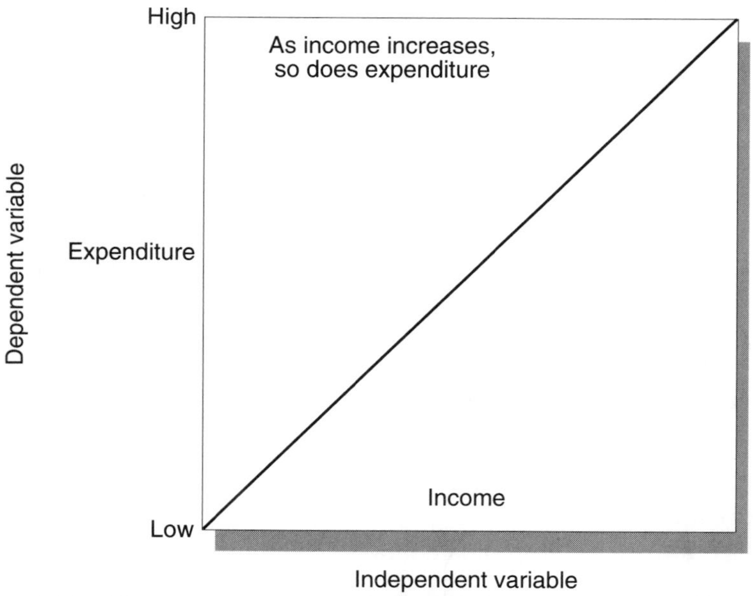

In marketing research tables, the independent variables are given on the top as columns. These are called *banners*. Dependent variables are given on the side as row variables and are called *stubs* (see Exhibit 14.2).

Exhibit 14.2 Example of Stubs and Banners			
Dependent variable (stub)	*Independent variable (banner)*		
Expenditure	*Income*		
	<$20 000	$20 000-39 900	$40 000+
Under $20 000			
$20 000-39 900			
$40 000+			

The purpose of this chapter is to provide the reader with a quick working knowledge of the most frequently used statistical measures in marketing research. No attempt has been made to explore the theoretical underpinnings of these measures, except at an intuitive level. A more theoretical discussion of these techniques can be found in Chapter 22.

SUMMARIZING THE DATA USING AVERAGES

The purpose of data analysis is to understand and interpret information contained in numbers. To do this effectively, we have to reduce the large set of data to a few summary figures. These summary figures can then be processed mentally. This principle applies even to apparently complex data analysis.

Averages are the main tool used in analyzing statistical data. We use them constantly: the average income of computer programmers, the average age of MBA graduates, the average amount spent on alcoholic beverages, and so on.

THE ARITHMETIC MEAN

What we commonly refer to as the average is call the *arithmetic mean* or simply the *mean* by statisticians. Let us consider an example. Twenty-one consumers rated a new brand of coffee on a 10-point scale. Their ratings are given below:

Example 1

Respondent #	1	2	3	4	5	6	7	8	9	10	11	12	13	14	15	16	17	18	19	20	21
Rating		6	3	7	5	6	4	4	6	7	3	5	9	6	4	2	7	5	5	8	6	9

To obtain the mean:

1. Sum all the observations; and

2. Divide the result by the sample size.

This can be written as follows:

Mean = Sum of observations/ Number of observations;

$$\bar{x} = \sum x / n$$

Where,

$\bar{x}$ = Mean (pronounced "x - bar")
Σ = Add together or sum (pronounced "Sigma")
x = Variable under consideration
n = Number of observations (sample size)

For Example 1:

$n = 21$
$\Sigma x = 117$
$\bar{x} = 117 / 4 = 5.57$

The mean is the most commonly used average. It is also the most useful. However, there are two other averages: the median and the mode.

THE MEDIAN

There are instances, as the following example shows, where the mean does not represent the true state of affairs. Consider the incomes of 10 individuals.

Example 2

Resp #	1	2	3	4	5	6	7	8	9	10
Income ($)	19 000	18 000	17 000	19 000	19 500	18 500	17 500	19 500	18 000	170 000

The average (mean) income of the above group is $33 600, although 9 out of 10 in this group earn under $20 000. The median is a measure that avoids this problem of extreme scores. The median is defined as the point in the middle. In other words, 50% of the respondents have a score above the median value and 50% of the respondents have a score below the median value.

To calculate the median:

1. Rearrange the scores in ascending (or descending) order.

2. Take the score of the respondent in the middle. This is the median.

3. If there is an even number of items, take the mean of the two middle items.

Median = Score attached to respondent $(n+1)/2$ when scores are ordered. *When the result ends in .5 such as 4.5, average the scores above and below, e.g., if the median is 4.5 average the score of the 4th and 5th respondents.*

Let us try this on Example 1:

1. Rearrange the 21 scores in an ascending order:

Order	1	2	3	4	5	6	7	8	9	10	11	12	13	14	15	16	17	18	19	20	21
Rating	2	3	3	4	4	4	5	5	5	5	6	6	6	6	6	7	7	7	8	9	9

2. The median of these 21 scores = $(21+1)/2 = 11$, or the 11th value which is 6. (Note exactly 10 respondents have scores above 6 and exactly 10 respondents have scores below 6.)

When the number of respondents is even, take the average of the middle two respondents. Suppose we have 20 respondents instead of 21:

Order	1	2	3	4	5	6	7	8	9	10	11	12	13	14	15	16	17	18	19	20
Rating	2	3	3	4	4	4	5	5	5	5	6	6	6	6	6	7	7	7	8	9

The median of these 20 scores = $(20+1)/2 = 10.5$ or the 10.5th value. To obtain the 10.5th value, we simply take the mean of the 10th and 11th scores ($[5+6/2] = 5.5$).

This calculation is especially important for Example 2. First, rearranging the 10 incomes:

Respondent	3	7	2	9	6	1	4	5	8	10
Income	17 000	17 500	18 000	18 000	18 500	19 000	19 000	19 500	19 500	170 000

Median = 18 750

Since there are an even number of respondents, the average of the middle two observations [($18 500 + $19 500)/2 = $18 750] is the median. As you can see, the median of $18 750 is more representative of the salaries of this group than is the average of $33 600.

THE MODE

In some cases neither the mean nor the median is appropriate. Suppose you are a manufacturer of a computer and you would like to introduce a model that will have the largest market. If you carry our a survey and average out the requirements of large and small companies, you may end up manufacturing a model that is too small for large firms and too large for small firms. The median will not help either. You need values that are applicable to most people. The mode is such a value.

The mode is defined as the most frequently appearing value in the data set. For example, suppose you ask nine of your friends how much they spent on eating out last month. You get the following answers:

Example 3

Respondent	A	B	C	D	E	F	G	H	I
Amount Spent ($)	80	200	50	50	20	100	100	50	100

The mode in this case is $100, since it is the most frequently occurring value. In other words, more people spend $100 per month than any other single amount.

The mode is the most frequently occurring value.

It is possible to get more than one mode for the same set of data. For example, if respondent E in the above example had said $50 instead of $20, we would have had two modal values: $50 and $100. Some data sets may have no mode. In example 2, there were three modes $18 000, $19 000 and $19 500. Obviously, the mode is not very helpful in this example.

MEASURING VARIABILITY

WHY AVERAGES ALONE ARE NOT ADEQUATE

The summary measures discussed so far (the mean, median and mode) are very important in understanding and analyzing the data. However, in many cases, they may be of limited value because they don't tell the whole story. Consider the following ratings of four brands by 10 respondents on a 10-point scale:

Respondent	1	2	3	4	5	6	7	8	9	10	Mean
Brand A:	5	5	5	5	5	5	5	5	5	5	5.0
Brand B:	1	1	1	1	1	9	9	9	9	9	5.0
Brand C:	1	2	3	4	5	6	6	7	8	9	5.0
Brand D:	3	4	4	5	5	5	5	6	6	7	5.0

The mean rating for each brand is 5. Yet the implications of these ratings are quite different. For example, Brand A is perceived to be an average product by all respondents, while Brand B evokes extreme reactions among consumers.

Brands C and D evoked a variety of responses. We need, therefore, measures that will give us more information about how the scores are distributed.

HOW VARIABILITY IN DATA IS MEASURED

There are several measures that give us an indication of the variability in our data. These are called measures of dispersion. In marketing research, four such measures are in common use. These are:

1. Range

2. Mean absolute deviation

3. Variance

4. Standard deviation

THE RANGE   The range is the difference between the largest and the smallest score. Thus, in the above example, for Brand A, the range is 0 (5 - 5), for Brands B and C it is 8 (9-1), and for Brand D it is 4 (7-3).

The range is the difference between the largest and the smallest score.

The range is not a very useful measure for two reasons:

1. It is extremely sensitive to one single large or small score. For example, if 100 respondents earn approximately $25 000 and one single respondent earns $150 000, the range would be $125 000. Yet if this one person with the high income was not in the sample, the range would be much smaller.

2. The scales used in marketing research are such that in most cases all the scale points would be used at least by some consumers. For instance, if you use a 5-point scale, it is almost certain that at least one person would use 1 and at least one person would use 5. So we are likely to end up with a range of 4, no matter how variable the scores are.

THE MEAN ABSOLUTE DEVIATION   The mean absolute deviation is a slightly more sophisticated measure of variability. To calculate the mean absolute deviation:

1. Calculate the mean.

2. Subtract the mean from each score.

3. Add all the deviation obtained in step 2, ignoring the negative signs.

4. Divide by the sample size.

When you ignore the sign of a negative number, you are converting the number into an absolute number (positive value). If you want to indicate an absolute number, you would write it between two vertical lines. Thus:

|-3| = 3
| 3| = 3

The formula for the mean absolute deviation is:

$$\sum |x - \bar{x}| \div n$$

Exhibit 14.3 Calculating the Mean Absolute Deviation: Some Examples

Respondent	1	2	3	4	5	6	7	8	9	10		Mean/ Mean Dvn.
Brand A:	5	5	5	5	5	5	5	5	5	5		5.0
MAD:		5 - 5| +	5 - 5| +	5-5| +	5-5| + . . . +| 5-5|								=	0/10 = 0
Brand B:	1	1	1	1	1	9	9	9	9	9		5.0
MAD:		1 - 5| +| 1 - 5| +| 1- 5| + |1-5| + . . . +| 9-5|								=	40/10 = 4
Brand C:	1	2	3	4	5	6	6	7	8	9		5.0
MAD:		1 - 5| +| 2 - 5| +| 3 -5| +| 4-5| + . . . +| 9-5|								=	21/10 = 2.1
Brand D:	3	4	4	5	5	5	5	6	6	7		5.0
MAD:		3 - 5| +| 4 - 5| +| 4 -5| +| 5-5| + . . . +| 7-5|								=	8/10 = 0.8

The mean deviation is a useful measure of variability, but it has some limitations. The most important limitation of the mean absolute deviation is that it treats different numbers differently; if a number is positive, it is left as it is, if a number is negative, it is changed into a positive number. This treatment, along with the fact that absolute values are somewhat awkward to manipulate mathematically, makes the mean absolute deviation unsuitable for statistical use.

THE VARIANCE   The conventional variance as defined below, overcomes the problem of positive and negative numbers by simply squaring each deviation from the mean.
    To calculate the variance:

1. Find the mean.
2. Subtract the mean from each score. (These are called *deviations*.)

3. Square each deviation. (These are called *squared deviations.* Also called *sum of squared deviations.*)
4. Add the squared deviations. (This is called the *sum of squares.*)
5. Divide it by (sample size -1).

The result is called the variance. Variance is one of the most useful measures for statistical work. The variance of a set of data points is usually symbolized as s^2. The formula for calculating the variance is:

$$s^2 = \sum(x - \bar{x})^2 / (n-1)$$

Exhibit 14.4 Calculating the Variance: Some Examples

Respondent	1	2	3	4	5	6	7	8	9	10	Mean Variance
Brand A:	5	5	5	5	5	5	5	5	5	5	5.0
Variance:	$(5-5)^2 + (5-5)^2 + (5-5)^2 + (5-5)^2 + \ldots + (5-5)^2$									=	0/9 = 0
Brand B:	1	1	1	1	1	9	9	9	9	9	5.0
Variance:	$(1-5)^2 + (1-5)^2 + (1-5)^2 + (1-5)^2 + \ldots + (9-5)^2$									=	160/9 = 17.8
Brand C:	1	2	3	4	5	6	6	7	8	9	5.0
Variance:	$(1-5)^2 + (2-5)^2 + (3-5)^2 + (4-5)^2 + \ldots + (9-5)^2$									=	61/9 = 6.8
Brand D:	3	4	4	5	5	5	5	6	6	7	5.0
Variance:	$(3-5)^2 + (4-5)^2 + (4-5)^2 + (5-5)^2 + \ldots + (7-5)^2$									=	12/9 = 0.75

The squaring of the deviations causes values very different from the mean to dominate the variance more than they would influence the mean absolute deviation. One problem with the variance is that it is not possible to relate it to the size of the mean since the variance is on a different scale (all numbers squared).

THE STANDARD DEVIATION   Standard deviation (symbolized as s) is the square root of the variance.

$$s = \sqrt{\frac{\sum(x - \bar{x})^2}{n-1}}$$

The standard deviation is an attempt to adjust for the squaring in the variance formula. You will see in Exhibit 14.5 that you can interpret standard deviation in relation to the mean as the coefficient of variation. This will indicate whether the variability in data is large or small.

Exhibit 14.5 Calculating the Standard Deviation: Some Examples

Respondent	1	2	3	4	5	6	7	8	9	10		*Mean Std. Dvn.*
Brand A:	5	5	5	5	5	5	5	5	5	5		5.0
Standard Deviation:	$(5-5)^2+(5-5)^2+(5-5)^2+(5-5)^2+\ldots+(5-5)^2$										$=$	$\sqrt{(0/9)} = 0$
Brand B:	1	1	1	1	1	9	9	9	9	9		5.0
Standard Deviation:	$(1-5)^2+(1-5)^2+(1-5)^2+(1-5)^2+\ldots+(9-5)^2$										$=$	$\sqrt{(160/9)} = 4.2$
Brand C:	1	2	3	4	5	6	6	7	8	9		5.0
Standard Deviation:	$(1-5)^2+(2-5)^2+(3-5)^2+(4-5)^2+\ldots+(9-5)^2$										$=$	$\sqrt{(61/9)} = 2.6$
Brand D:	3	4	4	5	5	5	5	6	6	7		5.0
Standard Deviation:	$(3-5)^2+(4-5)^2+(4-5)^2+(5-5)^2+\ldots+(7-5)^2$										$=$	$\sqrt{(12/9)} = 0.87$

To understand standard deviation, it may be helpful to calculate another measure called the coefficient of variation.

COEFFICIENT OF VARIATION The coefficient of variation expresses variability as a percentage of the mean.

$$\text{Coefficient of Variation}(CV) = (\text{Standard Deviation} \div \text{Mean}) \times 100$$
$$CV = (s \div \bar{x}) \times 100$$

Whenever the CV is high (for example greater than 25% or 30%), you should check the distribution to see if the data are more highly loaded above or below the mean (i.e., a lopsided or *skewed* distribution).

In our continuing example, the coefficient of variations for the four brands are:

Brand A: Mean = 5; Standard Deviation = 0	CV = (0/5) x 100	= 0
Brand B: Mean = 5; Standard Deviation = 4.2	CV = (4.2/5) x 100	= 84%
Brand C: Mean = 5; Standard Deviation = 2.6	CV = (2.6/5) x 100	= 52%
Brand D: Mean = 5; Standard Deviation = 0.87	CV = (0.87/5) x 100	= 17.4%

The coefficient of variation is 84% for Brand B but only 17.4% (less than one fourth) for Brand D. This means that the scores for Brand D are more consistent across respondents than scores for Brand B. This conclusion is somewhat obvious, since they are of the same magnitude as the standard deviations. This is because, in our example, we artificially set means for all brands to be the same. But that does not have to be so, and in reality the means are seldom the same. When the mean varies from brand to brand or from attribute to attribute, a low standard deviation may be associated with a large mean and a high standard deviation may be associated with a small mean. In such cases, comparing coefficients of variation rather than absolute standard deviations will lead to meaningful conclusions.

Exhibit 14.6 Calculating The Mean, Variance, Standard Deviation and Coefficient of Variation

Consumer (1)	Rating (x) (2)	Deviation $(x-\bar{x})$ (3)	$(x-\bar{x})^2$ (4)
A	8	(8-5) =3	3^2 =9
B	7	(7-5) =2	2^2 =4
C	7	(7-5) =2	2^2 =4
D	5	(5-5) =0	0^2 =0
E	5	(5-5) =0	0^2 =0
F	5	(5-5) =0	0^2 =0
G	5	(5-5) =0	0^2 =0
H	4	(5-5) =-1	-1^2 =1
I	4	(5-5) =-1	-1^2 =1
J	3	(5-5) =-2	-2^2 =4
K	2	(5-5) =-3	-3^2 =9
n =11	Sum(Σx) = 55		$\Sigma(x-\bar{x})^2$ =32

How To Calculate the Mean $(\bar{x})$

1. Calculate the number of respondents n.	n = 11
2. Sum the scores (x) to obtain Σx.	Σx = 55
3. Find the mean.	$\bar{x} = \Sigma x/n$ 55/11 = 5
	Mean $(\bar{x}) = \Sigma x/n$ = 5

How To Calculate the Variance (s^2)

1. Calculate how each score deviates from the mean.	$(x - \bar{x})$	Column (3)
2. Square each deviation score from Column(3).	$(x - \bar{x})^2$	Column (4)
3. Add all squared deviations.	$\Sigma (x - \bar{x})^2$	Total of Col.(4)
4. Divide the result by $(n - 1)$	$\Sigma (x - \bar{x})^2 / (n - 1)$	32/(11-1) = 3.2

Variance $(s^2) = \Sigma (x - \bar{x})^2 / (n - 1)$ = 3.2

continued

$$\text{Variance } (s^2) = \Sigma\, (x - \bar{x})^2 / (n - 1) = 3.2$$

How To Calculate the Standard Deviation (s)

1. Calculate the square root of the variance. $\sqrt{3.2} = 1.79$

$$\text{Standard Deviation} = s = \sqrt{\frac{\Sigma\, (x-\bar{x})^2}{n-1}} = 1.79$$

How to Calculate The Coefficient of Variation

1. Divide the standard deviation by the mean $1.79/5 = .358$
2. Multiply the result by 100 $358 \times 100 = 35.8\%$

$$\text{Coefficient of variation (CV)} = (s/\bar{x}) \times 100 = 35.8\%$$

GENERALIZING THE RESULTS

Suppose we survey 1000 Canadian adults and find that 35% of them read at least one newspaper every day. How accurate is this estimate of 35%? Could it be, for instance, as high as 45% or as low as 25%, if we measured everyone in the population?

SAMPLING AND NON-SAMPLING ERRORS

Marketing research data are subject to two types of error—sampling and non-sampling errors. When our questionnaire is not clear, when our interviews are not done properly, when we interview the wrong people and so on, our results are subject to *non-sampling errors.* These errors do not depend on the sample size. They are there because the research was not carried out the way it should have been. There is no easy way of consistently measuring the impact of all non-sampling errors. On the other hand, *sampling errors* are not avoidable but they are measurable. They come about because we survey only a few hundred respondents and try to generalize the results to several million people. We can make the sampling error as small as necessary (by taking larger and larger samples), but we cannot eliminate it, unless we survey everyone in our target group.

When we sample only a small fraction of the population, we sacrifice some accuracy. But how much? To understand this, we need another concept—*the margin of error.* The margin of error refers to the range within which the true result is likely to fall. Such ranges can be specified to any given level of probability. (The obtained percentage is called the *estimate.*)

The *true* percentage (the value we would have obtained if we had measured everyone in the population) is called the *parameter*. The margin of error is a statistical term. This concept might be more palatable if it were called the precision of the estimate.

For example, on the basis of statistical tests, we can state that 25% of all Canadians smoke cigarettes; the margin of error on this estimate is + or - 3% at the 95% level. This statement means that if we repeated the study a number of times with the same sample size and calculated the proportion of the sample that smoked and calculated the margin of error each time at the 95% level of confidence, such margins of error would include the true proportion of Canadians smoking 95% of the time.

When we talk about the margin of error, we refer strictly to the sampling error and not to other errors that may occur in our data. Questions with respect to the margin of error are posed as follows:

- In a survey of 1000 Canadians over the age of 18, 56% said they would vote for the Conservatives in the next general election. What is the margin of error?

Although the survey said that 56% would vote Conservative, if we had interviewed all Canadians over 18, we might have got a different answer. Given that we interviewed only 1000 Canadians, to what extent can we be wrong?

- In a product test with 300 consumers, the averaging rating for sweetness was 6.5. What is the margin of error?

If we had carried out the product test on every consumer in the target group instead of just 300, how far off would we be from our current results?

To answer these questions we need to understand the relationship between populations and samples. This is discussed in a later chapter.

GENERALIZING FROM A SAMPLE

Suppose we want to find out the percentage of teenagers in Canada who smoke. We can carry out a survey among 1000 teenagers in Canada. But how do we know that our results, based on just these 1000 teenagers, are really representative of all teenagers in Canada? How do we know that the results obtained through a sample will represent the universe (population)? This is the fundamental sampling problem. (As mentioned earlier, the true answer is called the *parameter* and the result obtained by us is called the *estimate*.)

To make any statement about the population from a sample, we must first make sure that our sample is chosen scientifically. This means that our sample should have been drawn using random sampling procedures: it can be a simple random sample, stratified random sample, multi-stage random sample or cluster sample using random sampling procedures. Provided we choose our sample using random procedures, certain generalizations can be made. It can be shown that if we plot all the means of all possible samples of a certain size from a population it will follow a bell-shaped curve called the *normal probability curve*. This result is called the *central limit theorem*. The practical implication of this finding is that it is possible to estimate how close our results are to the true mean by using a well-established and fairly straightforward procedure that relies on the normal probability distribution. This in turn generates what are known as confidence intervals and margins of error.

HOW TO CALCULATE THE MARGIN OF ERROR

STANDARD ERROR AND CONFIDENCE COEFFICIENTS   At this stage, we need another measure called the *standard error*. The standard error is simply the standard deviation divided by the square root of the sample size:

$$SE = s \div \sqrt{n}$$

For example, in a survey, the following results were obtained:

Sample mean = \$7 (\$7 per week spent on milk by households with one or more children between 1 and 18 years old).

Standard Deviation = 1.5

Sample Size = 100

What is the standard error?

$$SE = s / \sqrt{n} = 1.5 / \sqrt{100} = 1.5 / 10 = 0.15$$

The interpretation of the standard error is given below:

- Mean ± 1 Standard Error will contain the true mean 67% of the time
- Mean ± 1.65 Standard Error will contain the true mean 90% of the time
- Mean ± 1.96 Standard Error will contain the true mean 95% of the time
- Mean ± 2.56 Standard Error will contain the true mean 99% of the time.

(The above multipliers such as 1.65, 1.96, 2.56, etc., are called *confidence coefficients* and the corresponding percentages such as 90%, 95% and 99% are called *confidence levels*.)

We can then state that

- We can be 90% confident that the true mean will be between $6.75 and $7.25.

- We can be 95% confident that the true mean will be between $6.71 and $7.29.

- We can be 99% confident that the true mean will be between $6.62 and $7.38.

The *standard error for percentages* is calculated using the following formula:

$$\text{SE for percentages} = \sqrt{\frac{P(100 - P)}{n}}$$

Where P is % obtained in the survey.

Example: In a survey of 100 respondents, 30% said that they had bought Brand A last week. What is the standard error of this percentage?

P = 30%

(100 − P) = (100 − 30) = 70

n = 100 (Sample Size)

$$\text{SE} = \sqrt{(30 \times 70)/100} = \sqrt{(2100/100)} = 4.6$$

Substituting,

We can then say that we would be 90% confident that the true percentage of the population that bought Brand A was 30% ± 7.59 at the 90% level of confidence (7.59 was obtained by multiplying 4.6 by 1.65, the confidence coefficient for the 90% level of confidence).

ARE TWO GROUPS DIFFERENT?

The researcher is quite often interested in finding out whether two groups are different in their responses. Do men like baseball more than women do? Is a brand of soap preferred more in Vancouver than in Montreal? As before, our concern is to make sure that the observed difference is the result of genuine differences between the groups under consideration, and not the result of the size of the samples chosen.

HOW TO CALCULATE THE SIGNIFICANCE OF DIFFERENCES

As we saw earlier,

- **For variables:**   Standard Error $=$ Standard Deviation $/ \sqrt{n}$
- **For percentages:**   Standard Error $= \sqrt{[P(100 - P)] / n}$

We need to calculate one more statistic called the *standard error of difference*. The formula is:

$$\text{SE of difference } (\text{SE}_d) = \sqrt{\text{SE}^2{}_1 + \text{SE}^2{}_2}$$

where

$\text{SE}^2{}_1 = $ Squared standard error for group 1

$\text{SE}^2{}_2 = $ Squared standard error for group 2

To assess whether the obtained differences between the two groups are significant, calculate:

$$z = (\bar{x}_1 - \bar{x}_2) / \text{SE}_d$$

Where

$(\bar{x}_1 - \bar{x}_2) = $ The difference between the two groups (either differences in percentages or averages)

$\text{SE}_d = $ Standard Error of Difference

The value obtained using the above formula is statistically significant (i.e., the two groups are significantly different) if it exceeds

1.65 (for 90% level),

1.96 (for 95% level) or

2.56 (for 99% level).

The above formula is for the means. If you are working with percentages substitute P_1 and P_2 for $\bar{x}_1$ and $\bar{x}_2$ respectively. All other calculations and interpretations are identical. (See Example 2 below.)

Example 1

In a survey, respondents rated a new detergent on a 10-point scale. The following results were obtained:

	Vancouver	Montreal
Mean	6.30	5.70
Standard Error	0.17	0.23

Can we state with 95% certainty that the observed difference between the two cities is real and not due to sampling error?

We need to calculate:

$$z = \left(\bar{x}_1 - \bar{x}_2\right) / SE_d$$
$$= \left(6.3 - 5.7\right) \div \sqrt{0.17^2 + 0.23^2} = 0.6 \div \sqrt{0.0623} = 2.4$$

Since the obtained figure is larger than 1.96 (required for significance at 95% level), we can say that the product is rated differently (higher in this case) in Vancouver than in Montreal.

Example 2

In a survey, 40% in Halifax and 45% in Saint John said that they would vote Liberal. The sample size was 400 in Halifax and 325 in Saint John. Is the difference in results significant (i.e., real and not the result of random sampling variations) at the 95% level?

Difference in percentages :	5	$40\% - 35\% = 5\%$
Standard Error for Halifax :	6	$40 \times 60 \div 400 = 6$
Standard Error for Saint John :	7	$35 \times 65 \div 325 = 7$
Standard Error for difference :	9.2	$\sqrt{6^2 + 7^2}$

$$z = \left(P_1 - P_2\right) / SE_d$$
$$= 5 \div 9.2 = 0.52$$

Since the obtained value is much less than the critical value of a difference of 1.96 standard errors required for 95% level of significance, we conclude that the difference in obtained results is attributable to chance. (By convention the most frequently used levels of significance in marketing research are 90% and 95% levels. A significance level of less than 90% is virtually never used.)

OTHER TESTS OF SIGNIFICANCE

The most frequently carried out statistical tests in marketing research are the ones described above: margin of error for means, margin of error for percentages, the significance of difference between two means and the significance of difference between two percentages. The tests were discussed above in their simplest form; they are presented in Chapter 22 with a more extensive explanation. There are also other tests of significance: chi-squared tests for testing dependence, tests for comparing more than two groups at a time, tests for comparing ranked data and so on. They are also explained in Chapter 22.

CORRELATION

Is smoking related to lung cancer? Is income related to expenditure? Do people with higher education get better jobs? Is purchase intention related to buying behaviour? Questions like these can be answered by calculating a measure called correlation. Correlations range from -1.0 to + 1.0.

A very high positive correlation means that the two variables under consideration are highly related. For example, if we find a very high correlation (0.8 or more) between the number of cigarettes smoked and the incidence of lung cancer, then it would follow that as the number of cigarettes smoked increases, so does the incidence of lung cancer; conversely, as the number of cigarettes smoked decreases, so does the incidence of lung cancer. A correlation of 0.6 or more (but less than 0.8) would lead us to the same conclusion, but with a lower degree of certainty. A correlation of 0.4 or more (but less than 0.6) would still indicate an identifiable relationship. If the correlation is less than 0.4, but greater than 0.2, we would infer a weak relationship between the variables. A correlation that is between 0.0 to 0.2 indicates that the relationship, if it exists at all, is too weak.

A very high negative correlation (for example, -0.8) means that the two variables under consideration are highly—albeit negatively—related. For instance, if there is a negative relationship between regularity of exercising and the incidence of minor illness, the correlation between the two variables would be negative. The interpretation of the magnitude of negative correlations is similar to the interpretation of the magnitude of positive correlations.

The interpretation provided here is just a rule-of-thumb guideline. There is no magical difference between a correlation of 0.78 and another of 0.81. Another thing to bear in mind is that correlation does not mean causation. If smoking and lung cancer are correlated, it does not automatically follow that smoking *causes* lung cancer. It simply means that both these variables are related and it is up to the researcher to find out if the relationship is spurious or real. Relationships are spurious when two variables are highly correlated but not directly related to each other. For example, there might be a high correlation between the number of rats and the size of the human population in Canada. It might simply mean that, over time, both rat and human population have increased. The increase in rat population did not cause the increase in the human population or vice versa. A high correlation in such instances is called spurious.

There are several techniques available for calculating correlations. One of the most widely used methods is known as the Pearson product moment correlation. Calculation details are provided in Exhibit 14.7.

Exhibit 14.7 Example for Calculating the Pearson Product Moment Correlation

(x) Men	(y) Women	$x - \bar{x}$	$y - \bar{y}$	$(x - \bar{x})^2$	$(y - \bar{y})^2$	$(x - \bar{x})^2 \cdot (y - \bar{y})^2$
8	7	2.5	1.3	6.25	1.69	3.25
7	8	1.5	2.3	2.25	5.29	3.45
7	7	1.5	1.3	2.25	1.69	1.95
5	4	-0.5	-1.7	0.25	2.89	0.85
5	5	-0.5	-0.7	0.25	0.49	0.35
5	6	-0.5	0.3	0.25	0.09	-0.15
5	5	-0.5	-0.7	0.25	0.49	0.35
4	6	-1.5	0.3	2.25	0.09	-0.45
4	3	-1.5	-2.7	2.25	7.29	4.05
3	4	-2.5	-1.7	6.25	2.89	4.25
2	8	-3.5	2.3	12.25	5.29	-8.05
$\bar{x} = 5.5$	$\bar{y} = 5.7$			34.75	28.19	9.85

$$ r_{xy} = \frac{\dfrac{\sum\limits_{i=1}^{n}(x_i - \bar{x})(y_i - \bar{y})}{n-1}}{\sqrt{\dfrac{\sum\limits_{i=1}^{n}(x_i - \bar{x})^2}{n-1}}\sqrt{\dfrac{\sum\limits_{i=1}^{n}(y_i - \bar{y})^2}{n-1}}} $$

$$ r_{xy} = \frac{\dfrac{\sum\limits_{i=1}^{11}(x_i - 5.5)(y_i - 5.7)}{11-1}}{\sqrt{\dfrac{\sum\limits_{i=1}^{11}(x_i - 5.5)^2}{11-1}}\sqrt{\dfrac{\sum\limits_{i=1}^{11}(y_i - 5.7)^2}{11-1}}} = \frac{\dfrac{9.85}{10}}{\sqrt{\dfrac{34.75}{10}}\sqrt{\dfrac{28.19}{10}}} = \frac{0.985}{3.130} = 0.315 $$

Since this value is greater than zero, we'd say that men's scores and women's scores tend to change in the same direction. However, since 0.315 is relatively small, the correlation would not be very strong. A way of determining whether a measure of correlation is large or not is presented at the end of Chapter 22.

SUMMARY

1. **Dependent and independent variables:** In data analysis we examine the relationship among variables. When we examine the relationship between purchase intention and product ratings, for instance, our implied hypothesis is that purchase intent *depends* on how a consumer rates a product. Purchase intent is therefore called the *dependent variable* and the product attributes are the *independent variables*.

2. **Measures of central tendency (summary measures):** To develop a global understanding we need to summarize the data. Three summary measures are available to us: the arithmetic mean, the median and the mode.

   a. The *arithmetic mean or mean* = Sum of observations/Number of observations:

   $$\bar{x} = \sum x / n$$

   (where $\bar{x}$ = the mean, $\sum$ = sum, x = the values of the variable, n = the sample size)

   b. The *median:* To obtain the median, first order the scores from the highest to the lowest or from the lowest to the highest. When the number of respondents is an odd number, the median is the score attached to respondent $(n+1)/2$. When the number of respondents is an even number, the median is average of the scores attached to respondents $n/2$ and $(n+1)/2$.

   c. The *mode* is the most frequently occurring value in a distribution.

3. **Measures of variability:** Measures of variability calculate the extent to which scores within a distribution vary. The most commonly used measures of deviations are the range, the mean deviation, the variance and the standard deviation.

   a. The *range* is the difference between the largest and the smallest score.

   b. *Mean absolute deviation* = $\sum |x - \bar{x} V n$

   (where the vertical bars | | mean "ignore the signs" while summing.)

   c. The *variance* (s^2) = $\sum (x - \bar{x})^2 / (n - 1)$

   d. The standard deviation (s) is the square root of the variance

   $$s = \sqrt{\frac{\sum (x - \bar{x})^2}{n - 1}}$$

   Coefficient of variation expresses variability as a percentage of the mean.

   Coefficient of variation (CV) = (Standard Deviation X 100) + Mean

4. **Sampling and non-sampling errors:** Sampling errors arise because we measure only a small part (the sample) rather than everyone in the population. Practically all other errors (such as improper wording of questions, non-response and question ambiguity) are non-sampling errors. Sampling errors (and only sampling errors) can be measured by *margin of error* calculations. Margin of error does not refer to the total error. To calculate the margin of error, we need to calculate the standard error. The standard error is simply the standard deviation divided by the square root of the sample size:

$$SE = s + \sqrt{n}$$

Mean ± 1.65 standard error will contain the true mean 90% of the time; mean ± 1.96 standard error will contain the true mean 95% of the time. These ranges are often referred to as the margin of error. The multipliers such as 1.65, 1.96, are called *confidence coefficients* and the corresponding percentages such as 90%, 95% and 99% are called *confidence levels*.

(The SE for percentages = $\sqrt{\dfrac{P(100 - P)}{n}}$

where P = % obtained in the survey.)

5. **Tests of significance:** Tests of significance measure whether the obtained difference between two or more groups could be explained as having come about by chance (i.e. we used sample measures instead of measuring everyone in the population). To assess whether two groups are significantly different, we need to compute the standard error of difference.

   a. *SE of difference* (SE$_d$) = $\sqrt{SE^2_1 + SE^2_2}$

   where

   SE$^2_1$ = Squared standard error for group 1

   SE$^2_2$ = Squared standard error for group 2

   b. Calculate (*Obtained difference between groups 1 and 2) ÷ SE of difference*

   For the groups to be significantly different from each other, the obtained value in Step b should exceed the critical values of 1.96 (95% level of confidence) or 1.65 (90% level of confidence).

6. **Correlation:** Correlations measure the strength of relationship between two variables. They range from -1.0 to +1.0. A positive correlation means that the two variables under consideration are positively related, i.e., change in one variable is accompanied by change in the other variable in the same direction. A negative correlation means that the two variables under consideration are negatively related, i.e., change in one variable is accompanied by change in the other variable in the opposite direction.

NOW THINK ABOUT THIS

Complete the following calculations.

CALCULATING THE STANDARD ERROR AND TESTING FOR SIGNIFICANCE OF DIFFERENCES

11 men and 11 women rated a product on overall liking on a 10-point scale, where 10 =Like extremely well and 1 =Dislike extremely. Calculate, the margin of error at the 95% level of confidence. Did the women rate the product differently than the men did?

	Men	Women
	8	7
	7	8
	7	7
	5	4
	5	5
	5	6
	5	5
	4	6
	4	3
	3	4
	2	8
Sample Size (n)	11	11
Mean (x)	5.0	5.7

Exercise: Complete the following

Standard Deviation (s)	_____	_____
Standard Error (SE) = $s/\sqrt{n}$	_____	_____
Margin of error (95% level) = SE * 1.96	_____	_____

Calculating the significance of differences

1. Calculate the standard error of difference (SE_d)
   = (SE for men)^2+(SE for women)^2 _____ + _____

2. Calculate ($\bar{x}_1 - \bar{x}_2$) / SE_d _____

   _____   _____

3. The obtained value is =   _____

15 / Communicating: The Art of Report Writing

WHAT YOU WILL LEARN IN THIS CHAPTER

- What makes a marketing research report a top candidate for influencing decision-makers
- Why multiple exposure can be helpful in a report
- What the fog factor, gobbledegook and the income tax have in common
- To avoid overcommunicating
- Why you should think in terms of goals
- The basic principles of writing reports
- How to structure research reports for more effective communication

INTRODUCTION

Everything depends on the degree to which words and word combinations correspond to the world of impression ... Has not every one of us struggled for words although the connection between "things" was already clear?

Albert Einstein

Although the tabulation phase of marketing research will provide important insights into the information content of the survey data, it's often necessary to perform some further data manipulation in order to extract maximum value from the fieldwork. Chapter 22 is devoted to more extensive investigation of the data. However, data analysis is usually not enough to give value to the project. The information extracted from the respondents must be communicated to the reader in such a way that they can readily interpret the findings to help understand and solve their marketing problems.

This chapter is divided into two sections. Part A presents basic but very important principles of business communication. Naturally, a marketing research report is just one type of business communication and it can be improved markedly by relying on the following suggestions. Part B discusses the specifics of writing a marketing research report.

A. A SHORT COURSE IN BUSINESS COMMUNICATION

Human language is like a cracked kettle on which
we beat our tunes for bears to dance to,
when all the time we are longing to move the stars to pity.

Gustave Flaubert

BASIC PRINCIPLES OF BUSINESS COMMUNICATION

There are some basic principles that apply to almost all forms of business communications. These are given in Exhibit 15.1.

Exhibit 15.1   The Art of Communication

What the writer should do:

1. Use short words, short sentences and short paragraphs
2. Avoid gobbledegook
3. Use the active rather than passive voice
4. Use multiple exposure through visuals and other devices
5. Avoid overcommunicating

What impact it should have on the reader:

6. The reader should be able to locate important ideas quickly
7. The reader should find the format attractive
8. The reader should be presented with complete arguments

What the writer should ask himself:

9. Is my sentence achieving a goal? If not, what is it doing here?

10. Do I hope for an outcome? If so, is my writing geared to achieving it? If not, why am I writing this way?

Something to think about?

11. Simplicity is the ultimate sophistication

USE SHORT WORDS AND SHORT SENTENCES

Short words and short sentences are easy to read. They are also easy to understand. Many people seem to have difficulty in expressing themselves in simple language. Some may prefer to express themselves in a more complex way because of their superior linguistic skills. Some may actually feel that unless they use a large vocabulary and complex sentences, their writing may be considered juvenile. However, the important thing to remember is that there are actually two kinds of writing: one that is read for the enjoyment of the language where the content is of secondary importance, and one that is read for its content where nothing else is of any great significance.

> Your writing style, by definition, is peculiar to you. The problem is that it may often seem peculiar to your reader. Incorporating generally used techniques into your style enhances your writing's readability and reader acceptance.

In literature, the writer uses the content only as a vehicle to express his or her skills as a superior writer. The reader's enjoyment is derived from the way the writer expresses himself or herself and not necessarily from the content of the writing. For example, a poet can describe a tree. The reader learns nothing new in a physical sense and yet derives enjoyment because of the way a poet uses the words and images. This kind of writing is entirely different from business writing.

Business writing has a different set of rules. In the business world, time is precious. The reader wants to absorb the information effortlessly and in the shortest possible time. Short sentences and short words go a long way to achieving this objective.

Compare the following examples, which one communicates faster and better?

Original version:

In the UK and throughout the Western world a rapidly growing proportion of young people appears to be faced with almost certain prospect of periods of prolonged unemployment brought about by fundamental changes in the structure of industry and commerce. However, many young people currently in employment find that a lack of initial basic educational skills, together with a lack of access to training facilities at work, means that their ability to adapt to these changes is also very restricted.

(Broadcasting for Youth)

Revised version:

In the UK and the Western world, more and more people appear to be faced with the almost certain prospect of being unemployed for a long time. This is brought about by deep changes in the structure of industry and commerce. Even young people who have a job find that they cannot adapt easily to changes since they lack basic skills and have no access to training at work.

While the revised version can still be improved, it is definitely much better than the original.

It is also a good idea to use short paragraphs. This is particularly true of the first paragraph of a report. Short paragraphs are likely to be less intimidating to the reader than long, wordy ones.

While it is good to use short words, short sentences and short paragraphs, it should be borne in mind that rigidly following the formula "short words, short sentences and short paragraphs" might lead to writing that is monotonous and choppy. A good rule is to vary the length of words, sentences and paragraphs from time to time.

THE FOG FACTOR

At all stages of practising writing, you may want to compare the difficulty of different passages. Or you may want to rewrite some of your reports. The fog factor is a device that helps you compare the difficulty of two passages. To compute the fog factor of any piece of writing, use a sample of about half a page:

- Count the number of words with 3 or more syllables.
- Divide it by the number of sentences. The larger the fog factor, the more difficult the passage.

Short sentences and short words reduce the fog factor. Once again, however, please note that having too many short sentences makes the writing less smooth. What's needed is sentences short enough and simple enough to be understood but in a writing tone that's interesting and pleasant to read.

The rule "do not write it in one sentence if you can write it in two" is simply a way of saying keep your sentences short. Long sentences force many readers to read twice—thus wasting the reader's time.

AVOID GOBBLEDEGOOK

Avoid gobbledegook and jargon. Be concise. Use plain language. As *The Economist* put it elegantly, "Don't be stuffy or pompous."

Here is a passage from the Canadian income tax act:

Reduction of dividend tax on hand - in the case of a new corporation that has been a private corporation continuously from the time of the amalgamation to the end of any taxation year, for the purposes of computing the refundable dividend tax on hand (within the meaning assigned by subsection 129(3)), of the new corporation at the end of the taxation year, where a predecessor corporation had refundable dividend tax on hand immediately before the amalgamation, the amount by which the refundable dividend tax on hand at that time exceeds any dividend refund (within the meaning assigned by subsection 129(1)) of the predecessor corporation for its taxation year ending immediately before the amalgamation shall be added to the aggregate determined under subsection 129(3) shall be deemed nil where, had a dividend been paid by the predecessor corporation immediately before the amalgamation, subsection 129(1.2) would have applied to deem the dividend not to be a taxable dividend.

What does it mean? Or is the idea so complex that it cannot be expressed in straightforward English? Also note that this passage from the income tax act has a very high fog factor.

Purveyors of gobbledegook (particularly in the legal and accounting professions) tend to argue that the concepts they use cannot be precisely expressed using plain English. When we consider the fact that lawyers constantly argue over the interpretation of legal documents written in legalese and that different accountants interpret the Income Tax Act differently, it is hard to believe that use of gobbledegook somehow makes the meaning more precise. In all business communication, and most personal dialogue, the principal objective is to be precise; otherwise, people don't value what is being said and can't react as desired because they don't understand what is actually wanted.

Plain language and brevity is seldom out of place. As *The New York Times* noted:

> The Lord's prayer contains 56 words, 23rd psalm 118 words, the Gettysburg address 326 words and the Ten Commandments 297 words, while the U.S. Department of Agriculture directive on pricing cabbage weighs in at 15 629 words.

It is easy to fall into the trap of believing that jargon and complex expressions are inevitable in your area of expertise. The fact is there is no evidence to suggest that plain language is less precise than obscure language.

USE THE ACTIVE VOICE

In business, people often seem to prefer the use of passive to the active voice. For example:

- Commitments have been made for the availability of further funds (Passive)

better

- The management has made a commitment for the availability of additional funds (Active)

- Two meetings were held regarding the legal implications (Passive)

better

- The advertising department held two meetings regarding the legal implications (Active)

- It is suggested that the implications of this survey be considered seriously (Passive)

better

- We suggest that you consider the implications of this survey (Active)

While the passive voice has its uses, quite often it hides the person who is responsible for the action. Using the active voice wherever possible will increase the directness and force of your writing.

USE MULTIPLE EXPOSURE

When you express the same idea in more than one way to communicate better, you are using multiple exposure. Multiple exposure reinforces one's understanding because it is underlining an idea encountered. It also gives the reader a second change to understand the same idea.

In textbooks, multiple exposure is often achieved by summaries, marginal notes, etc. In research reports, it can be achieved in several ways; for example, executive summary, general summary and detailed findings sections of research reports repeat the same information; they differ mainly in the details they contain.

The most important thing to bear in mind in using multiple exposure is to make sure that it is not overused so that the reader finds it condescending or boring. There are several ways in which you can use multiple exposure effectively. In writing research reports, you may want to explore the possibility of using drawings and graphs in addition to written commentary. This might make the report easier to understand. Consider the following example:

Exhibit 15.2 Cream Cheese Market in Canada

Brand	Market Share (%)
Stodgie	70%
Dullo	21%
Others	9%

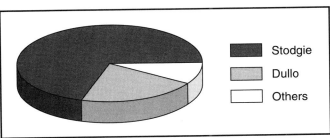

Stodgie Cream Cheese has a 70% share of the Canadian Market. The main competitor to Stodgie in this market is Dullo with 21% market share. A number of smaller brands account for the remaining 9%.

In the above example, multiple exposure was achieved by summarizing the information in three different ways: in words, numbers and picture. Yet, it is unlikely that an average reader would immediately notice that this is the case.

One of the most successful economics texts of all time, Samuelson's *Economics* (1980), uses multiple exposure very effectively. Exhibit 15.3 is an example from Samuelson's book. The graph illustrates an idea already discussed in the text and the explanation attached to the graph restates the same idea. Perhaps this is one of the major reasons for the book's enormous success.

Exhibit 15.3   Effective Use of Multiple Exposure: An Example

The saving-and-investment diagram has many applications. It shows that:
1st, Each dollar of investment can be "multiplied" into three dollars of income:

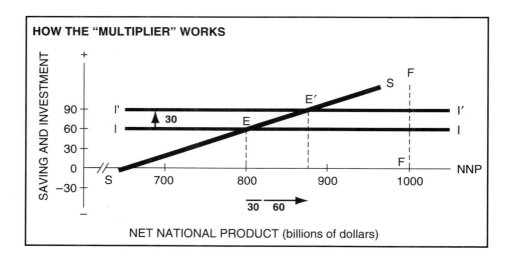

NET NATIONAL PRODUCT (billions of dollars)

New investment shifts II up to I'I'. E' gives the new equilibrium income, with income increasing 3 for each 1 increase in investment. (Note that the broken horizontal arrow is 3 times the length of the vertical arrow that shows the shift in investment, and is broken to show 2 for consumption respending for each 1 of investment.)

Paul A. Samuelson, and A. Nordhaus
1980   *Economics.* New York: McGraw Hill, 1980, p. 225.

The technique used by Paul Samuelson was initially brought to my attention by Professor A.S.C. Ehrenberg of the London Business School - CC

While it is not the intention of the authors to encourage mechanical multiple exposure in communicating, multiple exposure does have a place in business communication. If used properly, multiple exposure can compensate (at least in part) for the short attention span of the reader, reinforce what the reader has already understood and emphasize those points that need to be remembered.

AVOID OVERCOMMUNICATING

Overcommunicating is telling the reader what he or she already knows (or is likely to know). Here is an example of overcommunication:

> Stand the box in an upright position and remove the protective wrapper. Carefully open the top of the box. Pull the instrument out. Remove the cellophane wrapper. Put the instrument in a suitable place and connect it to an appropriate A.C. electrical outlet. Switch the instrument on.

Cut to the chase as quickly as possible. Overwriting bores and confuses the reader.

The writer could simply have said "unwrap the instrument and plug it in." In business writing, overcommunicating arises out of the writer's lack of confidence in the readers. The problem with this approach is that by carefully going through the steps that an average person would go through anyway, the writer might confuse the readers. Instead of simply opening the box and plugging in the instrument, the readers might spend time making sure that they have followed all the instructions. Furthermore, when the readers come to the part where they have to pay close attention, they may not do so, having been conditioned to the trivial instructions provided thus far. The way to avoid overcommunicating is to ask yourself the question: Is there a possibility of serious misunderstanding if this explanation is not provided?

Overcommunicating should be differentiated from multiple exposure. In using multiple exposure, we are emphasizing points that need to be emphasized; in overcommunicating, we are emphasizing points that don't need to be explained.

MAKE IT EASY FOR THE READER

It is the task of the writer to make it as easy as possible for the reader to find the information he or she needs, quickly and accurately. This can be achieved in a number of ways.

1. **Using subheadings:** Subheadings alert the reader to the next idea. They make it easy for the reader to find what he or she is looking for. Use subheadings whenever you can. Where possible, use subheadings that are idea-oriented rather than description-oriented. For example, subheadings used in this chapter (such as "Use Short Sentences", "Use Multiple Exposure") are idea-oriented and tell the reader the basic ideas behind each section. In contrast, subheadings such as "Sentence Length" and "Multiple Exposure" are descriptive titles. Idea-oriented titles serve as summaries, increase multiple exposure and therefore increase comprehension.

The report is written to be read quickly, understood easily and acted on effectively. Don't cloud the issues.

---

2. **Using numbers:** When paragraphs, sections or points are numbered, it makes it easy for the reader to follow the relationship among ideas discussed. Consider the following three versions:

Version 1

We can increase our market share by lowering our price, by increasing our promotional activity or by stepping up our distribution.

Version 2

There are three ways in which we can increase our market share. *One*, we can lower our price; *two*, we can promote our product heavily; or *three*, we can step up our distribution.

Version 3

We can increase our market share in three ways:
1. Lowering our price
2. Increasing our promotional activities
3. Stepping up our distribution

Most readers would find the information they need much more readily in the last two versions (especially the last one) than in the first version.

3. **Using chunking:** In Chapter 10 ("Looking"), we introduced the idea of chunking or breaking down the information into smaller logical units. This applies to written communication as well. Instead of expressing complex relationships among variables in one lengthy paragraph, you should break what you want to say into smaller logical chunks.

4. **Using suitable layouts:** The way the information is laid out can make it easy or difficult for the reader to follow what is being communicated.

Compare the following:

Version 1

Most secondary data come from three basic sources: Company records of sales, advertising expenditures, special promotions, etc., information that is collected by large organizations such as Statistics Canada or syndicated surveys like A.C. Nielsen, Predicasts and Frost & Sullivan in which information on products and brands in general is collected and distributed either free or for a fee.

Version 2

Most secondary data come from three basic sources:
- *Company records* of sales, advertising expenditures, special promotions, etc.
- *Information that is collected by large organizations* such as Statistics Canada; or
- *Syndicated surveys* like A.C. Nielsen, Predicasts and Frost & Sullivan in which information on products and brands in general is collected and distributed either free or for a fee.

The second version aids the reader by manipulating various visual aspects of written communication such as the use of indents, italics and bullets.

Use an Attractive Format

People often make judgments about your report before they read one word of it. Most of these judgments are subconsciously based on visual appearance. An attractive looking report is an invitation for the reader to read it. Unless the reader is waiting for the information that is contained in the report, a badly laid out report is less likely to be read.

As communications consultant, Sherry Sweetnam (1986), points out:

> In business, the standard for physical appearance for both people and inanimate objects is that they be tidy and clean, giving a sense of order and balance. We become suspicious when this standard is breached. We would question a consultant's professionalism if he or she walked into the office looking unkempt or too casually dressed. Likewise if ... [written communication] has an unorganized, unbalanced appearance, we are apt to distrust ... the message—let alone read it.

Principles discussed in the previous section—using subheadings, using numbers, using chunking and using suitable layouts—also tend to make the report visually attractive.

PRESENT THE READER WITH COMPLETE ARGUMENTS

Many report writers—either due to writer's block or laziness—present incomplete arguments. In market research reports, for instance, the researcher may write something like:

> When rating quality of service, customers rate a bank on the basis of their experiences with the person at the counter. In our survey, a large proportion of customers rated the tellers of XYZ bank very highly. Hence we can infer the quality of service provided by XYZ bank is high.

It is not clear whether it has been established either in this survey or in earlier ones that there is a relationship between the quality of perceived service and a customer's experience with the teller or whether it is an assumption made by the researcher. Incomplete arguments can mislead and frustrate the reader and therefore should be avoided.

WRITE WITH A PURPOSE

Business communication, according to Sherry Sweetnam (1986), has three purposes: to inform, to persuade and to create action. To make sure your report sticks to the point, you may want to assess each paragraph by these criteria: does this paragraph inform, persuade or aim to create action? If a paragraph is not accomplishing any of these three purposes, perhaps it should be cut. Of the three, the most difficult to identify are statements that inform. Almost any statement can be assumed to inform. How does one decide whether one is writing information statements or conveying purposeless information? When you are in doubt, an effective way of differentiating purposeless information from purposive information statements is to refer to your objectives. If the sentence has information that would help achieve the study objectives, then it is a valid information statement; if not, then perhaps it is a candidate for elimination.

Exhibit 15.4   Think in Terms of Goals

Purpose statements

Problem statements

Benefit statements

Information statements

Solution statements

Feel good statements

If a sentence is not achieving any goal, what is it doing in your report?

Every sentence in your report should have a purpose and should contribute to achieving your objectives.

WRITE FOR AN OUTCOME

Although marketing research reports are generally considered just to be providing information to the decision-maker, the researcher has to persuade the decision-maker of the validity of the findings and the correctness of the interpretation. The researcher is hoping for an outcome. The report has to be structured in such a way as to make the decision-maker appreciate the validity of the interpretation. In other words, the tools the researcher uses (language, style, arguments, analysis and interpretation) should not call attention to themselves.

The communicator should aim for seamless communication. Seamless communication is a way of communicating in which both the communicator and the receiver are involved in the outcome of the message. For example, when someone asks us what time it is, we simply respond with the time—we do not concern ourselves with how well the question was asked, whether it is grammatically correct, the motives of the other party, etc. What was attended to was the message and not the medium. Communications that are seamless (such as arguments that do not put up a barrier between the writer and the reader, writing that does not puzzle the reader, words that do not confuse the decision-maker) have a much better chance of achieving the intended outcome.

DON'T FOLLOW RULES MECHANICALLY

Writing is an art. Therefore, while the general rules discussed will improve your writing, the rules may not always work. For each rule, there may be several exceptions. We would like to emphasize that while you should pay attention to all the rules mentioned thus far, you should feel free to ignore them if necessary.

B. WRITING THE RESEARCH REPORT

Because the report is your contact with the decision-maker, whom you might never meet, it might be the most important part of your research project. Careful attention should therefore be given to writing the research report. Basic principles of writing marketing research reports that can be useful in this context are presented in this section. What we discussed in previous sections applies to all business communications. In this section we will concentrate on research reports in particular. There is, of course, considerable overlap between the two sections of knowledge.

BASIC PRINCIPLES OF WRITING REPORTS

KNOW YOUR AUDIENCE AND WRITE IN THEIR STYLE The key to providing analysis which satisfies the client is to think of his or her needs as expressed by the project objectives and your knowledge of what is wanted in terms of presentation format. Realize, also, that your direct client also has clients within his or her own organization. Address your client's internal communication needs. If possible, find out who is on the distribution list for the report and the format preferred within the organization. Remember, all of these people will be very busy. Put your report in a familiar style and the likelihood of your report being widely read increases greatly.

WRITING REPORTS THAT WILL BE READ AND USED Edward Stephens (1975:7) provides advice which is almost universal in its applicability, but is especially apt for marketing research:

> As a researcher, you have done something, investigated something, or observed something and want people to know about it. The people to whom you report have plenty of other things to read.

> As an author, you are competing for their attention just as the journalist or ad writer is competing with everything else the reader has to interest him. What you have learned should be quickly apparent to your reader.

The keys to readable and useful research findings are simplicity and conviction. Overly long reports are often not read. And the secret to having people read your report is to interest them with a punchy executive summary. Use five or six bullet points and cut out all the non-essentials. Always strive to answer the question: What will help my client the most? Answer this question successfully and then satisfy that need and your future is guaranteed to be bright.

A book written by Robert R. Updegraff called *Obvious Adams* (1980: 27-28) advanced the belief that successful marketing research and successful marketing decision-making is based on an open mind, the ability to discern the obvious, and obviously important, from the superficial.

The first test of obviousness I borrowed from Kettering of General Motors, who had it placed on the wall of the General Motors Research Building in Dayton: ***This problem when solved will be simple.***

The obvious is nearly always simple—so simple that sometimes a whole generation of men and women have looked at it without even seeing it. Whereas if an idea is clever, ingenious, or complicated, we should *suspect it*. It probably is *not* obvious.

The history of science, the arts and the great developments in the world of business, is a history of men stumbling upon simple solutions to complex problems. Mr. Kettering's wise proverb might be paraphrased. *"The solution when found will be obvious."*

Source: Robert R. Updegraff, *Obvious Adams: The Story of a Successful Businessman.* Louisville, Kentucky: The Updegraff Press (2564 Cherosen Road, Louisville Kentucky, 40205), 1980 Memorial Edition, pp.27–28)

Try to generate interest in your report. Insert tables and display charts and diagrams to underscore your point. Readers always yearn for something to break the monotony of pages and pages of prose.

The liberal use of subheadings is also very effective in report writing. Use subheadings to highlight key findings, new ideas, important points and words that need to be referenced. The subheadings help the reader to make progress through the report and they act as reference points while re-reading the report.

Exhibit 15.5 Keys to Effective Writing

Robert E. Kelley (1981: 194-95) offers the following suggestions for effective writing. These rules are more specific to report writing than those discussed in the first section of this chapter:

- **Know your audience**. Consider everyone who will read the report. What are their needs, backgrounds and preferences? How will they use the report? What can you assume they know and don't know? What style will increase reader acceptance?

- **Write your report in a positive tone**. Emphasize needed improvements and projected results; don't denigrate the client.

- **Write short reports, if possible**. Shorter reports not only appeal to busy clients but they also reduce the amount you must write. Longer reports provide greater opportunity for poor writing displays.

- **Break your report into sections**. Use headings and subheadings to focus the reader's attention.

- **Limit each topic to one page, if possible**. This forces you to write concisely, summarizing the major points of each topic and prevents the reader from confusing topics.

- **Avoid long, complex sentences and paragraphs**. They confuse or bore the reader. Lawyers refer to this as the KISS principle—"Keep It Simple, Stupid".

- **Avoid jargon, slang and unnecessary technical terms**. Write in plain language, use words familiar to the reader.

- **Use direct descriptive words rather than euphemisms**. For example, use the word "fired" instead of "he found himself out of a job."
- **Use the active voice, not the passive**. Action verbs portray the image you want.
- **Vary your sentence structure to avoid monotony.**
- **Use graphs, pictures, charts and tables when appropriate**. A well constructed graph often tells more than an entire written page. Keep complicated material in the appendix, while summarizing its content in the report.
- **Use numbers selectively**. Use absolute values, percentages or ratios, depending on their content in the report and their understandability. Recheck your numbers for accuracy.
- **Emphasize major points through indentations, underlinings, asterisks, bullets or capital letters**. Visually, the major points should jump out at the reader.

Your goal is a concise, punchy report that both informs and convinces the reader.

Reprinted with permission of Charles Scribner's Sons, an imprint of Macmillan Publishing Company from *Consulting: The Complete Guide to a Profitable Career*, by Robert E. Kelley.

STRUCTURE OF RESEARCH REPORTS

Research reports vary in their length, depth, format and style. Consequently, a universal format may not be suitable for all reports. However, to avoid each report's looking different, we can adopt a standard format and deviate from this, if we have some reason to do so.

BUT THEY'RE READING THE LAST PART FIRST! If they start from the back of your report and read forward, they're not wrong—you are. Human nature dictates that, in reading marketing research reports, the reader wants the punch line first. Remember, the sponsor decided to do the study to find answers to marketing problems. He did not want to buy marketing research. Marketing research is just the vehicle that provides better problem-solving ammunition. To satisfy this need to "find out what I've bought," always give the key findings up front in the executive summary. Limit the executive summary to two pages at most. The preferred style is to summarize the study in five to six bullet points on one page.

Make the executive summary informative and the last page won't have to be read first. Make it interesting and the whole report will be read, used and referred to often. If the client does read further, much more will be gleaned from the report by having read the executive summary first.

THE EXECUTIVE SUMMARY   The executive summary is the most important part of the report. It will be read first. It will be read intensely. In many cases, nothing else will be read.

The project sponsor has been waiting for several weeks (maybe months) for the answers which you know but he or she will only find out after getting the report. The yearning for information should be satisfied quickly, effectively and painlessly in the executive summary.

Provide the key findings in five to six bullet points. The writer might feel that this style does not fully explain the findings—and it doesn't. However, the reader will get the primary information quickly and will then be able to read into the findings sections for further elaboration.

Also, think in terms of your sponsor having to present your work to others within the organization. Somebody will be asked to present the information determined by the study on one overhead transparency slide. This will likely come from the executive summary.

Statements such as, "35% felt great relief from arthritis due to Brand S alfalfa tablets," should be made, rather than, "Of the 131 respondents who reported symptoms of arthritis during the study, 35% said that they had experienced great relief from those symptoms and they attributed this to having taken Brand S alfalfa tablets."

Keep it simple, short and punchy. Don't belabour points in the summary. And don't feel as if all of the intricacies need to be explained there, they don't.

Exhibit 15.6   Report Outline

The Outline of the report generally follows this sequence:

(Cover Letter)

Title Page

Executive Summary

Table of Contents

The Main Report

1 Background of the client, the industry and the problem area

2 The Marketing Problem/Opportunity

3 The Methodology of the Project

4 The Key Findings

5 Supporting Findings

6 Recommendations

Appendices

BACKGROUND OF THE CLIENT, THE INDUSTRY AND THE PROBLEM AREA   This section does not need to be long and detailed in most reports, because readers of technical reports are already familiar with the study background. It should provide a statement of the context within which the project has operated. It should also address the organizational needs that precipitated the project.

This section is not needed so much for the direct contact person within the sponsoring organization but rather for others who will not have detailed knowledge of the problem area but are concerned with the problem and its solution.

THE MARKETING PROBLEM/OPPORTUNITY   The most damning question of any marketing research project is, "Now, why did we do this project anyway?" The intention of the proposal is to guard against this question being asked by the direct project sponsor. This section of the report informs all those other readers of the problem context which the project addressed and, hopefully, provided insight on.

THE METHODOLOGY OF THE PROJECT   The research manager within the host organization will need this information in order to confirm the validity of the project to others in the organization. Other readers of the report might view this section as a boring diversion. If the methodology needs detailed explanation because of its complexity, then provide that material in an appendix and give only the basics in this section.

The methodology section should include the following:

- the nature of the marketing research process (whether it was a focus group, a field survey or both)
- the way in which the sample was selected and why
- the sample size and the accuracy provided by that size
- when the fieldwork was conducted
- where the fieldwork was conducted
- how the fieldwork was conducted
- the success of the fieldwork, i.e., the response rate, contact rate and so on
- any helpful comments on the researcher's feelings about the fieldwork

FINDINGS   This is the meat of the report. The reader who becomes sufficiently interested by the executive summary to read further probably skips directly to this section. In most reports, this section should be kept direct and uncomplicated.

Only important questions were included in the research questionnaire. Consequently, the client wants to know the respondents' answers to those questions. Satisfy the client's yearning by answering the following questions:

- *What was asked?*
- *What did they say?*
- *What does it mean?*

Concentrate on answering these questions in the most direct way possible. And, once again, remember that the person commissioning the study usually has the responsibility of communicating the research findings to others within the sponsoring organization. To aid in this communication process, plan your report around a carefully staged presentation consisting of several tables, charts and graphs. Some of the project findings will need to be stated within prose.

Try to use creative techniques of presentation to highlight the key findings. Some researchers prefer to display the key findings as one-page tables consisting of the question actually asked written within quotation marks at the top of the page, the table of numerical frequencies in the centre of the page and an interpretation at the bottom of the page or on the facing page. Naturally, not all findings, especially those from qualitative studies or those resulting from sophisticated analysis techniques, can be presented in this manner. Experienced researchers often expend considerable effort to find the best presentation for their projects. They find the results worth the effort. Exhibit 15.7 illustrates the use of text, numbers and graphs to present a lot of material in an understandable fashion.

It's good practice to state each objective (and sometimes the corresponding hypothesis), the corresponding question asked, the findings in numerical or diagrammatic form and the interpretation of the findings. *Brief* statements about statistical significance may be made for each key finding. However, in many reports, the more technical statistical information is better placed within the appendix.

Don't expect the client to dig into lengthy tabulations and the detailed statistical analyses to find answers to questions. When it's necessary to refer to statistical analyses of the data, it is often best to place this technical information in an appendix. When referring to an appendix from the body of the report, make sure that your references are accurate an that the appendix is easy to find. The reader should be rewarded in the appendix by finding explanations which are understandable and not expressed in jargon.

Every project will contain questions that needed to be asked but either were not of primary importance during the design phase or fell into that position after the findings were reviewed. This information should be treated in a manner similar to the key findings, except, perhaps, in a more abbreviated manner. Even though these are supporting findings, keep the reader's interest high through good communication of this information by presenting well-designed tables, charts, graphs and diagrams. Also, use the appendices for the technical material.

Exhibit 15.7 An Example from a Report on Business Attitudes

Most firms have not experienced any Free Trade effects yet, but expect to next year.

Confirmed: 63% of firms have not experienced any Free Trade effects so far 41% of firms expect no Free Trade impacts next year

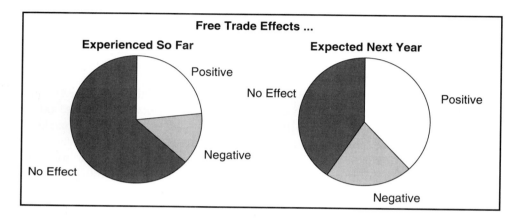

- most of those firms that have experienced positive impacts so far, expect positive impacts next year
- most of those firms that have experienced no impacts so far, expect no impacts next year .
- most of those firms that have experienced negative impacts so far, expect negative or no impacts next year

> Derived from a cross-tab of 'expected' effects by 'experienced' effects

- the presence of unions, the number of employees, Canadian or foreign ownership and whether located in Burlington or Hamilton-Wentworth made no differences in responses
- detailed findings are available in Appendix VI

> Derived from cross-tabs of 'experienced effects' and 'expected effects' by 'presence of unions,' 'number of employees,' 'ownership' and 'location.'

Discussion (verbatim comments):

"Selling to friends is better than enemies."

"The door's open for the south to go north, but there's no attitude, no desire for the north to go south."

"I've noticed a changed attitude in the U.S. towards foreign firms. They're more accepting of us."

> Data findings can be made 'more real' by extracting verbatim comments.

P. Brockman, K. Bulman, J. Kowal, and D. Pastoric.
"Business Attitudes in Hamilton-Wentworth & Burlington: A Survey of Executive Opinion."
Hamilton, Ontario: McMaster University M.B.A. Marketing Research Report, 1989.

MARKETING RECOMMENDATIONS   The recommendations section can be touchy for some organizations and researchers. Many sponsors say to the researcher, "Now give us your opinions. What do you think about our problem?" In many cases, the researcher will have valuable insights based on his intimate involvement with the project and the data, and on an objective consulting perspective. Sometimes that is just what the sponsor wants. However, there are sponsors who feel that the researcher's job is simply to report on the survey findings and that's all. These people will feel that any statements made by researcher will be based on partial, and sometimes wrong, information about the brand, the company and the market and, therefore, aren't worth hearing.

In both of the above situations, respect the opinion of the client. The researcher is paid to provide the information needed by the sponsor. Going further than requested can be detrimental to the usefulness of the report. Not going far enough might be seen as a lack of interest and involvement. Sometimes, this can result in a delicate balancing act. Try to be sensitive to such problems.

APPENDICES   The appendices are not an afterthought or a catch-all for leftovers. The appendices should be an important report component for the thoughtful research sponsor. Remember, the researcher is not involved on a daily basis with the business, product or services under scrutiny. Consequently, some important facets of the problem might escape the researcher but be discovered by the sponsor if enough information is presented in the appendices.

The appendices must be presented clearly and in a well-organized fashion. Label them and provide tabs to facilitate speedy retrieval of the appropriate appendix referred to from the body of the report. When testing a large number of hypotheses, try to summarize many pages of awkward statistical analyses into tables that are easy to read and that present the essence of what was found. Remember, the sponsors did not pay for a set of computer tables—they paid for answers.

Exhibit 15.8 Principles of Written Communication

1. Use short words.

2. Use short sentences.

3. Do not write it in one sentence if you can write it in two.

4. Use active voice rather than passive voice.

5. Use graphs to illustrate simple or dramatic ideas.

6. Use word "sign posts."

continued

7. The reader should be able to locate important ideas quickly.

8. The reader should find the format attractive.

9. The reader should not be presented with incomplete arguments.

10. Think in terms of goals:

Purpose statements

Problem statements

Benefit statements

Information statements

Solution statements

Feel good statements

If a sentence is not achieving any goal, what is it doing in your report?

11. Think in terms of outcomes.

If it is not contributing to your outcome, why are you writing it?

12. Simplicity is the ultimate sophistication.

SUMMARY

A report that communicates effectively and efficiently is the most important part of any project. When clients of consulting projects don't want to read a report because it's too intimidating or can't understand the report because it's poorly written or because the writing is too academic or technical, the whole project loses substantial if not complete value in the mind of the client.

A well written report combines an enticing executive summary, logical organizational structure, well presented facts with insight that appeals to the readers' experience, intellect and intuition. Any charts and tables must communicate crisply and quickly the marketing insights garnered from the survey data. Marketing recommendations must be based on practical knowledge of the client's business. If this can't be done, then it's probably better to leave the marketing recommendations out of the report. Supporting information and statistical analysis are best positioned in the appendices — this information usually interrupts and confuses the readers when presented in the Findings Section.

Now Think About This

1. Take one column out of a recent *Newsweek* magazine and calculate the fog factor. Now, take the same number of words out of your most recent report, assignment or paper for this course and calculate the fog factor. Which passage do you think was easier to read? Which had the lower fog factor?

2. Select several recommendations from a report that you have recently written. Were these passages written in the active or passive voice? If they were written in the passive voice, rewrite them in the active voice.

References

Kelley, Robert E.
1981 *Consulting: The Complete Guide to a Profitable Career*. New York: Charles Scribner's Sons.

Samuelson, Paul A. and A. Nordhaus
1980 *Economics, 13 ed*. New York: McGraw Hill.

Stephens, Edward
1975 "How to Write Readable Research Reports that Get Your Ideas Across" *Marketing News*. Chicago: American Marketing Association, March 14, 1975.

Sweetnam, Sherry
1986 *The Executive Memo*. New York: John Wiley.

Updegraff, Robert R.
1980 *Obvious Adams: The Story of a Successful Businessman*. 2564 Cherosen Road, Louisville; KY: The Updegraff Press, 1980 Memorial Edition

PART 5

How to Deal in Specialized Areas of Research

16 / Product Research

WHAT YOU WILL LEARN IN THIS CHAPTER

- To recognize a product testing situation
- To tell the difference between a paired comparison design and a proto-monadic design
- To identify which product test to use when orange drink crystals are being tested against orange juice
- To understand the nature of new product research
- To identify the different forms of simulated test market models

INTRODUCTION

Product research is a core area of marketing research for manufacturing firms. It's conducted by every large research firm and by most, if not all, medium-sized firms. There are also several smaller research firms that specialize in product testing and others that specialize in a new product research.

Campbell's Soup, Kellogg, General Foods, Nestlé and many others are continually concerned about whether people who eat their soup, cereal, coffee and frozen entrées like them better than they like the competition. Campbell's is likely to be interested in how close consumers perceive Campbell, Heinz, Lipton and Knorr soup brands to be on taste, saltiness, value and many other characteristics. London Life, Canada Life and Manufacturer's Life might like to identify which basic term life insurance policy provider is perceived to offer the best product for professional people.

Beatrice Foods is probably interested in whether people think there's any difference among the several brands of ice cream that Beatrice produces and markets. They'd probably also like to determine whether their premium ice cream is perceived to be the best by consumers and the reasons for that ranking. Beatrice might conduct this study as purely attitudinal research over the telephone or they might ask the questions of individuals after they have tasted Beatrice and competing ice cream brands.

A retail grocer such as Loblaws, A&P, Miracle Mart, SuperCentre or Food City would like to determine a picture of the landscape of competing food retailers in particular markets on the several dimensions on which supermarkets are evaluated by shoppers. This is often called the brand map for the product or service. A brand map derived using a procedure called correspondence analysis is presented in Exhibit 16.1. Which stores are seen as close substitutes on some characteristics, which are seen as different, which are perceived as better on price, which has the best produce, which has the best service and which has the best specials are the major questions addressed by this type of research. This might help the retailer to reposition an existing store to better compete in its retail area.

Exhibit 16.1   A Brand Map of Retail Grocery Stores in Midtown, Ontario

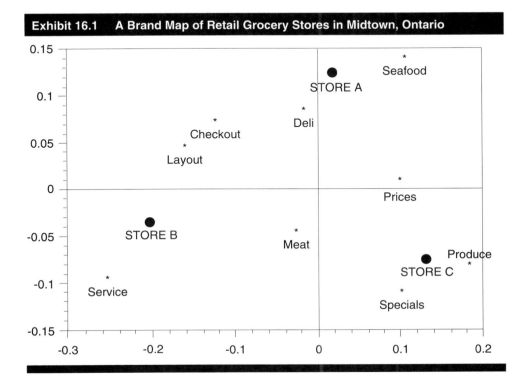

These brand maps can be constructed in a number of different ways to help marketers to understand the way shoppers see the brand marketplace on the several important attributes they use for choosing brands, stores or services.

For example, Store A in Exhibit 16.1 is seen as having the best deli, seafood, and checkout by shoppers. Store B is perceived to have the best service, while Store C is thought to have the best produce and specials. Store B and Store C are seen as both providing good meat, although Store C might have a very slight advantage. For Store C to gain a best meat image, it must compete against Store B. While Store C is perceived to have the best prices, it has substantial competition from Store A on this characteristic.

The questions that motivate product research are the following:

- How acceptable is our product to our target market?
- Do consumers prefer our brand more or less than the competitors' brands?
- Which formulation of our product should be developed to the stage of commercialization?
- What is the level of acceptance or preference for specific attributes of our brand?
- What is the market potential of our new product?

While the first four questions are typical of the area of product testing, the last is from new product research. These disciplines are somewhat related but are generally treated as separate research areas. While product testing is typically concerned with existing brands and is not predictive, new product research is conducted on new products or new brand variations and is typically intended to predict the future success or failure after market introduction.

> The product test is the most important thing the researcher does. We in marketing delude ourselves when we think our advertising, promotions, package graphics, shelf displays, and sales-force efforts match the product in importance. While our marketing skills get us our high trial levels, it is all—in the end analysis—merely incremental, for it is the product that largely generates its own repeat business and is the *sine qua non* of free enterprise (Reprinted by permission of Greenwood Publishing Group, Inc. Westport, CT, from *Danger: Marketing Researcher at Work*, by Terry Haller. Quorum Books, 1983, p.21).

Product testing is the older of the two disciplines. While new product research depends on some of the most sophisticated new analysis procedures, product testing relies on relatively straight-forward analysis. The images of the two disciplines are also different.

It is, therefore, perplexing that product research is considered the domain of the drudge, while other research tributaries assume the fulgid glamor of a Vegas lounge act. The cold truth is that if the product research is not performed with surgical precision and unassailable thoroughness, the rest of the research package might as well be forgotten. In fact, nothing in the entire marketing pantheon equates with the business of testing the product (Reprinted by permission of Greenwood Publishing Group, Inc. Westport, CT, from *Danger: Marketing Researcher at Work*, by Terry Haller. Quorum Books, 1983, p.21).

PRODUCT TESTING

In general, product testing research is any study in which the consumers' responses are influenced by exposure to or trial of a product. It's important that the respondents' reactions to the product based on usage be measured. The subjects must actually taste the new orange pop, often tasting competing brands as well. Or the manufacturer might have formulated several variations of the new frozen entrée and wants the respondents to try each and judge which recipe they like better. Great care must be used in these situations. The manufacturer must be careful that the pre-production product being tested on consumers will actually taste like the product which is produced on a production line. Kitchen-prepared samples might have an unfair advantage and misrepresent the market potential of the final product. Also, care must be taken when deciding on the location of the testing. Should the trial be conducted in a shopping mall that is convenient for the researchers and where the food preparation can be done properly and consistently for each respondent? Or should the subjects be given the food item to prepare naturally in their homes but perhaps not as the manufacturer would like the item to be cooked and served? These are serious questions that can, and have, influenced product testing findings.

The correct design of the product testing sampling and field methodology is often critical to the success of such a study. In its most basic form, the design of product testing means that equal numbers of people try each brand and that an equal number try Brand A first and try Brand B first. However, the sampling and field designs used in product testing can get very involved. Also, the execution of these complex designs requires well trained and highly disciplined field personnel. The study of these designs goes well beyond the intention of this chapter. Those who become deeply involved in product testing need a good practical and theoretical understanding of this topic, which is called the design of experiments in its formal setting. In fact, a very compact and useful definition of product testing is "a controlled experiment involving trial of the product."

Although product testing is used extensively by packaged goods firms, there remain some questions of product marketing that product testing does not answer:

- How the product will be sold?
- Whether the product will succeed or fail in the market?
- What market share gain should the product achieve after launch?

Product testing is based very much on the description of consumers' responses to perceptual and preference questions and does not rely on predictive modelling techniques to infer future events in the marketplace, as does new product research.

THE OBJECTIVES OF PRODUCT TESTING

When preparing to conduct a product test, the following questions must be asked when designing the project:

- Is product testing the appropriate application area? Can it achieve the project objectives?
- When should the product testing be conducted?
- Which products are to be included in the product test?
- What characteristics of the products, the consumers or the market will affect the procedure for the testing?
- What are the qualifications of the sample consumers?
- Where should the test be conducted?
- Which product testing procedure should be used?
- How will the findings be used by the marketers?

DECIDE WHEN PRODUCT TESTING IS APPROPRIATE

Product testing is when the consumer is asked to use the physical product and to express opinions regarding specific aspects of the product. For example, respondents might be asked to judge two formulations of a brand with respect to their saltiness, thickness or colour. Naturally, this can only be done if the subjects are able to see, smell and taste the product. In other words, product testing requires the respondent to use the product, preferably in as natural a way as possible. Product testing can indicate the degree of acceptance and preference for a brand but it cannot predict the sales level of a new product.

Product testing requires a finished product for execution since the respondents must use the actual product. Although in most cases, the product being tested has been on the market for some time, a finished product does not always mean the product that's on the supermarket shelf. In some tests, variations of the brand formulation are tested by the respondent to determine which is preferable. When this type of testing is done, the product is often prepared in the company's test kitchen rather than in the production setting. Care must be taken to ensure that the quality and characteristics of the tested product are the same as those that will appear in the retail store. Otherwise the test will be biased and may indicate that the "kitchen-cooked" product will be greatly preferred, but the result of production line cooking might not receive such a favourable rating from shoppers.

Reaction to the *product* is the job of product testing ... not reaction to the marketing activities. Consequently, the product is usually tested *blind*.

In most product tests the product is presented to the respondents blind, i.e., with no packaging and identity, since the intention is to get the response to the product itself without the influence of marketing factors. Consequently, there is usually no need for finished packaging for the test.

In fact, great care is often taken to disguise the identity of the brand. In some cases, this is very difficult. For example, it's felt by many that to experience a cigarette properly, the smoker should see the smoke exit from his or her mouth. To do this, the subject must not be blindfolded. But how is the cigarette brand to be hidden from the respondent? It is almost impossible to disguise the type of paper, the length of the filter and distinctive markings and still obtain a valid test. In other situations, the subjects can be blindfolded when they try the products in central location studies with little or no negative effect on their perceptions.

Blind tests are not given completely without information. Although the package is plain, there must be a category name, e.g., chicken soup, and there is a legal requirement that ingredients of edible products must be listed on the label. Also, when multiple products are to be tested, they must be identified in some way. In some cases the identification is "try first" and "try second" or "week one" and "week two," or sometimes an identity such as 726 and 842 are placed on the packages.

In order to eliminate all biases, really blind or double bind tests can be conducted. This means that neither those who are actually placing the product nor the respondents are aware of the identity of the brands.

If a brand is dominant in its category, it should be tested blind, otherwise its image of being the biggest and best will draw a biased response. If blind testing is not possible, for example, in the case of a laundry detergent with rainbow speckles, then a "monadic" test where the detergent is tested alone against a benchmark should be conducted (see later in this chapter).

Sometimes there are brands that are so different that they can't be compared to other brands. For example, while cola drinks can be compared among themselves, as can ginger ales and root beers, *Dr. Pepper* has no directly comparable competing beverage. *Dr. Pepper* might have to be tested monadically, i.e., by itself without reference to any other beverage.

WHEN SHOULD THE PRODUCT TESTING BE CONDUCTED?

Although product testing is usually executed on existing products and new product research is conducted on new products, the technique of product testing can be used for the assessment of acceptability and preference of a new product. The product testing approach can be used at almost any stage during the product life cycle (Exhibit 16.2).

Another consideration in product testing is the time of the year. When testing products it's necessary to consider the natural purchasing and use cycles of the product category. To conduct product tests at the wrong time of the year would inject bias into the findings, for example, testing of cold remedies during the summer or sun tan lotion during the winter can produce misleading findings.

Exhibit 16.2 The Life Cycle of Product Research

Stage of Product Life Cycle	Typical Research	Objectives
Product Idea or Concept	Concept Test	Test acceptability of concept (or alternative concepts)
Product Development	Product Test	Test acceptability of prototype, alternative formulations, unbranded product variations
Product Development (c)	Product/Concept Test	Test reactions to product(s) in relation to expectations generated by concepts
Pre-Launch	Simulated Test Market	Predict share and sales after launch
Launch	Home Use/ Extended Use Test	Evaluate all aspects of marketing mix (product, price, advertising, package, promotions, distribution, etc.)
Growth	Product Test	Test acceptability of product relative to competitive entries
Maturity	Product Test	Evaluate potential of brand or product among non-users. Test line extensions.
Decline (Revitalization)	Product Test	Re-examine all aspects of marketing mix. Isolate product and brand strengths and weaknesses.

WHICH PRODUCTS ARE TO BE INCLUDED IN THE PRODUCT TEST?

Sometimes product testing is conducted on only one product, although the majority of applications involve the testing of two or more products or brand variations. When testing two products, a decision must be taken as to whether two very similar or two quite different products should be tested together. Of concern in these cases is whether the consumer will be able to discriminate between two very similar brands or two similar formulations of the same brand. Of course, the very objective of the research project might be to identify whether consumers can tell the difference. In other cases, the intention might be to determine the perceived difference between the manufacturer's brand and the test brand.

WHAT CHARACTERISTICS OF THE PRODUCTS, THE CONSUMERS OR THE MARKET WILL AFFECT THE TESTING PROCEDURE?

Product testing is a research area that can be fully appreciated only after the researcher has had significant experience with a variety of products, use situations, types of consumers, markets and testing locations.

Product testing can never be exactly like actual product usage by the consumer. The testing situation always introduces some abnormality in comparison to the consumer's usual patterns of purchase consideration, purchase, usage and product reaction/assessment. This bias varies with the type of product, testing situation, type of consumer, etc.

Any product testing situation will be artificial. The challenge is to filter out as much as possible that might bias the findings and then make sure that the test is designed so that the biases are balanced, even though they can't be eliminated.

Even though quite elaborate research designs have been developed for product testing and product research in general, consumer reaction is still subject to bias as a result of the research conditions. Therefore, careful design considerations must be made prior to any product testing. Also, product testing responses cannot be taken as "absolute measures." Data from all product testing must be evaluated by the researcher in a comparative context.

WHAT ARE THE QUALIFICATIONS OF THE SAMPLE CONSUMERS?

Naturally, product testing is conducted among consumers comprising the brand's target market. There are several procedures for identifying market segments and deciding on the best target segment(s) for the brand. The sample size in product testing is quite small, usually between 100 and 300 respondents. However, the sampling requirements especially for in-home product testing, are typically quite demanding. The qualifications for obtaining the most appropriate respondents vary depending on the life-cycle stage of the brand and on the intentions of the product testing. Exhibit 16.3 provides rough guidelines for the selection of the respondents.

Exhibit 16.3 Selection of Respondents for Product Research

Product Research Challenge	Type of Respondent
New Brand	Current users of the category (stimulate trial)
Product Improvement/Cost Savings	Current users of the brand (maintain acceptance)
Evaluate Competitive Position	Current users of competitive brands (encourage switching)
Product Comparisons for Advertising	Current users of brand and competitive brands (government regulates comparative statements in advertising)
Product Preparation Change	Those responsible for food preparation in household
Household Reaction to Product	Spokesperson for household, frequently the buyer of product rather than end-user (e.g., disposable diapers, dog food)

Product improvements are typically made to attract new business to the brand. Since an improvement will satisfy those current customers who were satisfied with the existing product, the sampling will be conducted among those who are new business prospects. These people might be users of a particularly important competing brand or they could be light users of the existing brand.

Research can warn you when consumers show signs of finding an established product less desirable than it once was. Maybe they have noticed that you have been using cheaper ingredients; they usually do (Ogilvy, 1983:160).

When the reformulation is focused on cost reduction, it's critical to test one's own customers to be assured that they will not be dissatisfied with the change and leave for other brands. In these cases, the identity of the brand can become very critical to the test situation.

When testing a flavour of a product line, test only those who have a predisposition to that flavour. Don't ask those who dislike orange pop to try the flavour—they still won't like it.

WHERE SHOULD THE TEST BE CONDUCTED?

There are two questions under the overall location question:

1. In which geographic area to conduct the test?
2. Which test environment (or testing facility) to use for the test?

GEOGRAPHIC LOCATION   Regardless of the country in which the product test is being conducted, there can be significant regional disparities that will bias the testing results. Some of these differences might be based on the historical culture of that region. For example, Vancouver testing can produce different results from the same tests in Toronto, even though the ethnic profiles of respondents are similar.

Ethnic differences within the test region and between ethnic groups and regions will further complicate the interpretation of the findings. Careful definition of the qualifications of the respondents based on the intentions of the study and on the target market segment is mandatory to avoid confusion.

TEST ENVIRONMENT   The basic decision is whether to save money and time by testing in a central location or whether to test within the environment where the product would typically be used by the consumer.

CENTRAL LOCATION TESTING (CLT)   This is conducted typically in shopping malls. However, other situations can be used, such as a church basement or a school auditorium, when recruiting has been conducted previously by telephone or by mall intercept. The important aspect of the central location is that it is not the natural environment in which the respondent would actually use the product.

Although the testing might be done in the public area of the mall, most research would be conducted in the research firm's mall office which is more private and less distracting for the subject.

IN-HOME TESTING / ACTUAL USAGE SITUATION   This is typically the preferred testing situation when the advantages listed for central location testing are not important, but overcoming the disadvantages is important. The key benefit of in-home testing is that the respondent uses the product in a familiar way in the environment where that product is typically used.

Exhibit 16.4   Central Location Product Testing

Advantages:
- Usually less expensive and faster
- Can have more control over:
  - preparation method
  - serving temperature
  - quantity tested
  - side-by-side comparison of products requiring lengthy preparation time
  - disguising key basic product differences, such as orange juice or orange crystal beverage
  - order of presentation or sequence of presentation, e.g.:
    - Brand A (taste) Blind
    - Brand B (taste) Blind
    - Brand B (retasted) with brand name revealed
    - Brand A (retasted) with brand name revealed
- Necessary if limited product availability
- Essential if product not easily portable
- Necessary if truly blind testing is required
- Guaranteed product usage is needed
- Visual observation of respondent reaction
- Immediate respondent reaction via open-ended questions
- Ability to probe initial reactions

Disadvantages:
- Limitation of the amount of test product respondent can try at one time
- Time of day can influence response to some products
- Family influences on respondent impossible to measure
- Lacks random representation of target consumer
- Environment might influence taste perceptions

The selection of the test site is an important aspect of product testing. Different results between in-home and central location testing are not infrequent. Some commonly acknowledged differences are:

- Startling tastes/flavours tend to win in malls, while blander flavours tend to win in-house
- Respondents' senses tend to get tired after repeated usage in the mall
- Physical limitations of a product become more apparent during in-home testing.

Exhibit 16.5   In-Home Product Testing

Advantages:
- Product used in the natural environment
- Prepared and presented as would be if bought, not the way manufacturer thinks best
- Measures the reaction of the whole household
- Provides opportunity for repeated usage
- Longer trial (e.g., one week) versus single taste test in mall
- Reaction is based on cumulative experience

Disadvantages:
- More expensive and more time consuming
- Researcher loses control over the way in which the product is used.

The pros and cons of the testing environment must be considered carefully during the design of the research. Products can test quite differently in an absolute and relative fashion when presented in different environments.

WHICH PRODUCT TESTING PROCEDURE SHOULD BE USED?

Now for the controversy. Although most researchers will agree with most of the preceding statements, many will disagree on which testing procedure is best, or even which is the better one to use in a particular situation. However, there certainly are some guidelines based on experience and on basic research that can help significantly with the procedure selection decision.

Many researchers become quite emotional over the selection of a particular testing procedure. Unfortunately, although a great deal of product testing has been done, many of the reasons for selecting one technique over another are based more on historical precedence and professional opinion than on objectively identifying the benefits and problems with the various procedures under different test situations.

> The longest-running, loudest, and often most bitter debate in the annals of consumer research centers around the merits of paired comparison testing (A vs. B) and monadic testing (person gets only one product, A or B) (Haller, 1983:31).

The most commonly used designs are called monadic and paired comparison tests.

PURE MONADIC TEST   The monadic test is used in those situations where the product would be conspicuous if presented in comparison to another. For example, the brand might be the dominant brand and thus easily recognizable, or the brand might have distinctive form or features that would overshadow any other brand in a comparison test. The pure monadic test can often answer the question of acceptability of the brand but is not able to provide any information on comparative grounds. The key characteristics of the pure monadic design are:

- Only one product is tried by respondent and evaluated

- The findings are compared to norms or historical test data collected in an identical fashion, or to concurrent tests on other products

- Used when there is no logical comparison

SEQUENTIAL MONADIC   The sequential monadic design is characterized by a sequence of what would appear to be two conventional pure monadic tests. However, the respondents' exposure to the first test taints their perceptions of the product presented second:

1. Product 1 is tried by consumer and evaluated.

2. Product 2 is tried by consumer and evaluated.

3. Evaluations of product 2 are biased by exposure to and testing of product 1.

PAIRED COMPARISON   This method is used to evaluate product reformulations, new formulations, and the current product versus the competitive product. It is a very sensitive procedure where differences are emphasized, but for which absolute measures are not available. It tends to be more commonly used where a single dimension is to be evaluated.

1. Product 1 is tried by respondent, but not evaluated.

2. Produce 2 is tried by respondent.

3. Both products are evaluated in a comparative manner.

4. Half respondents will try product 1 first while other half will try product 2 first to equalize order bias. The order bias is not eliminated, just equalized.

5. Look for comparative preferences.

PROTO-MONADIC PAIRED COMPARISONS   The proto-monadic design is one of the most widely used designs in product testing. While providing monadic information on the brand tried first, it also garners comparison information from the consumers. None of these designs is best in the sense of being applicable to all product testing situations and being unfettered methodologically.

One snag is that the first interview casts its influence over the usage of the second product, and, even though you rotate your product sequence, the results are not exactly the same as the simple paired test. Another problem is that such a design characteristically produces too *much* information (Haller, 1983:34).

The distinguishing features of the proto-monadic design are:

1. Product 1 is tried and evaluated. The product along with instructions and an opinion evaluation form are placed in the respondent's home. The recording form asks for product usage details, overall rating of the brand and reasons for rating the product either positive or negative.

2. Product 1 is taken away and product 2 is introduced. The household is called one week later. The opinion recording form is collected along with the remaining product. The second product, instructions and questionnaire are then left to be used.

3. Product 2 is tried and evaluated. The household is called one week later and the opinion record is collected. Then, the respondent is questioned on the comparison between the two products to obtain preference information.

4. Half of respondents try product 1 first while half try product 2 first.

5. Product should be marked "first week" rather than "try first" to hide the fact that the respondent will be asked to try two products.

6. Key purpose is the paired evaluation, but absolute measures are also obtained.

The analysis first compares the first week responses between the two products. The product usage information can be analyzed in a straightforward manner. The opinion questionnaire data are analyzed monadically only on the first week answers. This information will highlight the attributes that are of primary interest to the subjects as well as to the manufacturer. However, the respondents are likely to concentrate on those important characteristics when using the second week brand, thereby biasing the findings. The paired evaluations will be helpful in assessing the relative preference for the brands (Exhibit 16.6).

TRIANGLE TEST   The triangle test is used to discern the difference between two products. The respondent is presented with two units of one product and one unit of another product. The subject is then asked to select the "different" product after all have been tried. The triangle test is often mistrusted by researchers. There are documented instances in which products that were clearly different could not be distinguished by respondents. Some feel that the task is too complex, too threatening, or the product interaction too strong to be reliable.

Exhibit 16.6	The Relative Benefits of Monadic and Paired Comparison Designs	
Type of Product Test	Pros	Cons
Monadic	• Consumers use products monadically in everyday life • With "normative" data, one has a benchmark to assess good vs bad	• Even though it's more realistic, no product testing situation is totally natural • Not very sensitive—bearing in mind the generally small absolute differences that exist between competing products
Comparative	• Highly discriminating • Differences between products are accentuated (appropriate in markets where technology advances in small steps) • Easy to determine whether consumers feel product is "better" than the competitor's or than own current brand • Easy to determine whether product is "different," e.g., when testing to see if brand can safely adopt a cheaper formula	• Far removed from the real world • Preference or difference judgments might be based on inconsequential differences —things that really won't matter to consumers when it comes to purchase • A "winning" product is not necessarily a "good" product —it needs to be judged against an established standard

HOW WILL THE FINDINGS BE USED

The use of data from product testing should always be in a comparative mode. The paired comparison procedures are obviously relative between the products. That is, consumers are saying, "This product is better than that one," not "This product is better than all similar products." However, the monadic testing also relies for proper assessment on comparison with established norms or other tests conducted separately. In other words, historical data are relied upon to assess consumers' input.

NEW PRODUCT RESEARCH

The importance of new brands to the prosperity of manufacturers of consumer products has grown tremendously during the last 20 years. On average, 15% of the current sales volume of North American firms is based on major new products introduced during the preceding five years and 32% is based on all new products. Sales and profits from new products are expected to increase in importance.

Since about 80% of all new product introductions for packaged goods fail and about one third of all new products achieving national distribution are subsequently withdrawn, those ambitious expectations stated in the previous paragraph will not become reality without substantial effort. Sophisticated marketing, marketing research and marketing modelling have become key allies of new product managers. New product evaluation models and laboratory test markets have become a regular part of brand managers' requests of their marketing research managers. The necessity of seriously and extensively investigating the process of new product introduction is now taken for granted in many firms.

While product testing requires usage of the product, new product research might not involve actual exposure to the product. In fact, the product might not be fully developed. New product research is quite varied in type and intention. When proposed variations of a new food item are tried on subjects, the new product research falls under product testing according to our earlier definition of product testing. However, much of the new product research involves attitudinal measures not based on the usage of the product but rather on exposure only to the marketing of the product, or first to the marketing to see if it can stimulate trial, and then to the product to see if it will motivate repeat usage. Also, when attitudes based on product usage are obtained in new product research, sometimes the strict design requirements used in product testing are not followed.

Marketing, marketing research and marketing modelling techniques for the creation, evaluation, introduction, tracking, and control processes have become more sophisticated in response to the challenges of increasing the success of new product marketing and of evaluating these opportunities at lower costs. Several new product evaluation models have been available for the past 10 to 20 years. The greatest amount of commercial activity in new product assessment models has occurred at the pre-test market stage of development through the use of simulated test market models.

SIMULATED TEST MARKETING

One of the greatest desires of new product managers is to have a procedure that will assess the market and financial feasibility of new products at as early a stage as possible in its life cycle. A procedure that was developed mainly in the late 1960's and 1970's for this purpose is the *simulated test market study* (STM). The exact beginning of this type of test is not formally identified because so many firms had the desire and took steps that could have led to the formal development of the STM. However, the Laboratory Test Market model of Yankelovich, Skelly and White gained prominence from the late 1960's.

> Using mathematical models, research can estimate the sales of new products, and the advertising expenditures required to achieve maximum profits. The Hendry, Assessor, Sprinter, ESP and News models are sufficiently reliable to tell you whether your product warrants the expense of test marketing. (About 60% of new products fail in test markets.) (Ogilvy, 1983:158)

The first of the STM's to gain substantial renown was the ASSESSOR model developed by Alvin Silk, Glen Urban and Management Decision Systems, Inc. (Silk and Urban, 1978). Because of the publication of Silk and Urban's 1978 article and subsequent articles (Urban and Katz, 1983; Urban, et al. 1983), ASSESSOR became the best known of the STM's in terms of its research methodology and the mathematics of its models. ASSESSOR is used to this day and competes with the other prominent STM models of BASES (Burke Marketing Research) and LITMUS (Yankelovich, Clancy, Shulman). ASSESSOR is currently owned by M/A/R/C Inc. and is called MACRO ASSESSOR.

LITMUS also became quite well known based on publications regarding its structure and mathematics (Blackburn and Clancy, 1982). Although the BASES model has not been as well documented in the academic literature (Lin, Pioche and Standen, 1982), it has gained a substantial reputation because of its quite extensive usage by major companies and through the committed marketing of Burke Marketing Research.

ASSESSOR, LITMUS, BASES and other STM's have somewhat similar field methodologies. These are:

- **Recruitment and Screening**: Subjects are recruited, usually in a central location, and are qualified for the study through a series of screening questions. While ASSESSOR screens on category usage, BASES usually does not.

- **Initial Questioning**: Respondents are asked a set of questions that indicates their category and brand usage, attitudes and preferences.

- **Advertising Exposure**: The subjects are exposed to advertisements about products in the category, including the new product, to force initial awareness. A short questionnaire is used to measure several dimensions of that advertising.

- **Shopping in "the Little Store"**: ASSESSOR and LITMUS respondents are encouraged to shop in a room called the "little store," that contains competing brands in the category. BASES respondents shop in an actual supermarket.

- **In-Home New Product Usage and Call-Back**: The respondents leave the central location with the new product, either because they bought it or it was given to them as a sample. The product is taken home and hopefully used by the respondents. The research firm calls the respondents back after approximately one to two weeks to determine if they have used the brand, to assess their opinions of the brand, to determine their preferences among competing brands and to identify their intention of purchasing the brand.

The manner in which the information is obtained, especially in the initial questioning and the call-back, and the nature of the responses is somewhat different among the STM's. However, they all aim to obtain an estimate of the market share of the brand or the sales estimate. In order to transform the data from the field interviews to market share and sales estimates, mathematical models relate the preference, opinion and usage information to the projected incidence of selecting the new brand in a retail store. Although the field methodologies are very similar, the prediction models are quite different.

ASSESSOR   The most distinctive feature of ASSESSOR has been its dual model format. Developed as an internal check, the data from the ASSESSOR fieldwork are processed through two models, each of which supplies an estimate of market share. The value of these two models is to provide a vehicle whereby a measure of internal reliability is calculated and by which any differences between consumer data and management judgment can be reconciled.

One of the models is called a *preference model* and it uses measures of comparison provided by the respondents. A critical component of the preference model is the "chip sheet." Respondents are asked to indicate their preferences among all pairs of brands in their awareness sets by dividing 11 imaginary poker chips between the brands in all the pairs. The preference information is then converted into purchase probabilities using the logit

Exhibit 16.7   Structure of the ASSESSOR Model

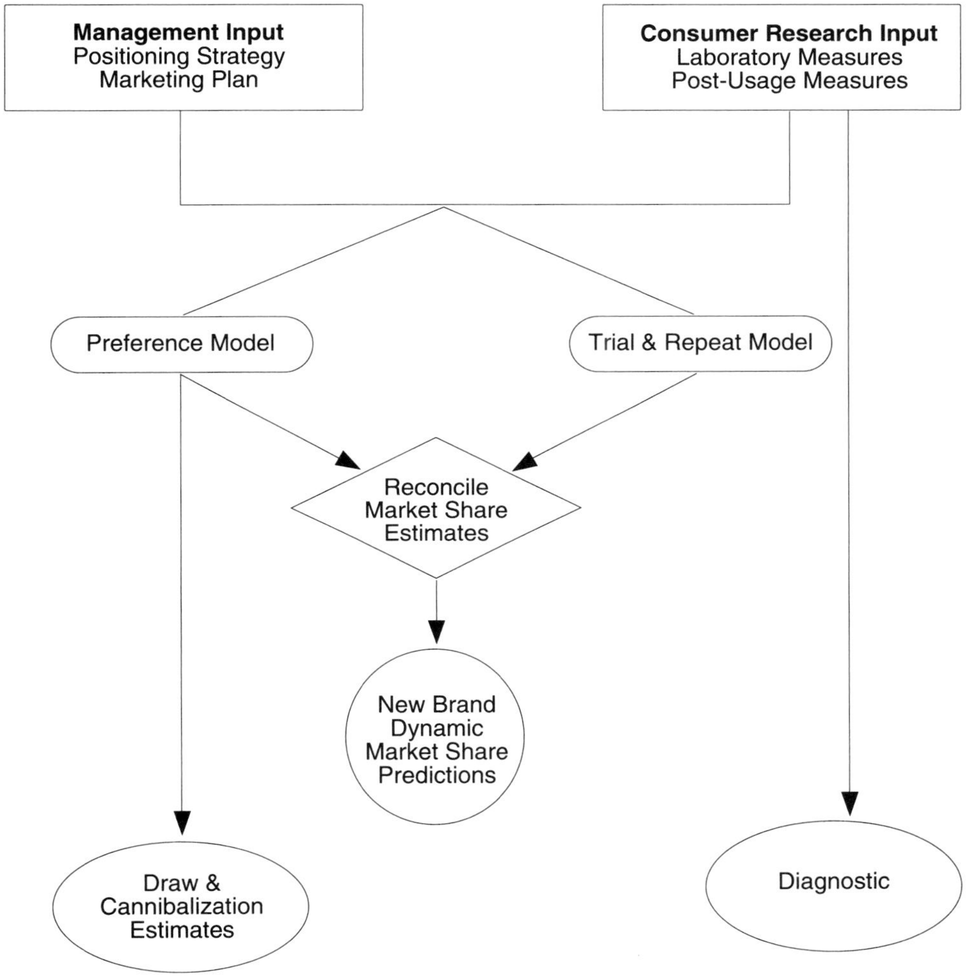

```
┌─────────────────────────┐          ┌─────────────────────────────┐
│   Management Input      │          │  Consumer Research Input    │
│  Positioning Strategy   │          │    Laboratory Measures      │
│    Marketing Plan       │          │    Post-Usage Measures      │
└─────────────────────────┘          └─────────────────────────────┘

        (  Preference Model  )            (  Trial & Repeat Model  )

                        ◇ Reconcile
                          Market Share
                          Estimates

                        ( New Brand
                          Dynamic
                          Market Share
                          Predictions )

 ( Draw &                                      ( Diagnostic )
   Cannibalization
   Estimates )
```

model of consumer choice. The purchase probabilities are then translated into the market share estimate.

The other model is a *trial and repeat model.* This model uses information regarding respondents' purchases in the laboratory store, and information obtained when subjects are called back after the in-home usage, including the subjects' decisions to order the new brand for home or mail delivery and their intention to buy the new brand in stores. Information from the company's marketing plan is also used to calculate the market share estimate.

In the trial and repeat model, a relatively direct and frequently used procedure is applied for calculating market share. The share estimate is obtained by multiplying the ultimate trial rate for the new brand by the ultimate repeat purchase for the new brand. The ultimate trial rate, or penetration, is a function of the probability of a consumer's making a first purchase of a new brand, the probability that a consumer becomes aware of the new brand and the probability that the new brand is available through the distribution channel to a consumer. This is illustrated in Exhibit 16.8

Exhibit 16.8   Calculations of the Trial/Repeat Model Based on Consumer Behaviour

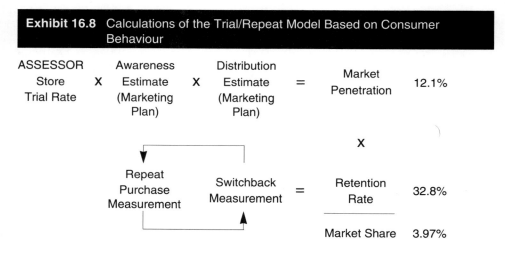

Where switchback is a measure of the likelihood of a respondent's switching back to the new brand after buying another.

In addition to the market share estimates, the client obtains the estimates of the source of the new brand's business. Cannibalization (business obtained at the expense of other brands from the same manufacturer) and draw (sales attracted from competitors) estimates are important to the marketing strategy and tactics for the new product. Diagnostic analysis is also performed on the responses. This involves a wide range of analysis from simple frequency distributions of the questionnaire responses to fairly sophisticated perceptual and preference analysis. ASSESSOR is now called MACRO ASSESSOR and is represented by M/A/R/C Inc.

LITMUS   Although the mathematical model on which LITMUS is built is quite different from the ASSESSOR model, the field methodology has a number of close similarities. Because the differences between the two models lie mainly in the mathematics, the LITMUS model will not be presented in depth in this chapter. The interested reader can refer to the paper by Blackburn and Clancy (1982). LITMUS is represented in Canada by The Creative Research Group.

BASES   While ASSESSOR depends heavily on theoretical and conceptual assumptions about the ways in which people respond to new products, BASES is supported by a large data base of past new product launches and relies on the premise that consumers' responses to any new product will be similar to their responses to previous new products in that category. Consequently, BASES relies on an extensive set of *norms* or normative data that are averages of the response of the market to previously launched new products. A big advantage of this procedure is that comparisons can be made to past successes and past failures to estimate the sales and market share of the new product.

BASES I combines a concept test with an empirically derived learning model, secondary information on expected year 1 distribution and adjustment indices to provide an initial estimated trial rate for the concept.

Respondents are intercepted in a shopping mall and shown a concept board consisting of a drawing of the concept product, product characteristics and benefits, and the price. The subjects are asked about their buying intentions, incidence of usage of existing brands, their likes and dislikes and other relevant diagnostics.

The client provides marketing plans and assumptions regarding the build up of distribution through retail stores, plans for media and advertising and trade and consumer promotions.

BASES I can also be used to simulate the effects on volume sales of changes in the marketing plan variables.

Research can get consumer reactions to a new product when it is still in the conceptual state. After one of our clients had invested $600 000 in developing a line of food products for senior citizens whose digestions were deteriorating, our research found a notable lack of enthusiasm among the old parties concerned. When I reported this disappointing news to the client, I was afraid that, like most executives faced with inconvenient research, he would argue with our methodology. I underestimated him. "Dry hole,"said he, and left the meeting (Ogilvy, 1983:160).

BASES II is a product/concept test that provides estimates of year 1 and year 2 sales volume and allows the simulation of the effect on sales of key marketing variables.

Shoppers recruited in mall intercepts are shown a finished concept board or commercial for the prototype product and asked for their purchase intentions along with other information. Those who show high potential to be triers are given the test product to try at home. After-usage responses are obtained through follow-up questioning regarding buying intentions, intended frequency of purchase, price/value assessments, liking or disliking and other diagnostic measures.

The rate at which shoppers will first repeat their initial trial purchase is estimated from the data. The repeat rate is based on correlations between price/value and like/dislike ratings and the rate of repeat purchase decay that BASES has validated on its own test results. BASES claims that this analysis procedure allows it to better estimate the volume potential of innovative new products.

In cases in which it does not know if the new product will attract new shoppers to the category, will cannibalize existing products of the manufacturer, or draw business away from competing brands, the SOVA (Source of Volume Analysis) model can be used. This analysis is based on consumers' relative preferences among alternative brands within the category or sub-category.

BASES III is a test designed to measure the response of shoppers to the new product when placed on store shelves. Store shoppers are intercepted and shown TV commercials or print ads for the new brand as well as for two other non-competing products. Respondents are then given 20% off coupons for the test product as well as for several others and allowed to continue with their shopping. The coupon redemptions form the basis for estimates of actual trial. Telephone call-backs are used to obtain after-usage information that will be used to estimate repeat purchase volume. Manufacturers' marketing plan variables are combined with the consumer data to estimate the rate of trial, first repeat purchase rates, average time between purchases, average trial units, average repeat units and quarterly retail sales volume. (BASES III is not offered in Canada.)

BASES IV monitors test markets and roll-out markets. The intention of BASES IV is to project test market results as soon as possible so that roll-out decisions can proceed quickly. A BASES II test is conducted several weeks prior to the test market to obtain current information as well as to recruit a panel of shoppers who will have been exposed to the product prior to the test market and can be used as a leading indicator during the test market.

Combining the panel data with those of the test market provides quicker estimates of the success of the product than would a test market alone, Burke suggests. (BASES IV is not available for use in Canada.)

> Research can save you time and money by 'reading' your competitor's test markets—even his cost of goods and profit margins. All the information is there to get, if you know where to find it (Ogilvy, 1983:161).

Burke states that BASES has been used on a wide selection of product categories and is quite accurate. BASES is purported to have estimated 71% of its test products within a 10% range of accuracy and nearly 100% within 20%. There are other Burke services such as Concept Design, PASS and Restager that can be executed in conjunction with BASES to enhance its usefulness to marketers.

SUMMARY

Product research is one of the most important applications of marketing research. Whether the task is to assess the potential of a new product or to determine the relative merits of two new variations of an existing product, product research contributes real value to the operation of the manufacturing and marketing firm.

Product research is split into:

- Product testing that is executed on existing products often through in-home or in-mall usage of the product and reporting on perceptions
- New product research that is conducted on product concepts and on products that have not yet been launched into the market place

Several consumer new product testing processes have become popular during the last 20 years:

- BASES, with several stages of analysis, from Burke Marketing Research
- ASSESSOR with its two parallel models, both preference and trial and repeat, from M/A/R/C Canada Ltd.
- LITMUS with its extended trial and repeat model and extensions from the Creative Research Group.

While Burke markets BASES I to provide market potential estimates at the concept stage, other research suppliers are striving to develop and commercialize competing techniques that will supply these precious early warning indicators as soon as possible after idea development and for as small a cost as possible.

Now Think About This

1. When conducting a product taste test on a beverage should the respondent be told the flavour of the beverage before tasting?

2. How can product testing and new product research be used together to provide more accurate estimates of product success or failure?

3. Discuss the pros and cons of ASSESSOR and BASES for analyzing new products.

4. Provide four reasons why simulated test market models might be better than test marketing. Why might STM's be worse?

References

Blackburn, J. and K. Clancy
1982 "LITMUS: A New Product Planning Model." in *TIMS/Studies in the Management Sciences* (ed. A. Zoltners), 18, 43-61.

Haller, Terry
1983 *Danger: Marketing Researcher at Work.* Westport CT: Quorum Books.

Horsnell, G.
1977 "Paired Comparison Product Testing When Individual Preferences are Stochastic: An Alternative Model." *Applied Statistics*, 26 (June), 162-172.

Johnson, Richard M.
(no date) "Simultaneous Measurement of Discrimination and Preference" Chicago: Market Facts.

Lin, Lynn Y. S., Alain Pioche, and Patrick Standen
1982 "New Product Sales Forecasting Recent BASES Model Experiences in Europe and in the United States." Presented to ESOMAR Conference, September 2, 1982.

Moore, William L.
1982 "Concept Testing." *Journal of Business Research*, 10, 279-94.

Morrison, Donald, G.
1981 "Triangle Taste Tests: Are the Subjects Who Respond Correctly Lucky or Good?" *Journal* of Marketing, 45 (Summer), 111-19.

Moskowitz, H.R., B. Jacobs, and N. Firtle
1980 "Discrimination Testing and Product Decisions." *Journal of Marketing Research*, 17 (February), 85-90.

Ogilvy, David
1983 *Ogilvy on Advertising.* Toronto: John Wiley & Sons Canada Limited

Silk, Alvin J., and Glen L. Urban
1978 "Pretest Market Evaluation of New Package Goods: A Model and Measurement Methodology." *Journal of Marketing Research*, 15 (May) 171-91.

Urban, Glen L., and Gerald M. Katz
1983 "Pre-Test-Market Models Validation and Managerial Implications." *Journal of Marketing Research*, 20 (August), 221-34.

Urban, Glen L., Gerald M. Katz, Thomas E. Hatch, and Alvin J. Silk
1983 "The ASSESSOR Pre-Test-Market Evaluation System." *Interfaces*, (December), 38-59.

Wierenga, B.
1974 "Paired Comparison Product Testing When Individual Preferences are Stochastic." *Applied Statistics*, 23 (September), 284-296.

17 / Communication Research

WHAT YOU WILL LEARN IN THIS CHAPTER

- To understand the different sequences of attitude and behavioural change that people go through for different types of products
- How different advertising strategies can be developed from an understanding of the attitude formation process
- That the choice of advertising research technique depends on the objective specified for the advertising
- About the laddering technique for developing advertising strategy and message content
- About the differences between theatre approaches and individualized testing
- How modern electronics is used to help test commercials
- What needs to be done to test the effectiveness of advertising

INTRODUCTION

Most communication research currently being conducted commercially pertains to advertising; therefore, the terms *communication research* and *advertising research* are often used interchangeably, although communication research is much broader in scope. In this chapter we will deal with communication research essentially as it relates to advertising.

WHAT IS ADVERTISING?

Advertising is the communication of a specific message to a large number of people. The message in an advertisement can be either product related or consumer related. The purpose of an advertisement is to persuade many consumers to buy a product or service. Sometimes the purpose of an advertisement can simply be to inform the consumers about the availability of a product or service, or it can be to create a favourable impression of the advertiser. Most advertising research tends to deal with how well the advertising is accomplishing the task of persuading a consumer to buy a product or a service. The main purpose of such research is to evaluate whether the advertisement is working.

> When I write an advertisement, I don't want you to tell me that you find it 'creative.' I want you to find it so interesting that you *buy the product*. When Aeschines spoke, they said, 'How well he speaks.' But when Demosthenes spoke, they said, 'Let us march against Philip.' (Ogilvy,David (1983), *Ogilvy on Advertising*, Toronto: John Wiley & Sons Canada Limited, p.7).

The immediate objective of any advertisement is to bring about a shift in consumers' perception, preference or behaviour that is favourable to the advertiser. Yet it is unrealistic to expect every single advertisement to accomplish this goal. In fact, every advertising campaign has a two-fold effect on the consumer: the short-term and the long-term.

The short-term effects of an advertising campaign would include the following: increasing product awareness; creating greater recognition of what the product has to offer; creating a positive image of the product such that it increases the probability of purchase; persuading the consumer to actually buy the product; persuading the consumer to buy the product again; and providing reinforcement of purchase satisfaction.

The long-term effects of advertising relate to creating and reinforcing a consistent and viable brand image. Brand image refers to the general perception of a brand as, for example, being expensive or inexpensive, being of low or high quality, being widely or not widely available, etc. Such brand image would imply a consistent and viable user image.

> Image means *personality*. Products, like people, have personalities, and they can make or break them in the market place. The personality of a product is an amalgam of many things–its name, its packaging, its price, the style of its advertising, and, above all, the nature of the product itself (Ogilvy, 1983:14).

HOW DOES ADVERTISING WORK?

No one has yet satisfactorily answered the question how does advertising work. In fact, there are people who maintain that the effects of advertisements are very different from what is usually supposed. Therefore all we are left with is a series of models that are simple formalizations of individual points of view as to how advertising is supposed to work. These models are neither right nor wrong. They are simply alternative ideas as to how advertising works, with little or no conclusive proof to support them. They are useful insofar as they provide a framework for testing advertising on certain criteria as formalized by a given model.

AIDA is one such model. According to this model, advertising results in Attention, which in turn may create an Interest among those whose attention is drawn to the advertisement. Such interest can create Desire culminating in Action (purchase of the product or service). Thus, according to this model, there can be no interest in the product if the ad was not noticed in the first place, no desire to buy the product if there was no interest, and no purchase of the product if there was no desire to own the product.

DAGMAR (Defining Advertising Goals for Measured Advertising Results) holds that the awareness of an advertisement leads to the comprehension of the message resulting in conviction eventually followed by action.

A third model holds that advertising simultaneously influences consumer attitudes (what they think) and behaviour (what they do). What consumers do influences what they think and what they think influences what they do. Yet another model holds that the process consists of the following steps in sequence: attention, communication, interest, adoption, purchase and reinforcement.

THE FCB GRID

What is now referred to as the FCB (Foote, Cone & Belding Advertising) Grid was developed by Richard Vaughn (1980) as a planning model portraying four primary advertising planning strategies shown in Exhibit 17.1, informative, affective, habitual and satisfaction. The most appropriate traditional and variant hierarchy-of-effects models are presented in each quadrant of the grid to indicate the sequence of behaviour and attitude change which is most likely to occur for products falling within those areas.

Exhibit 17.1 Foote, Cone & Belding Grid		
	Think	**Feel**
High Involvement	INFORMATIVE (Economic) Learn-Feel-Do	AFFECTIVE (Psychological) Feel-Learn-Do
Low Involvement	HABITUAL (Responsive) Do-Learn-Feel	SATISFACTION (Social) Do-Feel-Learn

THE INFORMATIVE STRATEGY—QUADRANT 1   Products that involve people in a rather lengthy process of perception, learning, attitude change and maturation and finally the purchase are said to be high involvement products. Quadrant 1 in Exhibit 17.1 presents the traditional hierarchy-of-effects model in an abbreviated format of learn, feel then do.

The hierarchy-of-effects model was discussed in Appendix 7C and is based on the work of Lavidge and Steiner (1961). At that time, it was presented as a basic listing of the types of attitudes that can be engendered in an individual and that could be the focus of marketing research. The concentration here is generally the same as in Appendix 7C. However, the hierarchy is also viewed in advertising as a set of possible objectives that the brand's advertising might be directed to achieve.

Initially, of course, shoppers are not aware of a new brand or service since it has not previously been offered to them. Correspondingly, the purpose of the advertising is to create the awareness in consumers' minds that the product is available for purchase. Many advertising campaigns during the early lifetime of a brand have an objective of creating awareness of the brand among at least a certain percentage of the target population. Advertising research at this stage would measure whether that objective had been achieved.

Exhibit 17.2   The Hierarchy-of-Effects Advertising Model

Unawareness
     Awareness
        Knowledge
           Liking
               Preference
                  Conviction
                     Purchase
                        Post-Purchase

Some advertising campaigns follow the hierarchy-of-effects with the intention of sequentially influencing the development of attitudes along the hierarchy until a purchase is made and then to enhance the post-purchase attitude change to be one of satisfaction and feeling that the best purchase had been made.

Advertising research at successive steps along the hierarchy would measure shoppers' knowledge of the characteristics, features and benefits of the brand, their liking for the brand and its attributes, their preferences for the brand among alternatives, and their conviction that the brand is the best brand for them to purchase, when the time comes to buy the product.

At some time, the opportunity might arise for the shopper to make the decision to buy or not to buy the brand. This is a behaviour, not an attitude. However, it's also very important to identify and question those who purchase the product, to record the circumstances of the purchase and their immediate reactions to the brand. The focus of research at this stage of the hierarchy is usually on the question "Did the ad work?" This is part of the overall objective of determining the effectiveness of advertising—which has been sought for as long as advertising has existed and is still not satisfactorily addressed in many cases.

After buying the brand, it's important for any manufacturer to monitor the consumer's reactions to the brand, both physically and mentally. Customer satisfaction with the purchase is extremely important to the continuing success of the brand and is a point of concern for the brand and advertising managers and for the advertising agency. Naturally, a satisfied customer is very likely to repeat that purchase in the future and it's less expensive to keep an existing customer than it is to attract a new customer. The process of creating ads that lead to product trial and creating products and ads that result in repeat purchasing are important objectives of any brand marketing function.

While the hierarchy represents a focus for advertising and advertising research, it does not encompass all of the needs for advertising research. For example, regardless of the stage in the hierarchy, there is the need for research to determine what to say (creative) and how to say it (production). Also, research is needed at the concept level, pre-production and post-production levels.

THE AFFECTIVE STRATEGY–QUADRANT 2   Those products and services that appeal to the basic feelings and visceral responses of the shopper are felt to be most effectively marketed by an affective strategy. This is portrayed in quadrant 2 of the FCB Grid (Exhibit 17.1). Products that appeal to a person's vanity, ego, self-involvement, subconscious and self-esteem perhaps require an advertising strategy that appeals more to the person's emotions. The affective quadrant hypothesizes a hierarchy where *feeling* is the first response, then *learning* about the product and finally the *doing* of purchasing the product. Products such as perfume, fashion clothing, lingerie, personal care prod-

Exhibit 17.3   FCB U.S. Grid Study

	THINK	FEEL
HIGH INVOLVEMENT	✔ Life Insurance ✔ 35mm Camera ✔ Motor Oil	✔ Family Car ✔ Perfume ✔ Complexion Soap
LOW INVOLVEMENT	✔ Liquid Household Cleaner ✔ Clothes Pins	✔ Greeting Card ✔ Popsicle

ucts, fun vacations and jewelry are felt to fall into this category (see Exhibit 17.3).

THE HABITUAL STRATEGY–QUADRANT 3   All of us buy a number of products the purchase of which we consider in a rational manner but that are of relatively low involvement. Perhaps most of what's bought on a typical grocery shopping trip falls into this category. The hierarchy proposed by Foote, Cone & Belding is one where the *purchase* is made relatively quickly because of the low importance (e.g., picking up a package of paper towels), then the consumer *learns* about the brand and finally develops some *feelings* or opinion about the brand. It's felt that products such as cleaning items, clothes pins and other product, which are often basic necessities and frequently rather boring to discuss, fall into this quadrant.

THE SATISFACTION STRATEGY–QUADRANT 4   The relatively minor articles that round out our lives and make them more pleasant are thought to fall into this strategy quadrant. Items like popsicles, candy bars, many food items, greeting cards, some basic clothing articles, beer, potato chips are life's little pleasures which take little effort to buy and are available to almost everyone. The sequence in the hierarchy proposed by FCB for this quadrant is one of buying first, then feeling and developing an attitude about the product and then learning about the product as much as is necessary, which is often very little.

The FCB Grid has been validated on over 20 000 consumer interviews in 23 countries (Vaughn, 1986). The research has confirmed the Grid and has been instrumental in relating the concepts of the Grid to other research on the hierarchy-of-effects and other areas such as right and left brain information processing and responses. Eight scales were developed for operationalizing involvement and think-feel (Ratchford, 1985):

- **Involvement**
  - Very important/unimportant decision
  - Lot/little to lose if you choose the wrong brand
  - Decision requires lot/little thought
- **Think**
  - Decision is/is not mainly logical or objective
  - Decision is/is not based mainly on functional facts
- **Feel**
  - Decision is/is not based on a lot of feeling
  - Decision does/does not express one's personality

- Decision is/is not based on looks, taste, touch, smell, or sound (sensory effects)

ADVERTISING DECISIONS

Advertising decisions cover the following areas:

1. What to say in an advertisement? (The Strategy)

2. Who to say it to? (The Target Audience)

3. How to say it? (The Creative Strategy)

4. How often to say it? (Minimizing Wear-out)

5. Where to say it? (The Media Strategy)

6. How much to spend? (Optimizing the Budget)

Although all the above are legitimate areas of investigation, most advertising research relates to refining and evaluating (1) and (3) above. The remaining areas are covered by secondary information, segmentation research, large-scale media usage studies and prior knowledge.

The advertisements that are evaluated can pertain to any media: radio, TV, newspapers, magazines, point-of-purchase, outdoor advertising or direct mail. Each medium has its own strengths and weaknesses and testing procedures will vary depending on the medium.

COMMUNICATION RESEARCH

Ideally, every advertisement or "communication" should have some stated objectives such as "to increase brand awareness among the target audience" or "to persuade consumers to use more of the brand advertised." Communication research is the systematic evaluation of how well these objectives have been accomplished through the advertisement. Communication research can test any aspect of the communication such as intrusiveness, appeal, transmission of information, influence on attitudes, memorability, persuasiveness, etc. (Measurement of audience size is not communication research.) The methods used can be qualitative, quantitative or both.

Communication research may be used for several purposes such as identifying possible creative opportunities and weaknesses, conserving media and production dollars, etc. It may be conducted at all stages of developing the creative approach for an advertising campaign:

1. Which basic approach to use? (Concept stage)

2. How to refine the selected approach? (Pre-production stage)

3. Did it work the way it is supposed to work? (Post-production stage)

Several dimensions may be measured in communication research. Some of the more common measures are brand recall, message recall, change in attitudes, brand or user image, purchase intent, diagnostic measures (strengths and weaknesses), etc. Questions that pertain to these measures do not necessarily have a standardized form. They may be open-ended or closed-ended, structured or unstructured, aided or unaided, scaled or non-scaled.

The usefulness of these measures is very dependent on the purpose for which they are collected. For example, how useful is the brand recall measure? If you believe in the DAGMAR model discussed earlier, you may want to collect the brand recall information since, according to this model, awareness is a critical variable. On the other hand, if you go by proven ideas, you may not care much for brand recall information since it has not been conclusively shown to be related to product purchase. In actual practice, the measures included in a communication research study depend on several factors: past studies, standard practice in a given industry or agency at any given time, researcher's notion of how advertising works, and the like.

RESEARCH TECHNIQUES

Some research techniques are common to all media. These techniques include focus groups, mall-intercept interviews and telephone tracking. Although these techniques have already been discussed, we will see here how some of them relate to advertising research.

Mall-intercept interviews can be used to evaluate measures such as brand and message recall, purchase intent, brand image and diagnostic information. Respondents can be asked to view an advertisement along with other ads and be tested for recall. Or the researcher may want to solicit comments on a given set of ads. This method also provides for splitting the sample into two groups (test and control) and for follow-up interviews, if necessary. Mall interviews are relatively inexpensive and it is not necessary to have finished commercials for testing purposes. The technique, however, is sensitive to the type of ad being tested and is subject to all other limitations of mall interviews.

Telephone tracking studies can be used to measure the effect of a given campaign by interviewing people before and after the campaign. Brand awareness, brand image, purchase interest and awareness of the advertisement are some of the aspects that can be measured. Its main advantage is that the test takes place in a natural setting rather than a shopping mall. Some disadvantages of this method are possible confusion of ads in question, uncontrolled exposure to ads and no control of extraneous factors related to campaign effectiveness. In addition, this procedure cannot be used effectively for diagnostic purposes. Most other tests are related to a specific medium.

The various methodologies that can be used are implemented and combined in ways that are suitable to the particular technique used at the time. The procedures described below give a general view of the types of studies that are used in advertising research.

LADDERING

Laddering is a relatively new procedure for assisting with the development of advertising strategy. (Reynolds, Cockle, and Rochon, 1990: Reynolds and Gutman, 1984). Laddering asks (and answers) the following questions:

1. How to tap into an individual's network of meanings?
2. How to explore this structure in terms of content or levels of abstraction and determine the linkages between these levels?
3. How to identify the common framework across respondents that can be used to summarize the data reflecting perceptual orientations across brands?
4. How to translate these perceptual orientations into advertising strategy?

The methodological goal of laddering is to build a common chart embracing all respondents' ladders that will serve as a reference point for defining important differences between respondents regarding:

1. To what ultimate common values the ladders connect;
2. The linkages between attributes and higher-level consequences and values;
3. The relation of products to the ladders, thereby providing implications for advertising strategy and product positioning.

The MECCAS (Means-End Conceptualization of Components for Advertising Strategy) model provides the analysis framework and methodology to work through a laddering exercise (see Exhibit 17.4)

The MECCAS Modelling Procedure can take one of several variations. The following three steps illustrate a procedure that is often used:

1. Obtain an exhaustive list of brands.
2. Form triads of the brands.
3. For pairs in each triad, there exist similarities and contrasts: "How could two of the three be the same?" "Which two of the destinations are different from the third?" "What causes the difference?" Find poles. "Which pole of the distinction is more preferred?"

The laddering process operates to force the consumer up the ladder of abstraction, i.e., to uncover the structural aspects of consumer knowledge as modelled by the means-end chain.

1. Ask consumers to rate the concepts they elicited in the triadic sort in terms of importance in a purchase decision.

2. "You mentioned that a concept was important (or unimportant) to you. *Why* is it important?"

3. Get answers to 2 and repeat "*Why* is that important to you?" until no further answers can be given.

4. Stretch out answers to enter the values areas.

Exhibit 17.4   MECCAS

(Means-End Conceptualization of Components for Advertising Strategy)

	Level	Definition
Values	Driving Force	The value orientation of the strategy; the end-level to be focused on in the advertising.
Traits	Leverage Point	The manner by which the advertising will "tap into," reach, or activate the value or end-level of focus; the specific key way in which the value is linked to the specific features in the advertising.
	Executional Framework	The overall scenario or action plot, plus the details of the advertising execution. The executional framework provides the "vehicle" by which the value orientation is to be communicated; especially the Gestalt of the advertisement; its overall tone and style.
Consequences	Consumer Benefit	The major positive consequences for the consumer that are to be explicitly communicated, verbally or visually, in the advertising.
Attributes	Message Elements	The specific attributes, consequences, or features of the product that are communicated verbally or visually.

Exhibit 17.5   The MECCAS Triadic Sorting

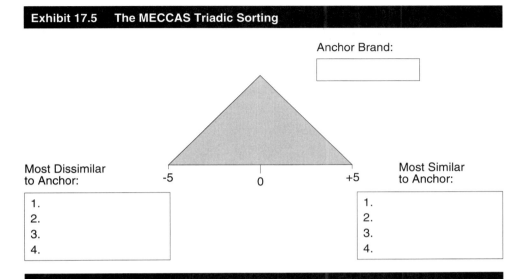

Laddering identifies the preferred anchor or pole brand of the initial triadic distinction and then sequentially probes through brands to determine why that distinction is important to the respondent. By following this procedure with the preferred pole at each level, a series of linkages connecting attributes to consequences and then to personal values is thereby uncovered.

The data analysis in laddering is quite extensive and seems to be growing in complexity as the area matures. The main steps in the data analysis are:

1. Content Analysis of all the elicited concepts resulting from the large number of laddering responses.

2. Categories of concept codes are developed that capture the essential aspects of most of the thoughts and responses expressed by subjects while completing the laddering tasks. Then each thought/response from each subject is assigned a category code. This procedure removes the idiosyncratic expressions of similar basic thoughts. Thus all laddering responses are now expressed in a set of standard concepts.

3. Structural Analysis
   • Identify the concepts of cognitive structure, the nodes, and the linkages among the concepts.
   • Construct a square matrix where the rows and columns are concept codes developed in the content analysis.
     • For a linked pair of concepts, an entry is recorded in a particular row/column cell each time the row concept preceded the column concept in the ladder responses, i.e., whenever the row concept was the probe stimulus that elicited the column concept, an entry is made into

- For a linked pair of concepts, an entry is recorded in a particular row/column cell each time the row concept preceded the column concept in the ladder responses, i.e., whenever the row concept was the probe stimulus that elicited the column concept, an entry is made into that cell. The total number of entries in any cell of the matrix corresponds to the number of times (across all subjects) that particular concept (row) directly elicited the other concept (column).
- The cell entries are converted to binary form: 0 if entry <=4; if entry >=5.

4. Value Structure Map
- The binary matrix is treated as a directed graph, a basis for representing the normative cognitive structure as a complex tree diagram.
- The value-level concepts are positioned at the top of the ladder while the more concrete attribute concepts are placed at the bottom.
- The ladder identifies the concepts that are normatively salient across most subjects and the major (most frequent) interconnections among those concepts.
- The concepts are ordered in a hierarchical fashion such that relatively

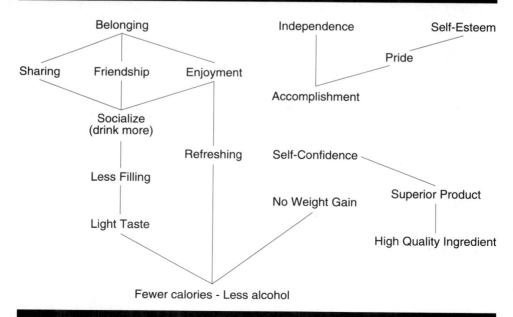

Exhibit 17.6 Hypothetical Hierarchical Value Map (HVM) for the Light Beer Category

From Reynolds and Rochon, in press.

concrete concepts like product attributes lead to more abstract concepts like consequences of use that in turn point to highly abstract end states like terminal values (see Exhibit 17.6).

CLUCAS COPY TESTING TECHNIQUE

Many advertising practitioners have viewed advertising research as a group of testing procedures that measures the attitudes of the audience prior to exposure to the commercial and then measures their attitudes after that exposure and compares the two sets of measurements to determine whether there has been a change that can be attributed to the commercial. These techniques treat what happens in a person's mind while watching the commercial as a *black box.* The measurements infer that a change has occurred in the black box, but they don't directly measure the workings of the black box itself.

The Clucas technique focuses directly on the task of trying to understand, measure and illuminate the processing of information through the black box. An anonymous commentator has remarked, "When you pay for television time, you rent people's minds for, say, 30 seconds at a time. Because that 30 seconds is the only thing you have control over, what happens second by second as the commercial unfolds is vital information to the advertiser." The Clucas technique attempts to understand what happens during those critical 30 seconds by measuring the following dimensions of the advertisement.

- **Oral Communication:**
  The script is written but is it heard? Some scripts are better than others and some parts of a script are better than other parts. Data are obtained on the per cent of the audience which heard each word of the script to compare to past norms of performance and to compare across the script being measured. The advertiser uses this information to smooth out the commercial and to improve it relative to other executions of the advertising message.

- **Visual Communication:**
  The advertiser usually has a heavier investment in the video production than in the script preparation. Consequently, it's important to know which parts of the visual message were seen and worked and which did not. The visual communication measures the percentage of people who can describe the different parts of the commercial, shot by shot.

- **Communication Objectives:**
  Since advertisers have different objectives for commercials, these objectives are specified and the commercial is tested to determine whether the objectives are being met. For example, if the creative process was

designed to focus viewers' attention on a portable television in the commercial at the end of scene one, then for the commercial to have achieved its objective, a higher percentage of viewers should have indicated that they did see that television. Clucas measures these scene objectives throughout the commercial.

- **Audience Response:**
  The black box theory implies that something happens in the viewer's mind when he or she sees the commercial. Have you ever commented on a commercial to yourself or criticized a commercial to someone else while it was playing? This is called *audience talk-back* and is quite vital to effective refinement of the commercial. Although the advertiser and agency encode the commercial with a specific message, the viewer might decode or interpret the commercial very differently than intended. These "stream of consciousness" data show the levels of audience response and the character of the audience involvement. The verbatim comments of the audience are analyzed by content to indicate common correct and incorrect interpretations of the message.

In addition to the above measures, scaled and closed-ended questions are used to determine the overall success of the commercial. This is done regarding:

- The commercial's success in accomplishing its communication objectives
- Brand recall
- Rating of a product in terms of how good it is on a six-point rating scale
- Entertainment value as measured on a six-point enjoyment scale
- Advertiser rating on a six-point scale
- Perceived selling effectiveness on a six-point scale

The scene-by-scene data and the quantitative overall measurements are compared to normative data by product category.

The field methodology for the Clucas technique is a "theatre approach." One hundred members of the target audience are shown program material with commercial clutters embedded in the program in a natural manner as usually seen on television. The moderator for the group focuses attention on the program rather than on the commercials. Questions are asked about the program, usually about one specific character, and then questions are asked about the commercial. To get more specific answers, the commercial is repeated scene by scene. After each scene, the respondents are asked questions regarding that scene that relate to the topics mentioned above. The summary questions are asked and the group is thanked and paid for their time.

THE DADSON COMPARE METHOD OF CREATIVE EVALUATION

The Dadson Compare Method evaluates advertising creative execution in terms of persuasion, communication and intrusiveness. Matched samples of 100 respondents each are selected from shoppers at mall locations. The experimental group views the commercial and is then asked questions regarding the brand advertised along the persuasion, communication and intrusiveness dimensions. The control group is asked the brand attitude questions but is not shown the commercial. The ratings from the matched samples are analyzed for differences between the control and experimental scores. The data can be compared to historical norms for most product categories.

THE PEAC SYSTEM

PEAC is generally recognized as the first organization to develop and perfect a portable instantaneous testing system. The PEAC system using hand-held microcomputers, provides second-to-second response to advertising and provides instantaneous viewing of the graphical results overlaid on the commercial.

The typical procedure for a PEAC test for TV or radio commercials is outlined below.

- **Recruitment:**
  Respondents are recruited from the intended target group for the commercial and invited to a central facility where the testing is conducted. Usually 20 to 30 shoppers are present at each testing. Because of the portability of the equipment, the testing can be flexibly relocated to be accessible to the respondents.

- **Introduction:**
  The respondents are informed of the general nature of the testing procedures and are shown how to use the hand-held response panels. The panels have five buttons labelled A, B, C, D and E, where the scale is usually "very positive" for A, "positive" for B, "neutral" for C, "negative" for D and "very negative" for E. The moderator can assign different scales to

the buttons should the need arise.

- **Preview Viewing of Commercials:**
  The commercials are shown to the respondents initially to familiarize them with the commercials and to reduce the order effects, first exposure effects and to help equalize prior familiarity. Respondents typically view and rate six to twelve commercials in a single pod.

- **Recall Questionnaire:**
  Brand recall and product recall questions are asked after the commercials have been viewed.

- **Second Viewing of Commercials Using the PEAC Hand-Held Units:**
  The moment-to-moment responses of the subjects to the commercials are obtained by their pushing the five buttons on the hand-held units. The respondents are encouraged to push the buttons as frequently as desired during the commercial. The responses are immediately sent to the personal computer and processed.

- **View Test Commercial in Isolation:**
  The shoppers' attention is focused specifically on the test material and they respond once again with the hand-held units.

- **Communication Questionnaire:**
  A questionnaire with open-ended questions is provided to test the credibility, confusion and relevance of the main and secondary messages.

- **Closed-ended PEAC Unit Questions:**
  The hand-held units are used by the respondents to provide answers to questions regarding their thoughts and feelings while viewing the commercials, product benefit statements, brand image statements, communications statements and socio-demographic questions. There are then 10 numbered buttons on the unit which are used to answer some of these questions.

- **Break** (optional):
  Discussion with client and data generated.

- **Focused Group Discussion:**
  A focused group discussion is held while the group views the PEAC Line graph superimposed on the test commercial. The PEAC Line moves dynamically into peaks of positive responses and valleys of negative responses to the commercial. The moderator stops the commercial frequently to obtain the group's explanation for the negative or positive feelings at those points in the commercial.

The PEAC system was developed in Canada and has now gained wide acceptance in the U.S. and in Europe as an instrument for the testing of television commercials and other marketing vehicles.

PERCEPTION ANALYZER

The Perception Analyzer is a method of measuring the creative value of a commercial second-by-second coincidental with the viewing of the commercial by the individual. A hand-held response meter is used by the subjects to respond to the test material on a real time, i.e., as it happens, schedule. The information is immediately available to the client in numerical and graphical format.

The fieldwork is conducted at mall sites with two to ten respondents or in single group studies ranging in size from 40 to 120 subjects. Multi-site studies can be conducted to obtain a regional or national profile with groups ranging up to 120 participants. Typically, respondents are screened and recruited by telephone and are invited to participate at accessible central sites where they are given an incentive of $50 or more.

The Perception Analyzer session is typically two hours in length and includes testing reviews of video or audio materials, one or two sessions where subjects perform a trade-off task among brands and product characteristics, and an evaluation of other advertising material. The last 30 to 45 minutes are devoted to discussions with participants.

The participants respond to questions by turning a dial on specially designed, developed and refined response meters that transmit the information directly back to a personal computer on the test site. The data are analyzed immediately and can be seen by the moderators and the client. The subjects' answers are completely anonymous and do not rely on their facility with oral communication, thereby enhancing the incidence of response from many who would have difficulty expressing themselves to their satisfaction.

The following is indicative of a typical interactive group session.

- **Participant Profile:**
  Attitudinal, behavioural and demographic information are obtained and can be used to analyze the commercial testing information by shopper segment.

- **Baseline Profile:**
  Categorical questions are used to elicit brand preference and intention to purchase information. A video tape of a typical walk down the aisle in a supermarket, for example, is shown to respondents. The are asked to indicate on their hand-held dials which sections of the display are most interesting and likely to attract their attention.

- **Reaction Profile:**
  The subjects view the target commercial and competitive commercials interspersed with a 20 minute clutter tape. Respondents' reaction to the test material, according to the criteria specified by the moderator, is reg-

istered through the hand-held dials. The evaluative criteria may be appeal, persuasiveness, believability, likability, and so on.

- **Post-Test Profile:**

  After responding to the clutter reel of commercials, respondents record their recall of the advertising and the perceived message using pencil and paper then use their dials to enter the written messages. The walk down the aisle video tape is shown a second time and subjects once again indicate which displays attract their attention.

  Each commercial is viewed two or three times and evaluated relative to the several different criteria. The comprehensive evaluative profile is stimulated by a battery of semantic scales.

- **Refocus:**

  Each commercial is shown a fourth time. The moderator then leads a discussion with the respondents examining those issues of interest to the viewing client.

Over 600 pieces of information can be garnered using this interactive testing procedure. Clients are able to view the information instantly and also to get reports after the data have been analyzed using appropriate statistical procedures. Although the Perception Analyzer is used most frequently to test television commercials, it is also used to test radio commercials, new products, animatic productions (roughed-out executions or animated drawings which are developed prior to incurring the expense of a full production of the commercial), broadcast talent, logos, movies and music.

DAY-AFTER-RECALL TEST (DAR)

The tests described so far are all intended to improve advertising prior to its being placed on the air or printed. There are, however, a number of procedures that are devoted to identifying whether the advertising as seen or read in the media was effective or not. The term *effective* can be misleading since it is related to the objective of the advertising which, as was discussed earlier, can vary from creating awareness through to convincing a purchaser that he made the right decision.

The principal rationale of those using the technique (DAR) is that if a commercial does not communicate anything, it can't sell anything. Thus, the commercial that communicates poorly should be discarded even though a high scoring commercial in itself cannot assure that all other elements of sales success are present (Miller, 1971:38).

One the most direct tests is called the *day-after-recall test*. The name is descriptive of the procedure. The day after a commercial is aired on television, respondents are called and asked if they viewed the program within which the commercial appeared the preceding day. If they did, they are asked to name the commercials that they remember appearing during that program. If they do not name the test commercial, they are asked in an aided fashion whether they saw the Whiskas commercial, for example. Viewers are also asked to mention the things that they remembered about the commercial. The percentages of viewers who correctly name the commercial and remember parts of it are compared to historical normative percentages that have been measured for commercials advertising products in the same product category. The Burke International Research Day-After-Recall Test is probably the best known of these procedures.

EIDETIC MOTIVATIONAL RESEARCH

Eidetic motivational research is quite different from most other marketing research procedures. It relies on the belief that each person perceives the world and objects in it through his or her idiosyncratic combination of senses and feelings. Separating the individual's perception through a dissection based on conventional verbal response to closed-ended questions does not capture the essence of the image formed by that person and on which that person makes decisions. Often eidetics refers to the "visual recall or internal imagery and encompasses the personal meanings of such visualizations" (Evering et al., 1990). Having respondents provide their total image of a brand or object based on the visual and verbal information provided by a television commercial is felt to keep the advertising impact closer to what is actually felt by the respondent and used to make shopping decisions.

MEASURING ADVERTISING EFFECTIVENESS

If it were possible, almost all advertisers would like to conduct studies which told them precisely that for every dollar spent on advertising they'd get $41.23 back in product sales. Unfortunately, this type of research has not been particularly effective in most areas of marketing.

The most frequent and critical questions asked of advertising managers are:

- How much should I spend?
- How should I spend it?
- Where should I spend it?

• When should I spend it?

An even more fundamental questions is "How effective is advertising in affecting sales?" Immediate sales results, even when totally measurable are, at best, an incomplete criterion of advertising effectiveness. In many cases, the most valuable effects of advertising may be experienced in the long term. However, if something is to happen in the long run, something must be happening in the short run that will ultimately lead to eventual sales results.

A logically correct specification of the effectiveness of advertising would entail a detailed account of the entire structure of the decision to buy and the various stages this decision breaks into as well as the nature of the influence that advertising makes at every stage of the decision process. For example, the decision to buy a brand is a complex process of an intention to buy in the product category, to acquire information about alterative product and brand choices, a planning phase, a choice of likely brand, and finally a decision to spend money on a specific brand. The simple result of product expenditures is the last step in a hierarchy of decisions that advertising can influence with many other variables at several junctions. Effectiveness as such is the result of where one measures the effect of advertising and in terms of what creative and business objective one chooses for the ad campaign. Measurement of the effectiveness of advertising should be seen as a series of tests instead of one standard measure that relates advertising dollars to sales.

The problems in the measurement of advertising effectiveness can be grouped into four major classifications:

1. The specification of goals or objectives;

2. Acquisition of the correct type of data;

3. Development of a correct framework (model) for analysis;

4. The development of suitable statistical procedures for the estimation and calibration of the model.

Not all of these problems are, however, explicity identified in each of the approaches used in advertising evaluation. The most common problem is the lack of appropriate data. But this is a trivial problem in comparison to the use of misspecified models. Naturally, a model that does not correctly reflect the information gathering, information processing and decision-making process used by consumers will not produce results that are generally usable.

There have been many attempts at developing econometric and time series models of the sales advertising relationship. Some of these projects have been successful but many have not achieved their objectives. One problem with this approach is that far too many resources have been devoted to the specification of lags and functional forms of the equations than to the underlying nature of the consumer decision-making processes involved in the system modelled and the structure of the model. Actually, the differences in the specification of goals and objectives of advertising among the various approaches can be easily related to the differences in the frameworks used.

Why Communication Research Can Seldom Predict the "Success of Advertisement"

• Creative strategy for copy and execution may change
• Objectives of the ad may not relate directly to sales
• Effects of ad may be delayed
• Research has no control over ad scheduling
• Ad strategy may be wrong or badly timed
• Product distribution may be poor
• Product may not live up to promise
• Competitors' activities
• Low category purchase level
• Residual effects of other advertising
• Advertising in other media

Although there have been studies that have achieved success in measuring the effectiveness of advertising in terms of sales and market share changes, the majority of such studies have not been able convincingly to represent the relationship between these two factors. Most of the reported successful studies have been in the consumer product sector. One successful application in the service sector is The Return-on-Advertising Model © (ROA Model ©) developed jointly by Marketing Decision Research Inc. and Econometric Research Limited. The ROA Model © was developed for a provincial government in Canada to estimate the effectiveness of tourism advertising through the modelling of the decision by tourists to take a pleasure trip to that province. The modelling process developed a comprehensive framework of the relationships among advertising expenditures and tourism expenditures and used linear structural modelling and econometric modelling and estimation procedures for evaluating the effectiveness of tourism advertising on a continuing basis.

The final model form used for estimation was developed in two steps:

• A causal model was constructed, tested and refined by using the LISREL procedure of structural modelling

• Econometric modelling was used to estimate the relationships indicated in the final structural causal model

Many relationships were investigated using the causal modelling and

Exhibit 17.7   A Model of the Tourist Choice to Visit Ontario

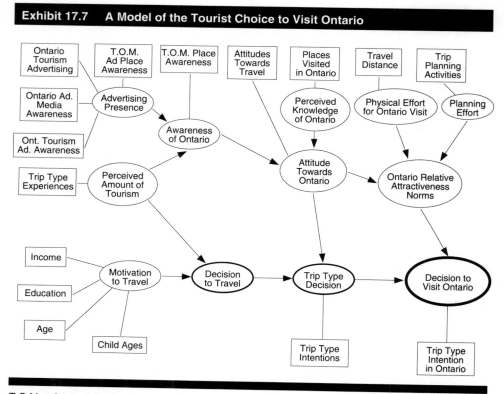

T.O.M. refers to 'top-of-mind' awareness.

econometric estimation procedures. The aim was to measure the responses of travel intentions to attitude, awareness, past trip history and socio-demographic factors. Many of the relationships investigated produced good to excellent indicators of fit of the models to the data. The initially proposed model of the decision to visit the province is shown in Exhibit 17.7.

The analysis procedure was able to reduce the "theoretically correct" model in Exhibit 17.7 to a smaller model that fitted the data better and allowed for estimation of the advertising effectiveness, shown in Exhibit 17.8.

While the modelling mathematics and the statistics of the estimation procedure used to arrive at the model in Exhibit 17.8 are beyond the scope of this book, the process is one that might provide some insights into the techniques that can be used for these types of problems.

Causal modelling was developed as a process and methodology to investigate causal linkages among adjacent structural components of a model and to build on those linkages from the basic primary independent variable model

Exhibit 17.8   A Reduced Model of the Tourist Choice to Visit Ontario

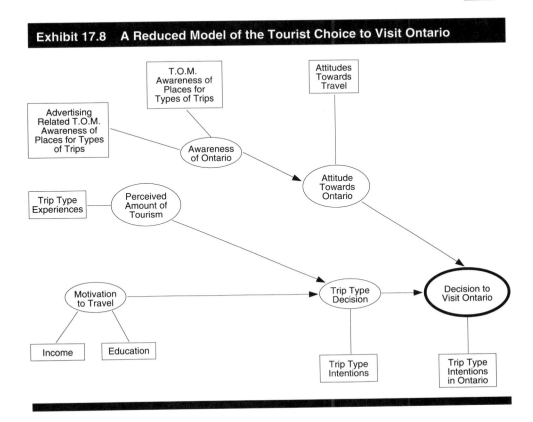

components to the higher-level dependent variables. Through the confirmation or invalidation of the causal relationships as they accumulate through the model, the overall causal structure is established among the model constructs. LISREL is a computer program designed to assist researchers to confirm or to refute hypothesized structural relationships in order to refine a model to fit the data better. The causal model refined using the LISREL analysis can provide the important basis for relating purchase behaviour to advertising through consumers' attitudes towards the product.

SUMMARY

Communication research is tremendously rich area of investigation within marketing research.

- It involves everything from focus groups to the most sophisticated modelling and statistical analysis.

- Advertising research is exciting because the testing done at the early stages might be reflected in the on-air commercial studied, and it can also be used to help identify the value of advertising which has existed in the marketplace for some time.

There are a number of common problems associated with communication research. These include:

- **Size**: Incremental effects of advertising are too small to measure with small samples
- **Money**: Dollars seldom available for proper sample size
- **Rigidity**: Client may insist on standard or pet techniques
- **Timidity**: Clients/agencies may demand data to make decisions automatic
- **Validity**: Seldom assessed

The future of communication research is likely to be even more exciting. New technologies such as the following are becoming more common:

- In-home UPC scanners
- In-home people meters
- Second-by-second TV ratings and single source data

More precise attitudinal and behavioural measures of response to advertising are likely to become common in the not-too-distant future as well.

NOW THINK ABOUT THIS

1. The text expands on models which can help explain the development of attitudes due to advertising in quadrant 1 of the FCB Grid. Develop a model which will help to explain more fully the process of quadrant 2.

2. Contrast the Clucas, PEAC and Perception Analyzer procedures for range of use, complication and face validity.

3. Discuss the ways in which the validity of Perception Analyzer technique could be assessed.

REFERENCES

Clucas, Eric

1990 Private Communication.

Evering, Henry, Ralph Evering, Robert Ricker, and Christian de Laet
1990 "Eidetic Organizational Development: Image Motivations and Systems Research." *Canadian Journal of Marketing Research*. 9, 14-32.

Kubursi, Atif A., David Butterfield, and Kenneth R. Deal
1990 *The Tourism Advertising Evaluation Model.* Toronto: Ontario Ministry of Tourism and Recreation.

Lavidge, R., and G.A. Steiner
1961 "A Model for Predictive Measurements of Advertising Effectiveness." *Journal of Marketing*, 25 (October), 59-62.

Miller, Don
1971 *Television/Radio Age*, May 31, 1971, p.38.

Ratchford, Brian S.
1985 "Operationalizing Involvement and Thinking/Feeling Dimensionality in the FCB Grid." Working Paper.

Reynolds, Thomas J. and Jonathan Gutman
1984 "Advertising is Image Management." *Journal of Advertising Research*, 24, No. 1 (February/March), 27-37.

Reynolds, Thomas J., Brian C. Cockle and John P. Rochon
1990 "The Strategy Imperatives of Advertising: Implications of Means-End Theory and Research Findings." *Canadian Journal of Marketing Research*, 9, 3-13.

Vaughn, Richard
1980 "How Advertising Works: A Planning Model." *Journal of Advertising Research*, 20, No. 5, 27-33.

Vaughn, Richard
1986 "How Advertising Works: A Planning Model Revisited." *Journal of Advertising Research*, (Feb/Mar), 57-66.

18 / Market Segmentation

WHAT YOU WILL LEARN IN THIS CHAPTER

- The importance of segmenting the market
- Different ways in which the market may be segmented
- To assess the special characteristics of the Canadian market with relation to market segmentation
- The difference between MVS and LVS methods
- To decide on the appropriate segmentation level for a given problem
- To choose a suitable technique for segmentation for a given problem

BASIC CONCEPTS

The problem of matching what the consumer wants with what the producer wants to sell is a perennial one. Even when there is a proven need for the product, the consumer has still to be informed and persuaded to buy the product. It is intuitively appealing to group consumers who have similar characteristics, wants and needs for the purpose of matching them with a product. The process of grouping consumers having something in common is called *market segmentation*. The matching of consumers and products through market segmentation has several implications that are not immediately obvious.

MAXIMIZING THE IMPACT OF LIMITED RESOURCES

Consider a product that can be consumed by anybody. No matter how universal the usage of a product appears to be—whether it be toothpaste, steak or books—it will not appeal to everyone. Denture-wearers are not likely to use toothpaste, vegetarians are not likely to eat steak and the functionally illiterate will not read books. While these are extreme examples, this principle is also true at a more common level. For example, expensive cars cannot be sold in large numbers to low income consumers; neither is a discount store likely to attract many millionaires to its annual sale.

To reach the total potential audience is obviously expensive. Canada may have a population of about 25 million people, but the bulk of sales for an expensive perfume may come from a small group of wealthier women who may number as few as one million. The manufacturer with an advertising budget of $25 million has two choices: reach every Canadian just once during the year, or reach the people who are most likely to buy the product 25 times during the same period. The conflict between reach and frequency is a common one. In general, when one of the two is preferred, the other suffers.

By restricting the advertising to selectively defined groups of consumers, the manufacturer may miss potential consumers who do not fall into pre-defined groups. But the underlying idea behind market segmentation is that losses due to such omissions will be more than offset by the increase in sales achieved within the defined target groups. The rationale is that the budget is limited and the audience is not and the best way to increase your profit is to concentrate your efforts in areas where the return on investment is the greatest.

AVOIDING THE NEGATIVE EFFECTS OF VISIBILITY

Even assuming that the manufacturer has an unlimited budget, it may not be a good idea to reach an audience that is, by and large, outside the potential market for the product. This is particularly true of prestige products. A prestige product cannot continue to be prestigious if its appeal is aimed at the mass market. Such an approach may affect the product in two ways: it may alienate current and potential consumers, and create hostility and derision among these who cannot afford it. Reaching people who are not in your market cannot always be considered a positive or even neutral exercise.

MINIMIZING UNPRODUCTIVE CONSUMER SUBSIDY

Let us compare the market for two products Alpha and Beta. Their consumer profile looks as follows:

Brand	Brand Conscious	Price Conscious
Alpha	85%	15%
Beta	10%	90%

If Beta decides to drop its price, it may have an immediate effect on Alpha in that some of the 15% of Alpha's consumers (price conscious group) may switch to Beta. Thus Alpha will see some erosion in its market share. However, if Alpha is not aware of the segmented nature of its consumers, it may decide to drop its price to compete with Beta. This strategy may be both expensive and counter-productive; expensive because Alpha's price strategy gives a price rebate to 85% of its consumers who did not care for it, and counter-productive because Alpha does not stand to gain much by its strategy (see Exhibit 18.1). Matters can get worse when Beta retaliates by lowering its price further. While the consumer is subsidized by both firms, both firms stand to lose overall in the game.[1]

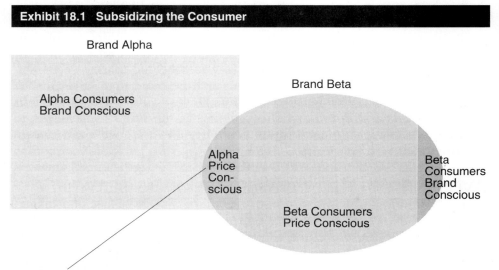

Exhibit 18.1 Subsidizing the Consumer

Brand Alpha

Alpha Consumers
Brand Conscious

Brand Beta

Alpha
Price
Con-
scious

Beta Consumers
Price Conscious

Beta
Consumers
Brand
Conscious

Only this part of Alpha's share will be affected by price changes. If Beta has already captured this segment, Alpha's retaliation (matching the price cut) is counterproductive because most of the remaining consumers are not influenced by price.

FINDING LARGE PROFITS IN SMALL NUMBERS

What do consumers want? When a marketer attempts to answer this question, he may find that many highly profitable product ideas are at the bottom of the list. If there is a market for a product among only one-half of one per cent of the population, an idea may not even be considered since the potential appears so trivial. But if the market is segmented and analyzed, the marketer may find a niche for a product that may have low potential volume but exceptionally high profits. Without segmenting the market, it is very difficult to determine whether the idea is an unpopular one in general, or a highly popular one among a small but identifiable group.

SEVEN WAYS TO SLICE THE MARKET

In broad terms, whenever we look at research results by different sub-groups—such as usage of a product among men, among women, among older people, among younger people and so on—we are indeed segmenting the market, albeit not formally. The terms *market segmentation*, however, applies to formal ways of dividing the market into identifiable sub-groups, usually made up of a combination of characteristics. It is a process of partitioning the market by gathering consumers with similar characteristics. The concept of similar characteristics, however, is not defined; consequently, markets can be segmented using any set of characteristics considered relevant for the market by the marketer and the researcher. Currently, seven different ways of partitioning consumers are popular (see Exhibit 18.2).

Exhibit 18.2 Seven Levels of Segmentation

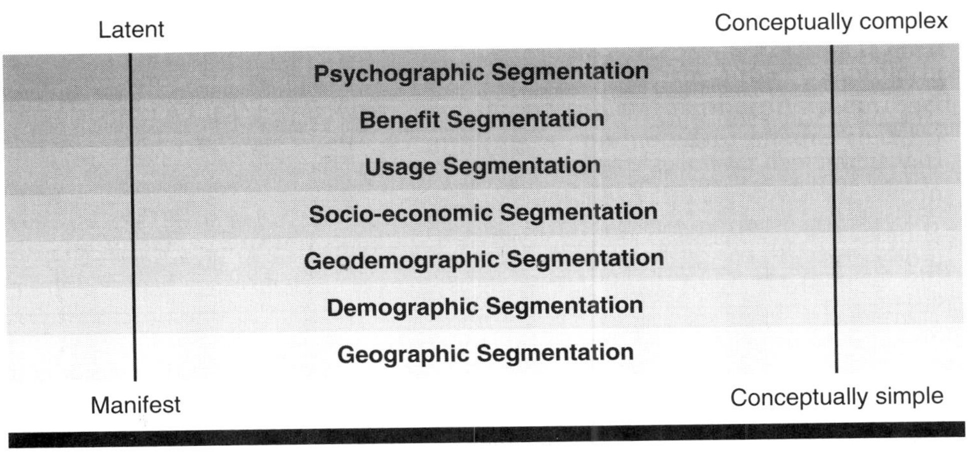

Latent   Conceptually complex

Psychographic Segmentation

Benefit Segmentation

Usage Segmentation

Socio-economic Segmentation

Geodemographic Segmentation

Demographic Segmentation

Geographic Segmentation

Manifest   Conceptually simple

GEOGRAPHIC SEGMENTATION   For most neighbourhood retail businesses, geographic segmentation is the most appropriate one. Neighbourhood retailers usually attract most of their customers from people in the immediate vicinity. Seventy-five per cent of those who frequent a convenience store, for example, are likely to live within a one mile radius.

DEMOGRAPHIC SEGMENTATION   For specialty stores, demographic segmentation may be more appropriate. Of importance to a women's imported shoe store can be the number of women above a certain level of income.

GEODEMOGRAPHIC SEGMENTATION   Geodemographic segmentation, which combines both geographic and demographic characteristics of a given area, is a popular way of segmenting the market. Such geodemographic segmentation can be pre-defined or custom-defined.

SOCIO-ECONOMIC SEGMENTATION   Socio-economic segmentation is indeed an extension of geodemographic segmentation. In addition to a person's demographics, his or her social class is taken into account. It is important to note here that people who belong to different social groups may exhibit different buying patterns, although they have the same economic status. Examples of this type of segmentation would include descriptions such as (what may be colloquially described as) "old money" or "upwardly mobile professional."

USAGE SEGMENTATION   The market can be segmented on the basis of heaviness of usage of a given category. Consumers who exhibit certain patterns of product usage are isolated for further study. In many product categories, a small percentage of consumers accounts for a large consumption volume. (This is often stated as the Pareto principle, or the 80-20 principle. In our example we may state that 20% of our consumers account for 80% of the consumption volume. The Pareto principle is not a scientific truth, but the pareto-type imbalance can be observed under a variety of marketing conditions.)

BENEFIT SEGMENTATION   Different groups of consumers may use the same product for different reasons. A visit to a restaurant may satisfy one's hunger or one's need to socialize; an after-shave lotion can be used either as a cosmetic or as an antiseptic. The marketer may want to segment the market on the basis of the main benefit package expected of a product by consumers. Such segmentation will help the marketer to position a brand more precisely, introduce a new brand or change the advertising strategy.

PSYCHOGRAPHIC SEGMENTATION   Consumers who belong to the same segment according to the criteria mentioned so far may still use different products. As a result their perception of the world–and hence their consumption habits and patterns–differ. Thus a person who considers himself frugal may not buy an expensive suit, although his geodemographic and socio-economic characteristics and benefit expectations may be no different from another who does. The reason for this is that these two consumers differ in their psychological orientation to the world around them.

Five of the above methods (geographic, demographic, geodemographic, benefit and psychographic segmentation) are described in greater detail in this chapter.

CHOOSING THE SEGMENTATION LEVEL

SEGMENTATION LEVELS AND LATENT VARIABLES   The seven ways of segmenting the marketing can also be seen as seven different levels of segmentation. Each level of segmentation from 1 to 7 adds complexity to the analysis. As we go from the lowest to the highest level of segmentation, the variables we analyze become less and less manifest and more and more latent.

Although achieving higher levels of segmentation requires greater skills of design, analysis and interpretation, it does not necessarily follow that those levels will provide the marketer with better marketing information. The decision about whether to use manifest variables or latent variables depends on the nature of the problem and the product under consideration.

For most generalized retail operations, manifest variable segmentation is more valuable and realistic, while for high-priced products with a narrow appeal, latent variable segmentation is likely to be more appropriate.

INAPPROPRIATE SEGMENTATION CAN BE COSTLY   Most segmentation procedures involve grouping people using some statistical criteria. Thus, no matter what variables are used, one is likely to end up with market segments that are different from a mathematical point of view. Yet if the segments do not relate to the product in question, then market segmentation is a futile exercise.

Sometimes the distortion can be very subtle. Assume a market for a product for which a manifest variable (income) and a latent variable (quest for status) are interrelated. If we segment the market according to the manifest variable (income), we will indeed find that income is related to consumption of this product. But while income is a necessary condition for the use of the product, it may not be a sufficient condition. The marketer may find that his effort to increase the market share of the product by appealing to people in a certain income group is not very successful, although segmentation indicated that heavy users of the product are from that group.

APPLYING OCCAM'S RAZOR   It is not always obvious what level of segmentation is appropriate for a given product. While this understanding comes with experience, sometimes no relevant prior knowledge exists. Under such circumstances it is appropriate to use Occam's razor and *start with the lowest level of segmentation and proceed to the next level only when that level is properly understood and found wanting.* Manifest variables should be analyzed and understood before one hypothesizes about the influence of latent variables.

STRATEGIC SEGMENTATION

Market segmentation can be used as a tool for strategic planning. A manufacturer may decide to use the results of market segmentation analysis in several ways. The most common of these uses are differentiation, concentration and atomization.

DIFFERENTIATION   The most common way of using market segmentation analysis is to identify the niche with the largest number of prospects and position the product there. This strategy, however, has some limitations. For instance, if this involves repositioning, there is a risk that we may not achieve the target position and in the process we may even lose our current market position. A better strategy might be to leave the current product as it is, but to introduce a new product to take advantage of the sub-segment of the existing market. Thus, when weight-conscious consumers wanted soft-drinks with fewer calories, most soft-drink manufacturers did not change the formulation of a successful product, but simply introduced a variation of it to cater to this sub-segment.

CONCENTRATION   Marketers using the concentration strategy may simply concentrate on one segment or even a sub-segment and may not be interested in profit opportunities that are open to them outside this segment. This is a less expensive strategy than differentiation and is suitable for makers of prestige items and businesses that have limited resources and whose main objective is to establish a strong reputation in one area rather than maximum profitability overall.

ATOMIZATION   This is segmentation carried to its extreme where products are designed to satisfy each potential customer. Makers of submarines, warheads, etc., fall into this category. Recent technology makes this a viable strategy in marketing mass market products. An example of this is a financial newsletter from the United States which is designed for each individual investor. Because information can quickly be retrieved from commercial databases, each subscriber gets a mass-produced, customized newsletter.

GEOGRAPHIC SEGMENTATION

The most obvious way of segmenting any market is by identifying where the buyers are. For many products, buyers tend to be concentrated in specific regions of the country. There is likely to be a greater per capita fish consumption in coastal regions than in other areas. The need for financial services is greater in economically developed parts of the country than in economically depressed regions.

GEOGRAPHIC SEGMENTATION FACTORS

In segmenting people geographically, one can use different factors depending on the product being marketed. Such factors would include geographic *territory* (e.g., Atlantic, Prairies), the *nature* of the area (urban or rural), the *size* of the area (e.g., cities with a population of 100 000 or more), population *density* (largeness of the market for a given geographic size), *climate* (e.g., the difference between Calgary and Victoria), *market scope* (global, national, provincial or local), and *standardized market measures* (such as primary marketing areas).

CANADIAN REALITIES

No major country in the world is geographically homogeneous. Disparities exist in consumption patterns, needs and wants. Canada is no different. In fact, the regional disparities are very striking in Canada. Consider these:

49th Parallel Plus 320 Kilometres:

- Canada is the second largest country in the world in terms of physical size, yet over two-thirds of its population live within 320 kilometres of the U.S. border. This would mean that the market runs east-west (rather than north-south) covering a narrow strip. Marketing activities should take this reality of Canadian geography into account.
- Less than one-twelfth of the land surface is occupied by farmland. Tremendous distances may have to be covered in marketing certain products and services.

Diverse Resources:

- There are marked regional differences in terms of resources: Alberta's oil industry, the Atlantic Provinces' fish industry, British Columbia's mining industry, etc., make the country's population mobile. Prosperity shifts from province to province depending on economic realities at any given time. As a result, workers tend to move from the less prosperous regions to the more prosperous ones. The average Canadian is highly mobile and is estimated to move residence 12 times in his or her lifetime.

Population: Concentration and Density:

- By concentrating on just two provinces—Ontario and Quebec— a marketer can reach nearly two-thirds of the Canadian market.
- Some of Canada's smaller provinces have the highest population densities.

Impact of Immigration:

- Canada's immigration and refugee policies bring an influx of people into the country on a continuous basis. The new arrivals do not distribute themselves evenly among the different regions of the country. For instance, 52% of Ontarians are foreign-born, while Western Canada contains the largest number of foreign-born people who immigrated prior to 1946. Consequently, the composition of consumers changes radically in different parts of the country.

Impact of Emigration:

- While seldom noticed by anyone, Canada's emigration is also very significant. It is estimated that in the first 120 years of Confederation for every four immigrants, there were three emigrants.

Large Urban Population:

- Canada's population is predominantly urban. Three cities—Toronto, Montreal and Vancouver—contain nearly 30% of the Canadian population. Cities with a population of 100 000 or more accommodate 55% of Canada's population.
- Larger urban areas also have more younger people, especially in the 20-40 age groups.

HOW GEOGRAPHY AFFECTS CONSUMPTION

The reason for geographic segmentation is that people who are grouped according to several of the criteria listed above tend to have different consumption patterns. These patterns are crucial to the marketer. Let us consider an example for each one of the above factors.

Geographic Territory:

As mentioned earlier, people who live in different regions tend to share patterns of consumption. In many cases, it may not be economical to transport certain items for consumption to other regions of the country.

Size of the Area:

Size of the area may be of particular interest to retail outlets. Certain items are consumed by a small proportion of the population. A high-fashion boutique, for instance, may appeal to just 1% of the population and hence not be cost-efficient in centres that have small populations.

Nature of the Area:

The nature of the area—urban or rural—can affect consumption patterns. For instance, there may be a greater need for insecticides in rural areas than urban areas. Urban residents are likely to dine out more often, and people who live on the outskirts of a city are likely to use automobiles more extensively.

Population Density:

This, once again, is very important for retail locations. Population density tells us how many consumers we may be able to reach within our retail trading zone (RTZ). The consumption patterns also tend to be different in centres with high population density.

Climate:

Canada`s climate—ranging from heavy snow in places like northern Alberta to intermittent rain in Vancouver and Victoria—shows extreme variety. The product one can market (snowblowers, umbrellas, insulation materials, clothing, etc.,) will depend on the local climate.

Market Scope:

Geographic segmentation will also depend on the scope of the market (as conceived by the marketer) or the nature of the product. Thus, the geographic market area may be *global* (multinationals), *national*, *provincial* (e.g., especially products and services that are federally regulated), or *local* (mostly retailers).

Market Area Measures:

Marketers use special measures such as Primary Marketing Areas (PMA) to isolate the market in which they want to concentrate their efforts. Such geographic classifications are even more extensive in the United States (e.g., Arbitron's Areas of Dominant Influence or ADI, A.C. Nielsen's A,B,C, and D market measures or DMA—Designated Market Areas).

Census Classifications:

Canada contains several identifiable sub-divisions such as regions, provinces, Census Metropolitan Areas (CMAs), Census Agglomerations (CAs) and Enumeration Areas (EAs). Statistics Canada, federal and provincial agencies, and several private sources provide information on such geographic units.

Multiple Classifications:

The above list provides a basic framework of the most commonly used dimensions of geographic classification. Effective geographic segmentation often incorporates several interlocking geographic dimensions.

The Problem of Contiguity:

One characteristic of segmentation that is more relevant to geographic segmentation than to any other type of segmentation is contiguity. For example, if two high-potential markets are separated by a small low-potential market, it may be desirable to include the intervening low-potential market as a part of one large segment along with the other two markets. In a case like this, the cost of dealing with two separate markets might be higher than dealing with one large market, a small part of which has low potential.

When is Geographic Segmentation Useful?

Geographic segmentation is useful only if one or more of the following criteria are met:

- There should be considerable cost savings in terms of movement of goods and services
- Consumers should show genuinely different consumption or product usage patterns
- The segmented portion should be a viable market for the contemplated product

Research into Geographic Segmentation

Geographic segmentation is usually carried out through secondary sources. The largest purveyor of geographic information (as it relates to marketing research) in Canada is Statistics Canada. Information is also available from other sources such as federal and provincial government publications and private publications. (For more details, refer to Chapter 24, Secondary Research.)

Demographic Segmentation

Segmenting consumers according to demographics—age, sex, education, income, occupation, household composition, etc.—is intuitively appealing. All standard cross-tabulations in marketing research acknowledge this by using demographic variables as the banner points (bases for looking at results as per sub-groups). Demographic information is routinely collected in consumer surveys, since buying decisions can be related to demographic variables. For instance, different products appeal to different age and occupational groups. Knowledge of these differences enables a marketer to target different products for different demographic groups (or the same product with different appeals to different demographic groups).

Availability of Demographic Information

Let us consider a situation in which we decide (either *a priori* or on the basis of research) that the segment which has the most potential for our product has certain demographic characteristics. Now, how do we find consumers who fit the demographic description? The most exhaustive set of information on demographics available in Canada is, of course, based on the census and is available from Statistics Canada. Demographic information is available for any given geographic sub-division of the country. For all practical purposes, the Enumeration Area (EA) is the smallest unit on which demographic information can be obtained. An EA consists of approximately 600 households. (The information is always provided in the aggregate for any given unit.) It is also possible to obtain demographic information on larger geographic units. Exhibit 6.4 shows how Canada is divided from a geographical point of view and how such divisions are defined. Demographics such as age, sex, marital status, mother tongue, citizenship, number of years of schooling, occupation and employment income are just some of the variables on which information is available.

USING DEMOGRAPHIC SEGMENTATION: AN EXAMPLE

Most marketers simply isolate the demographic characteristics of their current franchise and use them to segment their prospective market. However, to really utilize demographic segmentation effectively, it is preferable to start with the characteristics of the population and then match them with an existing or a potential product.

Consider, for instance, Canadian population growth. Statistics Canada estimates that for the 20 years ending in 2001, the population will grow by 16%. However, this growth will not be even across all age groups. The growth will be concentrated in two age groups: people who are 65 years or older and adults between the ages of 35 and 54. This information provided by organizations like Statistics Canada can be used to segment the market profitably, target the audience and create new products, if necessary. The two groups in which the largest growth is expected are potentially highly profitable segments.

Segment 1: Senior Citizens (Age 65+)

Size (by 2001): About 13% of the population

Type of Products with Specific Appeal: Medical services, drugs, travel, health related products, leisure items, income-oriented conservative financial products, nursing homes, special furniture, any product that relates to financial or physical security, etc.

Other Observations: Not only will this segment be about 50% bigger than it is now, but it will also live longer because life expectancy in general is on the rise. The people in this group are also likely to have a higher purchasing power.

Segment 2: Middle-Aged (Age 35-54)

Size (by 2001): One third of the Canadian population

Type of Products With Specific Appeal: Several luxury items, larger homes and cars, better furniture, expensive recreational items such as boats, investment products, purchases for younger people, etc.

Other Observations: In terms of purchasing power, this group represents considerable clout. It is a group that is in its peak earning period with considerable discretionary income. This group has more money to spend than the younger groups but is less security oriented than the older groups—an ideal target group for a marketer.

These two segments alone will cover about 45% of the Canadian population in the next 13 years. Products that are developed and marketed to these segments over the next few years will have a good chance of survival. In addition to marketing specific products, these demographic trends can also be used to tailor the message to the demographic groups. For instance, even the models used in advertising and the basic appeal used to lure the consumers can be matched to the expectations of these segments.

OTHER EXAMPLES OF DEMOGRAPHIC SEGMENTATION

Income is another prime demographic variable on which consumers may be segmented. Between the early 1970's and the early 1980's, the income of Canadian households showed a dramatic increase in terms of constant (80's) dollar (see Exhibit 18.3).

Exhibit 18.3 Increase in Canadian Household Incomes

	Early 1970's %	Early 1980's %
40 000+	6	29
35-40 000	8	10
25-35 000	25	22
15-25 000	27	21
Under 15 000	25	18

To a large part, this increase in household income can be attributed to both spouses working outside the home. The important point here is that higher real income results in higher purchasing power. A product that was to target households with an income of over $40 000 in 1970 would have seen its audience grow five-fold in a period of 10 years. Similarly, those products that are targeted to the lower income groups would have seen their market segment shrink during the same period. (This change in distribution may have left the relative standing of the segments unaffected. Nevertheless, higher real income does increase the purchasing power of the consumer).

Another major trend in demographics is the rise of single parent families. See Exhibit 18.4 for how they changed between the early 1970's and early 1980's.

Exhibit 18.4 Growth of Single Parent Families

	% Change	
	#	Income
Two-parent	22	30
1 parent - male	25	35
1 parent - female	59	18

Marketers may want to pay more attention to these segments, given the differences in their purchasing patterns and purchasing power.

These observations may sound obvious. However, it is not clear how many of these changes in demographic structure are taken into account by marketing researchers. We recently compared the demographic sections of several questionnaires and cross-tabulation of data for the past 15 years. As far as we can tell, the dramatic changes in income, family structure, etc., are hardly reflected either in the way questions are phrased or (more important-ly) in the way they are tabulated. Changing demographic patterns and hence the resultant segmentation may not be relevant to every study. But it appears doubtful that enough studies which could benefit from such an analysis are in fact paying sufficient attention to the changing demographic patterns and windows of opportunities in the marketplace.

GEODEMOGRAPHIC SEGMENTATION

Segmentation that combines geographical factors with demographic and socio-economic factors is known as geodemographic segmentation. While the three types of segmentation—geographic, demographic and socio-eco-nomic—can be used separately, if they are not combined, they are of limited value.

INCREASING THE UTILITY OF SEGMENTATION BY COMBINING DIFFERENT LEVELS

Geographic segmentation is inevitable when the market is limited either by its nature (retail establishment) or by law (for example, certain financial institutions). However, demographic and socio-economic segmentation—even when they are carried out independently of their geographic units—cannot be used effectively for marketing purposes unless we relate the segments back to geographic units. It is of little use to know that our product will appeal to consumers who are over 50 years old with an annual income of at least $50 000, if we do not know where to find them. Demographic segmentation, when not combined with other factors such as geographic and socio-economic factors, is of limited value.

DEMOGRAPHICS AND SOCIO-ECONOMIC FACTORS

Demographic factors relate to:

1. Variables relating to the size of the market
2. Sex
3. Factors relating to life cycle such as age
4. Nationality, religion and race

Socio-economic factors relate to:

1. Monetary factors
2. Home ownership factors
3. Social class

Although the distinction is not always clear-cut, in general, demographic characteristics are those inherent in the individual or in the family unit, while socio-economic characteristics are those acquired by the individual or the family unit. In some cases, socio-economic factors could be based on the marketer's judgment (e.g., the definition of "social class" will vary depending on who defines it). Some commonly used demographic and socio-economic factors are given in Exhibit 18.5.

Exhibit 18.5   Commonly Used Demographic and Socio-economic Variables

Commonly Used Demographics
- Population
- Number of households
- Size of the household
- Age
- Sex
- Marital status
- Nationality
- Religion
- Race

Commonly Used Socio-economic Variables
- Income
- Education
- Occupation
- Type of dwelling
- Home-owner/renter
- Mobility
- Social class

DATA COLLECTION

Geodemographic segmentation information is obtained in two different ways.

Method 1: Custom Segmentation:

In major usage and attitude studies, information is always collected about the consumer's demographic and socio-economic characteristics. These characteristics can be clustered (a statistical segmentation procedure discussed later) and related to product usage. This procedure not only helps us to identify the most profitable market segments but it also indicates the correlates of usage. For example, we may identify the following segment as potentially the most profitable one for our product: consumers with at least university education who are female with an annual income of at least $45 000. Market research surveys are seldom large enough to tell us where to find consumers who conform to the definition of this segment. However, we can obtain this information (for a fee) from Statistics Canada.

In some cases, the marketer may skip the marketing research survey and simply define the segments in demographic and socio-economic terms. While this is a valid technique for a pre-segmented product (when it is the intention of the marketer to market the product to a specific group), it can be risky for an established product if the marketer's definition of the market is at variance with reality.

Method 2: Pre-defined Segmentation:

The popularity of geodemographics has led several suppliers to create pre-defined segments based on geodemographics. Some of the major suppliers of such information in North America are given in Exhibit 18.6.

Exhibit 18.6 Some Major Suppliers of Geodemographics in North America

- CACI (ACORN)
- Claritas (PRIZM)
- Compusearch (Lifestyles)
- Donnelley Marketing Information Services
- Geographic Decision Support Systems (GDSS)
- Market Statistics
- National Decision Systems (FutureVISION)
- National Planning Data Corporation
- Urban Decision Systems
- Criterion (Texas)
- Demographic Research Company
- Dualabs
- The Glimpse Corporation
- Marketing Economics Institute

Except for Compusearch, all of the organizations listed in Exhibit 18.6 are based in the United States, but some are rumoured to have plans to start their operations in Canada.

HOW ARE PRE-DEFINED SEGMENTS CREATED? Typically, segments are created as follows: A basic unit for which census information is available—such as an enumeration area in Canada or zip code in the United States—is first chosen. A series of demographic and socio-economic characteristics for which census information is available is then selected to form the basis of geodemographic segmentation. A cluster is defined as all those geographic units that fulfill a set of pre-defined characteristics. Thus, for example, a given enumeration area (EA) may be classified as belonging to cluster A if, in that EA:

- 60% of the households have an income of at least $60 000
- Between 20% and 30% have a university education
- The incidence of households with children is between 15% to 25%
- Between 50% to 60% are apartment dwellers
- Over 75% of those employed are white collar workers

A wide ranging set of demographic and socio-economic characteristics is usually used in creating clusters. Currently, the most widely used pre-defined geodemographic segment is the one created by Compusearch under the name of "Lifestyles," which is really a census-based grouping of EAs. Despite what the name suggests, the clusters do not necessarily reflect the lifestyles of the individuals; they are simply the average demographic and socio-economic levels of the geographic units. The lifestyles of the individuals in a geographic unit are presumed to follow the combined characteristics of individuals for that unit. There are about 50 such lifestyles. A main advantage of pre-defined segments is that they provide a relatively low-cost analysis of the market for those who cannot afford to carry out custom research to define their market at precisely the individual level.

CURRENT TRENDS IN GEODEMOGRAPHIC SEGMENTATION

In recent years certain clear trends have emerged in the field of geodemographic segmentation.

Greater Sophistication in the Creation of Clusters:

Earlier systems of geodemographics were based on fewer variables with less sophistication in the way consumers were clustered. Current systems, on the other hand, are considerably more sophisticated. Some systems even have clusters that use a combination of characteristics at the individual level rather than at the geographic level, thus making the segments richer and far more meaningful from a marketing perspective.

Integration of Several Data Sources:

Another recent development is to merge several major studies (e.g., industry studies such as PMB Print Measurement Bureau or NADbank (Newspaper Audience Databank) with geodemographic clusters to enable the marketer to identify not only the demographics and socio-economic characteristics of a given geographic area but other information, such as media habits and purchase behaviour, as well. While the quality of information thus integrated is not necessarily guaranteed, integrated data bases provide us with a preliminary view of the possible relationships that can be exploited by the marketer.

MANIFEST VERSUS LATENT APPROACHES TO SEGMENTATION

The approaches to segmentation discussed so far (geographic, demographic and geodemographic) are known as *manifest approaches*. They are based on the attributes of the consumer about which there is general agreement. For instance, the fact that a person is a resident of Halifax, or a female, or a senior citizen is observable or easily definable. Manifest variables segmentation (MVS) approaches are based on observable variables such as sex or place of residence, or on factual details such as age or income. The remaining segmentation approaches are based on latent variables. Although it is very seldom discussed, latent variable segmentation (LVS) is theoretically very different from manifest variable segmentation and the distinction should be clearly understood to avoid misinterpretation of the results.

LVS approaches use variables that are elicited from the consumer. The responses are subjective, often unverifiable and subject to interpretation by the analyst. Consider the following typical questions:

- **Are you a friendly person?**

(Each consumer may have his or her own definition of what constitutes a "friendly person." The evaluation is essentially *subjective*.)

- **Do you frequently go to parties?**

(What does the word "frequently" mean? Even it is understood in the same way by most consumers, the answer is partially *unverifiable*.)

- **Do you consider yourself successful?**

(Many people may not admit that they are unsuccessful; people who consider themselves successful may not really be so; people who consider themselves unsuccessful may in fact be very successful on many objective criteria. Two problems are evident in questions like these: potentially false responses and misperceptions.)

Even if we ignore all the above problems, there is still a question of interpretation. For instance a consumer who answers positively to all people-oriented questions may be classified as "friendly" by one analyst but "extroverted" by another analyst. The marketing strategies that follow will depend on how the consumer is classified. Thus the segmentation is based on the subjective interpretation by the analyst.

CHARACTERISTICS OF LVS

LVS should be interpreted differently:

Given that LVS is beset with so many problems (subjective, unverifiable and potentially misleading responses, subjective and potentially misleading interpretation by the analyst) one might be led to believe the LVS is useless, misleading or both. Interestingly enough, LVS can be very useful. This might appear contradictory until we realize that latent variables can be interpreted very differently from manifest variables.

LVS need not relate to reality:

In working with manifest variables, we expect the answers given by the respondent to reflect the true state of affairs. For instance, if a respondent says that she earns between $45 000 and $50 000 a year, we assume that this answer is correct. In fact, such an assumption is often necessary for us to interpret the data intelligently. In work with latent variables, *there needs to be no relationship between what the respondents say and what they do.* For example, a person who answers that he is successful need not necessarily be successful in real life. What really matters is that the person said that he or she was successful. If this response correlates with buying behaviour in some way, then it is a valid measure for our purposes.

LVS relates to attitudes and not necessarily to behaviour:

The most critical thing to understand with latent variables used in market segmentation is that *we are measuring attitudes and not behaviour,* although the questions asked of the consumers may relate to their behaviour. We are simply not interested in what they are like, only in what they say they are like. Consequently the segments that a researcher comes up with may have no relationship with theoretically based segments, with similar names, in other disciplines such as psychology. A segment of "extroverts" obtained in a market segmentation study may bear no relationship to another segment of "extroverts" theoretically derived by a psychologist specializing in personality theories. Put in another way, in MVS the expected relationship is between a consumers' responses and reality, while in LVS the expected relationship is between consumers' responses and purchase behaviour and not necessarily with reality.

APPLICATION OF LVS METHODS

LVS methods are commonly used in the following areas:

- **Socio-economic segmentation:** Socio-economic segmentation is a hybrid of LVS and MVS variables. When socio-economic segmentation is not identical with geodemographic segmentation, it involves subjective labelling of consumers by the analyst. For instance, an upper socio-economic segment can be defined differently by different analysts: they can use different variables to arrive at this segment and they can use different cut-off points of the same variables. While the variables themselves may not be latent, the segments based on them can be.

- **Usage segmentation:** Usage segmentation can be derived either by MVS or LVS procedures. We may derive usage segments by using manifest variables such as heaviness of usage, or by using latent variables such as patterns of consumption (as stated by the consumer) or occasions of consumption of certain products. Usage segmentation works better when manifest rather than latent variables are used.

- **Benefit segmentation**: Benefit segments are derived on the basis of consumer expectations of benefits provided by a product. Such benefits can be currently or potentially available or can conceivably be added to the product. Benefit segmentation comes under the LVS group for various reason. For example, a consumer may not always state explicitly the benefit he expects to derive from a product (e.g., the real reason for buying a BMW may be perceived prestige value, but the consumer may state durability as the main benefit derived); or the benefit statements made by the consumer may just be rationalizations for buying the least expensive product.

- **Psychographic/lifestyle segmentation**: These strategies use latent techniques extensively. Consequently, their value depends heavily on those who designed the study and analyzed the data.

We can consider socio-economic segmentation as an extension of geodemographic segmentation and usage as an elementary form of benefit segmentation. Neither of these methods involves special techniques in terms either of data collection or analysis.

BENEFIT SEGMENTATION

Given the same product, different consumers will use it for different reasons. One consumer may buy a brand of toothpaste because it makes "your teeth sparkle" (*cosmetic*), another may buy the same brand to "fight cavities" (*prevention*), and a third may buy it because it was the one on sale (*price*). Daniel Yankelovich (1964) reported in the *Harvard Business Review* how Timex used this strategy effectively and increased its market share. Yankelovich's analysis showed that watch companies operated with little understanding of the benefits sought by consumers. Watch manufacturers had assumed that watches were jewelry items to be marketed as such through jewelers, using prestige claims in advertising. Yet only a third of the consumers really cared for such appeal. Nearly 7 out of 10 consumers bought watches based on price (23%), or durability and quality (46%). Timex decided to concentrate on these two segments—price and quality. Within a few years of adopting this benefit segmentation strategy, Timex became the largest watch company in the world.

A typical benefit segmentation study asks a series of questions (in a closed-ended scaled format) on the importance of product benefits to the consumer. See Exhibit 18.7 for examples.

Exhibit 18.7 Examples of Benefit Ratings

Please indicate how important it is to you that a toothpaste should...

	Very important				Not at all important		
Clean your teeth well	7	6	5	4	3	2	1
Get your teeth to sparkle	7	6	5	4	3	2	1
Prevent cavities	7	6	5	4	3	2	1
Be reasonably priced	7	6	5	4	3	2	1
... and so on.							

The responses are then grouped together using statistical procedures such as cluster analysis. These procedures group consumers who answered similarly to a set of attributes. For instance, we may find that a group of consumers who scored highly on attributes such as "Prevent cavities," "Keep gums healthy," "Reduce tartar build-up," forms a segment. This segment will then be named (e. g., "Health/Prevention") by the analyst and its characteristics identified. Let us assume that an analyst has identified four segments in the toothpaste market: sensory, cosmetic, health and price. A summary statement can then be prepared (see Exhibit 18.8) as to the nature and size of these segments.

Benefit segments can be used to isolate a marketing or advertising strategy. They can also be used to identify new product opportunities.

Exhibit 18.8   Hypothetical Segments (Toothpaste Market)

	Sensory	Cosmetic	Health	Price
Main benefit	Flavour, feel (cool)	Brightness of teeth	Cavity/decay prevention	Low price
Main demographics	Age under 10	Age 25-44 Singles	Age 45+ Married	Inc.< 25K Larger HH
Main features	Prefer special flavours/menthol	Smokers	Prefer special ingredients	Not brand loyal
Main geographic region	Larger cities	Quebec	BC	Rural
Main psychographic trait*	Hedonistic	Social	Concerned	Value
Size of segment (#)	23%	37%	18%	22%
Size of segment ($)	19%	41%	26%	14%

• Note all studies collect psychographic information.
The actual summary statements can be (and usually are) much more detailed than this.
Please note that these are fictitious data.

PSYCHOGRAPHIC SEGMENTATION

WHAT IS PSYCHOGRAPHICS?

Psychographic refers to the behavioural profiles of different consumers. These profiles are generally provided by consumers themselves. It is how they perceive themselves in different aspects of life. Such aspects would include *activities, interests* and *opinions*. Typically a series of statements is provided to the respondent. The respondent is required to indicate his or her agreement with each statement. Exhibit 18.9 shows examples of such statements.

Exhibit 18.9 Some Typical Psychographic/Lifestyle Statements (AIOs)

I am a homebody

I enjoy spectator sports

I'd rather spend my time outdoors

My greatest achievements are ahead of me

We should build a strong defence force

A woman is fulfilled only if she can provide a happy home for her family

Availability of social security programs makes people lazy

It is very important for me to feel that I am part of a group

There is too much government interference these days

I enjoy my work

I shop around for bargains

Another way of looking at psychographics is to view it as *personality of a consumer as expressed through his or her lifestyle.* But why study psychographics? The answer to this question is simply that consumption behaviour is part of a person's general behaviour and is influenced by his or her personality. A person's personality as it relates to consumption behaviour can be understood by studying his or her lifestyle. A market researcher should select those aspects of consumers' psychographics that may have a bearing on their response to products, packaging, advertising and public relations efforts. Such variables could encompass attitudes, opinions, self-concepts, interests, perceptions of products and their usage.

USES OF PSYCHOGRAPHIC RESEARCH

Psychographic measures are used for four primary purposes: to isolate the target market, to understand consumer behaviour, to gather strategic information and to minimize marketing risk.

Isolating the target market through AIOs:

The three main components of the psychological make-up—attitudes, interests and opinions or AIO—often lead the marketer to consumer segments that would not have been obtainable through other techniques, such as demographics or socio-economic segmentation. It is possible for a user segment to be totally indistinguishable in terms of demographics and other characteristics from a non-user segment and yet be dramatically different to terms of their AIO's. Psychographic measures enable us to identify and isolate such target segments.

Understanding consumer behaviour through underlying motivations:

Psychographic segmentation provides the answer to *why* a consumer buys a product or a brand. Other forms of segmentation (e.g., demographic segmentation, benefit segmentation) answer the questions *who*, *how* and *what* but not *why*. Psychographic segmentation implies a causal relationship between a consumer's psychographics and his or her buying behaviour. Therefore, the motivational connection between the two can be used in strengthening the image of a product (e.g., an advertising campaign designed to strengthen the benefit perceived by the target segment).

Product categories and psychographics:

Consider three categories of product: expensive products (e.g., Rolls Royce), discretionary products (e.g., jacuzzi) and indistinguishable products (e.g., toothpaste). In all these categories psychographics play an important role and provide valuable strategic information. Some consumers would never consider buying a Rolls Royce, no matter how much they earned, what demographic or socio-economic group they belonged to, or what benefit the car provided. They might simply consider the car ostentatious. Purchase of discretionary products, like a jacuzzi, could depend on a person's psychographics. When products are indistinguishable (for instance, toothpaste), psychographics could provide clues to brand usage. Such information could be used for strategic purposes: re-positioning a product, developing a promotional strategy, or exploring new marketing and distribution methods.

Minimizing risk through identification of crucial marketing variables:

When a product is introduced (unless it is a truly mass market product), it is important to identify the group of consumers who are likely to make it a success. A product can succeed even if the segment is very small, provided it is identified and targeted correctly. However, when the segment is small, it is important to understand how to motivate that segment to buy, since the latitude for error is minimal. In such cases, having psychographic information or not having it could make the difference between success and failure. Psychographics could minimize the risk of marketing to the wrong group, or of marketing to the right group with the wrong appeals.

MARKET SEGMENTS AND SCIENTIFIC THEORIES

Generally speaking, psychographic segments obtained in marketing research are not a contribution to psychological or sociological theories. Psychographic segments obtained by the market researcher have only one purpose: to enable the marketer to market the product better. Consequently a researcher may include any specific statement that would help achieve this purpose. People in a segment named "introvert" in a coffee study may bear no relationship to the personality profile of an introvert as defined by a psychologist on the basis of a battery of tests. In fact, the profile of an introvert in a coffee study may even be different from the profile of an introvert in an automobile study. All this really does not matter as long as the researcher can measure reliably whatever he or she is measuring within the context of measurement.

GENERALIZED SEGMENTS

Researchers have been striving to achieve overall segments that are constant across the population and across different marketing research studies and relate them to buyer behaviour. Psychographic segments are tailor-made for each product. The most ambitious of such efforts is the development of VALS (values and lifestyle) typology developed by SRI International of California. In Canada, Goldfarb and Thompson Lightstone market their own classifications.

VALS VALS classifies the population into nine different categories as follows:

- Need-Driven Groups
1. **Survivors** (4% of the U.S. adult population): Very poor, old, fearful, far removed from the cultural mainstream.
2. **Sustainers** (7%): Resentful, angry, street-smart, bordering on poverty, involved in the underground economy.

- Outer-Directed Groups
3. **Belongers** (35%): Content, conventional, aging, traditional and patriotic.
4. **Emulators** (9%): Young, ambitious, flashy, attempting to break into the system.
5. **Achievers** (22%): Prosperous, middle-aged, self-assured; "leaders and builders of the American dream."

- Inner-Directed Groups
6. **I-Am-Me** (5%): Very young, impulsive, exhibitionistic, narcissistic.
7. **Experiential** (7%): Direct experience seeking, artistic, inner-growth oriented, youthful.
8. **Societally conscious** (8%): Mature, successful, out to change the world.

- Combined Outer- and Inner-Directed Group

9. **Integrated lifestyle** (2%): Flexible, tolerant, understanding, psychologically mature, able "to see the big picture."

GOLDFARB   The Goldfarb Corporation classifies consumers into six categories:

1. **Day-to-day watchers** (27% of Canadian adults): Realistic, satisfied with what life has to offer. Early followers rather than leaders.
2. **Old-fashioned puritans** (15%): Conservative to the point of being defensive, traditional to the point of being inflexible, and indifferent to the point of being apathetic.
3. **Disinterested self-indulgents** (14%): Insular, self-centred, uninterested in the world's problems.
4. **Joiner-activists** (19%): Leading edge thinkers, non-conformists, shapers of current opinions, conceptually broad thinkers.
5. **Aggressive achievers** (13%): Confident, success-oriented, hungry in their quest for power and position.
6. **Responsible survivors** (12%): Confident about themselves and their abilities, cautious, non-risk-taking.

The original list on which these segments are based consists of 185 statements. However, a short version of just 20 statements serves as a proxy for the long version and the above six segments can be derived from the short version.

CANADIAN PROFILES   Thompson Lightstone & Associates have developed their own psychographic segments. The TL system uses a two-pronged approach. First, 21 statements covering nine product dimensions, such as innovativeness, attitudes to advertising, impulse buying, convenience, brand loyalty, health concerns, skepticism to advertising, etc., are presented to the consumer. This gives rise to six consumer segments:

1. Cautious shopper (16%)
2. Non-demanding shopper (14%)
3. Convenience shopper (14%)
4. Price/value conscious shopper (15%)
5. Secondary shopper (14%)
6. Born to shop (14%)

Second, 33 statements covering dimensions such as family values, self-confidence, career orientation, grooming, etc., are evaluated by the consumer. This gives rise to six different segments:

1. Modern/active (15%)
2. Contented striver (14%)

3. Traditional values (9%)
4. Empty nesters (15%)
5. Insecure (18%)
6. Home/family oriented (17%)

Canadian profiles are then created by merging the two sets:

1. Passive/uncertain (14%)
2. Mature market (12%)
3. Home economists (15%)
4. Active/convenience oriented (14%)
5. Modern shoppers (14%)
6. Traditional, home/family-oriented (15%)

(Please note that most of the results presented for the Canadian population are essentially as they apply to the PMB universe (see Chapter 20). It is assumed that the results for the general adult population will be similar.)

DO PSYCHOGRAPHIC SEGMENTS REALLY EXIST IN THE POPULATION?

When we compare the three segments which purport to measure the lifestyles/psychographics of consumers, it is obvious that the similarity among the three is less than striking. Who is right? If all are right, is one better than the other? There are no clear-cut answers to these questions. Psychographic/lifestyle statements do not uncover market segments that are there waiting to be uncovered. Rather, they simply group consumers on the basis of whatever the researcher thinks is important. The segments are a function of the original questions and the ability of the researcher to identify and name them, and not a function of objective reality.

This is not to say that such segments are of no value. The value comes out of the correlation between a given segment and buyer behaviour. To the extent that such correlations exist and can be proved to exist in a consistent manner, the segments are valuable. To the extent that there is no consistent relationship between product usage and buyer behaviour, the segments are of no value to the marketer, no matter how elegant and theoretically sound the statements and the statistical analyses that follow.

No matter what claims are made for a method's theoretical validity and statistical sophistication, if it can't be shown that there is a consistent empirical relationship between product usage and psychographic segments, the method is essentially useless to the marketer. It also follows that a particular system of segmentation that has worked for other products may not work very well for your product. To get the most out of segmentation research, it is important to be concerned more with consistent empirical relationships than with elegant theoretical models.

GUIDELINES FOR BUYING SEGMENTATION RESEARCH

If you commission segmentation research, you may want to bear the following in mind:

- Segments are constructs. They are formalized models of how people think and act.
- The model reflects a researcher's thinking on the subject. A different researcher can come up with a different model and therefore with different segments. The "template" used by the researcher determines the nature of the segments obtained.
- A theoretical basis for most of these models does not exist and when it does, it may be of little use to the marketer.
- The usefulness of any segmentation model is based on answers to two questions:
  1. Does it specifically relate to your product?
  2. Is it reliable (repeatable)?

ANALYTIC TECHNIQUES

UNLIMITED APPROACHES, LIMITED TECHNIQUES

We saw earlier how the market can be segmented in seven different ways. In fact, using a different paradigm, one could generate more segmentation levels. Hybrid segmentation approaches are also possible. Depending on one's theoretical orientation (and imagination), one could indeed conceive of a limitless number of ways to segment the market.

However, no matter what level or approach the researcher uses to segment the market, only a limited number of techniques are commonly used to group consumers. The techniques to be discussed here are not the only ones that can be used to segment the market, but one of the following approaches should be adequate for almost all segmentation problems encountered in marketing research.

Marketing segmentation can be carried out using an intuitive approach, a market structure approach, or a market partition approach. Exhibit 18.10 shows the analytic scheme appropriate to segmentation analysis.

Exhibit 18.10 Intuitive Approaches to Segmentation

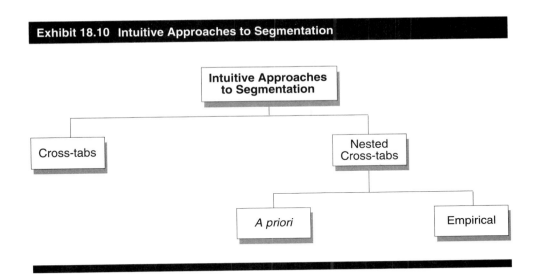

INTUITIVE APPROACHES

SUB-GROUPS AND NESTED SUB-GROUPS   Whenever we use cross-tabs which divide consumers into sub-groups (e.g., by sex, age, or mother tongue) to understand the market, we are indeed segmenting the market, although a simple cross-tab would hardly qualify as a segmentation technique.

A step above this approach is to classify respondents who fulfill a series of attributes rather than a single one. For example, we may group *women* between the ages of *20 and 35* who live in *larger cities*. This is known as the nested sub-group approach.

NESTED SUB-GROUPS: *A priori* and Empirical Nested sub-groups can be elicited in two different ways. The first approach uses *a priori* reasoning. The market is divided into segments of importance to the product at hand. This approach can be useful when the marketer already knows enough about the characteristics of the market. It is also useful when the market is segmented (e.g., geodemographic segmentation of the market by "off-the-shelf" suppliers) with no definite idea as to where and when such segments may be used.

The second method applies an empirical approach. A series of alternative nested sub-groups are initially cross-tabulated against critical marketing variables (such as product and brand usage); the alternative that produces the best sub-group distinction is then used in the full-scale tabulation of the data. (The initial alternatives for nested sub-groups are usually chosen on the basis of prior knowledge and theoretical expectations.)

The main advantage with the empirical approach is that the segments are almost certain to make sense. The disadvantage is that it allows a researcher to try a series of alternatives whether they make sense or not; since the likelihood of finding a relationship—sometimes by chance alone—increases with the number of alternatives tried. Using this approach, it is possible to end up with segments that appear relevant to the data on hand but are either not reproducible or not readily interpretable.

MARKET STRUCTURE APPROACHES

In some instances the marketer's interest is not necessarily in identifying the consumers who compose a given segment but just in understanding the structure of the market that can form the basis for strategic communication or unexploited opportunities in the marketplace. (The task of identifying the consumers who compose a given segment is reserved for subsequent research/analysis provided the market structure warrants further investigation).

Market structure can be analyzed in many different ways. Three commonly used multivariate techniques for this purpose are multidimensional scaling, discriminant analysis and correspondence analysis. (For a more complete description of these techniques, see Chapter 23, Advanced Data Analysis.)

MULTIDIMENSIONAL SCALING   When a number of brands are rated on key attributes, they can be plotted on a two-dimensional plane (or on more dimensions if warranted by the analysis) such that similar brands are grouped on the basis of similar ratings of these attributes. (The saliency—or the importance of a given attribute in distinguishing different brands—can also be inferred through this technique.) This provides a visual representation of the brands and attributes. This output is also commonly known as the *perceptual map* or the *brand map* (see Exhibit 18.11).

If we found that certain attributes were highly salient but no brands were placed along these dimensions, it would indicate potential opportunity for a new product. There likely is a market segment in need of a product. About 15 years ago most research indicated that there were many breakfast cereals (such as bran cereals) that catered to fibre conscious eaters, but not many brands in the category of nutritious, natural and healthy (such as "Harvest Crunch"). This pattern was clearly seen in perceptual maps in which the dimensions of "natural" and "healthy" appeared very salient but there were hardly any brands fulfilling these needs. Several brands were later introduced successfully to cater to this segment.

Exhibit 18.11 Multidimensional Scaling

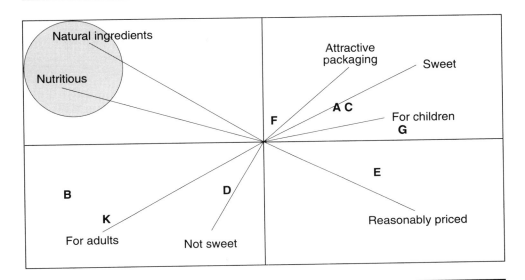

The above shows a typical two-dimensional map produced using the multidimensional scaling technique. Brands are indicated by letters (A, B, C, etc.). Note that several brands compete in two distinct segments based on age: a group of brands catering to children and another group catering to adults. No brands are perceived to be nutritious and natural (top left quadrant). It is quite probable that this represents a market segment whose needs are not catered to by the brands currently available in the market.

DISCRIMINANT ANALYSIS   In discriminant analysis, we can pre-define the segments and then identify the importance of different variables in contributing to the formation of that segment. Using this technique it is also possible to arrive at two-dimensional maps akin to those derived using multidimensional scaling (see Exhibit 18.12).

CORRESPONDENCE ANALYSIS   This technique is conceptually akin to multidimensional scaling. It could, for example, place demographic characteristics and brand usage on a two-dimensional plane (or on more dimensions if warranted by the analysis), as shown in Exhibit 18.13. Once again, if no brands are located around a demographic variable or set of variables, one could infer the existence of a market segment that has not been catered to by the products currently available in the market.

Exhibit 18.12 Discriminant Analysis

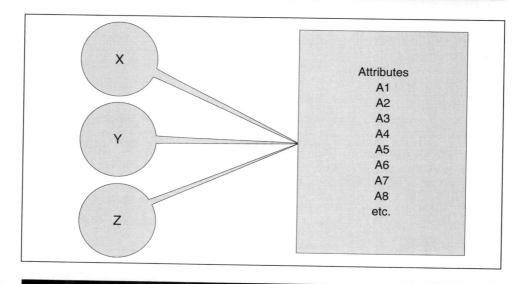

In discriminant analysis, the analyst (or the marketer) defines the segments (indicated as X, Y and Z in the above chart) based on product usage or some other characteristics relevant to the marketing objectives. The analyst also defines the variables that are assumed to influence these segments. The technique then identifies the nature of the relationship between the set of attributes (right side of the panel) and the segments by assigning weights to the attributes.

MARKET PARTITION APPROACHES

In market partition analysis, as opposed to structure analysis, we not only want to identify the existence of different segments, but we want to identify the characteristics of the members of each segment on variables not directly related to the segmentation process itself. For instance, using multidimensional scaling we could have identified the existence of a segment that would be a prime candidate for a nutritious, natural and healthy brand, but not the characteristics of those who make up this segment. We need to use different techniques to accomplish this.

There are two distinct approaches to partitioning the market: the dependence approach and the interdependence approach.

DEPENDENCE APPROACH   In the dependence approach, our aim is to partition the market using a dependent variable. For instance, we may decide to segment the market on the usage of a given product. The resultant segments,

Exhibit 18.13 Correspondence Analysis

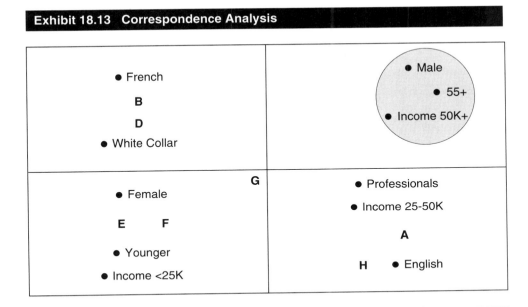

In the example above, note that the demographic segment that includes older, affluent males is not catered to by any of the brands currently on the market. Perhaps this segment does not use the product under consideration. Or - as is more often the case - this lucrative segment of the market has been left uncatered for. At the very least, a closer look at this segment is warranted. If there is potential, market partitioning techniques may be used to understand this segment in greater detail.

then, will relate directly to the usage of the product. The characteristics of these segments—if included in the analysis—will be assumed to be the variables contributing to the usage of the product.

INTERDEPENDENCE APPROACH   In the interdependence approach, we do not start with a dependent variable. The researcher simply uses all the variables considered relevant to the grouping of consumers for a given market. Although no dependent variable is used, the basic reasoning behind this approach is that, when consumers are grouped on relevant marketing variables, the resultant segments should also be correlated with the most potentially relevant dependent variables, such as product usage.

We discussed earlier how markets can be segmented using intuitive (subgroup and nested sub-group analyses) and market structure (multidimensional scaling, discriminant analysis, correspondence analysis) approaches. Although all approaches are useful, the widely preferred methods of segmentation concentrate on partitioning the market.

DEPENDENCE APPROACH TO SEGMENTATION

The dependence approach uses a criterion chosen by the researcher as the basis for segmentation. For example, the researcher may want to partition the market on the basis of product usage. The segments derived, then, will directly reflect the usage of the product. The characteristics of the segments will be assumed to be the variables contributing to the usage of the product. As in other analyses, we have to assume that the researcher has included all the relevant variables in the analysis.

While there may be other ways of partitioning the market using dependent variables, the most commonly used technique is the Automatic Interaction Detector, or AID for short.

AUTOMATIC INTERACTION DETECTOR (AID) The Automatic Interaction Detector, or AID, is a technique which groups people on attributes that contribute most to a dependent variable (see Chapter 23, Advanced Data Analysis). Here are some examples of problems that can be solved using the AID technique:

- What demographic characteristics combine to define readership segments in the newspaper market?

- What psychographic characteristics define different beer drinkers with common drinking patterns? What are their other characteristics such as demographics?

In AID we use several pieces of information (e.g., demographic traits) to explain one aspect of behaviour (e.g., purchase intention). The one aspect that we try to explain is called the *criterion variable*. The variables we use to explain the criterion variable are called the *predictor variables*. In AID, we simply input a criterion variable (like the ratings of purchase intention for a product) along with the predictor variables (like the demographics of the respondents). The technique then searches for the predictor variable that is most closely associated with the criterion variable (e.g., purchase intention) and divides the sample into two parts on that basis. Following this, the next most closely related predictor variable is selected and each of the two sub-groups are split in turn into two additional sub-groups. This procedure is repeated for all the remaining variables. Given a dependent variable (like consumption volume), AID repeatedly tries a number of independent variables (demographics, ratings, etc.) to determine which variable contributes most to the dependent variable. The groups obtained in this way are the market segments, some of which may be of interest.

The typical output we get is a "tree diagram" which groups people that contribute most to the dependent variable (see Exhibit 18.14). From this, we may infer:

- The relative importance of different variables
- The number of respondents who fall into the segments that may be of importance to the marketing strategist
- The hierarchy of relationship among variables

AID is a relatively simple type of segmentation analysis that has been available for about 25 years, but has been largely neglected by the market research industry. One reason may be that people have regarded segmentation as synonymous with complex analysis of scale batteries and for this purpose AID is less suitable.

AID is more appropriate when the potential predictor variables being investigated are situational or demographic variables rather than attitude or image scale items. The groups of people at the bottom of the roots are basically clusters defined by the hierarchical order of the splits that have defined them. This can be useful in forming the analysis categories for subsequent analysis. An additional advantage is that the final output is in a form that is easily understood by a marketing person (see Exhibit 18.14).

One main weakness of the method is that it requires a fairly large sample size because it splits the sample into two at each stage.

INTERDEPENDENCE ANALYSIS APPROACH TO SEGMENTATION

In interdependence analysis, the researcher does not specify a dependent variable. Instead, the researcher aims to find out how similar or different consumers are on the basis of a number of variables. Segments are formed by identifying people who answer a set of questions similarly. The most commonly used interdependent method is cluster analysis.

CLUSTER ANALYSIS   Cluster analysis refers to a group of techniques that are used in market research primarily to group consumers who are similar (see Chapter 23, Advanced Data Analysis). Thus we can group consumers who want similar benefits from a product, consumers who have similar demographics, consumers who have similar reading habits, and consumers with similar lifestyles, etc.

For a given set of variables, cluster analysis divides the respondents into several groups such that within any one group respondents are similar to one another in their responses to the variables. We are not specifically interested in one attribute at a time, but in similar *patterns* of ratings.

Exhibit 18.14 AID: An Example of Direct Marketing Response Rates by Segments

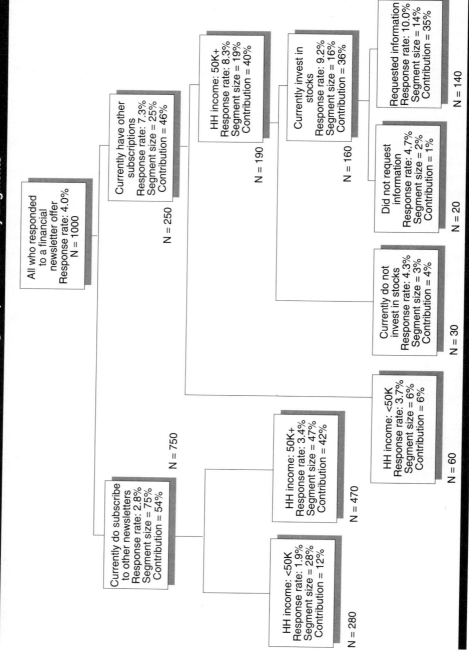

All who responded to a financial newsletter offer
Response rate: 4.0%
N = 1000

Currently have other subscriptions
Response rate: 7.3%
Segment size = 25%
Contribution = 46%
N = 250

HH income: 50K+
Response rate: 8.3%
Segment size = 19%
Contribution = 40%
N = 190

Currently invest in stocks
Response rate: 9.2%
Segment size = 16%
Contribution = 36%
N = 160

Requested information
Response rate: 10.0%
Segment size = 14%
Contribution = 35%
N = 140

Did not request information
Response rate: 4.7%
Segment size = 2%
Contribution = 1%
N = 20

Currently do not invest in stocks
Response rate: 4.3%
Segment size = 3%
Contribution = 4%
N = 30

HH income: <50K
Response rate: 3.7%
Segment size = 6%
Contribution = 6%
N = 60

Currently do subscribe to other newsletters
Response rate: 2.8%
Segment size = 75%
Contribution = 54%
N = 750

HH income: 50K+
Response rate: 3.4%
Segment size = 47%
Contribution = 42%
N = 470

HH income: <50K
Response rate: 1.9%
Segment size = 28%
Contribution = 12%
N = 280

Most market segmentation studies utilize cluster analytic techniques. The type of data used for this purpose tend to be either psychographic or attitudinal. Consumers may be asked to respond to a number of lifestyle questions (psychographics) or to rate the product benefits. Respondents may then be grouped into homogeneous clusters based on their lifestyles or on their product benefit ratings. Once the respondents are grouped into distinct segments, we may analyze the data further by cross-tabulating these segments against demographic characteristics, usage patterns, brand ratings, etc.

A wide range of techniques are included under the umbrella term *cluster analysis*. For example, the AID technique, Q technique, MCA analysis, hierarchial clustering, smallest space analysis and even factor analysis can be used to cluster people. (Although we treated AID as a distinct dependence method, it is in fact a cluster analytic technique, when we use the term to include all partitioning techniques).

Although all these techniques have one main purpose, classifying people (or occasionally variables), the final output might differ from technique to technique. The analyst is free to choose any level of clustering that would suit the objective of the research study.

GENERAL CONSIDERATIONS   There are several ways in which one can determine how close or far apart people are. For example, in determining how close two respondents are:

- We may consider all differences in attributes to be of equal importance; or
- We may consider larger differences to be more critical than small differences.

Several other assumptions are possible. Cluster analysis procedures will differ depending on the assumptions we make. Technically, different assumptions given rise to different distance functions. It is not necessary to know the intricacies of these distance functions to use cluster analysis. It may be stated in passing that most techniques make use of the Euclidean distance function.

The researcher should consider several factors while using cluster analytic techniques. First, different forms of cluster analysis may give different solutions since the criterion on which clustering is achieved may differ from technique to technique. Second, if the sample size is not large enough, we may end up with clusters with very small bases. Generalizations based on sample bases may turn out to be unreliable. Third, although most techniques have the same purpose (i.e., classifying people or variables), the logic of a given technique may make it inappropriate for a given problem.

Another serious consideration is the data base on which clusters are derived. Cluster analysis groups people on the variables the analyst manipulates (considers relevant). If those variables are in fact irrelevant, the groups derived on the basis of those variables will also be irrelevant.

In spite of the above caveats, cluster analytic techniques are useful in practice, especially in the area of segmentation research.

HOW MANY SEGMENTS?

No matter which method we use, we can derive as many segments as there are respondents. How do we know how many true segments there are in reality? There are mathematical criteria to let us know how many segments there are in our data. But unfortunately mathematical criteria may not coincide with consumer-driven segments.

One recent program by Richard Johnson uses a convergent approach, i.e., producing two different solutions at each level and comparing them to determine whether they are close. The most widely used approach is to identify several solutions and use the one that is most closely aligned with the marketer's objectives.

USEFULNESS OF SEGMENTATION

Almost every market research analysis, including cross-tabs analysis, assumes that different people react differently to products and services. Hence the usefulness of segmentation is beyond question. But what is open to question is how useful these sophisticated techniques are in identifying the segments. Although no definitive answer can be given to this question, many marketers find the segments produced by these techniques very usable. If appears that segmentation is more suitable for products with multiple benefits and images (such as beer and automobiles) than for products that have a strictly unitary utility function (such as refrigerators). However, these are broad generalizations. It is difficult to predict beforehand whether segmentation (especially latent variable segmentation) variety will prove to be useful for a given product.

SUMMARY

1. Market segmentation can
  - Maximize the impact of limited resources
  - Minimize the negative effects of visibility
  - Minimize unproductive consumer subsidy

2. Inappropriate segmentation can be costly since it may lead to erroneous marketing decisions. Therefore, one should be careful in choosing the appropriate segmentation level. The researcher should start with the lowest level of segmentation and proceed to the next level only when that level is properly understood and found wanting.

3. For most retail businesses, *geographic segmentation* is the most appropriate. Geographic segmentation is useful only if one or more of the following criteria are met:

   • There should be considerable cost savings in terms of movement of goods and services

   • Consumers should show genuinely different consumption or product usage patterns

   • The segmented portion should be a viable market for the contemplated product

4. *Demographic segmentation* may be more appropriate for specialized retail businesses. For example, a store selling women's imported shoes may be interested in the number of women above a certain level of income residing in the retail trading zone. Almost all marketing research cross-tabulations acknowledge the pre-eminence of demographic classification of consumers.

5. Segmentation which combines geographical factors with demographic and socio-economic factors is known as *geodemographic segmentation*. Geodemographic segments are created by identifying the demographic characteristics of very small geographic units (such as enumeration areas) and then combining similar units. Pre-defined geodemographic segments are available from several commercial sources.

6. Manifest variable segmentation (MVS) approaches are based on observable variables such as sex or place of residence, or on factual details such as age or income. Latent variable segmentation (LVS) approaches use variables that are elicited from the consumer. The questions evoke responses that are subjective, often unverifiable and subject to interpretation by the analyst. For example,

   • Are you a friendly person?
   • Do you frequently go to parties?
   • Do you consider yourself successful?

   Latent variables need not relate to reality. For example, when a respondent says that she is outgoing, we accept the response as true. In other words, we treat the response as an attitude rather than as behaviour. LVS methods are used in usage, benefit, and lifestyle/psychographic segmentation.

7. Different groups of consumers may use the same product for different reasons. *Benefit segmentation* identifies groups of consumers who use a given product for similar reasons.

8. *Psychographics* refers to the behavioural profiles of different consumers. These profiles are generally provided by consumers themselves. They are how they perceive themselves in different aspects of life. Such aspects would include activities, interests and opinions. A researcher may want to create unique psychographic/lifestyle segments for the product in question. Some research houses also offer "off-the-shelf" psychographic/lifestyle segments.

9. A variety of statistical techniques can be used to segment the market. Such techniques include sub-group and nested sub-group analysis (intuitive segmentation), discriminant analysis, multidimensional scaling and correspondence analysis (structural segmentation), AID (dependence analysis) and cluster analysis (interdependent analysis).

NOW THINK ABOUT THIS

1. Describe the seven most popular ways to segment the market.

2. Discuss the advantages and disadvantages of MVS versus LVS approaches.

3. Should a researcher create his or her own psychographic/lifestyle segments or accept generalized segments marketed by others? Why?

4. Outline the analytic techniques used in segmentation research.

REFERENCES

Yankelovich, D.
1964 "New Criteria For Market Segmentation." *Harvard Business Review*, (March-April).

NOTE

1. I am grateful to Mr. Ralph Thornicroft of The Clorox Corporation (San Francisco) for expounding this point very eloquently at various French restaurants around Toronto. - Chuck Chakrapani

19 / Pricing Research

BASIC CONCEPTS

There are several ways in which a product or service may be priced. While some pricing techniques can be established through marketing research, others cannot. Before understanding whether research can be used, we need to review the pricing techniques. (The term *product* is used in this chapter to include both products and services. *Product* may also refer to a brand, depending on the context.)

PRICE IS WHAT THE CONSUMER WILL PAY

In capitalist economies, products do not have intrinsic value. A bottle of perfume sells for several times the price of a litre of milk, but not because the intrinsic value of perfume is far greater than milk. The price of a product—when not controlled by regulatory agencies—is simply the value that the manufacturer or marketer has placed on the item. Price is driven by supply and demand.

Is there then a moral price? Is there a point beyond which a consumer is "ripped off" by a firm? While all of us feel that there is a fair price for a product, when we compare what a product's intrinsic value is to determine a fair price—such as the nutritional value of milk as opposed to a bottle of soda pop—it is obvious that there is no relationship between a product's price and its intrinsic value, no matter how we define these terms. Consequently, fair pricing and moral pricing become sociological and ethical concepts and are not particularly meaningful in a marketing context. There are only the prices consumers are willing to pay and the needs of consumers that products fulfill. All that a firm can do is to gauge the specific relationship between supply and demand in relation to the product it produces. (That is not to say that a firm should not have its own convictions on fair prices; but such considerations are extraneous to the basic capitalist environment.)

THE PARADOX OF PRICING AND POWER

Pricing is related to power. If the demand for a product is strong and profits are good, a firm is free to increase the price. The firm can also choose to decrease the price because it can afford to. The firm has the power to alter its price in any way it chooses. If the demand for a product is weak and profits are poor, the firm cannot increase the price because this might weaken demand even further. It cannot lower its price since there is a chance that the already poor profits might dwindle further. This partly explains why, during times of recession, weak competitors go out of business. Strong competitors can reduce their price to attract reluctant consumers. Weak competitors, on the other hand, might only succeed in lowering their already low profit margins.

THE ROLE OF RESEARCH

There are several instances in which research can be used to decide on the optimal pricing of a product. But, except in instances where the role of research is defined in advance, pricing decisions are often arbitrary. The main problem is that pricing decisions are made on estimates of cost that are often much firmer than the very uncertain estimates of the market. However, for most products it is the market—not the product or the cost of production—that ultimately guarantees the survival of the product and the attendant profits.

Pricing decisions can kill products that could have been potential winners. One common mistake relates to price elasticity: the belief that if prices were much lower, consumers would buy much more. Such economic truths are not universal and need to be tested in different contexts. Pricing decisions can have a very great impact on profitability, probably even more than sales volume.

CAN RESEARCH HELP?

If there is no fair price for a product and if moral pricing is an extraneous consideration, then price should be viewed within the context of the marketing environment. When viewed in this way, pricing is a function of three marketing variables: the product, the consumer and the competition. All three variables are potentially measurable through research. Consequently, research may be of help to the marketer.

The reasons for arriving at a given price are numerous and varied. Some methods are product-oriented, some market-oriented, and yet others competition-oriented. Marketing research is seldom relevant to product-oriented pricing techniques, partly relevant to competition-oriented techniques, and highly relevant to market-oriented techniques. Before discussing the research techniques and their applications, it might be worthwhile reviewing the main pricing techniques that are currently in existence.

THIRTEEN WAYS TO PRICE A PRODUCT

There are hundreds of ways in which one can price a product or a service. But the most commonly used techniques in business can be reduced to about a baker's dozen.

COST-ORIENTED PRICING

COST-PLUS PRICING   This strategy of simply adding the desired profit margin to the total costs is one of the least market-oriented strategies. As such, cost-plus pricing is found in less developed markets, markets where cartels exist, or markets where the producers have a monopoly. It may also be used in established industries where the price variations are minimal and the products are of comparable quality.

MARGINAL PRICING   Marginal cost pricing occurs when major buyers want a lower price in consideration of the volume of purchase. When such deals are made, the firm pools all fixed costs and calls them "contribution to overhead and profit." The firm may accept the lowest possible price. The rationale for this is that if all the variable costs are covered and if some small profit is generated on the basis of these deals, it would lower the general cost of running the business. Obviously, the marginal pricing technique can be considered only in instances where, (a) without marginal pricing the firm would lose the business; and (b) the marginal pricing is restricted and is not likely to affect other customers who pay higher prices.

MARKET-ORIENTED PRICING

ELASTICITY PRICING   Elasticity pricing is a way of pricing a product on the basis of market response to the price. When you decrease the price, will the demand go up or remain the same? Conversely, when you increase the price, will the demand go down or remain the same? When a product is price elastic (i.e., if you decrease the price $x\%$, your sales would go up by much greater than $x\%$), prices may be lowered in the hope that sales volume and total revenue will increase. It may also be used when the market is inelastic within a given range by increasing the price to the top of that range, thereby increasing the profitability of each unit.

SKIM PRICING   In skim pricing the unit price is set very high. Usually this is a short-term strategy. This strategy is suitable when there is patent protection (such as that obtained by the drug industry recently in Canada), high market-entry costs, technological innovation, product uniqueness, or short market life. One problem with skim pricing is that the high profit margin attracts competition.

SLIDE-DOWN PRICING   This is an intermediate strategy to get from skim pricing towards penetration pricing (see below). When skim pricing is used, it attracts competition because of the strategy's high profitability. As the competition moves in, the firm responds by decreasing its price to meet the challenge. Sometimes the price is periodically lowered to discourage the competition from moving in.

PENETRATION PRICING   This is the opposite of skim pricing in the sense that its main thrust is to increase the market share rather than the unit profitability. For instance, most Canadian supermarkets operate on low margins but depend on volume to be profitable.

Penetration pricing can be used to achieve maximum market share, to establish a position in the market when a firm is a new entrant in the field, to discourage other competitors from entering the market, and to grow at the expense of competitors who are not market-oriented in a price-elastic market.

SEGMENT PRICING   This strategy involves pricing the same product differently for different market segments. The idea behind this strategy is that different groups of consumers have different uses for the product and consequently derive different benefits from the same product. A market segment may or may not be elastic depending on the benefits derived from the product by that segment. For instance, identical telephone services are priced differently for the business and the residential markets. Another example would be where minor cosmetic changes are made to a product to market to a particular segment at a vastly increased price.

PRESTIGE PRICING   A product is deliberately priced high with a view to creating a quality image. Such pricing strategies are more common among high fashion items than common, everyday items.

FLEXIBLE PRICING   When a product's demand is volatile and when it is vulnerable to competitive challenges and changing demand levels, a firm may respond by changing the price of the product as and when the challenge arises.

PHASE-OUT PRICING   When a product line is trimmed or when the long-term trend in demand is declining, a firm may decide to price the product high and extract as much profit as possible.

COMPETITION-ORIENTED PRICING

PRE-EMPTIVE PRICING   Pre-emptive pricing is used to protect the firm's dominant position in the market. The product is priced such that competitors are discouraged from entering the market. For example, the price of a product can be dropped substantially, making it potentially less profitable for future competitors. This strategy is used when the firm senses that competitors are about to enter the market.

FOLLOW PRICING   This is the strategy of pricing the product by taking into account the market leaders. This strategy can be useful when a product is indistinguishable from other available ones and when extreme price differentials could evoke fierce responses from market leaders.

LOSS LEADER PRICING   This is a ploy in which a product is priced low (probably lower than the cost of production) to attract customers, who, once you get them, can be sold other products with normal or high profit margins. A variation of this is simply to offer incentives and discounts to attract consumers. But this strategy works only in the short-term since competitors tend to react with similar offers lowering the overall profitability in a segment. An example of this approach is the triple bonus points offered by most U.S. airlines to attract customers. If every airline offered similar plans, no one would have a competitive edge, only greater liability.

Pricing approaches are not mutually exclusive. For instance, there can be no market-oriented price that effectively ignores the competition and the product. Yet pricing can be approached from several different angles. Further, many variations, permutations and combinations of the above approaches are possible. This leaves us with the basic question of how we decide which to use.

There is always the real possibility that a product may fail at a lower price. For certain products, a lower price means—in addition to low profit margins—a smaller market share. An advantage offered to the consumer is not necessarily perceived as such by the consumer. If only the firm had known this in advance.

RESEARCH INTO PRICING

BASIC QUESTIONS ABOUT THE COMPETITION AND CONSUMERS

We need to ask some fundamental questions about the competition and consumers to make sense of the market's reaction to prices. Here are a few suggested questions:

About Competition:
- Are substitute products available?
- How is the competition likely to react to this price?
- Have competitors' pricing strategies affected your sales in the past?
- Have competitors' sales been responsive to price changes?

About Consumers:
- Does your product fill a basic need?
- How large is your market?

- How much will consumers pay?
- How much would they buy?
- Is the product price-sensitive?
- How is the product bought?
- What are the motives for buying this product?
- What saving can be passed on to the buyer?
- What new benefits can be provided?
- Is the product in the "shop around" category?
- Is there a general price awareness among consumers for this product?

Some of these questions can be answered by secondary research and general knowledge, some by standard panel data subscribed to by the firm, and yet others require ad hoc research. Some questions may require more than one approach.

USING THE APPROPRIATE STRATEGY

Given that there are so many ways of pricing a product (we have discussed 13 of them), which one should a marketer choose? Can research help the marketer decide what strategy to use? Having decided on a strategy, can research help the marketer choose the optimal price for the product? Is there a range of acceptable prices within which consumers are not price sensitive?

Doing research on pricing based on a poorly conceived strategy simply adds cost to an already expensive proposition. The marketer, therefore, has the responsibility of choosing the appropriate strategy for pricing before commissioning research. It is not uncommon for good products to disappear from the shelf as a result of a poorly conceived pricing strategy. In general, the pricing strategy would depend on factors such as corporate policy (e.g., "we will not be undersold"), competitive environment (e.g., ready availability of several competing brands in the market place), brand loyalty that is common for that category, profit margin to the retailer, and quality of the product.

However, there are some broad guidelines as to when to use different pricing level strategies. If you have a high quality product, if you can control the distribution, if you can stand behind your product, you may be able to use a *high price strategy*. This strategy works particulary well when you have a monopoly or when demand exceeds supply. *Moderate price strategy* should be used to hold the current market share in a mature market. *Low price strategy* is appropriate when your objective is to increase your market share and short-run volume. To be successful, you should be able to hold a low-cost position for a sustained period.

TEN COMMON FALLACIES ABOUT PRICE

Choosing an appropriate strategy would also depend on the marketer's perception of the dynamics of the marketplace. Some of the commonly held beliefs about the market place are fallacious and J. Nault identifies 10 of them:

1. **Consumer buys rationally**: Buying motives are often illogical, emotional and impulsive. The rational "economic man" is the creation of economists and can hardly be found in real life.

2. **Quality determines the price**: In reality, the reverse is often true. In many product categories, price is an indicator of quality. Quality can be used to determine the price only if an increased price leads to the perception of quality.

3. **Price can be soundly based on margin goal**: This approach, even when it works, can lead to pricing that does not relate to the market and can thus lead to opportunity losses.

4. **Recession favours low-price products**: Pricing research has not established this; it appears more likely that during a recession consumers look for value for money rather than for the cheapest product on the market.

5. **Consumers know the market prices**: Consumers do seem to know the prices of frequently purchased items and important durables such as automobiles. For most other items, consumers are hardly aware of the real prices.

6. **Wise pricing is relative to competition**: What is really important is the perception of target buyers and the value they see in the product. Such perceptions may or may not relate to the competition.

7. **New products are to be priced at today's cost of goods**: Costs are bound to increase considering that we live in an unstable economy.

8. **Only the market leader can control the price**: The fact is, in many cases, number two or three has more flexibility and initiative.

9. **Manufacturers control the retailers' selling price**: Very frequently powerful middlemen control the selling price and no pricing strategy will work the way the marketer expects unless the influence of the intermediaries is taken into account.

10. **Price low at entry, then increase once share goals are achieved**: A low entry price creates a price/value association in consumers which may become very difficult to change later on. The initial price positioning must be a long-term one.

PRICING STRATEGY AND RESEARCH

The relevance of research depends on the pricing strategy chosen (see Exhibit 19.1). For instance, when cost-plus pricing strategy is adopted, ad hoc research can hardly be of any help; if it is used at all, it is to predict the consequences of price changes rather than to effect or stall them. However, the role of research is not always obvious. Even when a more sophisticated pricing strategy is used, many corporations effect price changes while research is still under progress. While the researcher may be labouring under the impression that the findings are to be used to determine the optimum price for the product, management may have commissioned it for the purpose of understanding the underlying market dynamics.

Exhibit 19.1   Pricing Strategies and Research Orientation

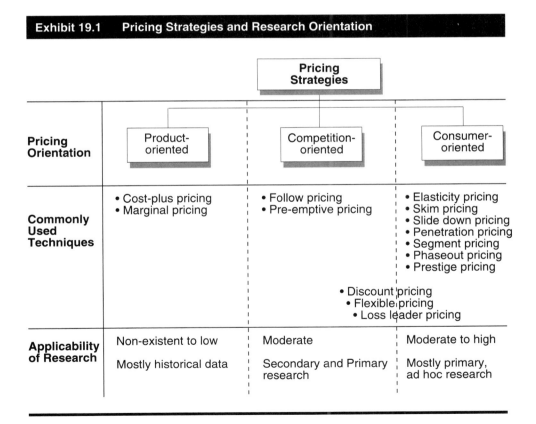

Pricing Orientation	Product-oriented	Competition-oriented	Consumer-oriented
Commonly Used Techniques	• Cost-plus pricing • Marginal pricing	• Follow pricing • Pre-emptive pricing	• Elasticity pricing • Skim pricing • Slide down pricing • Penetration pricing • Segment pricing • Phaseout pricing • Prestige pricing
		• Discount pricing • Flexible pricing • Loss leader pricing	
Applicability of Research	Non-existent to low Mostly historical data	Moderate Secondary and Primary research	Moderate to high Mostly primary, ad hoc research

Let us assume that we have overcome all these hurdles and avoided all the pitfalls and the marketer has considered alternative pricing strategies and has chosen the appropriate ones. Still the marketer (and the researcher) has to answer several questions before settling on an appropriate research technique.

1. **Is ad hoc research needed at all?** There are some instances in which research is not critical for pricing decisions. Products that are known to have high brand loyalty and low price elasticity, monopolistic brands with no major negative perception, brands that have inflexible cost-plus consideration, and mature brands considering price increase in line with general market trends fall into this category. While in almost all cases research can provide additional information, in some cases (as in the ones mentioned) research is used more to confirm what the marketer already knows than to gain insights into consumer behaviour.

2. **Can we use econometric models instead?** Econometric models which utilize economic variables to forecast the effect of price changes may be adequate in several situations. For instance, when a product is known to respond to changes in consumer disposable income, inflation rate, or competitive price environment, these factors can be built into a model and decisions can be based on the outcome as predicted by the model.

3. **Can secondary research be used instead?** A number of data sources readily available to the marketer may provide adequate indication as to the possible effects of price changes. Secondary sources, if properly used, may provide significant clues to the reaction of the market to price changes. Secondary data can also be incorporated into econometric models discussed in the previous paragraph. Some of the more common sources of secondary data are:
   - Competitive price lists
   - Competitive advertising expenditure
   - Competitive advertising and promotional literature
   - Customer feedback
   - Sales force feedback
   - Published literature on the product category
   - Professional and trade associations
   - Financial and annual reports of competitors
   - Government statistics
   - Statistics Canada reports, census data
   - Industry trend data (published sources/internal sources)
   - Product pricing trends (published sources/internal sources)

Note: Not all of these sources are available for each product; however, at least a few sources should be available for any given product.

DECIDING ON THE TYPE OF RESEARCH

Even if we decide to do ad hoc research, a number of decisions have to be made before deciding on the specific technique.

1. **Single brand versus multi-brand**: Price sensitivity can be tested for a single brand in isolation or in the context of competing brands. When a single brand is tested in isolation, certain assumptions are made about the market. The most critical of such assumptions is that the price change will be effected in a market whose environment is substantially the same as that obtained at the time of testing. In other words, the marketer implicitly assumes that the competitors will neither increase nor decrease their prices within the time frame under consideration. If they do effect a price change, the marketer further assumes their action will not have a substantial effect on the brand under consideration.

    How reasonable are these assumptions? Experience has shown that they are valid in some cases, especially in markets where brands cater to segments instead of competing directly. However, in cases where products are fairly similar and a wide choice is available to consumers, relative pricing may be the most important factor.

2. **Manifest versus latent approaches**: Response to pricing can be elicited either directly or indirectly. Indirect (latent) approaches have the advantage of eliciting responses that may be difficult for the consumer to give in response to direct questioning. Direct (manifest) approaches, on the other hand, are straightforward in that they establish a direct communication between the consumer and the researcher.

3. **Randomized versus sequential approaches**: When we use several brands in a price study, the brands can be presented at random or sequentially. In either case, we can control either for the effect of order or the context of presentation.

REPRESENTATIVE RESEARCH TECHNIQUES

The schematic Exhibit 19.2 shows these choices and representative research techniques that can be used when such choices are made. Specific research techniques that can be used include:

- Price sensitivity meter (PSM)
- Psychological pricing technique
- Buying response randomized test
- Randomized shop situation test
- Trade-off technique
- Dual matrix technique

All these techniques are either *product utility type* or *feature utility type*.

Exhibit 19.2   Pricing Research: Choosing an Appropriate Research Technique

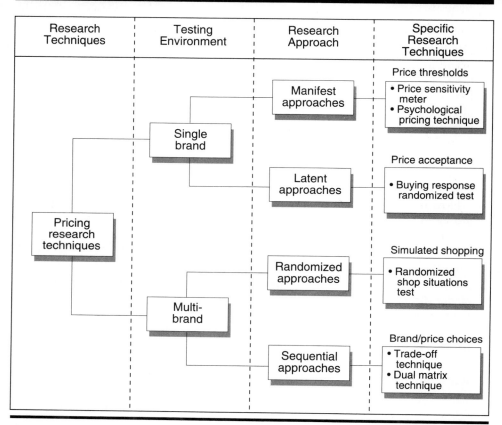

PRODUCT UTILITY MODELS   Product utility models assume that a consumer has some utility for a given product or brand and that this utility can be translated into monetary terms. As long as this utility does not fall below the utility for the price of the product, the consumer will continue to buy it. When the product utility falls below the price utility, the consumer will turn away from the product. Thus if the utility (in monetary terms) for a movie is $7 and if the current charge is $6.50, an increase in price up to $7 will simply increase the profitability and will have no effect on consumer behaviour. Any increase above this will witness a deterioration in sales. In other words, any product is price elastic but such elasticity may have a range within which an increase or decrease in price has no effect on consumer behaviour. Product utility models are used in cases where no added benefits are offered to the consumer for the higher price.

FEATURE UTILITY MODELS   Feature utility models assume that the utility of a product is nothing more than the sum of utilities for its individual features. Thus the utility for a personal computer is the sum of utilities for its different features such as memory, user friendliness, software availability and the like. When confronted with a choice situation, a consumer would choose the product with the highest utility. This model offers greater flexibility to the marketer:

- If the proposed price increase is lower than the utility currently derived by the consumer from the product, price can be increased with no effect on sales.

- If the proposed price increase is higher than the utility currently derived by the consumer from the product, the marketer has two alternatives: either reduce the cost of production by eliminating a feature that has a low utility to the consumer or add a feature with a high utility and increase the price. Feature utility models are used in cases where the marketer has the option of changing the product or the way it is positioned.

PRODUCT UTILITY RESEARCH TECHNIQUES

PSYCHOLOGICAL PRICING TECHNIQUE

Psychological pricing holds that consumers do not buy for two reasons: either the product is too cheap or it is too expensive. At each level of pricing, these two groups can be found. When we exclude these two groups from the total (potential) market, we arrive at potential buyers at different price levels. This is accomplished simply with the use of two questions:

- Above which price would you say that *you would definitely not buy* Brand A because it would be too expensive?

- Below which price would you say that *you would definitely not buy* Brand A because your would not trust its quality?

The analysis consists of (1) excluding "don't know" answers; (2) cumulating the percentages for each level starting from the lowest price for (i) those buying because it is not too expensive and (ii) for those not buying because it is too cheap; and (3) subtracting one percentage from the other. Step (3) gives the buying response at different levels (see Exhibits 19.3 and 19.4). The marketer may choose either the point at which the buying response is the highest or the point at which the aggregate profits are the highest, given the buying level.

Exhibit 19.3   Psychological Pricing: Price Acceptance

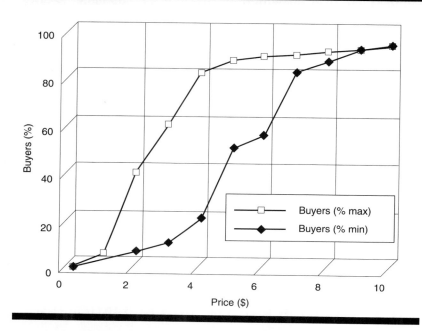

Exhibit 19.4   Psychological Pricing: Buying Response Curve

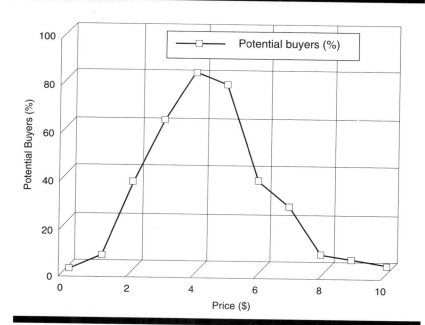

PRICE SENSITIVITY METER (PSM)

The price sensitivity meter (PSM) takes the psychological pricing technique a step further. Four questions are used:

- At what price would you consider this product to be cheap, yet of acceptable quality?
- At what price would you consider this product to be expensive, yet a possible purchase?
- At what price would you consider this product to be too expensive to consider buying?
- At what price would you consider this product to be too cheap to trust its quality?

Exhibit 19.5   PSM: Optimal and Indifference Prices

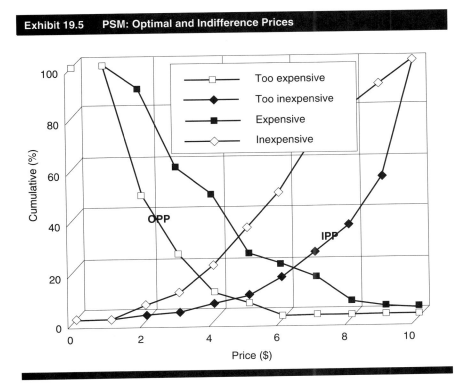

Exhibit 19.6   PSM: Buying Response Curve

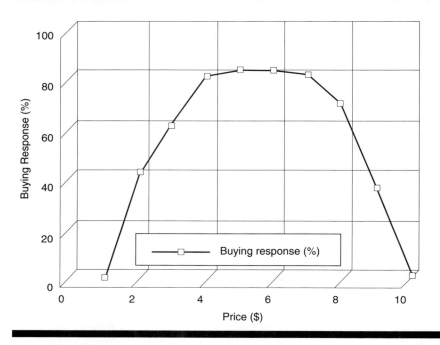

Initial analysis is similar to that of the psychological pricing technique (see Exhibits 19.5 and 19.6). Subsequent analysis includes inverting the expensive and inexpensive cumulative figures to obtain:

- **Optimal pricing point** (the point at which the consumer resistance is at its lowest, i.e., the point at which the "too expensive" and "too inexpensive" lines intersect)

- **Indifference pricing point** (the point at which receptivity is at its highest, i.e., the point at which the "inverted expensive" (not expensive) and "inverted inexpensive" (not inexpensive) lines intersect)

- **Point of marginal inexpensiveness or PMI** (the point below which there is a buyer reluctance because of quality concerns, i.e., the point at which the "too inexpensive" line intersects the "inverted expensive" line)

- **Point of marginal expensiveness or PME** (the point above which there is a buyer reluctance because of price, i.e, the point at which the "too expensive" line intersects the "inverted inexpensive" line)

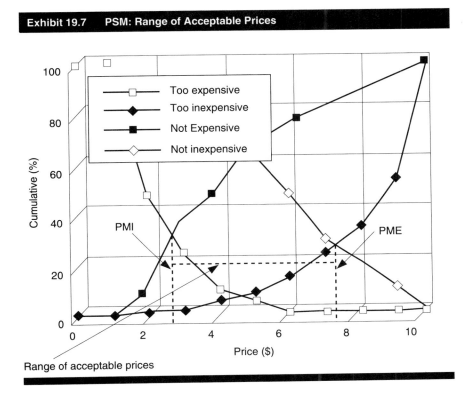

Exhibit 19.7   PSM: Range of Acceptable Prices

Range of acceptable prices

• **The range of acceptable prices** (the interval within which price change is not the major determinant of buying, i.e., the interval that is between PMI and PME).

Exhibit 19.7 illustrates these parameters.

RANDOMIZED TEST OF BUYING RESPONSE

This is yet another variation of the techniques discussed above. Here the consumer is presented several prices in a randomized order. The interviewer reads out each price and asks the respondent to choose one of three answers:

• Yes, would buy at that price
• No, it is too cheap
• No, it is too expensive

The resultant graphs show how elastic the product is, how soon it is perceived to be too cheap and how late it is perceived to be too expensive (see Exhibits 19.8 and 19.9).

Exhibit 19.8   Randomized Test: Non-buyers

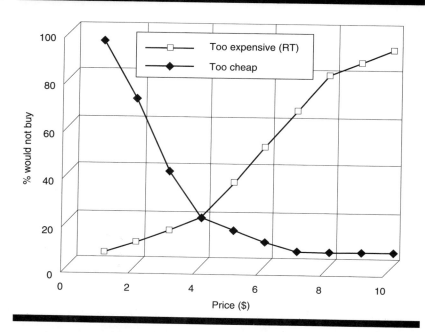

Exhibit 19.9   Randomized Test: Buying Response

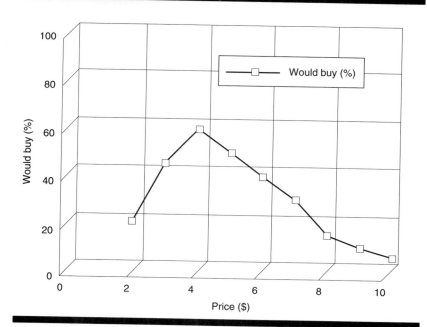

EXPERIMENTAL DESIGNS

Another fairly common method is to present different prices to different groups of consumers and ask how likely they are to buy the product at the given price. Each sub-sample is exposed to only one price. The results thus obtained can then be analyzed using analysis of variance techniques. The main problem with this technique is the initial disposition of the different sub-samples. This problem is particularly acute if the market is heterogeneous. On the positive side, if properly handled, the analysis can detect subtle relationships among different variables influencing price response.

SEQUENTIAL CHOICE TESTS (DUAL BRANDS x PRICES MATRIX)

When our aim is to identify the effect of marginal price changes on brand choice, we can use sequential choice tests. If we want to compare brands A and B, we can start at the same price level for both. The price is increased by a small amount each time to see at what level brand switching occurs.

> *Example:*
>
> Which brand would you buy if brand A and B are priced at $1?
>
> If the respondent says Brand A ask:
>
> > If Brand A is priced at $1.10 and B is priced at $1 which would you buy?
>
> If the respondent continues to say Brand A, ask:
>
> > If Brand A is priced at $1.20 and B is priced at $1 which would you buy?
>
> and so on.

In the actual test situation, the interviewers are given an easy-to-read matrix which guides them through the various alternatives depending on the answers (see Exhibit 19.10).

SEQUENTIAL CHOICE TESTS (MULTIPLE BRANDS x PRICES MATRIX)

This is an extension of the dual brands times prices technique. In a typical interview situation, the consumer is presented with several brands with the same price and is asked to choose one. The price of the chosen brand is changed to the next higher level and the consumer is asked to choose again. The brand that is chosen at the highest price is removed from the display and the test is continued until all the alternatives are exhausted.

Exhibit 19.10   Dual Brand X Prices Sequential Choice Matrix

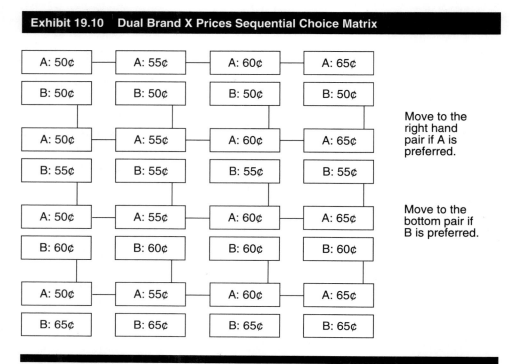

Move to the right hand pair if A is preferred.

Move to the bottom pair if B is preferred.

Interviewer Instructions: There are two brands (A and B) and several prices. Start with the pair at the top left hand box. Follow the line that connects consumer preference to the next pair.

The results are treated as trade-offs between prices and brands and the relative price sensitivity can be calculated. Thus we can plot (1) the percentage of times a brand was chosen at different prices levels, and (2) the percentage of times a brand was chosen from among all brands shown at that price (see Exhibits 19.11 and 19.12).

RANDOMIZED MULTIPLE CHOICE TESTS

The consumer is presented with a repertoire of competing brands at the market price along with the test brand at a given price. The consumer is asked to choose one. When this is done, the test brand is re-presented with a different price with the same repertoire of brands. In the general model, only the price of the test brand is changed following each choice. Different price levels of the test brand are introduced at random rather than in an ascending or descending order. The typical response curves are presented in Exhibit 19.13.

Exhibit 19.11   Sequential Choices: Market Shares

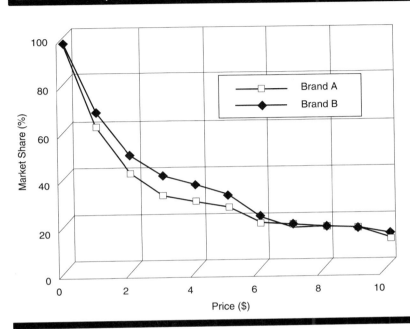

Exhibit 19.12   Sequential Choice: Buying Response

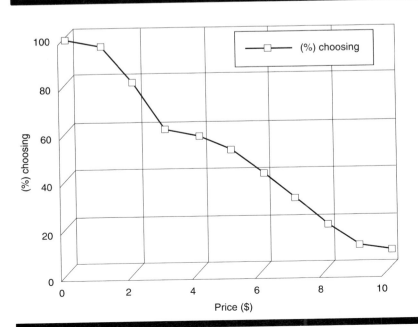

Exhibit 19.13   Randomized Multiple Choice: Brand Shares

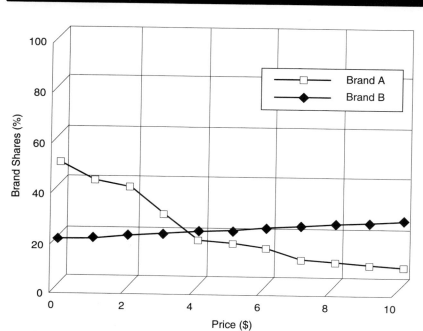

FEATURE UTILITY MODELS

Consider two offers by an airline to the same destination: plan 1 costs $250 but you have to commence your trip on a Sunday morning and return before the following Wednesday; plan 2 has no such restriction but costs $350. Which one would you choose? A class of popular models attempts to answer this question by hypothesizing that each consumer has some "use" for each major feature offered by each alternative, as well as for the price. The use that a consumer has for different features and for the price can be quantified on the same scale. The quantified usefulness is called a *utility*.

For instance, if the utility for $100 (the difference in cost between the two plans) is 0.8 and the utility for flexibility (travelling on any day and returning on any day) is 0.6, then the consumer would choose plan 1. A consumer who has a utility of 0.3 for $100 and a utility of 0.7 for flexibility would choose plan 2.

In the above example, the consumer is modelled to perceive a given brand not as one unit, but as a combination of features; each feature has a separate utility that can be exchanged with any other feature that has the same utility value. Because the utilities refer to different features of a product, these models can be referred to as *feature utility models*. These techniques assume that every consumer has some utility for each feature of a product. Purchase decisions are made on the basis of these utilities. However, a consumer is unaware of the utilities that he or she attaches to different features. All that consumers can do is to indicate their preferences for different brands or features. Fortunately, techniques are now available to break down an individual's overall preferences into utilities for each feature of the product. Representative techniques in this category are conjoint analysis and trade-off analysis.

CONJOINT ANALYSIS

Let us consider a consumer who is presented with a choice of two models of cars A and B. Further assume that the consumer has the utilities for different features as shown in Exhibit 19.14.

Exhibit 19.14   Utilities for Attributes

MPG	Utility	Warranty	Utility	Price	Utility
11-15	0.8	1 year	1.0	$20 000	1.9
16-20	1.2	2 years	1.1	$22 000	1.7
21-25	1.5	3 years	1.5	$24 000	1.5
26-30	2.0				

Model A gives 23 miles per gallon, has a one-year warranty and costs $22 000. Model B gives 20 miles per gallon, comes with a two-year warranty and has a price tag of $24 000. Which model would this consumer choose? If we look up the utilities for this consumer for different features we find that Model A has a total utility of 4.2 (1.5 + 1.0 + 1.7), while Model B has a total utility of 3.8 (1.2 + 1.1 + 1.5). Therefore, this consumer would choose Model A over Model B. If we are to sell Model B to this consumer, we should increase the total utility by at least 0.4, which can be done either by dropping the price to $20 000, or by increasing MPG to at least 26, or, if these are not possible, by increasing the warranty period to three years. From a theoretical point of view, it does not matter which change is made as long as it provides the required number of utilities. The manufacturer naturally will choose the alternative that is least expensive to provide.

But how do we know what these utilities are? After all, the consumer does not know what his or her utilities for different features are and consequently cannot tell the researcher. To determine utilities, the consumer is presented with different hypothetical models of cars. Some of these choices are shown below:

Model 1:   11-15 MPG / 1-year warranty / $22 000

Model 2:   16-20 MPG / 1-year warranty / $22 000

Model 3:   21-25 MPG / 1-year warranty / $22 000

Model 4:   26-30 MPG / 1-year warranty / $22 000

Model 5:   11-15 MPG / 2-year warranty / $22 000

Model 6:   16-20 MPG / 2-year warranty / $22 000

Model 7:   21-25 MPG / 2-year warranty / $22 000

Model 8:   26-30 MPG / 2-year warranty / $22 000

Model 9:   11-15 MPG / 1-year warranty / $20 000

Model 10:   16-20 MPG / 1-year warranty / $20 000

Model 11:   21-25 MPG / 1-year warranty / $20 000

and so on. (In the above example, a total of 36 combinations—4 x 3 x 3—are possible). The consumer is simply asked to rank the alternatives from the most desirable to the least desirable.

Given the ranks of various feature combinations, we need to infer utilities for individual features. Mathematically, this is achieved by decomposing the ranks given by the consumer. In the above example, the technique attempts to find 10 numbers corresponding to each feature alternative, i.e., four mileage alternatives, three warranty alternatives and three price alternatives as shown in the beginning of this section. These 10 numbers should fulfill the following objective: when the numbers corresponding to the features are combined for a model, they should follow the same ranking given by the consumer. This is achieved by computer through iterative procedures. Because each person may have a different utility for the same feature, the utilities are derived for each individual separately.

SOME PROBLEMS AND SOLUTIONS   While conjoint analysis is intuitively easy to understand and, therefore, easy to apply to real life research results, there are some problems.

THE MODEL MAY NOT BE APPROPRIATE   Conjoint analysis assumes that consumers not only have utilities for individual features of a product but they simply add all the individual utilities to arrive at a figure that represents the

Exhibit 19.15   Utilities for Attributes at Different Levels

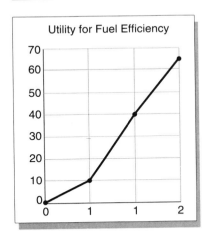

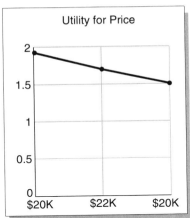

total utility for the product at a given price. This ignores the possibility that, in certain situations, the whole is greater than the sum of its parts. For example, in evaluating a job "good working conditions" may have a certain utility and "excellent salary" may have a certain utility. But a combination of both may have a utility that may be far higher than the sum of their individual utilities. These situations may arise in products in which certain features are traditionally assumed to be mutually exclusive.

The same feature may have different utilities in different products. For instance, extended warranty for a low priced car may have a lower utility than for a higher priced car. Conjoint analysis assumes that a given feature has the same utility in all products.

Under these circumstances, the fit of the model will be weak. When this happens we either have to try another model or interpret the findings cautiously. Since there is always a possibility that the model may not fit, it may be desirable to include as many realistic combinations of features as possible in the study so that they can be interpreted globally, even if we can isolate the effect of different features.

THE ATTRIBUTES MAY BE SUBJECTIVE   Sometimes attribute levels are worded in such a way that they don't mean the same thing to different consumers. For instance, "low quality," "medium quality" and "high quality" may mean entirely different things to different consumers and can provide misleading results. It is a good practice to use only those attributes and levels that are concrete and objective.

AVERAGING OF UTILITIES MAY HIDE A SEGMENTED MARKET   Although the utilities are derived on an individual basis, they are usually examined at the aggregate level. Consider a highly segmented market in which a particular feature has a very high utility for about 10% of the consumers but a low utility for others. By averaging out utilities for all the consumers, we may arrive at the conclusion that consumers do not consider the feature beneficial. We may miss a highly lucrative and segmented market. To avoid this, we may want to group similar utility patterns using segmentation techniques like cluster analysis. This is particularly true of products at the high end which usually appeal to a small, segmented but less price sensitive group of consumers.

THERE MAY BE TOO MANY COMBINATIONS   In our example we had three attributes and 10 levels (fuel efficiency—four levels, warranty—three levels, and price—three levels). If we present all combinations to the respondents for evaluation, we have 36 (4 x 3 x 3) combinations. This may be too much for a respondent, if we ask him to simply rank the alternatives. If, instead of three attributes, we have five attributes with three levels in each, we may have 243 combinations! If we want to use all combinations, the task will quickly become formidable. Fortunately, there are some solutions to this problem.

First, we can reduce the number of alternatives using a statistical technique known as the fractional factorial design. This procedure enables us to test fewer alternatives and yet come up with an estimate of utilities for each feature included in the study. Second, we may obtain some information by straightforward questioning rather than by conjoint analysis, thereby reducing the number of attributes measured by conjoint analysis. Third, we can use a pairwise trade-off approach, as described in the following section.

TRADE-OFF ANALYSIS

In trade-off analysis, consumers are presented with two choices at a time. For example, the consumer is asked a series of questions such as:

- Would you prefer a car that gives 23 mpg with a 1-year warranty? or
- Would you prefer a car that gives 20 mpg with a 2-year warranty?

Such questions may be relatively easier to answer than the menu approach we used earlier in which the consumer has to take into account several attributes at the same time. However, it can be argued that the menu approach simulates the real life decision-making alternatives better. Currently, the menu approach appears to be more widely used.

ANALYTIC TECHNIQUES

Several standard procedures can be used to analyze the results obtained using the research techniques outlined here. Some more commonly used techniques are:

- **Buying response curves**: The results from most of the above techniques can be analyzed by plotting buying response curves. Knowledge of elementary statistics such as standard deviation and standard error should be adequate to interpret the results.

- **Profit analysis curves**: When maximum total profit, rather than the highest achievable market share for a brand, is the main objective, the buying response figures should be weighted by profit per unit at different price levels. A further refinement of the procedure would be to add an additional weight to take into account the usage level. While it is important that the sample be representative for pricing tests, it is particularly critical when additional weights for volume and profitability are used.

- **ANOVA/Coded regression**: In models involving different brands and price levels, the data may be analyzed using analysis of variance/coded regression procedures. Almost any standard statistical package (e.g., SPSS, Systat, SAS) should be adequate for analytic purposes.

- **Trade-off/Conjoint analysis**: The techniques involving brand/price trade-offs can be analyzed using special techniques like monotonic analysis of variance or non-metric regression techniques. Many stand-alone programs are available for this purpose.

- **Segmentation analysis**: Techniques such as cluster analysis and hierarchical cross-tabulations may be used to identify market segments that are small but highly profitable.

DECISION ALGORITHMS

Now we are back to the original question: how to avoid the "price *du jour* syndrome," or how not to react to competition in a way that is against our long-term interests. With so many alternatives, so many research techniques available, what should we do? If research is an alternative, which technique should a researcher use? The following framework may provide some guidelines to the marketer and the researcher. These questions can be answered by the marketer and the researcher by systematically narrowing down the choices.

MARKETER'S DECISION ALGORITHM

1. Can past data be used? Are there sales records, past research studies that throw any light and provide enough input for pricing?
2. Can an econometric model be used (i.e., do we know that the product responds directly to economic conditions so that we do not have to carry out ad hoc studies)? If not:
3. Can the information required for pricing be obtained in other ways (such as industry figures, standards)? If not:
4. Are the variables involved in determining the price such that they are best measured and analyzed by marketing research techniques?

If the answer to the first three questions is no and to the fourth yes, the marketer may want to acquire the assistance of a researcher. At this stage, the decision-making process is temporarily transferred to the researcher.

RESEARCHER'S DECISION ALGORITHM

1. Should we just consider our brand or should we consider the competitive environment?
2. Does the product lend itself to direct questioning on price (e.g., computers) or do we need to use indirect questioning (e.g., prestige products)?

3. Is there an order effect in presentation? Do we use a randomized or sequential approach?

4. Among the techniques that are suitable, is there an aspect of the technique that would make it less suitable than others (e.g., interaction effect in conjoint analysis)?

5. Can 4 above be overcome by other means?

6. If more than one technique is suitable which is more cost-effective, faster and less error prone?

Choosing the appropriate technique based on the answers to the above questions will go a long way to choosing the right strategy that will result in consistent and profitable pricing.

SUMMARY

1. In a capitalist economy, price is determined by market forces of supply and demand rather than by cost of production. Market research can play a useful role in determining the optimal price for a given product.

2. Pricing may be cost-oriented, market-oriented or competition-oriented. Research can be useful in market- and competition-oriented pricing strategies. The basic pricing strategies are:

   - Cost-plus pricing
   - Marginal pricing
   - Elasticity pricing
   - Skim pricing
   - Slide-down pricing
   - Penetration pricing
   - Segment pricing
   - Prestige pricing
   - Flexible pricing
   - Phase-out pricing
   - Pre-emptive pricing
   - Follow pricing
   - Loss leader pricing

3. There are many common fallacies relating to pricing. J. Nault identifies the following:

- Consumer buys rationally
- Quality determines the price
- Price can be soundly based on margin goal
- Recession favours low price products
- Consumers know the market prices
- Wise pricing is relative to competition
- New products are to be priced at today's cost of goods
- Only the market leader can control the price
- Manufacturers control the retailers' selling price
- Price low at entry, then increase once the share goals are achieved

4. Before embarking on pricing research, you should consider whether ad hoc research is needed at all. You may decide to use econometric models or secondary data analysis instead. If you do decide to use ad hoc research, you will need to consider alternative approaches: single brand versus multibrand, manifest versus latent approaches, and randomized versus sequential approaches.

5. There are two basic types of pricing models:

- **Product utility models** (e.g., psychological pricing technique, PSM, randomized test of buying response, experimental designs, sequential choice tests, randomized multiple choice tests) assume that a consumer has some utility (a measure of importance) for a given product or brand and that the utility can be translated into monetary terms.
- **Feature utility models** (e.g., conjoint analysis, trade-off analysis) assume that a product's utility is the sum total of utilities for each of its features.

NOW THINK ABOUT THIS

1. Why is research seldom used in cost-plus pricing?

2. Thirteen pricing strategies are described in this chapter. Describe the strengths and weaknesses of each strategy.

3. What is the difference between product utility models and feature utility models? Describe conjoint analysis and price sensitivity meter. Under what conditions would you use these models?

20 / Media Research and Other Specialized Areas

WHAT YOU WILL LEARN IN THIS CHAPTER

- How media research works
- To name and describe some major media research studies in Canada
- To appreciate the complexities of media research
- Why different methodology is required for different media
- The most commonly used media research terms
- Some specialized areas of marketing research
- Why different techniques are used in different areas of specialization
- The particular characteristics of different areas of research

INTRODUCTION

If you are a market researcher, you could be involved in solving problems arising from different sectors of industry and business. Such sectors could include media audience measurements, pharmaceuticals, packaged goods, industrial products, political polling and other areas. No matter which area you work in, the general principles of research apply. In addition, each area of specialization has its own techniques to solve problems that are distinctive to that area. For instance:

- If you are interested in what toothpaste consumers use, you can interview them on any day of the week; but if you are interested in knowing what sections of a daily newspaper people read each day, your sample should be designed such that all days of the week are covered and you have a large enough sample each day.

- If you are interested in finding out people's political views, you can probably call them on the phone and administer a 15-minute long questionnaire; but if you are interested in knowing what doctors think of a new medical innovation, you may have to arrange with the doctor for a 15-minute interview.

- If you are interviewing consumers on a commonly used product, you may not need specialized interviews; but if you want to interview investment managers you may need people with specialized skills and knowledge.

- If you interview consumers of mass market products, you are likely to aggregate the data to understand the market; but if you interview industry leaders, you would probably analyze the interviews individually to identify the patterns and distinctiveness of responses.

Thus, depending on the area of study, the way you sample, the way you conduct the interview, the skills you need in an interviewer and the way you analyze can be very different. It is beyond the scope of the present book to expound these differences. The purpose of this chapter is simply to highlight some functional areas.

MEDIA RESEARCH

Media research as defined here refers to research carried out to measure the number of readers, viewers or listeners exposed to a given medium. Because such numbers are used for competitive purposes, it is important that the research be carried out rigorously. There are several methodological issues involved in media research. Discussion of such issues is beyond the scope of this book. However, descriptions of how some of these studies are carried out may give you an idea of the complexities and methodological issues involved in such studies. Commentaries are included to clarify some aspects of these studies.

Here is a description of some of the major media studies carried out in Canada:

- **Newspaper Readership Study:** NADbank studies (Newspaper Audience Databank) are carried out on behalf of member newspapers by the Newspaper Marketing Bureau. Sample size: 24 000 plus telephone interviews; carried out in over 30 different markets simultaneously. Rolling half sample (over 12 000) each year.

- **Magazine Readership:** PMB Print Measurement Bureau carries out magazine readership studies on an annual basis. PMB is sponsored by publishers, advertising agencies, and advertisers. Sample size: 8000 personal interviews per year.

- **Radio Listenership:** BBM (Bureau of Broadcast Measurement) carries out studies on behalf of broadcasters, advertisers and advertising agencies. Sample size varies from market to market. A household diary method is used to measure both radio and TV audiences. Individuals in a household record their tuning by daypart (described later).

NEWSPAPER READERSHIP STUDY: NADBANK'91

OBJECTIVES   NADbank (Newspaper Audience Databank) is the major study conducted for Canada's daily newspaper publishers. It is the largest private research study undertaken in Canada. The objectives of the study are to:

- provide a measure of Canadian daily newspaper audiences on a market-by-market basis;
- provide information on consumer shopping, product usage and purchase behaviour.

The study is carried out using Computer Assisted Telephone Interviewing (CATI) technology.

THE MARKETS   Thirty-two separate markets are dialled simultaneously and from 10 CLTs (Central Location Telephone facilities) in different cities across the country. In the past, approximately 24 000 NADbank interviews were conducted every 2 years. Starting in 1990, the study is to be conducted annually. The annual target will be approximately 12 000 interviews. Every year the oldest 12-months' interviews are discarded and a new year's added to provide a continuous sample of over 24 000 interviews.

Exhibit 20.1 Interviews by Market (per year; half sample)

CLT	Market	Market Quota	Total Quota
Halifax	Halifax	450	
	Moncton	225	
	Saint John	300	975
Québec City	Chicoutimi/Jonquière	225	
	Québec City	400	
	Trois Rivières/Shawinigan	300	
	Granby	225	1150
Montreal	Sherbrooke	300	
	Montreal	1300	
	Ottawa/Hull	500	2100
Toronto	Kingston	225	
	Toronto	750	
	Kitchener	400	
	Owen Sound-Grey Bruce	225	
	North Bay	225	1825
Hamilton	Hamilton	575	
	St. Catharines/Niagara	300	
	Brantford	225	1100
London	London	400	
	Windsor	400	
	Sault Ste. Marie	225	1025
Winnipeg	Winnipeg	400	
	Regina	400	800
Calgary	Medicine Hat	225	
	Calgary	400	625
Edmonton	Saskatoon	400	
	Edmonton	400	
	Red Deer	225	1025
Vancouver	Kamloops	225	
	Vancouver	500	
	Victoria	400	
	Prince George	225	1350

The interviews are conducted by Canadian Facts. Interviews were distributed to accommodate the CLT locations maintained by Canadian Facts.

INTERVIEWING SCHEDULE   Interviewing is carried out daily, Tuesday through Saturday, starting January 29 and finishing June 1. No interviewing is conducted on Sundays and Mondays.

Comment: The interviews are geared to weekday and weekend readership of newspapers. The critical newspaper readership question is "Did you yourself happen to read or look into yesterday's issue, that is ____ day's issue of (name of the paper)?" Thus Tuesday interviews measure Monday's readership and Saturday interviews measure Friday readership. Tuesday to Saturday interviews thus cover the entire week.

There are only two weeks when interviewing may not take place during this period: Easter week and the week of May 21, because of Victoria Day. Interviewing during these weeks is suspended if newspaper publication is affected.

Comment: Interviewing is suspended during holiday weeks to allow for people not being exposed to newspapers on a specific day and because readership patterns may be affected during holiday weeks.

SAMPLE DESIGN

Type of Sample: The study uses a true random digit dialling (RDD) sample. The sample is constructed first by identifying all working NNXs for the market and then inserting randomly generated numbers to represent the last four digits in a telephone number. The NNX (telephone exchange) represents the first three digits of the seven digits in a locally dialled telephone number. This type of sample yields substantial quantities of not-in-service and business numbers. Extensive pre-screening is done to eliminate most of these numbers. Approximately 56 per cent were found not to be eligible. Most of the numbers dialled, therefore, are working, residential numbers.

Sample Streams: The sample is split into four independent RDD sample streams, each with identical calling schedules. The release of sample streams is staggered to ensure that a new sample is available at different times throughout the study. Every four weeks a new sample stream is released until all four samples have been released. Each stream requires about seven weeks of dialling to achieve the required completion rates. Numbers which result in a refusal may require dialling over a greater number of weeks as they are suspended for two or three weeks when a refusal is encountered.

Comment: Sample streams have two purposes: to control the work flow, so that interviews are conducted at an even pace during the course of the interview period; they can also be used as replicated sub-samples.

Exhibit 20.2 Release of Sample Streams

Week of:		Stream A	Stream B	Stream C	Stream D
Jan 29	Wk01	Main			
Feb 5	Wk02	Main			
Feb 12	Wk03	Main			
Feb 19	Wk04	Main + Ref	Main		
Feb 26	Wk05	Main + Ref	Main		
Mar 5	Wk06	Main + Ref	Main		
Mar 12	Wk07	Main + Ref	Main + Ref	Main	
Mar 19	Wk08	Ref	Main + Ref	Main	
Mar 26	Wk09	Ref	Main + Ref	Main + Ref	
Apr 2			EASTER		
Apr 9	Wk10	Ref	Main + Ref	Main + Ref	Main
Apr 16	Wk11	Ref	Main + Ref	Main + Ref	Main
Apr 23	Wk12		Ref	Main + Ref	Main + Ref
Apr 30	Wk13		Ref	Main + Ref	Main + Ref
May 7	Wk14			Ref	Main + Ref
May 14	Wk15			Ref	Main + Ref
May 21			VICTORIA DAY		
May 28	Wk16			Ref	Main + Ref

Ref = Refusals

DAY OF WEEK CONTROLS   In newspaper audience research, it is important to understand readership patterns by day-of-week. For this reason samples must be controlled by day-of-week as well. Therefore, not only is the sample divided into four sample streams (as noted above), but each stream is also divided into five-day samples (Tuesday, Wednesday, Thursday, Friday, and Saturday). For example, a telephone number dialled on Tuesday will not be available for dialling again until next Tuesday. Only after four weeks of dialling numbers are they moved to other days of the week. (The only exceptions to this rule are appointments, refusals and household language barriers.) To maintain the representativeness of the sample it is important that as many completions as possible are achieved in the first four weeks of a sample.

Comment: The day-of-week balance is traditionally considered to be important in newspaper readership studies. The actual specification for this study stipulates that the day-of-week balance be maintained such that deviation for any given day does not exceed + or – 2 percentage points (i.e. 20 ± 2% of interviews for each interview day).

RESPONDENT SELECTION WITHIN THE HOUSEHOLD   A telephone sample represents only a "household sample." Because we want to interview only one individual per household, we have to take the sample selection process one stage further. We must randomly select a respondent within households of two or more qualified persons. There are a number of techniques we could use, but the simplest procedure is the most recent birthday technique. A respondent within a household is selected by asking to speak to the person who is 18 years of age or older and who had the most recent birthday in the household. The interviewer must speak to that person only. The qualifying person is to remain the same once the first screening is complete. Substitutions are not allowed.

Comment: Why do we bother screening for a respondent in each household? Certain persons are more likely than others to answer the telephone and certain persons are more interested than others in doing this type of interview. If we were to interview only these people, then we would not have a true representation of the general population. Sample selection techniques are particularly important when one tries to measure the incidence of something, such as the incidence of newspaper readership.

WHO DOES THE "HOUSEHOLD" INCLUDE/EXCLUDE?   A "household" includes all persons who reside in the private dwelling accessed by the telephone number you have dialled. These persons do not need to be related, but they must perceive themselves to be living in a "household." If the number you have dialled puts you in contact with persons living in an institution, or the telephone is located in a common area and many "households" have use of the telephone (such as a dormitory), then the number is non-residential.

RESPONSE RATES   This study demands a very high response rate. A response rate of 65% (with no substitutions allowed at the household or the respondent level) is specified for this study.

Comment: Compared to other marketing research studies, a response rate of 65% with no substitutions in NADbank'91 is very stringent. However, most media studies specify fairly high response rates. In fact, the NADbank'88 study specified and achieved a 70% response rate, one of the highest achieved anywhere in the world. It is less likely that such response rates will be achieved in the future. There are many reasons why very high response rates are hard to achieve: extensive use of answering machines (which enable the respondent not to answer the telephone at all), people mistaking research for selling and thus refusing to participate, use of cellular phones and other factors contribute to lowered response rates and to making the response rate calculations complex.

The two most important factors which allow us to increase the response rate are: the amount of time spent in the field; and, the degree to which call-backs are conducted to convert refusals.

"No reply's," "busy's," incomplete "appointments" and "refusals" all count toward the response rate calculation. In most studies we do not have the time to get through to these households. For NADbank we keep calling these numbers until a contact can be made.

The major reason for people refusing to conduct an interview is inconvenience. Once again the effort required to re-contact a refuser several times to conduct an interview at a more convenient time is too much for most studies. For NADbank it is important we re-contact these households several times in an attempt to catch a potential respondent at a better time. It is very important, therefore, that each household is approached in the best possible manner. There is a limited amount of sample we are able to use to achieve the desired completions. Our best chance of achieving the desired result is on the first contact with the eligible respondent.

SAMPLE RECYCLING PATTERNS   The computer is programmed such that it will control the calling patterns as per the following rules:

> Engaged will recycle every 30 minutes up to 3 times/day
> No reply will recycle every 90 minutes up to 2 times/day

REFUSALS (HOUSEHOLD AND RESPONDENT)

1st refusal — In streams 1 and 2, refusals are suspended for 3 weeks + 1 day. In streams 3 and 4, refusals are suspended for 2 weeks + 1 day.

2nd refusal —I n streams 1 and 2, refusals are suspended for 3 weeks + 1 day. In streams 3 and 4, refusals are suspended for 2 weeks + 1 day.

3rd refusal — Refusal suspended.

Respondent language barriers — Suspended immediately.

Household language barriers — See Household refusals. Suspended permanently after 3rd contact resulting in household language barrier.

Day-of-week patterns — Engaged, No response, Answering machine and Household language barriers are only called on designated day for the 1st four weeks for the stream. In weeks 5 and 6 these numbers are moved to the next calling day (e.g., Tues to Wed). In week 7 the numbers are available every day.

Comment: When a respondent refuses to participate, more attempts are made by skilled interviewers to convert the refuser into a respondent. Most refusals seem to happen because the respondent is contacted at an inconve-

nient time. Consequently, surveys with people who have refused previously (refusal surveys) are usually met with measurable success if carried out properly. To facilitate a favourable response, the respondent is called back at a later date on a different day. In order to manage dialling of refusals more closely, all telephone numbers which result in a refusal will be moved to a Refusal Survey for that market. As a result, each market actually has two questionnaires: main and refusal. The refusal questionnaire is identical to the main questionnaire.

REFUSAL CONVERSION   The most challenging aspect of this study is to develop a technique for convincing respondents who initially refuse to agree to participate on further contacts. Appointment scheduling, therefore, is a very important task. Many refusing respondents are unsure of the process (they are not sure why they are being approached, they are concerned about sales pitches, getting on mailing lists, etc.) and it is with these respondents that an interviewer's skills are most important. When re-dialling refusals, interviewers are encouraged to try different approaches in the first few seconds of contact, in an attempt to interest the respondent or make him or her feel more secure with the interview.

THE QUESTIONNAIRE   The NADbank questionnaire consists of the following sections:

- Introduction and household screening
- Media
- Daily newspaper readership
- Weekend newspaper readership
- TV publication readership
- Demographics
- Shopping behaviour and advertising flyers
- Vehicle ownership and maintenance
- Household possessions
- Household improvements
- Radio listening
- Vacation and business travel
- Leisure activities
- Alcohol use
- Financial products
- Proprietary questions

The questionnaire has been customized for each market; newspapers, store lists, etc., are specific to each market. The questionnaire will vary in length from 20 minutes to 30 minutes, depending on the number of proprietary questions included, the number of newspapers asked about (and whether these papers are residential or non-residential) and the respondent.

Comment: *A number of questions are asked about respondents' buying behaviour. This is then related to readership of newspapers.*

PMB READERSHIP STUDIES

PMB Print Measurement Bureau is a federally incorporated, non-profit, tripartite association of publishers, advertising agencies and advertisers. Its purpose is to provide its members with detailed information on the readers of specific consumer and business publications; their exposure to other media; ownership of consumer durables; use of products, brands and services; habits and lifestyles. It does this by conducting a nationwide research study and publishing the results annually.

HOW PMB CONDUCTS ITS STUDIES   During March to July and September to December of each year, PMB conducts over 8000 personal in-home interviews across Canada with people aged 12 years and over. The sample is based on a national household probability design. Toronto, Montreal and Vancouver are over-sampled, the remainder of the country being sampled according to population and certain economic criteria. What this means is that every household in Canada (with isolated exceptions, e.g., far North) has a pre-determined chance of being in the survey. Primary sample units are Census Enumeration Areas (EAs). Of the 42 000 EAs in Canada, PMB selects about 2000 with a probability of selection that takes into account the number of households in the EA. On average, 10 households are selected in each EA from which an average of 6.5 interviews are obtained. The respondent is chosen through the use of a selection grid that gives each person in the household an equal chance of being interviewed.

Two years' worth of data are combined to provide a rolling average for each annual report. Every year the oldest 12 months' interviews are discarded and a new year's interviews added. PMB'90 is based on interviews in 1988 and 1989 and has a sample size of 15 553.

READERSHIP METHOD   The readership of individual titles is collected in a personal interview. Respondents are shown a mock-up of a recent issue of each publication they claim to have read or looked into in the last six to eight months. After leafing through the mock-up, they are asked whether they have read or looked into that particular issue before. A yes answer constitutes a proven reader. A publication's readership is based on an aggregate of all people claiming this prior readership. To save time, issues are stripped down (skeletonized) to a maximum of ten spreads which serve as a memory trigger.

Other readership measures are also taken for each title. These include the number of times the particular issue is picked up, the total length of time the respondents spent reading it, and their degree of interest in the publications in general.

SINGLE SOURCE DATA COLLECTION A second questionnaire is left with respondents who have completed the personal interviews, to be picked up later. This self-completion questionnaire includes questions about products, brands and services respondents might have used, their ownership of consumer durables, leisure activities and lifestyles. It provides the data for PMB's product profile service.

The response rate to the product profile questionnaire is in excess of 80%, providing a sample base of 12 000 for PMB'90; to facilitate use of the data, an ascription process is used. Essentially this means that a respondent who has not provided information in the leave-behind is "married" to a similar respondent who has provided such information. This process results in one single media and product database.

OTHER MEDIA A considerable amount of general information on other media is collected in the personal interview. Among the questions asked:

- frequency of television viewing
- time spent watching television on weekdays, Saturdays and Sundays, and by time of day
- time spent watching non-commercial television
- frequency of listening to radio
- time spent listening to radio on weekdays, Saturdays and Sundays, and by time of day
- yesterday listening to radio
- yesterday reading of daily, Saturday and Sunday newspapers (not by name)
- personal miles driven in the past seven days and four weeks
- personal trips by public transit in the average week and the last three months
- frequency of reading community newspapers
- reading of community newspapers in the past seven days and the past month

In addition to questions on products and services, the product profile questionnaire includes further questions on other media. These cover:

- the way in which people read daily newspapers
- how much time, in total, they spend reading them
- the sections they look at
- their receipt of community newspapers
- numbers of separate days reading community newspapers
- time, in total, spent reading them
- level of interest in community newspapers
- types of television programs people like to watch
- times of day their programs are viewed
- types of radio programs listened to

RADIO LISTENING: BBM STUDIES

BBM Bureau of Measurement has been measuring radio listenership for over 40 years. The surveys are carried out in five steps:

1. *Selection of sample* BBM randomly selects telephone listings in each region.

2. *Household enumeration* Households are contacted by telephone and the number of persons aged 7+ is determined. At this stage, the sample is confirmed to be representative in size and location.

3. *Diary packages mailed* These contain diaries for every household member aged 7+ and also $0.50 in coin for each participant.

4. *Reminder telephone calls* Reminder phone calls are placed to all selected households just before the start of the survey week to verify the reception of diaries and to encourage participation. During the survey week, another call or reminder card urges cooperation and requests prompt return of the completed diaries.

5. *Computer calculations and projections* After the information from the diaries is transferred to computer tape, a succession of programs projects diary data to the population of each age/sex group in each sampling cell. The computers calculate average quarter hour and cumulative audience for "central area" and "full coverage" and perform all computations to produce the comprehensive Radio Station and Market reports, as well as the Radio Reach Reports.

Comment: *TV and radio are linear media. With print media, it is possible for a respondent to start anywhere (e.g., the last page), go anywhere (e.g.,* *the beginning) and flip back and forth. Broadcast media does not provide this flexibility. Hence the difference in methodology between print and broadcast measurements. Note that the respondent is provided with a diary to record his or her viewing. In readership studies, it is not important to know when a respondent reads a magazine or a newspaper. However, for TV and radio audience measurement it is important to know the pattern of viewership by time period.*

SELECTION OF SAMPLING HOUSEHOLDS   The basic source for the lists of households to be contacted is the telephone directory. The survey design specifies how many diaries are needed from each sampling unit or "cell." The first step is to determine how many households must be approached in each BBM cell in order to get the necessary number of diaries. Records of response rates and statistics on the number of people per family enable us to calculate how many households to contact in order to bring in the diaries we need.

Example

Tabulated diaries required	900
Response rate from diary mail-out	50%
Mail-out required (900 + 50%)	1800
Average persons per family (7 yrs +)	2.6
Families required for mail-out (1800 + 2.6)	692
Enumeration participation	75%
Directory listings required (692 + 75%)	923

Note: Unless otherwise stated, references to sample size always refer to the number of returned, completed diaries.

To ensure proper geographic distribution of the sample households within the entire sampling cell, the population or number of households served by each Post Office is examined. The number to be selected from each community is determined by matching it to the Post Office distribution as closely as possible. Following this, household selection is made on a random basis. The selected listings are postal coded, keyed into the computer and printed onto forms for the use of telephone interviewers.

HOW LARGE A SAMPLE IS NEEDED TO MEASURE RADIO STATION AUDIENCES? Generally speaking, the larger the sample, the greater the degree of accuracy. All estimates are subject to sampling error. Different demographic sub-groups, and different time blocks have different "relative errors."

The survey design and estimation vary from simple random sampling. They introduce "design effects" which influence all estimates. Important factors are the estimate type (AQH or cume, see Glossary), the demographic group for which the estimate is made, the length of the time block over which the AQH estimate is made, and the degree of weighting involved in the estimate. BBM has developed a list of these design effects, based upon experimental replication of the basic survey (BBM, 1984).

Comments: *AQH refers to Average Quarter Hour audience which represents the average number of listeners in any quarter hour over a specified period of time or days.*

REPORTING STANDARD   BBM does not report any audience data in its regular survey reports for any demographic group or market area that is based on a sample of less than 75 diaries, except in circumstances suggested in the paragraph above. This requirement helps to determine the sample size in any market across Canada. The larger and more competitive the market, the greater the need to report audience data for various demographic groups. Consequently, the size of the sample required is increased.

The following table (Exhibit 20.3) and example indicate the size of the tabulated sample needed for reporting each age break that can be provided in BBM reports. These sample sizes are based on the assumption that the response rates would be the same for all age segments in each market. The percentage of population given is for Canada; there can be significant differences in individual areas.

Exhibit 20.3	National Distribution of Population by Age Group		
Age group		% of population (7+)	Theoretical minimum sample to report (@75 min)
All Persons	7+	100.0	75
Adults	18+	79.7	94
Women	18+	40.6	185
	18-49	26.6	282
	18-34	17.2	436
	18-24	7.6	987
	25-59	24.7	304
	25-49	19.0	395
	25-34	9.6	781

Age group		% of population (7+)	Theoretical minimum sample to report (@75 min)
Men	18+	39.1	192
	18-49	27.1	277
	18-34	17.5	429
	18-24	7.8	962
	25-29	24.7	304
	25-49	19.3	389
	25-34	9.6	781
Teens	12-17	11.9	630
Children	7-11	8.4	893

Example
Women 18-34 are 17.2% of population 7+. Therefore, in an average market, if responses were proportionate for all age groups, a total tabulated sample of 436 or more should yield 75 diaries from women 18-34.

REQUIRED SAMPLE SIZE DEPENDS ON DATA TO BE REPORTED   While sample sizes are broadly related to population, the amount of detail to be reported also determines how many tabulated diaries are required from any market area.

THE REACH REPORT   Issued with the Fall Radio survey, this report gives weekly reach and weekly hours tuned to every radio station in over 300 reporting areas. The minimum aim is to report these data for all persons 7+ and adults 18+ in every area. To make sure that this result will be achieved, the minimum tabulated sample for each area in the full surveys is set at 130 diaries. A Spring Reach Report accompanies the Spring Radio Survey books. It samples about half of BBM's reporting markets and gives data for approximately 270 areas.

SAMPLES AND SURVEY FREQUENCY BY MARKET SIZE   The 130 diary minimum is for all areas in which no reported member radio station is located. For all areas in which a BBM member station is located, a minimum required sample is determined according to market size or area population. All radio markets are classified under one of four headings:

- **Major markets:** Census Metropolitan Areas with population of 500 000 or more. BBM targets for at least 1225 diaries returned by all persons 7+

from the primary coverage area, including 900 from the central area of the market. These markets are surveyed four times yearly.

- **Other major markets:** Those with a central area population of over 200 000. Target for returned diaries is 1775, including 1100 from the central area. These markets are surveyed in fall and spring.

- **Other competitive markets:** Those with a central area population of less than 200 000 with three or more stations. Target for returned diaries is 675, including 450 from the central area. These markets are surveyed in fall and spring.

- **Non-competitive markets:** Those with a central area population of less than 60 000, in which two or fewer stations operate. Target for returned diaries is 460, including 330 from the central area. These markets are surveyed every fall.

TELEVISION VIEWING: NIELSEN BROADCAST INDEX (NBI)

WHAT'S MEASURED? The NBI reports divide Canada into 42 separate designated market areas (DMAs) which collectively represent 99% of the total television viewers in Canada. Measurement period frequency varies market by market, with full coverage measurement periods—or sweeps—in November and March. Local area reports are distributed under the name "Nielsen Broadcast Index" (NBI). In addition, eight "Special Market" reports including two of the major English/French markets, plus three regional markets are produced. Special reports are also produced for Cancom audiences, Toronto DMA and Lethbridge Metro.

HOW IS IT MEASURED? A master list of homes covering the entire country is developed to select sample households for individual surveys. For a specific measurement, a sample of homes is randomly selected from this master list. These homes are then pre-contacted to secure cooperation prior to receipt of their television viewing diary. Each program viewed by the family over a one-week period is recorded in the diary. Once the diaries are returned, they are checked for completeness and the appropriate stations are credited with their viewing. The computer then matches the viewing records to the station program names and calculates the final Nielsen Television Rating.

WHAT IS REPORTED? Reports are divided into four comprehensive sections:

- **Daypart summary:** Audience viewing for each station across 20 different dayparts.

- **Daypart distribution:** An extension of the daypart summary which shows where a station attracts its audience (i.e., home markets versus spill markets)—available during sweep periods only.

- **Program averages:** Ratings and share data for all programs telecast during the measurement period in a convenient alphabetical listing.

- **Time period:** Program audience estimates for all reportable stations by half-hour segments (quarter-hour for news periods) which allows clients to monitor competitive activity.

Report Features

- **Cable share data:** Percentage of audience contributed by cable households. Can determine the impact of simulcasting on U.S. signals.

- **Trend share:** Current household share versus share for two previous sweep periods and one additional measurement period. Allows for a quick share trend analysis without opening another report.

- **Weekly reach:** Weekly cume data provided by daypart for each station under six demographic categories.

- **Spill ratings:** Household audience spill into adjacent DMAs for each station by daypart.

- **Audience distribution:** Indicates where a station's audience is derived from, by daypart (i.e., Metro Area, Home DMA, Adjacent DMAs).

- **Demographics:** Nineteen demographic categories

Households	
Viewers	2+
	18+
	18-34
	18-49
	24-54
Teens	12-17
	Girls
Children	2-11
Working Woman	Lady of the House
Men	18+
	18-34
	18-49
	25-54
Women	18+
	18-34
	18-49
	25-54

NETWORK PEOPLE METER SERVICE (NTI)

WHAT'S MEASURED? The Network service of A.C. Nielsen reports audiences for national and regional networks. Included are the conventional networks and the specialized cable-delivered broadcasters. Network reports provide viewing information 24 hours a day across the entire year. Due to the specialized recruitment procedure, a great deal more is known about the viewer. Finer demographic breaks on age, education, income and occupation provide excellent decision-making details. This breakthrough technology ensures that all viewing environments including multiple sets, VCRs, satellite and video signal sources are monitored precisely.

HOW IS IT MEASURED? Nielsen uses a panel sample of 1500 households which is representative of the country by geography, cable status, the presence of children under 18, age of household head, plus language. Respondents indicate their viewing through the use of a remote control unit. Viewing records are stored in a micro-computer and transmitted over phone lines between 3 and 6 a.m. to Nielsen's main computers in Markham, Ontario.

REPORT FEATURES Nielsen reports provide the following information.
- All networks alphabetical program listing
- All networks program season-to-date averages
- Individual network program rankings by demographic group
- Individual network day and time audiences
- Multiday program audiences
- Multiday program reach
- Network station line-ups

GLOSSARY OF SOME COMMONLY USED MEDIA RESEARCH TERMS

Cost per rating point (CPP). The cost of a media vehicle for reaching one per cent of the target group.

Cost per thousand (CPM). The cost of a media vehicle for reaching each 1000 of the target group.

Cumulative audience (Cume). See Reach.

Designated market area (DMA). A geographic area defined by A.C. Nielsen, based on area of primary television viewing.

Efficiency. The relationship between circulation (or audience) and media cost, commonly expressed as cost per thousand.

Frequency. The number of times that the average household or person is exposed to the advertising among those reached at least once in a specific period of time.

Gross cost. The cost of media including agency commission.

Gross rating point (GRP). The sum of the ratings achieved by a specific media vehicle.

HUT (Households using television). The percentage of all TV households in the survey area with one or more sets in use during a specific time period.

PUT (Persons using television). The percentage of all persons (or of all persons in a demographic category) in the survey area who are viewing television during a specific period of time.

Ratings. The audience of a particular TV or radio program or station at a particular time expressed as a per cent of the audience population.

Reach. The number or per cent of different homes or persons exposed at least once to a medium over a specific period of time. In broadcast measurement, **reach** is also referred to as **cumulative audience (cume)**.

Share. The audience of a particular television program or time period expressed as a per cent of the population viewing TV at that particular time.

Target audience. The portion of the total audience defined to be the most likely purchasers of the product, that is, the total audience excluding waste.

TRPs. The sum of ratings of a specific demographic segment may be called **Target Audience GRPs** or simple **TRPs.**

INTERNATIONAL MARKETING RESEARCH

The world is changing. Two trends are currently discernible. One, economic boundaries now exceed national boundaries. For instance, the European Community is the economic merger of most European countries creating one single market where there used to be several. The U.S.-Canada Free Trade Agreement may soon include Mexico, thereby creating another larger market. Two, the free market is expanding. For instance, East European countries are adopting capitalist ideas. This development creates challenges and opportunities around the world.

The newly created trading blocks increase competition within each block. Emerging market economies create new opportunities where there were none before. Consequently, it makes sense for many companies to expand beyond their national boundaries. Entering a new market involves obtaining information about that market. Thus, international marketing research is becoming increasingly important. However, there might be vital differences in marketing research procedures when one moves from one country to another. A researcher should be aware of potential areas of difference.

BASIC DATA AVAILABILITY

In Canada, we can obtain detailed road maps for every part of the country and obtain the demographic characteristics of any enumeration area. Such is not the case in every country. In some countries they can be obtained only with great difficulty. In other countries such information is not available at all. Your sampling design and weighting procedures will have to take this reality into account.

For conducting secondary research, a number of sources are available. The section on International Data in the chapter on Secondary Research lists some major information sources for international research.

If the researcher is interested in a particular country, the best way to start the research is by gathering secondary data that are freely available through that country's consulates and trade associations. Many capitalist countries welcome foreign investments and would provide this information for the asking.

INFORMATION TO BE GATHERED

Once you are in a market, you know your information needs. But it is more difficult to define your needs if you have yet to enter that market. These are some of the generalized factors you should investigate if you are interested in a market, but do not have enough information about it.

1. **Nature and Size of the Market:** How big is the market? How many consumers? What is their per capita income? If the per capita income is too low, is there an affluent segment in the market that can afford your product? How large is this segment? How fast is the market growing? There are several market factors to consider, such as:

   • Ethnic differences
   • Language
   • Social structure and diversity
   • Religious structure and diversity
   • Traditions
   • Climate and geography

- Channels of distribution
- Availability of media for advertising
- Literacy levels
- Income levels and patterns (segments)
- Institutional factors

Information on these topics can be obtained—usually without difficulty—by contacting the relevant government or trade authority in the country of interest.

2. **Buyer Behaviour:** Is your product suited to the market being contemplated? Some markets simply do not use some products even though buyers can afford them. Different blends of coffee or tobacco appeal to buyers in different countries. Brand names and advertising that one country may find appealing may be offensive to buyers in another country. Information on buyer behaviour may need primary research, although some secondary research information may be available from published sources.

3. **Cultural Factors:** This is closely related to buyer behaviour. What is prestigious, ostentatious or essential is decided by socio-economic conditions within a culture. However, these generalizations cannot be transported to another culture because socio-economic patterns do not necessarily generalize across different cultures. Work on cultural archetypes shows that to market a product successfully we not only need data on buyers' ability to pay but also on how they view different products and what they mean to them.

4. **Trade Restrictions:** Many countries have trade barriers. They may have imposed import duties and taxes on all imported goods or on selected items to protect local industry. They may also have restrictions on foreign ownership of companies that operate within their country. Such restrictions can reduce the profitability or even threaten the viability of marketing your product in a given country. This information can be easily obtained by contacting the relevant government or trade authority in the country of interest.

5. **Trade Incentives:** Some countries encourage foreign investments, especially if it is in an industry that is perceived to be beneficial to the country in question. Such incentives can increase your profitability. Again, this information can be easily obtained by contacting the relevant government or trade authority in the country of interest.

6. **Political and Legal Factors:** Political stability of the host country as well as the legal restrictions imposed by that country can affect the success of a product. A sovereign state can nationalize an industry without warning. It can impose restrictions on product formulation and marketing. These are, in effect, risk factors over which the marketer has no control.

Consequently, it is important to assess these factors before entering the market. Information of this nature can only be partly gleaned through research. One may need to employ special consultants to fully assess political and legal factors that are relevant to marketing.

INDUSTRIAL MARKETING RESEARCH

Industrial marketing research refers to research carried out on businesses as opposed to on individuals. *Business to business research* is another common name for industrial marketing research. Industrial marketing research uses secondary data extensively (see Chapter 24 Secondary Research). Even when primary research is carried out, it can be supplemented by reliable secondary data that are readily available.

HOW IS INDUSTRIAL MARKETING RESEARCH DIFFERENT?

Industrial marketing research differs from consumer marketing research in many ways.

TYPE OF PRODUCTS   Industrial products can be classified in many ways. Some of the commonly used criteria are:

1. **Price:** Is it a high end product or low cost product? High cost products are judged by more complex criteria than low cost products. Consequently, the type of research information collected will differ depending on the cost of the product. While this is also true of consumer products, very small orders for a high priced industrial product are enough to keep a supply business alive.

2. **The importance of the product:** How critical is the product from a functional point of view? How important is the product from an appearance point of view? When a product is critical to the operation of another product or service, the price tends to be inelastic (within bounds). The importance of a product to the appearance of another product or service (e.g., colour monitor for a word processor) can be elastic or inelastic depending on whether appearance itself is critical for the product or service in question. These aspects can be identified through industrial marketing research and negotiated later on.

3. **Distribution method:** Is it wholesale or is it direct? Distribution methods have a considerable impact on flexibility in terms of pricing, incentives

and other factors. Even if other things are equal, products can compete simply by the way they are distributed.

4. **Custom component:** Is it a standard product or does it involve custom engineering? Products that require custom engineering, such as defence equipment, need a different research approach from standard products. For custom products, the critical factor is the expertise that is required to match the customer need. For standard products, on the other hand, the critical factor is the quality of the product already produced. Long-term relationships are more common for custom products than for standard products. A wide range of products fall between these two categories— standard components customized to suit customer needs.

5. **Number of key customers:** Is the customer base large or is it narrow? The more specialized the product, the more narrow the customer base. To compensate, specialized products have fewer competitors.

6. **Expertise of purchasing agent:** Is it high (e.g., qualified engineer) or low? When skilled purchase agents are used, it is important that the research interviewer be knowledgeable. In consumer research, interviewers are not required to have any specialized skills.

   Thus the information requirements, nature of the interview, and type of interviewers to be used may depend on the product itself.

AVAILABILITY OF BACKGROUND INFORMATION   In consumer marketing research, when we approach a respondent, we collect extensive demographic information in addition to information on the topic we are interested in. In industrial marketing research, on the other hand, we do not necessarily collect the equivalent of demographic information for the company. The characteristics of the company are often available from other sources. For instance, if we are interested in the characteristics of public companies, extensive information, such as their size, turnover, profitability, SIC (Standard Industrial Classification code), etc., is already available.

SIZE OF THE SAMPLE   In consumer marketing research, we interview only a small fraction of the population. In industrial marketing research, it is not unusual to measure a large proportion of the population (sometimes everyone in the population). This is because, compared to consumer research, the population in industrial research tends to be much smaller.

INTERVIEWERS   For reasons discussed earlier, the interviewers tend to be more knowledgeable about the product in question and sometimes interviewers may be professionals themselves.

COST   Industrial marketing research often involves interviewing a specific person in an organization. This could mean identifying that person, making a personal phone call to make an appointment and other preliminary efforts before an interview can take place. In addition, the interviewer is likely to be better trained or more knowledgeable (compared to interviewers used in consumer research). It is also not uncommon to provide some incentive to the respondent. All this results in a higher cost per interview.

SAMPLE GENERATION   In consumer research, it is relatively easy to generate samples. This is usually done using Random Digit Dialling (RDD) or selecting EAs. In industrial research, a complete frame for a given target audience may not always be readily available. Even when the sample frame is available, the researcher may still have to do additional screening before locating the right respondent. While it is true that industry associations and directories provide a list of organizations, such lists may be incomplete and thus may introduce a bias. Even the sample frames provided by commercial sources (such as Dun and Bradstreet) are not complete in all instances.

WHO CARRIES OUT RESEARCH?   Not all the special factors mentioned above are applicable to all industrial marketing research studies. In fact, many industrial marketing research studies are structurally similar to consumer marketing research studies. When special factors do not significantly alter standard research procedures, many marketing research firms can handle the project competently. A few firms can also accommodate substantial deviations from standard research procedures. However, when the project involves specialized knowledge and requires specially qualified or highly informed interviewers, it is handled through consulting firms that specialize in that area of expertise.

POLITICAL POLLING

Political polling does not pose any major methodological problem to a competent researcher who is comfortable with probability sampling and weighting procedures. In fact, almost all major research houses in the country do some form of political polling. It is treated as a special topic in part because the media isolates some research houses (such as Goldfarb, Decima, Environics, Angus Reid) as "polling companies" as opposed to "marketing research companies." It is interesting to note that these polling companies claim that no more than 15% of their work has to do with political polling.

In political polling, the results are often used for decision-making purposes. Polling results are also often published which may arguably affect the fortunes of a political party. For these reasons, it is important that polling be carried out using acceptable research procedures. Most pollsters seem to produce results that are comparable, not a surprising observation given that polling is no different from other properly conducted surveys.

A major problem with political polling is that it is time sensitive. Most polling, therefore, is done over the telephone. Because it is time sensitive, respondents are seldom called back if they are unavailable for an interview when they are called the first time. The response rate achieved in these studies can be as low as 10 or 15%. To minimize bias, some researchers use lists of phone numbers covering different areas or telephone exchanges. The interviewer is then asked to obtain a minimum number of interviews from each area (or telephone exchange). While this procedure does not eliminate bias, it ensures that respondents come from different parts of the city being surveyed, thus minimizing one source of bias.

One of the current issues being debated in the media is whether political polling influences the way people vote and, if it does, whether political polling during elections should be banned altogether. Current research evidence shows that political polling exerts only limited influence in affecting the final outcome of elections (Adams, 1990).

PHARMACEUTICAL MARKETING RESEARCH

Pharmaceutical research, once again, is not very different from consumer research insofar as research methodology is concerned. Pharmaceutical firms use audit data (by IMS) and omnibus data (e.g., by Professional Studies, ISL Medical Studies and Schema Research), profiling series (Walsch), as well as ad hoc research data (e.g., Cooper Market Studies, Angus Reid Group, ISL Medical Studies).

A substantial amount of pharmaceutical research work is carried out with physicians (including specialists), pharmacists and related professionals. Procedurally it differs from consumer market research in that:

- Appointments are nearly always arranged over the telephone before the actual interviews are carried out.

- In most cases, respondents are offered an incentive to do the interview, a procedure rarely used in consumer marketing research.

- Sample sizes are much smaller. (So is the universe. For instance, there are only about 20 000 general and family physicians, about 1800 obstetricians and gynecologists, and about 500 dermatologists in Canada.)

- Samples seldom utilize probability selection procedures.

- Costs of conducting research is high. (As an example, during early 1991, the cost of a 20-minute interview was $75 in a general practitioner's office and $125 for 30 minutes with a specialist.)

Although small samples are used, some studies use multivariate analytic techniques such as perceptual maps, conjoint, factor and regression analyses.

SUMMARY

1. Media research has several special methodological problems. Such methodological problems depend on the medium being measured.

2. Most media studies use sophisticated sampling and weighting procedures.

3. Major Canadian media studies include NADbank (newspapers), PMB (magazines), BBM and Nielsen (radio and TV). To illustrate the complexity of design in most media studies, the NADbank study was described in detail.

4. International marketing research could involve extensive secondary research, primary research, as well as an understanding of the host market. Cultural, legal and government restrictions must also be taken into account.

5. Industrial marketing research is often characterized by
   • a smaller universe
   • lack of availability of a complete and reliable sample frame
   • expensive interviews
   • changing methodology depending on the nature of the product under consideration.

6. Political polling does not pose any special critical methodological issues. Because of its time sensitivity, the response rate tends to be low. All major polls use probability samples.

7. Pharmaceutical research typically uses professionals (such as physicians and pharmacists) as respondents. Samples tend to be smaller and the cost per interview higher.

NOW THINK ABOUT THIS

1. Compare the media studies described in this chapter. Identify the major differences in methodology among the different studies.

2. Why are the methodologies different depending on the medium?

3. Is it possible to use a common methodology for all media studies? If not, why not?

4. Compare and contrast the different specialized areas of marketing research. Is a well trained market research professional equipped to handle all specialized areas of research?

REFERENCES

Adams, Michael
1990 "Political Polling: Should it be banned?" *Canadian Journal of Marketing Research*, 9.

Arnold, Jon
1991 "Biz-to-biz Research is Rare in Canada, but Situation is Changing." *Marketing News*, 25 (5), March 4.

BBM
1984 *Battle of the Bounce*. BBM Bureau of Measurement, Toronto.

BBM
1986 *Why, What and How: A Guide to Measurement of Radio Audiences by BBM*. BBM Bureau of Measurement, Toronto.

Cummings, John
1988 "Industrial Marketing Research: Current Practices." *Canadian Journal of Marketing Research*, 7.

Newspaper Marketing Bureau
1990 *Technical Report, NADbank'90*. (Prepared by Canadian Facts, Toronto). Newspaper Marketing Bureau

1991 *Interviewers' Manual, NADbank'91*. (Prepared by Canadian Facts, Toronto).

PMB Print Measurement Bureau
1990 *What is PMB?* PMB Print Measurement Bureau, Toronto.

21 / Sampling Methods

THE BASIC QUESTIONS OF SAMPLE DESIGN

The design of a sampling procedure and the determination of the correct sample size are central to the marketing research project. Those who observe marketing research, but never really get involved in conducting any, often take the sampling for granted. They seem to realize that sampling happens, but don't always appreciate the reasons for different types of sampling scenarios or the motivation behind different size samples. Even fairly experienced marketing researchers may lack in-depth understanding of the details of sampling.

Sampling was presented at a basic level in Chapter 6. This chapter takes a moderate approach to the topic, building on the basics of Chapter 6. For an in-depth treatment of sampling, the reader must consult a book devoted to sampling. A particularly well developed practical approach is presented in *A Manual of Sampling Techniques* by R.K. Som (1973).

There are 10 main questions that must be addressed in any marketing research project:

1. Should a sample be taken?

2. How should the population be described?

3. What is the basic sampling unit?

4. What type of data collection procedure (field methodology) will be used?

5. How will an individual respondent be identified?

6. What is the incidence rate?

7. Are there group characteristics among the individual respondents?

8. How will cooperation be obtained from individual respondents?

9. What will be done about non-response?

10. How big should the sample be?

For some projects, the answers will be direct and easy; for others, a great deal of analysis may be required to address the questions to the satisfaction of all involved parties.

DEFINING POPULATIONS

The starting point for any sampling is the population that is the parent to that sample. The population usually does not pertain to everyone in Canada. For many marketing research studies, young children would not be a relevant segment of the population and would be excluded from the definition of a "qualified respondent." In most studies, the target population needs to be defined in a specific manner so that the researcher knows when a person from that population has been contacted. Proper definition of the target population is a matter of economy. If the target population is defined too loosely, then some people will be interviewed who can't provide the information necessary for the study. On the other hand, if the target population is defined too tightly then some parts of the universe that should be sampled will not be contacted through the sampling process.

THE SAMPLING UNIT

The unit of sampling is defined as that entity about which the answers will be relevant. In most projects, the individual is the appropriate sampling unit. However, in other cases, it may be the household that is of importance and an individual will not be able to provide the breadth of information that's necessary. Very often in industrial marketing research, the company or the organization is the critical sampling unit. The breadth of information required by the objectives and scope of the study will direct the researcher to properly define the sampling unit.

THE SAMPLING FRAME

After specifying the target population and the sampling unit, it's then necessary to be able to identify those sampling units for contact. The vehicle used for identification of the sampling units might be a telephone directory, street directory, city map showing residences on streets, organization membership lists, list of those who returned their warranty cards for an appliance, directory of manufacturers, a business directory, or many others. In fact, a sampling frame might be any list or combination of lists that help to identify the prospective respondents.

One problem with most lists that can be used for sample frames is that they are frequently inaccurate and not current. Even the telephone directory can only list those people who don't object to being listed and who had phone numbers before the closing date for the directory. Other lists are often less accurate than the telephone directory.

PROCEDURES FOR DETERMINING SAMPLE SIZES

CROSS-TAB REQUIREMENTS

A very high percentage of marketing research projects involve only cross-tabulation of the survey data. Sometimes these studies will perform a chi-square analysis of independence between variables. In these cases, the sample size required is determined in a more or less ad hoc fashion. The two sources of guidance are 1) the minimum cell size needed for the chi-square test of independence (or association); and 2) the number of breakdowns and sub-breakdowns which are likely to be made of the data.

A rule-of-thumb condition for using the chi-square test of independence is that at most 20% of the cells in the table can have an expected frequency of five or fewer and that no cell should have an expected frequency of less than one. Let's take a small example to illustrate the way in which the required sample size can be calculated. "Intention to purchase a brand" and "age groups" are two variables cross-tabbed in Exhibit 21.1. Suppose that a brand manager at a large Canadian packaged goods company were able to estimate the intention percentages based on his experience and on past studies of a similar nature. Also, suppose we were able to obtain the percentages of the target population in each of the three age categories. This might also have come from the past projects conducted for the company or perhaps from a Statistics Canada report. These two sets of percentages are called marginals, because they appear in the margins of the table. We can use these figures to calculate the expected frequencies for each of the cells in the table.

Exhibit 21.1 Marginal Distributions Used for Calculating Sample Size

Intention Levels	Age Groups 18 to 24	25 to 49	50 to 64	Total Percentages
Definitely will				35%
Probably will				30%
Might or might not				10%
Probably will not				15%
Definitely will not				10%
Total	30%	50%	20%	100%

The expected number of people from a sample who would end up in any cell in the table in Exhibit 21.1 can be calculated by multiplying the total marginal per cent (expressed as a decimal) that appears in the row corresponding to that cell by the corresponding column marginal per cent (expressed as a decimal) by the size of the sample. For example, the expected number of people from a sample of 500 who would say that they definitely will buy the brand and who are between 18 and 24 years old is:

0.35 x 0.30 x 500 = 52.5 people

This and the expected frequencies for the other cells of the table are shown in Exhibit 21.2.

Exhibit 21.2 Expected Frequencies Assuming a Sample Size of 500

Expected Frequency of Intention Levels	Expected Frequency of Age Groups			Total Percentages
	18 to 24	25 to 49	50 to 64	
Definitely Will	52.5	87.50	35.00	35%
Probably Will	45	75.00	30.0	30%
Might or might not	15	25.0	10.0	10%
Probably will not	22.5	37.50	50.0	15%
Definitely will not	15	25.0	10.0	10%
Total	30%	50%	20%	100%

Since the smallest expected frequency in Exhibit 21.2 is 10, then the chi-square rule-of-thumb is satisfied. In other words, the sample size is large enough to perform the chi-square test of independence between intention to purchase and age in the table in Exhibit 21.1 (after the sample data is collected). In fact, too large a sample size might have been taken if the objective were simply to satisfy the requirements of the rule-of-thumb and to minimize costs. What size sample should have been taken? How would you find out? The simplest way of determining the minimum sample size is to work in reverse. The smallest expected frequency, 10, was found when multiplying the smallest of the row marginals, 10%, by the smallest of the column marginals, 20%. In reverse, we can construct the simple inequality

$0.10 \times 0.20 \times n \geq 5$ or $n \geq 5 \div (0.10 \times 0.20) = 250$

Exhibit 21.3 Expected Frequencies Given the Minimum Sample Size

Expected Frequency of Intention Levels	Expected Frequency of Age Groups			Percentages	Total Frequency
	18 to 24	25 to 49	50 to 64		
Definitely will	26.25	43.75	17.5	35%	87.5
Probably will	22.5	37.5	15.0	30%	75
Might or might not	7.5	12.5	5.0	10%	25
Probably will not	11.25	18.75	7.5	15%	37.5
Definitely will not	7.5	12.5	5.0	10%	25
Total Percentages	30%	50%	20%	100%	
Frequency	75	125	50		250

So, the sample size is 250. With 250 respondents, we should expect the following numbers of respondents in each of the cells of the table, as shown in Exhibit 21.3.

Of course, the analysis performed in Exhibit 21.3 depends on the estimates of the marginal percentages being fairly accurate. This information would have to be known (or estimated) prior to the sample's being taken. If prior studies had been performed in that area or if pertinent secondary data were available, then the calculations could be done with very little effort. If good relevant data were not available, then preliminary estimates based on knowledgeable guesses would be needed to identify the likely smallest marginal row and column percentages. This information could be used to obtain fairly good sample size estimates. Since the calculations shown above are somewhat more conservative than is the chi-square rule-of-thumb (we required all cells to have an expected frequency of five or more), the sample sizes should be at least large enough. The other requirement of the chi-square test that no cells have an expected frequency of less than one is also satisfied by the procedure just explained.

The calculations above were performed on only two variables in a hypothetical study. However, almost any survey will have several variables of significant importance. In order to arrive at a sample size that would be useful, the calculations should be performed for several cross-tab combinations of the most important variables in the study and then the largest sample size should be selected.

BUDGET-BASED METHODS

Budget-based methods are the most widely used procedures for determining sample sizes. The reason for this is that many samples are not true random samples where everyone in the target population has an equal chance of being selected. Consequently, the statistical procedures are not appropriate and need not be used. Also, many small- to medium-size projects have relatively fixed budgets and regardless of what the sample size formulas may specify, the budget may not support that level of sampling. So the actual size of the sample is constrained by the budget.

Budget-based sample size calculation formulas are more basic than the sample size formulas for the statistical-based method, and even simpler than for the cross-tab procedure. However, the information needed for arriving at the numbers to enter into the equations is sometimes more difficult to develop. The basic formula for budget-based methods is:

Sample size = budget ÷ cost of one completed questionnaire

One reason the procedure gets complicated is that the "cost of one completed questionnaire" involves a fair bit of research unless the study is so routine that it's been conducted several times in the past and in a very similar fashion to the current case.

The cost to complete one questionnaire is often stated in practice as including all of the fieldwork. Sometimes that cost is quoted as also including questionnaire editing, coding, data entry and basic tabulation. The formula written above for sample size considers the cost of one completed questionnaire to cover all project costs including project design, questionnaire design, sample design, drawing of the sample, all fieldwork costs, data preparation, data processing, data tabulation, statistical analysis, report writing, report presentation, meeting time, professional fees and profit margin.

All of the costs that contribute to obtaining one completed questionnaire and reporting that (as well as others) to the client must be estimated based on the experience of the research supplier's staff and that of its suppliers (sub-contractors). Costs such as questionnaire editing, coding and data entry can be estimated fairly accurately by an experienced manager of field operations. The cost of actually getting one person to complete on questionnaire is sometimes fairly difficult to obtain. As in any area of cost estimation, the greater the experience, the better the cost estimate. One of the parameters of the cost estimate that is extremely important is the *incidence rate*.

The incidence rate is the percentage of the population that has the characteristics necessary to be considered a potential respondent. These characteristics might include age (25 to 39 years old), gender (female), family status (married, living with spouse, parent of at least two children under the age of 12), employment status (works at least 35 hours per week outside the home), and product usage (has dyed or coloured her hair at home during the past 12 months). You can imagine that it would be substantially more difficult to find 500 people with these specific characteristics than to find 500 heads of their households (either male or female) who are responsible for the main grocery shopping for the household.

Naturally, the screening or qualification questions must be asked at the beginning of the questionnaire. You have to make sure that you're talking to the correct people, otherwise the whole interview might be wasted. If the incidence rate is 30%, then three out of ten people who answer the telephone and answer the screening questions, for example, would qualify, on average. If the incidence rate is five per cent, then only five out of 100 of those who answer all of the qualifying questions would qualify to continue with the survey. The next problem would be to encourage those qualified people to complete the remainder of the questionnaire.

The conversion of an incidence rate into the sample size formula is fairly direct. Although quite simple formulas were used for response rates in Chapter 8, the classification of calls into different final states is often done in more detail. For example, the following categories are often used:

a. Completed interview

b. Ineligible to be interviewed

c. Eligible but refused to be interviewed

d. Undetermined refusals (refused before screener was completed)

e. Eligible callbacks (qualified had to be called back for interview)

f. Undetermined callbacks (had to be called back to get qualification)

g. Language barriers, illness, infirmity, etc.

h. No answer, busy

i. Not a residential number (business, government, etc.)

j. Number not in service or disconnected

k. Incorrect listing

The basic formula for different rates of field response are:

$$\text{Response Rate} = \frac{\text{(Number of completed interviews)}}{\text{(Number of sample units contacted)}}$$

$$\text{Contact Rate} = \frac{\text{(Number of sample units contacted)}}{\text{(Number of sample units identified)}}$$

$$\text{Completion Rate} = \frac{\text{(Number of completed interviews)}}{\text{(Number of sample units identified)}}$$

$$\text{Incidence Rate} = \frac{\text{(Number of sample unit contacts that qualify)}}{\text{(Number of sample unit contacts asked qualifying questions)}}$$

or

$$= \frac{(a + b + e)}{(a + b + c + e)} \text{ from the list of categories presented above.}$$

From the last formula, we can obtain:

Number of sample unit contacts asked qualifying questions

$$= \frac{\text{(Number of sample unit contacts that qualify)}}{\text{(Incidence rate)}}$$

This formula should be relabelled now as "Number of sample unit contacts to be asked qualifying questions," since we're at the stage of trying to decide how many names and/or telephone numbers have to be obtained in order to begin the fieldwork and be assured that the target number of completed interviews can be obtained. For example, if the proposal specified that 500 completed interviews would be delivered to the client, then a somewhat larger number of people would have to qualify to be interviewed, a larger number would have to be contacted and a still larger number of names would have to be given to the interviewers.

We define a *net response rate* as the percentage of qualified respondents who complete the survey interview. The rate is represented by

$$\text{Net response rate} = \frac{\text{Number of completed interviews}}{\text{Number of sample units contacted that qualify}}$$

Using this formula, we can see that if we need to complete 500 interviews and if the net response rate is 80%, the number of sample units which must qualify can be calculated as shown below.

$$\text{Number of sample units contacted that qualify} = \frac{500}{0.80} = 625$$

If the incidence rate is 20% and 625 units must qualify, then the number of sample units that must be asked the qualifying questions is calculated by

Number of sample unit contacts asked qualifying questions

$$= \frac{\text{(Number of sample units that qualify)}}{\text{(Incidence rate)}}$$

$$\text{Number of sample unit contacts asked qualifying questions} = \frac{625}{0.20} = 3125$$

In order to get the 3125 people who will be asked the qualifying questions, we must start with a larger number. This larger number will include those identified sample units who will refuse before the screening questions are completed; those who will have to be called back; those who will be disqualified due to language barriers, illness, etc.; those who will not answer their telephones; those numbers that will turn out to be business or government offices rather than private residences; those numbers not in service; and incorrect listings. In order to determine the number of sample units which must be identified, e.g., the total number of telephone numbers which must be provided to the interviewers, the 3125 must be adjusted by the contact rate as shown below.

Number of units identified

$$= \frac{(\text{Number of sample unit contacts to be asked qualifying questions})}{(\text{Contact rate})}$$

If the contact rate is 50%, the formula provides

Number of sample units identified = 3125 ÷ 0.50 = 6250

which is the total number of sample unit telephone numbers which must be provided in order to result in 500 completed interviews.

Another way of writing the last formula is

Number of sample units identified

$$= \frac{(\text{Number of sample unit contacts that qualify})}{(\text{Contact rate}) \times (\text{Incidence rate})}$$

This last equation is applicable in general. However, the estimates that go into the equation are point estimates, typically the average contact rate and the average incidence rate. The actual response rate might be above or below the average response rate. Estimates that are too high are okay but costly, while those that are too low will provide too small a sample size. The same comments apply to the average incidence rate. There are more extensive formulas that could be used to adjust for chance, but they will not be used in this chapter.

SAMPLE SIZE DETERMINATION WHEN ESTIMATING POPULATION PARAMETERS FROM SIMPLE RANDOM SAMPLES

When calculating the size of the sample using statistical techniques, two key study requirements come into the picture. These are the *precision* with which the population parameter, the true mean or the true proportion, is estimated and the *confidence* needed that the estimate of the population proportion is precise within the required limits. These concepts relate to a practice called *a confidence interval estimate of the true mean of the population* or of the true proportion of the population. These calculations are related to the *normal probability distribution.*

THE SAMPLING DISTRIBUTION OF THE POPULATION MEAN   The normal distribution is the most commonly used probability distribution in the area of statistical inference. The basic characteristics of the normal distribution pertain to its shape. It's quite common to measure distances away from the centre of the normal distribution (which is the mean, median and mode) in terms of standard deviation units. From the distribution shown in Exhibit 21.4, observe that 67% of the total area under the curve lies within one standard deviation unit from the mean, 80% lies within 1.282 standard deviation units, 90% lies within 1.645 standard deviation units and 95% lies within 1.96 standard deviations. At least one of these measurements will be used in almost every instance of statistical inference.

For example, if a shopper were observed to have spent $132.00 on groceries last week and if the mean spent on groceries for all shoppers were $122.00 and the standard deviation were $16.94, then that person's spending was 0.59 standard deviation units above the mean,

$$z = \frac{x - \bar{x}}{s} = \frac{\$132.00 - \$122.00}{\$16.94} = 0.59$$

Where x is the average from the sample observation, $132.00, $\bar{x}$ is the sample average, $122.00, and σ is the standard deviation of the sample.

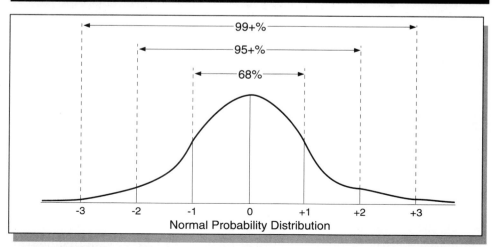

Exhibit 21.4   The Normal Probability Distribution

Normal Probability Distribution

This practice of converting distances expressed in physical units to distances expressed in terms of standard deviation units is quite helpful when doing two things, estimating parameters (e.g., means and proportions) and testing hypotheses about means and proportions.

When a sample is taken, some standard calculations are usually performed on the data. For example, the average amount that respondents said they spent on groceries during a week will be calculated. Or the proportion of respondents who said that they prefer *Tide* to *Cheer* are developed from the data. When either of these two numbers are computed, they are called *point estimates* of the true population values. For example, if the average amount spent on groceries last week by 250 respondents was $124.60, we would consider that mean amount of money spent on groceries by the population from which the sample was selected to be $124.60, or somewhat close to $124.60. The concept of "somewhat close" brings up the question of "How close do you want the point estimate of $124.60 to be to the true mean grocery expenditure level of the population?" That question can't be answered accurately but only in a statistical sense.

When estimating the true mean expenditure level of groceries during the previous week, the marketing manager might say that he wants the estimate to be accurate within $1.00. This is his personal desire. If the brand manager in the same firm were asked, she might say that she wants the estimate to be accurate within $5.00. The project can accommodate either request. The difference between meeting the request of the marketing manager and the desire of the brand manager lies in the sample size (this is largely constrained by the project budget as mentioned earlier).

Let's take the brand manager's request that the estimate of grocery spending be precise within $5.00. If we knew absolutely that the true mean grocery bill for the population from which the sample was drawn was $126.00 last week, we would know that the sample average of $124.60 was a bit low. Anyone having even the most basic feeling for probability would realize that this result is not too surprising since sample values tend to vary around the population values. They would also know that the sample average might just as well have been a bit above the true mean. In addition, they would also understand they would never really know whether the sample average was above or below the true population mean. However, they might feel that they would like some idea of how close the estimate is to the real value. In other words (statistical words), they would like to know how much *confidence* they have that the true population mean was within the $5.00 range around the sample average. This level of confidence might be 99%, 95%, 90%, 85% or any level they wanted.

The same view would be expressed about the proportion of the sample that stated they preferred *Tide* to *Cheer*. The brand manager might say that she would like to be 95% confident that the actual proportion of the population which preferred *Tide* fell within four percentage points of the sample percentage, which might be 65%. She's now stated all she has to in order for the research consultant to calculate a required sample size for that question.

The averages of all of the different samples of a certain size which could be drawn from a population can be tabulated and graphed so that their dispersion can be observed and understood. That graph is called the *sampling distribution* or simply the *distribution of sample averages*.

As an example of the sampling distribution, suppose that a population were defined to be the 10 adult children from one family that live in the area. Each adult child has his or her own family for which groceries must be bought. Suppose that we asked them how much they spent on groceries last week and they gave us the figures shown in Exhibit 21.5.

Exhibit 21.5   Weekly Grocery Spending of Population Units

Shopper	Amount Spent Last Week
Martha	$100
Anne	$110
Mary	$120
Kathy	$130
Mimi	$140
Linda	$150
Mark	$160
Jim	$170
Janice	$180
Barbara	$190

Suppose that we didn't want to ask all 10 people (the population) about their grocery spending. To make the task easier, we could simply randomly select two of the 10 as our sample. We'd then calculate the average and use it as our estimate of the actual mean amount spent on groceries by the 10 people.

A simple random sample of two of the people could be drawn from the population in Exhibit 21.5. There are altogether 45 combinations of two persons that could have been selected from that same population. Any one of the 45 samples shown in Exhibit 21.6 might have been the one that was actually drawn. For each sample an average, standard deviation, standard error, and lower and upper confidence limits can be calculated.

Exhibit 21.6   Statistics Based on all Samples of 2 from Population

	Average	Standard Deviation	Standard Error	Lower Limit	Upper Limit
Total Population	$145.00	$30.28	$9.57		
Anne and Martha	$105.00	$7.07	$5.00	$95.20	$114.80
Mary and Martha	$110.00	$14.14	$10.00	$90.40	$129.60
Mary and Anne	$115.00	$7.07	$5.00	$105.20	$124.80
Martha and Kathy	$115.00	$21.21	$15.00	$85.60	$144.40
Anne and Kathy	$120.00	$14.14	$10.00	$100.40	$139.60
Mimi and Martha	$120.00	$28.28	$20.00	$80.80	$159.20
Mary and Kathy	$125.00	$7.07	$5.00	$115.20	$134.80
Linda and Martha	$125.00	$35.36	$25.00	$76.00	$174.00
Anne and Mimi	$125.00	$21.21	$15.00	$95.60	$154.40
Mary and Mimi	$130.00	$14.14	$10.00	$110.40	$149.60
Linda and Anne	$130.00	$28.28	$20.00	$90.80	$169.20
Martha and Mark	$130.00	$42.43	$30.00	$71.20	$188.80
Mary and Linda	$135.00	$21.21	$15.00	$105.60	$164.40
Anne and Mark	$135.00	$35.36	$25.00	$86.00	$184.00
Mimi and Kathy	$135.00	$7.07	$5.00	$125.20	$144.80
Martha and Jim	$135.00	$49.50	$35.00	$66.40	$203.60
Mary and Mark	$140.00	$28.28	$20.00	$100.80	$179.20
Janice and Martha	$140.00	$56.57	$40.00	$61.60	$218.40
Linda and Kathy	$140.00	$14.14	$10.00	$120.40	$159.60
Anne and Jim	$140.00	$42.43	$30.00	$81.20	$198.80
Mary and Jim	$145.00	$35.36	$25.00	$96.00	$194.00
Barbara and Martha	$145.00	$63.64	$45.00	$56.80	$233.20
Janice and Anne	$145.00	$49.50	$35.00	$76.40	$213.60
Linda and Mimi	$145.00	$7.07	$5.00	$135.20	$154.80
Kathy and Mark	$145.00	$21.21	$15.00	$115.60	$174.40
Mary and Janice	$150.00	$42.43	$30.00	$91.20	$208.80
Barbara and Anne	$150.00	$56.57	$40.00	$71.60	$228.40
Mimi and Mark	$150.00	$14.14	$10.00	$130.40	$169.60
Kathy and Jim	$150.00	$28.28	$20.00	$110.80	$189.20
Mary and Barbara	$155.00	$49.50	$35.00	$86.40	$223.60
Janice and Kathy	$155.00	$35.36	$25.00	$106.00	$204.00
Linda and Mark	$155.00	$7.07	$5.00	$145.20	$164.80

continued

	Average	Standard Deviation	Standard Error	Lower Limit	Upper Limit
Mimi and Jim	$155.00	$21.21	$15.00	$125.60	$184.40
Barbara and Kathy	$160.00	$42.43	$30.00	$101.20	$218.80
Janice and Mimi	$160.00	$28.28	$20.00	$120.80	$199.20
Linda and Jim	$160.00	$14.14	$10.00	$140.40	$179.60
Barbara and Mimi	$165.00	$35.36	$25.00	$116.00	$214.00
Janice and Linda	$165.00	$21.21	$15.00	$135.60	$194.40
Jim and Mark	$165.00	$7.07	$5.00	$155.20	$174.80
Barbara and Linda	$170.00	$28.28	$20.00	$130.80	$209.20
Janice and Mark	$170.00	$14.14	$10.00	$150.40	$189.60
Barbara and Mark	$175.00	$21.21	$15.00	$145.60	$204.40
Janice and Jim	$175.00	$7.07	$5.00	$165.20	$184.80
Barbara and Jim	$180.00	$14.14	$10.00	$160.40	$199.60
Barbara and Janice	$185.00	$7.07	$5.00	$175.20	$194.80

The distribution in Exhibit 21.5 is called the distribution of the sample observations. The probability of randomly selecting any one of the siblings for the sample would be 0.10. The probability of any one pair being drawn into the sample is 1/45 or 0.022. The average spending per person based on samples of two people is listed in Exhibit 21.6 for each of the 45 pairs. The graph of those 45 averages is presented in Exhibit 21.7. This is called the distribution of the *sample averages* or the *sampling distribution*. That distribution has a mean equal to the mean of the spending of the 10 people and a standard error which is

$$\sigma_{\bar{x}} = \frac{\sigma}{\sqrt{n}}$$

where σ is the Greek letter sigma which is used to represent the standard deviation of the distribution of the 10 observations which constitute the population and n is equal to 2, the size of the sample, for this example. Throughout the remainder of this book, Greek letters will be used to indicate characteristics of the population while Roman letters will be used for characteristics of the sample.

Sampling distributions have certain characteristics. If the samples are large enough (generally stated in textbooks as at least 30, but in practice often taken to be at least 50, with 60-80 being more comfortable), the distribution of sample averages will be normally distributed, the mean will be the

Exhibit 21.7   Sampling Distribution of the Population of Two Person Samples

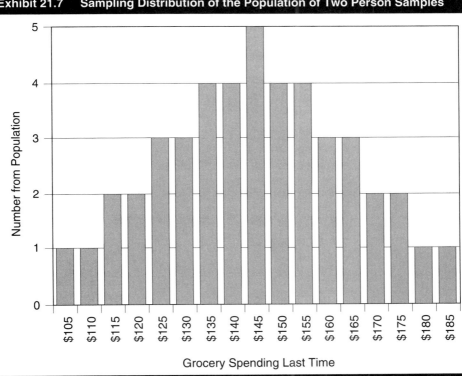

same as the true population mean, represented by μ, the Greek letter mu, and will have a standard deviation (called the standard error or the standard deviation of the sampling distribution) equal to the standard deviation of the distribution of individual observations, σ, divided by the square root of the sample size, i.e.

$$\sigma_{\bar{x}} = \frac{\sigma}{\sqrt{n}}$$

STATISTICAL INFERENCE WHEN ESTIMATING MEANS   Much of statistics is devoted to trying to *infer* characteristics of a population from the calculations made from sample data. Certain characteristics of the distribution of sample averages are very important to this inference process. One of these important practices is to be able to compare distances in physical units, say dollars, to a standard. This is done by using the standard deviation as the basic unit of measurement for the distribution of sample observations, and the standard error as a basic analysis standard of measurement for the distribution of sample averages, much as the dollar, franc, mile or kilometre are used in their respective areas. In statistical inference, the distance that an observed measure, the average of a sample, is from the true mean of the population is measured in terms of standard error units.

Statistical inference can most simply be illustrated by the exercise of estimating the population mean by setting up a *confidence interval* centred on the sample average and having a width based on the standard error. As can be seen from the graph in Exhibit 21.7, the distribution of the sample averages for grocery spending are approximately normally distributed. However, this was a fabricated example as you can see from the original distribution of spending amounts per person. For larger sample sizes and population sizes, the distribution of the sample averages will look very much like a normal distribution as long as the samples are large enough, generally larger than 30. In forming the 95% confidence intervals based on the sample averages from the many samples, it would be found that approximately 95% of those intervals included the true mean. The confidence intervals were calculated and listed in Exhibit 21.6 for this small sample. Calculations for the first confidence interval, i.e., for the sample of Anne and Martha, are:

$$
\begin{aligned}
\text{sample size} &= 2 \\
\text{sample average} &= \$105 \\
\text{sample standard deviation} &= \$7.07 \\
\text{confidence level} &= 95\% \\
\text{confidence coefficient} &= z_{1-0.95} = z_{0.05} = 1.96 \\
\text{standard error} &= \frac{\$7.07}{\sqrt{2}} = \$5.00
\end{aligned}
$$

lower limit of the confidence interval $= \$105.00 - 1.96 \times \$5.00 = \$95.20$
upper limit of the confidence interval $= \$105.00 + 1.96 \times \$5.00 = \$114.80$

Because of the small sample size of only two people, only about 69% (31 of the 45 samples) of the intervals include the true mean of $145.00.

As a second example, let's say that we want to estimate the amount of money that former customers of Firestone Canada spent on automotive service the last time that they took their cars to a garage. If the average automotive service price was $202.60 and if the standard deviation was $202.13, then we could be 95% confident that the true mean amount spent by all of the people in the population was between $189.66 and $215.44. The calculations are as follows:

$$\begin{aligned}
\text{sample size} &= 938 \\
\text{sample average} &= \$202.60 \\
\text{sample standard deviation} &= \$202.13 \\
\text{confidence level} &= 95\% \\
\text{confidence coefficient} &= z_{1-0.95} = z_{0.05} = 1.96 \\
\text{standard error} &= \frac{\$202.13}{\sqrt{938}} = \$6.60
\end{aligned}$$

lower limit of the confidence interval $= \$202.60 - 1.96 \times \$6.60 = \$189.66$
upper limit of the confidence interval $= \$202.60 + 1.96 \times \$6.60 = \$215.54$

Of course, the calculations shown above were based on the results obtained from a sample, a sample that was designed for a particular sample size. However, the topic of this section is calculating sample sizes. In order to get the sample sizes, we have to take what we ended up with and work the process backwards.

CALCULATING THE SAMPLE SIZE WHEN ESTIMATING MEANS   We discussed earlier the need for two parameters of the confidence interval to be specified. These are the precision, sampling error, or the half-width of the confidence interval, and the confidence level. Suppose that the marketing manager of Firestone had requested that the amount spent last time on automotive service be estimated within $5.00 and that he wanted to be 95% confident that the $10 wide interval included the true mean of the population from which the sample would be drawn. The requirements and information available would be:

$$\begin{aligned}
\text{precision} &= \$5.00 \\
\text{confidence level} &= 95\% \\
\text{confidence coefficient} &= z_{0.05} = 1.96 \\
\text{Precision} = 1.96 \times s_{\overline{x}} &= \frac{1.96\, s_x}{\sqrt{n}} \quad \text{or} \quad \$5.00 = \frac{1.96\, s_x}{\sqrt{n}}
\end{aligned}$$

Solving for the unknown sample size provides

$$n = \frac{1.96^2\, s_x^{\,2}}{\$5.00^2}$$

Now, it's obvious that there's one more step to go, to determine s_x. The difficulty is that s_x is based on the sample that has not yet been drawn. The only way around this problem is to obtain an estimate of s_x in some way. Formally, since s_x is the sample value which will eventually be known, we will be estimating the true population standard deviation of the distribution of sample observations, which is usually referred to as σ, the Greek letter sigma. To differentiate between the true standard deviation of the population, σ, from our preliminary estimate, we'll use the note σ' for the preliminary estimate. The actual formula that we'll use for estimating the size of the sample is

$$ n = \frac{z_\alpha^2 \sigma'^2}{e^2} $$

where e denotes the sampling error or precision and z_α is defined as the confidence coefficient corresponding to the 95% confidence level, or, conversely, the 5% level of risk. This 5% level of risk means that there is a 5% risk that the confidence interval will not include the true mean. This risk is often called the alpha (α) risk, or the risk of a Type I error. The concept of a Type I error will be explained later.

Actually there are several ways to get a preliminary estimate of the standard error. The best way is to have recently conducted a similar study where that standard error was calculated with confidence. Then that value would be used in the equation for σ'.

A second way to estimate σ is to conduct a small preliminary sample and use the calculated value of the sample standard deviation, s, as an estimate of σ. This can work well, but usually project sponsors want to get the main study underway without any undue delay or expense. This normally means no preliminary study to determine the sample size, accompanied by the refrain "let's just do it."

A third procedure is fairly easy and has been borrowed from machine design and other engineering applications. This involves the calculation of a tolerance interval. The tolerance can be identified in response to two simple questions. The first is "What's the least that you realistically think people would state for their last automotive service? The answer might be $20.00 (other than for a free inspection or redoing something under warranty). The second question is "What's the most that you realistically think that people would state as the cost of their last automotive service?" One thousand dollars might be good target value.

Now, from the earlier explanation of the normal distribution, we know that almost all of the area under the normal distribution lies within three standard deviations from the mean. In fact, 99.74% of all the area under the standard normal distribution lies within three standard deviations from the mean. The reasonable lower and upper tolerance limits are placed at the plus and minus 3 standard deviation points on the normal distribution graphed in Exhibit 21.8.

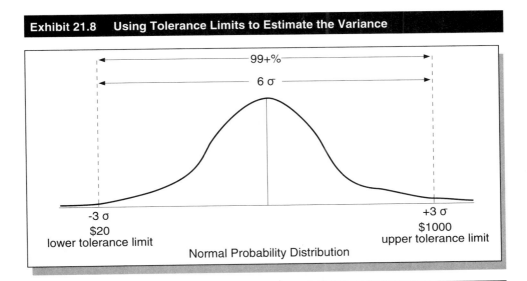

Exhibit 21.8   Using Tolerance Limits to Estimate the Variance

So, if $20 was given as a reasonable lower value and $1000 as a reasonable upper limit, then the range from $20 to $1000 spans an interval of six standard deviation units. If six standard deviations is $980 units wide, then one standard deviation is $166.33 wide. Then the sample size can be calculated:

$$n = \frac{1.96^2 \, \sigma_x'^2}{\$5.00^2} = \frac{1.96^2 \times \$166.33^2}{\$5.00^2} = 4252$$

If the desired precision were to estimate the true mean within $10.00 then,

$$n = \frac{1.96^2 \, \sigma_x'^2}{\$10.00^2} = \frac{1.96^2 \times \$166.33^2}{\$10.00^2} = 1063$$

Notice that when the precision is changed from $5.00 to $10.00, i.e., doubled, the sample size is cut from 4252 to 1063, i.e., one quarter of the former value. This will always be true.

THE COEFFICIENT OF VARIATION AND RELATIVE PRECISION   Sometimes, the client says that he wants to estimate the mean within 10%. In the problem above, if the precision was $10.00 and the mean was $200, then the precision was $10 ÷ $200 or 0.05 or 5% of the mean. In these types of situations where the precision is stated in a percentage term, the dispersion of the population is also stated in percentage terms. The coefficient of variation is the statement of the percentage dispersion as measured by the standard deviation divided by the mean:

$$CV = \frac{\text{standard deviation}}{\text{mean}} = \frac{\$166.33}{\$202.60} = 0.83 \text{ or } 83\% \text{ and}$$

if the relative precision were

$$R = \frac{\text{precision}}{\text{mean}} = 5\% \text{ then}$$

the formula could be stated as

$$n = \frac{z^2 \sigma'^2}{e^2} = \frac{z^2 \left(\dfrac{\sigma'^2}{\mu} \right)}{\left(\dfrac{e}{\mu} \right)^2} = \frac{z^2 CV^2}{R^2} = \frac{1.96^2 \times 0.83^2}{0.05^2} = 1059$$

which is very close to the previous result of 1063(different because of rounding).

CALCULATING SAMPLE SIZES WHEN ESTIMATING POPULATION PROPORTIONS Most survey research questions provide attribute type of data, i.e., nominal or ordinal data, rather than interval or ratio data. In other words, most questionnaires ask people to give a lot more "yes or no" or "which one do you like best?" or "do you strongly agree or not?" answers than responses that can provide continuous type data resulting in the calculation of means and variances. This means that the sample proportion rather than the mean is the more typical result of analyzing the data from a survey research question.

In the previous section, we investigated the sampling distribution of the mean of a continuous variable. Similar distributions exist for proportions. At the individual respondent level, a choice is made to answer yes or no to a question. When respondent number three chooses *yes*, the count is one yes vote. When respondent seven says *yes*, the vote goes up to two. And so on, until respondent 1050 says *yes* and we tally the yes votes and find that 365 of the 1052 respondents said *yes*, which gives a 0.347 proportion saying yes, or

34.7%. Since the sampled population might have been extremely large, maybe 500 000 people, many different samples of size 1052 could have been taken. The 0.347 was one of many possible proportions that could have occurred. In fact, there is a population of sample proportions that has a particular probability distribution. We sampled one of the proportions from that sampling distribution when we drew the sample of 1052 people and asked the question.

Proportions have a probability distribution as do means. The sampling distribution of the **population proportion** has a mean of π, the Greek letter pi, and a standard deviation of

$$\sigma = \sqrt{\frac{\pi(1-\pi)}{n}}$$

which is normally distributed, given that the value of the true population proportion, π, is known. On our way to determining the size of a sample from a population to estimate the population proportion, we first set up the formula for an interval estimate, which is

$$\pi \pm z_\alpha \sigma = \pi \pm z_\alpha \sqrt{\frac{\pi(1-\pi)}{n}}$$

If the manager wants to estimate the true proportion within four percentage points, then the error, or precision, would be specified as

$$e = z_\alpha \sqrt{\frac{\pi(1-\pi)}{n}}$$

Solving for the required sample size gives us the equation:

$$n = \frac{z_\alpha^2 \pi(1-\pi)}{e^2} = \frac{z_\alpha^2 \sigma'^2}{e^2}$$

for a large population where the sample is not a large percentage of the population size.

Once again, one of the problems is to determine the sample size, but the formula calls for the population proportion, π, to be used in the formula. This value of π isn't known prior to the sample being taken and has to be estimated in some way. If nothing whatsoever is known about the possible values of π, then the value 0.50 should be taken, since π (1-π) is maximized for π = 0.50, as shown in Exhibit 21.9. This assures a sample size that is at least

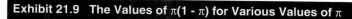

Exhibit 21.9   The Values of π(1 - π) for Various Values of π

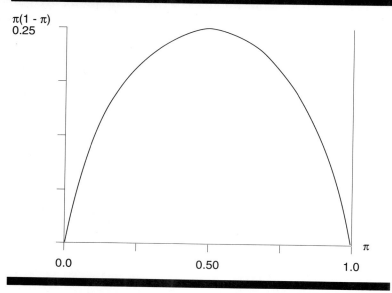

large enough. If the sample proportion could be estimated within an interval, then the value which is closest to 0.50 should be taken for the estimate of π. For example, if a preliminary estimate of the true proportion is between 0.20 and 0.35, then 0.35 should be the value used in the sample size calculations.

Suppose that the marketing manager at Firestone had identified the following question as being the most important of those in a questionnaire regarding the attitudes of past and present customers.

3. How likely are you to take your car back in the future to Firestone for servicing, repairs or tires? (Please check the box below.)

[ ]1   DEFINITELY WOULD TAKE BACK TO FIRESTONE

[ ]2   PROBABLY WOULD TAKE BACK

[ ]3   MIGHT OR MIGHT NOT TAKE BACK

[ ]4   PROBABLY WOULD NOT TAKE BACK

[ ]5   DEFINITELY WOULD NOT TAKE BACK TO FIRESTONE

Of particular importance to the marketing manager is the percentage of people who say that they would definitely take their car back to Firestone. In fact, he states that he wants to be 95% confident of being able to estimate the true percentage of all past customers who would definitely take their cars back to Firestone within four percentage points. The company has never conducted a study like this previously but the manager feels that at least 30% of Firestone's past customers should say that they definitely will return. With this information, we can calculate the required sample size considering this one question. The important parameters are:

Desired confidence level = 95%
Confidence coefficient = 1.96
Desired precision or sampling error = 0.04

Preliminary estimate of true population proportion was given as a minimum of 30% and a maximum of 50% by the marketing manager. If there is doubt in this range estimate, the preliminary estimate should be taken to be 50% to ensure at least a large enough sample size

$$= \pi' = 0.50$$

Preliminary estimate of true variance = $\pi'(1 - \pi') = 0.50(1 - 0.50) = 0.25$

$$n = \frac{z_\alpha^2 \pi(1-\pi)}{e^2} = \frac{1.96^2 \times 0.50 \times 0.50}{0.04^2} = \frac{3.84 \times 0.25}{0.0016} = 600.25 \cong 601$$

If the lower end of the interval, 30%, were taken as an estimate of π', then the sample size might have been too small, as is shown.

$$n = \frac{z_\alpha^2 \pi(1-\pi)}{e^2} = \frac{1.96^2 \times 0.30 \times 0.70}{0.04^2} = \frac{3.84 \times 0.21}{0.0016} = 504$$

If the desired precision were 3 percentage points then the sample size would be 1068, and if the desired precision were 2 percentage points then the sample size would be 2401. Notice that as the precision is cut in half, the sample size is quadrupled.

To complete this example, suppose that the survey resulted in 1036 people answering the question and 38.4% saying that they definitely would take their cars back to Firestone. The interval estimate of the true proportion of the population that would take their cars back to Firestone is:

$$p \pm z_{0.05}\, s_p \Rightarrow 0.384 \pm 1.96 \sqrt{\frac{0.384(1 - 0.384)}{1036 - 1}} \Rightarrow 0.384 \pm 0.0296 \Rightarrow$$

$$[0.3544 \text{ to } 0.4136] \text{ or } 35.44\% \text{ to } 41.36\%$$

The calculated precision of 2.96 percentage points is somewhat tighter than was required by the marketing manager. One reason is that the actual sample size was much larger than the required size of 601 for the 4 percentage point precision. However, it was a bit smaller than needed for the 3 percentage point error. An additional effect on the precision comes from the sample percentage being 38.4% rather than 50% that was used in the sample size calculations. Since $p(1-p)$ is smaller for $p = .384$ than for $p = 0.50$, then the standard error is smaller and consequently the half-width of the confidence interval is smaller.

DETERMINING SAMPLE SIZE FOR FINITE POPULATIONS   All of the calculations above assumed that the population was extremely large and that the sample was a relatively small percentage of the population. This is usually the case when taking a survey in practice. However, it makes sense that if the sample were, say, 75% of the size of the population, then we'd know a great deal about the population, regardless of the actual size of the sample. A rule-of-thumb in sampling says that in a case where the sample size is 10% or more of the population size, it's reasonable to expect that since we'll know a great deal about the population we shouldn't have to take quite so large a sample size.

   This logic corresponds to what's called in statistics the *finite population corrector*. This factor is represented by

$$\sqrt{\frac{N-n}{N-1}}$$

and is often denoted by FPC

   When applied to the formula for a confidence interval for the true population proportion, π, the expression is:

$$p \pm z_a \sqrt{\frac{p(1-p)}{n}} \sqrt{\frac{N-n}{N-1}}$$

   From the above expression, you can see that as the sample size n gets large relative to the population size N, then the finite population corrector is a fraction that gets smaller and smaller. In the limit of taking a census, since $n = N$, then the finite population corrector is zero and the sample proportion p is equal to π.

For example, if $N = 100\ 000$ and $n = 1,$

then the finite population corrector (FPC) =

$$FPC = \sqrt{\frac{100\ 000 - 1}{100\ 000 - 1}} = 1$$

If $N = 100\ 000$ and $n = 1000$, then

$$FPC = \sqrt{\frac{100\ 000 - 1000}{100\ 000 - 1}} = 0.995$$

If $N = 100\ 000$ and $n = 20\ 000$, then

$$\text{FPC} = \sqrt{\frac{100\ 000 - 20\ 000}{100\ 000 - 1}} = 0.894$$

If $N = 100\ 000$ and $n = 80\ 000$, then

$$\text{FPC} = \sqrt{\frac{100\ 000 - 80\ 000}{100\ 000 - 1}} = 0.447$$

If $N = 100\ 000$ and $n = 100\ 000$, then we have taken a census and

$$\text{FPC} = \sqrt{\frac{100\ 000 - 100\ 000}{100\ 000 - 1}} = 0.000$$

When the finite population corrector is factored into the formula for the sample size, the following expression is the result

$$n = \frac{z_\alpha^2 \pi(1-\pi)}{e^2 + \dfrac{z_\alpha^2 \pi(1-\pi)}{N}}$$

As an example, let's say that we want to estimate the true population proportion within 4 percentage points (0.04) with 95% confidence and that we know nothing about the true proportion, i.e., use $\pi' = 0.50$. Substituting those values into the equation that we had earlier for the sample size gives:

$$n = \frac{(1.96)^2 \times (0.50)(1 - 0.50)}{(0.04)^2} = 601$$

If we calculate the sample for various population sizes, we can construct the table in Exhibit 21.10.

Exhibit 21.10   The Relationship Between Population Size and Sample Size

Population Size	Sample Size
1 000 000 000	600.25 = 601
100 000 000	600.25 = 601
1 000 000	599.89 = 600
100 000	596.67 = 597
50 000	593.13 = 594
20 000	582.76 = 583
5 000	535.91 = 536

To many people, the table in Exhibit 21.10 is quite amazing. In a very real sense, the size of the target population has very little influence on the size of the sample. Going from a population of 1 billion people down to a population of 50 000 people reduces the necessary sample size by 7 people. Amazing, but true! Similar findings would be obtained for other values of the parameters, i.e., for various values of the confidence level, desired precision, estimate of π' and population size.

Similarly, in the case where the *mean* is being estimated, the sample size formula including the finite population corrector is

$$n = \frac{z_\alpha^2 \sigma^2}{e^2 + \dfrac{z_\alpha^2 \sigma^2}{N}}$$

and calculations similar to those illustrated above can be performed.

SAMPLE SIZE DETERMINATION WHEN TESTING HYPOTHESES

TESTING HYPOTHESES ABOUT MEANS In addition to calculating confidence intervals for the true means of distributions, researchers often begin with hypotheses regarding the true mean spending per week on groceries, the true mean age of the target market segment, the true mean amount spent last time on automotive service, and so on. Sometimes these hypotheses pertain to the means of two separate groups within the population. For example, did men and women spend the same amount of money on automotive service the last time, or do high income and low income people spend the same amount on groceries per week? Although these questions could be addressed with confidence intervals, testing of hypotheses is sometimes a more natural way of approaching the problem.

Hypothesis testing is used in formal statistical procedures as a matter of course. However, the process of stating and testing hypotheses does not always seem to be second nature to researchers and clients who don't have a firm statistical background. There is a certain logic and flow to the analysis of hypotheses that can be very attractive to even the beginning researcher. In most problem situations, the client has some preconceived notions of what the "truth" is in the marketplace. It might be that he or she expects that the mean spending of customers for groceries is at least $100.00 per week, or that high income earners spend more on auto service than do low income earners. These statements by the client of what he thinks is the truth can usually be stated as the alternate hypotheses in marketing research.

The alternate hypothesis is typically a brief statement of what the client believes to be true in the population regarding a certain attitude or behaviour. The opposite of the alternate hypothesis is the null hypothesis. Since the null hypothesis usually states what the client believes not to be true, you're actually hoping to find data that will allow you to say that the null is not true and consequently you must assert that the alternate hypothesis represents the true state of the variable.

We'll take two examples to show you what we mean. Suppose a client says he believes that the customers in his restaurant chain are generally middle-aged. You press him a bit further and he tells you that he would estimate the average age is 43 years old. In the questionnaire administered in the restaurant, the respondents are asked to indicate the year in which they were born. In statistical analysis, it's typical to state the beliefs of the client or the researcher in terms of the hypotheses, which are then tested by the analysis of the data. The hypotheses in this case would be:

null hypothesis	H_o: The average age is 43 years.
alternate hypothesis	H_a: The average age is younger or older than 43 years.

Notice that this is one of those cases where the state that is actually believed to be true is stated as the null hypothesis. This is most commonly found in situations where the null hypothesis is that one particular value is true, rather than a range of values. It's common to state a risk level or level of significance along with the null hypothesis. This indicates the chance that you'd be willing to take of incorrectly concluding that the mean age is either younger or older than 43 years when in fact it is 43 years old. This is also stated as the risk of rejecting the null hypothesis when it's really true, which is defined in statistics as a Type I error, or alpha risk.

The hypotheses above are stated in such a way that we are faced with a two-sided alternate hypothesis, that is, we don't care whether the average is greater than or less than 43, we're just interested in whether there is any difference. In a two-sided hypothesis test, we're testing against one specific numerical value for the null hypothesis. If the null hypothesis is rejected then the conclusion is that the true mean is different from the null hypothesized value, but we don't care in which direction that difference lies.

In the above example, the restaurateur might have stated that he felt that his customers were older than 43. Since the null hypothesis is often written as a statement that we'd like to refute, and the alternate is what we believe to be true, the hypotheses in this case would be:

H_o: The average age is 43 years or younger.
H_a: The average age is older than 43 years.

The risk of a Type I error is often stated to be 5% or 10% but could be stated as any chance of error with which the decision-maker is comfortable. This risk of a Type I error is also referred to as the level of significance or alpha risk. These hypotheses are stated in such a way that they will produce a one-sided test, that is, we're only concerned with whether the average is greater than 43 or not.

As another example, suppose that you want to test the hypothesis that the amount of money spent by tourists on food and beverage in restaurants in the Midland, Ontario area, while visiting the Ste-Marie Among the Hurons tourist attraction, is the same as the amount spent in restaurants in the Thunder Bay region while visiting Old Fort William. We're now testing whether two values are the same or different. The hypotheses would be:

H_0: mean spending in Midland area = mean spending in Thunder Bay area
H_a: mean spending in Midland area ≠ mean spending in Thunder Bay area

Once again, a level of Type I error would be stated for this two-sided test.

In each of the cases discussed above, a sample size must be determined. The process is somewhat similar to that used for confidence intervals. However, the logic and the calculations are a little more involved. In the first example above, the manager is betting that the mean is 43 years old. If the actual sample average is significantly different from 43, then he'd have to admit that he was wrong. The definition of *significantly different* is determined by the stated risk of rejecting the null hypothesis when it is true, that is, 5% risk of a Type I error. The diagram relating these parameters is presented in Exhibit 21.11.

Exhibit 21.11   The Critical Values for Testing a Two-Sided Hypothesis

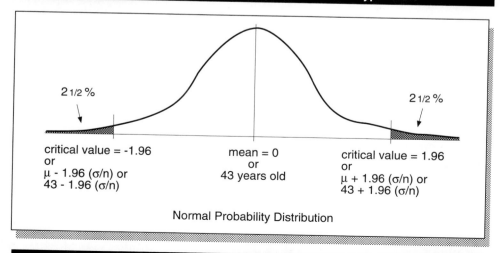

2 1/2 %

2 1/2 %

critical value = -1.96
or
μ - 1.96 (σ/n) or
43 - 1.96 (σ/n)

mean = 0
or
43 years old

critical value = 1.96
or
μ + 1.96 (σ/n) or
43 + 1.96 (σ/n)

Normal Probability Distribution

In Exhibit 21.11, the 5% risk of a Type I error is split evenly between the two tail areas of the normal distribution. The values that cut off these 2 1/2% areas in each tail are measured as being 1.96 standard error units away from the hypothesized mean of 43 or the standardized mean of 0. These positions are written as:

$$\pm 1.96\,\sigma_{\bar{x}} \text{ or } \pm 1.96\,\frac{\sigma}{\sqrt{n}}$$

So, in this example, *significantly different* becomes defined as a sample value more than 1.96 standard error units away from the mean. In contrast to the Type I error, there exists a Type II error which is the error of not rejecting the null hypothesis when it's actually false. In order to determine the sample size in an hypothesis testing situation, it's necessary to specify the risk of a Type II error that one is willing to accept.

As another example, let's suppose that you're the manager of a supermarket. One of your decisions is the number of checkouts to have open at any time. You have to decide how many clerks to schedule for a shift and then how many to put on checkout. About six months ago, you had some staff count the number of customers standing in line at any one time on a Saturday between 9:00 a.m. and 5:00 p.m. The average number of customers standing in line was 3.21 and the standard deviation was 0.75. You were informed by head office that this was within the limit of tolerance for shoppers, but that an average of 3.00 was best. However, you were also told that if the average became 3.50, then customers would get very upset about standing in line, some would leave their buggies and shop elsewhere while others would go through the line, but there would be a high level of dissatisfaction and a large percentage of those customers would never return to your store. Let's state the hypotheses as follows:

$$H_o: \mu = 3.00$$
$$H_a: \mu = 3.50$$

Let's say that if the testing concluded that the mean was 3.50 or higher then you had to open another checkout during that time. Because of the added cost, you wanted to limit your risk to 10% of scheduling another clerk when you really didn't need to. (This is the Type I error, rejecting the null hypothesis when it was not false.) On the other hand, you decided that you could only handle a 5% risk of not putting on another clerk when the lines were actually too long, that is, not rejecting the null hypothesis when in fact the lines were too long, a Type II error. These specifications are graphed in Exhibit 21.12. Understanding the basics of probability, you wonder whether the true number of customers waiting is 3.21, the best value of 3.00 or the longest permissible line of 3.50.

Exhibit 21.12 Specifying the Type I and Type II Errors for Sample Size Calculation

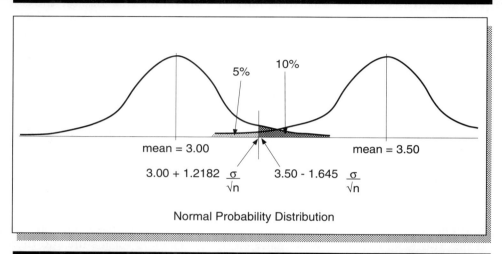

The point on the graph in Exhibit 21.12 where the line cuts off 10% of the right tail of the leftmost normal distribution curve, which has the mean of 3.00, and that also cuts off 5% in the left tail of the rightmost normal curve, which has a mean of 3.50, must be common to both curves. In order for this to happen, we must express this point as a distance above the 3.00 mean and as a distance below the 3.50 mean. (σ_0 is the standard deviation of the distribution with a mean of 3.00 and a σ^a is the standard deviation of the distribution with a mean of 3.50.).

$$3.00 + z_{0.10}\frac{\sigma_o}{\sqrt{n}} = 3.50 - z_{0.05}\frac{\sigma_a}{\sqrt{n}}$$

The equation can now be solved for the sample size that will satisfy the two requirements for risks of Type I and Type II errors. (Since our sample provided a standard deviation of 0.75, we will assume that this value is reasonable for both distributions and we'll take

$$n = \frac{\sigma^2\left(z_o + z_a\right)^2}{\left(\mu_a - \mu_o\right)^2}$$

$$n = \frac{0.75^2 \left(1.282 + 1.645\right)^2}{\left(3.50 - 3.00\right)^2}$$

$$n = \frac{0.5625 \times 8.567}{0.25} = 19.27 \approx 20$$

TESTING HYPOTHESES ABOUT PROPORTIONS   The determination of sample sizes for hypotheses involving proportions is performed in a very similar fashion to that illustrated above for means.

1. First, the hypotheses need to be stated.

2. The risk of a Type I error and the risk of a Type II error need to be specified.

3. The point between the null hypothesized proportion and the proportion of the alternate hypothesis that satisfies the two risk levels must be expressed as a distance above the smaller proportion and a distance below the higher proportion.

4. The two expressions are equated and solved for n, the needed sample size.

Suppose that you work in marketing research for a consumer packaged goods firm. The firm regularly creates and tests concepts for new products. Based on past tests, criteria have been established for testing the new concept. Let's say that for past new product concepts if the proportion of respondents in a concept test who said that they "definitely will buy" the new product was 0.25 or less, then the concept was scrapped. However, if the percentage who said that they definitely will buy was higher than 0.40, then the concept was advanced to the next stage of analysis. If the percentage was between 25% and 40%, the brand manager would give an order to conduct one more concept test and then make a formal decision regarding the future of the concept. The hypotheses can be stated as:

H_o: $\pi_o = 0.25$, $\alpha = 0.10$ (risk of Type I error, or alpha risk)
H_a: $\pi_a = 0.40$, $\beta = 0.05$ (risk of Type II error, or beta risk)

The graphs of the two probability distributions are shown in Exhibit 21.13. We will need to specify some value between 0.25 and 0.40 such that if the sample proportion is less than this "critical value" then we will reject the alternate hypothesis and if the sample proportion is larger than the critical value, then the null hypothesis is rejected.

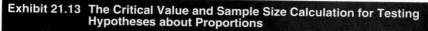

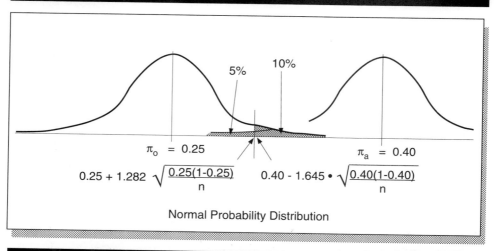

Normal Probability Distribution

The expressions can be stated for the critical value. The expression

$$\sum |x - \bar{x} V n$$

is the distance above the null hypothesized value of 0.25, while

$$0.40 - 1.645\sqrt{\frac{0.40(1 - 0.40)}{n}}$$

is a distance below the alternate hypothesized value of 0.40.

By equating the two expressions for the critical value, an equation for the sample size can be obtained.

$$n = \frac{\left[z_o \sqrt{p_o(1 - p_o)} + z_a \sqrt{p_a(1 - p_a)}\right]^2}{(p_a - p_o)^2}$$

$$n = \frac{\left[1.282 \sqrt{0.25(1 - 0.25)} + 1.645 \sqrt{0.40(1 - 0.40)}\right]^2}{(0.40 - 0.25)^2}$$

n = 83

This sample size will be large enough so that the Type I and Type II risks can both be satisfied.

SAMPLING PROCEDURES
STRATIFIED SAMPLING

Although simple random sampling theoretically provides samples that are similar to the parent population, that is, representative, this does not always happen. For various reasons, the most important being chance variation, one income group or one age category might be represented in the sample to a greater or lesser extent than it would be in the population. When the threat of an unrepresentative, although random, sample occurs, then the researchers might decide to ensure representativeness while maintaining random selection of respondents. What results is a process called stratified sampling.

The issue of representativeness is multifaceted. The project might require that each income category of the sample have the same percentage of respondents as does the population. This is called *proportionate stratified sampling*. However, many projects specify that the percentage of the sample drawn from a particular category be larger or smaller than the percentage of the population that falls within that category. This is called *disproportionate stratified sampling*.

There are very good reasons for specifying that the project sample be done in either the proportionate or disproportionate manner. As mentioned above, proportionate stratified sampling is conducted to ensure that the sample is similar to the population in terms of particular characteristics. Disproportionate stratified sampling is usually conducted so that categories that normally would be occupied by very small percentages of the population have large enough sample sizes for statistical analysis. In other words, you might need to analyze the sample in a category using statistical procedures that require a reasonably large sample size. If a proportionate sample were taken, the number of respondents in that category might be so small that the minimum sample size requirements could not be met. Also, it would be difficult to have much confidence in the findings from these small sample categories.

For example, Thompson Lightstone and Company Limited (TL) conducts an omnibus survey called *OmniTel*. The total sample size across Canada is 2000 respondents. If the sampling were proportionate to the population sizes, Ontario and Quebec would dominate the sample with larger numbers of respondents. However, the Atlantic provinces and the Prairie provinces would have very few respondents because of their relatively much smaller populations. Proportionately, the sample sizes would be:

Ontario	36%	720
Quebec	27%	540
Atlantic	9%	180
Manitoba/Saskatchewan	8%	160
Alberta	9%	180
British Columbia	11%	220
	100%	2000

TL does not draw a proportionate sample because of the small sample sizes which are seen above for the Atlantic provinces and the Prairies. They draw a disproportionate sample:

Ontario	25%	500
Quebec	25%	500
Atlantic	12.5%	250
Manitoba/Saskatchewan	12.5%	250
Alberta	12.5%	250
British Columbia	12.5%	250
	100%	2000

These sample sizes for each of the geographic areas are large enough to analyze statistically and to give confidence in the findings.

The determination of the sample size for proportionate or disproportionate stratified sampling is more involved than for simple random sampling. The simplest process is distributing the sample among several strata based on proportionate representation as measured by the population.

1. Specify the variable on which to stratify and decide on the number of categories.
2. Obtain a frequency distribution of the population based on that variable. (This information might be available from Statistics Canada or from your local department of economic development.)
3. Calculate the number of respondents to obtain from each stratum by specifying

$$n_s = \frac{N_s}{N} n,$$

where N_s is the number of population elements in stratum s, N is the total size of the target population and n is the size of the total sample.
4. Randomly select n_s respondents from each of the S strata of the determining variable.
5. Control the sampling to satisfy the stratified sampling requirements.
6. The analysis is then executed on the combined sample, usually, and sometimes on the individual strata.

DISPROPORTIONATE STRATIFIED SAMPLING   Determining the sample sizes in disproportionate stratified sampling situations is beyond the objectives of this book. The interested reader should consult a book that concentrates on sampling, such as Sudman (1976) or Som (1973).

WEIGHTING OF SAMPLE FINDINGS FROM DISPROPORTIONATE SAMPLING   Given all the reasons for sampling in a disproportionate manner, much of marketing research sampling is conduced in this manner, either by design or neglect. Consequently, it's necessary to have a procedure to follow when using the responses from such a sample. The problem with a disproportionate sample is that some or all of the findings can't be used exactly the way they appear in the initial tables printed out from the computer. The reason for this is that some of the groups in the sample are either over-represented or under-represented in the sample because of the dictates of the disproportionate sampling process. For example, if after sampling the lower income categories have disproportionately higher sample sizes then if left that way the analysis might abnormally represent the desires of the poor in the study findings.

The adjustment of the sample findings obtained from disproportionate sampling is called *weighting*. As the name implies, certain weights are applied to the sample output in order to adjust the influence of the data back to what it would have been if the sample categories had been represented in the same proportions as the sample frame categories.

A short example will illustrate the basics of weighting. Suppose that a sample of grocery shoppers in North Canoe, Orr, Ontario, revealed that the relation between their income levels and the amounts spent on groceries during their last main grocery trip are as tabled in Exhibit 21.14. The corresponding sample frequencies are provided in Exhibit 21.15.

Exhibit 21.14   Cross Tabulation of Income by Spending

(Percentages)

	Less than $40 000	$40 000 to #49 999	$50 000 to $59 999	$60 000 to $79 999	$80 000 or more	Total	Total Number
$60 or less	38%	21%	12%	8%	29%	21%	46
$61 to $99	27	26	20	31	10	24	52
$100 to $159	31	27	45	34	35	34	76
$160 or more	4	26	23	27	26	21	46
Total %	100%	100%	100%	100%	100%	100%	220
Total Number	45	47	49	48	31	220	
Income %	20.5%	21.4%	22.2%	21.8%	14.1%	100%	

Exhibit 21.15 Cross Tabulation of Spending by Income

(Frequencies)

			Income			
Spending	*Less than $40 000*	*$40 000 to #49 999*	*$50 000 to $59 999*	*$60 000 to $79 999*	*$80 000 or more*	*Total Number*
$60 or less	17	10	6	4	9	46
$61 to $99	12	12	10	15	3	52
$100 to $159	14	13	22	16	11	76
$160 or more	2	12	11	13	8	46
Total Number	45	47	49	48	31	220

If someone were to ask if the sample is representative of North Canoe Orr in terms of the income distribution, the answer would have to be no. Exhibit 21.16 below shows that the lowest two income categories are underrepresented, the middle income groups are about right and the upper income category is overrepresented. In order to adjust the sample, the proportions in each income category need to be adjusted to conform to the sample frame.

Exhibit 21.16 Determination of Weights

	Population Distribution North Canoe Orr, Ontario	*Sample*	*Weighting Calculation*	*Weight*
Less than $40 000	30%	20.5%	30% ÷ 20.5%	1.463
$40 000 to $49 999	25	21.4	25% ÷ 21.4%	1.168
$50 000 to $59 999	20	22.2	20% ÷ 22.2%	0.901
$60 000 to $79 999	20	21.8	20% ÷ 21.8%	0.917
$80 000 or more	5	14.1	5% ÷ 14.1%	0.355
Total	100%	100%		

Since there should have been 46.3% more people sampled in the lowest income category (less than $40,000), the impact of their responses should count 46.3% more heavily in the tabulation and in any other calculations based upon those data. The weights shown in Exhibit 21.16 are used to multiply the frequencies based on the lowest income group. So the 17 lowest income households which indicated that they spent $60 or less in groceries becomes 24.87 with weighting. (The calculation is: 17 x 1.463 = 24.87.) Naturally, the assumption is that if more of these folks had been sampled they would have said approximately what the sampled people reported. Similarly, the influence of the highest income earners is reduced by 64.3% by multiplying that row of Exhibit 21.17 by the weight of 0.357.

Exhibit 21.17 Weighting the Sample Findings

| | Income | | | | | |
Spending	Less than $40 000	$40 000 to #49 999	$50 000 to $59 999	$60 000 to $79 999	$80 000 or more	Total Number
$60 or less	24.87	11.68	5.41	3.67	3.20	48.83
$61 to $99	17.56	14.02	9.01	13.76	1.07	55.42
$100 to $159	20.48	15.18	19.82	14.67	3.91	74.06
$160 or more	2.93	14.22	9.91	11.92	2.84	41.82
Total %	100%	100%	100%	100%	100%	
Total Number	65.84	55.10	44.15	44.02	11.02	220.13*

*error due to rounding

CLUSTER SAMPLING

The purpose of cluster sampling is to reduce the cost of fieldwork, specifically the fieldwork of in-home personal interviews. If we were to draw a simple random sample of 500 households across the Metropolitan Toronto area, we'd expect there would be a fair distance between each of the selected households. The interviewer would have to drive to one house, conduct the interview, get back into her car, drive to the next interview, get back into her car, and so on. A lot of time would be wasted in travel from one household to the next.

Consider that although Toronto is quite diverse, it's probably possible to select a large number of geographic areas within Toronto that could be considered to be mini-Torontos in terms of their demographic or other characteristics. The boundaries for some of these areas might be quite odd looking in order to fashion the mini-Toronto. The interviewer could go to one of these areas, called a *cluster*, park her car, and then visit several households before having to drive to another cluster to conduct more interviews.

The procedure in single stage cluster sampling is:

1. Divide the sampling frame into collectively exhaustive and mutually exclusive clusters, each of which can be used as a microcosm of the parent population.

2. Randomly select a number of clusters to compose the sampled clusters.

3. Execute a census on the selected clusters.

Very complex sampling procedures can be performed. These are often referred to as multistage cluster sampling. The steps might include the following:

1. Divide the sampling frame into collectively exhaustive and mutually exclusive clusters, for example, areas of Toronto.

2. Randomly select a number of clusters to compose the sampled clusters.

3. Randomly select the second stage sampling unit within each cluster, for example, city blocks.

4. Interview everyone on the selected city blocks, or select a random sample or stratified sample of the households on those city blocks.

5. Select the person to interview from the household randomly or according to some specified selection criterion, (e.g., whose birthday comes up next).

The reader who is interested in the calculation of sample sizes in cluster sampling is referred to specialized books in sampling, such as Som (1973).

MALL-INTERCEPT SAMPLING

Mall-intercept sampling will be discussed separately because of the frequency of its use. This procedure is not a random sampling process. The people who comprise the mall sample self-select themselves to be in the study mall on that day and that choice puts them in the position where they might be stopped by an interviewer. Not all people who use shampoo, buy groceries, eat frozen desserts or buy tires shop in a shopping mall. The best that can be done is to select prospective respondents on a random basis, such as approach the fifth person past the tree. So, a mall-intercept sample is a convenience sample.

Since a mall-intercept sample is not a random sample, care must be taken with the data and the analysis. The determination of the sample size for mall studies can be conducted in all the ways that were reviewed earlier. However, since the sample is not random, projection to the population is not encouraged. It should be remembered that the statistical formulas for determining sample sizes depend on random samples being selected and might not be appropriate.

IDENTIFICATION OF SAMPLE RESPONDENTS

Identifying the sample respondents can be done in a wide variety of ways. The most obvious process for selecting a respondent in a mall study is to stop the tenth person through the southwest entrance to the Sherway Gardens Mall. He's right in front of you and easy to spot. Of course, if you need to interview only women over 50 years, then you can select every fifth of that bunch. Selecting telephone respondents or respondents for mail studies or for in-home personal interviews can be done in several ways. Business-to-business research respondents can be identified sometimes only by calling the company and asking for the person in charge of buying computers, for example.

Most random sampling schemes rely on lists of some sort. The list might be a telephone directory, street directory, a directory of manufacturing firms, a professional association membership list, a list of members of a particular group.

Telephone directories are often used to select a systematic random sample. For example, the November 1989 issue of the Metropolitan Toronto telephone directory contains 2013 pages, 5 columns on each page and about 120 names in each column. If you wanted to draw a sample of 500 respondents and you anticipated that all would be home and that half would comply, then you would need a list of 1000 names and numbers. To get these 1000 names and numbers, you know that you'll have to select one name from approximately every other page. To select a random starting page, you can randomly choose between one and two (flip a coin). To pick the sampling column from a page, choose a random number between one and five (roll a die, but eliminate six). Lastly, to select a name from the column, pick a random number between 1 and 120. Although this systematic selection technique is not completely random, it's close enough to qualify as a workable and efficient procedure.

One problem with selecting respondents from the telephone directory, is that some people have unlisted numbers, some got their numbers too late to be included in the directory and some moved after the directory was printed.

In cities in which the incidence of unlisted numbers is not too severe, the random selection process from the directory is very workable. In other cases, the researcher needs a more random procedure. For telephone studies, this can involve some form of random digit dialling.

Pure random digit dialling involves identifying all of the active exchanges in an area, say 525-x, 527-x, 529-x, and then generating the right four dialling digits randomly from the computer. This procedure will produce a random sample. However, the obvious problem of having to call some numbers which are not in use at the time of the project makes for a larger number of dead numbers for the interviewers to try.

An alternative to random digit dialling is the plus-n, plus-two or plus-one procedure, which was explained in Chapter 6. Then either two or one is added to the rightmost digit of the whole number. The randomly selected number of 525-7071 becomes 525-7072 under the plus-one technique or 525-7073 under plus-two. In either case, the newly formed number might or might not be in the telephone directory and it might or might not actually have been assigned to a household, so that some numbers will certainly be dead. However, since the root of each number was actually assigned and listed number, the chances that the plus-one number is in working order is much higher than it is for the random digit dialling process. This procedure will get around the problem of unlisted numbers and newly assigned numbers, except for those in new exchanges.

Street directories are used extensively in cluster sampling or for constructing sampling frames for particular areas of a city. *Mights Directory* for Metro Toronto and *Vernon's Directory* for Hamilton are two that might be very helpful to those who perform the sampling function. These directories list names, addresses, telephone numbers, and sometimes occupations and household sizes, on a street-by-street basis. For industrial marketing research, *Scott's Directory of Manufacturing* and the business directory developed by the local chamber of commerce or board of trade can be very helpful. There are many trade association and professional association directories that can also be very useful.

QUOTAS

Many marketing research projects require certain quotas of sample respondents to be satisfied. These may involve equal numbers of males and females or a specified number who earn above or below $50 000 to coincide with a stratification requirement. When these quotas are specified, a set of screening or filtering questions must be used at the beginning of the questionnaire to identify which category the respondent falls into. The tallies of group membership are kept and checked on a regular basis. Towards the end of the fieldwork, the tally sheet is referred to frequently in order to determine whether any quotas have been filled and require no more respondents. (Actually, during the beginning of the fieldwork, the tally might be kept based on the information contained in the questionnaire without resorting to screening questions. However, as the end is approached it will become necessary to screen on some characteristics in order to avoid over-satisfying the quota needs.)

STANDARD ERROR CALCULATIONS FOR COMPLEX DESIGNS

REPLICATED SUB-SAMPLES

In any of the complex sample designs, standard error calculations are a major computational problem. Replicated sampling is a procedure that simplifies this problem somewhat. The concept behind replicated sampling is quite straightforward. Instead of taking a simple random sample of 1000 people from Metropolitan Toronto, two unrelated simple random samples of 500 people each are drawn, or four samples of 250 each, or five of 200 each, or whatever number is desired.

Replicated sampling can be used with any sample design, whether simple random sampling, stratified sampling, cluster sampling or any variation of multistage sampling. The important characteristic is that the samples are drawn in the same methodological manner and are not interrelated.

The standard error calculation is addressed via the comparison of the sub-sample statistics. Summary statistics are calculated for each of the sub-samples. Then the variation among the sub-sample statistics is used to estimate the overall variation. The detailed calculations will not be presented here, but the interested reader is referred to Moser and Kalton (1971) and Deming (1960).

DESIGN EFFECTS (DESIGN FACTORS)

Some researchers carry out statistical testing as if the rules for random selection and subsequent use of statistical inference were met. However, caution should be used when performing statistical tests of significance and other tests that rely on sampling errors. The procedures used in texts on statistics and survey research often discuss significance tests assuming that the sampling is done in a simple random unrestricted manner. This is often not the case in survey practice.

The sampling error varies depending on the design of the sampling. For example, the variance of a simple random sample might be less than that of a multistage sample of the same size. The variance of a cluster sample might be greater than the variance of a stratified sample of the same size. If these variations exist and if the statistical tests of significance are executed as if simple random samples are taken, then major mistakes can result if adjustments are not made.

The precise formulas for standard errors of sampling distributions when complex sampling is used are quite complicated and tedious to execute in most situations. A procedure which has been recognized as a viable compromise between using the typically incorrect standard error assuming simple random sampling and the complicated formulas when complex sampling designs are used involves the use of what is called *design effects* or *design factors*. This process involves the calculation of the appropriate standard errors for a small range of the results, the calculation of the design effects for these results and the adjustment of the standard errors over the remaining range by the average of those design effects (Moser and Kalton, 1971).

For example, suppose that a complex multistage design were to be used that might involve cluster sampling and stratified sampling. The formulas for calculating the standard errors for such a design are quite complicated and the calculations are difficult. As a short cut to the complete calculations, the simpler standard error assuming that the same sample size were drawn in a simple random fashion is used. In its simplest form, the design effect is calculated as

$$\text{design effect} = (\text{design factor})^2$$

$$= \frac{\text{variance of sampling distribution for complex sample design}}{\text{variance of sampling distribution for simple random sample}}$$

or,

design effect

$$= \frac{(\text{standard error of sampling distribution for complex sample design})^2}{(\text{standard error of sampling distribution for simple random sample})^2}$$

The calculation of the design effect using the formulas above would be done after sampling to establish the design effect benchmarks. The design effect can then be used to adjust the simple random sampling result to the estimate of the complex design variance by using the formula as

$$\begin{matrix} \text{variance of sampling distribution} \\ \text{for complex sample design} \end{matrix} = \text{design effect} \times \begin{matrix} \text{variance of sampling distribution} \\ \text{for simple random sample} \end{matrix}$$

$$\begin{matrix} \text{standard error for complex} \\ \text{sample design} \end{matrix} = \text{design factor} \times \begin{matrix} \text{standard error for simple random} \\ \text{sample} \end{matrix}$$

Since the design effect is commonly greater than one, significance tests performed incorrectly using the variance assuming a simple random sample had been taken might incorrectly indicate significant differences, while if the correct but larger standard error were used then the difference would be found not to be significant. When actually performing the statistical testing, a design factor is often used. The influence of these design factors or design effects should be included in the testing through adjustment of the variances. This is particularly true of complicated designs such as stratified sampling, cluster sampling and, particularly, multistage sampling. In these cases, the standard error might be increased by a design factor of 1.5 or 2.0 (Worcester and Downham, 1986:347). These factors are in many cases arbitrary coefficients that have developed acceptance through usage.

Lydall (1955) presented the findings for the standard errors for several measures of the National Savings Survey of the Oxford Institute of Statistics. These showed that the design factors ($\sqrt{\text{deff}}$) were all greater than 1.00, in fact all in the range of 1.00 to 1.50.

The design factor is also used for estimating standard errors for higher level statistical parameters, such as regression coefficients and partial and multiple correlation coefficients. Kish and Frankel (1968) showed, based on five studies, that the $\sqrt{\text{deff}}$ (i.e., the design factor) for regression coefficients was 1.06 compared to 1.17 for means. The point of their exposition was that, even though the design effects vary, they are not negligible and their use in adjusting the standard error obtained in the more basic simple random sampling case is necessary so that the standard error for the more complicated designs is not underestimated.

BASIC USE OF THE DESIGN EFFECT   As was seen earlier, the simplest formula for determining the sample size for estimating the mean is derived from:

$$\text{Precision} = z_\alpha s_{\bar{x}} = z_\alpha \frac{s_x}{\sqrt{n}} = e$$

where $s_{\bar{x}}$ is the standard error of the complex design and s_x is the standard deviation of the complex design, z is the confidence and e is the precision or error or half-width of the confidence interval. Solving for the sample size, n, we get

$$n = \frac{z_\alpha^2 s_x^2}{e^2}$$

Since the calculations for the variance of the sampling distribution of the complex design would be very complicated to produce, the task is made somewhat simpler by estimating the variance of the simple random sample of the same size drawn from the population. The design effect is then used to adjust (usually increase) the variance for the simple random sample and then to obtain the sample size value.

$$n = \frac{z_\alpha^2}{e^2} s_x^2 = \frac{z_\alpha^2}{e^2} \text{deff } s_{srs}^2$$

Of course, since the deff is usually greater than one, the sample will be somewhat larger than will the sample drawn in a simple random unrestricted manner.

THE DESIGN EFFECT AND STRATIFIED SAMPLING   The design effect is proportional to the ratio of the sampling variance for the complex design to the sampling variance for a simple random sample of the same size. Essentially, simple random sampling is used as a benchmark against which to compare supposedly more efficient sample designs. For example, if the standard error for a simple random sample of 400 cases is 0.4562 and the standard error for a proportionate stratified random sample is 0.4437, then the design effect or deff is

$$\text{deff} = \frac{(0.4437)^2}{(0.4562)^2} = 0.9459$$

which means that the variance of the stratified sample is about 5.4% smaller than that of the same-sized simple random sample. This would indicate, of course, that the stratified design is more statistically efficient because of its smaller standard error.

The formula can also be used to indicate that to obtain precision from a simple random sample that's equivalent to the precision obtainable from the stratified sample of size 400, a sample of size 423 (i.e., 400/0.9459) is needed.

Since these design effects can be calculated only at the end of a study, their value is for planning future studies once the benchmark of the current study has been established.

THE DESIGN EFFECT AND QUOTA SAMPLING   In situations such as quota sampling, it is not possible to calculate sampling errors and perform traditional statistical testing because of the non-random manner in which the sample is drawn.

As an example, we'll introduce one additional concept, that of the homogeneity within cluster samples. A standard measure of this homogeneity is rho (ρ), a measure which has characteristics similar to those of the correlation coefficient. Rho ranges from -1 to $+1$, where 0 means that the heterogeneity within the cluster is equivalent to what it would be under random allocation of objects to the clusters, and $+1$ and -1 mean that there is perfect homogeneity within the cluster. (Negative values of rho are rarely observed in practice.) It's quite natural to have smaller clusters with substantial homogeneity while as the size of the cluster increase, it's typical that it becomes more diverse, i.e., more heterogeneous. Although it's possible to conduct a pilot sample to calculate rho, it is more typical that rho is established based on a full survey and then used in subsequent studies.

In stratification, the aim is to make each of the groups, i.e., each stratum, as homogeneous as possible internally. However, in cluster sampling the opposite is true. The intention is to make each cluster as diverse as the parent population. In fact, each cluster should be a micro-population similar to the parent.

The design factor can be related to the heterogeneity of the cluster, ρ, through a formula developed by Hansen, Hurwitz and Madow (1953),

$$\frac{s^2_{\bar{x} \text{ cluster}}}{s^2_{\bar{x} \text{ simple random}}} = 1 + \rho(\bar{n} - 1) = \text{design effect}$$

or

$$\frac{s_{\bar{x} \text{ cluster}}}{s_{\bar{x} \text{ simple random}}} = \sqrt{1 + \rho(\bar{n} - 1)} = \text{design factor}$$

where n is the average size of the sample from each cluster and the variances are those of the sampling distributions.

These design effects can be used in two ways. One is to estimate the variance of the cluster sample if the variance of the related simple random sample is known. The second is to estimate the size of the sample in situations where the design factors have been established. From the first equation above, the variance of the cluster can be estimated as

$$s^2_{\bar{x} \text{ cluster}} = s^2_{\bar{x} \text{ simple random}} \left[1 + \rho(\bar{n} - 1)\right]$$

or,

$$s^2_{\bar{x} \text{ cluster}} = s^2_{\bar{x} \text{ simple random}} \times \text{design factor}$$

When the homogeneity coefficient ρ, the variance of the sampling distribution for simple random sampling and the average cluster sample size are known, the variance for the cluster can be estimated.

SUMMARY

This chapter has presented the topic of sampling from a perspective meant to broaden and deepen the sampling knowledge which readers would have attained by studying Chapter 14. In particular the topic of sample size was handled in a fair bit of detail. Sample size calculation procedures were presented for:

• Cross-tabulation requirements
• Budget-based methods
• Estimating the true population mean of a variable
• Estimating the true population proportion of a variable
• Testing hypotheses about the population mean of a variable
• Testing hypotheses about the population proportion of a variable

Topics associated with the above sample-size calculation problems were also addressed. These include:

• The effect of the population size on the size of the sample, i.e., the finite population corrector
• Replicated samples
• The weighting of findings from disproportionate stratified sampling
• The use of the design effect for adjusting sample variances

In order to present the procedures for calculating the sample size, it was necessary to provide background information on the nature of the normal distribution, the sampling distribution, the standard error, and statistical inference. This was presented for both continuous distributions (interval and ratio scaled data) and for discrete distributions (nominal and ordinal data). This material will be essential for understanding the material presented in Chapter 22 and Chapter 23.

NOW THINK ABOUT THIS

1. Why is it important to consider the sample size prior to performing cross-tabulations?

2. Specify in detail the difference between the standard deviation of the distribution of observations and the standard deviation of the distribution of sample averages. What are the other names for the standard deviation of the distribution of sample averages?

3. What's the value of design factors in practical marketing research?

4. Why are the row with the smallest marginal relative frequency and the column with the smallest marginal relative frequency used when calculating the sample size in performing cross-tabulations?

5. Is the standard error usually smaller or larger than the corresponding standard deviation for a given distribution?

6. What's the primary reason why sample size calculations are usually somewhat easier when estimating population proportions than when estimating population means?

7. Give three examples of situations in which it would be preferable to take disproportionate stratified samples rather than proportionate stratified samples.

REFERENCES

Bryant, Barbara E.
1975 "Respondent Selection in a Time of Changing Household Composition." *Journal of Marketing Research*, May, 129-35.

Deming, W.E.
1960 *Sample Design in Business Research*. New York: Wiley.

Hansen, Morris W., William N. Hurwitz, and William G. Madow
1952 *Sample Survey Methods and Theory*. 2 vols. New York: Wiley.

Kish, L., and M.R. Frankel
1968 "Balanced Repeated Replications for Analytical Statistics." *Proceedings of the Social Statistics Section*, American Statistical Association, 2-10.

Lydall, H.F.
1955 *British Incomes and Savings*. Blackwell, Oxford: University of Oxford, Institute of Statistics, Monograph No.5.

Moser, C.A., and G. Kalton
1971 *Survey Methods in Social Investigation*. 2nd ed. London: Heinemann Educational Books Ltd.

Som, Ranjan Kumar
1973 *A Manual of Sampling Techniques* London: Heinemann Educational Books Ltd.

Sudman, Seymour
1975 *Applied Sampling*. New York: Academic Press.

Troldahl, Verling C., and Roy E. Carter, Jr.
1964 "Random Selection of Respondents within Households in Phone Surveys." *Journal of Marketing Research*, 1, May, 73.

Worcester, Robert, and John Downham
1986 *Consumer Market Research Handbook*. 3rd rev. ed. Amsterdam: North-Holland, p.347.

APPENDIX 21A

Sampling for the 1990 NADbank Study

INTRODUCTION

The Newspaper Audience Data Bank (NADbank) is initiated and funded by Daily Newspaper members of the Newspaper Marketing Bureau, Inc. (NMB). The overall objectives of this research are to:

- Provide a reliable survey measurement of Canadian daily newspaper audiences on a market-by-market basis
- Provide information on consumer behaviour, such as shopping, product usage, travel, leisure activities, etc.

The NADbank '90 survey employed a single measurement technique, telephone interviewing. The 1990 survey comprised a full sample comparable in size to earlier NADbank studies. The NADbank '90 data were collected using Canadian Facts' nationally integrated interviewing system, probably one of the largest computer-supported telephone interviewing systems in the world. With this system, all functions other than the asking of the questions and recording of the answers are controlled by computer. Sample management, sequence presentation, handling of recalls and appointments, and sequence of questions were electronically managed in the NADbank'90 survey.

OBJECTIVES

The specific objectives of the NADbank '90 survey were to provide information on the following:

- Average issue audience and reader characteristics of measured newspapers

- Duplication of average issue audiences between measured newspaper editions
- Cumulative readership of measured newspaper editions over a series of issues
- Information on receipt and place of reading for each measured newspaper
- Time spent reading daily newspapers
- Audience and reader characteristics of measured television listing publications
- Readership of sections, features or pages of special interest in a newspaper
- General newspaper reader patterns
- Exposure to other media
- Retail shopping habits
- Product usage and purchasing or ownership habits
- Social activities and attitudes

SAMPLING

SAMPLE UNIVERSE

The universe for this study was defined as all individuals 18 years of age and older, residing in private households with access to telephones, within each of the following specified CMA (census metropolitan area), CA (census area) and other geographically defined markets.

Moncton	CA
Saint John	CMA
Chicoutimi/Jonquière	CMA
Trois Rivières/Shawinigan	CMA/CA
Québec City	CMA
Granby	CA
Sherbrooke	CA
Montréal	CMA
Ottawa/Hull	CMA
Kingston	CA
Toronto	CMA
North Bay	CA
Kitchener	CMA
Owen Sound-Grey Bruce Area	CA/Counties

St. Catharines	CMA
Hamilton	CMA
Brantford	CA
London	CMA
Windsor	CMA
Sault Ste. Marie	CA
Winnipeg	CMA
Regina	CMA
Saskatoon	CMA
Calgary	CMA
Medicine Hat	CA
Edmonton	CMA
Kamloops	CA
Red Deer	CA
Prince George	CA
Vancouver	CMA
Victoria	CMA

Sample Method

The sample design specified was the Random Dialling (RDD) method. A random probability sample using RDD sample methods requires that

- Each exchange has an equal probability
- Each household with a telephone has an equal probability
- Each individual has a probability of the inverse of the number of qualifying people resident in the household

Sampling Operations

The following steps were undertaken in the preparation of the NADbank '90 sample:

1. Geographic stratification
2. Preparation of a list of exchanges in each of the defined areas
3. Random generation of telephone numbers using Canadian Facts' RRD (Random Digit Dialling) computer program
4. Daytime pre-screening of numbers to eliminate non-residential and not-in-service numbers

5. Random assignment of screened-in sample to sample streams A through E
6. Within each stream, sample was randomly divided into the five interviewing days (Tuesday to Saturday) and, within each day, the sample was then split into 10 replicates, i.e., similarly selected but separate samples
7. Household contact to determine postal information for flagged exchanges and in the Montréal market, to determine language information for the over-sample of non-French sample requirements
8. Random selection of one particular individual to be interviewed from each household

1. Geographic stratification

In order to facilitate disproportionate regional sampling requirements, the St. Catharines CMA, Owen Sound-Grey Bruce Area, and the Hamilton CMA were each stratified in two groups.

St. Catharines CMA	- St. Catharines CMA - Balance of CMA
Owen Sound-Grey Bruce Area	- Owen Sound CA - Balance of Grey Bruce counties (Excluding the townships of Huron, Kinloss, Culross, Carrick, Normanby, Egremont and Proton.)
Hamilton CMA	- Burlington Census Subdivision - Balance of Hamilton CMA

The Ottawa/Hull CMA and the Trois Rivières/Shawinigan CMA/CA were also geographically stratified prior to selection. For these two markets, sampling was on a proportionate basis. The strata were as follows:

Ottawa/Hull CMA	- Ottawa - Hull
Trois Rivières/Shawinigan CMA/CA	- Trois Rivières CMA - Shawinigan CA

2. Preparation of a list of operant exchanges

Each of the markets was defined in terms of three digit exchanges. As the boundaries of exchanges do not coincide with Statistics Canada boundaries, some exchanges are included that are in part outside the defined CMA, CA or other geographical universe. At the interviewing stage, postal code information was collected. This permitted the matching of postal codes to the area.

Using the Statistics Canada Postal Code Conversion File, the postal code linkage to census enumeration area (EA) was analyzed for each market. This analysis determined that the majority of postal codes can be classified as being inside or outside a market, with the exception of a small number of LDUs (local delivery units). A decision rule was established to exclude all overlapping LDUs whenever the universe coverage achieved without them was at least 98 per cent. With this criterion, the Market Area Screening program was able to screen approximately 95 per cent of households contacted using the postal code identification. For the remaining 5 per cent, classification was based on geographic location, as determined by questioning the respondent.

3. Creation of telephone numbers

Using the listed exchanges (3 digit prefix), random digit suffixes were generated by computer.

4. Pre-screening of gross sample

The gross samples were then pre-screened in order to eliminate the not-in-service and non-residential numbers. The gross sample was assigned to interviewing staff who made one daytime call to each number creating an initial net frame.

5. Random assignment of screened-in sample to sample streams A through E

The sample which was screened was then randomly allocated to each of the five sample streams, labelled A, B, C, D and E, of the study.

6. Sample assignment

The sample of screened-in telephone numbers was generated in five sample streams which in turn were allocated to five equal sub-samples for day-of-week control. Within each interviewing day, the sample was divided into replicates. The computer system controlled the presentation of the sample in terms of day-of-week recalls.

7. Postal code and language screening

Numbers pre-identified as requiring a special postal check were screened at the household contact stage.

In the Montréal CMA, there was a requirement for an over-sampling of "non-French." For the over-sample survey, households were screened at the household contact stage for "non-French" eligibility. Home language (language most often spoken in the home) was used to define "non-French." In areas where French and other languages were both used in the home, non-French was determined on the basis of mother tongue. If necessary, the language of interview was ultimately used to classify the respondent if such was not possible with the use of either home language or mother tongue.

8. Respondent selection

The recent birthday method was used to randomly select the one individual 18 years and over to be interviewed. No substitutions were permitted.

DATA COLLECTION

Interviewing Schedule

To make the interviewing logistically more manageable, the sample was divided into five sample streams, A through E. The calling pattern for each sample stream was staggered so that calling was started four weeks apart. Stream A started calling in week 1, stream B started in week 4, stream C started in week 8, and so on.

Interviewing Period

Interviewing commenced in all markets on Tuesday, January 23, 1990. The last interviewing day was July 10, 1990.

INTERVIEWING LOCATIONS

Ten CLTs (Central Location Telephone interviewing banks) were available for this study. Individual markets were assigned to a specific CLT according to proximity and capacity.

TRAINING PROCEDURES

All field supervisory and interviewing staff received extensive training prior to the start of data collection. A field manual was developed specifically for NADbank'90 by the project team. The manual was provided to each supervisor, monitor and interviewer working on the study prior to the formal field briefings.

The briefing/training session, in which all field personnel participated, covered the following activities

- An overall explanation of the study
- A detailed (page-by-page) review of the field manual with specific emphasis on the schedule

- The study design
- Household and respondent selection procedures
- Recording call outcomes
- The importance of minimizing refusals
- Monitoring procedures
- Questionnaire content
- Commonly asked respondent questions
- Mock interviews
- Daily reporting requirements

The NADbank field team was composed of approximately 250 staff, of whom about half worked on any given day.

FIELD EFFORT

Throughout the field period, all active telephone numbers were continuously dialled the maximum number of times. It is estimated that close to 600 000 calls were made.

A number was deactivated if it met any of the following eight conditions:

1. It was not in service.
2. It was non-residential number.
3. It was determined to be located outside the defined geographic area.
4. It was defined as a completed interview.
5. After the household/respondent had refused participation on four separate occasions. (All households and respondent refusals were treated as a separate survey and as such were assigned to a specially trained sub-group of interviewers in each CLT office. Every effort was made to complete an interview upon the initial contact. However, if this was not possible, then the refusal team was assigned the household.)
6. After encountering a language problem with different people within a selected household on four separate occasions. (Bilingual interviewers were used for the Montréal and Ottawa/Hull markets. In all other Québec markets, only French interviewers were used and in all other markets only English language interviews were accepted. When language problems were encountered, numerous attempts were made to speak with another household member in order to identify the eligible respondent and conduct an interview.)
7. If the chosen respondent was unavailable throughout the entire field period.
8. After a number had a minimum of 15 consecutive non-contact attempts across at least 10 weeks and on each sample day.

QUALITY CONTROL

Throughout the entire field period, stringent quality control procedures were continuously administered to ensure that the highest possible standards were met. In addition to the increased control the computer network provides to the telephone interviewing and sample management, the following control procedures were also operational:

- A continuous monitoring ratio of one to eight
- An overall supervisory ratio of just over one to six
- Daily verbal and electronic communication between each CLT and the national field controller
- Daily monitoring by the project team of the previous night's activity Periodic review of completions to date through the use of FACTS topline reports
- Daily meetings of the project team to review progress
- Periodic field visits to the CLT offices by members of the project team

CALL PLAN

The specifications required as equal a balance as possible of interviews by day of week during the survey period. To accommodate this objective, the calling conformed to a specified pattern. The call plan pattern provided in the NADbank specification is presented below.

Five equal sub-samples of random digit telephone numbers were created prior to commencing any fieldwork and were designated as "Tuesday," "Wednesday," "Thursday," "Friday," and "Saturday" samples for initial interviewing.

For the first four weeks, each day's sample was treated as belonging to a different universe. For example, a respondent from the sample designated for Tuesday was interviewed only on Tuesday should be interviewed on Tuesday unless a specific call-back time or another interviewing day is requested by the designated respondent.

For the fifth and sixth week, telephone interviews were moved one day forward (i.e., interviews designated for Tuesday were moved to Wednesday) if no prior contact with the designated respondent was established. From the seventh week, interviews were obtained on any day to achieve an equal total number of interviews in respect of each day of the week to permit an estimation of average issue weekday audiences.

Starting in the middle of the second or third week, as discretion dictated, attempts were made to recontact refusals and language problems on the "designated day plus one." After the fourth week, these too were opened up to dialling at any possible time.

The only exception to this design involved "callbacks at definite times on specific dates." From the beginning, these were attempted as arranged.

Every eligible number was to be dialled within the first two weeks.

With the exception of stream E, all issued telephone numbers adhered to the aforementioned call plan. In stream E, all numbers were released for dialling on any designated day one week earlier than specified. This change was made in order to maximize the interviewing effort in the final few weeks of the fieldwork.

ASCRIPTION AND WEIGHTING

In the event that information was missing, and the correct response could not be inferred from other data, the questionnaire was either rejected or a "not stated" category was assigned depending on the question. No inferences were permitted on any key readership questions relating to average issue readership or cume measures. In terms of eligible break-offs, all missing data were assigned a not stated category from the point of the break-off.

ASCRIPTION

Ascription is a mathematical technique used to achieve a complete data set. The application of the technique permits the projection of a sample to its universe without the application of weighting procedures that are different from those used in the main analysis. The technique ascribes missing data by assigning responses from a donor respondent to a recipient respondent with similar characteristics.

As in most other surveys, the most frequently refused question of importance is that concerning income. In order to provide meaningful projections on income (household and personal) all missing data within the two variables were ascribed. Within each market, Canadian Facts' ascription procedure matched respondents with similar characteristics and transferred the responses from donors to recipients. In situations where a match was not possible within a market, the recipient respondent was matched with a national donor. The variables used in the ascription model are as follows:

Household income
- Gender
- Occupation of head of household (within gender)

- Number of contributors to household income
- Age (within number of contributors)
- Average household income
- Average personal income (used as a control to ensure a respondent was not ascribed a household income that was less than his/her personal income)

Personal income
- Gender
- Occupation of respondent (within gender)
- Age
- Average personal income
- Average household income (used as a control to ensure a respondent was not ascribed a personal income that was greater than his/her household income)

Ascription was achieved by first calculating an average income for each respondent in a given market. This average was calculated using the midpoints. Three tables were then produced based on respondents with stated household incomes (i.e., Tables A, B and C). If a respondent did not state an income, an average income was assigned according to the matching attributes in Table A. If a respondent stated that his or her income was under or over $30 000 but refused to elaborate, an average income was assigned according to the matching attributes in Tables B or C accordingly.

If it was not possible to ascribe an income from the market tables, then the national tables were used to make a match. In the few cases where a match was not possible using all of the variables, then an estimate was made based on the limited information available. In no case was an income randomly assigned.

WEIGHTING PROCEDURES

Three basic weight schemes are applied to the data, household weighting, household conversion weighting, and individual weighting.

HOUSEHOLD WEIGHTING

The first level of weighting is applied to bring different sized households (within geographic area and language group in some markets) into proportion according to Statistics Canada 1986 household census data. The household weighting takes the form of size of household, within day of week, within geographic area or language. The day-of-week weighting brings into equal balance the Tuesday to Saturday sub-samples. The language groupings are defined as French and non-French. Home language is the variable used to define French and non-French. In cases where French and another language are both used in the home, assignment of language is determined on the basis of mother tongue. Individuals whose mother tongue is French and another language are assigned according to language of interview.

The household size groups were:

1 person
2 persons
3 persons
4 or more persons

Household weighting within day of week is applied within each CMA/CA market in total, except in the following cases:

1. Trois Rivières/Shawinigan CMA/CA—Trois Rivières CMA and Shawinigan CA weighted separately.
2. Montréal CMA—French, non-French.
3. Ottawa/Hull CMA—Ottawa and Hull weighted separately.
4. Owen Sound-Grey Bruce Area—Owen Sound CA and balance of Counties weighted separately.
5. St. Catharines CMA—St. Catharines CMA and balance of CMA weighted separately.
6. Hamilton CMA—Burlington and balance of Hamilton CMA weighted separately.

HOUSEHOLD CONVERSION WEIGHTING

Conversion of the household weighting constitutes the second level of weighting. This weighting adjusts for the fact that only one individual per household was interviewed. Design weights (inversely proportionate to the probability of being selected) are applied to correct the different chances of selection.

INDIVIDUAL WEIGHTING

After the conversion weights are applied, additional weighting is applied to correct for differential response rates across various age, sex, geographic and language groups within day of week. The age and sex groups were:

Males:

> 18-24 years
> 25-34 years
> 35-49 years
> 50-64 years
> 65 years and over

Females:

> 18-24 years
> 25-34 years
> 35-49 years
> 50-64 years
> 65 years and over

A language grouping applied only to the following markets:

1. Ottawa/Hull CMA—French, non-French
2. Montréal CMA—French, non-French

A geographic grouping applied only to the following markets:

1. Owen Sound-Grey Bruce Area—Owen Sound CA and balance of counties weighted separately.
2. St. Catharines CMA—St. Catharines CMA and balance of CMA weighted separately.
3. Hamilton CMA—Burlington and balance of Hamilton CMA weighted separately.

These various age, sex, and language groups within day of week are brought into proportion according to updated estimates of the latest Statistics Canada population counts. The population projections and adjustment weighting are carried out as one step.

POPULATION PROJECTION ESTIMATES—JUNE 1990

Population estimates were developed using the following sources:

1. 1986 Census estimates of population-age within sex within language.
2. 1989 post-census estimates for total market population counts and provincial sex and age detail updated to June 1990 assuming a growth factor similar to the previous year.

All projections are reported to the nearest hundred.

22/Statistical Analysis

- How to decide which statistical procedure to use when confronted with a research question and a set of data
- How to perform the calculations and to reach a conclusion
- How to analyze nominal and ordinal data using chi-square tests, asymmetric lambda, Z-tests, Mann-Whitney test, Kruskal-Wallis test, Friedman test, Kolmogorov-Smirnov test and Spearman Correlation
- How to analyze interval and ratio data using t-tests and analysis of variance

CHAPTER OVERVIEW

The statistical analysis techniques illustrated in this chapter are not exhaustive in their scope. This chapter presents those procedures that are used most often commercially in the analysis of marketing research data. The appendix to this chapter presents several techniques that are used less often but may be helpful in some situations. Although the presentation in this chapter is relatively basic, it's presumed that the reader has had a prior course in basic probability and statistics.

THE NATURE OF DATA

Chapters 9 through 14 introduced the basic ways of presenting and analyzing data for ease of understanding and for communicating that information to others. It's vital to understand the principles of those chapters before embarking on the trail of statistically analyzing the data. Statistical analysis of data which are not first understood is useless and expensive. The following quotation puts the data interpretation/statistical analysis problem in perspective.

Blind Data

Data leads a double life. Sometimes it's for analysis, sometimes it's for presentation. Although these two kinds of data may be similar, they're not quite the same—like identical cousins.

Data for analysis has an audience of one: the person looking at it. Data for presentation has an audience of many: all the people whom the analyst expects to see it.

Data for analysis is best when it's pared down to numbers and shapes alone; most of the context—the information about the information—is carried in the analyst's head. The analyst is looking for patterns, and patterns are obscured by detail. The patterns might be linear trends, three-dimensional shapes, clusters, or any of a dozen other types. The analyst must be prepared to find any one of them. After she has found a pattern, though, she must look at the elements in the data that cause the pattern, and discover whether the pattern is real and interesting. At this point, all the background information must be available to make the pattern's meaning clear.

The good analyst carries out most of the background information in her mind, and uses it to test the patterns as she analyzes. The situation for presentation is the reverse. All the relevant information must be instantly available. A person looking at the data from a new context must be able to see what it means before she can do anything with it. That means that all the information necessary to understand the data must be printed right there on the page with the data, or must be immediately accessible from the screen that is displaying the data.

And data presentation is not limited to presentation to other people: You may want to look at the data yourself in six months, and there's a good chance you won't remember what you did. Which means that when you're storing data, you must also store information about the data.

Here are a few tips to help you with each half of data's split personality.

For analysis:

- Many different programs exist to help analyze data. Few of them give you a chance to understand the background of the data. Always find out as much as you can about who collected the data, where it was collected, what time period it covers, what was studied, and what the viewpoint of the data collector was. If you have a different data set you can compare with the one you're using, do so; tracking down the reasons the two sets differ will give you valuable insight into what your data set means. And you can often find errors that might have thrown your analysis off. For example, using data collected once a year to project weekly trends is a no-no.

- Once you have all the information in your mind, use a program that lets you hide as much of it as possible. Programs generally let you put the information back in as necessary, but you need to keep from distracting yourself with preconceptions.

- Consider what techniques you want to use depending on what data you have. John W. Tukey's techniques of exploratory data analysis are helpful if you don't know where to start. Let the data tell you what it shows.

For presentation:

- Put all the information you can into the display. Always remember that tables and graphs get copied out of context. If you want to convey information, it must be present in the output.

- Remember your audience. Someone is going to read this, even if it's only your boss. The presentation must be aimed at somebody.

- Avoid the "Eureka!" problem. The display you see the answer in for the first time will probably not convey that answer to others who have not looked at all the earlier displays you have generated. Think carefully about the best way to show what you discovered and then use that method. In general, tables are good for quantitative results, charts and graphs for qualitative.

- Always think about what you would have wanted to know about the data before you started analyzing it, and make sure that information is available to those who are going to follow your analysis.

SOURCE: Reprinted from MacUser , December 1988. Copyright ©1988, Ziff Communications Company

DATA SCALES

In order to analyze survey research data statistically, the right statistical techniques must be used. To decide which methods to use, the type of data must be determined. This task is sometimes referred to as *identifying the information content of the data*. There are basically four levels of information content, nominal, ordinal, interval and ratio. It's quite common to classify the first two as discrete data and the second two as continuous data. Examples of the four levels are presented in Exhibit 22.1. The examples are from a questionnaire conducted for Firestone Canada in 1981, and are used with permission.

Exhibit 22.1   Scales of Measurement for Data Analysis

Nominal Data

Who decided where the car should go for this most recent service or purchase?

[ ] 1 I DID

[ ] 2 ANOTHER HOUSEHOLD MEMBER DID

[ ] 3 A FAMILY MEMBER WHO DOES NOT LIVE IN MY HOME DID

[ ] 4 SOMEONE OUTSIDE OF MY IMMEDIATE HOUSEHOLD AND FAMILY DID

Ordinal Data

4. Please write in the spaces below the most important reasons why you answered the way you did to Question 3 just above.

First most important reason _____

Second most important reason _____

Third most important reason _____

Interval Data (or often treated as such, although might not meet strict requirements

How important is having a source of automotive service which	*Extremely Important* 5	*Very Important* 4	*Important* 3	*Slightly Important* 2	*Of No Importance* 1
...allows you to talk to the mechanic?	[ ]	[ ]	[ ]	[ ]	[ ]

Ratio Data

Would you please write the <u>approximate cost</u> of this service or purchase on the line following?

$ _____.__

DATA ANALYSIS PROBLEMS AND SOLUTION PROCEDURES

WERE EACH OF THE ANSWERS GIVEN BY ABOUT THE SAME NUMBER OF PEOPLE?

In a mail survey which was conducted for Firestone Canada Inc. in 1981, the following question was asked:

In the past, did <u>you</u> ever experience the situation where your car was serviced incorrectly by <u>any</u> automotive service outlet?

[ ] 1 NO ················ > GO TO SECTION 3 ON THE NEXT PAGE.

[ ] 2 YES

|
|···· > What did you do about it the last time it happened?

    [ ] 1 I WENT ELSEWHERE TO HAVE THIS SAME REPAIR DONE AGAIN

    [ ] 2 I FIXED IT MYSELF

    [ ] 3 I DID NOTHING ABOUT IT

    [ ] 4 I COMPLAINED ABOUT IT AND THEY FIXED IT CORRECTLY

    [ ] I COMPLAINED ABOUT IT AND THEY DID NOT FIX IT CORRECTLY

    |····· > [ ] 5 THEN I WENT ELSEWHERE TO HAVE THIS SAME REPAIR DONE AGAIN

    [ ] 6 THEN I FIXED IT MYSELF

The distribution of respondents' answers to the questions are presented in Exhibit 22.2.

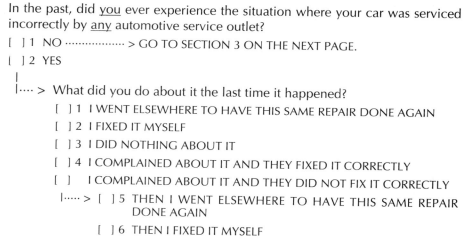

Exhibit 22.2

Q.2-6   What did you do about it (poor automotive service) the last time it happened?

Reaction to Poor Service	Observed From Survey	
	Number	Per cent
Went elsewhere	97	18%
Fixed myself	43	8
Did nothing	16	3
Complained and fixed correctly	279	52
2nd Complaint, then went elsewhere	79	15
2nd Complaint, then I fixed it myself	22	4
Total	536	100%

As discussed in Chapter 10, when presenting data in tables, usually only whole number percentages should be used. In this chapter, tables are often presented containing percentages expressed to one or two decimal positions. This was done so that readers can perform some of the calculations themselves to confirm their understanding of the techniques. Also, the computer programs usually print out the decimal positions.

It's natural for the reader to scan the preceding table and determine the most of the people (52%) said that they "complained about the poor automotive service and that it was then fixed correctly." (The most frequently stated answer is called the *mode*.) The next most frequently reported answer was that the respondent "went elsewhere to have that same repair done again." Since only 18% of the sample gave that second most frequent response, it's easy to conclude in this case that the six possible answers were not equally selected by the 536 respondents.

A quick visual inspection allows us confidently to conclude that the distribution above does not look uniform or random. Although in some cases visual inspection of tabled data shows obvious departures from the uniform distribution, in many situations the frequencies among the answers will be too close for the reader to conclude either that one number stands out from the others or that the distribution is uniform. Consequently, it's necessary to have a standardized statistical procedure that can be used to confirm the visual conclusions reached by the analyst and to help the analyst to reach a conclusion in those cases where the relative frequencies in the table are so close to one another that visual inspection of the table does not lead to a clear statement.

In general, *randomness* in the marketing research context means one of the following:

- that the respondents just didn't care which answers they gave and simply checked off answers randomly;
- that the respondents didn't have any clear preference among the answers and indicated one of several possible answers; or
- that an equal number of the respondents favoured each of the possible answers.

All three cases of randomness cited above lead to the situation where none of the possible answers stands out or takes on a particularly distinctive importance in the table.

THE CHI-SQUARE TEST FOR GOODNESS OF FIT   Before the data in any table can be analyzed, the information content type or type of data must be determined. In the preceding table, the data are nominal, i.e., the answers are simply verbal descriptions of various courses of action that could have been taken by respondents. There was no natural order to the answers. Since the information content of the data in the above example is nominal, then the chi-square test for goodness of fit could be performed on the data. The chi-square test is one of many statistical procedures classified as nonparametric statistical tests.

Nonparametric Statistical Procedures

A statistical method is nonparametric if it satisfies at least one of the following criteria:

1. The method may be used on data with a nominal scale of measurement.
2. The method may be used on data with an ordinal scale of measurement.
3. The method may be used on data with an interval or ratio scale of measurement, where the distribution function of the random variable producing the data is either unspecified or specified except for an infinite [*sic* indefinite] number of unknown parameters.

W.J. Conover, *Practical Nonparametric Statistics*, John Wiley & Sons, 1971.

Good research investigation of data begins with a set of two hypotheses. Each hypothesis is a possible conclusion that might be reached based on the subsequent statistical testing of the data. One set of research hypotheses for the question "What did you do about it (poor automotive service) the last time it happened? is:

The *null hypothesis*:

H_o: Consumer reactions to inadequate automotive service are uniformly distributed among the six categories listed above

The *alternate hypothesis*:

H_a: Consumer responses to inadequate automotive service are not uniformly distributed

As with many statistical tests, the chi-square test for goodness of fit basically determines whether there is a significantly large difference between the *observed* values which were found in the sample and those values which would be *expected* to be found if the null hypothesis of uniformly distributed responses were true.

The first step in the chi-square goodness of fit analysis involves determining what findings would be expected if the null hypothesis were true. In this case, the null hypothesis is that the distribution is uniform. Consequently, we would *expect* that an equal number of the 536 respondents who answered the question would have indicated each of the six possible answers. The expected frequency for each category is then 536 ÷ 6 = 89.33.

The next step in the chi-square test for goodness of fit is to calculate the difference between the frequencies for the answers provided by the respondents and those frequencies that would be expected to occur if the null hypothesis of a uniform distribution of answers were true. (It's very important to realize that the chi-square test is always performed on *frequencies* and never on percentages.) Next, those differences are squared and then the squared differences are divided by the corresponding expected or "if random" frequencies. The last step is to sum all the categories to obtain the total 539.54, which is called the chi-square statistic. The calculations would be as shown in Exhibit 22.3.

The mathematical formula for the chi-square test for goodness of fit is:

$$\chi^2 = \sum_{i=1}^{r} \frac{\left(\text{observed}_i - \text{expected}_i\right)^2}{\text{expected}_i}$$

where r = the number of rows or number of values of the variable

The calculated chi-square statistic 539.54 must then be compared to a critical value, i.e., some benchmark, to decide whether the data follow a random distribution or whether there's a pattern to the responses.

Exhibit 22.3

Q. 2-6   What did you do about it (poor automotive service) the last time it happened?

Reaction to Poor Service	Observed From Survey		Expected If Random	Difference	Difference Squared	Difference Squared ÷ 'If Random'
	Number	Percent	Number			
Went elsewhere	97	18%	89.33	7.67	58.82	0.66
Fixed myself	43	8	89.33	−46.33	2146.47	24.03
Did nothing	16	3	89.33	−73.33	5377.29	60.20
Complained and fixed	279	52	89.33	189.67	35974.71	402.72
2nd Complaint went elsewhere	79	15	89.33	−10.33	106.71	1.19
2nd Complaint fixed myself	22	4	89.33	−67.33	4533.33	50.74
Total	536	100%	535.98*			539.54

* Error due to rounding.

The critical chi-square value is 11.07 for a 5% level of risk and five degrees of freedom. The number of degrees of freedom for this test is calculated as the number of categories, 6 here, minus 1, which gives the five degrees of freedom. (The critical values of chi-square are obtained from a table of chi-square values for various numbers of degrees of freedom and for several levels of risk of a Type I error. A Type I error occurs when the null hypothesis is rejected incorrectly, i.e., when it was really not false.) The 5% level of risk is a very commonly used value for hypothesis testing. Although a 10% level of risk is also used often, especially in practice, levels of risk higher than 10% are used much less frequently. This means that if the null hypothesis is rejected when the calculated chi-square is greater than 11.07 (for five degrees of freedom), then there is a 5% risk that the conclusion is incorrect. In other words, concluding that the responses to the six answers in the above example are not uniform might be wrong. However, there is only a 5% risk (at most) that the distribution would, in fact, be uniform when the data produced a chi-square statistic of 11.07. Since the calculated chi-square of 539.54 is so much greater than 11.07, the risk of incorrectly rejecting the null hypothesis is very close to zero. (The number of degrees of freedom is calculated as the number of categories minus one, i.e., df = 6 − 1 = 5.)

The chi-square test for goodness of fit can be applied to a wide range of data. Regardless of the information content of the data, i.e., nominal, ordinal, interval or ratio, the chi-square test can be performed. However, using the chi-square test on higher level data, i.e., ordinal, interval or ratio data, might not extract the full amount of information from those data. Consequently, the analyst should always be searching for the most effective test to use with a certain type of data.

IS THERE ANY RELATIONSHIP BETWEEN TWO VARIABLES?

One of the most common actions in the analysis of survey data is to present the data in a table called a cross-tab. The purpose of cross-tabulating data is often to present the distribution of the values of a particularly important variable over two or more divisions or sub-groups of the sample. For example, it might be of interest to investigate whether the values of one nominal variable are the same or different between men and women, or among several income groups, or among several groups describing the levels of consumption of a product.

In addition to the benefit of being able to present a table of data, it's necessary to test statistically whether the two variables composing the tables are related to one another. Assuming that the data have only nominal properties, the chi-square test of independence would be the correct procedure to follow.

THE CHI-SQUARE TEST OF INDEPENDENCE   Suppose that Firestone wanted to investigate whether men and women react differently to the situation in which their cars are serviced incorrectly. Taking the table presented earlier and breaking the sample into two groups, men and women, provides the frequency table in Exhibit 22.4 followed by the table of column per cents. In this case, we could be asking whether a person's reaction to poor automotive service might be related to the person's gender. There would be an implication that the variable "reaction to poor service" might be the dependent variable (or effect) and the "gender" is the independent variable (or the cause or influencing factor). Notice in the second table in Exhibit 22.4 that the per cents are being added across the values of the dependent variable for each of the two groups.

Exhibit 22.4

Q. 2-6   What did you do about it (poor automotive service) the last time it happened?

Consumer's Reaction to Poor Automotive Service Broken Down by Gender (Frequencies)

Reaction to Poor Service	Gender		Total
	Male	Female	
Went elsewhere	65	30	95
Fixed it myself	31	11	42
Did nothing about it	11	5	16
Complained and they fixed it	201	70	271
2nd Complaint/went elsewhere	55	23	78
2nd Complaint/fixed myself	18	4	22
Total	381	143	524

Consumers' Reaction to Poor Automotive Service Broken Down By Gender (Column Per Cents)

Reaction to Poor Service	Gender		Total
	Male	Female	
Went elsewhere	17%	21%	18%
Fixed it myself	8	8	8
Did nothing about it	3	3	3
Complained and they fixed it	53	49	52
2nd Complaint/went elsewhere	14	16	15
2nd Complaint/fixed myself	5	3	4
Total	100%	100%	100%
Base	381	143	524

"Are the patterns of responses between the two groups the same or different?" is a common but important question to ask of data which are split into groups.

The null and alternate hypotheses pertinent to the above situation are:

H_0: Customers' reaction to poor automotive service and gender are statistically independent

H_a: Customers' reaction to poor automotive service and gender are not statistically independent

The concept of statistical independence has a precise definition in probability. In the context of the example above, statistical independence means that if the null hypothesis were true, then the probability of the joint occurrence of any level of reaction to poor automotive service and either gender group could be calculated according to the following formula:

P(Reaction = i and Gender = j) = P(Reaction = i x P(Gender = j)

where i is used to represent any row of the above table and
j is used to represent any column of the table.

For example

P("Went elsewhere" and "Male") = (95 / 524) x (381 / 524) = (0.1813) x (0.7271)

The expected frequency would then be

P("Went elsewhere" and "Male") x Sample size = 0.1813 x 524 = (95 x 381) / 524 ≈ 69.07

Continuing in this fashion, the remaining expected frequencies in the table in Exhibit 22.5 can be obtained.

Exhibit 22.5   Consumers' Reaction to Poor Automotive Service Broken Down by Gender

Reaction to Poor Service	Observed Frequencies Gender		Expected Frequencies Gender	
	Male	Female	Male	Female
Went elsewhere	65	30	69.07	25.93
Fix it myself	31	11	30.54	11.46
Did nothing about it	11	5	11.63	4.37
Complained and they fixed	201	70	197.04	73.96
2nd Complaint/elsewhere	55	23	56.71	21.29
2nd Complaint/fixed myself	18	4	16.00	6.00
Total	381	143	380.99	143.01

If the null hypothesis of independence were not true, then the formula used above to calculate the expected frequencies would not be correct. The key question is, "Is it reasonable that the observed frequencies could have been produced under the situation proposed by the null hypothesis or are they simply due to random variation?"

The testing procedure is actually quite straightforward. It involves measuring the differences between the actual observed frequencies produced by the sampling and the expected frequencies calculated based on the null hypothesis of statistical independence. The chi-square test of independence may be used to test the assumption of statistical independence.

Exhibit 22.6   Consumers' Reaction to Poor Automotive Service Broken Down by Gender

Reaction to Poor Service	Males Observed – Expected = Diff			Females Observed – Expected = Diff		
Elsewhere	65	– 69.07 =	–4.07	30	– 25.93 =	4.07
Fixed myself	31	– 30.54 =	0.46	11	– 11.46 =	–0.46
Did nothing	11	– 11.63 =	–0.63	5	– 4.37 =	0.63
Complained and fixed	201	–197.04 =	3.96	70	– 73.96 =	–3.96
2nd Complaint/elsewhere	55	– 56.71 =	–1.71	23	– 21.29 =	1.71
2nd Complaint/fixed myself	18	– 16.00 =	2.00	4	– 6.00 =	–2.00

Although a basic feeling for the differences between the observed and expected values can be obtained by scanning the table in Exhibit 22.6 and observing the relatively small values of the differences, a more formal manner of combining the differences is necessary. The chi-square formula typically used is:

$$\chi^2 = \sum_{i=1}^{r}\sum_{j=1}^{c} \frac{\left(\text{observed}_{ij} - \text{expected}_{ij}\right)^2}{\text{expected}_{ij}}$$

where r = the number of rows and c = the number of columns in the table.

$$\chi^2 = \frac{(65-69.07)^2}{69.07} + \frac{(31-30.54)^2}{30.54} + \frac{(11-11.63)^2}{11.63} + \frac{(201-197.04)^2}{197.04} + \frac{(55-56.71)^2}{56.71} + \frac{(18-16)^2}{16} +$$

$$\frac{(30-25.93)^2}{25.93} + \frac{(11-11.46)^2}{11.46} + \frac{(5-4.37)^2}{4.37} + \frac{(70-73.96)^2}{73.96} + \frac{(23-21.29)^2}{21.29} + \frac{(4-6)^2}{6} = 2.433$$

Using the above formula, the chi-square value of 2.433 is obtained. The calculated value of 2.433 must be compared to some critical chi-square value in order to reach a conclusion regarding the null hypothesis, i.e., whether customer reaction to poor automotive service and gender are statistically independent or not. For this example, the tabled critical value of chi-square for a 5% level of risk and for five degrees of freedom [(6 rows -1)] x (2 columns -1)] is 11.07. Since the calculated chi-square statistic of 2.433 is smaller than the critical value of 11.07, the proper conclusion is that customer reaction to poor automotive service is not related to the customer's gender. In other words, regardless of whether a dissatisfied customer is male or female, the reaction to poor automotive service is about the same.

Computer-based statistical packages conduct the above analysis and provide indicators for reaching conclusions regarding the hypotheses. Two popular statistical packages are SPSS and SYSTAT. Theses packages would have returned a p-value, or probability value, of 0.787. This value of 0.787 should be interpreted as the level of risk of incorrectly rejecting the null hypothesis of statistical independence between customer reaction to poor automotive service and gender. Since the maximum level of risk of incorrectly rejecting the null hypothesis is normally set at 5% or 10% and since the analysis indicates that the risk level is 78.7%, the risk is clearly too high and one should not reject the null hypothesis. In other words, the differences evident in the data table could be due to chance alone and cannot be interpreted as evidence of a relationship between the variables under study.

ANOTHER EXAMPLE OF THE CHI-SQUARE TEST OF INDEPENDENCE   As another example, let's investigate a question that was part of a study conducted for Shaklee Canada Inc. in 1986 among a cross-section of Canadians in major urban areas. Shaklee Canada Inc. markets food supplements, household cleaning products and cosmetics under the Shaklee brand name. The intention of the study was to determine whether Canadians' perceived level of health and sense of well-being were influenced by their consumption of vitamins, minerals and other food supplements. Assume for this example that the data have only nominal properties (although we know that they are at least ordinal). Presenting scaled attitude measures in cross-tabs and analyzing the relationships using the chi-square test is a typical first step in data analysis.

One of the important questions asked regarding perceived health improvements was:

Q.3.5   Would you say that brand of food supplement which you just mentioned (AS BEING THE MOST HELPFUL) has had a great improvement, good improvement, moderate improvement, minor improvement or no improvement in your health?

GREAT IMPROVEMENT IN HEALTH	5
GOOD IMPROVEMENT	4
MODERATE IMPROVEMENT	3
MINOR IMPROVEMENT	2
NO IMPROVEMENT AT ALL	1
	104

The table in Exhibit 22.7 cross-tabulates the level of improvement in health which respondents perceived that they enjoyed because of taking a food supplement by usage group membership. The four groups were Shaklee Canada sales leaders, Shaklee food supplement users, those who used other brands of food supplements and those who were non-users of a specific core group of five food supplements.

Exhibit 22.7   Perceived Level of Improvement in Health by Food Supplement Usage Group

Perceived Health Improvement	Shaklee Leaders	Shaklee Users	Other Brands	Non-User	Total
Great	73%	33%	13%	20%	37%
Good	24	34	26	17	28
Moderate	2	20	34	33	20
Minor	0	10	15	22	10
None	1	3	12	8	5
Total	100%	100%	100%	100%	100%
Base	143	165	154	36	498

Since the sales leaders were so dramatically positive and since there were so few of those who were classified as non-users of five specified food supplements, we will concentrate on only two of the groups in the Shaklee study, Shaklee users and users of other brands. Then the question could be asked, "Are the attitudes of these two groups the same with respect to perceived improvement in their health?" (Or, are the distributions for perceived health improvement the same for the two groups?) Now, how can the question be answered? As we've seen above, many of these statistical questions can be answered in more than one way. We shall continue in the same manner as we did above for the Firestone example.

Exhibit 22.8	Observed and Expected Frequencies of Perceived Level of Improvement of Health By Usage Group				
	Observed Frequencies			Expected Frequencies	
Perceived Health Improvement	Shaklee Users	Other Brands	Total	Shaklee Users	Other Brands
Great	55	20	75	38.79	36.21
Good	56	40	96	49.66	46.34
Moderate	32	53	85	43.97	41.03
Minor	17	23	40	20.69	19.31
None	5	18	23	11.90	11.10
Total	165	154	319		

The null and alternate hypotheses pertinent to the situation in Exhibit 22.8 are:

H_o: Perceived health improvement and usage group are statistically independent

H_a: Perceived health improvement and usage group are not statistically independent

If the null hypothesis were true, then the probability of the joint occurrence of any level of health improvement and either usage group could be calculated according to the following formula:

P(Improvement = i and Usage = j) = P(Improvement = i) x P(Usage = j)
where i is used to represent any row of the above table and
j is used to represent any column of the table.

For example,

P (great improvement and Shaklee user) = (75/319) x (165/319)
= (0.2351) x (0.5172)
= 0.1216

The expected frequency would then be

P(great improvement and Shaklee user) x Sample Size
= 0.1216 x 319 ≈ 38.79

Continuing in this fashion, the remaining expected frequencies in Exhibit 22.8 can be obtained. A table of the differences between the observed and expected values is presented in Exhibit 22.9.

Exhibit 22.9 Calculating the Differences between the Actual Observations and the Expected Values

Perceived Health Improvement	Shaklee Users Observed – Expected =		Diff	Other Brands Observed – Expected=		Diff
Great	55 –	38.79 =	16.21	20 –	36.21 =	–16.21
Good	56 –	49.66 =	6.34	40 –	46.34 =	–6.34
Moderate	32 –	43.97 =	–11.97	53 –	41.03 =	11.97
Minor	17 –	20.69 =	–3.69	23 –	19.31 =	3.69
None	5 –	11.90 =	–6.90	18 –	11.10 =	6.90

The chi-square formula for this example is:

$$\chi^2 = \frac{(55 - 38.79)^2}{38.79} + \frac{(56 - 49.66)^2}{49.66} + \cdots \frac{(18 - 11.10)^2}{11.10} = 32.09$$

Using the above formula the chi-square value of 32.09 is obtained. The tabled critical value of chi-square for a 5% level of risk and for four degrees of freedom [(5 rows - 1) x (2 columns - 1)] is 9.49. The calculated chi-square statistic of 32.09 is greater than the critical value of 9.49. Therefore, the proper conclusion is that perceived health improvement and usage group are related variables.

A computer-based statistical package such as SPSS or SYSTAT would have returned a p-value, or probability value of 0.0000. This value of 0.0000 should be interpreted as the level of risk of incorrectly rejecting the null hypothesis of statistical independence between perceived health improvement and usage group.

In conclusion, there is a relationship between perceived level of health improvement and usage group. The chi-square value does not indicate the direction of the relationship. Logic dictates that health improvement would be the dependent variable and that usage group would be the independent variable. A statistic called *asymmetric lambda* gives an indication whether the independent variable of usage group could be used to predict the value of the dependent variable, perceived health improvement. Asymmetric lambda will be discussed later in this chapter. For reference, the value of asymmetric lambda in this example is 0.0583, indicating a fairly weak dependency of perceived health improvement on usage group.

Care must be taken with the chi-square test since the sample size affects the magnitude of the calculated chi-square value. Even though the proportions in a chi-square table might stay the same, a larger sample will produce a larger value of chi-square. It's a well known fact, in statistical circles, that if all of the frequencies in a cross-tab are multiped by a constant, say k, then the value of chi-square is also multiplied by k.

HOW STRONGLY ARE TWO VARIABLES RELATED?

In this section, the relationship between perceived health improvement from taking a food supplement and the gender of the respondent from the Shaklee Canada study is investigated to illustrate the procedure for measuring whether a relationship exists, and then whether it's strong enough to be useful. Gender is, of course, a natural nominal variable. However, perceived health improvement is at least ordinal in measurement properties. In fact, a scale such as this would typically be considered to be interval when analyzed in most commercial studies. For illustration in this example, perceived health improvement will be treated as nominal. Later examples in this chapter will exploit this variable's measurement properties more fully.

Exhibit 22.10 Perceived Improvement in Health Due to Food Supplement by Gender

Frequencies

Perceived Health Improvement		Gender		Total
		Female	Male	
Great	5	60	22	82
Good	4	68	34	102
Moderate	3	56	41	97
Minor	2	22	26	48
None	1	11	15	26
Total		217	138	355

continued

Percentages

Perceived Health Improvement		Gender		Total
		Female	Male	
Great	5	27.65%	15.94%	23.10%
Good	4	31.34	24.64	28.73
Moderate	3	25.81	29.71	27.32
Minor	2	10.14	18.84	13.52
None	1	5.07	10.87	7.32
Total		100.00%	100.00%	100.00%
Base		217	138	355

Pearson chi-square = 15.39 df = 4 Probability = 0.0040

Asymmetric lambda (row dependent) = 0.0277

The note in Exhibit 22.10 provides two of the statistics which are available from most computer-based statistical packages. The findings above indicate that there is a relationship at the 0.4% level of risk between perceived improvement in health and gender.

The asymmetric lambda value of 0.0277 implies that the relationship is relatively weak between the two variables. Asymmetric lambda ranges between values of 0.0 and 1.0, where 0.0 means that the relationship is such that the independent variable is ineffective in helping to predict the values of the dependent variable. A value of 1.0 means that if you knew a value of the independent variable, then you could accurately predict the corresponding value of the dependent variable. The general procedure for calculating asymmetric lambda is:

1. Arrange the cross-tab so that the dependent variable is the row variable and the independent variable is the column variable.

2. Select the largest values in each of the columns of the table (including the total column) and combine as follows:

$$\frac{\text{Sum of largest values in columns of body of table} \quad \text{Minus} \quad \text{Largest value in total column}}{\text{Total sample size} \quad \text{Minus} \quad \text{Largest value in total column}} = \text{Asymmetric lambda (row dependent)}$$

$$\text{Lambda} = \lambda_b = \frac{\sum_{k=1}^{C} \max f_{jk} - \max f_{.k}}{N - \max f_{.k}}$$

where max f_{jk} = maximum frequency in the rows of column k,

max $f_{.k}$ = maximum frequency among the row totals in the marginal column

C = the number of columns in the body of the table (not counting the marginal column)

N = the total sample size represented in the table.

The asymmetric lambda value for this example was calculated as follows:

$$\text{Lambda} = \lambda_b \left[(68 + 41) - 102 \right] / (355 - 102) = 0.0277$$

This value of lambda implies that the rate of error in predicting the value of the dependent variable, perceived health improvement, is reduced by 2.77% when information about the independent variable, usage group, is used to help with the prediction.

Another way of calculating lambda is to compare the error in predicting the value of the dependent variable in the absence of any information regarding the values of the independent variable with error in predicting the dependent variable when knowing the values of the independent variable. Suppose that one of the 355 respondents in the earlier table was selected at random and that you know absolutely nothing about that person. If you were asked to provide that person's perceived improvement in health due to having taken food supplements, what would you say? Since most of the respondents reported that they had felt a "good level of health improvement," you should follow the odds and give "good improvement" as your answer. The probability of your answer being correct is 102/355 or 0.2873. Of course, the chance of your answer being in error is 253/355 or 0.7127.

If you had information about the respondent's sex, then your prediction should have been for a good level of health improvement for females and a moderate level of health improvement for males. Consequently, the "error after," i.e., error after utilizing the information conveyed by the independent variable of gender, would be

Error after = [(271–68) + (138–41)]/355 = 246/355 = 0.6930

The difference between the before and after rates of error is

Error before–Error after = 0.7127–0.6930 = 0.0197

Comparing the difference in error to the "error before" gives

(Error before–Error after) ÷ Error before = 0.0197 ÷ 0.7127 = 0.0277 or a 2.77% decrease in error of predicting the dependent variable, perceived level of health improvement, if information about the independent variable, respondent's gender, is known and used for the prediction.

ANOTHER EXAMPLE: COMBINING THE CHI-SQUARE TEST AND ASYMMETRIC LAMBDA   In the Shaklee study, the relationship between the perceived level of knowledge of nutrition and the perceived health improvement was important to investigate. The research question was whether level of knowledge about nutrition had any influence on a person's perceived level of health improvement due to having taken food supplements. Although both of the variables in the following analysis have ordinal properties, they will be treated as if they were only nominal by the chi-square test.

The question about nutrition knowledge was:

Q.15   Would you say that you, personally, are very well informed, fairly well informed, or not very well informed about nutrition?

VERY WELL INFORMED	3
FAIRLY WELL INFORMED	2
NOT VERY WELL INFORMED	1

Although these are two ordinal variables, the research question can be answered partly by using a chi-square analysis of the cross-tabulation of the two variables. The cross-tab relating perceived health improvement to nutrition information appears in Exhibit 22.11.

Exhibit 22.11   Perceived Level of Information About Nutrition

Frequencies

Perceived Health Improvement	Not Very Well Informed	Fairly Well Informed	Very Well Informed	Total
Great	6	26	50	82
Good	8	60	34	102
Moderate	4	62	31	97
Minor	2	31	15	48
None	1	15	10	26
Total	21	194	140	355

continued

Percentages

Perceived Health Improvement	Not Very Well Informed	Fairly Well Informed	Very Well Informed	Total
Great	28.57%	13.40%	35.71%	23.10%
Good	38.10	30.93	24.29	28.73
Moderate	19.05	31.96	22.14	27.32
Minor	9.52	15.98	10.71	13.52
None	4.76	7.73	7.14	7.32
Total	100%	100%	100%	100%
Base	21	194	140	355

Pearson chi-square = 25.34 df = 8 Probability = 0.0014

Asymmetric lambda (row dependent) = 0.0711

The conclusion would be that knowledge of nutrition and perceived health improvement are related, but weakly. The probability value of 0.0014 indicates that there is only a 0.14% risk that perceived level of health improvement and nutrition knowledge are actually not related. The asymmetric lambda value of 0.0711 implies that the error of predicting the perceived level of health improvement is reduced by 7.11% if information regarding the respondent's perceived level of information about nutrition is used.

ARE TWO PERCENTAGES THE SAME OR DIFFERENT?

Sometimes the focus of attention in a table might be on the percentages of respondents from two different groups who gave one particular value of the dependent variable. These would be referred to in some situations as the *top box scores* or percentages. In these cases, the focus of the statistical testing is concentrated on the size of the difference between the two scores or percentages. A relatively simple and straightforward test that would be applicable here would be the Z-test for the differences between two percentages. This test assumes that an underlying normal distribution describes the data. Consequently, the Z-test should not be used for sample sizes less than 30 where normality cannot be established.

Let's investigate the difference between Shaklee users and users of other brands of food supplements. The table in Exhibit 22.12 was used in the previous section. It provides the percentage of each usage group that reported each of five levels of perceived health improvement due to having taken food supplements.

Exhibit 22.12 Perceived Level of Improvement in Health by Food Supplement Usage Group

Perceived Health Improvement	Shaklee Leaders	Shaklee Users	Other Brands	Non-Users	Total
Great	72.73	33.33	12.99	19.44	37.35
Good	24.48	33.94	25.97	16.67	27.51
Moderate	2.10	19.39	34.42	33.33	20.08
Minor	0.00	10.30	14.94	22.22	9.64
None	0.70	3.03	11.69	8.33	5.42
Total	100.00%	100.00%	100.00%	100.00%	100.00%
Base	143	165	154	36	498

Very often, the marketing manager is most interested in differences among the groups with regard to the most positive rating. In this case, let's concentrate on great improvement in health as the top box scores. The non-users will be discarded because of the very small sample. Shaklee leaders will also be bypassed here because of their dramatically higher score in the top box. Focusing on Shaklee users and other brand users, notice in the table in Exhibit 22.13 that 33.33% of the Shaklee users felt that they had experienced a great improvement in health, while 12.99% of the other brand users said that they had benefited from a great improvement in health.

Exhibit 22.13 Top Box Scores for Health Improvement by Respondent Group

Perceived Health Improvement	Shaklee Leaders	Shaklee Users	Other Brands	Non-Users	Total
Great	72.73%	33.33%	12.99%	19.44%	37.35%
Base	143	165	154	36	498

Our research question is, "Is the percentage of Shaklee users who reported a great improvement in health significantly different from the percentage of other brand users who indicated the same level of health improvement?" In a case like this, the basic hypotheses to be tested are:

$H_o : \pi_{Shaklee} = \pi_{Other}$, alpha risk = 0.05

$H_a : \pi_{Shaklee} \neq \pi_{Other}$

Since $p_{Shaklee} = 0.3333$ and $p_{Other} = 0.1299$

then $p_{difference} = 0.3333 - 0.1299 = 0.2034$

Is this difference of 0.2034 large or small? Whether 0.2034 is a large or small number must be judged relative to the size of the standard error. In this example, the null hypothesis was that the true proportion of Shaklee users feeling great improvement in health was equal to the true proportion of other brand users reporting great improvement. Consequently, since the variance is calculated as

$$s_p^2 = \frac{p(1-p)}{n}$$

and since the two proportions were hypothesized to be equal, the variance of the difference between the two proportions is

$$s_{p_1-p_2}^2 = p(1-p)\left(\frac{1}{n_1} + \frac{1}{n_2}\right)$$

where $p = \dfrac{0.3333 \times 165 + 0.1299 \times 154}{165 + 154} = 0.235$

$$s_{p_1-p_2}^2 = (0.235)(1 - 0.235)(1/165 + 1/154) = 0.0023$$

and the standard deviation $s_{p_1-p_2} = 0.048$. The Z-statistic calculated below measures the difference between proportions that actually occurred (0.235) and the difference that was expected based on the null hypothesis (0.00). This difference is expressed relative to the standard deviation of 0.048.

$$z = \frac{(p_1 - p_2) - (\pi_1 - \pi_2)}{s_{p_1-p_2}}$$

$$= \frac{0.2034 - 0}{0.048} = 4.238$$

Using a 5% level of risk, then the Z-statistic of 4.238 must be compared with the value of 1.96, which is obtained from a table of standard normal deviates.

Since $Z = 4.238 > Z = 1.96$, the null hypothesis of equal percentages of both groups feeling great improvements in health can be rejected and the alternative of unequal percentages is confirmed.

The above example was used to illustrate in general the approach to testing the difference between two percentages. In the Shaklee study, the actual null hypothesis was that the percentage of Shaklee users who would report a great improvement in health due to taking food supplements would be at least as large as the percentage of other brand users who would indicate a great improvement. To confirm that the Shaklee users in fact reported a great improvement in health in significantly larger numbers than did other brand users, a one-tailed test was performed. The Z-statistic was calculated as 4.238, as above. Using the 5% level of risk in a one-tailed test would require that the statistic be compared to a critical value of 1.645. Since $Z = 4.238 > Z = 1.645$, the superior benefits felt by Shaklee users were confirmed.

ARE TWO MEANS THE SAME OR DIFFERENT?

At least a few questions intended to measure the respondents' attitudes regarding some object are included in most marketing research surveys. Many of the attitude measurement techniques produce answers on scales that are often assumed to be at least interval in their information content. When survey research data are of the interval or ratio types, then it's permissible to analyze those data using almost any statistical procedure in existence. There is a broad range of statistical analysis procedures available for interval and ratio data, with almost no restrictions on whether the data must be interval or ratio. These parametric procedures include Z-tests, t-tests, analysis of variance, regression, correlation, discriminant analysis, factor analysis, cluster analysis, and many others. In addition to the parametric techniques, any of the nonparametric procedures may be used on the interval and ratio data.

The Shaklee Canada study of food supplements will provide a good example for the illustration of the procedure known as an *independent samples t-test*. The first example treated in this section was drawn from the Shaklee study and is directed at testing whether the respondents' perceived level of health prior to taking the food supplement identified as being most helpful is different from the perceived level of health after having taken the food supplement for a period of time. The two questions asked in the questionnaire appear below.

6. Now, please think back to the time just before you started taking the food supplement brand which you just mentioned. Please rate your health at that time on a scale that goes from 1 to 10, where 1 means very poor health and 10 means excellent health at that time.

	Very Poor								Excellent	
State of Health Before Supplements	1	2	3	4	5	6	7	8	9	10

Next, please rate the state of your health after you took the food supplement brand just mentioned for the length of time which you told me you took it for. Again, use a scale where 1 means very poor health and 10 means excellent health.

	Very Poor								Excellent	
State of Health After Supplements	1	2	3	4	5	6	7	8	9	10

One obvious question that should be asked about the data is whether the respondents perceived that their level of health changed from the time before they began taking food supplements until the time of the survey. Since each of the respondents will have provided an answer to each of these two questions in sequence, the scores must be treated as being dependent or related measures. A concern in a situation such as this is that the answer to the latter question would have been formulated with the answer to the earlier question in mind and, consequently, the two values would be related. In other words, if only the second question had been asked, then the answers might have been different from those answers which were received to that second question when it was asked sequentially after the first question. The analysis to answer the question of the relationship between the before and after perceived states of health will be addressed in the next section through a *paired t-test*.

A second research question might lead to the investigation of whether men and women reported any difference in their perceived levels of health after having taken the food supplement for a period of time. Since the way one gender answered the above question does not seem to have influenced the way the other gender answered, we'll investigate the relationship assuming that the two groups, men and women, provided independence responses.

As a preliminary level of analysis leading up to the *independent sample t-test*, the cross-tabulation of the data will first be presented and analyzed using the chi-square test. The tabled responses are presented in Exhibit 22.14

The results from the chi-square test of independence between the two variables are presented in Exhibits 22.15 and 22.16. The findings are inconclusive because of the warning that appears in Exhibit 22.16 regarding the expected frequency in the cells of the frequency table. (That rule of thumbs says that no more than about 20% of the cells should have an expected frequency of less

Exhibit 22.14 Perceived Health After Having Taken Food Supplements for a Period of Time, Broken Down by Gender

		Column Percentages Gender				Frequencies Gender		
Perceived Health		Male 1	Female 2	Total		Male 1	Female 2	Total
Very	1	0.71%	0.00%	0.28%	1	1	0	1
poor	2	0.00	0.00	0.00	2	0	0	0
	3	0.71	0.46	0.56	3	1	1	2
	4	2.13	1.38	0.56	4	3	3	6
	5	5.67	4.61	5.03	5	8	10	18
	6	14.18	8.76	10.89	6	20	19	39
	7	19.86	17.97	18.72	7	28	39	67
	8	35.46	40.09	38.27	8	50	87	137
Excel-	9	9.93	17.05	14.25	9	14	37	51
lent	10	11.35	9.68	10.34	10	16	21	37
Total		100.00%	100.00%	100.00%	Total	141	217	358

than five.) Six of the 18 cells (33.3%) in the expected frequency table corresponding to Exhibit 22.14 have expected frequencies of less than five. (You should confirm that this is true.) Consequently, although the chi-square statistic might provide some indication of the existence or non-existence of a relationship between perceived health after having taken food supplements and gender, caution should be followed in supporting that conclusion. (Notice in Exhibit 22.14 that no one gave an answer of 2 on the 10-point scale. SPSS automatically collapsed the table to nine rows and two columns. Consequently, there were 8 degrees of freedom and 18 cells in the table in Exhibit 22.14. The unaltered table is presented in Exhibit 22.14 for completeness.)

Exhibit 22.15 SPSS/PC+ Analysis of Perceived Health Example

Cross-tabulation: HLTHASUP
by SEX

Chi-Square	D.F.	Significance	Min E.F.	Cells with E.F.<5
8.33638	8	.4013	.394	6 OF 18 (33.3%)

Statistic	Symmetric	With HLTHASUP Dependent	With SEX Dependent
Lambda	.00552	.00000	.01418

Number of Missing Observations = 252

Exhibit 22.16 SYSTAT Analysis of Perceived Health Example

WARNING: MORE THAN ONE-FIFTH OF FITTED CELLS ARE SPARSE (FREQUENCY <5)

SIGNIFICANCE TESTS ARE SUSPECT

Test statistic	Value	DF	Prob
Pearson chi-square	8.336	8	.401

Coefficient	Value	Asymptotic STD Error
Lambda (row dependent)	.0000	.00000

There are several other statistical tests that can be executed on the data tables in Exhibit 22.14. One of the most important tests to perform on this data might be the t-test to identify whether a statistically significant difference exists between the mean perceived health of males and the mean perceived health of females. Since the answers of the females to the perceived health question did not depend on the answers given by the men, and viceversa, this would be termed an *independent samples t-test*.

The null and alternate hypotheses would be stated in words as:

H_o: The mean health of males is the same as the mean health of females

H_a: The mean health of males is not the same as the mean health of females

In statistical notation, the hypotheses would be:

H_o: $\mu_{males} = \mu_{females}$

H_a: $\mu_{males} \neq \mu_{females}$

Usually the level of acceptable risk of incorrectly rejecting the null hypothesis of no difference between males and females and concluding that the mean health of males is different from the mean health of females is stated along with they hypotheses. In textbooks, the level of risk of this so-called Type I error is most often stated to be 5% or 0.05. In practice, the level of risk that is printed out from the statistical analysis is stated in the findings as the "level of risk of the test." For example, the following analysis will be seen to indicate that the mean levels of perceived health of males and females are significantly different at the 6.4% level of risk. The calculations for this test are presented below.

The t - statistic is calculated from $t = \dfrac{\overline{x}_m - \overline{x}_f}{s_{\overline{x}_m - \overline{x}_f}}$

where the standard error is $s_{\overline{x}_m - \overline{x}_f} = \sqrt{s_p^2\left(\dfrac{1}{n_m} + \dfrac{1}{n_f}\right)}$

and

where $s_p^2 = \dfrac{\displaystyle\sum_{i=1}^{n_m}\left(x_{mi} - \overline{x}_m\right)^2 + \sum_{i=1}^{n_f}\left(x_{fi} - \overline{x}_f\right)^2}{n_m + n_f - 2}$, called the pooled variance.

The average perceived health of males can be calculated by adding together the values given by the 141 males in the sample and dividing by that sample size of 141, for example:

$$\overline{x}_m = \frac{x_{m1} + x_{m2} + \cdots + x_{m,141}}{141}$$

Since the data have been summarized in categories in Exhibit 22.15, the calculation in this case would be performed as follows

$$\overline{x}_m = \frac{1 \times 1 + 3 \times 1 + 4 \times 3 + 5 \times 8 + 6 \times 20 + \cdots + 10 \times 16}{141} = 7.504$$

Similarly,

$$\overline{x}_f = \frac{1 \times 0 + 3 \times 1 + 4 \times 3 + 5 \times 10 + 6 \times 19 + \cdots + 10 \times 21}{217} = 7.793$$

The pooled variance estimator is

$$s_p^2 = \frac{345.086 + 389.588}{141 + 217 - 2} = 2.064$$

where the p subscript stands for pooled.

$$s_{\overline{x}_m - \overline{x}_f} = \sqrt{2.064 \times \left(\frac{1}{141} + \frac{1}{217}\right)} = 0.155$$

$$t = \frac{(7.504 - 7.793) - 0}{0.155} = -1.86$$

SPSS, a statistical package available for both mainframe and personal computers, provides the following information in Exhibit 22.17 that's useful for comparing the means of the two groups.

Exhibit 22.17   SPSS/PC+ t-test for Two Independent Samples

Independent samples of SEX

Group 1: SEX EQ   1.00   Group 2: SEX EQ   2.00

t-test for: HLTHASUP

	Number of Cases	Mean	Standard Deviation	Standard Error
Group 1	141	7.5035	1.570	132
Group 2	217	7.7926	1.343	091

		Pooled Variance Estimate			Separate Variance Estimate		
F Value	2-Tail Prob	t value	Degrees of Freedom	2-tail Prob	t value	Degrees of Freedom	2-tail Prob.
1.37	0.039	−1.86	356	.064	−1.80	265.80	.073

The left side of Exhibit 22.17 furnished the statistics that help to test whether the variances of the two groups are the same or different. Since the F-Value to the left in Exhibit 22.17 corresponds to a risk of 3.9%, the hypothesis of equal variances can be rejected. Consequently, the "Separate Variance Estimate" would be used to obtain the t-test value of −1.80 and the risk of 7.3%.

The personal computer statistical package, SYSTAT, provides the analysis in Exhibit 22.18.

Exhibit 22.18   SYSTAT t-test for Two Independent Samples

INDEPENDENT SAMPLES T-TEST ON HLTHASUP GROUPED BY SEX

GROUP	N	MEAN	SD
2.000	217	7.793	1.343
1.000	141	7.504	1.570

SEPARATE VARIANCES T = 1.800 DF = 355.9 PROB = .073

POOLED VARIANCES T = 1.850 DF = 356   PROB = .064

The conclusion from these t-tests is that there is not a significant difference between males and females with respect to perceived health after having taken the food supplements for a period of time. This conclusion is based on the assumption that the maximum acceptable level of risk of a Type I error is 5% and that the variances of the two distributions are not significantly different. If the two variances were not statistically different, then the pooled variances t-test would be used. In this example, the conclusion would still be that the male and female perceptions would be the same regardless of which variance calculation was used in the t-test.

As another example, we'll once again investigate the perceived improvement in respondents' health due to having taken a food supplement broken down by gender. The question, as described earlier in this chapter, is presented again below.

Q.3.5 Would you say that brand of food supplement which you just mentioned (AS BEING THE MOST HELPFUL) has had a great improvement, good improvement, moderate improvement, minor improvement or no improvement in your health?

Exhibit 22.19 Perceived Improvement in Health due to Food Supplement, by Gender

Perceived Health Improvement	Gender		Total	Gender		Total
	Female	Male		Female	Male	
Great	27.65%	15.94%	23.10%	60	22	82
Good	31.34	24.64	28.73	68	34	102
Moderate	25.81	29.71	27.32	56	41	97
Minor	10.14	18.84	13.52	22	26	48
None	5.07	10.87	7.32	11	15	26
Total	100.00%	100.00%	100.00%	217	138	355

Analysis of the data in Exhibit 22.19 provides the following results:

1. There is a relationship between perceived improvement in health and gender at the 1% level of significance. This finding is based on the chi-square analysis displayed below.

Pearson chi-square = 15.39 df = 4 Probability = 0.0040

2. The relationship is very weak, since lambda indicates only a 2.77% reduction in error to predict the value of health improvement based on knowing the person's gender;

Asymmetric lambda (row dependent) = 0.0277

3. The two distributions are different as indicated by a Kolmogorov-Smirnov test (see the appendix to this chapter).

Exhibit 22.20   Calculations for Kolmogorov-Smirnov Test

| Perceived Level of Health Improvement | Cumulative Percentages Gender | | Difference |
	Female	Male	
Great	27.65%	15.94%	11.17
Good	58.99	40.58	18.41
Moderate	84.80	70.29	14.51
Minor	94.94	89.13	5.81
None	100.00%	100.00%	100.00%

$$\text{K-S D statistic} = |18.41 \div 100| = 0.1841$$

$$\text{The critical K-S D value} = 1.36 \times \sqrt{(217 + 138) \div (217 \times 138)} = 0.148$$

Since the K-S D statistic of 0.184 is greater than the K-S critical value of 0.148, then it can be concluded that the distribution of responses of the females in the sample to their perceived improvement in their health is different from the distribution of the males' answers to the question, at the 5% level of risk.

Exhibit 22.21   Top Box Scores for Gender by Perceived Health

| Perceived Level of Health Improvement | Gender | | Total |
	Female	Male	
Great	27.65%	15.94%	23.10%

4. The top box scores are statistically different. The top box scores for this problem are listed in Exhibit 22.21. The basic question is whether the percentage of females (27.65%) who felt that they had experienced a great improvement in health due to food supplements is significantly different from the percentage of males who reported the same level of improvement (15.94%). The calculations follow.

$$p_{females} = 0.2765 \qquad p_{males} = 0.1594 \qquad p_{difference} = 0.1171$$

The pooled proportion reporting a great improvements is $p = 0.2310$

$$s^2_{p_f - p_m} = (0.231)(1 - 0.231)\left(\frac{1}{217} + \frac{1}{138}\right) = 0.0021 \text{ and } s_{p_f - p_m} = 0.046$$

The Z-statistic is $Z = \dfrac{0.1171 - 0}{0.046} = 2.54$, larger than the critical value of 1.96 for 5% risk

Therefore, the conclusion is that the percentage of females in the study who reported a greatly improved level of health due to having taken food supplements is significantly different from the percentage of males in the study who reported the same level of health improvement.

Since the table clearly shows that the percentage for females (27.65%) is larger than the percentage for males (15.94%), the alternate hypothesis might be stated that the percentage of females in the population who perceive that they have received a greater improvement in their health due to having taken food supplements is larger than the corresponding percentage for males. The hypotheses stated symbolically would be:

H_o: $\pi_f \leq \pi_m$, $\alpha = 0.05$
H_a: $\pi_f > \pi_m$

The critical Z-statistic would still be calculated to be 2.54 and since that value is still greater than the critical Z-value of 1.645, the null hypothesis would be rejected once again. The conclusion would be that the percentage of females who perceived a higher level of health due to having taken food supplements is greater than the corresponding percentage of males.

5. The mean level of health improvement for females is greater than for men. Up to this point in the analysis, the data have been treated as nominal for the chi-square test and the Z-test and as ordinal for the K-S test. However, in most practical commercial analyses the data would also be treated as if the attitude scale had interval properties. Assuming interval properties allows us to ask one more question, "Was the mean level of perceived health improvement different between the women and the men in the study?" The hypotheses would be:

H_o: $\mu_f = \mu_m$, $\alpha = 0.05$
H_a: $\mu_f \neq \mu_m$

The output from the SYSTAT statistical analysis package presented in Exhibit 22.22 provides the information we need.

Exhibit 22.22 T-test for Mean Difference Between Genders' Perceived Health (SYSTAT)

Independent Samples T-test On Perceived Improvement in Health
Grouped By Gender

Group	N	Mean	Std.Dev.
Female 2	217	3.664	1.135
Male 1	138	3.159	1.222

Separate Variances T = 3.895 df = 276.0 Prob = 0.000
  Pooled Variances T = 3.959 df =   353 Prob = 0.000

SPSS, another statistical package, provides the t-test information given in Exhibit 22.23.

Exhibit 22.23 T-test for Mean Difference Between Genders' Perceived Health (SPSS)

T-TEST/GROUPS SEX (1,2)/VARIABLES SUPPIMPR.
Independent samples of Sex

Group 1: Sex EQ   1.00   Group 2: Sex EQ   2.00

t-test for: SUPPIMPR, Perceived Improvement in Health Due to Food Supplement

	Number of Cases	Mean	Standard Deviation	Standard Error
Group 1	138	3.1594	1.222	0.104
Group 2	217	3.6636	1.135	0.077

	Pooled Variance Estimate			Separate Variance Estimate		
F Value	2-Tail Prob.	t Value	Degrees of Freedom	2-Tail Prob.	t Value	Degrees of Freedom	2-Tail Prob.
1.16	.335	−3.96	353	0.000	−3.89	276.01	0.000

Using the pooled variances t-test, the proper conclusion is that the mean perceived level of health improvement of women, 3.664, is significantly different from the mean perceived level of health improvement of men, 3.159, at the 0.05% level of risk. Therefore, the null hypothesis should be rejected. If a one-tailed test had been performed on the above data, the conclusion would have been to reject the null hypothesis and conclude that the mean for females is significantly higher than the mean for males.

ARE THE MEANS OF TWO RELATED SAMPLES THE SAME OR DIFFERENT?

There are many types of questions that can lead to testing the strength of the association between two attitudes which are related in some manner. The first example treated in the last section was drawn from the Shaklee study and is directed at testing whether the respondents' perceived level of health prior to taking the food supplement identified as being most helpful is different from the perceived level of health after having taken the food supplement for a period of time. The two questions asked in the questionnaire are repeated below.

6. Now, please think back to the time just before you started taking the food supplement brand which you just mentioned. Please rate your health at that time on a scale that goes from 1 to 10, where 1 means very poor health and 10 means excellent health at that time.

	Very Poor								Excellent	
Health State of Health Before Supplements	1	2	3	4	5	6	7	8	9	10

Next, please rate the state of your health after you took the food supplement brand just mentioned for the length of time which you told me you took it for. Again, use a scale where 1 means very poor health and 10 means excellent health.

	Very Poor								Excellent	
Health State of Health After Supplements	1	2	3	4	5	6	7	8	9	10

Put yourself in the situation of answering these two questions in a telephone interview. The first question is asked and you provide the answer 6. Then the interviewer asks about your level of health after having taken the food supplement. It's quite likely that you think about the answer 6 given for the first part of the question and then develop your answer to the second part relative to that 6 answer. What you've done is to relate your second answer to your first answer. If you had been asked about your level of health after having taken food supplements without having first been asked about your health before food supplements, your answer to that after question might have been different.

The objective of this question was to identify whether there was a significant difference between the respondents' health after and before the food supplement usage. The null hypothesis would be that there is no difference and the alternate hypothesis would be that there is a difference between the two perceived levels of health.

H_0: $\mu_D = 0$, $\alpha = 0.05$
H_a: $\mu_D \neq 0$

Where the D in the above hypotheses signifies the difference between the before and after perceived levels of health. To determine whether there is any difference, the *paired t-test* is the most appropriate measure, if the necessary assumptions are met. The output in Exhibit 22.24 from SPSS investigates the relationship discussed above.

Exhibit 22.24 Paired t-test for Perceived Health Before and After Taking Food Supplements (SPSS).

Paired samples t-test: HLTHBSUP Perceived Health Before Food Supplements
HLTHASUP Perceived Health After Food Supplements

Variable	Number of Cases	Mean	Standard Deviation	Standard Error
HLTHBSUP	358	5.9972	2.057	0.019
HLTHASUP	358	7.6788	1.442	0.076

(Difference) Mean	Standard Deviation	Standard Error	2-Tail Corr.Prob.	t Value	Degrees of Freedom	2-Tail Prob.
−1.6816	2.014	0.016	0.380 0.000	−15.80	357	0.000

Exhibits 22.25 and 22.26 illustrate the two ways of obtaining a paired t-test from SYSTAT. Exhibit 22.25 shows the paired t-test obtained from the STATS module while Exhibit 22.26 provides the output from the MGLH module of SYSTAT for executing a paired t-test.

Exhibits 22.24 and 22.25 present the paired t-test results in the most conventional manner. Both procedures provide information that leads to the conclusion that the perceived level of health after having taken food supplements is significantly different from the perceived level of health prior to having taken food supplements. This statement is based on the t-test value of 15.80 which is significantly larger than the 5% risk critical value of 1.96. In fact, the tabled two-tailed probabilities are 0.000 indicating that there is

Exhibit 22.25 Paired t-test for Perceived Health Before and After Taking Food Supplements (SYSTAT—STATS Module)

The Following Results Are For:

Sample = 1.000

Paired Samples T-test on Hlthbsup   Vs   Hlthasup With 358 Cases

Mean Difference =   −1.682
Sd Difference =   2.014
T = 15.800   Df = 357   Prob = 0.000

Exhibit 22.26 Paired t-test for Perceived Health Before and After Taking Food Supplements (SYSTAT—MLGH Module)

252 CASES DELETED DUE TO MISSING DATA.
NUMBER OF CASES PROCESSED: 358

DEPENDENT VARIABLE MEANS
     HLTHBSUP   HLTHASUP
      5.997   7.679

HYPOTHESIS
TEST OF HYPOTHESIS

SOURCE	SS	DF	MS	F	P
HYPOTHESIS	1012.302	1	1012.302	249.632	0.000
ERROR	1447.698	357	4.055		

an extremely small risk (less than 0.1% risk) that the conclusion of there being a significantly large difference between the two means is not true.

In Exhibit 22.26, the most important statistics for drawing a conclusion about the relationship between the two related sets of data are the F-ratio of 249.632 and the Probability value of 0.000. This information is presented above in the form of an analysis of variance table (ANOVA). However, the ANOVA analysis is equivalent to a paired t-test due to the way in which the SYSTAT input statements were composed. In fact, the F-ratio is equal to the square of the T-value in this case. The Probability value of 0.000 implies that the F-ratio is extremely high and that the null hypothesis of no difference between the two mean perceived levels of health should be rejected. The information in these exhibits might be a little misleading regarding the calculation of the paired t-test value. Although the means of the two variables are printed in the exhibits, the paired t-test value is not calculated on the difference between those two means. The calculation is based on the mean of the differences between each respondent's answers on the two related questions.

Exhibit 22.27   Calculations for a Paired t-test

Case	Perceived Health Before Supplement	Perceived Health After Supplement	Difference in Perceived Health
1	7	8	$1 = d_1$
2	4	7	$3 = d_2$
3	9	9	$0 = ...$
4	7	8	1
5	5	6	1
6	5	7	2
7	6	8	2
8	4	4	0
9	7	9	$2 = d_9$
10	6	7	$1 = d_{10}$
Sum			$13 = \sum d_i$

For these 10 cases in Exhibit 22.27, the average of the differences between each respondent's perceived health before and after having taken food supplements is

$$\bar{x}_D = \frac{1+3+0+1+1+2+2+0+2+1}{10} = \frac{13}{10} = 1.3$$

where D stands for the differences between the two related answers. To complete the analysis, the standard deviation and then the standard error of the differences in perceived health are calculated. Both the average of the differences and the standard error of the differences are used in the following paired t-test statistic,

$$t_r = \frac{\bar{x}_D - 0}{s_D / \sqrt{n}}$$

If the t_r value is greater than the critical t-value obtained from the table of the Student's t-distribution for a specified level of risk and the proper number of degrees of freedom, then the null hypothesis of no difference between the two measurements is rejected. Otherwise the null hypothesis is not rejected.

For the example above on all 358 cases as extracted from SPSS,

$$\overline{x}_D = 1.682, \quad s_D = 2.014, \quad s_{\overline{x}_D} = \frac{2.014}{\sqrt{358}} = 0.106 \quad \text{and} \quad t_r = \frac{\overline{x}_D - 0}{s_D / \sqrt{n}} = 15.80$$

Since the critical value of t is

$$t_{(\alpha = 0.05, \, df = 358 - 1)} = 1.96$$

and since the calculated t-value is so much larger, the null hypothesis should be rejected and the conclusion would be that there was a significant change in the perceived health of the respondents between the time before they started taking food supplements and the time of the survey. The analysis for a one-tailed test would have produced the conclusion that the perceived health after taking food supplements was significantly higher than was the perceived health before taking the supplements.

ARE THE MEANS OF THREE OR MORE GROUPS THE SAME OR DIFFERENT?

When the analysis question is, "Are the means different among the three groups?", then the t-test becomes awkward to use since tests would have to be performed between group 1 and groups 2, group 1 and group 3, and between group 2 and group 3. Fortunately, a procedure called the *analysis of variance* addresses the comparison of the means of an interval- or ratio-scaled variable among three or more groups. We saw in the preceding section that when comparing the means of two groups, the independent samples t-test and the analysis of variance (ANOVA) provide the same results.

Fairly early in the Shaklee questionnaire, the following question was asked to obtain respondents' perceived level of health before any questions were asked directly about their usage of food supplements.

Q.41   Now I'd like you to use a scale from 1 meaning very poor health to 10 meaning excellent health. Please give me a number between 1 and 10 to indicate your state of health <u>right now</u>.

VERY POOR HEALTH				FAIR HEALTH					EXCELLENT HEALTH
1	2	3	4	5	6	7	8	9	10

The findings in the Shaklee study for the respondents' perceived health at the time of the survey were analyzed in more detail to determine whether respondents who were identified as having used Shaklee food supplements reported different results from those who said they had used other brands of food supplements, and from those who used no food supplements, according to the study definition. Because of the 10-point attitude scale, the level of measurement of perceived health was assumed to be interval-scaled, therefore allowing for application of ANOVA.

The hypotheses for this example are:

$H_0 : \mu_{Shaklee} = \mu_{Others} = \mu_{Non}, \propto = 0.05$
H_a: not all means are equal

The output from SPSS/PC+ and from SYSTAT are presented in Exhibits 22.28 and 22.29. Although Exhibit 22.28 is from SPSS/PC+, the output from SPSS-X Release 3.1 for the IBM VM/CMS mainframe computer produces exactly the same table.

Exhibit 22.28 Analysis of Variance for Differences in Perceived Health Among Three Groups (SPSS/PC+)

ONE WAY

Variable   HELTHNOW
By Variable   GROUP
Analysis of Variance

Source	D.F.	Sum of Squares	Mean Squares	F Ratio	F Prob.
Between Groups	2	23.0725	11.5362	4.3677	0.0131
Within Groups	607	1603.2292	2.6412		
Total	609	1626.3016			

Group	Count	Mean	Standard Deviation	Standard Error	95 Pct Conf Int for Mean	
Grp 1	185	7.5243	1.5985	.1175	7.2925 To	7.7562
Grp 2	203	7.0542	1.6356	.1148	6.8278 To	7.2805
Grp 3	222	7.3874	1.6376	.1099	7.1708 To	7.6040
Total	610	7.3180	1.6341	.0662	7.1881 To	7.4480

continued

Multiple Range Test
LSD Procedure
(*) Denotes pairs of groups significantly different at the .050 level

Variable   HELTHNOW

		G G G
		r r r
		p p p
Mean	Group	2 3 1
7.0542	Grp 2	
7.3874	Grp 3	*
7.5243	Grp 1	*

Exhibit 22.29   Analysis of Variance for Differences in Perceived Health Among Three Groups (SYSTAT)

The Following Results Are For:
   Sample = 1.000
2 Cases Deleted Due To Missing Data.

Dept Var: HELTHNOW   N:610   Multiple R: .119   Squared Multiple R: .014

Analysis of Variance

Source	Sum-of-squares	DF	Mean-square	F-ratio	P
Group	23.072	2	11.536	4.368	0.013
Error	1603.229	607	2.641		

The information from the computer outputs in Exhibits 22.28 and 22.29 indicates that there is a statistically significant difference among the mean perceived levels of health of the three groups of respondents at the time of the survey. This conclusion is based on the F-ratio of 4.368 and on the F Prob or P = 0.013. The P-value of 0.013 indicates that there is less than a 1.3% risk that in fact there is not a significant difference among the three mean levels of perceived health.

The F-ratio and P-value indicate that some difference exists among the three means. However, they do not signify whether all three means are different from one another, whether one mean is different from the other two, or whether some other difference pattern exists.

From the matrix at the end of the SPSS output in Exhibit 22.28, it appears that Group 1 (Shaklee users) is different from Group 2 (other brand users), and that Group 3 (non-users) is significantly different from Group 2.

The remaining implication is that the perceived health of Shaklee users was not significantly different from that of non-users of food supplements.

SUMMARY

The organization format for the chapter has been focused on providing the analysis technique that coincides with a certain type of data. Of course, to use this organizational format, one must know the type of data that are contained in the questionnaires received from the field. The ability to identify whether data have nominal, ordinal, interval or ratio properties might be somewhat difficult for the beginning researcher, but this task becomes much easier with practice.

The basic tools of statistical analysis of marketing research have been presented in this chapter. The purpose was to provide an explanation of those techniques most commonly used in marketing research practice. Certainly, some of the procedures presented in the chapter are used much more than others. For example:

- the chi-square test for goodness of fit is used only occasionally;
- the chi-square test of independence is used in almost every study;
- the asymmetric lambda is not used much in practice, but is integral to the analysis of relationships between two nominal variables;
- the Z-test for the difference between two percentages is used frequently;
- the t-test for the difference between two independent means is used quite often;
- the paired t-test is also used frequently; and
- analysis of variance is used fairly often.

The appendix to this chapter introduces several analysis procedures called nonparametric techniques that are used with nominal or ordinal data. Although these procedures are not used very frequently in practice, they can provide statistical rigor in situations where the more standard procedures are not applicable.

The experienced researcher will want to investigate and use more advanced analysis procedures that will be helpful in teasing more information out of the data. However, the ability to understand the basic data and to present them clearly to others, with or without high powered statistics, is the critical differentiating factor between the sophisticated data analyst and the uninspired practitioner.

NOW THINK ABOUT THIS

1. When there are two variables, the data are nominal and it's necessary to determine whether there's any relationship between the two variables, which analysis procedure should be used?

2. When three groups of people rank several brands according to their liking of those brands, which technique should be used to analyze the data?

3. When each person in a sample is asked to rank order several brands according to their price/quality value, which statistical test is more appropriate?

4. If a large sample can be grouped into two parts and if each person indicates whether he or she will buy the brand, how would you determine whether there's any difference between the two groups in terms of their intention to buy the brand?

5. List the requirements for using the paired t-test.

6. How can the difference between interval and ratio data be determined?

7. When using SPSS or SYSTAT, why is it necessary to test the two-tailed test directly?

8. If interval-scaled data for a sample which could be split into four groups were analyzed by analysis of variance in SPSS, how would you determine whether there's any difference among the groups. If you found that there was a difference, how would you identify which groups are different and which groups are similar?

9. When doing an independent samples t-test in SPSS, of what value is the F-test information which is provided?

10. What's the key difference between the Mann-Whitney and the Kruskal-Wallis tests should be used?

23 Advanced Data Analysis: The Art of Using Special Techniques

WHAT DOES *MULTIVARIATE ANALYSIS* MEAN?

Multivariate means analyzing several variables at one time or together. How many variables exist among those that we want to analyze and how many are used only as "grouping factors"? Is one variable associated with, related to, or dependent on several others? How are the several variables related among themselves? What is the information content of each of the variables?

The key aspects for understanding multivariate analysis are:

- One data set is the focus of the attention
- Respondents are asked to provide responses on several characteristics, attributes or facets of an object at one time or simultaneously
- The principal attention of the analysts is on the simultaneous relationships among the several variables of focus

"Objects" refer to a brand, a company name, a product characteristics, persons, or anything about which respondents can be asked to provide answers. For example, respondents might be asked to consider the brands (i.e., objects) of orange juice with which they are familiar. After being asked to identify the brand which they drink most often, the subjects are asked to rate that brand on the following five characteristics: sweetness, ability to quench thirst, vitamin C content, value, and pulp content. Although the researcher's interest might initially be focused on each of the five variables, that focus is very quickly altered to consider how the brand rated overall, i.e., considering all five variables together. Since the buyer will make a purchase decision on the brand as a whole, the simultaneous consideration of all variables is the most natural way of trying to interpret the data so as to assist the marketing management to make better decisions regarding the brand.

HIDDEN RELATIONSHIPS IN DATA

In marketing research we often examine pairs of attributes such as *price and sales* or *overall liking and purchase intent.* If we find that whenever the price is high sales are down, we can conclude that increased price results in decreased sales. Similarly, if consumers who score high on overall liking also score high on purchase intent, we may infer that liking leads to purchase intent.

But there may be more to these concepts than meets the eye. For example, suppose we discover a relationship between the price of a product and its sales. If, in addition to price, we see that other variables, such as availability and quality, are also correlated with sales, then how do we know which variables are more important? How do we know that quality is not simply a function of availability? Suppose consumers rate a bank on 20 different attributes such as *fast service, reliable service, courteous service, modernity, friendliness,* etc., might it be possible that these 20 different dimensions are simple expressions of just three underlying factors such as good service, modernity and efficiency? If a minority group is poorly paid, is it because it is being discriminated against or is it because it is not as well educated or as experienced as other minority groups? In other words, when we simply consider two variables at a time, we quite often look at only the *manifest relationships*. However, the *latent relationships* among attributes are often of greater importance in marketing research than the manifest relationships. Latent relationships are particularly relevant when we study multivariable relationships. For example, when we analyze the interrelationships among say 20 or 30 variables simultaneously, the relationships are seldom manifest, they are usually latent.

When analyzing data sets that contain a large number of latent variables, special research and analytical techniques are usually needed to tease out the hidden relationships in data. This chapter provides an introduction to a variety of such techniques used in marketing research. The main purpose of the chapter is to provide a panoramic view of the various techniques available to the researcher to solve marketing research problems. (Providing a thorough statistical presentation of the use and interpretation of the techniques presented in this chapter is beyond the scope of this book.)

SIMPLE AND MULTIPLE LINEAR REGRESSION ANALYSIS

Regression analysis is an important area in marketing research, as it is in many areas in which survey data are collected with the purpose of determining relationships between sets of variables. Regression analysis is a very broad topic. In this section, we'll investigate the basic logic of regression by studying simple linear regression and then extend that understanding by studying an example of multiple regression.

Regression analysis is a technique that enables us to understand the relationship between one particular variable and a set of other variables. Here are a few examples:

- How is purchase intent affected by customer perceptions of the product as expressed by their ratings on product attributes?

- How is readership of a magazine related to social class characteristics as measured by a set of demographic traits?

- How are sales affected by distribution, seasonality, inflation and other such factors?

Regression analysis enables us to understand the nature, direction and strength of such relationships.

THE MAJOR RESULTS OF REGRESSION

1. The relationship between the dependent variable and the independent variables. Multiple regression analysis yields an equation of the form (for example):

Overall liking = 0.8 x rating on sweetness

+ 0.6 x rating on flavour

+ 0.3 x rating on colour

...

+ 0.2 (intercept)

The values of overall liking are treated as if they depend on the ratings on sweetness, ratings on flavour and ratings on colour that were provided by the respondents. By convention, overall liking is called the *dependent variable* or *criterion variable* and the rating on sweetness, rating on flavour and rating on colour are called the three *independent variables*. The numbers in the above equation (0.8, 0.6, 0.3 ...) are called *regression coefficients* (B coefficients). They are simply weights assigned to each rating, depending on the contribution of each characteristic to explain overall liking. If you wanted to predict a person's overall liking, then you would multiply that person's rating on each of the above variables by the corresponding regression coefficient and add them up. The resultant number is that person's predicted rating on overall liking.

2. The relative importance of variables. The technique also provides a measure known as *beta coefficients* (standardized B coefficients). Beta coefficients indicate the relative importance of the variables. For example, a variable with a beta coefficient of 0.6 is twice as important as another variable with a coefficient of 0.3.

3. The strength of relationship. Regression analysis also yields a measure known as R^2 (coefficient of determination) which measures the amount of "variance explained." Suppose in the earlier example that we conducted a regression analysis where we investigated the relationship between overall liking and the rating on sweetness, rating on flavour and rating on colour. If the resulting analysis showed us that the coefficient of determination (R^2) is 0.85, that would mean that the rating on sweetness, rating on flavour and rating on colour would explain 85% (0.85 x 100) of the variation in the values of overall liking obtained from the sample. If you could accurately predict a person's overall liking by plugging that person's rating of the brand on sweetness, flavour and colour, then the R^2 would be 1.00. On the other hand, if those three predictor variables provided absolutely no help in predicting overall liking, the coefficient of determination would be zero.

There are several different procedures available to carry out multiple regression analysis. The two most commonly used techniques are *stepwise* and *simultaneous* methods. In stepwise forward regression, each independent variable is entered sequentially depending on its ability to explain variance of the dependent variable. The one variable that explains the most variation in the values of the dependent variable is added first. Then the second most powerful variable is added, then the third, and so on. In simultaneous regression, all the independent variables are entered at one time. The researcher might then identify those predictor variables which are most valuable for prediction and re-run the regression including only those most effective variables.

WHEN TO USE REGRESSION ANALYSIS

Use regression analysis when

- you want to determine the influence of one or more variables on a given variable
- all your variables (both criterion and predictors) are interval-scaled. (Some predictor variables may be nominal-scaled. These variables are called *dummy variables.*

WHAT YOU GET OUT OF REGRESSION ANALYSIS

The regression analysis technique:

- provides an equation that shows that variables are important in contributing to the dependent or criterion variable
- identifies the relative importance of each of the independent or predictor variables
- determines how much variance is explained by the independent variables that significantly influence the dependent variable
- provides an equation that can be used to predict the values of the criterion variable if the values of the predictor variables are known.

A PRACTICAL APPLICATION OF REGRESSION ANALYSIS

As an example of regression analysis, we'll refer to a study conducted for Firestone Canada Inc. during 1981. The intention of this study was to determine the perception of Firestone automotive service among a sample of Firestone's past customers, to determine the preferences for various characteristics of automotive service, and to develop a profile of the way in which the respondents think of automotive service. Two components of that study are presented in Exhibits 23.1 and 23.2. The respondents were asked 13 questions regarding their perceptions of various characteristics of automotive service pertaining to the last time they had their cars serviced at Firestone. Those statements are listed in Exhibit 23.1 as they appeared in the questionnaire.

Exhibit 23.1 Perceptions of Last Automotive Service at Firestone

2. Remembering back to this **most recent** service or purchase occasion at a **Firestone** store, please check the boxes below which indicate whether you strongly agree, somewhat agree, neither agree nor disagree, somewhat disagree or strongly disagree with each of the following statements.

	STRONGLY AGREE 1	SOMEWHAT AGREE 2	NEITHER AGREE NOR DISAGREE 3	SOMEWHAT DISAGREE 4	STRONGLY DISAGREE 5
All services were done correctly	[ ]	[ ]	[ ]	[ ]	[ ]
The mechanic was courteous	[ ]	[ ]	[ ]	[ ]	[ ]
Car did not run well afterwards	[ ]	[ ]	[ ]	[ ]	[ ]
Work was done on time	[ ]	[ ]	[ ]	[ ]	[ ]
Service manager was trustworthy	[ ]	[ ]	[ ]	[ ]	[ ]
The bill was unreasonably high	[ ]	[ ]	[ ]	[ ]	[ ]
The waiting area was comfortable	[ ]	[ ]	[ ]	[ ]	[ ]
Staff was courteous and helpful	[ ]	[ ]	[ ]	[ ]	[ ]
The location was inconvenient	[ ]	[ ]	[ ]	[ ]	[ ]
The mechanic was competent	[ ]	[ ]	[ ]	[ ]	[ ]
Excellent credit terms	[ ]	[ ]	[ ]	[ ]	[ ]
Convenient business hours	[ ]	[ ]	[ ]	[ ]	[ ]
They provided prompt attention	[ ]	[ ]	[ ]	[ ]	[ ]

(Some of the statements above are presented as negative statements. During the analysis, the scales were all converted to be positive. Also, the scale was changed in the computer so that it ran from 1 meaning strongly disagree to 5 being strongly agree. In the data analysis, the 13 questions were labelled V075 to V087.)

The respondents were then asked to indicate their intention to take their cars back to Firestone for further servicing in the future.

Exhibit 23.2   Intention to Return to Firestone

3. How likely are you to take your car back in the future to Firestone for servicing, repairs or tires? (Please check a box below.)

     [   ] 1   DEFINITELY WOULD TAKE BACK TO FIRESTONE

     [   ] 2   PROBABLY WOULD TAKE BACK

     [   ] 3   MIGHT OR MIGHT NOT TAKE BACK

     [   ] 4   PROBABLY WOULD NOT TAKE BACK

     [   ] 5   DEFINITELY WOULD NOT TAKE BACK

(For statistical analysis, the scale in this question was transformed in the computer to run from 1 being definitely would not take back to 5 meaning definitely would take back. In the data analysis, this question is labelled V088S.)

The two question types found in Exhibits 23.1 and 23.2 occur fairly often in marketing research projects. Of course, one basic question that the researchers can ask is whether there is a relationship between customers' perceptions of their last automotive service and their intentions to go back to Firestone in the future. With the questions in their present form, the problem can be approached with regression analysis.

Before beginning the analysis, the researchers might have some idea of which aspects of automotive service (predictor variables from Exhibit 23.1) might be most strongly related to a customer's intention to return to an automotive service outlet (the question presented in Exhibit 23.2). These preconceived notions of promising relationships are important to lead the researchers in rewarding directions rather than wasting time on analysis that would be judged obviously fruitless by anyone working in the marketing of automotive service. Although these basic practical feelings about relationships are critical to the efficient analysis, the regression analysis approach begins with a basic null hypothesis that the perceptions of the customers are not all related to their intentions to return. The alternate hypothesis is that some combination of the perceptual variables is related to the intentions of the customers to return. These alternate hypotheses are what "make sense" to the knowledgeable practitioner.

The marketing researcher would usually begin the analysis by working with the total set of 13 independent variables and then eliminating those that are not strongly related to the dependent variable, intention to return, and finally distilling the independent variables to that subset which are most strongly related to the dependent variable. The basic practical reason for this is to end up with the information necessary to develop an advertising platform or, perhaps, a service improvement program. Both of these activities should be focused on only a few truly important characteristics of automotive service, not the full 13. Naturally, an advertising campaign that tries to convey information about 13 aspects of automotive service would be confusing to customers. But a campaign based on two to four important criteria for evaluating a garage could be quite effective for the advertiser.

We will treat the full set of 13 independent variables in the next subsection on multiple regression. However, in order to present the fundamental logic and important basic components of regression, we'll first treat the simple regression case of testing whether one particular independent variable is related to the dependent variable. To make this very simple, let's just take the first of the questions from Exhibit 23.11, "Do you agree or disagree that all services were done correctly?" A real benefit of beginning with simple regression is that it has a direct visual analogue. The data area tabled in Exhibit 23.3 and plotted in Exhibit 23.4.

Exhibit 23.3 Frequency Table of Intention to Return (V087S) by All Services Were Done Correctly (V075S)

| Values of V088S | Values of Variable V075S | | | | | |
	1	2	3	4	5	Total
5	0	0	12	64	284	360
4	5	20	19	123	167	334
3	9	13	10	46	66	144
2	12	29	4	12	0	57
1	24	15	0	0	0	39
Total	50	77	45	245	517	934

The graph corresponding to the data resulting when two variables are measured on similar five-point scales is not very exciting. However, these types of variables are quite often found in marketing research studies. The data from the table in Exhibit 23.3 are graphed in Exhibit 23.4. The larger and darker points correspond with greater frequencies for the two corresponding values of variables. For example, the two value combinations with the fewest respondents reporting those values (other than zero) are V075S=3, V088S=2 and V075S=1, V088S-4, while the most dense combination is V075S=5, V088S=5 where the respondents strongly agreed that all services were done correctly and that they would definitely take their cars back to Firestone. Since the visual intention of simple linear regression is to fit a straight line to the scatter of data points, a straight regression line was overlaid to the points in Exhibit 23.4.

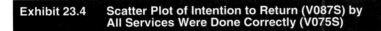

Exhibit 23.4   Scatter Plot of Intention to Return (V087S) by All Services Were Done Correctly (V075S)

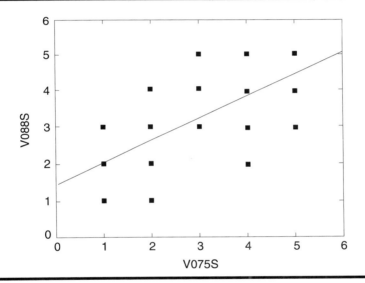

Although it's probably fairly easy for most people to envision that the line would be drawn from lower left to upper right for this scatter of points, it would be quite difficult in most situations to visually find the line that best fits the scatter. In fact, before we could even attempt to find that best line we would need some criterion for what would qualify as a *best fit* regression line. The best fit criterion for regression is achieved by a methodology called the *least squares* approach. Basically, this is similar to adjusting the line through the scatter of points until the sum of the distances from the points above the line to the line is equal to the sum of the distances from the points below the line to the line. In order to obtain the best fitting regression line, one of many computer programs would be used except when working with very simple data bases.

Of course, the equation of a straight line is

$$y = a + bx$$

where y is the dependent variable intention to return to Firestone and x is the independent variable of whether all services were done correctly the last time service was obtained from Firestone. The a in the equation is the value that indicates where the line intersects the y-axis and b is the slope of the regression line. The parameters a and b are the main numbers produced by the statistical analysis conducted by computer. For the data from the Firestone study, the regression results in Exhibits 23.5 and 23.6 were obtained from a computer program.

Exhibit 23.5   Analysis of Variance of the Regression

SOURCE	SUM-OF-SQUARES	DF	MEAN-SQUARE	F-RATIO	P
REGRESSION	464.116	1	464.1169	699.202	0.000
RESIDUAL	618.643	932	0.664		

Exhibit 23.6   Regression Coefficients and Tests

DEP VAR: V088S   N: 934   MULTIPLE R: .655   SQUARED MULTIPLE R: .429
ADJUSTED SQUARED MULTIPLE R: .428   STANDARD ERROR OF ESTIMATE: 0.815

Variable	Coefficient	Std. Error	Std. Coeff	Tolerance	T	P(2- Tail)
CONSTANT	1.477	0.098	0.000	.	14.991	0.000
V075S	0.600	0.023	0.655	1.000	26.442	0.000

A regression analysis such as this can be performed using one of many statistical computer programs available for personal computers as well as for mainframe computers. Each of the statistical programs is capable of providing a substantial amount of analysis. We'll concentrate on the most important information that would be extracted from the computer printouts to help the researcher answer the basic question of whether intention to return can be predicted from perceived service. (There are several statistical aspects of regression analysis that will not be covered here because of their technical nature.)

The first piece of information we'll consider is the actual estimate of the regression equation. From Exhibit 23.6, we can select the values of the constant, a, and the slope coefficient, b. These values are 1.477 and 0.600, respectively. The regression equation can now be written as

$$y = 1.477 + 0.600x$$

Notice that the y intercept of 1.477 coincides roughly with the place where the line intercepts the V088S axis in Exhibit 23.4. The slope of 0.60 can be interpreted as the increase in intention to return to Firestone for each one point increase in agreement that all services were done correctly during the last service at Firestone. Assuming that this regression line exactly fits the data (an unrealistic situation when working with survey data), if we knew the level of agreement that all services were done correctly then we could also know that person's intention to return to Firestone just by substituting his or her value for V075S into the regression equation. So if V075S were equal to 4 then V088S, intention, would be equal to 1.477 + 0.600 x 4 or 3.877.

At this point, it could be argued that a person's intention score can't be 3.877, it would have to be either 3 or 4, so that 3.877 is not realistic. This is true. In fact, some would state that regression should not be executed on this type of data since it is not truly interval- or ratio-scaled, i.e., it's not *continuous* data. True again, in the strict sense. However, this type of data is almost routinely subjected to regression analysis in marketing research practice. Some of the strict rules of formal statistics might be violated, but using regression analysis in this way has been shown to be robust and is common practice in marketing research.

Now that we've interpreted how the regression line would be identified from the analysis, we should determine whether that regression line is at all useful in explaining the variation of data values between the two variables. Regression will almost always provide an equation. However, the truly important component of the analysis is identifying whether that equation can be used to help understand the respondents' attitudes or behaviour. The basic question of whether there is or is not a relationship between the perceptual variables (the independent or predictor variables) and the intention to return variable (the dependent or criterion variable) is addressed by the analysis of variance table presented in Exhibit 23.5.

The information contained in Exhibit 23.5 is labelled "Analysis of Variance of the Regression." There are several pieces of information that indicate the value of the regression analysis in helping to explain why the values of the dependent variable are different for various values of the independent variables. The analysis of variance table presents the F-ratio statistic and its corresponding level of significance "P," as labelled in Exhibit 23.5.

The F-ratio indicates the degree to which the independent variables influence the variance calculation for the dependent variable, V088S in this example. In general, the larger the value of the F-ratio, the stronger is the influence of the independent variable(s). The P value indicates the likelihood that a conclusion stating that the dependent variable is related to or dependent upon the independent variables is in fact false. In Exhibit 23.3 this P value of 0.000 implies that the chance is extremely small that the dependent variable is not related to the set of independent variables, in this case just one.

Three additional values that indicate the strength of the relationship between the dependent variable and the independent variable(s) are presented in the first two lines of Exhibit 23.6. These are the "multiple R," the "adjusted squared multiple R" and the "standard error of estimate." Since there is only one independent or predictor variable in this regression, the multiple R is the simple Pearson correlation coefficient. Since this value is positive, we can feel comfortable that as a customer's agreement increases that all services were done correctly so his or her intention to return to Firestone for automotive service also increases. The values of the multiple R can range from –1.0 to +1.0. A value of 0.0 means that there is no relationship between the points.

The squared multiple R is the square of the Pearson correlation coefficient and is also called the coefficient of determination. This value can vary between zero and one, with values closer to one better than values closer to zero. The value of 0.429 in Exhibit 23.6 is a moderately strong value that indicates a fairly reasonable ability of the independent variable, V075S, to explain the variation in the values of the dependent variable, V088S. This squared multiple R actually denotes the proportion of variation in the dependent variable which is accounted for, or explained by, the independent variable. In this case about 42.9% of the variation in the values of customers' intentions to return are explained by their agreement or disagreement that all services were done correctly the last time.

The squared multiple R can be formulated in general as

$$R^2 = \frac{\text{explained variation}}{\text{total variation}} = 1 - \frac{\text{unexplained variation}}{\text{total variation}}$$

As stated earlier, if R^2 is zero then there is no relationship between the variables and if R^2 is equal to 1.0 then there is a perfect linear relationship. Rather than wondering whether a value of R^2 between 0 and 1 indicates a strong relationship or not, a statistical test is available that can provide a statistical answer with very little effort. This is the same test which was used at the end of Chapter 22 when the Spearman correlation coefficient was discussed. The null hypothesis is that $R^2 = 0$. The appropriate t-test formula is

$$t = \frac{R\sqrt{n-2}}{\sqrt{1-R^2}}$$

For this example, the calculation is

$$t = \frac{0.655\sqrt{934 - 2}}{\sqrt{1 - 0.429}} = 26.46$$

This value can be checked as you would check any t-test value. The number of degrees of freedom is $n-2$ or 932. For a 5% level of risk and a one-tailed test (we're only concerned whether R^2 is greater than 0) the t-distribution test value is 1.645. Since 26.46 is so much greater than the critical value of 1.645, we can safely conclude that there is a significant relationship between customers' perception that all services were done correctly and their intention to return to Firestone.

The adjusted squared multiple R of 0.428 indicates the proportion of variance we can expect to explain when using this regression model with a new sample drawn from the same population. It adjusts the squared multiple R by the sample size and the number of predictor variables.

Another important statistic from Exhibit 23.6 is the *standard error of estimate*. This statistic is used when predicting a value of the dependent or criterion variable that would result from a particular value of the independent or predictor variable. For example, we saw earlier that if a customer said that he or she somewhat agreed (value 4) that all services were done correctly last time, then the regression equation would predict that the customer would give a value of 3.877 for his or her intention to take the car back to Firestone for service. As we saw in Chapters 21 and 22, this point estimate for the intention would often be accompanied by an interval estimate based on a standard error. The standard error used for this calculation in regression is called the standard error of estimate and is provided as one of the numbers in the computer output of Exhibit 23.6 and of nearly every computerized regression analysis. The calculation for a confidence interval estimate of the intention to return which coincides with a person's somewhat agreeing that all services were done correctly is provided by many statistical programs. Exhibit 23.7 shows the confidence intervals for many values of the independent variable smoothed to provide what are called *confidence bands* around the regression line. Notice that the confidence band is closest to the regression line when the value of V075S is at its mean of 4.18 and becomes wider as the values of V075S diverge from the mean. This is because our knowledge of the relationship is best at the mean and becomes less accurate at the extreme values. Users of regression should always be cautious of making inferences about the dependent variable based on the high and low values of the predictor variable and should never extend the regression beyond the range of the sample data.

Exhibit 23.7   95% Confidence Bands Around the Regression Line

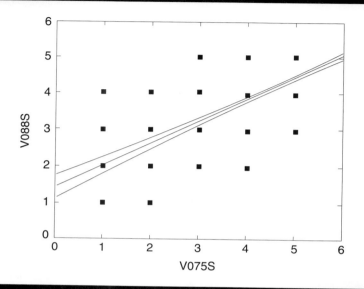

The standard error of estimate is also used as a measure of the goodness-of-fit of a regression. One of the objectives of executing a regression is to minimize the standard error of estimate. However, the benefit of using this measure is enjoyed primarily when executing multiple regression, as we will see shortly.

After investigating the tests related to whether the overall regression analysis is valuable, it's necessary to consider the information regarding the individual regression parameters. The lower part of Exhibit 23.6 provides this information. Let's focus on V075S, the only predictor variable in the regression at this stage. Previously, we saw that the coefficient given in the V075S row of Exhibit 23.6 provides the value that multiplies V075S in the regression equation. The next column displays the standard error of the regression coefficient for V075S.

A useless regression is one that has a regression line that is horizontal or nearly so since the value or y stays the same regardless of the value of x that is substituted into the regression equation. The coefficient of V075S is 0.600 in Exhibit 23.6 and many people might conclude that the value is very close to zero. However, the regression must be expressed in relative units, i.e., in standard error units, before it's compared to zero. In fact, this method of analysis will lead us into performing a t-test on the regression coefficient.

Before explaining this t-test we need to introduce the concept of the *true regression relationship* between the variables, i.e., that which would result if the complete data set from the population were analyzed, this is denoted by

$$y_i = \alpha + \beta x_i + \varepsilon_i$$

The parameter σ is the true vertical axis intercept if we were working with the population data and β is the true slope. The parameter ε, epsilon, is the difference between the actual value of y in the data set and the predicted value of y_i for a given value of x_i when using the equation $y_i = a + \beta x_i$. This Σ is typically referred to as the residual, i.e., the amount left over which can't be explained after the value of y was predicted from the regression equation from a value of x.

Often, this testing is represented as a formal hypothesis testing situation where hypotheses are established for the regression coefficient. To test whether the variable is useful or not involves determining whether the slope coefficient for that variable is equal to zero or statistically different from zero. For example,

$$H_o: \beta = 0 \qquad , \text{risk} = 0.05$$
$$H_a: \beta \neq 0$$

The t-test for the coefficient of x is represented as

$$t = \frac{b - \beta}{s_b}$$

where s_b is the standard error of the regression coefficient. For the Firestone example, the calculation for the t-test to determine whether that coefficient of 0.600 from Exhibit 23.6 is close to zero or significantly different from zero is given below,

$$t = \frac{0.600 - 0.000}{0.023} = 26.087$$

The difference between this value and the t-value of 26.442 in Exhibit 23.6 is due to rounding. This t-value is found to be larger than the critical t-value of 1.96 for a 5% level of significance. The appropriate conclusion is that the coefficient of 0.600 for V075S is significantly different from zero. This information along with R^2 and F-ratio values from Exhibits 23.5 and 23.6 provide strong evidence that there is a significant relationship between Firestone customers' agreement that all services were done correctly during the last service and their intention to return to Firestone for automotive service. The relationship is such that the higher the level of agreement that the service was done correctly, the greater the tendency for the respondents to report higher levels of intention to return to Firestone.

MULTIPLE REGRESSION

The simple linear regression presented in the previous section investigated the relationship between one predictor variable and one criterion variable. In marketing research practice, there might be several questions (predictor variable candidates) which are hypothesized to be related to another question (the criterion variable) and that could help to explain respondents' attitudes or behaviour as measured by that question. In this section, we'll present the basics of multiple regression, the procedure that is used to analyze the relationship between several predictor variables and one criterion variable.

In the last section, we selected as the sole predictor or independent variable the first of the variables coinciding with the questions listed in Exhibit 23.1 that were intended to measure respondents' perceptions regarding their last service experience. This was variable V075S and it was intended to measure whether Firestone customers felt that all the services which should have been performed on their cars during their last service at Firestone had been done correctly. The overall conclusion of the last section was that V075S was substantially helpful in explaining the variation in respondents' reported intentions to return to Firestone. In this section, we will investigate V075S as well as the other 12 questions pertaining to the respondents' perceptions about their last service visits to Firestone stores. Before beginning any statistical analysis, the researcher should have hypothesized that certain variables are likely to be related to some other variable(s). There should not be a wholesale act of throwing everything into the computer and then taking everything that the computer gives back. In the Firestone study, the researchers had legitimate bases for hypothesizing that any or all of the 13 perceptual variables were related to customers' intentions to return to Firestone for further car servicing. Typically, the research procedure begins by regressing all of the hypothesized predictor variables on the criterion variable, identifying which are likely to be useful for understanding and predicting the criterion variable and then extending the analysis to the smaller subset that looks most promising. This process may continue until the smallest set of significantly useful variables has been isolated. This procedure can be executed based on the researcher's decision regarding the best set of variables to investigate or a procedure called stepwise regression can be used. If stepwise regression is used, the regression should be re-run on the set of final variables decided upon in order to ensure that the correct calculations are performed.

Exhibits 23.8 and 23.9 present the computer output for the regression involving all 13 predictor variables and the criterion variable, V088S.

Exhibit 23.8 Analysis of Variance of the Regression

SOURCE	SUM-OF-SQUARES	DF	MEAN-SQUARE	F-RATIO	P
REGRESSION	394.788	13	30.368	49.343	0.000
RESIDUAL	390.198	634	0.615		

Exhibit 23.9 Regression Coefficients and Tests

DEP VAR: V088S   N: 648   MULTIPLE R: 0.709   SQUARED MULTIPLE R: 0.503

ADJUSTED SQUARED MULTIPLE R: 0.493   STANDARD ERROR OF ESTIMATE: 0.785

VARIABLE	COEFFICIENT	STD ERROR	STD COEF	TOLERANCE	T	P(2 TAIL)
CONSTANT	0.054	0.219	0.000		0.246	0.806
V075S	0.367	0.037	0.400	0.478	9.870	0.000
V076S	0.036	0.044	0.029	0.601	0.807	0.420
V077S	0.034	0.027	0.043	0.681	1.271	0.204
V078S	0.021	0.035	0.021	0.647	0.602	0.547
V079S	0.157	0.039	0.149	0.561	3.990	0.000
V080S	0.085	0.028	0.098	0.785	3.086	0.002
V081S	0.006	0.028	0.007	0.838	0.221	0.825
V082S	-0.058	0.051	-0.047	0.465	-1.140	0.255
V083S	0.046	0.024	0.055	0.934	1.888	0.060
V084S	0.070	0.038	0.068	0.555	1.817	0.070
V085S	0.001	0.036	0.001	0.763	0.039	0.969
V086S	-0.026	0.038	-0.023	0.685	-0.675	0.500
V087S	0.215	0.044	0.199	0.482	4.942	0.000

The F-ratio from Exhibit 23.8 indicates the degree to which the independent or predictor variables influence the variance calculation for the dependent or criterion variable, V088S in this example. In general, the larger the value of the F-ratio, the stronger is the influence of the predictor variables. The P value indicates the likelihood that a conclusion stating that the criterion variable is related to or dependent upon the predictor variables is in fact false. In Exhibit 23.8 this P value of 0.000 implies that the chance is extremely small that the dependent variable is not related to the set of predictor variables.

Two additional values that indicate the strength of the relationship between the criterion variable and the predictor variables are presented in the first two lines of Exhibit 23.9. These are the "adjusted squared multiple R" and the "standard error of estimate." The "adjusted squared multiple R" value of 0.493 in Exhibit 23.9 is a moderately strong value indicating a fairly reasonable ability of the 13 predictor variables to explain the variation in the values of the criterion variable.

The standard error of estimate with a value of 0.785 at the top of Exhibit 23.9 is a measure of the variation of the residual or error terms of the regression around zero. The effectiveness of the predictor variables in explaining the variation in the values of the criterion variable can be monitored by how close the remaining unexplained variation, as measured by the standard error of estimate, is to zero. When performing a regression analysis, the researcher often attempts several times to improve on the effectiveness of the regression. After each attempt, whether the standard error of estimate has decreased in value or increased is a good indication of whether the current analysis is better or worse, respectively, than the previous analyses.

Comparing these indicators of goodness-of-fit of the multiple regression equation (now representing a plane rather than a simple straight line) to the cloud of sample data points relative to the fit of the simple linear regression presented in Exhibits 23.5 and 23.6, we can see that the adjusted squared multiple R has improved from 0.428 to 0.493 and the standard error of estimate has improved (decreased in value) from 0.815 to 0.785. Also in Exhibit 23.9, the column of regression coefficients provides the numbers to write the regression equation. For this example, we can write the regression equation as

V088S = 0.054 + 0.367 V075S + 0.036 V076S + 0.034 V077S + 0.021 V078S + 0.157 V079S + 0.085 V080S + 0.006 V081S – 0.058 V082S + 0.046 V083S + 0.070 V084S + 0.001 V085S – 0.026 V086S + 0.215 V087S

Although we saw from the analysis of variance in Exhibit 23.8 that the regression was "significant," i.e., worthwhile from a statistical point of view, we should ask if we can't make the analysis better. Better in this case means to improve the "fit" of the regression to the scatter of points formed by the criterion and predictor variables or to maintain a constant or better fit while reducing the complexity of the regression equation, i.e., eliminating some of the predictor variables. We saw that the fit of the regression equation improved somewhat in going from having only V075S in the equation to having all 13 variables present. However, we need to investigate the contribution of each of the predictor variables to the regression.

The resources for eliminating variables from the regression equation are contained in the sixth and seventh columns of the table in Exhibit 23.9. The t-values and their corresponding values of P(2 tail) can be used to decide which of the predictor variables to keep in the regression equation and which can be deleted. The t-values contained in the sixth column are similar to the t-values produced from t-tests. Essentially, the t-values in the sixth column measure the distance in standard error units that each of the variable's coefficients is away from zero. If a coefficient were equal to zero, we could conclude that there is no relationship between that predictor variable and the criterion variable. If a 5% level of significance were used, then for this example the critical t-value would be approximately 1.96 for concluding whether to keep the variable in the equation or not.

Starting with V075S, we can see that the corresponding t-value in Exhibit 23.9 is 9.870 and the P(2 tail) is 0.000. These values indicate that V075S should be kept in the equation at this stage. Now look at V076S which has a t-value of 0.807 and a P(2 tail) of 0.420. This information directs us to drop V076S from the regression equation. Continuing, we find that V079S, V080S, V087S, and once again, V075S should be kept in the regression. We can see that because of p-values above the critical level of significance of 5%, V077S, V078S, V081S, V082S, V083S, V084S, V085S, V086S and, repeating, V076S should be dropped from the equation. The regression has been re-run with the five most promising predictor variables in the equation and the results are presented in Exhibits 23.10 and 23.11.

Exhibit 23.10 Analysis of Variance

(Non-Significant Variables Deleted from the Full Set of 13 Variables)

SOURCE	SUM-OF-SQUARES	DF	MEAN-SQUARE	F-RATIO	P
REGRESSION	510.116	4	127.529	217.781	0.000
RESIDUAL	483.108	825	0.586		

Exhibit 23.11 Regression of the Five Significant Variables on V088S

DEP VAR: V088S   N: 830   MULTIPLE R:0.717 SQUARED MULTIPLE R: 0.514
ADJUSTED SQUARED MULTIPLE R: 0.511   STANDARD ERROR OF ESTIMATE 0.765
175 cases deleted due to missing data

VARIABLE	COEFFICIENT	STD ERROR	STD COEF	TOLERANCE	T	P(2 TAIL)
CONSTANT	0.179	0.140	0.000		1.283	0.200
V075S	0.406	0.027	0.440	0.695	15.105	0.000
V079S	0.192	0.031	0.183	0.665	6.150	0.000
V080S	0.107	0.022	0.123	0.922	4.872	0.000
V087S	0.212	0.031	0.198	0.720	6.934	0.000

The F-ratio of 217.781 in Exhibit 23.10 is still significant. In addition, in Exhibit 23.11 the standard error of estimate has decreased from 0.785 to 0.765 and the adjusted squared multiple R has increased from 0.493 to 0.511. Although these changes might not seem very substantial, the fit of the regression equation to the data has improved, while the number of predictor variables has dropped from 13 to four. Since simplicity along with explanatory power is the objective of regression analysis, the steps that have led to the last solution in Exhibit 23.11 have been worthwhile. In concluding this multiple regression example, it must be mentioned that *outlier* values, i.e., those with rather extreme values in comparison to the averages, have been eliminated to improve the fit of the equations. The elimination of outliers is a common practice in statistical analysis.

In summary, we can state that respondents' perceptions regarding whether all services were done correctly, the service manager was trustworthy, the bill was unreasonably high, and whether they provided prompt attention, are related to whether they intend to take their cars back to Firestone for service in the future. The regression equation relating these variables is

$$y = 0.179 + 0.406 \ V075S + 0.192 \ V079S + 0.107 \ V080S + 0.212 \ V087S.$$

The values that any former customer of Firestone provides for the four predictor variables can be substituted in the above equation to provide a prediction of that person's intention to take his or her car back to Firestone for automotive service. The predicted value would be a number between 1 and 5 on the intention scale. There will be research situations in which the interest lies in predicting into which groups the population might be divided. In these cases, discriminant analysis would be preferable to regression. Discriminant analysis is presented in the next section.

DISCRIMINANT ANALYSIS

Many marketing research surveys gather information pertaining to the demographics of the consumers as well as ratings on product attributes. Such information is often used to predict the probable purchase behaviour of the consumer. Discriminant analysis is a technique that identifies the importance of different variables in determining whether a consumer belongs to a particular group or not. Discriminant analysis might be used to accomplish the following tasks:

- Given a person's demographic characteristics, can we determine the possibility of his or her being a reader of *The Toronto Star*?
- Given a consumer's ratings of attribute importance of a product, we could attempt to predict whether he or she will use Brand X.

- We could try to identify the relative importance of different attribute ratings in determining whether the consumer will prefer Brand A to Brand B.

In discriminant analysis, we get an equation similar to that in regression analysis. By substituting the actual ratings of the independent variables in the equation, we should be better able to classify the respondent as being a member of one group or another. The accuracy of the classification is also determined by the technique.

A HISTORICAL EXAMPLE

Some years ago, Frederick Mosteller, a Harvard professor, faced a rather intriguing problem. The problem related to the authorship of a few papers which had been published as *The Federalist Papers* over 150 years earlier. The authorship of some of these papers was in dispute: they had been written either by James Madison or by Alexander Hamilton. Both Madison and Hamilton had held high political office at about the same time. Madison was the President of the United States and Hamilton was the Secretary of the United States Treasury. Both held similar political views and both wrote about similar political matters. Their personal histories were also similar and they were about the same age. To thicken the plot, they did not sign their papers and later each claimed sole authorship of the disputed papers.

Mosteller started with an assumption that sounded reasonable: different authors use common words at different rates. He selected the five words most frequently used by Madison and Hamilton. The words were *and, in, of, the* and *to*. By analyzing the known writings of Madison and Hamilton, Mosteller arrived at the frequency with which each author used these five words. Using discriminant analysis, he was able to assign a weight to each of the five words. These weights were later used to determine the authorship of the disputed *Federalist Papers*. (Incidentally, Madison was the winner although he wasn't around to know it.)

At first blush, this story appears irrelevant to marketing research. But, in fact, the problem is very similar to several marketing research problems. Mosteller tried to find out whether a piece of writing belonged to Madison or Hamilton on the basis of their other writings. In marketing research, a similar situation arises when we try to find out whether a person would buy Brand A or Brand B, on the basis of his or her ratings of *other* variables or based on personal characteristics. In the next section, we'll try to predict whether Firestone Canada customers will or will not return to Firestone for automotive service based on their perceptions of various aspects of automotive service during their last visit to Firestone.

TWO-GROUP DISCRIMINANT ANALYSIS OF THE FIRESTONE EXAMPLE

Suppose that Firestone Canada wanted to predict whether people intended to return to Firestone for automotive service or whether they intended not to return. The five-point intention-to-return scale presented in Exhibit 23.2 could be reframed as a two-point scale where 1 meant that the person had said either that they definitely would not return (previously the value 1) or probably would not return (previously 2) and where 2 meant that they either definitely would return (previously 5) or probably would return (previously 4). The midpoint on the scale was not included so that we can better discriminate between those who expressed either negative or positive intentions.

For this initial example, only two of the 13 predictor variables will be used to help determine whether an individual will or won't return to Firestone for automotive service. These two variables are the customers' perception regarding whether the services were done correctly during the last service at Firestone and whether they provided prompt attention.

For illustrative purposes, the answers to the three relevant questions provided by 20 past Firestone customers are listed in Exhibit 23.12. Ten of the customers said that they would not return, while then said that they would return to Firestone for automotive service.

Exhibit 23.12	A Sample of 10 People from the Firestone Example for Two-Group Discrimination		
Person Number	Intention V088SC	All Services Done Correctly V075S	They Provided Prompt Attention V087S
1	Won't Return	1	5
2	Won't Return	1	4
3	Won't Return	1	3
4	Won't Return	2	3
5	Won't Return	2	4
6	Won't Return	4	4
7	Won't Return	1	1
8	Won't Return	2	1
9	Won't Return	2	2
10	Won't Return	3	1
11	Will Return	5	5
12	Will Return	2	4
13	Will Return	5	5

continued

Person Number	Intention V088SC	All Services Done Correctly V075S	They Provided Prompt Attention V087S
14	Will Return	5	5
15	Will Return	5	4
16	Will Return	5	3
17	Will Return	4	3
18	Will Return	5	5
19	Will Return	5	5
20	Will Return	5	5

Now that the five-point, intention-to-return to Firestone (V088S) scale has been redefined as a two-point scale, (V088SC), regression analysis should no longer be used to find the relationship between intention to return and perceptions of the last Firestone visit. However, two-group discriminant analysis is well suited to this task.

The graph in Exhibit 23.13 shows the scatter of points for respondents' perceptions that all services were done correctly and that prompt attention was provided. The circles are the will return points while the squares are the won't return points.

Exhibit 23.13   Scatter Graph of V075S and V087S

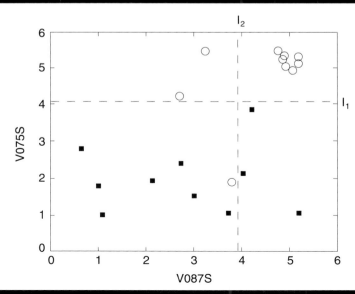

Discriminant analysis produces a function representing a line that is intended to separate the groups of points according to the criterion variable, in this case intention to return to Firestone. We can see from Exhibit 23.13 that a line perpendicular to the V076S axis, labelled l_1, does quite a good job of separating the points except for one of the will return points, which falls below the horizontal cutting line. The line perpendicular to the V087S axis, labelled l_2, does a fairly good job of discriminating between the groups of points. However, three points of each type fall in the wrong areas and would be misclassified if we were to use the cutting line that intersects the V087S axis.

The discriminant analysis approach develops an equation for a line which will best separate the two groups of points. In this case, that line will be some linear combination of V075S and V087S which has the greatest discriminating ability for this set of 20 observations.

Discriminant analysis is available as part of most large statistical analysis programs. This is true of both the mainframe and personal computer versions of SPSS, SAS, BMDP and SYSTAT. These computer programs provide a substantial amount of output for the discriminant analysis of a data set. In order to illustrate discriminant analysis for this example, we'll try to keep the amount of computer data output to the minimum level necessary to understand the procedure.

As in regression analysis, it's necessary to know which of the predictor or independent variables are effective in relating to the criterion or dependent variable. This information will be provided by a series of univariate F-tests. Exhibit 23.14 provides the table of univariate F-tests for the Firestone data.

For each of the perception variables, both the explained sum of squares (i.e., due to the variable) and the unexplained or error sum of squares are provided. The degrees of freedom are divided into the sums of squares to provide the MS (mean squares) or estimates of variance. The F-ratios are calculated by dividing the MS due to the variable by the error MS for that variable. For example, the F-ratio of 37.925 for V075S was calculated by dividing 36.450 by 0.961. The P values are the probabilities that F-values of the sizes listed could have been produced solely by chance by the base distributions. The higher the F-ratios and the lower the P values, the better is the predictive power of the variable in the relationship. We can see from Exhibit 23.14 that both V075S and V087S are valuable predictor variables.

The P values are used to decide whether a perception variable should be kept in the analysis or not. The P values are levels of risk of Type I errors. Suppose that a person had selected a 5% level of risk of a Type I error as his or her decision criterion, if the P value for a variable is smaller than 0.05, i.e., 5%, then the variable should be kept in the analysis. This is true for both the variables in Exhibit 23.14 for the Firestone case.

Exhibit 23.14 Univariate F Tests

Variable		Sum of Squares	Degrees of Freedom	Mean Squares	F-Ratios	P
V075S		36.450	1	36.450	37.925	0.000
	Error	17.300	18	0.961		
V087S		14.450	1	14.450	9.966	0.005
	Error	26.100	18	1.450		

As an overall measure of the strength of the relationship between the independent variables and the dependent variable, we'll refer to Exhibit 23.15. The results of three statistical tests are shown in that table: the Wilk's Lambda, Pillai Trace and the Hotelling-Lawley Trace. Each of these tests provides information about the effectiveness of the set of two predictor variables in explaining the dichotomous criterion variable. For each of these measures, the Prob-values are compared to the risk level specified, say 5% risk. If the Prob-value is less than the 5% risk, as it is here, the conclusion is that the relationship is significant and (barring other statistical problems such as interrelationships among the variables) should provide the ability to predict whether a person would or would not return to Firestone.

Exhibit 23.15 Multivariate Test Statistics

Test Statistic	Value of Test Statistic	F-Statistic	Degrees of Freedom	Prob
Wilk's Lambda	0.286	21.212	2, 17	0.000
Pillai Trace	0.714	21.212	2, 17	0.000
Hotelling-Lawley Trace	2.496	21.212	2, 17	0.000
Chi-Square Test of Residual Roots	21.275		2	0.000

Exhibit 23.16 lists information that will help to predict whether each individual customer is likely to return to Firestone or not.

Exhibit 23.16 Discriminant Coefficients and Loadings

Canonical correlations   0.845

Dependent variable canonical coefficients
Standardized by conditional (within groups) standard deviations

V075S	0.885
V087S	0.396

Canonical loadings (correlations between conditional dependent variables and dependent canonical factors)

V075S	0.919
V087S	0.471

Group classification function coefficients

	1	2
V075S	1.789	4.495
V087S	1.808	2.793

Group classification constants

1	2
− 4.923	−17.318

Most discriminant analysis programs generate values or scores for each of the respondent cases to help predict the group to which that respondent would probably belong. This information is presented in Exhibit 23.17.

The factor values in Exhibit 23.17 are obtained from substituting the data from the two predictor variables into the discriminant function. The factor scores are used to help assign each person to one or the other of the two groups formed from the criterion variable, intention to return. These two groups are won't return and will return. Those respondents whose factor scores are negative are predicted not to return, while those whose factor scores are positive are predicted to be in the will return group. The distance (1), distance(2), prob(1) and prob(2) values are also used for predicting the group to which each respondent will belong.

Exhibit 23.17 Discriminant Scores Calculated for Each of the 20 Cases

Case	Factor	Distance (1)	Distance(2)	Prob(1)	Prob(2)	Group	Predict
1	−1.588	2.121	3.744	0.992	0.008	1.000	1.000
2	−1.917	1.416	3.674	0.997	0.003	1.000	1.000
3	−2.246	0.950	3.790	0.999	0.001	1.000	1.000
4	−1.343	0.188	2.843	0.982	0.018	1.000	1.000
5	−1.014	0.997	2.659	0.954	0.046	1.000	1.000
6	0.792	2.293	0.712	0.085	0.915	1.000	2.000
7	−2.903	1.693	4.502	1.000	0.000	1.000	1.000
8	−2.000	1.512	3.779	0.998	0.002	1.000	1.000
9	−1.671	0.683	3.238	0.993	0.007	1.000	1.000
10	−1.097	1.951	3.222	0.964	0.036	1.000	1.000
11	2.024	3.528	0.559	0.002	0.998	2.000	2.000
12	−1.014	0.997	2.659	0.954	0.046	2.000	1.000
13	2.024	3.528	0.559	0.002	0.998	2.000	2.000
14	2.024	3.528	0.559	0.002	0.998	2.000	2.000
15	2.024	3.528	0.559	0.002	0.998	2.000	2.000
16	1.367	3.164	1.348	0.016	0.984	2.000	2.000
17	0.464	2.142	1.345	0.200	0.800	2.000	2.000
18	2.024	3.528	0.559	0.002	0.998	2.000	2.000
19	2.024	3.528	0.559	0.002	0.998	2.000	2.000
20	2.024	3.528	0.559	0.002	0.998	2.000	2.000

Exhibit 23.18 illustrates the discriminant function that is used to categorize the points. When the group 2 points, except for case 12, are projected onto the discriminant axis, they lie above the discriminant line and fall on the positive segment of the discriminant axis. The group 1 points, except for case 6, fall on the negative segment of the discriminant axis.

For the distance values in Exhibit 23.17, the distance value which is smaller indicates the group membership, while the prob-value which is higher directs the group assignment. For example, case 1 has a negative factor score, a Distance(1) value which indicates that the case is closer to group 1 than to group 2 and the Prob(1) which indicates that the probability is 0.992 that the person will not return and only 0.008 that he or she will return. With all this evidence, it's quite easy to assign respondent 1 to the won't return group. It turns out that this prediction is exactly what the respondent

Exhibit 23.18   The Discriminant Function

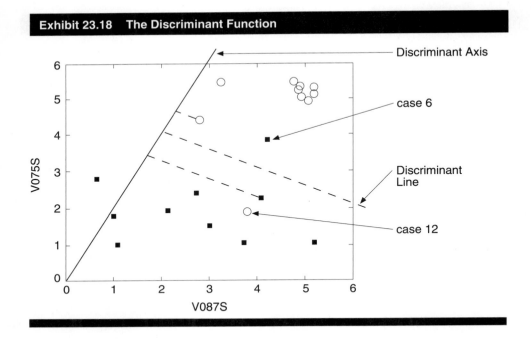

said in response to the intention to return question which provided V088SC (see Exhibit 23.12). So the discriminant analysis was successful in predicting group membership for case 1.

Look through Exhibit 23.17 and see that cases 2 through 5 and 7 through 10 were correctly assigned to group 1, i.e., the Predict values and the Group values are both 1. Case 11 and cases 13 through 20 were also correctly classified, however, these assignments were to group 2. We can now see that there were two incorrect classifications. These were cases 6 and 12. Although the discriminant analysis indicated that person 6 will return and person 12 won't return, the answers given by the respondents were the opposite of the predictions.

This process of keeping tally of correct versus incorrect assignments is one way of judging the efficacy of the discriminant analysis. This information is typically presented in a *confusion matrix*. The confusion matrix for this small subset from the Firestone data set is tabled in Exhibit 23.19. It shows that the analysis is 90% effective in using the respondents' perceptions of whether the services were done correctly and whether they received prompt attention to predict whether the people will or will not return to Firestone for automotive service.

The illustration presented is changed in one way when conducted in practice. Instead of using the complete sample for the analysis, usually about one

Exhibit 23.19 Confusion Matrix for Firestone Discriminant Example (column per cents)

	Won't Return	Will Return	Sample Total	Size
Won't Return	90%	10%	50%	10
Will Return	10	90	50	10
Total	100%	100%	100%	
Sample Size	10	10		20

half of the sample is randomly selected for the discriminant analysis calculations. The discriminant analysis scores (factor scores) are then calculated for the *hold-out sample*, or fresh sample, and their group membership is predicted. The predictive success as seen on the hold-out sample is reported in the confusion matrix and is taken as the primary indication of the ability of the discriminant function to categorize sample respondents correctly based on their answers to the questions asked to produce the predictor variable values.

Discriminant analysis enables us to answer specific questions such as:

- Which of the variables (e.g., ratings, demographics) is strongly related to usership?
- Can we reduce the number of variables and yet have all the information relevant to usership?
- How important are these variables in relation to one another?
- How well do the variables discriminate the user from the non-users? How accurate is the predicted classification?

Discriminant analysis can be extended to problems involving more than two groups. For example, the problem may be to predict which of the four brands of a product a consumer is likely to use. Multiple discriminant analysis is designed to tackle such problems but will not be presented in this book.

FACTOR ANALYSIS

WHAT IS FACTOR ANALYSIS?

You might have seen questionnaires which contained a large number, say 27, of attitude and opinion questions. Have you ever asked yourself, "When a woman's going to buy a jar of jam, does she really use all of these dimensions in making her selection from the supermarket shelf?" Of course it would take forever for the woman to make her way through her grocery list if she evaluated each and every item on, say, 15 to 40 criteria. You'd expect that some of those 27 product characteristics, for example, mean about the same thing. They probably do. Factor analysis is just a procedure whereby we can determine which of those 27 attitudes mean about the same thing. Perhaps you'd end up with only three distinctly different and important criteria (factors) for selecting jam. Or maybe only two important criteria (factors) for choosing among frozen dinners. Factor analysis refers to a group of techniques that is concerned with identifying the similarity of meaning among a large number of variables and reducing that large number of variables to fewer variables or factors that have distinctly different meanings. Suppose you asked consumers to rate a number of microcomputers on 25 variables, such as high quality, high compatibility, expense, wide variety of options, scope for expansion, state-of-the-art technology, knowledgeable sales staff, excellent after sales service, etc. Although consumers might give your their ratings on 25 such attributes, it is quite possible that many of these dimensions are interrelated. Assume, for example, that a consumer differentiates computers on quality, then attributes such as *high quality, high compatibility, expense, wide variety of options, state-of-the-art technology, scope for expansion*, etc., could be measuring the same underlying dimension, quality. Factor analysis is a formal statistical method that reduces a large number of attributes to a smaller group of related dimensions known as factors.

An intuitive understanding of the technique can be gained by a geometric presentation. Suppose consumers rate a department store on *courteous service* and *personalized service*. Furthermore, those who rate the store highly on *personalized service* also rate it highly on *courteous serv*ice; similarly those who rate it low on one attribute also rate it low on the other attribute. Now we can create a new attribute or factor by combining the two attributes and calling them a new name, good service. In other words, a factor is simply a combination of related variables. The purpose of factor analysis is to find optimum combinations of variables that are related. Given this framework, we may achieve our purpose by using a variety of mathematical procedures (principal components analysis, common factor analysis, etc.), rotations (varimax, quartimax, etc.) and assumptions.

Although factor analysis can be used for more sophisticated model building, it is widely used in marketing research for data reduction purposes. The most commonly used method is principal components analysis followed by varimax rotation.

It is possible to extract as many factors as there are variables. But using too many factors defeats the purpose of using factor analysis, which is data reduction. In general, mathematical criteria are applied to identify the most appropriate number of factors. However, good common sense and a deep understanding of the domain being studied are very important for deriving a good factor analysis solution to a marketing problem.

WHEN TO USE FACTOR ANALYSIS

You can use factor analysis when you have a large number of variables, and you want to group them into a smaller number of factors. In general, the variables used in factor analysis are expected to be interval-scaled. Factor analysis can be used to identify related and redundant attributes. It can also be used as a preliminary technique leading to more complex analysis.

FACTOR ANALYSIS OF THE FIRESTONE EXAMPLE OF CUSTOMER PERCEPTIONS OF LAST SERVICE

The regression and discriminant analyses used data obtained from Firestone customers' perceptions of their last experience with automotive service at a Firestone store. The questionnaire measured customers' perceptions of the service they received using 13 variables. These were presented in Exhibit 23.1 and are reproduced in Exhibit 23.20 for your convenience.

| **Exhibit 23.20** Perceptions of Last Automotive Service at Firestone |

2. Remembering back to this **most recent** service or purchase occasion at a **Firestone** store, please check the boxes below which indicate whether you strongly agree, somewhat agree, neither agree nor disagree, somewhat disagree or strongly disagree with each of the following statements.

	STRONGLY AGREE 1	SOMEWHAT AGREE 2	NEITHER AGREE NOR DISAGREE 3	SOMEWHAT DISAGREE 4	STRONGLY DISAGREE 5
All services were done correctly	[ ]	[ ]	[ ]	[ ]	[ ]
The mechanic was courteous	[ ]	[ ]	[ ]	[ ]	[ ]
Car did not run well afterwards	[ ]	[ ]	[ ]	[ ]	[ ]
Work was done on time	[ ]	[ ]	[ ]	[ ]	[ ]
Service manager was trustworthy	[ ]	[ ]	[ ]	[ ]	[ ]

continued

	STRONGLY AGREE 1	SOMEWHAT AGREE 2	NEITHER AGREE NOR DISAGREE 3	SOMEWHAT DISAGREE 4	STRONGLY DISAGREE 5
The bill was un-reasonably high	[ ]	[ ]	[ ]	[ ]	[ ]
The waiting area was comfortable	[ ]	[ ]	[ ]	[ ]	[ ]
Staff was courteous and helpful	[ ]	[ ]	[ ]	[ ]	[ ]
The location was inconvenient	[ ]	[ ]	[ ]	[ ]	[ ]
The mechanic was competent	[ ]	[ ]	[ ]	[ ]	[ ]
Excellent credit terms	[ ]	[ ]	[ ]	[ ]	[ ]
Convenient business hours	[ ]	[ ]	[ ]	[ ]	[ ]
They provided prompt attention	[ ]	[ ]	[ ]	[ ]	[ ]

(Some of the statements above are presented as negative statements. During the analysis, the scales were all converted to be positive. Also, the scale was changed in the computer so that it ran from 1 meaning strongly disagree to 5 being strongly agree. In the data analysis, the 13 questions were labelled V075 to V087.)

In order to have better insight into the ways in which people perceive automotive service and make decisions regarding their choices for future service, a thorough understanding of the responses to the above questions could be very helpful. A significant amount of understanding has already been obtained by executing the regression and discriminant analyses. The understanding of most topics is usually enhanced if the domain of the topic can be simplified. When reading the list of 13 variables in Exhibit 23.20, you might have thought that some of the variables have somewhat similar meanings. For example, if "all services were done correctly," variable V076S, then you would think that "the car ran well afterwards," variable V077S. Also, how much difference do you think customers would identify between "the mechanic was courteous," variable V076S, and the "staff was courteous and helpful"? This situation in which more than one variable might have similar meanings to respondents arises in many marketing research studies. The key role of factor analysis in these situations is to identify those variables that have similar meanings.

Factor analysis is one of the easier multivariate procedures to use and to interpret. A major difference between factor analysis and regression and discriminant analysis is that all of the variables in factor analysis are treated as being the same type of variable, i.e., there is no criterion variable/predictor variable(s) split in the set of variables. All the variables in the factor analysis can be considered to be simply a set of variables which might have something in common. The task for the analysis is to determine which variables are perceived to have similar meanings and what those variables have in common.

The first step in factor analysis is to determine which variables will be factored. In the Firestone study, there were six distinct groupings of variables from the whole questionnaire that were each submitted to factor analyses to help identify simpler interpretations of the findings. One of those groupings of variables was the respondents' perceptions of their last service at Firestone as represented by the 13 variables in Exhibit 23.20. Compared to the other sets of variables from the Firestone study that were factor analyzed, this grouping provided the most successful simplication through factor analysis. Success in this case relates to identifying fewer factors than the number of variables that account for a substantial amount of variation in the scores of the variables and that also have a relatively simple and meaningful interpretation.

The second step is to select the procedure for factor analyzing the set of variables. The two procedures most often used are principal component analysis and common factor analysis. Although in many situations the results of these two methods are very similar, many practitioners prefer the principal components procedure because its solutions tend to have more consistency than those from common factor analysis. We will focus our attention in this section on the principal components technique.

The third step is to perform the quantitative analysis and the fourth step is to interpret the results of the analysis. The results from a computerized factor analysis are presented in Exhibit 23.21.

Exhibit 23.21 Computer Output of Factor Analysis of Firestone Service

A. CORRELATION MATRIX TO BE FACTORED

	V075S	V076S	V077S	V078S	V079S
V075S	1.000				
V076S	0.347	1.000			
V077S	0.469	0.143	1.000		
V078S	0.356	0.299	0.159	1.000	
V079S	0.479	0.465	0.177	0.398	1.000
V080S	0.270	0.200	0.383	0.210	0.210
V081S	0.227	0.171	0.050	0.180	0.219
V082S	0.414	0.550	0.189	0.403	0.540
V083S	0.034	0.043	0.164	0.029	0.086
V084S	0.594	0.443	0.234	0.283	0.429
V085S	0.198	0.267	-0.015	0.168	0.272
V086S	0.228	0.285	0.017	0.263	0.289
V087S	0.400	0.396	0.160	0.544	0.443

	V080S	V081S	V082S	V083S	V084S
V080S	1.000				
V081S	0.115	1.000			
V082S	0.205	0.304	1.000		
V083S	0.167	0.063	0.112	1.000	
V084S	0.170	0.247	0.405	0.054	1.000
V085S	0.001	0.239	0.277	0.052	0.315
V086S	0.109	0.261	0.361	0.089	0.370
V087S	0.212	0.299	0.580	0.107	0.374

	V085S	V086S	V087S
V085S	1.000		
V086S	0.412	1.000	
V087S	0.278	0.421	1.000

B. LATENT ROOTS (EIGENVALUES)

1	2	3	4	5
4.438	1.484	1.061	0.954	0.857
6	7	8	9	10
0.761	0.721	0.595	0.554	0.505
11	12	13		
0.424	0.339	0.307		

C. COMPONENT LOADINGS

	1	2	3
V082S	0.762	0.090	-0.030
V087S	0.739	0.119	0.035
V079S	0.716	0.012	-0.153

continued

V075S	0.701	−0.317	−0.250
V084S	0.696	0.001	−0.153
V076S	0.660	0.080	−0.171
V078S	0.606	−0.006	−0.148
V086S	0.559	0.395	0.272
V077S	0.369	−0.727	0.012
V080S	0.381	−0.573	0.210
V083S	0.162	−0.259	0.809
V081S	0.433	0.218	0.280
V085S	0.461	0.477	0.219

D. VARIANCE EXPLAINED BY COMPONENTS

1	2	3
4.438	1.484	1.061

E. PER CENT OF TOTAL VARIANCE EXPLAINED

1	2	3
34.142	11.412	8.164

F. ROTATED LOADINGS

	1	2	3
V075S	0.750	0.301	−0.020
V079S	0.683	0.094	0.245
V084S	0.667	0.097	0.229
V082S	0.650	0.110	0.394
V076S	0.640	0.015	0.248
V087S	0.594	0.115	0.443
V078S	0.590	0.082	0.186
V083S	−0.271	0.686	0.450
V077S	0.366	0.684	−0.249
V080S	0.258	0.671	−0.023
V086S	0.292	−0.024	0.676
V085S	0.231	−0.144	0.643
V081S	0.198	0.089	0.516

G. VARIANCE EXPLAINED BY ROTATED COMPONENTS

1	2	3
3.461	1.560	1.963

H. PER CENT OF TOTAL VARIANCE EXPLAINED

1	2	3
26.622	11.998	15.098

continued

I. FACTOR SCREE PLOT
EIGENVALUES

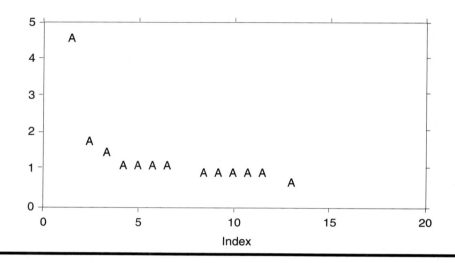

Index

There is substantial amount of interpretation related to the output from a factor analysis, as is true of the other multivariate procedures. Some of the key points will be discussed in a summarized form, not because of their lack of importance but rather to keep the discourse relatively short.

1. The two most important pieces of information are the "rotated loadings" in Exhibit 23.21F and the "per cent of variance explained" in Exhibit 23.21H.

2. Principal components analysis operates on either the correlation matrix or the covariance matrix of the variables. The correlation matrix is presented in Exhibit 23.21A. Notice those pairs of variables having high correlations in that table. These associations form the basis of the operating methodology for the analysis and will surface again in the component loadings and rotated component loadings tables.

3. The "latent roots (eigenvalues)" of Exhibit 23.21B provide an indication of the relative strength of the sequence of solutions to the problem. The first eigenvalue of 4.438 is substantially larger than the second eigenvalue of 1.484. This indicates that the solution with the first component (which is also referred to as the first factor) will provide much more explanation than the second component. Component 2 will provide more explanation than component 3 will, and so on.

Exhibit 23.21B contains 13 eigenvalues. This means that we could arrive at a solution that contains 13 components or factors. However, it would be self-defeating to consider such a solution since our objective is to reduce the number of dimensions (variables or components), not to keep them the same. Typically, the researcher would specify some stopping rule for the computer program to follow. Usually, this is provided in terms of a cut-off value for the minimum eigenvalue, often a value of 1.00, or a maximum number of components or factors, very often between 2 and 4.

4. The "component loadings" are provided in Exhibit 23.21C. For each variable in the left column, read across the row and find the largest number. This number is called the component loading (or factor loading) and helps to identify the variable with a specific component. Most of the variables will be strongly related to one particular component. These loadings have been sorted in Exhibit 23.21C so that those which relate most strongly to component 1 are listed first, then to component 2, and so on.

The eight variables listed first load most strongly on component 1. For example, V082S has a loading of 0.762 on component 1, 0.090 on component 2, and -0.030 on component 3. The loading of 0.762 indicates that V082S will be related to component 1 and to the other variables that load strongly on component 1, such as V087S.

5. The variance explained by each of the components is listed in Exhibit 23.21D. Notice that these values are identical to the eigenvalues. Since the computational purpose of principal components is to explain the maximum amount of variance using the smallest number of components, we'd like to see large amounts of the total variance of 13 accounted for by these 3 principal components. Comparing the total variance explained by the first 3 components, 6.983, to the total variance of 13 indicates that 53.7% of the total variance is accounted for by those three components.

6. The "per cent of total variance explained" presented in Exhibit 23.21E simply expresses the variance for each of the 3 principal components relative to the variance explained by the total set of 13 components. For example, 34.142% is the variance explained by component 1, 4.438, divided by the total variance for the 13 components, 13.000. Sometimes, these per cents are calculated as the variance explained by component 1 divided by the variance explained by that set of 3 components, i.e., 4.438 divided by 6.983 = 63.6%. This indicates that out of the variance explained by these three components, component 1 accounts for 63.6% of the explanatory power.

7. Very often, the researcher directs the computer program to try to improve on the solution by rotating the axes of the dimensions represented by the components. Visually, this would be similar to moving your camera in such a way that you'd get a more expressive photograph of your subject. Although it's more of a movement rather than a focusing, typically a

clearer explanation of the similarity among subsets of variables is obtained after the rotation.

The rotated component loadings are presented in Exhibit 23.21F. The variables which loaded onto each of the principal components are listed in Exhibit 23.22. After considering the similarities among each set of variables, the interpretations for each component were written. These component labels will vary in wording somewhat depending on which researcher is doing the analysis. There's nothing in the computer program indicating which words are used for each component. The researcher needs to develop the labels so that they make sense within the context of the problem and for the uses which will be made of the analysis. Notice that V083S, convenience of the location, was not used in Exhibit 23.22. Notice in Exhibit 23.21F that V083S had a loading of 0.686 on component 2 and a loading of 0.450 on component 3. Also, the interpretation of convenient location did not coincide with the value interpretation of component 2 and although it was somewhat similar to the variables that loaded onto component 3, the loading allocation would have been somewhat violated by assigning V083S to component 3. Consequently, V083S was dropped from the analysis.

8. The per cent of total variance explained by the rotated components is presented in Exhibit 23.21G and H for each of the 3 principal components relative to the variance explained by the total set of 13 components. These are interpreted in a fashion similar to that explained in step 6 above. For example, 26.622% is the variance explained by component 1, 3.461, divided by the total variance for the 13 components, 13.000. Out of the variance explained by the first three components, the per cent of variance explained by component 1 is 3.461 divided by 6.984 or 49.6%.

9. Exhibit 23.21I shows a graph called a "factor scree plot." It provides some basic information on the number of components that are likely to be valuable in explaining the set of points. In the scree plot, we can see that the eigenvalue drops substantially from the first to the second, much less from the second to the third, about the same amount from the third to the fourth and then stays about level from the fourth to the seventh. This diagram helps to confirm our choice to maintain a three component solution to this problem.

The interpretation of the three principal components present in Exhibit 23.22 is the main result from this principal components factor analysis. This information can be used by itself to help understand people's perceptions of automotive service. It could be used to help develop an advertising or automotive service campaign and in conjunction with other analyses. For example, the information from a factor analysis can be saved in the data file and then used within a regression or discriminant analysis.

Exhibit 23.22　Variables Which Relate to the Principal Components

Three Principal Components

Service and Attention	Value	Comfort and Convenience
All services were done correctly	Car ran well afterwards	Convenient business hours
Service manager was trustworthy	The bill was not unreasonably high	Excellent credit terms
The mechanic was competent		The waiting area was comfortable
Staff was courteous and helpful		
The mechanic was courteous		
They provided prompt attention		
Work was done on time		

(Some of the statements above are presented as negative statements. During the analysis, the scales were all converted to be positive. Also, the scale was changed in the computer so that it ran from 1 meaning strongly disagree to 5 being strongly agree. In the data analysis, the 13 questions were labelled V075 to V087.)

CLUSTER ANALYSIS

Cluster analysis refers to a set of techniques that is used in market research primarily to divide a sample of consumers into two or more groups, where the people in each group are similar in terms of some important characteristics. Thus, for example, we can group consumers who want similar benefits from a product, consumers who have similar demographics, consumers who have similar reading habits and consumers with similar lifestyles.

At a basic level of analysis, the data are often analyzed for readily identifiable and pre-identified groups like men and women, French-speaking and

English-speaking, younger and older. However, there may be occasions when such simple groupings of respondents may not be adequate. We may want to identify people who are similar in their response to several questions. In other words, we are not specifically interested in one attribute at a time, but in similar patterns of ratings or similar patterns of demographics. Also rather than forcing the nature of the groups on the data, cluster analysis is used to determine the variables used to construct the groups.

Given a set of variables we are interested in, cluster analysis divides the respondents into several groups such that within any one group respondents are similar to one another in their responses to the given variables but are substantially different from respondents in other groups. (Although cluster analysis procedures exist that produce overlapping clusters, this discussion will cover only exclusive clusters.) Cluster analysis also identifies the respondents within each group. This identification can be used for further analysis of data, perhaps by discriminant analysis.

A wide range of techniques is included under the umbrella term cluster analysis. For example, the AID technique, Q technique, MCA analysis, hierarchical clustering, k-means clustering, smallest space analysis and even factor analysis can be used to cluster people.

WHERE CLUSTER ANALYSIS IS USED

Most market segmentation studies utilize cluster analytic techniques. The types of data used for this purpose tend to be either psychographic or attitudinal. Consumers may be asked to respond to a number of lifestyle questions (psychographics) or to rate the product benefits. Respondents may then be grouped into homogeneous clusters based on their lifestyles or on their product benefit ratings. Once the respondents are grouped into distinct segments, the data may be analyzed further by cross-tabulating these segments against demographic characteristics, usage patterns, brand ratings, etc.

Though all these techniques have one main purpose—classifying people (occasionally variables)— the final output may differ from technique to technique. For example, hierarchical clustering produces a tree diagram known as a *dendrogram*. This is very similar to the "tree" produced by AID. In hierarchical cluster analysis, the total sample is repeatedly broken into smaller categories. The analyst is free to choose any level of clustering that would suit the objective of the research study.

The researcher should consider several factors when using cluster analytic techniques. First, different forms of cluster analysis may give different solutions since the criteria on which clustering are achieved may differ from technique to technique. Second, if the sample size is not large enough, the end result may be clusters with very small bases. Generalizations made on small sample bases may turn out to be unreliable. Third, although most techniques have the same purposes (i.e., classifying people or variables), the logic of a particular technique may make it inappropriate for a given problem.

Another serious consideration is the data base on which clusters are derived. Cluster analysis groups people on the variables the analyst manipulates (considers relevant). If those variables are in fact irrelevant, the groups derived on the basis of those variables will also be irrelevant.

In spite of the above caveats, cluster analytic techniques are useful in practice, especially in the area of segmentation research. Other applications of cluster analysis include model fitting, data reduction, and hypothesis testing.

CLUSTERING TECHNIQUES

Q-type factor analysis bases its groupings on the intercorrelations between the means and standard deviations. Cluster analysis separates the respondents (points) based on the distances between scores (ratings) of the respondents on the several variables.

Cluster analytic techniques can be viewed as being of two types, agglomerative and divisive. The agglomerative procedures begin with the individual subjects and combine more and more respondents in a rolling procedure until everyone has been assigned to a group. The divisive techniques work in reverse. They start with the total sample and then split the sample over and over again until they arrive at the individual case level.

Another way of classifying clustering procedures is by the manner in which the clusters are constructed. The two main classes are the hierarchical methods and the partitioning method. While hierarchical methods are represented by a tree or dendrogram, partitioning methods are not. While hierarchical methods can work in either the agglomerative or divisive manners, partitioning procedures work in an agglomerative way. The analyst specifies the number of clusters desired prior to the analysis. If three clusters are specified, the partitioning technique then chooses three cases that are as different from the centre of the cases as possible and also as different from each other as possible. It then assigns all the rest of the cases to the "seed" case which is closest to it and such that the within groups sum of squared deviations is minimized.

In a simplified presentation of cluster analysis, we'll explain the six principal phases of cluster analysis by means of a short example. We'll then expand the example and illustrate cluster analysis with an example that is more realistic.

PHASE 1: THE DATA

Cluster analysis is a technique used to group or cluster objects together according to some criterion. The objects to be clustered can be almost anything. Many marketing research studies use the individual respondent as the object and end up grouping people together in clusters. Often the variables that are used in the analysis are attitudinal or usage variables where the responses are on an itemized response scale. The table in Exhibit 23.23 has been extracted from a study that was conducted for Firestone Canada in 1980 regarding automotive service. The study was conducted among past customers of Firestone drawn from Montreal, Toronto, Hamilton–Burlington, Winnipeg, Edmonton and Vancouver. From the total 1036 respondents, five cases were selected for this illustration of cluster analysis. In one part of the questionnaire, the customers were asked about the importance they place on 21 facets of automotive service; two of these are shown in Exhibit 23.23.

Exhibit 23.23 Importance of Automotive Service Characteristics to Firestone Customers

How important is having a source of automotive service which...	OF NO IMPORTANCE	SLIGHTLY IMPORTANT	IMPORTANT	VERY IMPORTANT	EXTREMELY IMPORTANT
	1	2	3	4	5
...always gets the job done right the first time?	[ ]	[ ]	[ ]	[ ]	[ ]
...has a pick-up and delivery service or loaner car?	[ ]	[ ]	[ ]	[ ]	[ ]

Exhibit 23.24 The Attitudes of Five Firestone Customers Regarding the Importance of Service Being Done Right the First Time (V145) and Having Pick-Up and Delivery Service or a Loaner Car (V152)

Customer Number	V145	V152
1	1.00	2.00
2	3.00	5.00
3	1.00	5.00
4	2.00	4.00
5	1.00	3.00

Since cluster analysis is often treated in a graphical manner, we'll start with a graph of the raw data, i.e., the importance which those five Firestone customers put on the two attributes mentioned above, represented as V145 and V152. Each of the points in Exhibit 23.25 is the plot of the corresponding case from Exhibit 23.24. The dashed lines in Exhibit 23.25 are the pairs of points; the distances denoted by the lengths of those dashed lines will be used when choosing which cases to cluster together and the order in which the clustering progresses.

Exhibit 23.25   Graph of Firestone Customer Importance Attitudes

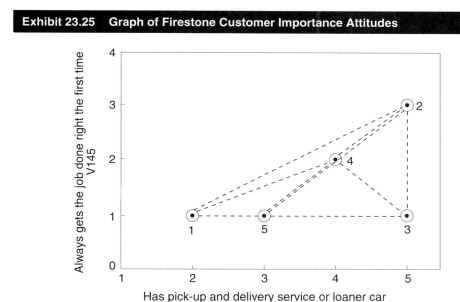

PHASE 2: TRANSFORM THE DATA

Transformation of the data matrix to some other format is a step that is often taken in cluster analysis. However, there is controversy over whether the data should be left in their original form or whether they should be standardized or "ipsatized."

Standardization is a procedure whereby the scores produced for each variable over all of the respondents are adjusted by their means to be centred on zero and to have a standard deviation of one. This is accomplished simply by subtracting each variable's mean from all of the scores (this step is called normalizing) and then by dividing each of the normalized scores by the standard deviation for that variable. This is the more common transformation of the data that is performed for clustering. The standardized importance scores for the five respondents selected from the Firestone data base are shown in Exhibit 23.26.

Exhibit 23.26 Standardized Importance Scores		
Case	V145	V152
1	−0.75	−1.54
2	−1.75	1.03
3	−0.75	1.03
4.	0.50	0.17
5.	−0.75	−0.69

In some studies, the individual respondents may have very different ranges of score values which they use for answering the questions. For example, on a 10-point scale, one subject might use only the interval from 5 to 8 for answering. Another respondent might use the range from 3 to 9. Since the answers of the latter will have greater variability, the "implicitly restricted scales" of the two subjects might need to be adjusted for there to be good comparability among the group. This process is called *ipsatizing* (Gurwitz, 1987). While standardization adjusts data to the mean and variation of the variable, ipsatization alters the scores of each respondent to the mean and variation of that person over the questions of interest. The ipsatized scores of the five Firestone respondents are listed in Exhibit 23.27.

Exhibit 23.27 Ipsatized Importance Scores		
Case	V145	V152
1	−0.71	0.71
2	−0.71	0.71
3	−0.71	0.71
4	−0.71	0.71
5	−0.71	0.71

In some situations, such as that presented here, the standardization and ipsatization of data provide no benefits for the data analysis. In this case, the data will be analyzed in their original form as shown in Exhibit 23.24.

PHASE 3: COMPUTING THE SIMILARITY–DISSIMILARITY MATRIX

All of the many cluster analysis techniques group objects together based on their similarity or dissimilarity using some measure of the distance between objects. In this example, we'll be using a very simple procedure for performing that grouping task. The similarity between objects, cases or people in this example, will be calculated on the straight line distance or Euclidean distance between the points as presented in the graph of Exhibit 23.25.

PHASE 4: CLUSTERING THE OBJECTS

The procedure used for this example is called the unweighted pair-group method using arithmetic averages. This is a basic cluster analysis method that requires only simple arithmetic yet is fairly often used in actual applications. Of course, with the availability of a wide range of statistical procedures for personal computers, the data analyst usually has several different procedures that can be used with little if any concern about the speed of calculation. Consequently, the major concern must be with the appropriateness of the technique to the data being analyzed.

CLUSTER STEP 1   Cluster those two points that are closest, or most similar, together in one cluster. From the similarity matrix of Exhibit 23.28, the smallest number larger than zero is 1.000. This is the distance between cases 1 and 5. Identify in the graph of Exhibit 23.25 that these are the physically closest cases.

Exhibit 23.28   Similarity (Euclidean Distance) Matrix Based on V145 and V152

Case	1	2	3	4	5
1	0.000	-	-	-	-
2	3.606	0.000	-	-	-
3	3.000	2.000	0.000	-	-
4	2.236	1.414	1.414	0.000	-
5	1.000	2.828	2.000	1.414	0.000

Now that cases 1 and 5 have been found to be the most similar, they will be considered to be one cluster for the remaining calculations. This cluster will be denoted by {15}. The distances between each of the remaining separate points and the centre of cluster 1 can be calculated as averages:

$$dist[2-\{15\}] = \frac{1}{2}(d_{21}+d_{25}) = \frac{1}{2}(3.606+2.828) = 3.217$$

$$dist[3-\{15\}] = \frac{1}{2}(d_{31}+d_{35}) = \frac{1}{2}(3+2) = 2.5$$

$$dist[4-\{15\}] = \frac{1}{2}(d_{41}+d_{45}) = \frac{1}{2}(2.236+1.414) = 1.825$$

The condensed similarity matrix is shown in Exhibit 23.29.

Exhibit 23.29 Reduced Similarity (Euclidean Distance) Matrix Based on V145 and V152

	2	3	4	15
2	0.000	-	-	-
3	2.000	0.000	-	-
4	1.414	1.414	0.000	-
15	3.217	2.500	1.825	0.000

CLUSTER STEP 2   The smallest value in the reduced similarity matrix will identify the next cluster. In Exhibit 23.29, the smallest distance between each of the single points and the cluster {15} is tied at 1.414. This is the value denoting the similarity between point 2 and point 4 and the similarity between points 3 and 4. When a tie such as this occurs, either of the two values can be selected randomly to constitute the next cluster. Let's choose cases 3 and 4 for the next cluster, which will be denoted by {34}. The revised cluster diagram appears in Exhibit 23.30. There are now two clusters of two points and one cluster of a single point.

The new revised similarity matrix must now be calculated using the new cluster {34}, the first cluster {15} and the independent case 2.

The revised similarity matrix is presented in Exhibit 23.31.

$$dist[2-\{34\}] = \frac{1}{2}(d_{23}+d_{24}) = \frac{1}{2}(2.000+1.414) = 1.707$$

$$dist[2-\{15\}] = \frac{1}{2}(d_{21}+d_{25}) = \frac{1}{2}(3.606+2.828) = 3.217$$

$$dist[\{15\}-\{34\}] = \frac{1}{4}(d_{13}+d_{14}+d_{53}+d_{54})$$

$$= \frac{1}{4}(3.00+2.000+2.236+1.414) = 2.163$$

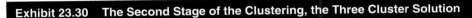

Exhibit 23.30   The Second Stage of the Clustering, the Three Cluster Solution

Exhibit 23.31 Revised Similarity (Euclidean Distance) Matrix Based on V145 and V152

	2	34	15
2	0.000	-	-
34	1.707	0.000	-
15	3.217	2.163	0.000

CLUSTER STEP 3   The next step is to decide whether the clustering will proceed any further. In some computer programs for clustering, the analyst is asked for the number of desired clusters and the procedure stops when that number of divisions has been reached. If we had specified three clusters, the work would now be finished. But let's continue until all of the clusters are identified.

Of course, the smallest remaining similarity value of 1.707 is between case 2 and cluster {34}. This means that we now include case 2 in a cluster that will be denoted as {234}. The diagram in Exhibit 23.32 shows the remaining space of similarities.

Exhibit 23.32   The Two Cluster Solution

CLUSTER STEP 4   We are now at the end of the clustering for this set of data, except for grouping all five cases together. The only remaining similarity calculation is:

$$dist\left[\{15\} - \{234\}\right] = \frac{1}{6}\left(d_{12} + d_{13} + d_{14} + d_{52} + d_{53} + d_{54}\right)$$
$$= \frac{1}{6}\left(3.606 + 3.000 + 2.236 + 2.828 + 2.000 + 1.414\right) = 2.514$$

The remaining similarity matrix becomes the 2 by 2 matrix in Exhibit 23.33 showing the similarity between the last two clusters that are then blended into the one cluster which includes all of the original five objects.

Exhibit 23.33   The Final Reduced Similarity Matrix

	15	234
15	0	–
124	2.514	0

Another way of viewing the steps we followed in forming the clusters is shown in the tree diagram or dendrogram in Exhibit 23.34.

Exhibit 23.34   Tree Diagram of the Clustering Sequence

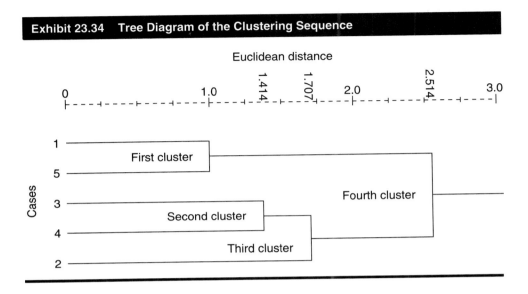

PHASE 5: REARRANGING THE RAW DATA AND SIMILARITY MATRICES

Additional visual insight into the sequences of the clustering decisions can be obtained if the raw data matrix is arranged in the order in which the objects were selected to be joined into clusters. The original order in which the numbers 1 through 5 were assigned to the objects might have been random or they might simply have been assigned in the order in which the respondents' questionnaires were completed and numbered. The matrix in Exhibit 23.35 has been developed based on the more relevant information pertaining to similarities among the objects.

Exhibit 23.35   Raw Data Matrix Arranged by Similarity

Case	V145	V152
1	1.00	2.00
5	1.00	3.00
4	2.00	4.00
3	1.00	5.00
2	3.00	5.00

The similarity matrix can also be rearranged in the order in which the points were drawn into the clusters. When this is done, the smaller similarity values are along the main diagonal of the matrix, while those values farthest away from the diagonal are the largest, i.e., the least similar.

Exhibit 23.36 Rearranged Similarity (Euclidean Distance) Matrix Based on V145 and V152

	1	5	4	3	2
1	0.000	-	-	-	-
5	1.000	0.000	-	-	-
4	2.236	1.414	0.000	-	-
3	3.000	2.000	1.414	0.000	-
2	3.606	2.828	1.414	2.000	0.000

The most similar pairs of cases tend to be placed near the diagonal while the most dissimilar are farthest away from the diagonal of the matrix.

PHASE 6: COMPUTATION OF THE COPHRENETIC CORRELATION COEFFICIENT

This last step of the cluster analysis develops a measure of how closely the tree diagram of the clustering matches the original similarity matrix. To arrive at this measure, the similarity matrix and the values that forced the clustering are compared and a similarity value called the Pearson correlation coefficient is calculated.

Exhibit 23.37 Similarity (Euclidean Distance) Matrix Based on V145 and V152

	1	2	3	4	5
1	0.000	-	-	-	-
2	3.606	0.000	-	-	-
3	3.000	2.000	0.000	-	-
4	2.236	1.414	1.414	0.000	-
5	1.000	2.828	2.000	1.414	0.000

At each of the stages of clustering there was one value that triggered the development of the next cluster. Those values produce the cophrenetic matrix which is shown in Exhibit 23.38. The values in the cophrenetic matrix are obtained from the tree diagram (Exhibit 23.34). To get the value for cell (5,1) follow the base of tree from where the line from case 1 begins as far as is necessary to be able to trace back to the base of case 5. Read off the value of 1.0 on the scale above the tree. For cell (4,3), trace from the base of case 3 as far to the right as necessary to be able to follow a branch back to case 4. The value on the scale corresponding to the connection between cases 3 and 4 is 1.414. The other values are found in similar manner.

Exhibit 23.38 The Cophrenetic Matrix of the Values which Drove the Clustering

	1	2	3	4	5
1	0.000	-	-	-	-
2	2.514	0.000	-	-	-
3	2.514	1.707	0.000	-	-
4	2.514	1.707	1.414	0.000	-
5	1.000	2.514	2.514	2.514	0.000

Exhibit 23.39 Comparison of the Similarity and Cophrenetic Matrices

	Similarity Matrix	Cophrenetic Matrix
(2,1)	3.606	2.514
(3,1)	3.000	2.514
(4,1)	2.236	2.514
(5,1)	1.000	1.000
(3,2)	2.000	1.707
(4,2)	1.414	1.707
(5,2)	2.828	2.514
(4,3)	1.414	1.414
(5,3)	2.000	2.514
(5,4)	1.414	2.514

To determine the degree of congruence between the calculated similarities and the values which drove the clustering, the Pearson correlations can be calculated. The Pearson correlation between the original similarity matrix and the cophrenetic matrix, i.e., the two columns of numbers in Exhibit 23.39, is 0.692 for this example. This indicates a reasonable but not outstanding representation between the tree and the similarities among the cases as represented by the similarity matrix. Since the values of the Pearson correlation coefficient can range from -1 to +1, where 0 means no correlation, the correlation value of 0.692 is in the right direction and is reasonably good for this illustration.

K-MEANS CLUSTERING OF THE FIRESTONE EXAMPLE

The Firestone example was used above to illustrate an agglomerative hierarchical procedure. As was mentioned earlier, there are many different procedures for clustering points. K-means clustering is a partitioning rather than a hierarchical process.

The analyst either has a good preliminary idea of the number of clusters which he or she wants to extract from the data or is willing to guess a preliminary number. This number of clusters will be produced from the analysis. Although in many cases the clustering from a hierarchical procedure and from K-means clustering will coincide, in some cases the clustering will be different in a number of ways. At this stage, the knowledge, experience and intuition of the analyst become important in deciding which cluster is most appropriate to use for the study.

For the Firestone example with five cases, the K-means clustering procedure from SYSTAT produced the table in Exhibit 23.40 when two clusters were specified.

As you can see, the same two clusters have been obtained that were extracted using the hierarchical procedure, i.e., clusters {15} and {234}. In addition, some useful statistical information is presented. In the top section of Exhibit 23.40, the variables V145 and V152 are listed together with a table which looks very much like an analysis of variance table. For each variable, the F-ratios and the corresponding PROB values indicate the value of the variables in forming the clusters. Because the PROB value for V152 is below 0.05 we could conclude that V152 was instrumental in this clustering. Using the same reasoning, we could also conclude that V145 was not terribly useful in this analysis and perhaps another variable should have been used for the clustering. This points out another task in cluster analysis, i.e., the decision regarding which variables to use in the clustering calculations.

Exhibit 23.40   Computer Analysis of Cluster Problem, 5 Cases

SUMMARY STATISTICS FOR 2 CLUSTERS

VARIABLE	BETWEEN SS DF	WITHIN SS DF	F-RATIO	PROB
V145	1.200 1	2.000 3	1.800	0.272
V152	5.633 1	1.167 3	14.486	0.032

CLUSTER NUMBER: 1

MEMBERS   STATISTICS

CASE	DISTANCE	VARIABLE	MINIMUM	MEAN	MAXIMUM	ST.DEV.
2	0.75	V145	1.00	2.00	3.00	0.82
3	0.75	V152	4.00	4.67	5.00	0.47
4	0.47					

CLUSTER NUMBER: 2

MEMBERS   STATISTICS

CASE	DISTANCE	VARIABLE	MINIMUM	MEAN	MAXIMUM	ST.DEV.
1	0.35	V145	1.00	1.00	1.00	0.00
5	0.35	V152	2.00	2.50	3.00	0.50

When performing the K-means cluster analysis on the 1036 cases from the Firestone file for the two variables V145 and V152, the results presented in Exhibit 23.41 were obtained. In this output, two clusters were specified and both variables 145 and 152 were shown to contribute significantly to the clustering of the respondents. The table in Exhibit 23.41 illustrates that the assignment of each respondent to a cluster can be seen from the computer output.

The foregoing discussion of cluster analysis has treated the topic at a very basic level. However, the procedure used in the Firestone example of five cases could be used on a larger data set. In fact, that procedure is very often used in practice.

Exhibit 23.41   Computer Solution for 2 Clusters, 1036 Cases

SUMMARY STATISTICS FOR 2 CLUSTERS

VARIABLE	BETWEEN SS	DF	WITHIN SS	DF	F-RATIO	PROB
V145	3.304	1	287.092	1018	11.717	0.001
V152	1435.647	1	501.328	994	2846.507	0.000

CLUSTER NUMBER: 1

MEMBERS   STATISTICS

CASE	DISTANCE	VARIABLE	MINIMUM	MEAN	MAXIMUM	ST.DEV.
1	0.16	V145	1.00	1.22	4.00	0.49
4	0.72	V152	1.00	1.99	3.00	0.83
5	0.73					
6	0.22					
8	0.73					
9	1.26					
11	0.16					
...	....					
1032	0.72					
1033	0.16					
1034	0.22					

CLUSTER NUMBER: 2

MEMBERS   STATISTICS

CASE	DISTANCE	VARIABLE	MINIMUM	MEAN	MAXIMUM	ST.DEV.
2	0.46	V145	1.00	1.34	5.00	0.58
3	0.46	V152	4.00	4.44	5.00	0.50
7	0.46					
10	0.62					
13	0.46					
17	0.46					
24	0.56					
25	1.66					
...	....					
1026	0.56					
1035	0.39					
1036	0.46					

SUMMARY

Multivariate analysis is used regularly in practical marketing research. However, it is certainly not used on every project. Many projects do not produce data that are conducive to multivariate analysis and many others do not have the budget that would support this level of effort.

We investigated the four main multivariate procedures in this chapter:

1. Linear regression is used when relating a set of variables that the researcher hopes to use to predict a criterion variable. The set of predictor variables are all or mostly of the interval or ratio type, while the criterion variable is interval or ratio.

2. Discriminant analysis is also used for predictive purposes. The main difference between regression and discriminant analysis pertains to the nature of the criterion variable, it is a dichotomous or multichotomous grouping variable in discriminant analysis.

3. Factor analysis is directed at simplifying a set of variables by finding similar interpretations among subsets of the variables.

4. Cluster analysis is a wide variety of procedures which work mainly to allocate people into groups based on some pertinent criterion.

NOW THINK ABOUT THIS

1. Sketch out a potential real life application regression, discriminant, factor and cluster analysis based either on your work experience or on an extension of a case that you might have studied in a marketing course.

2. Write a paragraph explaining the relative merits of regression analysis and two-group discriminant analysis.

3. To some people, factor analysis and cluster analysis seem to be interchangeable. There are some situations where either procedure can be used. Find situations where both factor analysis and cluster analysis can be used.

REFERENCE

Gurwitz, Paul M.
1987 "Ipsative Rescaling: An Answer to the Response Set Problem in Segmentation Analysis." *Journal of Advertising Research*, June/July.

24 / Secondary Research

WHAT YOU WILL LEARN IN THIS CHAPTER

- What secondary research is and how it can help the researcher
- The sources of secondary data
- How to do internal research
- What information is available from the federal government
- What data are collected by Statistics Canada and how to obtain them
- The type of information that may be obtained from provincial governments
- Some of the major private sources of secondary data in Canada
- What secondary sources are available for international research

INTRODUCTION

The main purpose of this book is to enable the reader to obtain a quick working knowledge of marketing research—what it is and how it is done. The book (especially the first 15 chapters) concentrates almost exclusively on these aspects. When you design and carry out a survey or focus group, you are said to be conducting primary research. In some cases, it is not necessary to carry out primary research because the information you are looking for may already be available, either in full or in part, from other sources. When you look for information from other sources you are said to be conducting secondary research. Researchers—and even more importantly those who commission research—should first scan the field to see if at least some of the required information is available from published and private sources.

SOURCES OF SECONDARY DATA

Secondary data come from two sources, internal and external. Either or both of these sources need to be consulted depending on the nature of information that is required.

INTERNAL SECONDARY DATA   These include sales force reports, cost of marketing, records of sales, advertising expenditures, product performance, marketing research done in the past, and the like.

EXTERNAL SECONDARY DATA   These come from three different sources. The first source is governments, federal, provincial and municipal. They provide a wide variety of secondary data. The second source is non-profit organizations such as industry associations and marketing boards. Part of the mandate of many of these organizations is to disseminate information. The third source is organizations that collect primary and secondary data for the explicit purpose of selling this information to those who require them.

Some of these sources are identified in this chapter. The sources are not exhaustive. However, they cover a wide spectrum of available information.

INTERNAL SECONDARY SOURCES

Internal data consist of information that is available within the organization. Such information may be obtained from different departments or might be resident in the files of the department that needs the information.

INTERNAL RECORDS

Internal records keep track of several variables of interest, such as advertising expenditure, sales volume, promotional efforts, success and failures of products. The main sources of such information are accounting and marketing records. While the information may not always be available in the form the researcher wants, internal records can be a rich source of information that might either eliminate the need to carry out some research projects or make a proposed research project much more effective.

SALES FORCE AND MARKETING INTELLIGENCE

Many firms employ their sales force to collect information that can be used as input to marketing intelligence. The sales force is already in the field, knows the market and can be cost effective data collectors. However, it should be remembered that a sales force is not trained to collect data in an unbiased way. Marketing intelligence gathered through the sales force can be effective provided it is used cautiously, with an awareness of its limitations and possible biases. The sales force should be informed of the dual use of the data and trained in proper data collection procedures.

RESEARCH REPORTS

Records of primary marketing research projects that have been carried out in the past can serve as secondary data for the current project. Such reports may be of immense value to the researcher. It may be worth reviewing the archives of the company for any research reports that may have a bearing on a proposed research project. In addition, companies may also have a variety of secondary data collected from external sources (to be discussed later).

Many corporations, especially the large ones, keep extensive records. But they are not necessarily centralized. Valuable information is often kept in different departments, making it difficult to provide an overview of all the information that is available from different sources within an organization. Larger organizations should construct a centralized data bank of all completed and in-progress marketing research projects as well as available secondary information. It is important for a researcher to explore the availability of different types of information within the organization, either from a centralized source or from different departments.

EXTERNAL SECONDARY SOURCES
FEDERAL GOVERNMENT/STATISTICS CANADA

CENSUS INFORMATION   The federal government provides extensive marketing information at a (relatively) low cost. Most information comes from the census data. Exhibit 24.1 shows the different types of census data collected by Statistics Canada.

If you want to know the characteristics of Canadians living in any part of the country, you can get detailed information. In fact, such information can be purchased at the enumeration area level. (An enumeration area consists of about 600 persons.) Thus, for example, if you are doing retail location research, you can get a detailed breakdown of demographic characteristics of people who live in a given area. Alternatively, you can also identify the enumeration areas containing concentrations of people with incomes above a certain level (or people with a certain age group or households of a certain size).

Exhibit 24.1   Census Data Collected by Statistics Canada

Census of Canada

Conducted once every decade. Some information is checked every five years. Census collects population and demographic data by geographical areas. Information is obtained on gender, age, race, citizenship, educational levels, occupation, employment status, family status, and income of inhabitants.

Census of Housing

Collects information on housing conditions such as the value of the dwelling, type of dwelling, year built, number of rooms, and ethnic origin of occupants.

Census of Manufacturers

Conducted each year. Covers major industries. Information is collected on value of products produced by industry, cost of materials and equipment, number of establishments, and wages paid to employees.

Census of Agriculture

Conducted every five years. Information is gathered on the number of farms, number, age, and gender of people residing in farms, value of farm products sold, number of tractors, number of livestock, presence of running water and electricity, and the value of farm products sold.

Census of Minerals

Data collected from mining companies including number of employees, wages, hours worked, quantities produced, cost of materials and supplies, and types of equipment used.

Statistics Canada publishes the *Market Research Handbook* and the *Canada Yearbook*. Both these publications summarize information that are of interest to market researchers. Exhibit 24.2 shows a page from the *Market Research Handbook*. One can also subscribe to *Statistics Canada Daily*, which lists the reports that are released on a daily basis.

ECONOMIC INFORMATION   Statistics Canada also publishes extensive economic statistics: gross domestic product; how personal income is earned and spent; personal expenditure on consumer goods and services; government revenues and expenditures; consumer price index; labour force characteristics and wages; statistics on the stock markets, construction industry, agriculture, mining and energy, transportation and communications, etc. *The Canada Economic Observer* summarizes these data.

Exhibit 24.2 Market Research Handbook

Table 3-60. Independent Retailers Sales, Ranked by Selling Area, by Kind of Business and Store Location, 1986

Tableau 3-60. Ventes des détaillants indépendants, classement selon la superficie de vente, selon le genre de commerce et le genre d'emplacement, 1986

Kind of business and quartiles / Genre de commerce et quartiles	Selling area Lower quartile values / Superficie de vente Valeur minimum du quartile		Average annual sales / Ventes annuelles moyennes	Average sales per / Ventes selon la superficie moyenne		Type of store location / Genre d'emplacement				
	Square foot / Pied carré	Square metre / Mètre carré		Square foot / Pieds carrés	Square metre / Mètres carrés	On street / Sur rue	Shopping centre - Centre commercial			
							Neighbourhood / de quartier	Community / Communautaire	Regional / Régional	Indoor mall / Mall intérieur
			$'000	$	$	%	%	%	%	%
All kind of business - Total - Tous genre de commerce										
Top 25% - Supérieur 25%	2,700	251	2,210	331	3,567	89.0	11.0	-	-	-
Upper middle 25% - Intermédiaire supérieur 25%	1,600	149	754	364	3,917	95.0	5.0	-	-	-
Lower middle 25% - Intermédiaire inférieur 25%	990	92	463	384	4,130	80.0	15.0	5.0	-	-
Bottom 25% - Inférieur 25%			223	413	4,445	79.0	16.0	-	-	5.0
Weighted average - Moyennes pondérées			911	348	3,747	86.0	12.0	1.0	-	1.0
Bakery products stores - Boulangeries-pâtisseries										
Top 25% - Supérieur 25%	912	85	283	201	2,165	50.0	14.0	-	12.0	24.0
Upper middle 25% - Intermédiaire supérieur 25%	600	56	199	265	2,850	67.0	16.0	-	12.0	6.0
Lower middle 25% - Intermédiaire inférieur 25%	300	28	162	361	3,889	77.0	15.0	1.0	7.0	-
Bottom 25% - Inférieur 25%			92	402	4,327	84.0	6.0	11.0	-	-
Weighted average - Moyennes pondérées			182	263	2,830	70.0	13.0	3.0	8.0	7.0
Fruit and vegetable stores - Fruits et légumes										
Top 25% - Supérieur 25%	1,500	139	1,053	517	5,561	100.0	-	-	-	-
Upper middle 25% - Intermédiaire supérieur 25%	1,100	102	304	239	2,569	100.0	-	-	-	-
Lower middle 25% - Intermédiaire inférieur 25%	900	84	252	257	2,771	100.0	-	-	-	-
Bottom 25% - Inférieur 25%			240	658	7,083	91.0	-	-	-	9.0
Weighted average - Moyennes pondérées			440	397	4,278	97.0	-	-	-	3.0

Kind of business and quartiles / Genre de commerce et quartiles	Selling area Lower quartile values / Superficie de vente Valeur minimum du quartile		Average annual sales / Ventes annuelles moyennes $'000	Average sales per / Ventes selon la superficie moyenne		Type of store location / Genre d'emplacement				
	Square foot Pied carré	Square metre Mètre carré		Square foot Pieds carrés $	Square metre Mètres carrés $	On street Sur rue %	Neighbourhood de quartier %	Community Communautaire %	Regional Régional %	Indoor mall Mall intérieur %
Grocery stores, more than 15% meat - Épiceries, plus de 15% de viandes										
Top 25% - Supérieur 25%	1,600	149	547	211	2,270	94.0	6.0	-	-	-
Upper middle 25% - Intermédiaire supérieur 25%	1,000	93	367	285	3,068	97.0	2.0	1.0	-	-
Lower middle 25% - Intermédiaire inférieur 25%	740	69	242	275	2,960	98.0	2.0	-	-	-
Bottom 25% - Inférieur 25%			181	363	3,913	98.0	2.0	-	-	-
Weighted average - Moyennes pondérées			334	254	2,736	97.0	3.0	-	-	-
Grocery stores, less than 15% meat - Épiceries, plus de 15% de viandes										
Top 25% - Supérieur 25%	4,920	457	4,416	497	5,347	77.0	20.0	2.0	-	1.0
Upper middle 25% - Intermédiaire supérieur 25%	3,000	279	1,715	457	4,916	95.0	5.0	-	-	-
Lower middle 25% - Intermédiaire inférieur 25%	1,600	149	778	352	3,785	97.0	3.0	-	-	-
Bottom 25% - Inférieur 25%			594	529	5,691	97.0	2.0	2.0	-	-
Weighted average - Moyennes pondérées			1,870	469	5,052	91.0	7.0	1.0	-	-
Meat markets - Marchés de viandes										
Top 25% - Supérieur 25%	1,040	97	646	388	4,180	98.0	2.0	-	-	-
Upper middle 25% - Intermédiaire supérieur 25%	625	58	351	414	4,458	81.0	13.0	-	5.0	-
Lower middle 25% - Intermédiaire inférieur 25%	400	37	411	801	8,617	88.0	10.0	3.0	-	-
Bottom 25% - Inférieur 25%			174	648	6,978	79.0	18.0	-	2.0	-
Weighted average - Moyennes pondérées			392	482	5,190	86.0	11.0	1.0	2.0	-

See Sources and Notes at the end of this Section.
Voir sources et notes à la fin de la section.

Source: This information provided through the cooperation of Statistics Canada. Readers wishing further information may obtain copies of related publications by mail from Publication Sales, Statistics Canada, Ottawa, Ontario K1A 0T6, by phone at 1-613-951-7277 or national toll-free 1-800-267-6677. You may also facsimile your order by dialing 1-613-951-1584.

STATISTICS CANADA

STATISTICS CANADA REFERENCE CENTRES   You may personally visit Statistics Canada reference centres in the following Canadian cities:

- St. John's, NF
- Halifax, NS
- Montréal, PQ
- Ottawa, ON
- Toronto, ON
- Winnipeg, MN
- Regina, SK
- Edmonton, AB
- Vancouver, BC

You may benefit from several services offered through these reference centres:

- **Inquiry services:** You may contact these offices in person or by phone or mail to obtain statistical information.
- **Consultancy services**: You can get assistance on data problems.
- **Data distribution and promotion services**: You may place orders for statistical publications, microfiche, tapes and census area maps.
- **Education services**: Publishes useful information on how to find and use statistical information.

STATISTICS CANADA CATALOGUE   *Statistics Canada Catalogue and Current Publications Index* issued by Statistics Canada lists numbered publications released by Statistics Canada. Publications include statistical data on primary industries, manufacturing, transportation, communication, commerce, employment, population, and general topics. Catalogued publications contain some of the following information:

- Statistical data
- Reference material to assist understanding
- Special studies
- Statistics Canada's services and operations

CANSIM DATA   CANSIM (Canadian Socio-economic Information Management System) is a computerized data base that has two modules:

1. **Times Series Module** which contains a wide variety of current and historical socio-economic information. This module contains:
   - system of national accounts
   - prices and price indexes
   - labour

- manufacturing and primary industry
- capital and finance
- construction
- merchandising and services
- external trade
- transportation
- agriculture and food
- population estimates and projections
- health and welfare

2. **Cross Classified Module** which contains cross-classified data in the fields of demography, education, health and justice. The CANSIM cross-classified module can be obtained from CANSIM host service bureau, Datacrown Inc., Ottawa.

MICROFILM   Statistics Canada provides census data and other information including all current serial publications of the external trade division on microfilm. A complete set of all Statistics Canada publications (going back to those listed in the Dominion Bureau of Statistics 1918-1960) are available through Micromedia Ltd. (telephone (416) 593-5211).

MACHINE READABLE DATA   Statistics Canada also provides extensive data on computer tapes. Such tapes include:

1. User summary tapes which contain tabulated data since 1961; they are more detailed than printed reports.
2. Public use sample tapes which provide access to records of unidentifiable individual respondents commencing with the 1971 census.
3. Spatial reference tapes containing supplementary geographical data commencing with the 1971 census.

LISTING OF SUPPLEMENTARY DOCUMENTS   This includes technical and discussion documents, working papers and memoranda. The material included in this listing can be tentative and speculative in nature, such as research reports that are not officially endorsed by Statistics Canada.

PROVINCIAL AND MUNICIPAL GOVERNMENTS

PROVINCIAL GOVERNMENTS   Provincial governments also publish a large variety of documents that are of use to market researchers. Because different provinces produce different publications, the researcher may have to determine the publications that are relevant to the province he or she is interested in. In some provinces each ministry publishes its own material; in other provinces there is a department of publications. Provincial governments provide statistical information on agriculture, ecology, education, health, industry, mining, tourism and general information. The scope of all such information is naturally confined to the province that publishes it. Provincial governments also publish educational material that may be of interest to market researchers. Most of the publications and project reports at the federal, provincial and municipal levels are considered to be public information and are accessible to the public.

Municipal Governments   Large municipal governments also publish reports that are relevant to their municipalities. Again, different municipalities publish different information. The economic development departments in municipal governments publish those reports which are usually most relevant to marketing researchers.

Chambers of Commerce   Most major towns and cities have chambers of commerce or boards of trade. Chambers of commerce are established to promote the business interest of the communities in which they operate. If you are interested in information pertaining to a given city or town, the chamber of commerce is a good place to start. Information provided by most chambers of commerce includes:

- **Economic facts** such as sales figures of retail stores
- **Demographic profiles** such as the distribution of age, sex, family size, etc.
- **Employment statistics** such as average weekly earnings
- **Government profiles** including revenues and expenditures
- **Quality of life factors** such as climate, cultural and recreational outlets, housing starts, etc.

The chamber of commerce publications can be obtained directly from chambers. They can also be found in public libraries.

Private Sources: General Information

Many private organizations provide information that is of use to the market researcher. Here are a few examples. *The Financial Post* publishes *Canadian Markets* which provides detailed information about individual markets. Exhibit 24.3 shows a page from *Canadian Markets*. The Conference Board of Canada publishes the *Handbook of Canadian Consumer Markets* which provides a wide range of useful data. *Sales & Marketing Management* magazine publishes an annual survey of purchasing power. *Canadian Trade Index*, published by the Canadian Association of Manufacturers, provides information on manufacturers' income and the economic sector and is a good source for export-oriented marketing research.

Exhibit 24.3 Canadian Markets

Toronto CMA

Income:
27% Above National Average
Pers'l Income, 1991 $87,322,276,000
% Canadian Total   18.08
Per Capita $22,800

Population:
June 1, 1991   3,822,400
% CanadianTotal   14.26
% Change, '22-'91   22.10
Average Annual Growth Rate   2.02%

Market:
Retail Sales, 1991   *$37,455,480,000*
% Canadian Total   17.50
Per Capita $9,800

POPULATION
1986 Census:
Total..3,427,165
  Male...................................1,674,545
  Female................................1,752,620

Age Groups:	Male	Female
Under 4	119,800	113,835
5-9	109,670	104,435
10-14	113,125	106,790
15-19	127,565	122,190
20-24	160,565	161,920
25-29	164,705	170,370
30-34	145,100	155,985
35-39	142,545	149,300
40-44	113,510	115,735
45-49	95,925	96,855
50-54	90,815	90,025
55-59	85,970	86,675
60-64	72,675	81,330
65-69	49,890	60,510
70-74	37,945	50,955
75+	44,740	85,695

MARITAL STATUS
1986 Census: (Age 15+)
Single (never married) 797,620
Married (includes separated) 1,706,885
Widowed.......................................163,125
Divorced...91,880

MOTHER TONGUE
	1986 Census	% Total
English	2,395,150	73.62
French	43,845	1.35
Dutch	15,470	0.48
Chinese	94,210	2.90
German	52,785	1.62
Greek	45,955	1.41
Hungarian	19,575	0.60
Indo-Pakistani	25,745	0.79
Italian	193,205	5.94
Japanese	5,105	0.16
Korean	10,380	0.32
Polish	37,965	1.17
Portuguese	78,035	2.40
Scandinavian Languages	4,720	0.15
Ukrainian	29,130	0.90
Vietnamese	8,875	0.27
Other	193,200	5.94

BUILDING PERMITS
	1989	1988 $000	1987
Value	10,019,310	8,784,102	7,523,113

HOUSING
1986 Census:
Occupied Private
  Dwellings, Total 1,199,800
  Owned 699,370
  Rented 500,390
  Single detached 517,705
  Apartment, 5 or more
    storeys 338,495
  Movable dwellings 395
  Other dwellings 343,195

FAMILIES
1986 Census:
Families in Private
  Households, Total 906,385
  Husband-wife families...............791,135
Lone-parent families 115,245
Average number persons
  per family 3.1
Average number children
  per family 1.3

PRIVATE HOUSEHOLDS
1986 Census:
Private Households, Total..........1,199,800
Population in private
  households 3,378,740
Average number per
  household 2.8

AVERAGE HOUSEHOLD EXPENDITURES
	1991
Food	$8,060
Shelter	9,693
Clothing	3,781
Transportation	7,349
Health & Personal Care	2,148
Recr'n, Read'g, & Education	3,744
Taxes & Securities	14,708
Other	9,414
Total Expenditures	58,897

CAPITAL EXPENDITURES
(Manufacturing)	1990	1989 $ millions	1988
Total exp.	3,579.2	3,636.2	3,687.3
Capital exp.	2,665.1	2,742.8	2,832.0
Construction	482.2	379.3	358.8
Mach. & equip.	2,182.9	2,363.5	2,473.2
Repair exp.	914.1	893.4	855.3
Construction	160.7	145.8	131.4
Mach. & equip.	753.4	747.6	723.9

MANUFACTURING INDUSTRIES
	1986	1981
Plants	8,429	7,072
Employees	391,761	350,554
	$000's	
Salaries, wages	10,129,127	6,615,421
Mfg. materials cost	28,276,258	19,589,663
Mfg. shipments, value	50,501,032	33,679.033
Total value added	22,952,479	15,065,258

NEW VEHICLE REGISTRATION
	1989
Cars, domestic	133,883
Cars, imported	56,455
Small Trucks, domestic	58,374
Small Trucks, imported	9,585
Medium & heavy trucks	6,402

INCOME
1986 Census: (1985 income)
Average employment income:	$
Male	33,781
Female	21,277
Average census family income	46,573
Average household income	43,025

LEVEL OF SCHOOLING
1986 Census:
Population, 15 years+ 2,732,375
Less than Grade 9 376,925
Grades 9-13...............................1,054,385
Trades/non-university 643,180
University, without degree 280,560
University degree.........................377,310

LABOR FORCE
1986 Census:
Males:
In the labor force 1,079,595
Employed...................................1,027,785
Not in labor force 242,965
Participation rate:.............................81.63
15-24 years 73.43
25 years+ 83.91
Females:
In the labor force 900,250
Employed......................................842,980
Not in labor force 509,555
Participation rate:.............................63.86
15-24 years 71.43
25 years+ 61.95

Other organizations provide continuous information on a subscription basis. A.C. Nielsen Company provides bimonthly data on product sales, retail prices, display space, inventories and promotional activities of competing brands of food stores and drug stores. The data are collected on a continuous basis from a sample of food stores and drug stores. Another example is the *Decima Quarterly* (of Decima Research) which tracks public opinion on a number of topics on a quarterly basis.

There are several business guides, directories and indexes that are of interest to the market researcher from time to time. Some of these are:

- *Canadian Trade Index*: This is published annually by the Canadian Manufacturers' Association. It contains a classified list of products manufactured in Canada, geographical and alphabetical listing of manufacturers.

- *Fraser's Canadian Trade Directory*: Alphabetical list of manufacturers, list of trade names, listings of foreign firms and their agents/distributors.

- *Canadian Urban Trends—National Perspective*: This guide, published by Copp Clark Pitman/Ministry of State for Urban Affairs is revised from time to time. It provides tables, charts, maps and text describing the economic and social impact of urbanization.

Private Sources: Specific Information

Private sources also provide information that is specific to a given field of inquiry. Exhibit 24.4 shows some common information sources. The listing is meant to be representative but not exhaustive. You will note that an impressive proportion of the sources listed come from a single supplier, Maclean Hunter. Almost all data in these publications refer exclusively to Canadian markets.

Exhibit 24.4 Sources of Specialized Information

Information	Available From	Comments
Advertising		
Report on Advertising Revenue in Canada	Maclean Hunter	Gross and net revenues of broadcasting, newspapers and other printed media (annual).
Canadian Advertising Rates and Data (CARD)	Maclean Hunter	Addresses, advertising rates, circulation, mechanical requirements, ownership of major broadcast and print media (monthly).

continued

Information	Available From	Comments
National List of Advertisers	Maclean Hunter	Organizations involved in national advertising, key personnel, advertising budget and media used (annual).
Automotive Areas Sales Guide Automotive After	Maclean Hunter	Motor vehicle registration by to census divisions. Repair shops, special Market service outlets, new dealers, automotive jobbers and service stations.
Aviation Canadian Aviation Report	Maclean Hunter	Statistics on aerospace industry, imports and exports, commercial airlines, passenger loads, freight and licences.
Canada Report on Canada	Maclean Hunter	Historical data on Canada: population, income, GNP, construction and manufacturing forecasts, economic indicators (annual).
Handbook of Canadian Consumer Markets	The Conference Board of Canada	Population, labour force and employ ment, income, expenditures, production and retail trade and consumer and industry price indexes. Collected from different sources. Trends, distributions and projections (biennial).
Bank of Canada Review	Bank of Canada	Monetary aggregates and fiscal policy, chartered banks, interest rates, selected economic indicators, labour markets, prices, income and costs, external trade and Canadian balance of international payments (monthly).
Canadian Outlook: Economic Forecast & Provincial Outlook: Economic Forecast	The Conference Board of Canada	Consumer expenditures, housing, government investment, trade, employment, labour, costs, prices, markets and budgets. Comparative tables (both quarterly).
Canadian Economic Observer	Statistics Canada	National accounts, labour markets, prices, domestic trade, merchandise trade, manufacturing, construction, agriculture, mining and energy, transportation and communications, financial markets, demography, and provincial and international comparisons (monthly).

continued

Information	Available From	Comments
Canadian Markets	Financial Post	Estimates and figures for population, households, personal disposable income and retail sales, Buying power index for individual markets. Extensive data on specific markets (annual).
Clothing		
Report on Canadian Apparel Industry	Maclean Hunter	Consumer expenditure for men's, women's and children's clothing. Information on manufacturing, imports and exports (annual).
Construction		
Building Material Sources	Maclean Hunter	Buying groups, national distributors, hardware wholesalers, brand names, associations and executives (annual).
Real Estate Development Annual	Maclean Hunter	Real estate developers, investors, lenders and development-related organizations (annual).
Drugs/Pharmaceuticals		
Canadian Drug Store Report	Maclean Hunter	Pharmaceutical sales by province, city and major urban areas. Number of pharmacies by province. Sales of specific products (annual).
Electronics		
Audioscience Canada's Annual Canadian Hi-Fi Buyers Catalogue	Maclean Hunter	Listing of all available products, manufacturers and representatives (annual).
Canadian Electronic Market	Maclean Hunter	Electronic market including imports, exports and net production.
Electronic Data Processing (EDP)		
Canadian Datasystems Reference Manual	Maclean Hunter	EDP organizations, suppliers and products (annual).
Canadian Salary Survey	Maclean Hunter	Average salaries of EDP professionals by province and by city.

continued

Financial

Directory of Pension Fund Investment Services	Maclean Hunter	Information on trust companies, insurance companies and corporate investment counsellors. Data on asset mix, number of clients and size of pension fund assets managed by each.
Mutual Fund Sourcebook	Financial Times	Information on all open-ended funds. Addresses, phone numbers, portfolio managers and performance records.

Food Industry

Directory of Restaurants and Fast Food Chains in Canada	Monday Report on Retailers	Information on 600 retailers with more than three outlets. Addresses, personnel listing, advertising, franchising and financial data (annual).
Food Industry Economic Review and Forecast	Maclean Hunter	Forecasts for different industries in the food and beverage sector. Historical data, performance figures.

Packaging

Canada's Packaging Market	Maclean Hunter	Data on the packaging market, including production, imports and exports.

Retailing

Canadian Directory of Shopping Centres	Monday Report on Retailers	All shopping centres over 4600 sq. metres. Information on owners, managers and tenants. Traffic data, rents and market population (annual).
Directory of Retail Chains in Canada	Monday Report on Retailers	Retail chains with more than three outlets. Addresses, personnel listing, merchandise range, financial status, lease and expansion information (annual).

INTERNATIONAL DATA

The current trends—Eastern Europe moving toward a market economy, U.S.-Canada free trade agreement, the emergence of the European Community, to name a few—indicate a movement towards an expanded, capitalist-oriented global market. Consequently, a Canadian researcher may require access to information in other countries. Specific secondary data may be obtained easily for developed countries, but accurate information is somewhat harder to come by for less developed countries.

Here are some sources that cover several countries:

- *International Marketing Data and Statistics*: Contains marketing-oriented statistical information including consumer spending and households for 132 countries around the world. Published annually by Euromonitor.

- *European Marketing Data and Statistics*: Contains statistical marketing information on 30 countries of Eastern and Western Europe. Comparative tables include population, employment, production, trade, the economy, standard of living, size of the market, and health. Published annually by Euromonitor.

- *World Index of Economic Forecasts*: Provides information on 370 organizations, including forecasts, plans and surveys for over 100 countries. Published by Gower Publishing.

- *The World Economic Survey:* This survey attempts to provide a basis for appraising the current trends in the world economy, especially as these affect the progress of less developed countries. Published by the Office for Development Research and Policy Analysis, Department of International Economic and Social Affairs, the United Nations.

- *The World Tables*: A compendium of economic and social data for a number of countries. Information provided includes economic data for each country, derived indicators for selected years for inter-country comparisons and demographic and social data. Published by The World Bank.

- *Demographic Trends 1950-1990*: This is a study of demographic and labour force trends over the period 1950-1990. It is based upon the historical information provided to the OECD by member countries. The changes in population and labour markets are presented by age and sex. A number of graphs are included to facilitate comparison among different countries. Published by OECD.

- *World Studies*: This provides information on growing markets, world price situation for a given product, political factors affecting markets, role of multinationals and trend forecasts. *World Studies* is available from Predicasts Inc.

SECONDARY DATA AS SAMPLING FRAMES

Although we have so far treated secondary data as providing research information, there is another important use for secondary data. Secondary data can be used as the sampling frame for specific types of research. For instance, if you want to survey mutual fund managers, you can use the *Mutual Fund Sourcebook* mentioned earlier. If you would like to interview businesses of a certain size in a given sector, Dun and Bradstreet may have a list of these businesses. The *Canadian Almanac and Directory*, published annually by Copp Clark Pitman Ltd., contains a variety of lists—TV stations, libraries, financial institutions, schools and colleges, government directory, etc. Such lists can be invaluable and save considerable cost and time for researchers attempting to carry out research in a specific field.

ADVANTAGES AND DISADVANTAGES OF SECONDARY DATA

While secondary data have a number of advantages, they should be used with caution for several reasons. This section briefly points out the advantages and the disadvantages of secondary data.

ADVANTAGES OF SECONDARY DATA

- **Secondary data are relatively inexpensive**: Even if you have to pay hundreds of dollars for a privately published directory, it is still much less expensive than obtaining the information in any other way.
- **Secondary data save time**: Primary research takes time. Secondary data provide the information now. When time is a critical factor, secondary data may prove very useful.
- **Secondary data enhance the quality of primary research**: In some cases, secondary data can provide all you need to know thus saving your organization the cost of doing primary research. In other cases, secondary data may provide partial information thus reducing the cost of research. In addition, because an analysis of incomplete secondary data focuses on what we need to know to achieve our objectives, it enhances the quality of research.
- **Secondary data may be the only way to obtain information**: In some cases the cost of doing primary research is so prohibitive (for example, demographic characteristics of Canadians, economic trends around the world) as to make it an unrealistic method of collecting data. In such cases, secondary data are the only available alternative.

DISADVANTAGES OF SECONDARY DATA

- **Secondary data may be flawed**: An internal research report written a few years ago may have used a defective methodology. For instance, the sample on which the findings were based may have been drawn from a biased sample of respondents. The model used to project economic growth may be inadequate; it might have left out some important parameter. Data provided for comparison purposes in a compendium may not really be comparable because of the different assumptions used. For instance, the U.K. measures unemployment differently from Canada and it may be misleading to compare the two figures directly. Directories put out by different associations may not necessarily question the veracity of the information provided by its members.

- **Secondary data may be biased**: Different organizations may have their own biases in the way they collect data. These biases are not easily identifiable. Projections provided by certain industries tend to paint a rosy picture, even when the outlook is not very bright.
- **Secondary data may not be appropriate**: The secondary data may appear similar to what you want to find out, but in fact they may not be adequate to fulfill your objectives. For example, you may be interested in finding out Canadian attitudes to beer drinking; the secondary data you have may deal with the same topic but might have included only male respondents over 25 years of age. Secondary data may be outdated. If you want to find out the attitudes of people towards investing, a survey done in April 1987 (before the stock market crash) may not reflect today's attitudes towards investing.

USING SECONDARY DATA

The use of secondary data is limited only by the researcher's imagination. Whenever you are called upon to do a research project, you may want to familiarize yourself first with the information that is available. Secondary data sources can be extremely valuable as long as you take into consideration their limitations. The case study below shows how secondary data were used to accomplish the objectives of a research project.

MARKET FEASIBILITY STUDIES USING SECONDARY DATA: A SHORT CASE STUDY

A product called The Bookkeeper was developed by a Canadian company in 1984 to help people keep track of their household financial picture. When cheques were written and deposited, the amounts were to be entered into The Bookkeeper keyboard. The Bookkeeper then stored the information and printed out a record of transactions when requested to do so. The Bookkeeper was to be designed to be sufficiently attractive to be placed in a convenient position near to the entrance door, or in the kitchen or den area. It was anticipated that household dollars used to buy The Bookkeeper would either be transferred from other purchases to The Bookkeeper or would be drawn from new discretionary income within the household.

A basic feasibility study was required since shares were to be offered for sale through a prospectus. Naturally, the prospective investors needed an indication of the possible market potential of the product.

One step in the analysis was to identify the potential sources of household funds that could have been redirected by the household from other uses to purchase The Bookkeeper. In order to identify the dollar potential for redirection to The Bookkeeper, the product assortment on which those dollars might have been spent had to be identified and secondary data sources needed to be procured to help estimate those amounts. Since there was not enough time and money for collecting any primary information on the product potential, secondary sources were used exclusively.

Several sources were investigated to provide the necessary information:

- "World Markets Show Renewed Vigur as U.S. Leads the Way," *Electronics Week*, July 23, 1984;
- "Electronics Industry Survey," *Standard & Poor's Industry Surveys*, July 1984;
- "The Number Game," *Microcomputer News*, August 1984;
- "The Bookkeeper Company Business Plan 1984," The Bookkeeper Company, 1984;
- "1984 World Markets Forecast Data Book," *Electronics Magazine*, McGraw Hill Publications, January, 1984;
- U.S. Bureau of the Census, "Money Income of Households, Families and Persons in the United States: 1982," February 1984, Series P-60, No. 142, Washington, D.C., 1984;
- U.S. Bureau of the Census, "Statistical Abstract of the United States: 1982-83," Washington, D.C., 1982.

The secondary sources provided information on the sizes of similar markets, basic data on the size of target market segments, and the amounts of money spent on similar products. It was found that the U.S. market for microwave ovens was 11.6 million units in 1981, and that the market for calculators and personal computers for 1984 was estimated to be $718.3 million and $575 billion, respectively. It was estimated that the calculator market would grow by 11% by 1987. The demand for personal computers would grow by 300% by 1987, ... developing into a $25 billion market (U.S. Bureau of the Census, 1984).

The next step was to construct various scenarios of what would be likely to happen in terms of market response. One of the scenarios is presented in Exhibit 24.5. Given the information available, it was thought that money might be redirected from the purchase of microwave ovens to buy The Bookkeeper. If this were to happen, then the extent of the change in spending had to be identified. In the realistic scenario, it was estimated that 0.5% of those who earned less than $15 000 would buy The Bookkeeper, that 1% of the families earning $15 000 to $24 999, that 5% of the $25 000 to $34 999, and 10% of the $35 000 and over households would buy. If that happened, then approximately $24 185 000 in revenue would be attracted to the product.

A pessimistic scenario was formulated in which smaller percentages of redirected dollars were hypothesized to produce $16 292 500 in Bookkeeper revenue. An optimistic scenario estimated that larger percentages of the dollars spent on microwave ovens would be redirected to The Bookkeeper, producing an estimated revenue of $63 370 000.

Exhibit 24.5 Predicted Revenue of The Bookkeeper

Family Income 1979		Less than $15 000	$15 000 to $24 999	$25 000 to $34 999	$35 000 and more
No. of Families		19 919 000	36 596 000	11 961 000	11 750 000
No. of Families Using Microwaves		2 100 000	3 500 000	3 000 000	3 000 000
Realistic Scenario	Total	1/2% Buy	1% Buy	5% Buy	10% Buy
Sales	345 500	10 500	35 000	120 000	180 000
Revenue	$24 185 000	$735 000	$2 450 000	$8 400 000	$12 600 000
Pessimistic Scenario	Total	1/4% Buy	1/2% Buy	2% Buy	5% Buy
Sales	232 750	5 250	17 500	60 000	150 000
Revenue	$16 292 500	$367 500	$1 225 000	$4 200 000	$10 500 000
Optimistic Scenario	Total	1% Buy	2% Buy	10% Buy	20% Buy
Sales	991 000	21 000	70 000	300 000	600 000
Revenue	$69 370 000	$1 470 000	$4 900 000	$21 000 000	$42 000 000

Other scenarios were developed in order to gain a well rounded perspective on the market potential of The Bookkeeper. Estimates of the revenue which might be drawn away from colour televisions sales, personal computers, calculators, tape recorders and other consumer electronics were used in the scenario analyses. This information was analyzed in a personal computer spreadsheet such as LOTUS or EXCEL.

The scenario feasibility analyses were performed at a very preliminary stage in the development of The Bookkeeper. Inherent in the estimated revenue figures were assumptions that the remaining development engineering would be successful; that financial backing for the project would be forthcoming; that The Bookkeeper could be manufactured for costs used in the assumptions of market attraction; that competent management and marketing personnel would be hired and that they could take the product successfully to market; and that consumers would find The Bookkeeper to be a beneficial product to purchase for the price.

Preliminary feasibility studies such as that discussed above are performed for most new products and for products that are imported from foreign markets and commercialized in Canada. Although there are many parts of the scenario build-up that might not happen just as estimated, the speed and the relatively low cost of feasibility studies conducted on secondary data encourage many companies to use this process as the initial stage of project assessment.

SUMMARY

1. When you gather information from published and unpublished sources rather than by designing a special study, you are said to collecting secondary data. Secondary research can save time and money.
2. Secondary data come from two sources: internal records of the company, such as advertising expenditure, sales figures, etc.; and external data, such as industry statistics and commercial data bases.
3. Statistics Canada is the largest purveyor of information relevant to market researchers.
4. For specialized research, a variety of secondary data can be obtained from private sources.

NOW THINK ABOUT THIS

1. You work for a company that manufactures expensive perfume. You decide that your target market consists of urban women whose household income is $60 000 and above. How would you estimate the size of this market?

2. A U.S.-based electronics manufacturer wants to start a Canadian operation. What secondary sources should the manufacturer consult before the
   plans are finalized?
3. Should you consult secondary sources before starting *any* primary
   research? Under what conditions would secondary research be most useful?

REFERENCES

U.S. Bureau of the Census
1982   "Statistical Abstract of the United States: 1982-82." Washington, D.C.

U.S. Bureau of the Census
1984   "Money Income of Households, Families and Persons in the United
       Sates: 1982." February 1984, Series P-60, No. 142, Washington, D.C.

25 / Legal Issues in Marketing Research

INTRODUCTION

Market research is not simply used to obtain information to provide input to marketing decisions. Several large organizations use marketing research figures to support claims of superiority (for instance, Coke versus Pepsi), or for use in litigation (to prove or disprove a certain claim) or to provide damages. Revenue Canada even used surveys to decide whether toothpaste is taxable or not. Survey results are used in civil and criminal cases as evidence. There is even a case where a client sued a research house (for instance *Yankelovich, Skelley and White* v. *Beecham*).

Given this scenario, a market researcher may be well advised to be aware of the principles that are relevant to the legal status of survey research in general. This chapter is largely based upon the papers written by Stitt and Huq (1988) and Bereskin (1988).[1] Although the material is general in nature, particular emphasis is given to the laws of the Province of Ontario. This chapter should not be considered a definitive guide to the topic; rather, it should be viewed as an overview of relevant principles as they currently exist. Since neither of the authors is a legal expert, the exposition should not be considered rigorous. For any specific legal problem, it is wise to seek advice from a member of the legal profession.

ADMISSIBILITY OF SURVEY RESULTS AS EVIDENCE

AT COMMON LAW

At the present time, there are no statutory provisions—either in Canada or Ontario Evidence Acts—that deal specifically with survey results as evidence. Their admissibility is found in the common law. Common law is based on decisions by judges, as opposed to decisions laid down in parliamentary legislation (statutory law). Two common laws govern the admissibility of survey evidence: the hearsay rule and the opinion evidence rule.

HEARSAY   Hearsay refers to evidence that is secondhand; that is, the evidence is not based on the personal knowledge of the witness, but is repetition of what the witness has heard from others. When the intention is just to state that a statement was in fact made, then it is not hearsay. For example, if Jones tells Smith that David stole a car, Smith cannot repeat Jones' statement as proof that David stole a car. However, Smith can repeat Jones' statement as a fact that such a statement was made by Jones, if it happens to be relevant for some reason. The reason for this position is that the witness (Smith in this example) is under oath and can be cross-examined while the third party (Jones) is not under oath and cannot be cross-examined on the statement (that David stole the car).

This means that market research evidence will be considered hearsay and will not be admitted if it is submitted to establish the truth of the statements made by the respondents and the respondents are not available for cross-examination. The greater the number of intervening parties in the survey process, the greater the likelihood of the survey data's being considered hearsay.

According to Cooke (1985) a sequence of events should occur for a typical survey to be considered accurate and fair:

- The interviewer must correctly either enter on the questionnaire what the respondent said or code it into a pre-coded list

- The coder must code the open-ended responses correctly
- The keypunch operator must punch the response correctly
- The programmer must program the computer correctly
- The computer must be functioning properly
- The expert must interpret the findings properly

In a typical survey, statements made by the respondents will pass though several persons. In the process, the initial statements become hearsay built on hearsay, if submitted to prove the truth of statements made by the originator.

However, there are several exceptions to the hearsay rule. Such exceptions are generally based upon two factors. First, no other evidence may be available (i.e., if the evidence is not admitted in its hearsay form, the court will have to adjudicate without it) and second, a substitute for cross-examination available to test the reliability of evidence.

EXCEPTIONS TO THE HEARSAY RULE

PUBLIC DOCUMENTS   Survey evidence does not necessarily fulfill the above conditions. An exception that may be relevant pertains to public documents. The leading test for a public document in Ontario was set out in *Finestone* v. *The Queen* (1953). This test requires that:

1. the survey must have been made by a public officer pursuant to a public duty to record and deal with matters which it was his duty to record;
2. the judicial proceedings must be public; and
3. the survey must be available to the public and brought into existence for that purpose.

Surveys conducted by research houses, government agencies and other organizations do not generally come within the definition of a public document as described above. The main reason for this is that such surveys are not conducted by a public officer pursuant to a public duty to record.

Therefore, under the hearsay rule, surveys conducted by a private entity will not be admitted into evidence in an Ontario court if they are submitted to prove the truthfulness of the statements made by the respondents, unless the respondents themselves appear in court.

There are no exceptions to the hearsay rule under which the survey data could arguably be rendered admissible. If, however, the survey evidence is offered merely to show that certain statements were made by the interviewees, then such evidence is not hearsay, and may be admitted (The court will still require proof that the statements were made. Such proof could take various forms, e.g., testimony of interviewers or affidavits sworn by the interviewees or interviewers.)

EXPERT OPINION EVIDENCE   The second common law doctrine relevant to the admissibility of survey research evidence is the opinion evidence rule. According to this rule, a witness may testify concerning only the facts of which he has personal knowledge and not concerning his opinions. Any inferences or conclusions to be drawn from the witness's perceptions are matters solely for the trier of fact. Private surveys breach this rule because survey results are usually introduced into court through opinion evidence.

However, a major exception to the opinion rule permits an "expert witness" to state his opinion, where his opinion or inference arises from a special skill he possesses and the subject matter of the inquiry is such that inexperienced persons are unlikely to prove capable of forming a correct judgment upon it without such assistance (for example, *R* v. *Fisher*, 1961). A market research witness in this instance offers opinions on the interpretation and significance of the survey results in person or in the form of a written submission. The results of the survey are not introduced into court as a list of individual responses of the various persons surveyed, but rather the results of the survey are collated and introduced in the form of conclusions of the survey results.

In general, the evidence of an expert should be useful, moderate, disinterested, fair and strictly professional (*R* v. *DeTonnacourt*, 1956). In the case of survey evidence, expert opinion will be admitted where the witness is shown to be a market research expert, and his or her testimony will be helpful to the trier of fact.

Assuming that the market researchers who conduct surveys for commercial clients are highly qualified and their testimony will be necessary to explain the survey results to a court, opinion evidence should be admissible under the expert opinion exception to the opinion evidence rule.

A major concern regarding the admissibility of expert opinion arises when the opinion is based on hearsay evidence. It has now been accepted that an opinion based on hearsay should be admitted and that the hearsay concern should be dealt with in deciding how much weight to give the opinion. In the *City of Saint John* v. *Irving Oil Co., Ltd*, (1966), an expert witness conducted interviews with 47 persons regarding the value of a parcel of land. Although the comments of those 47 persons were hearsay evidence and not admissible, the expert was permitted to give his opinion on the value of the land based on those interviews.

The dangers posed by the hearsay element would be addressed by the trier of fact in deciding how much weight to give the opinion. Thus, it is likely that expert opinion evidence will be admissible even where it may be based on or involve the interpretation of survey results. The hearsay concerns will be addressed by limiting the weight given to the expert's opinion, and not by making the evidence inadmissible.

JUDICIAL ATTITUDES

To ascertain the current judicial attitudes towards survey research, we may examine three specific types of proceedings: trade marks, passing-off, and obscenity cases.

TRADE MARKS

In the area of trade mark litigation, surveys are frequently carried out on a representative sample of the target population to determine whether a particular trade mark is recognized by the public or whether it would cause confusion with a similar trade market. For example, does the trade mark "Toys Я Us" lead to confusion with the trade mark "Kids r Us" (*Toys Я Us Inc.* v. *Canarsie Kiddie Shop*, 1983)?

There are two kinds of confusion in trademark surveys: product confusion and source confusion. Product confusion arises when a product's name, trademark or packaging is so similar to that of another product that consumers are likely to confuse one product with the other. Source confusion arises when a product by one manufacturer is actually a line extension of another manufacturer. Product confusion is easier to test than source confusion. It is not easy to test source confusion without first planting an idea in the mind of respondents; the respondent may not have thought of it but for the survey.

In trade mark surveys, the nature of the determination to be made is to prove that certain views are held by the public. The comments of the interviewees are not introduced as evidence to prove the truthfulness of their statements, but to show that they were made. Consequently, the hearsay rule is usually not breached.

For instance, in *Canadian Schenley Distilleries Ltd* v. *Canada's Manitoba Distiller Ltd.* (1975) the judge stated:

> In my view the admissibility of survey evidence and the probative value of that evidence when admitted is dependent on how the poll was conducted, the questions asked, how they were asked, and how they were framed and what purpose the evidence is to be used for. There will be no objection to evidence being admissible when the poll is put forward not to prove the truth of the statements it contains but merely to show the basis of an expert's opinion, or as in the present instance, an assessment of the results of the survey.

This view has been accepted in several subsequent Canadian cases.

The most important basis for admitting the evidence, therefore, is that the responses of the interviewees are not being admitted as statements to prove the truth of the matters asserted, but to prove that those views are held. A court will also want to be satisfied that the survey was fairly and scientifically conducted. In this respect, Daniel Bereskin (1988) identifies eight specific factors (among others) that are important:

1. **The universe** The study should identify and examine the proper universe. The survey respondents should be drawn from the target market in terms of demographic and geographic and other relevant characteristics.

2. **The sample** The sample chosen from the relevant universe should be representative. While in the strictest sense this would mean a probability sample, in practice this type of sample can seldom be carried out under survey conditions. It is therefore advisable to label the sample as a "modified probability sample" (assuming that the sample was indeed chosen using probability sampling procedures).

3. **The questionnaire** The questions should address the correct legal issues and the wording should be clear, unambiguous and unbiased. Nor should the sequencing of questions be subject to any bias.

4. **The implementation** The person or persons who carry out the survey and interpret the results must be experts. While it might be easy for an experienced person to qualify as an expert, it is not likely that any one single person has all the necessary expertise in every aspect of research such as design, sampling design, fieldwork, computing and statistical analysis. Therefore, it is normal to have the person who is in charge of the project (who, in effect, supervises the experts) explain and defend the project.

5. **The data** The data must be accurately reported. This involves several aspects. For instance, pre-coding of open-ended questions should be justifiable. Similarly, the grouping of variables should be logical. Statistical procedures should be error-free and relevant.

6. **The sampling plan and execution, questionnaire and fieldwork** These should follow accepted norms and standards. Recorded cases do not tend to define such standards. Consequently, generally accepted industry standards and objective procedures should prove adequate. However, most surveys involve several compromises and trade-offs. The expert should be aware of such trade-offs and their implications for the results.

7. **The research should be independent** The survey should be carried out independently and lawyers involved in the case should not appear to have influenced the formulation of the questionnaire, the survey methodology or the interpretation.

8. **The survey should be double blind** Neither the respondents nor the interviewers should know who the client is or what the objectives of the study are.

What these principles imply is that when the researcher uses accepted research procedures (the basic principles of which are described in this book) and takes additional care because of the sensitive nature of litigation, the evidence may be admissible.

The British approach to the issue of survey data in trade mark cases and the hearsay rule is similar to that followed by the Canadian courts. The case of *GE (General Electric) Trade Mark* (1969) established the admissibility of survey data in trade mark cases. A company known as GEC had applied to have the trade market *GE* removed from the trade marks registry on the grounds that it was likely to cause confusion between GE and GEC. In order to demonstrate the likelihood of confusion, a survey of the general public was conducted. The admissibility of the survey evidence was challenged in court. The court, however, accepted the survey evidence, although it did not discuss the basis of its admissibility.

American courts have long accepted the admissibility of survey data for the purpose of determining the public's state of mind. In a 1951 case (*United States* v. *88 Cases More or Less Containing Bireley's Orange Beverage*), a government survey was admitted as evidence of the state of mind of consumers regarding the contents of a particular bottle. Twelve years later, in *Zippo Manufacturing Co.* v. *Rogers Imports Inc.* (1963), the court pointed to the superiority of evidence provided through a properly conducted scientific survey over statements of experts or a limited number of witnesses provided by either party. According to Robert Lavidge (1985), a common use of survey data now includes determination of whether a term is generic, whether trade marks are confusing, and the secondary meaning of a trade mark or design.

PASSING-OFF

Passing-off is a form of misrepresentation. It is:

- a misrepresentation,
- made by a trader in the course of trade,
- to prospective customers of his or ultimate consumers of goods or service supplied by him,
- which is calculated to injure the business or good will of another trader (in the sense that this is a reasonably foreseeable consequence), and
- which causes actual damage to a business or goodwill of the trader by whom the action is brought, or will probably do so.

An example of passing-off would be when a manufacturer imitates the highly distinct packaging style of another established brand (for instance refer: *Perrier* v. *Canada Dry*, 1983, Re *Carson* v. *Reynolds*, 1980, *Molson* v. *Labatt*, 1985.

The use of survey evidence to establish public opinion or attitude in passing-off cases is similar to that in trade mark cases. Survey evidence will be admitted in Canadian and British courts (see *Lego System Aktieselskab And Another* v. *Lego M.O. Lemelstrich Ltd.*, 1983) to establish that two trade marks, slogans or designs are causing confusion in the public mind. The general principles that were discussed in the previous section (trade marks) regarding sound research practices also apply to passing-off cases.

OBSCENITY

Obscenity is defined on the basis of community standards. Consequently, in obscenity cases survey results that measure community standards and attitudes are frequently admitted. Consider the case of *R.* v. *Prairie Schooner News Ltd. and Powers* (1970). The case revolved around the possession of obscene written matter for the purpose of publication, distribution and circulation. The accused submitted the results of an opinion poll to establish the relevant community standard regarding obscenity. The evidence was rejected by the trial judge (and later by the Court of Appeal) because the person conducting the poll was not considered an expert in the science of opinion research or on the subject of obscenity. Furthermore, the universe was inappropriate and the sample selection was not based on scientific principles. The court outlined three conditions under which survey evidence establishing public views on obscenity could be admissible:

- **Relevant universe:** selection of the proper segment of population whose characteristics are relevant to the community being studied;
- **Proper coverage:** sample representative of Canada and not drawn from a single city; and
- **Adequate sample units:** a sample of a large enough size so that reasonable conclusions may be drawn from the survey results.

If these criteria are met, the court said, then survey results may be admissible as evidence of public state of mind, attitude or belief. American courts have been accepting surveys under these conditions in obscenity cases for a number of years.

The above guidelines were followed in a subsequent case. In *R.* v. *Times Square Cinema Ltd.* (1971), the Ontario Court of Appeal rejected the survey evidence submitted by the accused to establish contemporary standards of community tolerance of sexual exploitation, because the surveys in question were deemed unsatisfactory and unrepresentative of community standards. The reasons for rejection were that the sample was too narrow and the interviewees were not sufficiently objective or impartial to be representative of the relevant population. The court also suggested that such evidence might be admissible in other cases if the survey were properly conducted.

In both cases, the court felt that survey evidence could be useful and admissible where

- the witness was an expert,
- he or she could establish that the poll was based on scientific principles, and
- the trial judge instructed the jury (if any) that the expert's opinion was to be disregarded if the expert could not demonstrate that the poll was based on sound principles.

LIABILITIES FOR INACCURACIES IN PUBLISHED SURVEY RESULTS

Can a survey sponsor or user be liable for inaccuracies contained in the survey? Let us focus on the situation in which an organization uses survey results to promote its (business) interests publicly through advertising or other communications. In this respect, the provisions of the *Federal Competition Act* and the *Ontario Business Practices Act* concerning misleading advertising and unfair business practices are most pertinent. (The next two sections are quoted directly from Stitt and Huq's original manuscript.)

COMPETITION ACT

The following discussion is based on the assumption that a survey sponsor will use the survey data in advertisements to promote its goods or services. The relevant provisions of the *Competition Act* are set out below:

36.(1) No person shall for the purpose of promoting directly, or indirectly, any business interest, by any means whatever

a. make a representation to the public that is false or misleading in a material respect;

b. make a representation to the public in the form of a statement, warranty of guarantee of the performance, efficacy or length of life of a product that is not based on an adequate and proper test thereof, the proof of which lies upon the person making the representation;

c. make a representation to the public in a form that purports to be

i. a warranty or guarantee of a product, or

ii. a promise to replace, maintain or repair an article of any part thereof or to repeat or continue a service until it has achieved a specified result.

In order for liability to exist under section 36, it must first be established that the survey sponsor has placed an advertisement outlining the survey results for the purpose of promoting its business interests. Since the advertisement would likely be placed with a view to increasing the sales and revenues, this requirement is easily satisfied. Next, for liability to exist under subsection (a), the advertisement must be false or misleading to the public in a material respect. Although "material" is not defined in the Act, this term is generally understood to mean that the inaccuracy must not be a trifling one, but rather must be one which would undermine the very results of the survey. That is, for the survey sponsor to be liable under this subsection, the survey would have to be fundamentally wrong in some major respect. A few incorrectly recorded responses or inaccuracies of a few percentage points would not be sufficient to create liability under this section if not material; and the survey sponsor could probably avoid prosecution for minor inaccuracies under this section by including a disclaimer to the effect that the results are accurate within x percentage points. The only way in which the survey sponsor would be in contravention of this section would be if the survey were grossly inaccurate or deficient.

Under subsection (b), liability would arise for example, if the advertisement (in the form of a statement to the public) regarding the efficacy of the survey sponsor's products as advertised were made on the basis of inadequate or improper testing. The same considerations apply here as with respect to subsection (a). That is, unless a survey has been conducted in an entirely improper and inadequate manner (e.g., inaccurate recording of answers), there may not be any liability under this subsection 36(1).

Therefore, liability under the *Competition Act* will arise only if a survey is conducted so improperly that it is grossly inaccurate and such survey is used to promote business interests of the survey sponsor. If the survey is properly conducted and there are only slight inaccuracies, as are commonly present in most surveys, and a qualifying statement is made to this effect, then it is unlikely that liability would ensue under the *Competition Act*.

BUSINESS PRACTICES ACT (ONTARIO)

The *Ontario Business Practices Act* prohibits a person from engaging in an unfair practice. The Act defines a series of "unfair practices" in section 2, set out below:

Unfair Practices - For the purposes of this Act, the following shall be deemed to be unfair practices:

a. a false, misleading or deceptive consumer representation including, but without limiting the generality of the foregoing, b. a representation that the goods or services have sponsorship, approval, performance characteristics, accessories, uses, ingredients, benefits or quantities they do not have ...

For a survey sponsor to be liable for inaccuracies in surveys under this section, it would have to be shown that "there has been a representation that the services have benefits which they do not have." That is, 1) the survey sponsor would have to make representations that certain benefits would result from using one's product or service, 2) such a representation would have to be incorrect. In order to show that the representation was incorrect, it would have to be demonstrated that the survey on which the representation was based was completely inaccurate. Only if both of the above criteria were satisfied would there be liability under the *Business Practices Act*.

Thus, it is unlikely that a survey sponsor will be liable under the *Ontario Business Practices Act* for inaccuracies in its surveys unless

1. representations are made that using the survey sponsor's product or service will result in certain benefits,
2. such representations are incorrect, and
3. such representations are based on inaccurate surveys.

HOW TO CONDUCT A STUDY TO INCREASE THE LIKELIHOOD OF ITS ADMISSIBILITY

Considering the time and expense involved in conducting a survey, one would like to increase the likelihood of its admissibility in courts. The exact requirements may of course vary from court to court. However, Stitt and Huq (1988) offer 11 guidelines that they consider to be the "common denominator" concerns.

1. The sample of the public tested should be representative of the universe being tested.
2. The sample tested should be large enough to form reasonable conclusions.
3. The questions should not be "leading" or "weighted" and should be as free from bias as possible.
4. Responses to questions should occur in a narrative form (as opposed to a yes or no format).
5. In the alternative, where answers are "translated" into various codes, and not recorded in a narrative form, as many codes as possible should exist (as opposed to "Yes" or "No").
6. All answers given to the interviewers should be disclosed.

7. Sound interview procedures should be followed by competent interviewers who have no knowledge of the litigation or the purpose of the survey.

8. The precise instruction given to the interviewers should be disclosed.

9. The data gathered should be accurately reported.

10. The data should be analyzed in accordance with accepted statistical principles.

11. The objectivity of the entire process should be assumed.

CONCLUSIONS

- **Hearsay:** Survey results will not be admissible at common law if they are merely "hearsay." A statement is hearsay if it is offered to prove the truth of the matter asserted by someone else who does not appear in court. Thus, if surveys sponsored by an organization are submitted to prove that statements made by the respondents are true, such evidence will be hearsay and not admissible.

- **Proof that certain statements were made:** If survey results are submitted to show that certain statements were made, then the surveys will be admissible. The evidence can take various forms such as the testimony of the interviewers or affidavits sworn by the interviewers or interviewees. It will usually be necessary to tender expert opinion evidence regarding the conclusions to be drawn from the survey. Opinion evidence is not admissible at common law under the opinion evidence rule. However, there is a recognized exception for "expert opinion evidence" where it can be shown that the witness is an expert in a recognized field of expertise and that his or her testimony is both necessary and helpful to the court to interpret the results of a survey. Expert opinion evidence will also be admissible even if it is based on hearsay evidence, but it will be given less weight than if it had been based on non-hearsay statements.

- **Statutory provisions:** No statutory provisions governing the admissibility of hearsay evidence currently exist in Canada. The only statutory restrictions are those limiting the number of expert witnesses who may be called (limitation of five under the *Canadian Evidence Act* and limit of three in the *Evidence Act (Ontario)* unless leave of the court or leave of the opposing party is granted).

- **Trade mark and passing-off cases:** Survey evidence is generally admissible in trade mark and passing-off cases when it is submitted to establish public opinion or public state of mind. There is no breach of the hearsay rule because survey data are introduced only to establish that a certain view is held by a particular segment of the public and not to prove that the statements made by interviewees are true. Survey evidence is therefore admissible in such cases as long as the court is satisfied that the survey has been fairly and scientifically conducted. This view is also held in Great Britain and the United States. Expert opinion evidence is also admissible in trade mark cases where the witness is an expert in market research and offers testimony that is helpful to the court.

- **Obscenity:** Public opinion surveys are also frequently admitted in obscenity cases to establish community standards existing with respect to obscenity. The judicial approach to survey material in such cases is to admit it where the survey has been properly conducted. Expert opinion evidence will only be admitted, however, where the witness is an expert in market research and in the field of obscenity.

- **Liability:** With respect to liability, under the *Competition Act* liability for inaccuracies in surveys will exist under the misleading advertising sections of the Act (s.36) only if the survey results are advertised with a view to promoting the survey sponsor's business interests and the survey is conducted so improperly that it is grossly inaccurate. If only slight inaccuracies exist and a statement is made that the survey may be inaccurate within a few percentage points, then it is unlikely that any liability would exist under the Act.

Under the *Business Practices Act*, liability for inaccuracies contained in surveys would exist only if the survey sponsor has made a representation that its products or services have benefits which they do not in fact have and those representations are based on surveys that are completely inaccurate.

Legal opinions are not static. They change with time and each new case may have a nuance that is distinct. Therefore, this chapter should not be considered exhaustive or definitive. The purpose of the chapter is to provide a perspective on the criteria frequently considered by the courts with respect to the proper conducting of a survey and, should the occasion arise, the principles that will determine the admissibility of evidence with respect to survey results per se or expert opinion evidence thereof.

SUMMARY

1. Currently, there is no federal statutory provision that deals with survey research as evidence. Survey research would come under the category of hearsay (what the witness had heard others say), which is generally inadmissible.

2. There are two exceptions to the above observation. Survey evidence may be offered to show that certain statements were made by the interviewees, and as expert evidence by research specialists.

3. Survey evidence is generally admissible in trade mark and passing-off cases when it is submitted to establish public opinion or public state of mind.

4. Survey evidence is generally admitted in obscenity cases to establish community standards with respect to obscenity.

5. Liability for inaccuracies contained in surveys will exist when the results of an improperly conducted survey are advertised in the promotion of a product and no mention is made of the margin of error relevant to that study.

6. For survey results to be admissible, the research project should adhere to industry standards and be technically sound.

NOW THINK ABOUT THIS

1. Collect a few advertisements that claim product superiority on the basis of survey research. What conditions should the claims satisfy to be upheld in court?

2. How does hearsay evidence relate to survey research?

3. Discuss the status of survey results with respect to trade mark and obscenity cases.

4. Marketing research surveys almost always contain inaccuracies. Under what conditions does liability arise?

REFERENCES

Bereskin, D.R.
1988   "The Use of Surveys in Legal Trade Mark Litigation." *Canadian Journal of Marketing Research*, 7, pp. 49-58.

Cooke, Mike
1985   "The Admissibility of Survey Data as Evidence in Courts of Law." *Journal of the Marketing Research Society*, 27(3), July 1985, p. 157.

Lavidge, Robert J.
1985   "Survey Research In Trade Mark Cases." Chicago Bar Record, Vol. 66 (January-February, 1985), p. 236.

Stitt, M.J. and N. Huq
1988   "The Legal Status of Survey Research." *Canadian Journal of Marketing Research*, 7, p. 42-48.

REFERENCES TO LEGAL CASES

Boyle-Midway (Canada) Ltd. v. Parkas Arpad Hommonay, [1977], 27 C.P.R. (2nd) 178

Canadian Schenley Distilleries Ltd. v. Canada's Manitoba Distillery Ltd. 25 C.P.R. (2nd) 1 at p. 9

Carling Breweries Ltd. v. Molson Companies Ltd. et al [1985], 1 C.P.R. (3rd) 191 at 198

Carson v. Reynolds [1980],115 D.C.R. (3rd) 139

City of Saint John v. Irving Oil Co. Ltd. [1966] S.C.R. 581

Cordon Bleu International Ltée v. S.G. Bradley Co. Ltd [1979] 60 C.P.R. (2nd) 71

Finestone v. The Queen (1953), 107 C.C.C. 93, [1953] 2 S.C.R. 107

GE Trade Mark [1969] R.P.C. 418; [1970] R.P.C. 339 C.A.; [1973] R.P.C. 297 (H.C.)

Lego System Aktieselskab and Another v. Lego M.O. Lemelstrich Ltd., Fleet Street Reports [1983] 155

Molson Companies Ltd. v. John Labatt Ltd. [1985], 1 C.P.R. (34) 494

Perrier (Société Anonyme) v. Canada Dry Ltd. (1983), 70 C.P.R. (2d) 61

R. v. Fisher [1971], O.W.N. 94

R. v. DeTonnacourt [1956], 18, W.W.R. 337 (Man. C.A.)

R. v Prairie Schooner News Ltd. and Powers [1970], 75 W.W.R. 585 (Man. C.A.)

R. v. Times Square Cinema Ltd [1971],3 O.R. 688

Standard Oil Co. v. Moore, 251 F.2d 188

Stringfellow and A.N.R. v. McCain Food (GB) Limited and ANR, Fleet Street Review [1984], 175

NOTE

1. The bulk of this chapter borrows heavily from two sources, Stitt and Huq (1988) and Bereskin (1988). Mary Jane Stitt is with Blake Cassels and Graydon, Toronto and Nicky Hutt is with Minden, Grass, Grafstein and Greenstein, Toronto. Daniel R. Bereskin is with Rogers, Bereskin and Parr, Toronto. We gratefully acknowledge their indirect contribution to this chapter. We also express our thanks to the *Canadian Journal of Marketing Research* for permission to use this material.

Marketing Research Firms in Canada

The listing below is based on the *Directory of Canadian Marketing Research Organizations 1991* published by the Professional Marketing Research Society in Canada. We have added a few more firms to this listing. Although the list is not exhaustive, it includes a wide range of firms which account for the bulk of commercial marketing research conducted in Canada. The list is non-evaluative. Inclusion here does imply endorsement. Similarly, non-inclusion here does not mean non-endorsement.

Although we have listed more than 100 organizations, many of them are very small (fewer than 5 employees). Some of the organizations listed are full-service research houses while others specialize in functional areas such as fieldwork, computer tabulation of data or focus moderation.

Many large organizations may have offices in several cities across Canada. Only the main offices are listed here.

Company Name	Yr. Open	# of empl.	Address	City	Prov.	P.C.	Phone
A. C. Nielsen Company of Canada Limited	1944	1030	160 McNabb St.	Markham	ON	L3R 4B8	416-475-3344
ABM Research Ltd.	1979	23	17 Madison Avenue	Toronto	ON	M5R 2S2	416-961-5511
AdMonitor International Inc.(1)	1985	36	#285-144 Front St. West	Toronto	ON	M5J 2L7	416-591-6655
Alywne Graham Research	1989	2	550 Jarvis Street, Suite 427	Toronto	ON	M4Y 1N6	416-924-1847
Andover Research Associates Inc.	1986	6	1183 Finch Avenue West, Suite 205	Downsview	ON	M3J 2G2	416-665-6699
Angus Reid Group, Inc.	1979	68	160 Bloor Street East, Suite 1300	Toronto	ON	M4W 1B9	416-324-2900
Applied Consumer & Clinical Evaluations	1986	22	2445 Dunwin Drive	Mississauga	ON	L5L 1T1	416-828-0493
Applied Marketing Statistics	1981	4	3080 Yonge St., Suite 4054	Toronto	ON	M4N 3N1	416-488-0790
BBM Bureau of Measurement	1944	335	1500 Don Mills Rd., Suite 305	Don Mills	ON	M3B 3L7	416-445-9800
Baar & Associates Ltd.	1981	3	6223 Centre Street North	Calgary	AB	T2K 0V2	403-221-9600
Barbara Campbell Recruiting Ltd.	1982	6	38 Purple Sageway	Willowdale	ON	M2H 2Z5	416-495-8240
Brenda Farrell & Associates Ltd.	1985	28	410-675 West Hastings Street	Vancouver	BC	V6B 1N2	604-682-7626
Burak Jacobson Research Partners Inc.	1981	24	11 Church St., Suite 400	Toronto	ON	M5E 1M2	416-363-5111
Burke International Research (2)	1965	63	1075 Bay St., 3rd Floor	Toronto	ON	M5S 2X5	416-924-5454
Burwell Hay	1986	14	121 Willowdale Avenue, Suite 100	Toronto	ON	M2N 6A3	416-733-4466
Business Generation Group	n/a	1	30 Wroxeter Avenue	Toronto	ON	M4K 1J6	416-466-9191
Butler Research Associates Inc.	1984	13	2221 Yonge St., Suite 100	Toronto	ON	M4S 2B4	416-487-4144
C.S.U. Market Field Services Inc.	1981	10	7030 Woodbine Avenue, Suite 102	Markham	ON	L3R 1A2	416-474-1770
Calgary Research Bureau, Inc. (3)	1986	10	#141, 6815-8th Street N.E.	Calgary	AB	T2E 7H7	403-279-5835
Camelford Graham Research Group	1988	13	2345 Yonge St., Suite 212	Toronto	ON	M4P 2E5	416-440-1016
Canada Market Research Ltd.	1976	23	1235 Bay Street, Suite 300	Toronto	ON	M5R 3K4	416-964-9222
Canadian Facts	1932	155	1075 Bay St., 3rd Floor	Toronto	ON	M5S 2X5	416-924-5751
Cantest Interviewing Services Ltd.	1981	8	2857 Lawrence Avenue East, Suite 12	Scarborough	ON	M1R 2S9	416-266-4561
Chapter Three Marketing Research Service	1983	15	245 Victoria Avenue, Suite 500	Westmount	PQ	H3Z 2M6	514-931-0848
Cogem Research Inc.	1972	24	1420 Sherbrooke St. Ouest	Montreal	PQ	H3G 1K5	514-845-9221
Commins, Wingrove	n/a		160 Eglinton Avenue E., Suite 320	Toronto	ON	M4P 3B5	416-482-0625
CompuSearch Market & Social Research	n/a		330 Front St. W., Suite 1100	Toronto	ON	M5V 2B7	416-348-9180
Consumer Contact Limited	1970	50	2450 Victoria Park Avenue	Willowdale	ON	M2J 4A2	416-493-6111
Consumer Vision Inc.	1988	10	14 Prince Arthur Ave, Suite 107	Toronto	ON	M5R 1A9	416-967-1596
Contemporary Research Centre (4)	1970	30	2221 Yonge St., Suite 503	Toronto	ON	M4S 2B4	416-486-2043
Contract Testing Inc.	1985	12	241 Clarence Street, Suite 26	Brampton	ON	L6W 4P2	416-456-0783
Cooper Research Limited	1974	11	170 The Donway West, Suite 206	Don Mills	ON	M3C 2G3	416-449-9289
Coopers & Lybrand Consulting Group	1955	230	145 King St. W., Suite 2300	Toronto	ON	M5H 1V8	416-869-1130
Corporate Research Associates Inc.	1978	12	2695 Dutch Village Rd., Suite 700	Halifax	NS	B3L 4M6	902-421-1336

Company	Est.	No.	Address	City	Prov.	Postal Code	Phone
Creative Research Group Limited	1971	64	100 Sheppard Ave. E., Suite 700	Toronto	ON	M2N 6N5	416-250-8500
Criterion Research Corp.	1982	36	103-1661 Portage Avenue	Winnipeg	MB	R3J 3T7	204-788-4845
DJC Research	1978	30	920 Yonge Street, Suite 720	Toronto	ON	M4W 3C7	416-928-0826
Dadson Research Inc.	1973	5	335 Renfrew Drive, Suite 101	Markham	ON	L3R 9S9	416-513-7413
Dash Software Ltd.	1979	2	1667 Warren Drive	Mississauga	ON	L4W 2X1	416-624-8343
Decima Research	1979	88	1 Eglinton Ave. E., 7th Floor	Toronto	ON	M4P 3A1	416-483-1724
Decision Marketing Research Limited	1974	10	661 Queen Street East	Toronto	ON	M4M 1G4	416-469-5282
Deloitte & Touche	1975	30	386 Woolwich Street	Guelph	ON	N1H 3W7	519-822-1090
Dun & Bradstreet Canada	1857	24	5770 Hurontario Street	Mississauga	ON	L5R 3G5	416-568-6158
Edmonton Research Bureau Inc. (5)	1986	10	4644A-99th Street	Edmonton	AB	T6E 5H5	403-434-9409
Eidetics Motivational Research	1968	18	43 Eglinton Ave. E., Suite 506	Toronto	ON	M4P 1A2	416-481-6419
Ellen Karp Research	1989	2	1177 Yonge Street, Suite 106	Toronto	ON	M4T 2Y4	416-921-4513
Elliott Research Corporation Limited	1936	38	One Valleybrook Dr., Suite 400	Don Mills	ON	M3B 2S7	416-391-1844
Environics Research Group Limited	1970	33	45 Charles St. E.	Toronto	ON	M4Y 1S2	416-964-1397
F. Greenbaum & Associates	n/a	1	148 Stibbard Avenue	Toronto	ON	M4P 2C3	416-322-4881
Focal Research Consultants Ltd.	1987	9	6300 Lady Hammond Rd., Suite 700	Halifax	NS	B3K 2R6	902-454-8856
Gadd International Research	n/a	1	23 Lee Avenue	Toronto	ON	M4E 2N8	416-699-4299
Gallup Canada Inc.	1941	48	180 Bloor Street West	Toronto	ON	M5S 2V6	416-961-2811
Generations Research Inc.	1986	43	20 Eglinton Ave. W., Suite 1104	Toronto	ON	M4R 1K8	416-489-6282
Gillian Tuffin Research Ltd.	1984	12	2323 Yonge St., Suite 807	Toronto	ON	M4P 2C9	416-488-7998
Goldfarb Consultants	1965	55	4950 Yonge Street, 17th Floor	Willowdale	ON	M2N 6K1	416-221-9200
Gordon Crowe Associates	1985	3	60 Lascelles Boulevard	Toronto	ON	M5P 2E2	416-481-9490
Group Centre	1974	12	8595 Rue St. Denis	Montreal	PQ	H2P 2H4	514-389-7423
Group Innova Inc.	1981	8	4269 St. Catherine St. W., Suite 700	Westmount	PQ	H3Z 1P7	514-937-8786
Hall & Hall Associates Limited	n/a	1	305-10459 Resthaven Drive	Sidney	BC	V8L 3H6	604-656-5655
ISL International Surveys Ltd.	1985	11	151 Placer Court	Willowdale	ON	M2H 3R5	416-495-0909
InfoGroup Inc.	1986	46	Mezzanine, 744 West Hastings	Vancouver	BC	V6C 1A5	604-682-0285
InfoSpan Inc.	1985	5	385 The West Mall, Ste. 257	Etobicoke	ON	M9C 1E7	416-626-1062
Innovative Marketing Inc.	1970	21	40 Eglinton Ave. E., Suite 203	Toronto	ON	M4P 3A2	416-440-0310
Insight Canada Research Inc.	1985	24	101 Yorkville Ave., 3rd Floor	Toronto	ON	M5R 1C1	416-921-0090
Insights Inc.	1979	38	546 Adelaide St. N.	London	ON	N6B 3J5	519-679-0110
Insignia Marketing Research Inc.	1990	8	399 Elm Road	Toronto	ON	M5M 3W3	416-481-6963
J.E. Clucas & Associates Inc.	1967	11	101 Placer Court, #205	Willowdale	ON	M2H 3H0	416-498-7000
J.P. Samuels Research Inc.	1985	4	47 Wellpark Boulevard	Agincourt	ON	M1V 1A6	416-298-4734
John Yerxa Research Inc.	1986	10	4644A-99th Street	Edmonton	AB	T6E 5H5	403-435-1123
Julie Schwartz & Associates	1988	3	120 Eglinton Ave. E., Suite 200	Toronto	ON	M4P 1E2	416-487-3681

Firm	Year	No.	Address	City	Prov.	Postal Code	Phone
Karom Group (The)	1986	25	2323 Yonge Street, Suite 802	Toronto	ON	M4P 2C9	416-489-4146
King Consulting & Research International	1990	4	28 Ferndale Avenue	Toronto	ON	M4T 2B3	416-963-9044
Kubas Consultants	1977	6	3080 Yonge Street, Suite 3020	Toronto	ON	M4N 3N1	416-487-7040
LMS Market Research	1988	3	987 Cermonial Drive	Mississauga	ON	L5R 2Z8	416-568-2158
Lang Research Inc.	1990	5	405 The West Mall, Suite 700	Etobicoke	ON	M9C 5J1	416-622-3944
Legendre Lubawin Goldfarb Inc.	1990	2	1172 St-Mathieu	Montreal	PQ	H3H 2H5	514-937-2079
Les Recherches en Marketing	1984	7	800 est, de Maisonneuve, Suite 210	Montreal	PQ	H2L 4L8	514-844-3331
Longwoods Research Group Limited (The)	1978	16	145 Adelaide St. W., Suite 300	Toronto	ON	M5H 3H4	416-861-9880
MBA Research	n/a	1	189 First Avenue	Toronto	ON	M4M 1X3	416-463-0270
Macdonald & Associates Consultants	1987	6	3-1750 The Queensway, Suite 1343	Etobicoke	ON	M9C 5H5	416-761-6030
Market Facts of Canada Limited	1962	80	77 Bloor St. W., Suite 1200	Toronto	ON	M5S 3A4	416-964-6262
Market Focus Inc.	1977	4	72 Steeles Ave. W., Suite 206	Thornhill	ON	L4J 1A1	416-764-1412
Market Research Professionals	n/a		82 Normark Drive	Thornhill	ON	L3T 3R1	416-764-1155
Marketbeat Consulting Inc.	1990	2	434 Clarence St., Suite 200	London	ON	N6A 3M8	519-433-1133
Marktrend Research Inc.	1980	28	Suite 303, 2930 Arbutus Street	Vancouver	BC	V6J 3Y9	604-731-8281
McIntyre & Mustel Research	1980	19	820-1441 Creekside Drive	Vancouver	BC	V6J 4S7	604-733-4213
Med-Pro Research	1989	2	22 Waggoners Wells Lane	Thornhill	ON	L3T 4K3	416-889-9480
Neuman Marketing Research	n/a		1231 Yonge St., Suite 209	Toronto	ON	M4T 2T8	416-960-5201
New Service Alliance (The)	1986	21	Suite 1203, Atrium on Bay, 595 Bay	Toronto	ON	M5G 2C2	416-581-0200
Numerix Data Analysis	1990	9	2323 Yonge St., Suite 804	Toronto	ON	M4P 2C9	416-489-4147
Opinion Place	1970	8	66K-1485 Portage Ave.	Winnipeg	MB	R3G 0W4	204-783-5160
Paul D. Allen and Associates Limited	1978	8	615 Mount Pleasant Rd., Suite 327	Toronto	ON	M4S 3C5	416-480-0530
Plunkett Communications Inc.	1989	2	525 Adelaide St. W., Suite 400	Toronto	ON	M5V 1T6	416-941-9555
Price Waterhouse	1908	70	1 First Canadian Place, Suite 3300	Toronto	ON	M5X 1H7	416-863-1133
R.I.S. Christie Data Collection Co.	1970	18	14 Verral Avenue	Toronto	ON	M4M 2R2	416-778-8890
Research Dimensions	1978	21	1155 Yonge St., 6th Floor	Toronto	ON	M4T 1W2	416-967-6161
Research House Inc.	1977	21	273 Eglinton Ave. E.	Toronto	ON	M4P 1L3	416-488-2328
Research Management Group	n/a		90 Eglinton Avenue E., Suite 405	Toronto	ON	M4P 2Y3	416-485-0773
Research Spectrum Limited	1976	1	56 Leuty Avenue	Toronto	ON	M4e 2R4	416-691-1555
Research Systems Corporations	1971	0	8 Midtown Drive, Suite 193	Oshawa	ON	L1J 8L2	416-623-0872
Robert Boutilier and Associates	1988	1	3698 Southwood St.	Burnaby	BC	V5J 2E6	604-433-2441
Rotenberg Research	1967	11	5 Laureleaf Road South	Willowdale	ON	M2M 3A3	416-223-2038
Ruston/Tomany & Associates Ltd.	1978	16	111 Elizabeth St.	Toronto	ON	M5G 1P7	416-977-1533
Schema Research Ltd.	1978	7	220 Duncan Mills Rd., Suite 206	Don Mills	ON	M3B 3J5	416-449-8686
Southam Marketing Research Services	1968	11	1450 Don Mills Road	Don Mills	ON	M2B 2X7	416-442-2070
Standard Research Systems	1980	2	26 Soho St., Suite 402	Toronto	ON	M5T 1Z7	416-340-1722

Starch Research Services Limited	1958	2	9 Gervais Dr., Suite 309	Don Mills	ON	M3C 1Y9	4416-391-2468
Susan Rose Marketing Research	1989	2	434 Grosvenor Avenue	Westmount	PQ	H3Y 2S4	514-939-1378
Sylvestre Marketing Inc.	1972	10	276 rue Sherbrooke ouest	Montreal	PQ	H2X 1X9	514-284-0878
T.R. Mills & Associates Inc.	1990	4	Interchange House, 3019 Harvester Rd	Burlington	ON	L7N 3G4	416-681-2090
Tabhouse Data Processing Services	1990	9	1726 Silverthorn Square	Pickering	ON	L1V 5C6	416-831-9760
Tandemar Research	1986	26	208 Bloor St. W., Suite 200	Toronto	ON	M5S 2T8	416-925-4444
Target Research Ltd.	1986	10	19 MacGregor Ave.	Toronto	ON	M6S 2A1	416-763-4651
Technalysis Inc.	1982	6	120 Eglinton Ave. E., Suite 602	Toronto	ON	M4P 1E7	416-487-3900
Tele-surveys Plus Inc.	1990	30	1015 Beaver Hall Hill, Suite 417	Montreal	PQ	H2Z 1S1	514-392-4702
The Advisory Group Inc.	1984	21	1122-4 Street S.W., Suite 310	Calgary	AB	T2R 1M1	403-264-2440
The Telephone Room	1990	12	2323 Yonge St, Suite 801	Toronto	ON	M4P 2C9	416-322-7520
The Tilwood Group Inc.	1970	11	161 Eglinton Ave. E., Suite 701	Toronto	ON	M4P 1J5	416-483-8707
Thompson Lightstone & Company	1977	61	1027 Yonge St., Suite 100	Toronto	ON	M4W 2K9	416-922-1140
Torrington-Promark & Associates Inc.	1987	1	3 Findlay Ave.	Toronto	ON	K1S 2T8	613-235-6655
Vantage Research Group Inc.	1989	7	2005 Sheppard Ave. E., Suite 100	Willowdale	ON	M2J 5B4	416-490-0131
Viewfacts	1980	65	875 Don Mills Rd.	Toronto	ON	M3C 1V9	416-449-1012
Viewpoints Research Ltd.	1986	6	404-115 Bannatyne	Winnipeg	MB	R3B 0R3	204-943-9253
Visions Etudes Qualitatives	1988	8	800 est, de Maisonneuve, Bureau 210	Montreal	PQ	H2L 4L8	514-844-7058
Westmount Research Consultants Inc.	1984	15	29 Park Rd.	Toronto	ON	M4W 2N2	416-920-8030

Focus Group Facilities in Canada

The facilities in this section is based on Focus Group Facilities in Canada, produced by the Qualitative Research Division (QRD) of the Professional Marketing Research Society. As with the listing of marketing research firms, the listing should be considered wide-ranging and representative rather than exhaustive.

Company Name	Address	City	Prov.	P.C.	Phone	Availability
DJC Research	255 Morningside Ave., Suite 323	Scarborough	ON		416-928-0826	D,E,W
Elliott Research	Promenade Mall, Bathurst & Hwy 7	Thornhill	ON		416-391-1844	D,E
Marktrend Marketing Research Inc.	2930 Arbutus St., Suite 303	Vancouver	BC		604-731-8281	D,E,W
Thompson Lightstone & Co.	Bramalea City Centre	Bramalea	ON		416-922-1140	D,E,W
Visions	800 est de Maisonneuve, Suite 210	Montreal	PQ		514-844-7058	D,E,W
Omnifacts Research Ltd.	130 Water St.	St. John's	NF	A1C 6E6	709-754-2442	D,E,W
Atlantic Survey Centre, Research Assoc.	1 Church Hill, Suite 200	St. John's	NF	A1C 6J9	709-753-0202	D,E,W
Omnifacts Research Ltd.	33 Ochterloney St., Suite 230	Dartmouth	NS	B2Y 4P5	902-466-6050	D,E,W
Focal Research Consultants Ltd.	6300 Lady Hammond Rd., Suite 700	Halifax	NS	B3K 2R6	902-453-6000	D,E
Corporate Research Associates Inc.	2695 Dutch Village Rd., Suite 700	Halifax	NS	B3L 4M6	902-421-1336	D,E,W
Impact Research	437 Grande-Allee Est	Quebec	PQ	G1R 2J5	418-647-2727	D,E,W
Som Inc.	969 Rte de L'Eglise, Bureau 300	Ste Foy	PQ	G1V 3V4	418-653-8225	D,E,W
Intervision Marketing	3490 Dundurand	Rosemount	PQ	H1X 1N1	514-687-5856	D,E,W
Espace Marketing Inc.	487 Est, Boul St. Joseph	Montreal	PQ	H2J 1J8	514-286-8274	D,E,W
Groupe Centre	8595 St. Denis	Montreal	PQ	H2P 2H4	514-389-7423	D,E,W
Createc+	206 Pine Avenue East	Montreal	PQ	H2W 1P1	514-844-1127	D,E,W
Robert Sylvestre Marketing	276 Sherbrooke St. W.	Montreal	PQ	H2X 1X9	514-284-0878	D,E,W
SEROM Recherche-Sondage Inc.	3405, St. Urbain	Montreal	PQ	H2X 2N2	514-842-1433	D,E,W
Recherche 007	41 Sherbrooke St. E., Suite 007	Montreal	PQ	H2X 3V8	514-499-8417	D,E,W
Avril Marketing	163 St. Paul St. E., Suite "C"	Montreal	PQ	H2Y 1G8	514-397-1458	D,E,W
Som Inc.	1450 City Councillors, Bureau 790	Montreal	PQ	H3A 2E6	514-982-6077	D,E
I.N.C.I. Inc.	500 sherbrooke O., Suite 250	Montreal	PQ	H3A 3C6	514-288-2123	D,E,W
Solumar/Market Facts of Canada	1200 McGill College, Bureau 1660	Montreal	PQ	H3B 4G7	514-875-7570	D,E
C.R.O.P.	651 Notre-Dame O., Bureau 500	Montreal	PQ	H3C 1H8	514-875-8086	D,E,W
IDM Research Inc.	1324 Sherbrooke St. W., Suite 200	Montreal	PQ	H3G 1H9	514-844-2511	D,E,W
Angus Reid Group	160 Bloor St. E., Suite 1300	Toronto	ON	M4W 1B9	416-964-1226	D,E,W
Angus Reid Group	1440 St. Catherine St., Suite 405	Montreal	PQ	H3G 1R8	514-875-5200	D,E,W
Legendre Lubawin	1172 St. Mathieu	Montreal	PQ	H3H 2H5	514-489-8417	D,E,W
Contemporary Research Centre	2155 Guy St., Bureau 1080	Montreal	PQ	H3H 2R9	514-932-7511	D,E,W
Decision Marketing (QC) Inc.	4269 Ste Cahterine O, Bureau 700	Westmount	PQ	H3Z 1P7	514-933-0598	D,E,W
Groupe Innova Inc.	4269 Catherine O., Bureau O	Westmount	PQ	H3Z 1P7	514-937-8786	D,E,W
Focus Two (Chapter Three Market Res)	245 Victoria, Suite #20	Westmount	PQ	H3Z 2M6	514-931-0848	E,W
Opinion Search	600-124 O'Connor St.	Ottawa	ON	K1R 5M9	613-230-9109	D,E,W
Factor Research Group	294 Albert St., Suite 604	Ottawa	ON	K1P 6E6	616-234-8960	D,E,W
Optima Consultants	251 Bank St., Suite 400	Ottawa	ON	K2P 1X3	613-236-2998	D,E,W

Research House Inc.	Portage Place, 1154 Chemong Rd.	Peterborough	ON	K9H 7J6	416-488-2328	D,E,W
Contract Testing Inc.	241 Clarence St., Suite 26	Brampton	ON	L6W 4P2	416-456-0783	D,E,W
Urban Associates	940 Main Street W	Hamilton	ON	L8S 1B1	416-525-7168	D,E,W
Research House	Warden Woods Mall, 750 Warden Ave.	Scarborough	ON	M1L 4R7	416-488-2328	D,E,W
Vantage Research Group Inc.	2005 Sheppard Ave. E., Suite 100	Willowdale	ON	M2J 5B4	416-490-0131	D,E
C.S.U. Market Field Services Inc.	6464 Yonge St., N4/N5	Willowdale	ON	M2M 3Z4	416-474-1770	D,E,W
Intertab-A	Suite 700, 100 Sheppard Ave. E.	Toronto	ON	M2N 6N5	416-250-8511	D,E,W
Elliott Research Corporation Limited	One Valleybrook Dr., Suite 400	Don Mills	ON	M3B 2S7	416-391-1844	D,E
Viewfacts	875 Don Mills Rd.	Toronto	ON	M3C 1V9	416-449-1012	D,E,W
Eidtics Motivational Research	43 Eglinton Ave. E., Suite 506	Toronto	ON	M4P 1A2	416-481-6419	E,W
Research House Inc.	273 Eglinton Ave. E.	Toronto	ON	M4P 1L3	416-488-2328	D,E,W
Face to Face	2323 Yonge St., Suite 808	Toronto	ON	M4P 2C9	416-488-8318	D,E,W
Camelford Graham Research Group	2345 Yonge St., Suite 212	Toronto	ON	M4P 2E5	416-440-1016	D,E,W
Generations Research Inc.	Edison Centre, 2345 Yonge St., #710	Toronto	ON	M4P 2E5	416-489-6282	D,E,W
Research Management Group	90 Eglinton Avenue E., Suite 405	Toronto	ON	M4P 2Y3	416-485-0773	D,E
Decima Research	1 Eglinton Ave. E., 7th Floor	Toronto	ON	M4P 3A1	416-483-1724	D,E,W
Innovative Marketing Inc.	40 Eglinton Ave. E., Suite 203	Toronto	ON	M4P 3A2	416-440-0310	D,E,W
Shaw MacLeod Associates	124 Eglinton Ave. W., Suite 200	Toronto	ON	M4R 2G8	416-480-0000	D,E,W
Butler Research Associates Inc.	2221 Yonge St., Suite 100	Toronto	ON	M4S 2B4	416-487-4144	D,E,W
Research Dimensions	1155 Yonge St., 6th Floor	Toronto	ON	M4T 1W2	416-967-6161	D,E
Sessions (A Division of QRI)	497 Davenport Rd.	Toronto	ON	M4Y 2W7	416-966-8500	D,E,W
Focus Canada	55 St. Clair Ave. W., Suite 127	Toronto	ON	M4V 2Y7	416-922-0438	D,E,W
Kubas Consultants	1 St. Clair Ave. W., Suite 1100	Toronto	ON	M4V 2Z1	416-960-5030	D,E,W
Thompson Lightstone & Company	1027 Yonge St., Suite 100	Toronto	ON	M4W 2K9	416-922-1140	D,E,W
Infocus Qualitative Research Services	920 Yonge St., Suite 727	Toronto	ON	M4W 3C7	416-928-1562	D,E,W
Burak Jacobson Research Partners Inc.	11 Church St., Suite 400	Toronto	ON	M5E 1M2	416-363-5111	D,E,W
Insight Canada Research Inc.	101 Yorkville Ave., Suite 301	Toronto	ON	M5R 1C1	416-921-0090	D,E,W
ABM Research Ltd.	17 Madison Avenue	Toronto	ON	M5R 2S2	416-961-5511	D,E
Canada Market Research Ltd.	1235 Bay Street, Suite 300	Toronto	ON	M5R 3K4	416-964-9222	D,E,W
A.R.A. Consultants	102 Bloor St. W., 9th Floor	Toronto	ON	M5S 1M8	416-961-1474	D,E,W
Market Facts of Canada Limited	77 Bloor St. W., Suite 1200	Toronto	ON	M5S 3A4	416-964-6262	D,E
Research House	Woodbine Mall, Hwy 27/Rexdale Rd	Rexdale	ON	M9W 6K5	416-488-2328	D,E,W

Availability: D = Days, E = Evenings, W = Weekends

Company	Address	City	Prov.	Postal Code	Phone	Availability
Weaver, Tanner, Miller	300 Ardelt Ave.	Kitchener	ON	N2C 2L9	519-578-5910	D,E,W
Insights Inc.	546 Adelaide St. N.	London	ON	N6B 3J5	519-679-0110	D,E,W
Cormark Communications Inc.	750 Baseline Rd. E.	London	ON	N6C 2R5	519-673-1380	D,E,W
Results Group	Suite 300, 326 Broadway Ave.	Winnipeg	MB	R3C 0S5	204-947-2705	D,E,W
Angus Reid	Suite 1900, 155 Carlton St.	Winnipeg	MB	R3C 3H8	204-949-3100	D,E,W
Opinion Place	66K-1485 Portage Ave.	Winnipeg	MB	R3G 0W4	204-783-5160	D,E,W
The Cor Group	1840 McIntyre St.	Regina	SK	S4P 2P9	306-359-3371	D,E,W
Public Attitude Tracking Services	#104-845 Broad St.	Regina	SK	S4P 3G1	306-949-5702	D,E,W
Consumer Interviewing Services	401-220 3rd Avenue S.	Saskatoon	SK	S7K 1M1	306-652-5160	D,E,W
Baar & Associates Ltd.	6223 Centre Street North, Suite 300	Calgary	AB	T2K 0V2	403-295-1534	D,E,W
Dunvegan Field Services	Suite 580, 707-7 Ave. S.W.	Calgary	AB	T2P 0Z3	403-269-6833	D,E,W
Angus Reid Group, Inc.	#670, 140-4 Avenue S.W.	Calgary	AB	T2P 3N3	403-237-0066	D,E,W
Heffring Research Group	999-8th Street S.W., Suite 630	Calgary	AB	T2R 1J5	403-228-9100	D,E,W
Marktrend Research Inc.	1207, 11th Avenue S.W., Suite 650	Calgary	AB	T3C 0M5	403-229-9716	D,E,W
Criterion Research Corp.	101-10155 114 St.	Edmonton	AB	T5K 1R8	403-423-0708	D,E,W
J.M.P. Marketing Services	1685 Ingleton Ave.	Burnaby	BC	V5G 4L8	604-294-3424	D,E,W
Brenda Farrell & Associates Ltd.	410-675 West Hastings Street	Vancouver	BC	V6B 1N2	604-682-7626	D,E,W
Vancouver Focus	200-839 Cambie St.	Vancouver	BC	V6B 2P4	604-689-5511	D,E,W
Infogroup Inc.	The Mezzanine, 744 West Hastings St.	Vancouver	BC	V6C 1A5	604-682-0285	D,E,W
Angus Reid Group	1600-355 Burrard St.	Vancouver	BC	V6C 1A6	604-682-1645	D,E,W
Scali, McCabe, Sloves	Suite 700, 1550 Alberni St.	Vancouver	BC	V6C 1A3	604-669-4444	E,W
Campbell Goodell Consultants Ltd.	1755 West Broadway, Suite 502	Vancouver	BC	V6J 4S5	6044-736-2081	D,E,W

Availability: D = Days, E = Evenings, W = Weekends

PMRS: The Rules of Conduct and Good Practice

WHAT IS PMRS?

The Professional Marketing Research Society (PMRS) is an association of Canadian marketing research professionals, although any marketing researcher anywhere in the world can become a member of PMRS. Associate membership of the Society is open to all interested individuals. PMRS has seven chapters across the country, runs a monthly newsletter *Imprints* and *Canadian Journal of Marketing Research*. It organizes evening meetings, seminars and educational courses throughout the year.

RULES OF CONDUCT AND GOOD PRACTICE

PMRS members abide by the society's *Rules of Conduct and Good Practice* which is periodically revised and voted upon by the members. The latest available version was published in 1984 and is reprinted with the permission of the Professional Marketing Research Society.

Rules of Conduct and Good Practice (1984)

INTRODUCTION

This document is currently divided into two chapters: Chapter A—For The General Professional Marketing Research Society Membership and Chapter B—For The Qualitative Research Division Membership. Within each chapter are a number of sections and each section may include two types of statements:

1) *Rules of Conduct* are considered mandatory; their violation could result in disciplinary action on the part of the Society as per the Constitution.

2) *Good Practice* guidelines represent an *ideal* toward which members should strive.

In the reading of this document, and for all purposes thereof, all references to and use of the masculine gender shall be deemed to be references to and use of the feminine gender where appropriate in the course of the affairs of the Society.

The acceptance of marketing and social "research" as a reliable source of information and, hence, its growth as a profession, depends upon the confidence of the business community and the public in the integrity of those professionally engaged in this type of work.

Membership in the Professional Marketing Research Society (PMRS) implies acceptance of—Chapter A Rules of Conduct and Good Practice, and membership in the Qualitative Research Division implies acceptance of both Chapter A and B. *Members of the Society undertake to refrain from any activity likely to impair confidence in marketing research in general and to comply with whatever general professional practices may be laid down from time to time by the Society.*

A) FOR THE GENERAL P.M.R.S. MEMBERSHIP

I. THE RESPONSIBILITY OF THE MEMBERS TO THE PUBLIC

Most marketing research depends on the co-operation of "respondents" either in their personal or in their business capacity. Marketing researchers, therefore, have a direct responsibility to ensure that respondents are in no way embarrassed or hindered in other ways as a result of any "interview"*. The purpose of interviewing respondents shall be limited to the finding out of information or observation of reactions relevant to the research problem at hand. Every possible attempt should be made by members to ensure a continuing climate of goodwill, responsibility and trust. A meticulous standard of good manners with respondents should be maintained and everything should be done to leave respondents positively disposed to marketing research.

*See Appendix 3A for definitions.

Rules of Conduct

1.1 Interviewing may not be used as a disguise for selling or developing sales leads, nor for deliberately influencing the opinions of those interviewed.

1.2 Any statement or assurance given to a respondent in order to obtain co-operation shall be factually correct and honoured.

1.3 No procedure or technique shall be used in which the respondent is put in such a position that they cannot exercise their right to withdraw or refuse to answer at *any stage* during or after the interview. Any request of the respondent to terminate the interview must be granted and, if he so requests, any information already given must be deleted.

1.4 The interviewer should explain to all respondents at the commencement of the interview, when applicable, the presence and purpose of any one-way mirror or audio/visual monitoring equipment.

1.5 The identity of individual respondents shall not be revealed by the "practitioner"* to the "client"* or anyone other than persons belonging to the organization of the practitioner concerned (either by supplying lists of individual respondents or by passing on answers to questions linked to the names of the individual respondents even when the client has supplied the original list of potential respondents) and members are entitled to give respondents such an assurance.

Exceptions to the aforesaid rule may be made in the following instances:
i) if the consent of respondents has been obtained before revealing their names to the client,

ii) if disclosure of these names is essential for the data processing, for verification of the original research, or to carry out further research. In such instances, however, the practitioner responsible for the original interview must insist that all the Rules of Conduct in this document are observed by all parties involved, via appropriate instructions in writing.

1.6 Interviewers must carry with them identification from the organization they represent for all face-to-face interviewing. Interviewers must identify themselves by name and organization in an introductory statement on *all* interviews. If requested by the respondent, the interviewer should provide the name, address and/or telephone number of the organization they represent. This information should be clearly indicated on any questionnaire handed out to respondents.

1.7 No respondent should be pressured into testing products which he does not want to try. Product information such as ingredients lists and instructions including the name, address and/or telephone number of the practitioner should be available where possible.

1.8 Before children under the age of 12 are *interviewed*, or asked to complete a questionnaire, the permission of a parent, guardian, or other person responsible for them, such as a teacher, shall be obtained. In obtaining this permission the interviewer shall allow the responsible person to see or hear the nature of the *interview*

*See Appendix 3A for definitions.

in sufficient detail to enable a reasonable person to reach an informed decision, e.g. not only should the subject matter of the *interview* be described, but any sensitive, embarrassing or complex questions should also be brought to the attention of the responsible person.

1.9 If computerized telephone interviewing techniques (e.g. collecting data or conducting an interview via taped message with no human interviewer) are employed, the type of machinery that automatically disconnects or "frees the line" when the respondent hangs up the phone, must be used.

Good Practice

1.10 A potential respondent who has initially refused to take part in a study should not be contacted for the same study on more than one subsequent occasion in person or by telephone. Any second call should be conducted by a specially trained interviewer or (field) supervisor (i.e. *not* the original interviewer).

1.11 It should be recognized that when communicating with any member of the public it is important that the materials used are appropriate in terms of content and wording to that particular public.

1.12 "Overly-long questionnaires"* should be avoided at all costs. If the respondent asks, interviewers should indicate to the respondent a reasonably accurate estimate of the duration of the interview. When appropriate interviewers should make appointments for interviews in advance when interviewing representatives of companies or other organizations.

1.13 The practitioner should inform the local authorities (e.g. police, security, etc.) before carrying out interviews under circumstances or about topics which might make the public suspicious or cause them to report the interviewer's activities.

1.14 If a respondent is interviewed as a party of a study, the practitioner should not deliberately seek an additional interview with this specific respondent unless re-interviewing is required by the study's design or unless the respondent's permission was obtained during the initial interview (and each subsequent interview).

1.15 Incentives should be avoided where possible for quantitative studies. Even when incentives are used, they should be offered as a small token of appreciation (e.g. lottery tickets and small gift items).

1.16 When interviewing 12 to 15 year old respondents discretion should be used when addressing sensitive subject matter or information (e.g. delete "household income" questions, etc.)

II. THE RESPONSIBILITY OF CLIENTS TO PRACTITIONERS

Rules of Conduct

2.1 In some instances potential clients ask for competitive bids from two or more practitioners, and when properly done, such practice is completely within the Rules of Conduct. However, certain conditions are essential to meet the standards of proper practice. These include:

i) Whenever a client asks more than one practitioner for a "proposal"* or "cost estimate"*, this fact and the number of proposals or cost estimates being requested must be communicated to the practitioners concerned. For any study, *the practitioner is then entitled to indicate in advance that he will request payment for the cost of preparing such a proposal or cost estimate.*

ii) During and following the proposal or cost estimate process, both the client and the practitioner must respect the confidentiality of each party's technical input or ideas. Specifically, in a competitive situation, no unique technique or idea included in a practitioner's proposal may be used by the prospective client in conjunction with another practitioner unless an appropriate payment has been made. (See 2.1 i) above.) Additionally, in a competitive situation, all unaccepted proposals in whole or in part remain exclusively the property of the originating practitioner unless an appropriate charge has been made. (See 2.1 i) above.) Conversely, no unique technique or idea included in a prospective client's specifications during the proposal or cost estimate process may be offered to other prospective clients by the practitioner without the originating client's approval.

2.2 Reports provided by a practitioner are the property of the client and are normally for the use within the client company or associated companies (including the client's agents). If a wider circulation of the results of the study, either in whole or in part is intended, the following minimum standards of disclosure should be adhered to in order that there will be an adequate basis for judging the reliability and validity of the results reported:

i) The client should ensure that dissemination of the study findings will not give rise to misleading interpretations and that the study findings will not be quoted out of their normal context.

ii) If a practitioner's name is to be used he must be consulted prior to dissemination of findings and is entitled to refuse permission for its name to be used in connection with the study until the practitioner has approved the exact form and contents of the dissemination.

iii) For all reports of survey findings the client has released to the public, the client must be prepared to release the following details on request: sponsorship of the survey; dates of the interviewing; methods of obtaining the interviews (in-home, telephone or mail); population that was sampled; size of sample; size and description of the sub-sample, if the survey report relies primarily on less than the total sample; exact wording of questions upon which the release is based; an indication of what allowance should be made for sampling error; and the percentage upon which conclusions are based.

2.3 Unless otherwise agreed and provided that the practitioner has followed the stipulated procedures and all reasonable precautions have been taken, the client is responsible for any damages sought by the public as a result of using any product or material supplied by the client. Additionally, when testing products or materials, proper usage instructions will be provided by the client and any cautions necessary for normal sale, must be highlighted (e.g. possible allergic

*See Appendix 3A for definitions.

reactions) and a listing of ingredients will be made available by the client where it is appropriate.

Good Practice

2.4　Clients have a responsibility to provide practitioners with enough information about a project for the latter to do a professional job. Specifically, clients should provide insight, preferably in writing, into the following areas:

　　i)　A statement of the research problem or, if unable to define the research problem, a perspective on the problem in terms of its general background.

　　ii)　A statement of the type of decision(s) that is likely to be influenced by the research results or the uses to which the research results will be applied.

　　iii)　A broad indication of the budget available.

2.5　When requesting proposals some indication should be provided as to how the successful proposal will be determined. Factors which might be used to determine the organization selected could include:

　　i)　Innovative approaches to solving the problem under review.

　　ii)　Ability to provide the necessary information—gathering and analysis resources—personnel, facilities, equipment, etc.

　　iii)　Relevant experience of the research firm.

　　iv)　Background/experience of individuals to be assigned to the work.

　　v)　Recognition of the limitations of the research.

　　vi)　Cost.

2.6　Clients should provide a prompt notification to all proposers once a selection has been made on a proposal or cost estimate.

2.7　Clients should only request a reasonable number of competitive proposals or cost estimates (e.g. 2 to 4) on any given project.

2.8　Clients should not assume that the contingency cost range included in some research proposals or cost estimate (e.g. +/- X%) may be applied to changes in the research specifications. Changes in specifications may be justification for revising the original estimate.

III. The Responsibility of Practitioners to Clients

Rules of Conduct

3.1　Research specifications, such as background, objectives and technical approaches or ideas, provided by a client or potential client remain the property of the client and contents may not be revealed to third parties without the client's permission. (See Section 2.1)

3.2　Unless authorized by the client, the practitioner will not reveal to respondents, interviewers or any other person not directly concerned with the study, the identity of the client, including the fact that he had undertaken or considered undertaking research in a particular area, confidential material relating to the study or the results of any study commissioned exclusively for that client.

3.3. If any aspect of a project is to be sub-contracted to another practitioner, the originating practitioner is obliged to inform the client before committing to the project.

3.4 When the same project is carried out on behalf of more than one client or two or more projects are combined in one interview, the practitioner is obliged to inform each client concerned that another client exists and to inform each client of the *generic* subjects addressed by the other client's project before the client commits to the project.

3.5 "Primary"* and "secondary"* "records"* are the property of the practitioner. The practitioner is entitled to destroy primary records one year from the end of the field work (providing secondary records are adequate to enable reconstruction of the results) and to destroy secondary records two years from the end of the field work without reference to the client. The preferred method of destruction is shredding on premises. If the client wishes exceptions to this, he must make special arrangements with the practitioner. The practitioner must provide reasonable access to the client on non-syndicated studies, to the completed questionnaires or data forms, cards/tapes provided the client bears the reasonable cost of preparing any duplicates or masking individual identity.

3.6 Unless otherwise specifically made clear that this practice will not be followed, the practitioner will automatically "verify"* or "monitor"* a minimum of 10% of each interviewer's completed interviews.

The practitioner will inform the client, prior to commencement of the study, the proposed nature of the verification* or monitoring* including the proportion of each interviewer's interviews to be covered. Upon request from the client, the practitioner is obliged to disclose the results of the verification. If verification of an interviewer's completed interviews suggests problems, verification must be done until there is firm evidence of either valid or invalid work. If the interviews appear to be invalid, 100% of the interviewer's interviews must either be rejected or replaced. In this case, the practitioner is obliged to inform the client immediately of these problems with verification.

3.7 For each survey, a practitioner will provide the following information, where applicable to the client (either in a report or in supporting documentation if a formal report is not being prepared):

i) Copy of questionnaire, interviewers' instructions and visual exhibits.

ii) The name of organization for which the study was conducted and name of organization conducting it, including sub-contractors.

iii) The specific objectives of the study.

iv) The dates on or between which the fieldwork was done and the time periods of interviewing.

*See Appendix 3A for definitions.

v) The universe covered (intended and actual) including details of the sampling method and selection procedures.

vi) The size and nature of the sample and details of any weighting methods used.

vii) The contact record based on the last attempt to obtain an interview, with the exception of mall surveys and quota samples where it is not appropriate.

viii) The method of recruitment when prior recruitment of respondents is undertaken.

ix) The method of field briefing sessions.

x) Weighted and unweighted bases for all conventional tables, clearly distinguishing between the two.

xi) A statement of response rates, how they were calculated, and a discussion of possible bias due to non-response.

xii) The method by which the information was collected e.g. mall intercept, telephone, etc.

xiii) The details of any incentives provided to respondents.

xiv) Sources of desk research.

xv) An adequate description of verification or monitoring procedures and results of the same.

xvi) The detail of any special statistical methods used in the analysis of the results.

3.8 The practitioner will limit the information supplied to prospective clients regarding their experience, capacities and organization to a factual and objective description.

3.9 When changes are made to the specifications of a study by either the practitioner or the client, the practitioner should inform the client of any fee changes at the time the specifications are revised.

3.10 A practitioner will conduct a study in the manner agreed upon. However, if it becomes apparent in the course of a study that changes in the plans should be made, the practitioner is obliged to make his views (including cost estimates) known to the client immediately.

3.11 A practitioner is obliged to allow clients to verify that work performed meets all contracted specifications and to examine and be present at all operations of the practitioner's organization relevant to the execution of the study.

Good Practice

3.12 The practitioner should make known any current involvement in the same general subject area before accepting a project. However, exclusive use of a practitioner over a given time period may be established only be special arrangements between client and practitioner.

3.13 When reporting findings of a study in either written or oral form, the practitioner should make a clear distinction between the objective results and their own opinions and recommendations.

3.14 The practitioner should provide to the client in the report, or a supporting document to fieldwork, tables, etc., in addition to the items listed in 3.7.

    i)   A discussion of any aspects of the research which may bias the results.

    ii) An assessment of the reliability of the sources used in desk research.

    iii) The name(s) of the individual(s) responsible for the study and report.

    iv) A list of sampling points used in the study (upon request).

3.15 The practitioner will assist the client in the design and execution of effective and efficient studies. If the practitioner questions whether a study design will provide the necessary information, the practitioner should make his own reservations known.

3.16 During and following the proposal or cost estimate process, cost quotations may be made public without the practitioner's permission, as long as an individual quotation cannot be associated with a given practitioner.

3.17 A practitioner will not use the names of clients in promotional material without the express permission of the client.

IV. GENERAL RULES OF PRACTICE FOR MEMBERS

Rules of Conduct

4.1 Members shall not try to turn to account or to use the fact of their membership in PMRS as evidence of particular professional competence, except insofar as membership implies the member subscribes to the Rules of Conduct and Good Practice.

    Unless authorized by the executive, members, when talking to the "press" or media representatives, should request that their membership in PMRS not be included in any subsequent articles or media reports to avoid their personal views or options being confused with those of PMRS.

4.2 Members recognize that marketing and social research is more an art than a science. It therefore follows that what is practical, sound and useful to clients is frequently more a matter of judgement than of definite rules and regulations.

    It is because such judgement follows from experience within the field that members of the Society believe they have a responsibility to their respective clients and management to point out the limitations of marketing research as appropriate.

    Members of the Society will do everything possible to extend and maximize the use of marketing and social research. They will also discourage research which, in their best judgement, is considered inadequate, inappropriate or subject to providing misleading information for the problem at hand.

4.3   Members commissioning market or social research work with a practitioner known not to be bound by these Rules of Conduct and Good Practice, shall ensure that the practitioner is familiar with its content and agrees in writing to abide by them.

Good Practice

4.4   When considering interviews with small populations that are likely to be of interest to other researchers, members should be especially careful to minimize the total number of interviews conducted to avoid "over researching" such populations. For the same reason, members interested in such populations should attempt to undertake syndicated research projects within those populations.

B) FOR THE QUALITATIVE RESEARCH DIVISION MEMEBERSHIP

V. RESPONSIBILITY TO THE PUBLIC

Rules of Conduct

5.1   Any statement or assurance given to a respondent in order to obtain co-operation shall be factually correct and honoured.

5.2   The respondent shall be allowed to remain anonymous or, in special circumstances where this is not possible, the respondent should be informed when being recruited, that his responses may not be anonymous.

5.3   Qualitative interviews must not be used for selling or developing sales leads and, for this reason, surnames and/or addresses and telephone numbers may not be supplied to the client. The interview itself should not be used by the client to deliberately try to influence the opinions of those interviewed.

5.4   Most marketing research depends upon the co-operation of respondents. All persons involved in a qualitative research project, therefore, have a direct responsibility to ensure that respondents or potential respondents are not embarrassed in any way.

5.5   Members must not harass, badger, grill or belittle any member of the public either while trying to recruit for or during the conducting of any qualitative study. Clearly, behaviour cannot be precisely defined but sincere and consistent efforts to show respect to the respondents are, nevertheless, a mandatory requirement of the Society's Rules of Conduct and Good Practice.

5.6   The respondent's right to withdraw, or to refuse to co-operate at any stage, shall be respected.

5.7   The *moderator* must explain to all respondents at the commencement of the interview (group or individual in-depth), where appropriate,

    i)   the presence and purpose of the one-way mirror;

    ii) the presence and purpose of the video-camera;

iii) the presence and purpose of the tape recorder;

iv) the confidentiality of the respondents' names and addresses.

Good Practice

In conjunction with the above Rules of Conduct:

5.8 The *client* has a particular responsibility to ensure that the moderator does not (or is not asked to) exceed "acceptable" limits or "harassment" of respondents. The client has an equal responsibility for their own attitude and behaviour (and that of other persons present at the invitation of the client), not only in front of the respondent but also when watching the interview in a separate location. In addition, if exposed to the respondent, the client should be careful not to introduce unsuitable bias by their reactions or comments.

5.9 It is the responsibility of the recruiter to ensure that the respondent is properly qualified for inclusion in the study. Recruiters also have a responsibility to explain to participants in the study exactly what is expected of them: for example, the importance of punctuality, the likely full length of the interview period, the date, time and exact location (with details of parking, nearest public transit stop, etc.), whether they will be asked to taste food or beverages, the payment (and any associated terms), whether or not smoking will be allowed during the group. It is a good idea if this information is confirmed in writing or through a follow-up, reminder telephone call.

5.10 The moderator has a responsibility to keep the session within the time limits specified to respondents on the occasion of their recruitment.
 The moderator has the responsibility of ensuring that all respondents have an equal opportunity to participate in the discussion. If the offensive language or behaviour of one respondent inhibits other respondents from fully participating, the moderator may have to ask the offending participant to leave.

5.11 No respondent should be pressured into taste testing any products which he does not want to try. Ingredient lists should be available if requested.

5.12 The issue of payment to participants who arrive too late to be included in the discussion should be clarified by the recruiter, moderator and/or client prior to commencement of the study. Since the fault is often not solely that of the respondent, it is suggested that some payment should always be made. (How much and who actually picks up that cost is a matter for negotiation between parties involved; it is suggested that at least half the promised amount be paid.)

VI. Other Responsibilities of the Recruiter

Rules of Conduct

6.1 The following Rules of Conduct are *assumed to be in operation* for any qualitative research undertaken by members of QRD, *unless changes* to any or all of the Rules have *been discussed and agreed to by all parties involved in the research study.*

i)   All respondents must meet usage/trial/ownership standards including type of brand, frequency of use/trial or other time limits specified for the study.

ii)   All respondents must meet demographic specifications for the study, including marital status, age, sex, income, occupation, household composition, etc.

iii)   No respondents (nor anyone in their immediate families or households) may *work* in an occupation that has anything to do with the topic area (whether wholesale, retail, sales, service or consultant) nor in advertising, marketing, marketing research, public relations or the media (radio, television, newspaper, etc.) nor *may respondents themselves ever have worked in such occupations.*

iv)   No respondent may be recruited who has attended, *in the past five years,* a focus group discussion or in-depth interview on the *same general topic* as defined by the moderator.

v)   No respondents should be recruited who *know each other* for the same study, unless they are in *different groups, or interviews, that are scheduled back-to-back.*

vi)   No respondent may be recruited who has attended a group discussion or in-depth interview *within the past year.*

vii)   No respondent may be recruited *who has attended five or more focus groups or in-depth interviews ever, unless he/she has not attended a group discussion/in-depth interview in the past five years.*

viii)   At least *one half* of the respondents recruited for each group/study involving in-depth interviews must never have attended a group discussion or in-depth interview before.

ix)   All respondents must have been living in the specified market area for at least the past two years.

x)   All respondents must be able to speak and read in the language of the group or study being conducted.

Good Practice

6.2   Before accepting a project, it is important that the recruiter clearly understands the moderator's (or client's) specifications; the recruiter has a responsibility to query any points of confusion and to highlight potential problems.

Once accepted, instructions should be followed explicitly. No changes to the agreed upon questionnaire should be made without prior approval from the moderator or client. Any information given to respondents (for example, the topic, whether there will be taste testing, etc.) must have been approved beforehand.

If problems in recruiting arise, the moderator (or client) should be advised immediately.

6.3   Recruiters have a responsibility to make every effort to ensure that all recruited respondents comply with specifications detailed for the project and that they turn up at the correct place, at the right time, being fully aware of what is expected of them. Confirmatory/reminder re-screening should, where possible, be conducted by someone other than the original recruiter.

Screening questionnaires used in the recruitment should be made available to the moderator in advance of the research sessions.

VII. OTHER RESPONSIBILITIES OF THE MODERATOR

A) TO THE RECRUITER

Rules of Conduct

7.1   To protect the respondents, persons recruited for a specific study should be used by the moderator only for that study and not be recalled to participate in another qualitative study without permission of the original recruiter.

Good Practice

7.2   The moderator should clearly define (preferably in writing) the complete specifications for the study to the recruiter (e.g. specific usage/trial/ownership standards; demographic specifications, etc.) as well as what, if anything, the respondent can be told about the topic, or session, in advance. In addition the moderator should obtain confirmation that the recruiter will follow the accepted Recruiting Guidelines of the Qualitative Research Division.

B) TO THE CLIENT

Rules of Conduct

7.3   When responsible for recruiting, the moderator must obtain an agreement from the client regarding recruitment specifications, supervise the recruiting for the study and ensure that recruitment goals are met (or provide an explanation when they are not met).

Unless otherwise agreed, the client can assume that the moderator will listen to taped interviews, or work from "transcripts," when preparing the analysis.

7.5   Each report should include a standard statement emphasizing the non-projectability of the results. Specifically, reports should not include precise percentaged results unless it is made clear at that point in the report, that the result applied only to those respondents and is not necessarily true of the population at large; proportions may be used (e.g. one-third).

7.6   Each report should also contain a copy of the recruiting questionnaire and details of respondent qualifications together with a copy of the discussion outline, and, if possible, any materials used as stimuli during the interview.

7.7 All material relating to clients must remain confidential to persons wholly or substantially employed by the moderator, unless otherwise authorized by the client.

Unless authorized to do so by the client, the moderator should not reveal to recruiters or respondents nor any other person not directly concerned with the work of the study, the name of the client commissioning the study.

Good Practice

7.8 The moderator must ensure that the client understands the non-projectability of qualitative research to the population at large before embarking upon the project.

7.9 The moderator has responsibility to ensure that he has a clear understanding of the problem and the reasons why the research is being undertaken. A discussion outline should be provided for perusal by the client well in advance of the first session.

7.10 The moderator must remain objective and observe rigorous neutrality (except when playing the devil's advocate) while conducting the group session and when preparing the report/analysis.

VIII. OTHER RESPONSIBILITIES OF THE CLIENT

Note: In some circumstances, the client may directly arrange for the recruiting. In such circumstances, the "client" is required to assume the responsibilities to the recruiter outlined in Sections 3.1 and 3.2.

Good Practice

8.1 *One* person at the *client* company should take responsibility for the final liaison with the moderator.

8.2 The moderator should be given every opportunity to understand the problems to be researched and should be included as early as possible in the planning stages of the project.

8.3 An outline of the research objectives and the immediate use to which the qualitative research learning will be put should be provided, in writing, for the moderator. This briefing document should be approved by *all* members of the client team before being given to the moderator.

It is helpful if key members of the client team (e.g. product managers, agency personnel as well as marketing research personnel) can be available for follow-up discussion of this briefing. Examples of all stimuli to be used (e.g. product, advertising, packaging, etc.) should ideally be available for review well in advance of the first interviewing sessions.

Specifications regarding the screening criteria should be agreed upon and, preferably, confirmed in writing.

8.4 Response to the moderator's suggested "discussion outline" should be provided as quickly as possible, to allow time for further discussion. The client should ensure that all issues currently under evaluation are included in the discussion outline.

8.5 The client has a responsibility, in agreeing to the proposed cost of the study, to ensure that the moderator understands:

i) whether a written analysis is required, and by what date

ii) whether the client expects to be given tape recordings of the proceedings

iii) whether the client requires transcripts of proceedings

iv) whether simultaneous translation is required for groups in a language other than English

v) how many copies of the report/presentations of the results, etc., are required.

8.6 The client with responsibility for the study (see 8.1 above) should, wherever possible, watch all qualitative research sessions. Where this is impossible, the client should attend the first session so that the moderator can obtain clarification of any unexpected issues.

Clients watching qualitative research sessions should do so with appropriate seriousness and decorum.

Source: Reprinted with permission of the Professional Marketing Research Society of Canada.

Appendix 3A

Definitions

1) "Research" refers to any examination or collection of information.

2) The term "respondent" refers to any individual, organization or group of persons to whom the practitioner approaches, either directly or indirectly, to collect information.

3) The term "interview" refers to any form of contact intended to generate information from a respondent (see #2 above).

4) The term "client" shall be understood to include any individual, organization, institution, department or division—including any belonging to the same organization as the practitioner—which is responsible for commissioning a research project.

5) The term "practitioner" shall be understood to include any individual, organization, department or division, including any belonging to the same organization as the "client" (see #4 above), which is responsible for or acts as a consultant on all or part of a research project.

6) An "overly-long questionnaire" may vary in length of time depending on variables such as subject matter, the number of open ended questions and the frequency of use of complex scales. As a general guideline, the following are generally considered "overly-long":

A personal interview in-home	over 60 minutes
A telephone interview	over 30 minutes
A mall-intercept interview	over 30 minutes

7) The term "proposal" refers to a practitioner submission that requires his recommendations as to technique, sampling or other design facets as well as a cost estimate.

8) The term "cost estimate" refers to a practitioner's submission that provides a cost estimate based on specifications provided by the client.

9) The term "primary records" refers to the most comprehensive record of information on which a research project is based e.g. completed questionnaires, taped recordings of interviews, etc.

10) The term "secondary records" is any record of information on which a research project is based apart from primary records (see #9 above) e.g. computer input, coding and editing instructions, etc.

11) The term "records" refers to both primary and secondary records collectively (see #9 and #10 above).

12) The term "verify" refers to the process of re-contacting an original respondent to confirm that the interview was in fact done and that selected aspects of the interview were carried out in the manner prescribed by the questionnaire and instructions.

13) The term "monitor" refers to the process of a supervisor listening to an interviewer interview a respondent.

APPENDIX 4

Statistical Tables

Table 1 Selected Percentiles of the X^2 Distribution

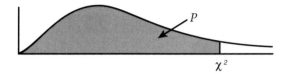

Values of χ^2 corresponding to P

υ	$\chi^2_{.005}$	$\chi^2_{.01}$	$\chi^2_{.025}$	$\chi^2_{.05}$	$\chi^2_{.10}$	$\chi^2_{.90}$	$\chi^2_{.95}$	$\chi^2_{.975}$	$\chi^2_{.99}$	$\chi^2_{.995}$
1	.000039	.00016	.00098	.0039	.0158	2.71	3.84	5.02	6.63	7.88
2	.0100	.0201	.0506	.1026	.2107	4.61	5.99	7.38	9.21	10.60
3	.0717	.115	.216	.352	.584	6.25	7.81	9.35	11.34	12.84
4	.207	.297	.484	.711	1.064	7.78	9.49	11.14	13.28	14.86
5	.412	.554	.831	1.15	1.61	9.24	11.07	12.83	15.09	16.75
6	.676	.872	1.24	1.64	2.20	10.64	12.59	14.45	16.81	18.55
7	.989	1.24	1.69	2.17	2.83	12.02	14.07	16.01	18.48	20.28
8	1.34	1.65	2.18	2.73	3.49	13.36	15.51	17.53	20.09	21.96
9	1.73	2.09	2.70	3.33	4.17	14.68	16.92	19.02	21.67	23.59
10	2.16	2.56	3.25	3.94	4.87	15.99	18.31	20.48	23.21	25.19
11	2.60	3.05	3.82	4.57	5.58	17.28	19.68	21.92	24.73	26.76
12	3.07	3.57	4.40	5.23	6.30	18.55	21.03	23.34	26.22	28.30
13	3.57	4.11	5.01	5.89	7.04	19.81	22.36	24.74	27.69	29.82
14	4.07	4.66	5.63	6.57	7.79	21.06	23.68	26.12	29.14	31.32
15	4.60	5.23	6.26	7.26	8.55	22.31	25.00	27.49	30.58	32.80
16	5.14	5.81	6.91	7.96	9.31	23.54	26.30	28.85	32.00	34.27
18	6.26	7.01	8.23	9.39	10.86	25.99	28.87	31.53	34.81	37.16
20	7.43	8.26	9.59	10.85	12.44	28.41	31.41	34.17	37.57	40.00
24	9.89	10.86	12.40	13.85	15.66	33.20	36.42	39.36	42.98	45.56
30	13.79	14.95	16.79	18.49	20.60	40.26	43.77	46.98	50.89	53.67
40	20.71	22.16	24.43	26.51	29.05	51.81	55.76	59.34	63.69	66.77
60	35.53	37.48	40.48	43.19	46.46	74.40	79.08	83.30	88.38	91.95
120	83.85	86.92	91.58	95.70	100.62	140.23	146.57	152.21	158.95	163.64

Adapted with permission from *Introduction to Statistical Analysis* (2nd ed.) by W.J. Dixon and F.J. Massey, Jr., McGraw-Hill Book Company, Inc., 1957.

Table 2   The Standard Normal Distribution

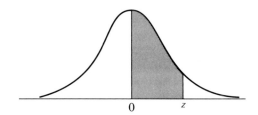

z	.00	.01	.02	.03	.04	.05	.06	.07	.08	.09
0.0	.0000	.0040	.0080	.0120	.0160	.0199	.0239	.0279	.0319	.0359
0.1	.0398	.0438	.0478	.0517	.0557	.0596	.0636	.0675	.0714	.0753
0.2	.0793	.0832	.0871	.0910	.0948	.0987	.1026	.1064	.1103	.1141
0.3	.1179	.1217	.1255	.1293	.1331	.1368	.1406	.1443	.1480	.1517
0.4	.1554	.1591	.1628	.1664	.1700	.1736	.1772	.1808	.1844	.1879
0.5	.1915	.1950	.1985	.2019	.2054	.2088	.2123	.2157	.2190	.2224
0.6	.2257	.2291	.2324	.2357	.2389	.2422	.2454	.2486	.2517	.2549
0.7	.2580	.2611	.2642	.2673	.2704	.2734	.2764	.2794	.2823	.2852
0.8	.2881	.2910	.2939	.2967	.2995	.3023	.3051	.3078	.3106	.3133
0.9	.3159	.3186	.3212	.3238	.3264	.3289	.3315	.3340	.3365	.3389
1.0	.3413	.3438	.3461	.3485	.3508	.3531	.3554	.3577	.3599	.3621
1.1	.3643	.3665	.3686	.3708	.3729	.3749	.3770	.3790	.3810	.3830
1.2	.3849	.3869	.3888	.3907	.3925	.3944	.3962	.3980	.3997	.4015
1.3	.4032	.4049	.4066	.4082	.4099	.4115	.4131	.4147	.4162	.4177
1.4	.4102	.4207	.4222	.4236	.4251	.4265	.4279	.4292	.4306	.4319
1.5	.4332	.4345	.4357	.4370	.4382	.4394	.4406	.4418	.4429	.4441
1.6	.4452	.4463	.4474	.4484	.4495	.4505	.4515	.4525	.4535	.4545
1.7	.4554	.4564	.4573	.4582	.4591	.4599	.4608	.4616	.4625	.4633
1.8	.4641	.4649	.4656	.4664	.4671	.4678	.4686	.4693	.4699	.4706
1.9	.4713	.4719	.4726	.4732	.4738	.4744	.4750	.4756	.4761	.4767
2.0	.4772	.4778	.4783	.4788	.4793	.4798	.4803	.4808	.4812	.4817
2.1	.4821	.4826	.4830	.4834	.4838	.4842	.4846	.4850	.4854	.4857
2.2	.4861	.4864	.4868	.4871	.4875	.4878	.4881	.4884	.4887	.4890
2.3	.4893	.4896	.4898	.4901	.4904	.4906	.4909	.4911	.4913	.4916
2.4	.4918	.4920	.4922	.4925	.4927	.4929	.4931	.4932	.4934	.4936
2.5	.4938	.4940	.4941	.4943	.4945	.4946	.4948	.4949	.4951	.4952
2.6	.4953	.4955	.4956	.4957	.4959	.4960	.4961	.4962	.4963	.4946
2.7	.4965	.4966	.4967	.4968	.4969	.4970	.4971	.4972	.4973	.4974
2.8	.4974	.4975	.4976	.4977	.4977	.4978	.4979	.4979	.4980	.4981
2.9	.4981	.4982	.4982	.4983	.4984	.4984	.4985	.4985	.4986	.4986
3.0	.4987	.4987	.4987	.4988	.4988	.4989	.4989	.4989	.4990	.4990

SOURCE: John E. Freund, *Statistics: A First Course*, 3/E, ©1981, pp.442-423. Reprinted by permission of Prentice-Hall Inc., Englewood Cliffs, New Jersey.

Table 3   The *t* Distribution

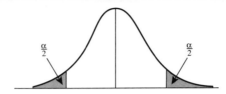

Two-tail area (α)		.20	.10	.05	.02	.01
d.f.	1	3.078	6.314	12.706	31.821	63.657
	2	1.886	2.920	4.303	6.965	9.925
	3	1.638	2.353	3.182	4.541	5.841
	4	1.533	2.132	2.776	3.747	4.604
	5	1.476	2.015	2.571	3.365	4.032
	6	1.440	1.943	2.447	3.143	3.707
	7	1.415	1.895	2.365	2.998	3.499
	8	1.397	1.860	2.306	2.896	3.355
	9	1.383	1.833	2.262	2.821	3.250
	10	1.372	1.812	2.228	2.764	3.169
	11	1.363	1.796	2.201	2.718	3.106
	12	1.356	1.782	2.179	2.681	3.055
	13	1.350	1.771	2.160	2.650	3.012
	14	1.345	1.761	2.145	2.624	2.977
	15	1.341	1.753	2.131	2.602	2.947
	16	1.337	1.746	2.120	2.583	2.921
	17	1.333	1.740	2.110	2.567	2.898
	18	1.330	1.734	2.101	2.552	2.878
	19	1.328	1.729	2.093	2.539	2.861
	20	1.325	1.725	2.086	2.528	2.845
	21	1.323	1.721	2.080	2.518	2.831
	22	1.321	1.717	2.074	2.508	2.819
	23	1.319	1.714	2.069	2.500	2.807
	24	1.318	1.711	2.064	2.492	2.797
	25	1.316	1.708	2.060	2.485	2.787
	26	1.315	1.706	2.056	2.479	2.779
	27	1.314	1.703	2.052	2.473	2.771
	28	1.313	1.701	2.048	2.467	2.763
	29	1.311	1.699	2.045	2.462	2.756
	30	1.310	1.697	2.042	2.457	2.750
	40	1.303	1.684	2.021	2.423	2.704
	60	1.296	1.671	2.000	2.390	2.660
	120	1.289	1.658	1.980	2.358	2.617
	α	1.282	1.645	1.960	2.326	2.576

Source: Paul Hoel, *Elementary Statistics*, 3rd ed. John Wiley & Sons, Inc. New York, 1971.

Table 4 Selected Percentiles of the *F* Distribution

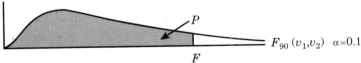

$F_{90}(v_1, v_2)$ $\alpha = 0.1$

v_1 = degrees of freedom for numerator

v_2 = degrees of freedom for denominator

v_2 \ v_1	1	2	3	4	5	6	7	8	9	10	12	15	20	24	30	40	60	120	∞
1	39.86	49.50	53.59	55.83	57.24	58.20	58.91	59.44	59.86	60.19	60.71	61.22	61.74	62.00	62.26	62.53	62.79	63.06	63.33
2	8.53	9.00	9.16	9.24	9.29	9.33	9.35	9.37	9.38	9.39	9.41	9.42	9.44	9.45	9.46	9.47	9.47	9.48	9.49
3	5.54	5.46	5.39	5.34	5.31	5.28	5.27	5.25	5.24	5.23	5.22	5.20	5.18	5.18	5.17	5.16	5.15	5.14	5.13
4	4.54	4.32	4.19	4.11	4.05	4.01	3.98	3.95	3.94	3.92	3.90	3.87	3.84	3.83	3.82	3.80	3.79	3.78	3.76
5	4.06	3.78	3.62	3.52	3.45	3.40	3.37	3.34	3.32	3.30	3.27	3.24	3.21	3.19	3.17	3.16	3.14	3.12	3.10
6	3.78	3.46	3.29	3.18	3.11	3.05	3.01	2.98	2.96	2.94	2.90	2.87	2.84	2.82	2.80	2.78	2.76	2.74	2.72
7	3.59	3.26	3.07	2.96	2.88	2.83	2.78	2.75	2.72	2.70	2.67	2.63	2.59	2.58	2.56	2.54	2.51	2.49	2.47
8	3.46	3.11	2.92	2.81	2.73	2.67	2.62	2.59	2.56	2.50	2.50	2.46	2.42	2.40	2.38	2.36	2.34	2.32	2.29
9	3.36	3.01	2.81	2.69	2.61	2.55	2.51	2.47	2.44	2.42	2.38	2.34	2.30	2.28	2.25	2.23	2.21	2.18	2.16
10	3.29	2.92	2.73	2.61	2.52	2.46	2.41	2.38	2.35	2.32	2.28	2.24	2.20	2.18	2.16	2.13	2.11	2.08	2.06
11	3.23	2.86	2.66	2.54	2.45	2.39	2.34	2.30	2.27	2.25	2.21	2.17	2.12	2.10	2.08	2.05	2.03	2.00	1.97
12	3.18	2.81	2.61	2.48	2.39	2.33	2.28	2.24	2.21	2.19	2.15	2.10	2.06	2.04	2.01	1.99	1.96	1.93	1.90
13	3.14	2.76	2.56	2.43	2.35	2.28	2.23	2.20	2.16	2.14	2.10	2.05	2.01	1.98	1.96	1.93	1.90	1.88	1.85
14	3.10	2.73	2.52	2.39	2.31	2.24	2.19	2.15	2.12	2.10	2.05	2.01	1.96	1.94	1.91	1.89	1.86	1.83	1.80
15	3.07	2.70	2.49	2.36	2.27	2.21	2.16	2.12	2.09	2.06	2.02	1.97	1.92	1.90	1.87	1.85	1.82	1.79	1.76
16	3.05	2.67	2.46	2.33	2.24	2.18	2.13	2.09	2.06	2.03	1.99	1.94	1.89	1.87	1.84	1.81	1.78	1.75	1.72
17	3.03	2.64	2.44	2.31	2.22	2.15	2.10	2.06	2.03	2.00	1.96	1.91	1.86	1.84	1.81	1.78	1.75	1.72	1.69
18	3.01	2.62	2.42	2.29	2.20	2.13	2.08	2.04	2.00	1.98	1.93	1.89	1.84	1.81	1.78	1.75	1.72	1.69	1.66
19	2.99	2.61	2.40	2.27	2.18	2.11	2.06	2.02	1.98	1.96	1.91	1.86	1.81	1.79	1.76	1.73	1.70	1.67	1.63
20	2.97	2.59	2.38	2.25	2.16	2.09	2.04	2.00	1.96	1.94	1.89	1.84	1.79	1.77	1.74	1.71	1.68	1.64	1.61
21	2.96	2.57	2.36	2.23	2.14	2.08	2.02	1.98	1.95	1.92	1.87	1.83	1.78	1.75	1.72	1.69	1.66	1.62	1.59
22	2.95	2.56	2.35	2.22	2.13	2.06	2.01	1.97	1.93	1.90	1.86	1.81	1.76	1.73	1.70	1.67	1.64	1.60	1.57
23	2.94	2.55	2.34	2.21	2.11	2.05	1.99	1.95	1.92	1.89	1.84	1.80	1.74	1.72	1.69	1.66	1.62	1.59	1.55
24	2.93	2.54	2.33	2.19	2.10	2.04	1.98	1.94	1.91	1.88	1.83	1.78	1.73	1.70	1.67	1.64	1.61	1.57	1.53
25	2.92	2.53	2.32	2.18	2.09	2.02	1.97	1.93	1.89	1.87	1.82	1.77	1.72	1.69	1.66	1.63	1.59	1.56	1.52
26	2.91	2.52	2.31	2.17	2.08	2.01	1.96	1.92	1.88	1.86	1.81	1.76	1.71	1.68	1.65	1.61	1.58	1.54	1.50
27	2.90	2.51	2.30	2.17	2.07	2.00	1.95	1.91	1.87	1.85	1.80	1.75	1.70	1.67	1.64	1.60	1.57	1.53	1.49
28	2.89	2.50	2.29	2.16	2.06	2.00	1.94	1.90	1.87	1.84	1.79	1.74	1.69	1.66	1.63	1.59	1.56	1.52	1.48
29	2.89	2.50	2.28	2.15	2.06	1.99	1.93	1.89	1.86	1.83	1.78	1.73	1.68	1.65	1.62	1.58	1.55	1.51	1.47
30	2.88	2.49	2.28	2.14	2.05	1.98	1.93	1.88	1.85	1.82	1.77	1.72	1.67	1.64	1.61	1.57	1.54	1.50	1.46
40	2.84	2.44	2.23	2.09	2.00	1.93	1.87	1.83	1.79	1.76	1.71	1.66	1.61	1.57	1.54	1.51	1.47	1.42	1.38
60	2.79	2.39	2.18	2.04	1.95	1.87	1.82	1.77	1.74	1.71	1.66	1.60	1.54	1.51	1.48	1.44	1.40	135	1.29
120	2.75	2.35	2.13	1.99	1.90	1.82	1.77	1.72	1.68	1.65	1.60	1.55	1.48	1.45	1.41	1.37	1.32	1.26	1.19
∞	2.71	2.30	2.08	1.94	1.85	1.77	1.72	1.67	1.63	1.60	1.55	1.49	1.42	1.38	1.34	1.30	1.24	1.17	1.00

Adapted from *Biometrika Tables for Statisticians*, Vol. 1 (2nd ed), edited by E.S. Pearson and H.O. Hartley, Cambridge University Press, 1958. Reproduced by permission of the Biometriika Trustees.

continued

$$F_{95}(v_1, v_2) \qquad \alpha = 0.05$$

v_1 = degrees of freedom for numerator

v_2 = degrees of freedom for denominator

v_2 \ v_1	1	2	3	4	5	6	7	8	9	10	12	15	20	24	30	40	60	120	∞
1	161.4	199.5	215.7	224.6	230.2	234.0	236.8	238.9	240.5	241.9	243.9	245.9	248.0	249.1	250.1	251.1	252.2	253.3	254.3
2	18.51	19.00	19.16	19.25	19.30	19.33	19.35	19.37	19.38	19.40	19.41	19.43	19.45	19.45	19.46	19.47	19.48	19.49	19.50
3	10.13	9.55	9.28	9.12	9.01	8.94	8.89	8.85	8.81	8.79	8.74	8.70	8.66	8.64	8.62	8.59	8.57	8.55	8.53
4	7.71	6.94	6.59	6.39	6.26	6.16	6.09	6.04	6.00	5.96	5.91	5.86	5.80	5.77	5.75	5.72	5.69	5.66	5.63
5	6.61	5.79	5.41	5.19	5.05	4.95	4.88	4.82	4.77	4.74	4.68	4.62	4.56	4.53	4.50	4.46	4.43	4.40	4.36
6	5.99	5.14	4.76	4.53	4.39	4.28	4.21	4.15	4.10	4.06	4.00	3.94	3.87	3.84	3.81	3.77	3.74	3.70	3.67
7	5.59	4.74	4.35	4.12	3.97	3.87	3.79	3.73	3.68	3.64	3.57	3.51	3.44	3.41	3.38	3.34	3.30	3.27	3.23
8	5.32	4.46	4.07	3.84	3.69	3.58	3.50	3.44	3.39	3.35	3.28	3.22	3.15	3.12	3.08	3.04	3.01	2.97	2.93
9	5.12	4.26	3.86	3.63	3.48	3.37	3.29	3.23	3.18	3.14	3.07	3.01	2.94	2.90	2.86	2.83	2.79	2.75	2.71
10	4.96	4.10	3.71	3.48	3.33	3.22	3.14	3.07	3.02	2.98	2.91	2.85	2.77	2.74	2.70	2.66	2.62	2.58	2.54
11	4.84	3.98	3.59	3.36	3.20	3.09	3.01	2.95	2.90	2.85	2.79	2.72	2.65	2.61	2.57	2.53	2.49	2.45	2.40
12	4.75	3.89	3.49	3.26	3.11	3.00	2.91	2.85	2.80	2.78	2.69	2.62	2.54	2.51	2.47	2.43	2.38	2.34	2.30
13	4.67	3.81	3.41	3.18	3.03	2.92	2.83	2.77	2.71	2.67	2.60	2.53	2.46	2.42	2.38	2.34	2.30	2.25	2.21
14	4.60	3.74	3.34	3.11	2.96	2.85	2.76	2.70	2.65	2.60	2.53	2.46	2.39	2.35	2.31	2.27	2.22	2.18	2.13
15	4.54	3.68	3.29	3.06	2.90	2.79	2.71	2.64	2.59	2.54	2.48	2.40	2.33	2.29	2.25	2.20	2.16	2.11	2.07
16	4.49	3.63	3.24	3.01	2.85	2.74	2.66	2.59	2.54	2.49	2.42	2.35	2.28	2.24	2.19	2.15	2.11	2.06	2.01
17	4.45	3.59	3.20	2.96	2.81	2.70	2.61	2.55	2.49	2.45	2.38	2.31	2.23	2.19	2.15	2.10	2.06	2.01	1.96
18	4.41	3.55	3.16	2.93	2.77	2.66	2.58	2.51	2.46	2.41	2.34	2.27	2.19	2.15	2.11	2.06	2.02	1.97	1.92
19	4.38	3.52	3.13	2.90	2.74	2.63	2.54	2.48	2.42	2.38	2.31	2.23	2.16	2.11	2.07	2.03	1.98	1.93	1.88
20	4.35	3.49	3.10	2.87	2.71	2.60	2.51	2.45	2.39	2.35	2.28	2.20	2.12	2.08	2.04	1.99	1.95	1.90	1.84
21	4.32	3.47	3.07	2.84	2.68	2.57	2.49	2.42	2.37	2.32	2.25	2.18	2.10	2.05	2.01	1.96	1.92	1.87	1.81
22	4.30	3.44	3.05	2.82	2.66	2.55	2.46	2.40	2.34	2.30	2.23	2.15	2.07	2.03	1.98	1.94	1.89	1.84	1.78
23	4.28	3.42	3.03	2.80	2.64	2.53	2.44	2.37	2.32	2.27	2.20	2.13	2.05	2.01	1.96	1.91	1.86	1.81	1.76
24	4.26	3.40	3.01	2.78	2.62	2.51	2.42	2.36	2.30	2.25	2.18	2.11	2.03	1.98	1.94	1.89	1.84	1.79	1.73
25	4.24	3.39	2.99	2.76	2.60	2.49	2.40	2.34	2.28	2.24	2.16	2.09	2.01	1.96	1.92	1.87	1.82	1.77	1.71
26	4.23	3.37	2.98	2.74	2.59	2.47	2.39	2.32	2.27	2.22	2.15	2.07	1.99	1.95	1.90	1.85	1.80	1.75	1.69
27	4.21	3.35	2.96	2.73	2.57	2.46	2.37	2.31	2.25	2.20	2.13	2.06	1.97	1.93	1.88	1.84	1.79	1.73	1.67
28	4.20	3.34	2.95	2.71	2.56	2.45	2.36	2.29	2.24	2.19	2.12	2.04	1.96	1.91	1.87	1.82	1.77	1.71	1.65
29	4.18	3.33	2.93	2.70	2.55	2.43	2.35	2.28	2.22	2.18	2.10	2.03	1.94	1.90	1.85	1.81	1.75	1.70	1.64
30	4.17	3.32	2.92	2.69	2.53	2.42	2.33	2.27	2.21	2.16	2.09	2.01	1.93	1.89	1.84	1.79	1.74	1.68	1.62
40	4.08	3.23	2.84	2.61	2.45	2.34	2.25	2.18	2.12	2.08	2.00	1.92	1.84	1.79	1.74	1.69	1.64	1.58	1.51
60	4.00	3.15	2.76	2.53	2.37	2.25	2.17	2.10	2.04	1.99	1.92	1.84	1.75	1.70	1.65	1.59	1.53	1.47	1.39
120	3.92	3.07	2.68	2.45	2.29	2.17	2.09	2.02	1.96	1.91	1.83	1.75	1.66	1.61	1.55	1.50	1.43	1.35	1.25
∞	3.84	3.00	2.60	2.37	2.21	2.10	2.01	1.94	1.88	1.83	1.75	1.67	1.57	1.52	1.46	1.39	1.32	1.22	1.00

Name Index

Subject Index